W9-CSE-602

GUIDE TO THE AMERIKANSKY RUSSKY VIESTNIK

VOLUME I: 1894-1914

GUIDE TO THE
Amerikansky Russky Viestnik

VOLUME I: 1894-1914

James M. Evans

CARPATHO-RUSYN RESEARCH CENTER

Fairview, New Jersey 1979

Publication of this volume was made possible through the generous support of His Grace, the Most Reverend Stephen J. Kocisko, D.D., Metropolitan Archbishop of Pittsburgh.

Copyright © by the Carpatho-Rusyn Research Center
All rights reserved
ISBN 0-917242-05-x
Library of Congress Catalog Number 79-55333
Printed in the United States of America

The Carpatho-Rusyn Research Center, Inc., established in 1978, is a non-profit cultural organization registered in the State of New York. The Center sponsors the publication and distribution of books, articles, and a quarterly newsletter about Carpatho-Rusyns in Europe and the United States.

For Patricia

PREFACE

The concept of a guide to the <u>Amerikansky Russky Viestnik</u> originated
in a proposal put forth by the members of the advisory committee to the
Carpatho-Ruthenian Microfilm Project at its October 22, 1976 meeting in
Pittsburgh, Pennsylvania. This committee, in conjunction with the Immigration History Research Center (IHRC), University of Minnesota, was
responsible for the collection and microfilming of all existing Carpatho-
Rusyn immigrant serial publications and almanacs. The project was
supported by a grant from the Metropolitan Byzantine Rite Province and
matching funds from the National Endowment for the Humanities. A description of this collection, which includes over 60 titles and information on
access to microfilm copy, is contained in <u>Carpatho-Ruthenian Microfilm</u>
<u>Project: A Guide to Newspapers and Periodicals</u> (St. Paul: IHRC, University
of Minnesota, 1979), compiled by Dr. Frank Renkiewicz.

To augment this microfilm project, the advisory committee decided to
commission the compilation of a guide to one of the major Rusyn immigrant
serial publications. Such a guide would constitute an invaluable aid to
scholars and students of Rusyn immigration history, cultural life, genealogy,
and religion. The exact character of the guide was allowed to develop as
the project progressed; however, an initial consensus suggested that the
volume would consist of a series of abstracts or short synopses of selected
articles and features taken from the pages of the newspaper. These abstracts,
together with precise reference to the location of the complete article in
the newspaper, would be arranged in chronological order under certain
general topics.

The committee selected the <u>Amerikansky Russky Viestnik</u>, one of the largest, oldest and more complete of the Rusyn serials available in the microfilmed collection, as the focus of the project. The <u>Viestnik</u> is also of considerable importance due to its prominence during the early years of immigration in the late nineteenth and early twentieth centuries.

In November 1976, this writer conducted a two-week pilot study to explore the feasibility of preparing a guide to the <u>Amerikansky Russky Viestnik</u>. After the successful conclusion of the pilot project, work on the present <u>Guide</u> began in earnest in December 1976. Due to the amount of material extracted, a decision was made to publish the <u>Guide</u> in two volumes. It was and is the hope of those involved with the project that this <u>Guide</u> and its succeeding volume will set a precedent for other scholars and, as such, encourage the preparation of similar works on Rusyn serials in the current microfilmed collection.

The production of any work having the scope of this volume depends on the coordinated efforts of many individuals. Indeed, the author has enjoyed assistance from a number of distinguished persons throughout the project's three-year duration, all of whom deserve my sincere appreciation.

First, I wish to extend my special gratitude to His Grace, the Most Reverend Stephen J. Kocisko, D.D., Metropolitan Archbishop of Pittsburgh, for his personal interest in and beneficial efforts on behalf of the project.

The guidance of the project's two consultants, Mr. E. Kasinec, Harvard University Research Bibliographer and Librarian, and Dr. Paul R. Magocsi, Harvard University Senior Research Fellow, has been of primary importance in this pioneering effort. Mr. Kasinec's seemingly inexhaustible ability to deal with the numerous details and difficulties inherent in a project of this sort has been invaluable. Dr. Magocsi's assistance as editor-consultant, especially his advice and direction during the publication phase of the project, is greatly appreciated.

I am indebted to Dr. Frank Renkiewicz, formerly Research Associate at the Immigration History Research Center and coordinator of this project, for the support and guidance rendered during the project's crucial early phase. My grateful thanks must also be extended to Professor Omeljan Pritsak, Director of the Harvard Ukrainian Research Institute, for placing at my disposal the excellent research facilities of the Institute on whose premises work on the Guide was conducted.

Several other persons have contributed significantly to the successful completion of this project: Dr. Bohdan Strumins'kyj, Slavic linguist associated with the Harvard Ukrainian Research Institute, provided invaluable assistance with the often perplexing nuances of Carpatho-Rusyn dialects; Dr. Zack Deal, III, author of the Guide's second volume, assisted greatly with the organization and presentation of the material; Mrs. Dorothea Donker single-handedly typed the final press-ready version of this manuscript; and last, but not least of all, my wife, Patricia Schiedler, was a constant and reliable source of advice, insight, and support during the last three years.

It is my hope and sincere desire that this Guide will facilitate as well as encourage the study of the Rusyn-American immigrant experience, an experience which is an inseparable part of our own American heritage.

J.M.E.

Cambridge, Massachusetts
August 1979

CONTENTS

Guide to the Amerikansky Russky Viestnik

Volume I: 1894-1914

INTRODUCTION

Volume I of the Guide to the Greek Catholic Union's Amerikansky

Russky Viestnik (ARV) is designed to facilitate the location and retrieval

of information from microfilmed volumes III through XXIII (1894-1914).[1]

During this period, the ARV contained a wealth of material relating to the

immigration and settlement of Carpatho-Rusyns in America during the nine-

teenth and early twentieth centuries.

Carpatho-Rusyns emigrated from their ancestral homes in the northern

Carpathian Mountain regions of Austria-Hungary to the United States,

usually because of the poverty and privation they were suffering under the

feudal economy of the Austro-Hungarian Empire. The majority of the Rusyns

who came to America during these years were from areas in the Kingdom of

Hungary which now comprise part of northeastern Czechoslovakia and the

Transcarpathian oblast' of the Ukrainian Soviet Socialist Republic.

The Rusyn immigration coincided with a period of tremendous growth

in American industry. Most immigrants, who were usually male and of an

agrarian background, were able to find employment as unskilled laborers

in factories or coal mines in the industrial regions of the northeast and

north central United States. Although low by American standards, a Rusyn

immigrant's wages could provide ample support for his family in Europe and,

upon his return there, the funds necessary to purchase land. For these

reasons, Rusyn immigrants viewed their stay in America as a temporary means

to ease their poverty-stricken existence in Europe. However, many were to

---

[1]This Guide does not include volumes I-II (1892-1893), VI-IX (1897-
1900), and XIV (1905), which were not available for microfilming.

remain in America, where they obtained permanent jobs, enjoyed a standard of living that had been hitherto beyond their reach, and experienced the social freedom and mobility unique to this country. As a result, colonies of Rusyn immigrants sprang up in industrial centers like Pittsburgh, New York City, and Detroit, as well as in the anthracite coal-producing regions of eastern Pennsylvania, West Virginia, and Ohio.

Rusyn immigrants found life in America vastly different from the familiar close-knit life of the village in Europe. As they sought employment and made daily contact with Americans and immigrants of other nationalities, there was little opportunity to continue practicing Rusyn language and customs. However, as Rusyn communities developed, their Greek Catholic parishes became centers of Rusyn immigrant life, playing an important role in the preservation of their unique native tongue and national customs.

Although the church fulfilled both spiritual and social needs of Rusyns, the immigrants still had few guarantees for their physical welfare. Because Rusyn workers were usually employed in the most hazardous forms of industrial labor and were victims of frequent industrial accidents, their mortality rate was very high. As the sole supporter of his family in Europe, the immigrant worker's demise would mean acute hardships for his poverty-stricken dependents.

To remedy this situation, the Rusyns followed the example of other immigrant nationalities in America and formed fraternal life insurance organizations. Members of these organizations paid a nominal monthly fee to the organization's treasury, which in turn promised to pay a sum of money to the member's beneficiary in case of death. Since these organizations were formed on the basis of nationality, their local branches, like the Greek Catholic parishes, served to bring Rusyn immigrants together and to reinforce the native language and customs of the Rusyn immigrants.

The first, largest, and most influential fraternal life insurance organization established by Rusyn immigrants was the Greek Catholic Union of Rusyn Brotherhoods (Sojedinenije Greko Kaftoličeskich Russkich Bratstv), popularly known as the "Sojedinenije" and hereafter referred to as G.C.U. This organization, founded by Rusyn laity and Greek Catholic clergy on February 14, 1892 in Wilkes Barre, Pennsylvania, was chartered:

> To spread love and friendship amongst the Ruthenian Greek Catholic people in America; provide material aid to members and their heirs in case of death; provide for ways and means necessary for the education of the people both in the national and religious requirements and to aid churches and schools; if material conditions permit, aid to the injured and indigent. [2]

In the early years, the G.C.U. tried to represent the cultural and religious interests of all Rusyn immigrants in America. However, from the beginning, the G.C.U. had to compete for members from other Slavic fraternal organizations, especially the First Catholic Slavic Union (established 1890) and the Pennsylvania Slovak Roman and Greek Catholic Union (established 1892). An additional problem for the G.C.U. was the internal factionalism and discord which developed among members over political issues and personal views. By 1894, a group of members from the Austrian province of Galicia were disenchanted with the purpose and direction of the G.C.U. under the leadership of Rusyns from Hungary and withdrew to form their own fraternal organization: the Rusyn National Union (Rus'kyj Narodnyj Sojuz), hereafter the R.N.U. Increasingly

---

[2] Michael Roman, ed., Jubilee Almanac of the Greek Catholic Union of the U.S.A. (Munhall, Pa.: Greek Catholic Union Press, 1967), p. 35.

oriented to the Ukrainian national movement, the R.N.U. became the G.C.U.'s chief antagonist on issues concerning nationality and the American Greek Catholic Church. Throughout the first twenty years of its existence, the G.C.U.'s leadership and policies prompted members and clergy to leave and to form alternative organizations, though none of these ever rivalled the size and power of the G.C.U.[3]

The G.C.U. was comprised of numerous lodges scattered throughout the eastern industrial and anthracite coal-producing regions of the United States. The communication link for this network of lodges as well as for the Rusyn immigrant communities was the organization's newspaper, the Amerikansky Russky Viestnik. From the first issue of March 17, 1892, the ARV served as an important source of news in Carpatho-Rusyn dialect for the immigrant communities. The paper provided national, international, and labor news, G.C.U. lodge and Greek Catholic parish information, a forum for reader commentary, short stories and poetry, as well as articles concerning the ever volatile issues of church and national identity.

The ARV quickly became the G.C.U.'s most effective instrument in obtaining the Rusyn community's support for its policies concerning church affairs and the nationality issue among immigrants in America. Although the ARV was chartered to represent the official word of the G.C.U., the newspaper more properly reflected the opinions and judgements of its editor-in-chief. The first influential editor was Paul Jurievich

---

[3] Paul R. Magocsi, "Carpatho-Rusyns in the United States," manuscript p. 24. This work appeared in Vojvodinian Rusyn translation in Nova dumka, VIII, 20-22 (Vukovar, Yugoslavia, 1979), pp. 67-73, 97-100 and will appear in a revised version in the Harvard Encyclopedia of American Ethnic Groups (Cambridge, Mass.: Harvard University Press, 1980).

Zsatkovich, who held the post from 1892-1914. Zsatkovich (1852-1916) immigrated to America in 1891 from a Rusyn village in Bereg county, Hungary, where he had been employed as a government notary. After coming to the United States, he became a charter member of the G.C.U. and he served as the organization's Supreme Recording Secretary and co-editor of the ARV, representing the Rusyn faction from Hungary. When several Rusyns from Austrian Galicia split from the G.C.U. to form the R.N.U. in 1894, Zsatkovich became the sole editor of the newspaper, a position he held until his resignation in 1914.

As editor-in-chief, Zsatkovich wrote most of the articles and commentaries published in the ARV. Thus, much of the controversy and polemics attributed to the G.C.U. concerning religious and national issues had their source in the opinions penned by Zsatkovich. His views often reflected the conservatism of the G.C.U.'s supreme officers and its magyarone Greek Catholic clergy and clerical supporters. Since some G.C.U. members neither supported Zsatkovich nor agreed with his opinions, attempts were repeatedly made to unseat him as editor at the G.C.U.'s stormy biannual conventions. However, Zsatkovich always rallied suffi-cient support to maintain a twenty-year tenure as editor-in-chief.

The ARV was a weekly, published every Tuesday until 1894, and every Thursday thereafter. A unique feature of the ARV was its publication in two versions: a Carpatho-Rusyn recension of Russian using the pre-1918 Cyrillic orthography, and a Latin script version of a Rusyn dialect heavily influenced by Eastern Slovak Šariš dialects. For the most part, the newspaper was published in these two versions as separate editions with readers subscribing to one or to the other.

Both editions were eight pages, with occasional special editions of twelve to sixteen pages usually published prior to the G.C.U.'s General Conventions and when the G.C.U. lodge directory (adressar) was included. Abbreviated four-page additions also appeared, generally when the editor-in-chief was officially representing the ARV at major events, such as conventions, church congresses, or meetings.

From the first editions in 1892 through 1895, and again, from 1904 to 1906, the two versions of the newspaper were combined and published as a single edition. In these years the length of the paper was twelve pages, with special editions of sixteen pages. From 1904 to 1906, articles in Cyrillic and Latin script were juxtaposed in columns on the same or following pages. In addition, an equivalency table of Cyrillic and Latin letters appeared in each edition.[4]

*   *   *

This Guide lists a selected number of articles and features pertaining to Rusyn life in Europe and America, and it focuses particularly on the problems of church affiliation and national identity that afflicted Rusyn-American communities over a twenty-year period. The material was chosen with the aim to facilitate future study of the following topics: (1) the Rusyn nationality issue; (2) the Greek Catholic Church; (3) the social, political, and economic life of Rusyns in Europe and America; and (4) Rusyn public opinion and reaction to current events.

The entries are classified into six major categories. Entries in the first five categories are arranged chronologically according to their date

---

[4] See entry number 5085 in this Guide.

of publication; entries in the sixth category are arranged alphabetically. Each entry has been assigned a four-digit number. The first digit represents the major category wherein the entry appears; the following three digits indicate the entry's individual number within its particular category. For example, the number 2389 means that it is entry 389 within Category 2.

The first category, the <u>Amerikansky Russky Viestnik</u>, consists of 93 entries pertinent to the <u>ARV</u> and other serial publications. Of particular interest are the articles concerning the editorship of these publications.

The second category, the Greek Catholic Union, contains 554 entries concerning the G.C.U. and other fraternal organizations. This includes official statements, minutes from meetings and conventions, and commentary on fraternal organizations and insurance matters as well as articles on the polemics between the G.C.U. and other fraternals.

The third (and largest) category contains 888 entries devoted to the Greek Catholic Church in Europe and America. This section covers a wide range of subject matter, from the issue of the Orthodox "schism" and the struggles to establish an American Greek Catholic eparchy, to the question of nationality and how this divided Greek Catholics. Other entries concern church dedications and anniversaries, clergy transfers, official decrees, and pastoral letters from the Greek Catholic hierarchy.

The fourth category, Rusyn Social Issues and Development, is a collection of 641 articles and reader commentary on a variety of topics related to the social, political, and economic life of Rusyn immigrants in America and Europe. The foremost concerns during this period were labor problems, the political situation in Europe and America, the changes in American immigration laws, Rusyn-American communities and their activities, and social mores among Rusyn-Americans. There was also frequent commentary on other immigrant groups as well as the nationality issue among Rusyns.

Topics relating to Rusyn Culture and Education comprise the 204 entries in the fifth category. These include commentaries on the preservation of Rusyn culture in America, the value of education especially in Greek Catholic parish schools, and the growth of Rusyn national consciousness in America and Europe. Other entries refer to Rusyn prose, poetry, and folksongs published in the ARV and to reviews of books and concerts.

The sixth and final category, Rusyn Individuals (or Personalia) is an alphabetical list of 685 clergy and other prominent persons about whom biographical information is given. These names were compiled from the G.C.U. necrology listings (1894-1902), biographical articles, and letters to the editor.

Titles of articles and features have been taken for the most part from the Cyrillic script version of the ARV. Three systems for transliterating Cyrillic script titles into Latin script were considered: the international system for Russian; the international system for Ukrainian; and the ARV system.[5] Each of these systems alone fails to render the uniqueness of the Carpatho-Rusyn dialects in Cyrillic script; therefore, the following has been developed for this Guide:

---

[5]Ibid.

А,а	—	A,a	Л,л	—	L,l	Ч,ч	—	Č,č
Б,б	—	B,b	М,м	—	M,m	Ш,ш	—	Š,š
В,в	—	V,v	Н,н	—	N,n	Щ,щ	—	ŠČ,šč
Г,г	—	H,h	О,о	—	O,o	Ь,ь	—	'
Д,д	—	D,d	П,п	—	P,p	Ъ,ъ	—	"
Е,е	—	E,e	Р,р	—	R,r	Ы,ы	—	Ŷ,ŷ
Ж,ж	—	Ž,ž	С,с	—	S,s	Э,э	—	Ė,ė
З,з	—	Z,z	Т,т	—	T,t	Ю,ю	--	Ju,ju
И,и	—	Y,y	У,у	—	U,u	Я,я	--	Ja,ja
I,i	—	I,i	Ф,ф	—	F,f	Ѣ,ѣ	--	Î,î
Й,й	—	J,j	Х,х	—	Ch,ch	Ѳ,ѳ	--	Ṫ,ṫ
К,к	—	K,k	Ц,ц	—	C,c			

Entries appear in several formats. For the majority of articles and commentaries, the author is listed first (or [N.N.] if anonymous), followed by the transliterated title and an English translation in brackets. Whenever the title does not adequately convey the content of the article, a brief annotation is provided.

For entries referring to letters to the editor, the author's name, letter's place of origin (if Europe, the Slavic rendition is followed by the Hungarian name in brackets and the Hungarian county[6]), and the date of letter, if available, is given. This information is generally followed by an annotation. When letters are titled, the title is listed, followed by the English translation in brackets and, if necessary, an annotation.

Each entry includes a source citation which indicates the volume, issue, and page number reference. This citation is located directly

---

[6]Names of villages and towns in the Rusyn counties of Hungary have been cited from Czechoslovak Government statistics, Statistický lexikon obcí v Republike československé, vol. 3; Slovensko; vol. 4: Podkarpatská Rus (Prague: Státní úřad statistický, 1927-1928).

beneath the entry at the right margin of the page. For example,

III (10): Mar 20, 1894; C-1, L-2&3 refers to the following elements:

Volume Number	Issue Number	Date of Issue	Page Number(s) in Cyrillic Script Edition	Page Number(s) in Latin Script Edition
III	10	Mar 20, 1894	C-1	L-2&3

Because issues appearing from 1904 to 1906 were published in a
combined edition, the designations "C" and "L" before page numbers are
unnecessary, since articles were duplicated in Cyrillic and Latin script
usually on the same page. For example, XV (31): Aug 23, 1906; 6,7
refers to:

Volume Number	Issue Number	Date of Issue	Page Number(s)
XV	31	Aug 23, 1906	6,7

Many articles listed in the Guide were serialized, consisting of
parts usually published in consecutive issues. Due to the length of
some of these serializations, the citations have been rendered in an
abbreviated form. For example, Parts I-VI, XXI (23-28): Jul 4-Aug 8, 1912
refers to:

Volume Number	Issue Numbers	Dates of Issues
XXI	23-28	Jul 4-Aug 8, 1912

Entries have also been assigned a code letter to further distinguish
the article by form and content. The code letter(s) appearing at the left
margin adjacent to the source citation mean the following:

A -- Article	Lit-Prose -- Literature, prose
Ad -- Advertisement, notice, invitation, unofficial request	N -- Necrology
	Nr -- News report
B -- Biography	O -- Official decree, document declaration, minutes, statistics
E -- Editorial	
Fs -- Folk Song	P -- Photograph
L -- Letter to the editor (America)	Pro -- Proverb
	R -- Report (Spravoyzdanie)
LE -- Letter to the editor (Europe)	Req -- Request (official)
Lit-Play -- Literature, play	Tab -- Table
Lit-Poetry -- Literature, poetry	

Family names of individuals in this Guide have been taken in most cases from the Latin script edition of the ARV.[7] Where it has been possible to check, this form has proved to be the spelling used today by relatives of these people. Where names did not appear in the Latin script edition, the names have been transliterated from Cyrillic according to the system reproduced above.

Since it is probable that Rusyn immigrants were known in this country by the Anglo-American rendition of their Slavic first names, in most cases this is the form in which they appear in the Guide. Some of the frequently used Anglo-American names and their Slavic equivalents are as follows:

---

[7]An exception has been made with the names of Greek Catholic clergy. Whenever possible, the names of clergy will be rendered as they appear in the necrology listing of the 1977 Directory of the Byzantine Ruthenian Metropolitan Province (Pittsburgh: Chancery Office, 1977).

Alexander	Aleksandr
Alexis	Aleksij, Alexij
Andrew	Andrej, Andro
Ann	Anna
Anthony	Antal, Antonij, Anton
Barbara	Varvara
Basil	Vasilij, Vasyl', Vasyl'ko
Constantine	Konstantyn
Cyril	Kyryll
Dimitri	Demeter, Dymytrij
Edward	Eduard, Edvard
Elias	Ilii, Ilko, Ylij, Ylija
Elizabeth	Elizabeta, Elyzaveta
Eugene	Eugenij, Evhenij
Eugenia	Eugenija, Evhenija
Eve	Eva
George	Heorhij, Jurij
Gregory	Hrehor, Hryhorij
Helen	Helena
Hilarion	Ylarion
Ignatius	Ihnat
Irene	Irenka, Iryna
Ivan	Ivan
Jacob	Jakob, Jakub
John	Ioan, Ioann, Joan
Joseph	Iosyf, Josef, Jozef
Julius	Julij
Julia	Julija
Katherine	Katharina, Kataryna
Lenora	Leonora
Louis	Lajoš, Ljudvyh
Lucas	Lukač
Mary	Maria, Marija
Margaret	Marhareta
Matthew	Matias, Mattej, Mattias

Michael	Michel, Mychayl
Nicephor	Nykyfor
Nicholas	Nikol, Nikolaj, Nykolaj
Paul	Pavel
Pauline	Paulina, Pavlyna
Peter	Petr, Petro
Simon	Seman, Simeon, Symeon
Sofia	Sofija
Stephen	Stefan
Suzanne	Zuzanna
Thaddeus	Teddeij, Tadejus
Theodore	Fedor, Teodore
Theodosius	Teodozij, Theodozij
Theodosia	Teodosija
Thomas	Foma, Toma, Tomaš
Veronica	Veronyka
Victor	Vyktor
Vladimir	Vladymir, Volodymyr
Xenia	Ksen'ja

To aid the reader further, three appendices are included. The first is a listing by term of G.C.U. supreme officers and their tenure from 1892 through 1914. This listing was compiled from the ARV and G.C.U. almanacs. The second and third appendices consist of membership and financial statistics taken from the ARV. These statistics represent only the aggregate G.C.U. membership and financial position. Source citations are provided to enable the reader to consult the ARV for more precise information regarding individual lodges. The reader will note that through the years these statistics have been published on a sporadic basis and in a variety of formats.

ABBREVIATIONS AND ACRONYMS

Abbreviations

Co.	--	Company
Dr.	--	Doctor
et al.	--	and others
n.d.	--	no date
N.N.	--	no name
n.p.	--	no place
o.s.	--	old style (Julian Calendar)
O.S.B.M.	--	Order of Saint Basil the Great
St.	--	Saint
V.R.	--	Very Reverend

Months of the Year

Jan	--	January		Jul	--	July
Feb	--	February		Aug	--	August
Mar	--	March		Sep	--	September
Apr	--	April		Oct	--	October
May	--	May		Nov	--	November
Jun	--	June		Dec	--	December

Organizations

ARV   --   Amerikansky Russky Viestnik (organ of the G.C.U.)

G.C.U.   --   Greek Catholic Union (Sojedinenije Greko Kaftoličeskich Russkich Bratstv)

F.C.S.U.   --   First Catholic Slovak Union (Prvá Katolícka Slovenská Jednota)

N.S.U.   --   National Slovak Union (Národný Slovenský Spolok)

P.R.G.C.U.   --   Pennsylvania Roman and Greek Catholic Union (Pennsylvanská Slovenská Rímsko a Grécko Katolícka Jednota)

R.N.U.   --   Rusyn National Union (Rus'kyj Narodnyj Sojuz)

U.M.W.   --   United Mine Workers of America

Y.M.C.A.   --   Young Men's Christian Association

States

AL -- Alabama	ME -- Maine	OK -- Oklahoma
CA -- California	MN -- Minnesota	PA -- Pennsylvania
CO -- Colorado	MO -- Missouri	VA -- Virginia
CT -- Connecticut	MT -- Montana	WA -- Washington
IA -- Iowa	NJ -- New Jersey	WI -- Wisconsin
IL -- Illinois	NM -- New Mexico	WV -- West Virginia
IN -- Indiana	NY -- New York	WY -- Wyoming
MA -- Massachusetts	OH -- Ohio	

Chapter 1

Amerikansky Russky Viestnik

1001   [N.N.]; "Balamučenie sredi naroda" [Confusing the people]
　　　　Rusyn nationality as discussed in <u>Svoboda</u> article.

　　　　A   III (6): Feb 6, 1894; C-2&3

1002   Rev. Cornelius Laurisin. Shenandoah, PA, Jan 8, 1894.
　　　　Commentary on <u>Svoboda</u>.

　　　　A   III (7): Feb 20, 1894; C-2

1003   [N.N.]; "Pojasnenija k statii, 'Balamutam', soobščennoj v Džerzi
　　　　Siti vychodjaščoj hazetî, <u>Svoboda</u>" [Commentaries on the
　　　　article, 'To confusers', published in the Jersey City news-
　　　　paper, <u>Svoboda</u>]

　　　　A   III (8): Feb 27, 1894; C-4&5

1004   Red.; "Yskry" [Sparks]
　　　　Column of editorial commentary on articles printed in <u>Svoboda</u>.

　　　　E   III (10): Mar 13, 1894; C-3
　　　　　　　　　　　　　　　III (31-32): Sep 13-20, 1894; C-3
　　　　　　　　　　　　　　　III (43): Dec 6, 1894; C-3
　　　　　　　　　　　　　　　III (46): Dec 27, 1894; C-3

1005   Ju.; "1892--17 Marta--1894" [1892--March 17--1894]
　　　　Commemorates the second anniversary of the <u>ARV</u>.

　　　　E   III (11): Mar 20, 1894; C-1, L-9&11

1006   [N.N.]; "Otpovîd' <u>Svobodî</u> na stychotvorenie v 15-om eja numerî:
　　　　'Popa nam nanjaly'" [Answer to <u>Svoboda</u> with respect to a poem
　　　　appearing in issue # 15, 'They hired a priest for us']
　　　　See: 5011.

　　　　A   III (16): Apr 17, 1894; C-2

1007   [N.N.]; "Pojasnenie na 'žalostnoe vozrŷdanie' <u>Svobodŷ</u> podannoe v
　　　　12-eja numerî pod zahlaviem 'Pryklad Bajdužnosty'"
　　　　[A commentary on 'Grievous Sobbing' in the 12th issue of
　　　　<u>Svoboda</u> under the title, 'An example of apathy']

　　　　A   III (18): May 15, 1894; C-4&5

1008   Paul Jurievich; "V zaščytî pravdŷ!" [In defense of truth!]
　　　　Commentary on <u>Svoboda</u>.

　　　　E   III (19): May 22, 1894; C-issue
　　　　　　　　　　　　　　　　　　　　　　　　　　supplement

1009   [N.N.]; "Čto-to o Hazetî" [Some facts about the newspaper]

  Part I: ARV: An important source of news for Rusyn-Americans.

         III (25): Jul 17, 1894; C-6

  Part II: Importance of newspapers for the Rusyn immigrant
  community.

         III (26): Jul 24, 1894; C-6

  Part III: ARV: Purpose and direction as a Rusyn-American
  newspaper.

         III (27): Jul 31, 1894; C-6

  Part IV: ARV: Fulfilling needs of the Rusyn immigrant
  community.

         III (28): Aug 14, 1894; C-6

  Part V: ARV: Its function.

         III (29): Aug 21, 1894; C-6

  Part VI: Information on publishing ARV as a weekly.

  A   III (30): Sep 4, 1894; C-6

1010   [N.N.]; "Koe-čto Svobodî. Samochval'ba y napadenie" [Something
  to Svoboda. Boastfulness and aggressiveness]

  Purpose and aspiration of Svoboda.

  A   III (26): Jul 24, 1894; C-4

1011   Vasilievich; "Otkrovennŷy mnînija o napravleniy y stremlenijach,
  Am. Russkoho Vîstnyka" [Candid opinions on the direction and
  aims of the ARV]

  Parts I - II: III (40-41): Nov 15-22, 1894; C-2, L-1

  Part IV: III (43): Dec 6, 1894; C-2&3, L-13

  A

1012   "Uvîdomlenie y Prošenie Redakciy" [Information and notification
  from the Editor]

  1895 ARV changes.

  O   III (44): Dec 13, 1894; C-5, L-1

1013   Redakcija; "Ot Redakciy" [From the Editor]

  G.C.U. main and ARV publishing offices moved from 417 S. Wyoming
  St. to 111 Hickory St. in Scranton, PA.

  O   III (47): Jan 2, 1895; C-4

1014   Ju.; "O čem mŷ zavse pyšem" [What we usually write about]

   ARV: direction and aims.

   E   IV (3): Jan 31, 1895; C-2, L-9

1015   [N.N.]; "Čužiy v Pensyl'vaniy" [Foreigners in Pennsylvania]

   Commentary on a Pennsylvania legislative bill that would
   discourage immigration to the state.

   A   IV (7): Feb 28, 1895; C-4

1016   [N.N.]; "1892 17-ho marta 1895" [1892-March 17, 1895]

   Commemorates the third anniversary of the ARV.

   A   IV (9): Mar 14, 1895; C-4&5, L-1

1017   [N.N.]; "Neslychannaja bezoclyvost'" [Unheard of Myopia]

   Criticizes the goals of Svoboda.

   A   IV (19): May 30, 1895; C-2&3

1018   [N.N.]; "Otpovîd' Svobodî" [Answer to Svoboda]

   A   IV (35): Sep 19, 1895; C-5

1019   N.; Hazleton, PA, Oct 3, 1895

   Commentary on Rev. Gregory Hruška's article, "Ščo vin jè?"
   [Who is he?] in Svoboda.

   L   IV (38): Oct 10, 1895; C-3

1020   John Smith and Paul Jurievich Zsatkovich; "Objavlenie y uvîdomlenie
   redakciy y yzdatel'stva Am. Russkaho Vîstnyka" [Declaration
   and information from the editor and publisher of the ARV]

   Request funds to support ARV.

   Req   V (2): Jan 23, 1896; C-1, L-1

1021   Redakcija y Yzdavatel'stvo; "Vo Vseobščoe vnymanie, perenesenie
   redakciy y knyhopečatny (drukarny) yz Skrenton, Pa., v Nju
   York. Otkrŷtie Russkoho Êmyhrantnoho Doma y Russko-Narodnoho
   Banka v Nju Yorkî" [General notice, transfer of the editorial
   and printing offices from Scranton, PA, to New York City.
   Opening of the Rusyn emigration house and Rusyn-National Bank
   in New York City]

   Beginning March 1, 1896, ARV offices will be located at 14th
   street, avenue A, New York City.

   O   V (6): Feb 20, 1896; C-1, L-1

1022   [N.N.]; "Svoboda východyt yz obščepoleznŷch predmetov y
vozvraščaetsja 'vo svoja sy'" [Svoboda turns away from
generally useful articles and returns to 'its own [prejudiced
tirades]']

     Commentary on the objectives of Svoboda.

     A   V (13): Apr 16, 1896; C-3

1023   [N.N.]; "Nîskol'ko slov jako otpovîd' na statiju Svobodŷ: 'Hadky
po konvenciy Sojuza y Soedynenija" [Several words in answer
to the article in Svoboda: 'Reflections after the Convention
of the Sojuz and Soedynenie]

     A   V (28): Jul 30, 1896; C-4&5, L-4

1024   [N.N.]; "Otče, otpusty ym, ne vydjat bo čto tvorjat!" [Father,
forgive them, they know not what they do!]

     Commentary on Svoboda. Comparison of views held by the ARV
and Svoboda.

     A   V (29): Aug 6, 1896; C-2&3, L-2

1025   Ju.; "Nova russkaja hazeta" [New Ruthenian newspaper]

     Commentary on the appearance of the Pravoslavnŷj Russkij
Vîstnyk [New York].

     E   V (36): Sep 24, 1896; C-2&3, L-2&3

1026   Rev. Augustine Laurisin; "Krutarstvo" [Roguery]

     Differences between the ARV and Svoboda concerning the
reporting of religious-national issues.

     A   V (37): Oct 1, 1896; C-2

1027   [N.N.]; "Dijavol'skija yntryhy" [Diabolical intrigues]

     Commentary on Svoboda.

     A   V (41): Oct 29, 1896; C-2&3, L-2&3

1028   Nicholas Skazko; Jersey City, NJ, Oct 19, 1896

     Commentary on Svoboda and the ARV.

     L   V (41): Oct 29, 1896; C-3

1029   [N.N.]; "Ostanovymsja--ne dal'še!" [Let us stop--no further!]

     Controversy concerning Rev. Cornelius Laurisin, which began
a series of polemical exchanges between the ARV and Svoboda,
are explored in this two part series.

     Parts I-II   V (42-43): Nov 5-12, 1896; C-2&3,
                                       L-2&3

     A

1030   Nicholas Skazko; Jersey City, NJ, Nov 7, 1896

        Commentary on Svoboda.

        L   V (43): Nov 12, 1896; C-4&5, L-4&5

1031   [N.N.]; "O Kalandaru" [About the Almanac]

        Commentary on the G.C.U. yearly almanac.

        A   V (44): Nov 19, 1896; L-2

1032   J.B.; "Jak yz Savlov dîlajut sja Pavly" [How Sauls have become
        Pauls]

        Commentary on Svoboda's recent articles on church and religion.

        A   X (2): Jan 24, 1901; C-2, L-2

1033   X.Y.; "Čym sja hornec' natjahne, tŷm eho vsehda čuty!" [A pot will
        always smell of what is put into it!]

        Svoboda on topics of church and religion.

        A   X (3): Jan 31, 1901; C-3, L-2

1034   [N.N.]; "1892-17-ho marta-1901" [1892-March 17-1901]

        Commemorates the ninth anniversary of the ARV.

        A   X (9): Mar 14, 1901; C-4, L-4

1035   J.L.; "Krytyka na Krytyku" [Criticism of Criticism]

        Commentary on Svoboda's criticism of the G.C.U. Almanac.

        A   X (12): Apr 4, 1901; C-2&3, L-2&3

1036   [N.N.]; "Nova russka hazeta v Amerykî" [New Rusyn newspaper in
        America]

        Endorses new Galician-Rusyn publication, Pravda, published
        at 428 E 72 Street, New York City.

        A   XI (13): Apr 10, 1902; C-3

1037   Michael Cupik; McKeesport, PA; Jul 20, 1902

        Commentary on the supporters of the newspaper, Slovenski
        American.

        L   XI (26): Jul 24, 1902; C-2&3

1038   [N.N.]; "Naš Kalendar" [Our Almanac]

        1903 G.C.U. Almanac.

        A   XII (2): Jan 22, 1903; L-2

1039　[N.N.]; "Novaja Hazeta" [New Newspaper]

　　　　Clergy-edited newspaper, Cerkovnaja Nauka.

　　　　A　　　　　　　　　　　XII (9): Mar 12, 1903; C-2, L-2

1040　[N.N.]; "Sluchajme dobrŷch sovîtov, dobrŷch rad" [Let us hear
　　　　good counsel, good advice]

　　　　The ARV's importance as a Rusyn-American newspaper.

　　　　A　　　　　　　　　　　XII (43): Nov 19, 1903; C-4, L-4

1041　[N.N.]; "Naš Kalendar" [Our Almanac]

　　　　1904 G.C.U. Almanac.

　　　　A　　　　　　　　　　　XIII (3): Feb 4, 1904; C-2, L-2

1042　[N.N.]; "Den' 17-ho marta" [Day of March 17]

　　　　Commentary on the twelfth anniversary of the ARV.

　　　　A　　　　　　　　　　　XIII (9): Mar 17, 1904; C-2, L-2

1043　Redakcija; "Ot Redakciy" [From the Editor]

　　　　The mailing of 12,000 G.C.U. 1904 Almanacs.

　　　　O　　　　　　　　　　　XIII (10): Mar 24, 1904; C-4, L-4

1044　Redakcija; "Od Redakcii" [From the Editor]

　　　　Announces the transfer of the G.C.U.-ARV offices from New York
　　　　City to Pittsburgh, PA.

　　　　O　　　　　　　　　　　XIII (26): Aug 18, 1904; 2

1045　Žatkovich; "Otkrovennŷy slova dobrî zasluženoho pryznanija"
　　　　[Sincere expressions of a well deserved acknowledgement]

　　　　The G.C.U. annual almanac.

　　　　E　　　　　　　　　　　XV (6): Feb 22, 1906; 2, 3

1046　[N.N.]; "Šlebodny Orel perestal lîtaty" [Šlebodní Orel has ceased
　　　　publication]

　　　　Technical and editor/staff difficulties are cited as the
　　　　reasons for the discontinuation of this newspaper, printed in
　　　　east Slovak dialect.

　　　　A　　　　　　　　　　　XV (10): Mar 22, 1906; 2, 3

1047　Ž.; "Den' 17 ho Marta" [Day of March 17]

　　　　Commemorates the fourteenth anniversary of the ARV.

　　　　E　　　　　　　　　　　XV (10): Mar 22, 1906; 4, 5

1048   Redakcija; "Ot Yzdatel'stva <u>Amer. Russkoho Vîstnyka</u>" [From the
       publisher of the <u>Amerikansky Russky Viestnik</u>]

    a. Explains the reason for an abbreviated edition of issue 20.

    b. Beginning July 1, 1906 subscribers have the choice of
       receiving an all Cyrillic script version or a combined
       Cyrillic-Latin script edition of the <u>ARV</u>.

    O   XV (20): Jun 7, 1906; 1, 2

1049   Julius Csarnovich; "Zaslato. Otvît <u>Bratstvu</u> na eho očernenija
       brechny" [Answer to <u>Bratstvo</u> to its calumnies and falsehoods]
       Letter to the Editor.

       Commentary on the organ of the P.R.G.C.U., <u>Bratstvo</u>.

       A, L   XV (30): Aug 16, 1906; 2, 3

1050   Paul Ju. Žatkovich; "Nîskol'ko otkrovennŷch slov do počt. Bratstv
       y do každoho, kotoroho dîlo ynteressuet yly ynteressovaty
       možet" [A few words to the honorable lodges and to everyone
       who is interested or could be interested]

       Commentary on the future financial status of the <u>ARV</u> and
       G.C.U. print shop.

       E   XV (39): Oct 18, 1906; 2, 3

1051   Redakcija; "Ot Redakciy" [From the Editor]

       Requests each subscriber to the <u>ARV</u> to order either the
       Cyrillic or Latin script version of the newspaper.

       Req   XVI (1): Jan 17, 1907; C-4, L-4

1052   Paul J. Žatkovich; "Naš Kalendár" [Our Almanac]

       1907 G.C.U. Almanac.

       E   XVI (3): Jan 31, 1907; L-2

1053   J.K.; "Holos na predyslovie H-na P. Ju. Žatkovyča umîščenoe v
       Mîsjacoslovî 'Soedynenija Hr. Kat. Russkych Bratstv' na hod
       1907" [Commentary on the preface [by] Paul Ju. Zsatkovich
       which appears in the 1907 Almanac of the G.C.U.]

       A   XVI (10): Mar 21, 1907; C-4, L-4

1054   Rev. Orestes Zlockij; "Bezlyčnost' <u>Svobody</u>" [The impudence of
       <u>Svoboda</u>]

       Commentary on an article concerning the ARV in <u>Svoboda</u>, # 38.

       A   XVI (38): Oct 10, 1907; C-2&3, L-2&3

1055   Rev. Theophane A. Obushkevich; "Otkrŷtoe pys'mo k o. O. Zlockomu"
       [Open letter to Rev. O. Zlockij]

       Commentary on Rev. Zlockij's commentary on an article in
       Svoboda, #38.

       A   XVI (42): Nov 7, 1907; C-4, L-4

1056   Paul J. Žatkovich; "Naš Kalendar!" [Our Almanac!]

       1908 G.C.U. Almanac.

       E   XVII (3): Jan 30, 1908; L-4

1057   Rev. N. Stecovich; "Nîskol'ko slov o hazetî Svoboda" [A few words
       about the newspaper Svoboda]

       Commentary on the trouble Svoboda causes among American Greek
       Catholics with its provocative articles.

       A   XVII (20): Jun 18, 1908; C-4, L-4

1058   Alexander Horoschak, et al.; "Protest protyv tendencijnoj statiy
       Svobodŷ 'chto slidue' a vmîstî y otvît na siju" [Protest
       against the tendencious Svoboda article: 'Who's next' along
       with an answer to it]

       Commentary by the Perth Amboy, NJ church council to an article
       in Svoboda, #36, concerning the union of all Rusyn-Americans
       as Ukrainians.

       A   XVII (32): Sep 10, 1908; C-4&5, L-4

1059   P. Ju. Zsatkovich; "Terroryzacija protyv hl. redaktora orhanu
       'Soedynenija'--Amer. Russkoho Vîstnyka" [Terrorism against
       the editor-in-chief of the organ of the 'Soedynenie'--ARV]

       The verbal attacks by Ukrainian nationalists against
       Zsatkovich. Several letters documenting this attack included.

       E   XVII (36): Oct 8, 1908; C-4&5, L-2&3

1060   Redakcija; "Jakym skvernŷm oružiem vojuet Svoboda v uspîch 'Sojuza'
       y ukraynstva" [The nefarious weapon Svoboda uses fighting on
       behalf of the 'Sojuz' and Ukrainianism]

       The use of falsified letters to the editor of Svoboda, pur-
       portedly written by G.C.U. lodges dissatisfied with G.C.U.
       policy towards Bishop Ortynsky.

       E   XVIII (1): Jan 14, 1909; C-3, L-2

1061   Redakcija; "Naš Kalendar" [Our Almanac]

       1909 G.C.U. Almanac.

       E   XVIII (2): Jan 21, 1909; L-4

1062 [N.N.]; "Nova amerykansko-ukraynska hazeta" [A new American-
Ukrainian newspaper]

Clergy newspaper, Dušpastyr [New York] edited by Rev.
P. Ponjatyšyn.

A   XVIII (5): Feb 11, 1909; C-2&3, L-2

1063 G. Koleszar; Yonkers, NY

Commentary on Dušpastyr.

L   XVIII (38): Oct 7, 1909; C-3, L-2

1064 P. Ju. Ž.; "1892 - 17, marta - 1910" [March 17, 1892 - 1910]

Commentary on the eighteenth anniversary of the ARV.

E   XIX (10): Mar 17, 1910; C-4, L-4

1065 "Uhro-russkaja publyka protyv najnovîjšoj akciy uhorsko-ukraynsko-
rutenijanskych vitčikiv" [Uhro-Rusyn public against the
latest action of the Uhro-Ukrainian-Ruthenian clergy]

Series of letters to the editor commenting on articles in the
newspaper Rusin.

Parts I-IV: XIX (25-28): Jul 14-Aug 14, 1910;
                                                    C-2, L-2
L

1066 [N.N.]; "Jak sudjat druhiy hazety o The Ruthenian" [How other
newspapers judge Rusin]

Reprint of an article about Rusin and its editors taken from
Pravda [Olyphant, PA], # 27, July 21, 1910.

A   XIX (27): Jul 28, 1910; C-3, L-2

1067 [N.N.]; "Nîskol'ko otkrovennŷch slov o novoj ukraynsko-rutenijanskoj
hazetŷ The Ruthenian" [Several candid words about the new
Ukrainian-Ruthenian newspaper, Rusin]

Parts I-IV: XIX (29-32): Aug 11-Sep 1, 1910
A

1068 U.R.D.; "Farysejstvo, zaprodatel'stvo Hanulja & Ko. dorohoju svoj
ukraynsko-rutenijanskoj hazetky The Ruthenian" [Pharisaism
and betrayal of Hanulya and Co. through their Ukrainian-
Ruthenian newspaper, Rusin]

Parts I-V: XIX (33-37): Sep 8-Oct 6, 1910;
                                                    C-4, L-2,4

Part VI: XIX (39): Oct 20, 1910; L-2&3
A

1069   Nicholas Vančo, et al.; Bridgeport, CT; Sept 29, 1910

Commentary on <u>Rusin</u> editor, Rev. V. Gorzo.

L   XIX (38): Oct 13, 1910; C-3, L-3

1070   Michael Jurko; Cleveland, OH; Nov 10, 1910

"Skvernaja taja-to ukraynskaja polytyka y cîla ej banda"
[The filthiness of these Ukrainian politics and of all of
its gang]

Commentary on the Rusyn-Ukrainian polemics allegedly caused
by <u>Rusin</u>.

L   XIX (44): Nov 24, 1910; C-2&3, L-2&3

1071   Joseph Fecko; Gary, IN; Mar 30, 1911; Emil Sarady; Gary, IN;
April 4, 1911

"Zaslato" [Letter to the Editor]

Condemns a "false" letter to the editor in <u>Rusin</u> which has
caused considerable polemics among Rusyns in Gary.

L   XX (12): Apr 6, 1911; C-2&3, L-2&3

1072   O.; "Duchoborcŷ-Cerkovnoborcŷ" [Deniers of the spirit-deniers of
the church]

Commentary on Revs. Joseph P. Hanulya and Valentine Gorzo,
editors of <u>Rusin</u>.

A   XX (12): Apr 6, 1911; C-4&5, L-2

1073   O.; "Sluhy Chrystoviy" [Servants of Christ]

Commentary on the editorship of <u>Rusin</u>.

A   XX (17): May 18, 1911; C-2&3, L-2

1074   Rev. E. Kubek; "Pričiny bezuspîšnosti" [The reasons for lack of
success]

Commentary on <u>Rusin</u> under the editorship of Rev. Hanulya.

Parts I-V: XX (23-27): Jul 6-Aug 3, 1911;
                                                    C-4, L-4

Part VI: "O. Hanulja y: no $$-dollariki" [Rev. Hanulya and
dollars]

                        XX (29): Aug 17, 1911; C-4, L-4

Part VII: "Ne tak Hospoda, nît! No objektivno i čestno"
[Not so gentlemen, no! But objectively and honestly]

                        XX (30): Aug 24, 1911; C-4&5, L-4

A

1075 John Borč; Mingo Junction, OH

    Commentary on Rusin.

    L   XX (25): Jul 20, 1911; C-3, L-3

1076 [N.N.]; "Novŷj patent. Vynajšly O. Horzov y O. Hanulja, manadžer y redaktor Rutenijana" [A new patent. Inventors Revs. Gorzo and Hanulya, manager and editor of Rusin]

    Commentary on Rusin and its editors.

    A   XX (47): Dec 21, 1911; C-4&5, L-4

1077 [N.N.]; "Lyteratura" [Literature]

    Commentary on the Rusyn-Slovak press in America. Lists prominent fraternal organizations and their publications.

    A   XXI (2): Jan 25, 1912; C-4&5, L-4

1078 Theodore Glagola; "Novoe Čudo" [New miracle]

    Commentary on editors of Rusin, Revs. Hanulya and Gorzo.

    A   XXI (11): Mar 28, 1912; C-4&5, L-2

1079 N.F. Mamroch; Dorchester, VA; May 13, 1912

    "Otkaz Ruthenian-ovy" [Reply to the Rusin]

    Commentary on Rusin and its editor, Rev. J. Hanulya.

    L   XXI (13): Apr 18, 1912; C-3

1080 V.D.; "Nîskol'ko otkrovennŷch slov o hazetî Rutenijan y ob eho redaktorî" [Several frank words about the newspaper, Rusin, and about its editor]

    A   XXI (31): Aug 29, 1912; C-2&3, L-2

1081 Paul J. Zsatkovich; "Ot Redakciy" [From the Editor]

    The 1913 G.C.U. Almanac.

    E   XXI (39): Oct 24, 1912; C-4, L-4

1082 Basil Ducar; "Otpovid' čysto O. Hanulî, redaktoru Ruteniana" [A frank response to Rev. Hanulya, editor of Rusin]

    Commentary on Rusin's position concerning the nationality issue.

    A   XXI (41): Nov 7, 1912; C-2, L-2

1083 Basil Ducar; "Rutenijan-u, eho redaktoru y eho korrespondentu v al'bom" [To Rusin, its editor and its correspondent to their diary]

    Commentary on Rusin and its policies.

    A   XXII (8): Mar 6, 1913; C-2&3, L-2

1084   [N.N.]; "Voprosŷ do tîch, kotorŷch možet sie kasatysja, y mohut
       daty ob"ektyvnoj otpovîdy" [Questions to those whom this
       may concern and who can give objective answers]

       Commentary on Rusin.

       A   XXII (11): Mar 27, 1913; C-2, L-2

1085   Redakcija; "Ot Redakciy Orhana 'Soedynenija'" [From the editor
       of the organ of the 'Soedynenie']

       Concerning the change in procedures for submitting material
       for publication by the ARV print shop.

       O   XXII (26): Jul 17, 1913; C-4, L-4

1086   P. J. Ž.; "1892 - 17-ho marta - 1914" [March 17, 1892 - 1914]

       Commentary on the twenty-second anniversary of the ARV.

       E   XXIII (10): Mar 19, 1914; C-4

1087   Paul J. Zsatkovich; "Proščal'noe slovo" [Farewell word]

       Parting editorial by ARV editor-in-chief after twenty-two
       years of service to the G.C.U.

       E   XXIII (22): Jun 25, 1914; C-4&5

1088   Michael J. Hanchin; "Ot Redakciy" [From the Editor]

       First editorial of ARV's new editor-in-chief. Reiterates the
       important role of the G.C.U. in preserving Rusyn culture in
       America.

       E   XXIII (23): Jul 2, 1914; C-4&5

1089   Joseph Palkabla; Donora, PA

       Commentary on former ARV editor-in-chief, Paul J. Zsatkovich.

       L   XXIII (26): Jul 23, 1914; C-3

1090   Andrew Hric; Duquesne, PA

       a. Commentary on the new editor-in-chief, Michael J. Hanchin.
       b. The plight of war orphans in Maramaroš County, Hungary.

       L   XXIII (26): Jul 23, 1914; C-3

1091   [N.N.]; "Ukrayncam ne ljubytsja" [Ukrainians don't like it]

       ARV viewpoint on articles in recent editions of Svoboda on
       what constitutes the Ukrainian nation.

       E   XXIII (29): Aug 13, 1914; C-4

1092   [N.N.]; "<u>A.R. Vîstnyk</u> vyključen yz staroho kraja?" [Has the <u>ARV</u> been banned in the old country?]

Concerning the rumors, reported in <u>Rusin</u>, that the <u>ARV</u> has been banned by the Hungarian Government.

A   XXIII (46): Dec 10, 1914; C-4

1093   [N.N.]; "Vyključenŷy hazetŷ" [Banned newspapers]

Commentary on the article in <u>Rusin</u>, # 49, that the <u>ARV</u> has been banned in Hungary.

A   XXIII (46): Dec 10, 1914; C-5

Chapter 2

Greek Catholic Union

2001   Basil Havrillo & Simon Kvasnyak; De Lancey, PA, Jan 6, 1894.

Gratitude extended to G.C.U. for help received in obtaining
Rev. J. Szabov as pastor of the De Lancey parish.

L   III (3): Jan 16, 1894; C-3, L-13

2002   [N.N.]; "Vŷselenie Halycyskych y Uhorskych Rusynov v Ameryku y ych
sorhanizovanie" [The immigration of Galician and Uhro-Rusyns
to America and their organization]

Part V: The individuals and societies responsible for
establishing churches and founding the G.C.U. in America.

A   III (4): Jan 23, 1894; C-2, L-13

2003   [N.N.]; "Protokol, zasîdanija čynovnykov 'Soedynenija Hr. kat.
Russk. Bratstv' proyschodyvšoho v Skrenton, Pa. 30-ho januara
1894" [Minutes of the G.C.U. officers' meeting in Scranton,
PA, January 30, 1894]

Part I: III (6): Feb 6, 1894; C-4&5, L-10

Part II: III (7): Feb 20, 1894; C-4, L-9

O

2004   [N.N.]; "A jak sudjat doma v starom kraju o nas y o našom
'Soedyneniju'" [How those at home in the old country view us
and our 'Soedynenie']

A   III (11): Mar 20, 1894; C-2&3

2005   Ju.; "Rešytel'nyi slova v spravî relihijno-narodnoho zabezpečenija
Amerykanskoj Rusy" [Decisive words on the matter of preserving
the religious-national heritage of American-Rusyns]

Part IV: "Ob orhanyzacijach y napravlenijach voobšče"
          [About organizations and their trends, in general]

                             III (15): Apr 17, 1894; C-2, L-13

Part V: "O Soedyneniju Hr. kat. Russkych Bratstv"
          [About the G.C.U.]

                             III (16): Apr 29, 1894; C-4&5, L-13

E

2006   Rev. Cornelius Laurisin; "Ot Komyteta rjadjaščoho usporjadženiem
Hol. Konvenciy" [From the organizing committee of the General
Convention]

Instructions and directions for delegates to the second G.C.U.
General Convention.

O   III (19): May 22, 1894; C-1

2007   [N.N.]; "Trykratnoe slava y ščyroserdečnŷj pryvît Hosp. Delehatam
        'Vtoroj Holovnoj Konvenciy Soedyn. Hr. kat. Rus. Bratstv'!"
        [Thrice glory and sincere greetings to the honorable delegates
        to the second General Convention of the G.C.U.!]

        A   III (19): May 22, 1894; C-1, L-9

2008   Cato.; "Perehljad Sobŷtij pred 'Holovnoju Konvencieju'" [Preview
        of events prior to the convocation of the General Convention]

        A   III (19): May 22, 1894; C-2&3, L-13

2009   [N.N.]; "Toržestvo vtoroj Holovnoj Konvenciy "Soedynenija Hr. kat.
        Russk. Bratstv'" [Celebration of the second General Convention
        of the G.C.U.]

        A, P   III (20): Jun 12, 1894; C-2&3, L-9&10

2010   John A. Smith, et al.; "Vsîm Bratstvam naležaščym do 'Soedynenija'!
        Počtennŷy y dorohiy brat'ja!" [To all lodges belonging to the
        'Soedynenie'! Dear, Honorable brethren!]

        Resolutions of the G.C.U. second General Convention.

        O   III (20): Jun 12, 1894; C-4, L-13

2011   Ju.; "Yspŷtanija s vtoroj Hol. Konvenciy našoho 'Soedynenija'"
        [Experience of the second General Convention of our
        'Soedynenie']

        E   III (21): Jun 19, 1894; C-2, L-13

2012   [N.N.]; "Ot holovnoho upravytel'stva Soedynenija Hreko. kat.
        Russkych Bratstv 'Cyrkular' Vsîm Poč̌t. Bratstvam naležaščym
        do 'Soedynenija'" [From the Supreme administration of the
        G.C.U. 'a circular' to all honorable members belonging to the
        'Soedynenie']

        a. George Wretyak has been appointed Supreme Treasurer.
        b. Warns lodge members to beware of trouble-causing Galicians.

        O   III (25): Jul 17, 1894; C-4, L-13

2013   Ju.; "Tolkovanija v spravach sumîstnych cerkovno-narodnŷch našych
        ynteressov" [Interpretations of our common religious-national
        interests]

        Part IX: G.C.U.: its function in the Rusyn-American immigrant
        community.

        E   III (30): Sep 4, 1894; C-2

2014   [N.N.]; "Slovo ot Redakciy" [Editorial]

        Publication of the protocol and proceedings of the G.C.U.
        second General Convention.

        E   III (32): Sep 20, 1894; C-4

2015 John Smith, et al.; "Trymîsjačnŷj rachunok 'Soedynenija Hr. kat.
Russkych Bratstv' ot 1-ho Junija do 1-ho Sept., 1894"
[Tri-monthly account of the G.C.U. from June 1 to September 1,
1894]

R   III (34): Oct 4, 1894; C-4, L-9

2016 A--O.; "Rosčet (Rachunok) 'Soed. Hr. kat. Rus. Bratstv'"
[Account of the G.C.U.]

From June 1, 1893 to June 1, 1894.

R   III (35): Oct 11, 1894; C-2, L-13

2017 [N.N.]; "Prazdnyk sv. Otca Našeho 'Nykolaja', patrona 'Soed. Hr. kat.
Russkych Bratstv', slîdovatel'no-že 'Amerykanskoj Rusy'!'"
[Feastday of our Holy Father Nicholas, patron of the G.C.U.,
and thus patron of American-Rusyns!]

A   III (44): Dec 13, 1894; C-1&4, L-9&10

2018 [N.N.]; "Rozsčet 'Soedynenija Hreko. kat. Russkych Bratstv' ot 1-ho
Sept. do 1-ho Decem., 1894" [Accounts of the G.C.U. from
September 1 to December 1, 1894]

R   III (44): Dec 13, 1894; C-4, L-10

2019 [N.N.]; "Vpečatlinija yz slučaja toržestvennaho prazdnovanija
prazdnyka Sv. Otca Nykolaja, patrona Soedynenija Hreko kat.
Russkych Bratstv" [Impressions on the occasion of the
glorious celebration of the feast day of Saint Nicholas,
patron of the G.C.U.]

A   III (45): Dec 20, 1894; C-2&3, L-13

2020 Ju.; "Vrednŷy y nedozrîlŷy mnînija y ubîždenija našeho naroda k
Bratstvam y Orhanyzaciy" [The harmful and immature opinions
and convictions of our people with regard to the lodges and
the Organization]

Part I: "Cîvylyzacija y Rusynŷ." [Civilization and the Rusyns]

IV (5): Feb 14, 1895; C-3, L-3&4

Part II: "Čto-že est' pryčynoju tomu mŷ Rusynŷ ne možem
sorhanyzovatys' podobno zdîšným obrazovanným narodnostjam"
[Why can't we Rusyns organize ourselves like other educated
peoples here]

E   IV (6): Feb 21, 1895; C-2&3, L 1

2021 Ju.; "Nedostatok narodnaho čuvstvija, Separatyzm y Korystoljubie,
jako prepjatstvija polnomu y uspîšnomu sorhanyzovaniju našych
Rusynov" [A lack of national consciousness, separatism and
self-interests are the obstacles preventing the complete and
successful organization of Rusyns]

E   IV (7): Feb 28, 1895; C-2, L-3

2022   Ju.; "Ešče o prepjatstvijach polnoho y uspišnoho sorhanyzovanija
       našych Rusynov" [More on the obstacles preventing the com-
       plete and successful organization of Rusyns]

       E   IV (8): Mar 7, 1895; C-2&3, L-3&4

2023   [N.N.]; "Rozsčet, 'Soedynenija Hreko. Kat. Russkych Bratstv' ot
       1-ho Decembra, 1894 do 1-ho Marta, 1895" [Accounts of the
       G.C.U. from December 1, 1894 to March 1, 1895]

       R   IV (9): Mar 14, 1895; C-4, L-1

2024   [N.N.]; "Všîm Bratstvam naležaščym do 'Soedynenija' [To all
       Lodges belonging to the 'Soedynenie']

       The creation of a special fund to provide a financial grant
       from the G.C.U. for the establishment of future Greek
       Catholic Churches in America.

       O   IV (10): Mar 21, 1895; C-4, L-1

2025   Ju.; "Ob uslovijach odnoj chorošoj Orhanyzaciy" [Several words
       on the conditions of a fine Organization]

       Information on the status of the G.C.U.

       E   IV (13): Apr 14, 1895; C-2,6

2026   [N.N.]; "Všîm Počt. Čynovnykam 'Soedynenija' y Všeč. Otcam
       Svjaščennykam" [To all honorable officers of the 'Soedynenie'
       and all honorable fathers]

       The G.C.U. supreme officers meeting held in Hazleton, PA,
       June 11, 1895.

       O   IV (19): May 30, 1895; C-4, L-4

2027   Rev. Corn. Laurisin; "Uvîdomlenie Holovnaho Sekretarja 'Soedynenija
       Hreko Kat. Russkych Bratstv' o ročnom dîystvovaniy y položeniy
       ětoj Orhanyzaciy, takže o zamîčanija dostojných rasporjaženijach
       y pryključenijach. Otčytano podčas čynovnyčeskaho zasîdanija,
       otbŷvšahosja 11-ho junija 1895 v Hazleton, Pa. Vŷsokopočtennoe
       zasîdanie! Všečestnîjšiy Otcŷ! Vysokopočtennŷy Čynovnyky!"
       [Information from the chief secretary of the G.C.U. about the
       annual operation and situation of this organization, also
       about the noteworthy directives and events. This was read
       at the supreme officers' conference held on June 11, 1895 in
       Hazleton, PA. Honorable assembly! Honorable fathers!
       Honorable officers!]

       Part I: IV (21&22): Jun 20, 1895; C-9&10,
                                                            L-9&10

       Part II: IV (23): Jun 27, 1895; C-4&5, L-4
       O

2028   Anthony Kostik, et al.; "Rosčet (Rachunok) 'Soedynenija Hreko kat.
        Russkych Bratstv' ot 1-ho Junija, 1894 do 1-ho Junija, 1895"
        [Accounts of the G.C.U. from June 1, 1894 to June 1, 1895]

        R   IV (21&22): Jun 20, 1895; C-10, L-10

2029   [N.N.]; "Vpečatlînija yz povoda čynovnyčeskaho zasîdanija otbŷvšahosja
        11-ho junija 1895, v Hazleton, Pa." [Impressions of the [supreme]
        officers' meeting held on June 11, 1895 in Hazleton, PA]

        A   IV (21&22): Jun 20, 1895; C-11, L-10

2030   Rev. John I. Sabo; "Protokol, čynovnyčeskaho zasîdanija 'Soedynenija
        Hr. kat. Russkych Bratstv' poderžaemoho dnja 11-ho junija 1895
        v Hazleton, Pa." [Minutes of the G.C.U. [supreme] officers'
        conference held on June 11, 1895 in Hazleton, PA]

        O   IV (23): Jun 27, 1895; C-5, L-4&5

2031   Ju.; "Mnînija ob Orhanyzacijach y ob ych obezpečeniy" [Thoughts about
        organizations and insuring their existence]

        A six part series on the G.C.U. and other insurance-fraternal
        organizations.

        Part I: IV (28): Aug 1, 1895; C-2, L-2

        Part II: IV (29): Aug 8, 1895; C-2, L-2

        Part III: "Smutnŷy poslîdstvija v slučaî raspadenija odnoj
        Orhanyzaciy" [Sad consequences in the case of the disintegra-
        tion of an Organization]

                        IV (31): Aug 22, 1895; C-2, L-2

        Part IV: "Sredstva obezpečajuščiy" [Preventive Measures]

                        IV (32): Aug 29, 1895; C-2, L-2

        Part IV (cont.): "Rasuždenija y mnînija o žertvoljubiy"
        [Judgements and opinions about self-sacrifice]

                        IV (33): Sep 5, 1895; C-2, L-2

        Part V: "Postojannŷj Raspoložytel'nŷj Fond" [Permanent
        Available Fund]

                        IV (34): Sep 12, 1895; C-2, L-2

        Part V (cont.): "Jak možno najskorše y najlehčajše ymîty nam
        'Post. Rasp. Fund'?" [How can we most quickly and easily have
        a 'Permanent Available Fund'?]

                        IV (35): Sep 19, 1895; C-2, L-2

        Part V (cont.): "Tolkvanija uslovij" [Interpretation of
        conditions]

                        IV (36): Sep 26, 1895; C-2, L-2

        Part VI: "Ob admynystraciy 'Post. Rasp. Funda'" [On the
        administration of the 'Permanent Available Fund']

        E   IV (38): Oct 10, 1895; C-2

2032   [N.N.]; "Ne reklama! Ne humbuh! Ne obman! No ščyroe y staratel'noe uvîdomlenie y napomynanie do vsîch čestnych našych Hr. Kat. Russkych Brat'ev žyvuščych v Amerykî!" [Not an advertisement! No humbug! Not a hoax! But sincere and careful information, reminder to all our honorable Greek Catholic Rusyn brethren, who are living in America!]

G.C.U. information on insurance benefits and claims.

A   IV (30): Aug 15, 1895; C-2&3, L-2&3

2033   [N.N.]; "Rozsčet, 'Soedynenija Hreko kat. Russkych Bratstv' ot 1-ho Junija do 1-ho Septembra, 1895" [Accounts of the G.C.U. from June 1 to September 1, 1895]

R   IV (36): Sep 26, 1895; C-4, L-4

2034   Basil Zdyňak; St. Louis, MO; Oct 16, 1895

Advocates the purchase of land by G.C.U. for Rusyn homesteads, churches and schools.

L   IV (40): Oct 25, 1895; C-2&3, L-2&3

2035   [N.N.]; "Zabotlyvost' 'Soedynenija' ob ěmyhrantnom zavedeniy (domî) y o narodnom bankî" [The Soedynenie's concern for the emigrant institution (house) and the national bank]

Two G.C.U. projects: Emigrant institution and a Rusyn national bank.

A   IV (41): Oct 31, 1895; C-2&3, L-2

2036   [N.N.]; "Soveršylos'! Nad sud'boj Russkoho ěmyhrantoho doma y Russko--narodnoho banka rîšeno. Dîjstvytel'nŷj rezul'tat pochval'noho dîjstvovanija 'Soedynenija Hr. kat. Russkych Bratstv' v spravî vozvŷšenija narodnoj česty y dokazanija vyščych humanystyčeskych čuvstv. Pervŷy userdnŷy žertvŷ, dannŷy na pokupku sobstvennoho doma dlja ěmyhrantnoho zavedenija" [Accomplishment! The fate of the Rusyn emigration institution and Rusyn-national bank has been decided. Actual result of the laudable action of the G.C.U. in the realm of lifting up national honor and proving higher humanitarian motives. The first zealous donations have been given for the purchasing of our own building for the emigration institution]

A   IV (46): Dec 4, 1895; C-2, L-2

2037   [N.N.]; "Den' sv. Otca Našeho Nykolaja, Patrona 'Soedynenija Hreko kat. Russkych Bratstv'" [Day of our Holy Father Nicholas, Patron of G.C.U.]

Information on the growth of the G.C.U. and churches during the previous year.

A   IV (48): Dec 19, 1895; C-1&2, L-1&2

2038   [N.N.]; "Trymîsjačnŷj rozčet (rachunok) 'Soedynenija Hreko kat. Russkych Bratstv.' Ot 1-ho Sept. do 1-ho Decembra, 1895" [Tri-monthly accounting of the G.C.U. from September 1 to December 1, 1895]

R   IV (49): Dec 26, 1895; C-4, L-4

2039   [N.N.]; "Russkij Èmyhrantnŷj Dom y Russko Narodnŷj Bank v Nju Iorkî" [Rusyn emigration house and Rusyn National Bank in New York City]

A   V (6): Feb 20, 1896; C-2, L-2

2040   Rev. Cornelius Laurisin; Shenandoah, PA; Feb 12, 1896

A court judgment against a former G.C.U. lodge in Shamokin, PA for $678.00 in back dues.

L   V (6): Feb 20, 1896; C-5, L-4&5

2041   John Smith; "Otpovedez New Yorkskim Slovakam gr. kat. vierovyznania" [Answer to the New York Slovak Greek Catholic faithful]

Clarifies the G.C.U. position regarding the emigration house and national bank in answer to a letter to the editor in Slovenski Novini [New York], # 586.

A   V (7): Mar 5, 1896; L-2&3

2042   [N.N.]; "Nebud'me ravnodušnŷmy v vospomoščestvovaniy bîdnŷch cerkvej" [Let us not be indifferent towards the relief of poor churches]

G.C.U. favors establishment of a special fund for relief-support of financially troubled churches.

A   V (9): Mar 19, 1896; C-3, L-2&3

2043   John Smith; "Otpovîd' na stat'ju, 'Pryčynok do ystoriy našoj zrîlosty,' — se ystorija russkoho Èm. Domu v Nju Yorku — pojavyvšujusja v 10-om sehoročnom numerî hazetŷ Svoboda" [Answer to the article, "On the History of our Maturity," that is, the history of the Rusyn emigration house in New York City, which appeared in the 10th issue of the current edition of Svoboda]

A   IV (10): Mar 26, 1896; C-4&5

2044   [N.N.]; "Pred hlavnoju Konvencieju 'Soedynenija'" [Prior to the general Convention of the 'Soedynenie']

Third general G.C.U. Convention.

A   V (11): Apr 2, 1896; C-2, L-2

2045   Paul Jurievich Žatkovich; "Predpoložennŷ (proektovanŷ) peremînŷ v hlavnŷch statutach 'Soedynenija Hr. kat. Russkych Bratstv'" [Projected changes in the main statutes of the G.C.U.]

Parts I-V: V (14-18): Apr 23-May 21, 1896

E

2046 [N.N.]; "Trykratnoe Slava y ščyroserdečnyj pryvît vsečestnîjšym
otcam y počt. hosp. delehatam III hlavnoj konvenciy
'Soedynenija Hr. kat. Russkych Bratstv', otbŷvajuščojsja v
Nju Yorkî 26, 27 y 28-ho maja 1896" [Thrice glory and
sincere greetings to reverend fathers and delegates to the
Third General Convention of the G.C.U. taking place in New
York City on May 26, 27, and 28, 1896]

A   V (18&19): May 21, 1896; C-1, L-1

2047 [N.N.]; "Hlavnoe Sobranie (Konvencija)" [General Meeting
(Convention)]

Description of events during the third general convention of
the G.C.U. in New York City, May 26-28, 1896.

A   V (20): Jun 4, 1896; C-2, L-2

2048 [N.N.]; "Ot holovnoho upravytel'stva Vsîm Počtennŷm Bratstvam
naležaščym do 'Soedynenija'!" [From the supreme administration to all honorable lodges belonging to the 'Soedynenie'!]

Resolutions adopted at the third general convention of the
G.C.U. in New York City, May 26-28, 1896.

O   V (23): Jun 25, 1896; C-4, L-4

2049 [N.N.]; "Nedostatok pravoj syly, ènerhiy y postojannosty u našych
ljudej v dîlach orhanyzacijnŷch" [Our peoples' inadequate
strength, energy and constancy in the affairs of the organi-
zation]

Part I: V (31): Aug 20, 1896; C-2, L-2

Part IV: "Pervŷy časŷ prozjabanija narodnaho našeho razvytija"
[The first times of stagnation of our people's development]

Beginnings of the G.C.U. and how the organization helped change
the apathy of the first Rusyn immigrants in America toward
their nationality heritage.

A   V (35): Sep 17, 1896; C-2, L-2

2050 [N.N.]; "Žertvŷ bezzabotlyvosty (bajdužnosty)" [Victims of indif-
ference]

Rusyns who will not join the G.C.U.

A   V (31): Aug 20, 1896; C-2&3, L-2&3

2051 Rev. Augustine Laurisin; "Konkurencija" [Competition]

G.C.U.: the "best" fraternal organization for all Rusyn-
Americans.

A   V (33): Sep 3, 1896; C-2, L-2

2052   Paul Jurievich Žatkovich; "Objasnenie" [An Explanation]

Official account (in opposition to a report in Svoboda) of
G.C.U. supreme secretary, Rev. Cornelius Laurisin's alleged
abuse of authority during G.C.U. third general convention.

E   V (33): Sep 3, 1896; C-4&5, L-5

2053   John Smith; "Ot Hlav. Upravytel'stva Soedynenija Hreko Kat. Russk.
Bratstv. Vo vnymanie vsîm počtennŷm bratstvam naležavšym do
'Soedynenija'! Počtennomu Bratstvu Sv. Petra y Pavla, čyslo
v Soed. 14 v Pytsburh, Pa." [From the Supreme Administration
of the G.C.U. Attention all honorable lodges which belong to
the 'Soedynenie'! To honorable lodge #14, Saints Peter & Paul
in Pittsburgh, PA]

Commentary on those who rebel against the G.C.U. hierarchy and
policies, starting rival fraternal organizations and creating
a situation of confusion among Rusyn immigrants in America.

O   V (34): Sep 10, 1896; C-2, L-2&3

2054   Rev. Augustine Laurisin; "Otpovîd' na 'Otverte pys'mo' Rev.
I. Konstankevyča, soobščennoe v 38-om numerî Svobodŷ"
[Answer to the 'open letter' by Rev. J. Konstankevič, pub-
lished in issue #38 of Svoboda]

The differences between the G.C.U. and R.N.U.

A   V (36): Sep 24, 1896; C-2, L-2

2055   J. A. [Žinčak] Smith; "Ot Hlavnaho Predsîdatelja Soedynenija
hr. kat. Russkych Bratstv. Vsîm počtennŷm Bratstvam naležaščym do 'Soedynenija'!" [From the Supreme President of
G.C.U. to all honorable lodges belonging to the 'Soedynenie'!]

Account of financial aid to the Wilkes Barre, PA, parish.

O   V (36): Sep 24, 1896; C-4, L-4

2056   Rev. Alexander Dzubay; "Ot Predsîd. Hlavn. Nadz. Komysiy
'Soedynenija', otvît na cylkuljar O. K. Lavryšyna [From the
President of the Supreme Overseeing Commission of the
'Soedynenie', answer to Rev. C. Laurisin's circular]

The controversy caused by Rev. Cornelius Laurisin's circular
during the third general G.C.U. convention.

O   V (38): Oct 8, 1896; C-2&3, L-2&3

2057   Rev. Theodore Damjanovics; "Napominatelné slova jednoho z naš'ych
horlivych duchovnikov" [Admonishing words from one of our
zealous priests]

The scandal, polemics and protests stemming from controversy
that occurred during the third general G.C.U. convention involving G.C.U. supreme secretary, Rev. Cornelius Laurisin.

A   V (39): Oct 15, 1896; L-2&3

2058   [N.N.]; "Proces 'Soedynenija' s Šamokynskym Bratstvom Sv. Kyrylla
       y Metodija" [Lawsuit of the 'Soedynenie' with Shamokin, PA,
       lodge of Saints Cyril and Methodius]

       Chronicles the legal battle to obtain back dues from the
       Shamokin, PA lodge, which seceeded from the G.C.U. on May 7,
       1894 to form a new fraternal organization, Rusyn National
       Union.

       A   V (40): Oct 22, 1896; C-2

2059   John Olšavski; Mahanoy City, PA; Nov 1, 1896

       "Publičnoe pys'mo do brat'ev našych hr. kat. Rusynov v
       Centralia, Pa." [Public letter to the Greek Catholic Rusyn
       in Centralia, PA]

       A Rusyn's opinion concerning the polemics between the G.C.U.
       and the R.N.U.

       L   V (42): Nov 5, 1896; C-4&5, L-4&5

2060   John Duda, et al.; Centralia, PA; Nov 3, 1896

       The polemics between the G.C.U. and the R.N.U.

       L   V (43): Nov 12, 1896; C-5, L-5

2061   [N.N.]; "Čynovnyčeskoe Zasîdanie, 'Soedynenija'" [(Supreme)
       officers' meeting of the 'Soedynenie']

       Meeting on December 8, 1896 at 1:00 p.m. in Trenton, NJ.

       A   V (46): Dec 3, 1896; C-2, L-2

2062   [N.N.]; "Mnoho nam ešče dîlaty" [There is still much for us to do]

       Outlines the problems of organizing Rusyn-Americans in the
       G.C.U.

       A   V (46): Dec 3, 1896; C-2, L-2

2063   [N.N.]; "Uradnicka schudza 'Sojedinenija'" [Supreme officers'
       meeting of the 'Sojedinenie']

       Meeting on December 8-9, 1896 in Trenton, NJ.

       A   V (48): Dec 17, 1896; L-2

2064   [N.N.]; "Prazdnovanija Prazdnyka Sv. Otca Nykolaja Patrona
       'Soedynenija'" [Celebration of the feastday of Holy Father
       Nicholas, Patron of the G.C.U.]

       Information on the annual growth of the lodges and churches.

       A   V (50): Jan 6, 1897; C-2, L-2

2065 [N.N.]; "XX Stolîtie" [Twentieth Century]

Past achievements and future goals of the G.C.U.

A   X (1): Jan 17, 1901; C-4, L-4

2066 [N.N.]; "Nužnoe dlja našych Bratstv" [Necessary for our Lodges]

Protecting the G.C.U. and its lodges from the danger of bankruptcy.

A   X (3): Jan 31, 1901; C-2&3, L-2

2067 [N.N.]; "Koe-čto ob Orhanyzacijach a o našej osobenno (smotry stat'ju v nrî 46 sej hazetŷ myn. hoda)" [A few words about organizations and about ours particularly (see the article in issue 46 of last year's newspaper [ARV])]

Part I: X (5): Feb 14, 1901; C-4, L-4

Part II: X (10): Mar 21, 1901; C-4, L-4

A

2068 Rev. D. Polivka; "De-ščo o Kanadî, myssijach, myssionarach ta y otverta vodpovîd' do radykalov!" [A few words about Canada, missions and missionaries there and a frank answer to radicals!]

Commentary on the R.N.U.'s attempt to organize Rusyn-Canadians.

Parts I-II: X (9-10): Mar 14-21, 1901; C-4, L-4

A

2069 Nikolaj; "Skromnŷja prymîčanija na stat'ju 'Koe-čto ob orhanyzacijach voobšče a o našej osobenno'" [Frank comments on the article 'A few words about organizations and about ours particularly']

A   X (12): Apr 4, 1901; C-4, L-4

2070 P.; "Jubylejnoe toržestvo odnoho našeho Bratstva" [Anniversary celebration of one of our lodges]

10th year anniversary of Brooklyn, NY lodge #1.

A   X (15): May 2, 1901; C-2&3, L-2

2071 [N.N.]; "Konvencija 'Narodnoho Slov. Spolku'" [National Slovak Union Convention]

Convention in Philadelphia, PA, June 3-8, 1901.

A   X (21): Jun 13, 1901, C-4, L-4

2072 [N.N.]; "Ročnoe Čynovnyčeskoe Sobranie 'Soedynenija'" [Annual (Supreme) Officers' Meeting of the 'Soedynenie']

Meeting in Buffalo, NY, June 25-26, 1901.

Part I: X (22): Jun 20, 1901; C-4, L-4
Part II: X (23): Jul 4, 1901; C-4, L-4

A

2073   [N.N.]; "Bol'še duchovnykov buntuet protyv 'Soedynenija'" [More
           clergy are instigating against the 'Soedynenie']

           Why many of the Greek Catholic clergy, including the apos-
           tolic visitor, are against the G.C.U. ARV charges that the
           anti-G.C.U. sentiment is the result of a conspiracy begun
           by the editors of Slovenski American.

           A   XI (23&24): Jul 10, 1902; C-1&2

2074   Rev. Alexis Holosnyay; "Protokol ročnaho Čynovnyčeskaho zasîdanija
           'Soedynenija' Hr. Kat. Russkych Bratstv otbŷvšahosja v Bufalo,
           N. Io. dnja 25-ho y 26-ho jun'ja 1901" [Minutes of the annual
           (Supreme) officers' meeting of the G.C.U. in Buffalo, NY June
           25-26, 1901]

           Part I: X (23): Jul 4, 1901; C-2&3, L-2&3

           Parts II-III: X (25-26): Jul 18-25, 1901; C-2, L-2

           O

2075   I.S. Leščišin; Sharon, PA; Jul 1, 1901

           The G.C.U. and future of Rusyns in America.

           L   X (25): Jul 18, 1901; C-3, L-3

2076   [N.N.]; "Naša Orhanyzacija y zapadnŷe Štaty" [Our organization and
           the western states]

           The growth of the G.C.U.

           A   X (27): Aug 1, 1901; C-2, L-2

2077   Redakcija; "V blahosklonnoe vnymanie vsîm brat'jam prynadležavšym
           do 'Soedynenija', hlavnîe že počt. urjadnykam Bratstv"
           [To favorable attention to all brothers belonging to the
           'Soedynenie' particularly to all honorable officers]

           The change in procedure in notifying the editor's office of
           address changes and the mailing of the ARV to members.

           O   X (27): Aug 1, 1901; C-4, L-4

2078   [N.N.]; "Assekuracija robotnykov" [Insurance of workers]

           Discussion of worker life and liability insurance.

           A   X (29): Aug 15, 1901; C-4, L-4

2079   [N.N.]; "Nîskol'ko slov o svîtskom blahosostojaniy" [A few words
           about temporal well-being]

           Why all Rusyn-Americans should join and support the G.C.U.

           A   X (32): Sep 5, 1901; C-2&3

2080 Basil Miklusčak; Duquesne, PA; Sep 2, 1901

      A new women's G.C.U. lodge.

      L   X (33): Sep 12, 1901; C-3, L-3

2081 [N.N.]; "Anarchysm y Radykalŷ" [Anarchy and Radicals]

      Condems the R.N.U. as a "radical" organization.

      A   X (34): Sep 19, 1901; C-2&3, L-2

2082 [N.N.]; "Teoretyčnŷ Anarchystŷ" [Theoretical Anarchists]

      Condems the R.N.U. as a radical organization.

      A   X (35): Sep 26, 1901; C-2, L-2

2083 [N.N.]; "Neprošenoe opekunstvo" [Uninvited guardianship]

      Involvement of other ethnic organizations and newspapers (listed) in Rusyn-American affairs.

      A   X (35): Sep 26, 1901; C-4, L-4

2084 Michael Juhas; "Ot Hlavnoho Predsîdatel'stva 'Soedynenija Hr. kat. Russk. Bratstv'" [From the supreme president of G.C.U.]

      a. Lodge #178 in Hawk Run, PA will be suspended unless delinquent dues are sent to G.C.U. main office.

      b. All subscribers to ARV are required to submit their correct addresses for subscription renewal.

      c. Creation of special fund for the General Convention, supported by contributions from all lodges.

      O   X (36): Oct 3, 1901; C-6, L-6

2085 [N.N.]; "Neprošenŷ opekunŷ No. II" [Uninvited guardians No. II]

      Commentary on other ethnic organizations' interference in Rusyn national-religious affairs. See: 2083.

      A   X (38): Oct 17, 1901; C-4, L-4

2086 [N.N.]; "Komu prynadležyt posmertna zapomoha" [To whom should posthumous help be given]

      The safeguards taken to ensure that insurance benefits be sent to the proper person in case of death.

      A   X (42): Nov 14, 1901; C-2&3, L-2

2087 [N.N.]; "Opasnŷe predvodytely" [Dangerous leaders]

      Commentary on Rev. Gregory Hruška and the founding of the R.N.U.

      A   X (42): Nov 14, 1901; C-4, L-4

2088 [N.N.]; "Ot hl. Uradu 'Soedyn. Hr. kat. Russk. Bratstv vsîm Počtennŷm Bratstvam prynadležavšym do 'Soedynenija' y vsîm Blahočestyvym Hr. kat. Rusynam y Rusynkam v Amerykî žyvuščym!" [From the Supreme Administration of the G.C.U. to all honorable lodges belonging to the 'Soedynenie' and to all honorable Greek Catholic Rusyns who live in America!]

Announces special activities to celebrate the feastday of St. Nicholas.

O   X (45): Dec 5, 1901; C-6, L-6

2089 [N.N.]; "Prazdnyk sv. Otca Nykolaja, Patrona 'Soedynenija'" [Feastday of St. Nicholas, patron of the 'Soedynenie']

The growth of the G.C.U.

A   X (47): Dec 19, 1901; C-1, L-1

2090 [N.N.]; "Prazdnovanie Prazdnyka Sv. O. Nykolaja" [Celebration of the feastday of St. Nicholas]

A   X (48): Dec 26, 1901; C-2, L-2

2091 "Toržestvo našych Bratstv po povodu Prazdnyka sv. O. Nykolaja, Patrona 'Soedynenija'" [Celebration of our lodges on the occasion of the feastday of St. Nicholas, Patron of the 'Soedynenie']

Series of letters to the Editor by various lodges relating local St. Nicholas day celebrations.

L   X (49): Jan 2, 1902; C-2, L-2

2092 [N.N.]; "Dîlo našej Orhanyzaciy" [The cause of our organization]

Requests continual support for the G.C.U. in light of past years' successes.

A   X (49): Jan 2, 1902; C-4, L-4

2093 [N.N.]; "Prystupajte do bratstva!" [Join a lodge!]

The function of the G.C.U. and why every Rusyn-American should belong to it.

Parts I-II: XI (2-4): Jan 30-Feb 6, 1902; C-2

A

2094 [N.N.]; "Dîla našeho 'Soedynenija'" [Affairs of our 'Soedynenie']

Statistical information on the growth of the G.C.U. with commentary on this organization's role in preserving Rusyn national heritage.

A   XI (6&7): Feb 27, 1902; C-4

2095 Redakcija; "Nîskol'ko slov k spomoščestvovaniju russkych unyversytetskych studentov v Halyčynî" [Several words about the
assistance of Rusyn university students in Galicia]

E   XI (6&7): Feb 27, 1902; C-4

2096 Michael Juhas, A.B. Bessenyey; "Ot Hl. Upravytel'stva 'Soedynenija
Hr. Kat. Russkych Bratstv', vsîm Počtennŷm Bratstvam do Soedy-
nenija prynadležavšym" [From the Supreme Administration of the
G.C.U. to all honorable lodges belonging to the 'Soedynenie']

Announces the convocation of the VII G.C.U. General Convention
in Johnstown, PA, July 24-27, 1902.

O   XI (8): Mar 6, 1902; C-6

2097 [N.N.]; "Postojannaja bor'ba" [Constant struggle]

Concerning the G.C.U.'s membership drive.

A   XI (9): Mar 13, 1902; C-2

2098 "Holosŷ o našoj Konvenciy" [Opinions about our convention]

Lodge projects and payment of debts.

Parts I-IV: XI (17-21): May 15-Jun 12, 1902; C-3&6
L

2099 Stephen Janošy; Bradenville, PA; May 11, 1902

Rusyn-Americans who will not join the G.C.U.

L   XI (18): May 22, 1902; C-2&3

2100 [N.N.]; "Nesčastija y syla velykych orhanyzaciy. Polnoe obezpečenie
est' edyno v orhanyzacijach velykych" [Accidents and the
strength of large organizations. Complete insurance coverage
is only in large organizations]

Commentary on fraternal organizations, in particular, the N.S.U.

A   XI (19): May 29, 1902; C-4

2101 George Macko; Dunbar, PA; May 17, 1902

The competition between the lodges of different fraternal
organizations in Dunbar.

L   XI (20)· Jun 5, 1902; C-2

2102 Paul Jurievich Žatkovich; "Počtennŷm našym čytateljam, osobenno že
Vsîm počtennŷm našym Bratstvam y počtennŷm ych členam y
členkynjam!" [To our honorable readers, especially to all our
honorable lodges and their honorable members!]

Pre-convention editorial expresses the hope for continual
support of the G.C.U.

E   XI (21): Jun 12, 1902; C-4

2103   [N.N.]; "S namy Boh! Da budet Svît!" [God is with us! Let there
be light!]

Introduction to the special convention edition, issue #21.

A, P   XI (21b): Jun 12, 1902; C-1

2104   [N.N.]; "Desjat' lît v žyzny našoj Orhanyzaciy" [Ten years in the
life of our organization]

A brief history of the G.C.U. with biographical sketches of
current G.C.U. officials.

A, P   XI (21b): Jun 12, 1902; C-2&3

2105   [N.N.]; "Nîskol'ko otkrovennŷch našych prymîčanij holosam o našoj
VII Hl. Konvenciy" [Several frank comments to opinions about
our VII General Convention]

The poor response of the lodges in preparing special projects
in celebration of the tenth year anniversary of the G.C.U.

A   XI (21b): Jun 12, 1902; C-3&4

2106   [N.N.]; "Ymenoslov Hl. Uradnykov v ysteceniy 10 lît" [Rollcall of
Supreme Officers during the past ten years]

List of past G.C.U. officers with dates of their tenure.

A   XI (21b): Jun 12, 1902; C-8

2107   [N.N.]; "VII Hlavna konvencija 'Soedynenija'" [Seventh General
Convention of the 'Soedynenie']

Part I: XI (22): Jun 26, 1902; C-1&2

Part II: "Protokol" [Minutes] XI (23&24): Jul 10, 1902; C-9&10

Part III: "Protokol" [Minutes] XI (26): Jul 24, 1902; C-6

O, P

2108   [N.N.]; "Naša orhanyzacija y našy svjaščennyky" [Our organization
and our priests]

Part I: XI (23&24): Jul 10, 1902; C-4&5

Part II: XI (26): Jul 24, 1902; C-4

A

2109   [N.N.]; "Ot novoyzbrannoho Hl. Uradu 'Soedynenija hr. kat. Russkych
Bratstv'. Vsîm počt. bratstvam do Soedynenija prynadležavšym!"
[From the newly elected supreme officers of the G.C.U. To all
honorable lodges belonging to the 'Soedynenie'!]

List of new officials and commentary on continuing the work in
furthering religious-national unity among Rusyn-Americans.

A   XI (23&24): Jul 10, 1902; C-7

2110   "Holosy protyv novoho dvyženija napravlennoho protyv našeho
      'Soedynenija.' Publyčnyj protest" [Opinions against the
      new movement aimed against our 'Soedynenie.' Public protest]

      Series of letters to the editor commenting on relations be-
      tween the G.C.U. and Družestvo as reported in <u>Slovenski</u>
      <u>American</u>.

      L   XI (26): Jul 24, 1902; C-2&3

2111   [N.N.]; "Velykoe Fiasko yly: Naprasna-daremna ahytacija nĭkotorych
      duchovnykov protyv 'Soedynenija'" [Great Fiasco or: the
      futile agitation of some priests against the 'Soedynenie']

      The formation of a new organization for Slovaks and Rusyns
      called "Družestvo."

      A   XI (27): Jul 31, 1902; C-2&3

2112   [N.N.]; "Nĭskol'ko otkrovennŷch slov k teperîšnoj-našoj sytuaciy"
      [A few open words about our current situation]

      The G.C.U.'s recent conflicts with the Apostolic Visitor and
      some of the clergy.

      A   XI (27): Jul 31, 1902; C-4

2113   Hl. Urjad; "Ot hl. Urjadu 'Soedynenija' Vsîm počt. bratstvam v
      laskavoe vnymanie" [From the Supreme Administration of the
      'Soedynenie.' Attention all honorable lodges]

      List of new G.C.U. officers and instructions for correspond-
      ing with them.

      O   XI (27): Jul 31, 1902; C-6

2114   Nicholas Pačuta; "Ot Hlavnoho pys'movodytelja 'Soedynenija'"
      [From the supreme recording secretary of the 'Soedynenie']

      a. Lists names and addresses of various newspapers and
          publishers acceptable to the G.C.U.
      b. New format introduced for lodge secretaries in reporting
          vital statistics on lodge members.

      O   XI (27): Jul 31, 1902; C-6

2115   [N.N.]; "Skrantonskaja konvencija" [Scranton Convention]

      Proceedings of a July 22, 1902 convention in Scranton, PA,
      sponsored by the Apostolic Visitor, Hodobay, to discuss the
      formation of a new fraternal organization, "Družestvo."

      A   XI (28): Aug 7, 1902; C-2&3

2116   [N.N.]; "V sebezaščyt" [In self-defense]

      Reply by editors of <u>Slovenski American</u> to a recent <u>ARV</u> letter
      to the editor. See: 2110.

      A   XI (29): Aug 14, 1902; C-2

2117 [N.N.]; "Otčajanaja zloba hlavných faktorov" [Desperate malice of the main managers]

The opposition the G.C.U. has received from Slovenski American.

A   XI (29): Aug 14, 1902

2118 [N.N.]; "Rady oproverženija zlobných klevet" [To refute malicious slander]

Refutes the claims by unnamed critics that the G.C.U. is a bankrupt organization.

A   XI (29): Aug 14, 1902; C-3

2119 Michael Juhas; "Ot hl. predsîdatelja 'Soedynenija hr. kat. Russkych Bratstv'" [From the supreme president of the G.C.U.]

Any member or lodge of the G.C.U. that joins the new organization, "Družestvo" will be suspended from the G.C.U.

O   XI (29): Aug 14, 1902; C-6

2120 [N.N.]; "Rev. John Szabó"

Reprint of a letter to the editor by Rev. John Szabó published in Görög Katolikus Szemle [Užhorod], which comments on the beginning of another fraternal organization, "Družestvo."

Parts I-II: XI (30-31): Aug 21-28, 1902; C-2&4

2121 [N.N.]; "Mest' nîkotorých duchovnykov y buduščnost' našeho naroda v Amerykî" [Vengeance of some priests and the future of our people in America]

The recent polemics between the G.C.U. and several Greek Catholic priests.

Part I: XI (32): Sep 4, 1902; C-2

Part II: XI (34): Sep 18, 1902; C-2

Part III: XI (37): Oct 9, 1902; C-2

Part IV: XI (39): Oct 23, 1902; C-2

2122 I.K.; Pittsburgh, PA; Sep 15, 1902

The G.C.U. and the new organization Družestvo.

L   XI (34): Sep 18, 1902; C-3

2123 Paul Jurievich Žatkovich; "Pros'ba do vsîch Bratstv do Soedynenija prynadležavšych" [Request to all lodges belonging to the 'Soedynenie']

Requests financial contributions for a striking workers' fund.

E   XI (35): Sep 25, 1902; C-2

2124   Michael Fedorko; Pittsburgh, PA; Sep 15, 1902

        Commentary on lodges and members of the G.C.U. who want to join Družestvo.

        L   XI (35): Sep 25, 1902; C-2

2125   Nicholas Pačuta; "Ot hl. pys'movodytelja 'Soedynenija'" [From the supreme recording secretary of the 'Soedynenie']

        New by-laws regarding the admittance of new members, reporting members' deaths, where insurance money should be sent upon a member's death.

        O   XI (35): Sep 25, 1902; C-5

2126   Joseph Polkabla; Leisenring, PA; Oct 3, 1902

        The G.C.U. relief-aid fund for striking miners.

        L   XI (37): Oct 9, 1902; C-4

2127   Michael Juhas; "Počtennŷm Bratstvam y členam 'Soedynenija!'" [To the honorable lodges and members of the 'Soedynenie'!]

        The murder of lodge member, Michael Čorej, the night of April 26-27, 1902 during an Easter procession at the Greek Catholic Church in Freeland, PA. See: 4174.

        O   XI (38): Oct 16, 1902; C-2

2128   Nicholas Pačuta; "Ot hl. pys'movodytelja 'Soedynenija'" [From the supreme recording secretary of 'Soedynenie']

        The application process for new members.

        O   XI (38): Oct 16, 1902; C-7

2129   [N.N.]; "Po bor'bî" [After the struggle]

        The preservation of Rusyn faith and nationality by the G.C.U.

        A   XI (40): Oct 30, 1902; C-2

2130   Nicholas Pačuta; "Ot hl. pys'movodytelja 'Soedynenija' počt. urjad-nykam Bratstv vo vnymanie" [From the supreme recording secretary of the 'Soedynenie,' attention honorable member lodges]

        The new policy regarding the reporting of members' deaths by the lodges.

        O   XI (41): Nov 6, 1902; C-7

2131   [N.N.]; "Rev. Džan Sabo opjat' napal nas" [Rev. John Szabo attacked us again]

        Reprint of a letter to the editor of <u>Görög Katolikus Szemle</u> [Užhorod], #44, November 2, 1902 by Rev. John Szabo commenting on the meeting of the G.C.U. in church affairs.

        L   XI (42): Nov 13, 1902; C-2&3

2132   [N.N.]; "Prosjat o zapomohu" [They request help]

Jessup, PA G.C.U. lodge requests donations for local striking Rusyn miners.

Req   XI (44): Nov 27, 1902; C-2

2133   Michael Juhas, et al.; "Ot Hl. Urjadu 'Soedynenija' Hreko kat. Russk. Bratstv'" [From the Supreme Administration of the G.C.U.]

a. The importance of maintaining the G.C.U. as the only Greek Catholic Rusyn fraternal organization.
b. Requests all members to contribute 25¢ to the reserve fund.
c. Requests lodges to observe St. Nicholas Day with special celebrations.

O   XI (45): Dec 4, 1902; C-6

2134   [N.N.]; "Prazdnyk Sv. Otca Nykolaja y naše 'Soedynenija'" [Feastday of St. Nicholas and our 'Soedynenie']

A   XI (46): Dec 11, 1902; C-2

2135   [N.N.]; "Prazdnyk Sv. O. Nykolaja" [Feastday of St. Nicholas]

A   XI (47): Dec 18, 1902; C-1

2136   [N.N.]; "Nîskol'ko vospomynanija dostojnŷ zamîčanija yz ystoriy Prazdnyka sv. O. Nykolaja, jako Patrona 'Soedynenija'" [Several comments worthy of remembrance from the history of the Feastday of St. Nicholas, patron of 'Soedynenie']

A   XI (47): Dec 18, 1902; C-2

2137   [N.N.]; "Obchoždenie Prazdnyka sv. O. Nykolaja Pokrovytelja--Patrona 'Soedynenija'" [Celebration of the Feastday of St. Nicholas, patron of 'Soedynenie']

A   XI (48): Dec 25, 1902; C-2

2138   [N.N.]; Hazleton, PA; "Zaslato" [Letter to the Editor]

Commentary on:

a. the G.C.U.
b. Very Rev. Andrew Hodobay
c. Slovenskj denník

L   XI (48): Dec 25, 1902; C-2

2139   "Dopysŷ o poprazdnovaniju našymy Bratstvamy Prazdnyka Sv. O. Nykolaja" [Letters to the Editor concerning the celebration of St. Nicholas Feastday by our lodges]

Part I: XI (48): Dec 25, 1902; C-2&3

Part II   XI (49): Jan 1, 1903; C-2&3

L

2140 Nicholas Pačuta; "K počtennŷm urjadnykam y urjadnyčkam našych Bratstv" [To the honorable officials of our lodges]

Commentary by the supreme recording secretary of the G.C.U. on the beginning of the new year.

O   XII (2): Jan 22, 1903; L-2
                              XII (2&3): Jan 29, 1903; C-2

2141 John Ihnat, Vanderbilt, PA; Jan 1, 1903

Concerning a Rusyn-American's transferring to three different G.C.U. lodges.

L   XII (2&3): Jan 29, 1903; C-3
                              XII (2): Jan 22, 1903; L-3

2142 Michael Juhas, et al.; "Protokol" [Minutes]

G.C.U. controllers meeting held in Braddock, PA, December 19-20, 1902.

O   XII (2&3): Jan 29, 1903; C-9&10
                              XII (3): Jan 29, 1903; L-2

2143 [N.N.]; "Hlavna nadzeratel'na komysija y Hlavnŷj sud 'Soedynenija'" [Supreme Overseeing Commission and Supreme Court of the 'Soedynenie']

Parts I-II: XII (4-5): Feb 5-12, 1903

A

2144 [N.N.]; "V zaščytî dostoynstva y russkoho charaktera našeho 'Soedynenija' y v zaščytî avktorytetu y povahy redaktorstva orhana 'Soedynenija'" [In the defense of honor and the Rusyn character of our 'Soedynenie' and in the defense of the authority and dignity of the editorship of the organ of the 'Soedynenie']

G.C.U. future after the troubled VII General Convention.

Part I: XII (5): Feb 12, 1903; C-4, L-4

Part II: XII (6): Feb 19, 1903; L-2&3; and
                              XII (6&7): Feb 26, 1903; C-9&10

2145 Michael Juhas, Peter Dzmura; "Vsîm počtennŷm Bratstvam do 'Soedynenija' prynadležavšym do laskavoj vîdomosty!" [To the notice of all honorable lodges belonging to the 'Soedynenie']

The payment of current and late dues to the G.C.U. treasurer.

O   XII (6&7): Feb 26, 1903; C-6
                              XII (7): Feb 26, 1903; L-7

2146   Michael Juhas; "Ot Hl. Predsîdatelja 'Soedynenija'" [From the
        Supreme President of the 'Soedynenie']

        a. Procedure for paying dues to the main office.
        b. Necessity of having the correct address for the mailing
            of the ARV and yearly almanac.
        c. Request financial reports from all lodges in time for
            the monthly accounting.

        O   XII (10): Mar 19, 1903; C-7, L-7

2147   Michael Turčik, et al.; Bridgeport, CT; May 2, 1903

        Seeks information concerning a former G.C.U. lodge secretary,
        Michael Katus, who absconded with $52.08 of the Bridgeport
        lodge's funds.

        L   XII (16): May 7, 1903; C-3, L-3

2148   Redakcija; "Hlavna Uradnicka Schodza 'Sojedinenija'" [Supreme
        Administrators' meeting of the 'Sojedinenie']

        Meeting held June 17-18, 1903 in Trenton, NJ.

        E   XII (21): Jun 11, 1903; L-4

2149   [N.N.]; "Jak otbŷlos' Hl. Čynovnyčeskoe Zasîdanie našoho 'Soedy-
        nenija'?" [What happened at the Supreme officers' meeting
        of our 'Soedynenie'?]

        Meeting on June 17-18, 1903 in Trenton, NJ.

        A   XII (22): Jun 25, 1903; C-2, L-2

2150   [N.N.]; "Protokol" [Minutes]

        Supreme G.C.U. officers' meeting held in Trenton, NJ, June
        17-18, 1903.

        Parts I-V: XII (22-26): Jun 25-Jul 23, 1903
        O

2151   Michael Manko; Brooklyn, NY; Jun 30, 1903

        Various Rusyn attitudes regarding the G.C.U.

        L   XII (25): Jul 16, 1903; C-3, L-3

2152   [N.N.]; "Horî Brat'ja!" [Upwards brethren!]

        The growth of the G.C.U.

        A   XII (25): Jul 16, 1903; C-4, L-4

2153 Nicholas Pačuta; "Ot Holovnoho Predsîdatelja 'Soedynenija.' Vsîm
Počtennŷm Bratstvam vo vnymanie" [From the Supreme President
of 'Soedynenie.' Attention all honorable lodges]

Announces the resignation of G.C.U. secretary A.B. Bessenyey.
Following the editorial is a statement by A.B. Bessenyey.

O   XII (33): Sep 10, 1903; C-3, L-3

2154 [N.N.]; "Dvum panam ne možno naraz služyty" [It is not possible to
serve two masters at once]

Rusyn-Americans belonging to both the G.C.U. and other fraternal organizations.

A   XII (34): Sep 17, 1903; C-4, L-4

2155 Michael Juhas, Nicholas Pačuta; "Ot Hlavn. Urjadu 'Soed.'" [From
the Supreme Administration of the 'Soedynenie']

Announces thirteen changes in procedure in reporting financial
accounts, membership changes and the filing of official docu-
ments relating to new members, new lodges and deceased members.

O   XII (40): Oct 29, 1903; C-6, L-6

2156 [N.N.]; "Razluky meždu Orhanyzacijamy" [The differences between
organizations]

The G.C.U. compared to other fraternal organizations.

A   XII (41): Nov 5, 1903; C-4, L-4

2157 Redakcija; "Nîskol'ko slov k statiy 'Razluky meždu Orhanyzacijamy'"
[A few words about the article 'Differences between Organizations']

E   XII (42): Nov 12, 1903; C-4, L-4

2158 Michael Juhas, et al.; "Ot Hlavn. Urjadu 'Soed.'" [From the
Supreme Administration of the 'Soedynenie']

St. Nicholas Day celebrations among the lodges.

O   XII (45): Dec 3, 1903; C-2, L-2

2159 Nicholas Pačuta; "Ot zastupca hl. sekretarja 'Soedynenija.' [From
the temporary supreme secretary of the 'Soedynenie']

List of lodges who haven't paid their dues and a reminder to
those to do so prior to the beginning of the now year.

O   XII (47): Dec 17, 1903; C-2&3, L-3

2160 [N.N.]; "Naše 'Soedynenija' y eho prepjastvija" [Our 'Soedynenie'
and its obstacles]

G.C.U.'s aspirations and efforts to organize all Rusyn-Americans.

A   XII (47): Dec 17, 1903; C-4, L-4

2161   Michael Juhas, et al.; "Ot Hl. Kontrol. 'Soedynenija'" [From the
       supreme controllers of the 'Soedynenie']

       List of financial actions accomplished by the G.C.U.'s
       Controllers during 1903.

       O   XII (47): Dec 17, 1903; C-7

2162   "Po Prazdnyku Sv. Otca Nykolaja, Pokrovytelja — Patrona 'Soedyne-
       nija'" [After the feastday of St. Nicholas, patron of the
       'Soedynenie']

       Report on the fund raising efforts of local lodges celebrating
       St. Nicholas Day.

       A   XII (48): Dec 24, 1903; C-4, L-4

2163   "Prazdnovanie prazdnyka Sv. Otca Nykolaja, Patrona našoho 'Soedy-
       nenija' našymy Bratstvamy" [Celebration of the feastday of
       St. Nicholas, patron of our 'Soedynenie' by our lodges]

       Series of letters to the editor from various lodges relating
       local St. Nicholas Day celebrations.

       L   XII (50): Jan 7, 1904; C-2&3, L-2&3

2164   Michael Salontay; Cleveland, OH; Dec 28, 1903

       Rusyns joining the G.C.U.

       L   XIII (1): Jan 21, 1904; C-3, L-3

2165   [N.N.]; "Resul'tat mîsjaca Sv. Nykolaevskoho" [Result of the month
       of St. Nicholas]

       The result of the G.C.U. membership drive between December 20,
       1903 - January 20, 1904.

       A   XIII (2): Jan 28, 1904; C-2, L-2

2166   Michael Juhas; "Pros'ba hl. predsîdatelja 'Soedynenija' do vsîch
       bratstv" [Request of the Supreme President of the 'Soedynenie'
       to all lodges]

       Requests donations for a G.C.U. standard-emblem.

       Req   XIII (10): Mar 24, 1904; C-2, L-2

2167   Michael Juhas, Nicholas Pačuta; "Ot hlavn. Uradu 'Soed.'" [From
       the Supreme Administration of the 'Soedynenie']

       Reminds lodges to pay all debts to the main office prior to
       May 31, 1904 when the annual general accounting begins.

       O   XIII (15): May 5, 1904; C-6, L-6

2168 Michael Juhas; "Ot predsîdatelja 'Soedynenija'" [From the president of the 'Soedynenie']

Requests $2.00 donations from all lodges for the new G.C.U. banner.

Req   XIII (17): May 19, 1904; C-2, L-2

2169 Mary Gmitrov, et al.; Clairton, PA; May 8, 1904

The formation of a Clairton G.C.U. Women's Lodge.

L   XIII (17): May 19, 1904; C-2&3, L-2

2170 Michael Juhas, Nicholas Pačuta; "Ot Hlavn. Urjadu 'Soed. Hr. kat. Russkych Bratstv'" [From the Supreme Administration of the G.C.U.]

Information concerning the VIII General G.C.U. Convention held in Trenton, NJ, June 18-23, 1904.

O   XIII (17): May 19, 1904; C-6, L-6

2171 [N.N.]; "Pred VIII Hl. Konvencieju 'Soedynenija'" [Prior to the VIII General Convention of the 'Soedynenie']

The program of the VIII General Convention.

A   XIII (19): Jun 2, 1904; C-2, L-2

2172 Michael Juhas; "Ot Hl. Presîd. 'Soed.'" [From the Supreme President of the 'Soedynenie']

Answers charges of incompetency from a fellow member.

O   XIII (21): Jun 16, 1904; C-2, L-2

2173 Joseph Bakoš; Cleveland, OH; Jun 19, 1902

The Cleveland G.C.U. lodge's fifth anniversary celebration.

L   XIII (22): Jun 23, 1904; C-2&3, L-3

2174 P. K.; New Castle, PA; Jun 25, 1904

Commentary on an article about the G.C.U. and its president. Michael Juhas, in Slovenské noviny [Hazleton].

L   XIII (23): Jun 30, 1904; C-3, L-3

2175 "Holosŷ o Konvenciy" [Opinions about the Convention]

Series of letters to the editor from various lodges reporting on special projects, paying old debts, etc. prior to the beginning of the VIII General G.C.U. Convention.

Part I: XIII (24): Jul 7, 1904; C-2&3, L-2&3

Part II: XIII (25): Jul 14, 1904; C-3&6, L-3&6

L

2176   Michael Juhas; "Ot Hl. Predsîd. 'Soed.'" [From the Supreme Presi-
        dent of the 'Soedynenie']

        Instructions for delegates arriving in Trenton, NJ for the
        VIII General G.C.U. Convention.

        O   XIII (24): Jul 7, 1904; C-6, L-6

2177   Žatkovich; "Na kanunî VIII hl. Konvenciy 'Soedynenija'" [On the
        eve of the VIII General Convention of the 'Soedynenie']

        The convention in Trenton, NJ, July 18-22, 1904.

        E   XIII (25): Jul 14, 1904; C-2, L-2

2178   [N.N.]; "VIII Hl. Konvencia našoho 'Sojedinenija'" [VIII General
        Convention of our 'Sojedinenie']

        A   XIII (26): Aug 18, 1904; 2,3

2179   [N.N.]; "Protokol" [Minutes]

        Protocol of the VIII General G.C.U. Convention held in Trenton,
        NJ, July 18-23, 1904.

        Parts I-XII   XIII (27-39): Aug 26-Nov 17, 1904; 2,3
        O

2180   [N.N.]; "Ne est'-ly to bezčel'nost'?" [Is this not impudence?]

        G.C.U.'s difficulty in organizing Rusyn-Americans in face of
        opposition from other national organizations.

        A   XIII (31): Sep 22, 1904; 6

2181   [N.N.]; "Poslîdovanija dostojnoe dîlo" [A cause worthy of continua-
        tion]

        The G.C.U.'s VIII General Convention.

        A   XIII (36): Oct 27, 1904; 4,5

2182   Michael Juhas; "Ot hlavnoho predsîdatelja 'Soedynenija.' Otkrŷtoe
        Pys'mo k vsîm Clenam y Clenkynjam prynadlezašcym k 'Soedy-
        neniju'" [From the Supreme President of the 'Soedynenie.'
        An open letter to all members belonging to the 'Soedynenie']

        The rumors circulating among members over the financial
        troubles of the organization.

        O   XIII (38): Nov 10, 1904; 6,7

2183   [N.N.]; "Svjato--Nykolaevskij mîsjac'" [St. Nicholas Month]

        G.C.U. activities during St. Nicholas Month, December 19,
        1904 - January 19, 1905.

        A   XIII (40): Nov 24, 1904; 4

2184   [N.N.]; "Ot hl. upravyt. 'Soedyn. hr. kat. russkych Bratstv'"
       [From the Supreme Administration of the G.C.U.]

       Outline of activities parishes and lodges should engage in
       while observing St. Nicholas Month.

       O   XIII (41): Dec 1, 1904; 9,10

2185   Mike L. C.; Gypsie, PA; Dec 7, 1904

       Rusyn immigrant workers who will not join the G.C.U.

       L   XIII (43): Dec 15, 1904; 2,3

2186   Rev. Joseph Hanulya; "Prazdnovanie pamjaty Sv. O. Nykolaja, Myr
       Lykijskych Čudotvorca!" [Celebration of the memory of St.
       Nicholas -- the miracle worker of Lycian Myra]

       Statistics on the growth of the G.C.U.

       A   XIII (43): Dec 15, 1904, 4,5

2187   "Prazdnovanie Prazdnyka Sv. O. Nykolaja, Patrona 'Soedynenija'"
       [Celebration of the feastday of St. Nicholas, patron of the
       'Soedynenie']

       Series of letters to the editor from various lodges relating
       local St. Nicholas Month celebrations.

       Part I: XIII (45): Dec 29, 1904; 9,11

       Part II: XIII (46): Jan 5, 1905; 9,11

       Part III: XIII (47): Jan 12, 1905; 2,3

       L

2188   Rev. M. Jackovich, et al.; "Protokol" [Minutes]

       Minutes of the annual G.C.U. Controllers meeting held in
       Braddock, PA, December 27-30, 1904.

       O   XIII (47): Jan 12, 1905; 4,5

2189   Helen Marinčik; "Nîskol'ko slov k našym Ženskym Tovaryščestvam a
       k vsîm sestram Rusynkam" [Several words to our women's lodges
       and to all Rusyn sisters]

       The role of women in the G.C.U.

       O   XV (2): Jan 25, 1906; 4,5

2190   Rev. M. Jackovich, et al.; "Protokol" [Minutes]

       Minutes of the G.C.U. Controllers meeting held in Braddock,
       PA, February 26-28, 1906.

       O   XV (8): Mar 8, 1906; 3

2191 [N.N.]; "Amerykanskij Mad'jarskij Sojuz" [American Magyar Union]

Activities of a Cleveland, OH based fraternal organization, founded February 27, 1906.

A   XV (8): Mar 8, 1906; 4,5

2192 [N.N.]; "Nîskol'ko slov o delehatach y ych vol'bach" [A few words about the delegates and their elections]

The procedure for choosing delegates to the G.C.U.'s IX General Convention.

A   XV (9): Mar 15, 1906, 2,3

2193 Nicholas Pačuta; "Ot hol. sekretara" [From the supreme secretary]

Requests all lodges to submit an account of dues to the main office prior to April 30, 1906.

O   XV (9): Mar 15, 1906; 6,7

2194 Michael Juhas; "Ot hol. Predsîdatelja 'Soedynenija Hreko Kat. Russkych Bratstv" [From the supreme president of the G.C.U.]

Information and regulations concerning the various activities for the IX General G.C.U. Convention.

O   XV (10): Mar 22, 1906; 6

2195 John Uhrin, et al.; "Proektŷ ot Hreko Kat. Russkoho Bratstva Sv. Ioanna Krestytelja č. v 'Soedyneniju' 26, sostavlennŷy na rjadnom sobraniju--mytynhu 18-ho dnja marta 1906" [Proposals from the G.C.U. lodge of St. John the Baptist, number 26 in the 'Soedynenie,' which were drafted at the lodge's regular meeting on March 18, 1906]

Part I: XV (10): Mar 22, 1906; 6,7

Parts II-VIII: XV (13-19): Apr 12-May 24, 1906

O

2196 [N.N.]; "Charakter našeho 'Soedynenija'" [The character of our 'Soedynenie']

The past, present and future of the G.C.U.

A   XV (11): Mar 29, 1906; 2,3

2197 John Uhrin, et al.; "Protest"

Protest of lodge 26 against the guidelines and regulations for the IX G.C.U. General Convention written by G.C.U. president, Michael Juhas. See: 2194.

O   XV (13): Apr 12, 1906; 6,7

2198   Michael Juhas; "Ot Holovnoho Predsîdatelja 'Soedynenija'" [From
        the supreme president of the 'Soedynenie']

        Information on the IX General G.C.U. Convention.

        O   XV (15): Apr 26, 1906; 4,5

2199   Helen Marinčik; "Nîskol'ko ščyro-sestryčných slov do ženskych hr.
        kat. russkych Tovaryšestv, prynadležaščých do 'Soedynenija'"
        [A few sincere-sisterly words to the women Greek Catholic
        lodges belonging to the 'Soedynenie']

        Proposes involvement of the women lodges in drafting resolu-
        tions and in planning projects for the IX General G.C.U.
        Convention.

        O   XV (16): May 3, 1906; 2,3

2200   John Uhrin; Homestead, PA; May 14, 1906

        "Zaslato" [Letter to the Editor]

        Answers charges of corruption in the G.C.U. controllers'
        committee.

        L   XV (18): May 17, 1906; 2

2201   Ann Svirbel', et al.; "Protest"

        Issue of delegate selection to the IX G.C.U. General Convention.

        A   XV (18): May 17, 1906; 2,5

2202   Paul Ju. Zatkovich; "Ix Hol. Konvencija našeho 'Soedynenija'"
        [IX General Convention of our 'Soedynenie']

        Part I: XV (18): May 17, 1906; 4,5

        Part II: XV (19): May 24, 1906; 1,2,3

        Part III: XV (20): Jun 7, 1906; 1,2,3

        E

2203   [N.N.]; "Bud'me na storoży" [Let us be on (our) guard]

        The internal troubles in the G.C.U. which made the IX General
        Convention controversial.

        A   XV (21): Jun 14, 1906; 4,5

2204   [N.N.]; "Protokol" [Minutes]

        Minutes of the IX G.C.U. General Convention held in Wilkes
        Barre, PA, May 28-31 and June 1-2, 1906.

        Parts I-VI: XV (21-26): Jun 14-Jul 19, 1906

        Parts VII-X: XV (30-33): Aug 16-Sep 6, 1906; 9,10,11

        O

2205   [N.N.]; "Orhanyzovanie hr. kat. russkych dîtej" [Organization of Greek Catholic Rusyn children]

The organization of juvenile lodges to instill and foster consciousness of the national-religious heritage in future G.C.U. members.

A   XV (22): Jun 21, 1906; 4,5

2206   Ž.; "Podražanija dostojnoe dîlo" [A cause worthy of imitation]

The business organizing and management capabilities of controllers John Uhrin and Rev. A. Holosnyay.

E   XV (24): Jul 5, 1906; 2,3

2207   Paul Jurievich Žatkovich; "Novŷj termyn srok" [The new term]

The newly elected supreme officials of the G.C.U. assuming office July 7, 1906.

E   XV (24): Jul 5, 1906; 4,5

2208   [N.N.]; "Uznanie y otlyčenie zasluh" [Recognition and appreciation of achievements]

The past achievements of John Uhrin, president-elect of the G.C.U.

A   XV (25): Jul 12, 1906; 2,3

2209   John Uhrin; "Ot hol. predsîdatelja 'Soedynenija Hr. Kat. Russkych Bratstv'" [From the supreme president of the G.C.U.]

    a. Reminds all newly-elected officials to prove their U.S. citizenship before taking office and the need to post an insurance bond (amounts specified per office).
    b. Notice to special committees of a special meeting on Monday, July 16, 1906 (committees named).

O   XV (25): Jul 12, 1906; 11

2210   Rev. Nicholas Chopey; "Vstupnoe slovo hl. duchovnoho upravytelja 'Soedynenija'" [First word of the spiritual director of the 'Soedynenie']

The G.C.U.'s role in preserving Rusyn faith and nationality in America.

O   XV (26): Jul 19, 1906; 4,5

2211   [N.N.]; "Sytyzenskij-horožanskij parahraf" [Citizenship paragraph]

The adoption of paragraph 19 into the G.C.U. by-laws which states that each supreme officer of the G.C.U. must be an American citizen.

A   XV (27): Jul 26, 1906; 4,5

2212 [N.N.]; "Protokol" [Minutes]

> Minutes of the G.C.U. supreme officers' meeting held in
> Homestead, PA July 17-19, 1906.
>
> O   XV (27): Jul 26, 1906; 6,7

2213 John Uhrin, et al.; "Protokol" [Minutes]

> Minutes of the G.C.U. supreme officers' meeting held in
> Homestead, PA July 16-17, 1906.
>
> O   XV (27): Jul 26, 1906; 9,10,11

2214 John Uhrin; "Vsîm č. hol. urjadnykam vo laskavoe vnymanie"
> [Attention all honorable supreme officers]
>
> The citizenship clause, #19, in the G.C.U. by-laws.
>
> O   XV (28): Aug 2, 1906; 4

2215 John Uhrin; "Vozzvanie y pros'ba do vsîch č. Bratstv prynadleža-
> ščych do 'Soedynenija'" [Notice and request to all honorable
> lodges belonging to the 'Soedynenie']
>
> The new affiliate of the G.C.U.--G.C.U. Juvenile Lodges.
>
> O   XV (28): Aug 2, 1906; 9,10

2216 John Uhrin; "Vsîm č. Bratstvam prynadležaščym do 'Soedynenija'"
> [To all honorable lodges belonging to the 'Soedynenie']
>
> Answers the critics of the citizenship clause, paragraph 19
> in the G.C.U. by-laws. More precise explanation of the law.
>
> O   XV (29): Aug 9, 1906; 2,3

2217 John Uhrin; "Počt. h-nu Mychalu Juhasu bŷvšomu dyrektoru, menadžeru
> y kassieru drukarny y hazetŷ, orhanu 'Soedynenija'" [To honor-
> able Mr. Michael Juhas, former director, manager and treasurer
> of the printing office and newspaper, organ of the 'Soedynenie']
>
> Requests former G.C.U. president, Michael Juhas, to account for
> $2,797.52 received for the ARV during his tenure.
>
> O   XV (30): Aug 16, 1906; 6,7

2218 John Uhrin; "Ot hol. predsîdatelja 'Soedynenija Hreko Kat. Russkych
> Bɩatstv'" [From the supreme president of the G.C.U.]
>
> a. The division among the lodges over the U.S. citizenship
>   requirement for supreme officers (paragraph 19 of the
>   by-laws).
> b. Reminds lodges that Michael Juhas has not yet made an
>   accounting of funds from the ARV that disappeared during
>   his tenure as G.C.U. president.
>
> O   XV (31): Aug 23, 1906; 4

2219 [N.N.]; "Otvît h-nu Ioannu Tacakovu na eho dopys', kotoru podal do
Bratstva, orhanu 'Pens. Slov. Ednoty' v n-rî 8 s dnja 16-ho
avhusta 1906, pod zahlaviem 'Treba sozvaty mymorjadnu konvenciju a Žatkovyča y Uhryna doloj" [Answer to Mr. John Tacakov
and his letter to the editor, which was published in Bratstvo,
Organ of the P.R.G.C.U., #8, August 16, 1906 under the title
"A special convention should be convoked; Žatkovich and Uhrin
must go away!"]

A   XV (31): Aug 23, 1906; 6,7

2220 "Mnînija na ahytaciju vedenu protyv proekta y rasporjaženija hol.
predsîdatelja 'Soedynenija' h-na Ioanna Uhryna kasatel'no
sytyzenskoho parahrafa y yzdanija orhanu" [Opinions about
the agitation against the plan and decree of 'Soedynenie'
president, John Uhrin, concerning the citizenship paragraph
and publication of the organ]

Letters from various lodges expressing their opinion on the
controversial citizenship clause adopted at the IX G.C.U.
General Convention.

L   XV (31): Aug 23, 1906; 6,7

2221 John Uhrin; "Počtennŷm Bratstvam, Bratskym urjadnykam y starŷm hol.
urjadnykam, kotorŷch to moe pys'mo kasaetsja" [To honorable
lodges, lodge officers and former supreme officers, whom my
letter concerns]

a. Requests all former supreme G.C.U. officers to correct any
   accounts with the clerk at the IX General Convention should
   disagreement over the amounts arise.
b. Commentary on the recent agitation against the president
   and ARV editor over various decrees considered in the best
   interest of the organization.
c. The G.C.U. Juvenile branch.
d. The dual edition of the ARV.

O   XV (32): Aug 30, 1906; 6

2222 Michael Klaczik, et al.; Duquesne, PA, Aug 28, 1906

The G.C.U. Juvenile Lodges.

L   XV (34): Sep 13, 1906; 2,3

2223 John Šestak-Svistak, Sr.; Malý Lipnik [Kishárs]; Sáros County,
Hungary, Jul 25, 1906.

Thanks the G.C.U. for benefit money sent to parents of John
Šestak-Svistak, who died in an industrial accident in America.

L E   XV (35): Sep 20, 1906; 2,3

2224 John Uhrin; "Ot hol. predsîdatelja 'Soedynenija' Hreko Kat. Russkych Bratstv'" [From the supreme president of the G.C.U.]

    a. Requests financial support for the G.C.U. Juvenile branch.
    b. Requests from George Nemčik (lodge #24 in Eckley, PA), who is on trial for the self-defense murder of an attacker, for contributions to defray court fees and help maintain his family.

Req   XV (35): Sep 20, 1906; 6,7

2225 John Uhrin, Nicholas Pačuta; "Počtennŷm brat'jam-tutoram y sestram-tutoram Junošeskych Bratstv, prynadležaščych do 'Soedynenija!'" [Honorable brother and sister tutors of the Juvenile Lodges belonging to the 'Soedynenie!']

The statutes in organizing Juvenile Lodges.

O   XV (37): Oct 4, 1906; 2

2226 [N.N.]; "Velyka neblahodarnost' vîrnykov, yly lučše, štuky 'dykych fylosofov'" [The ingratitude of the faithful, or better, the crafts of 'wild philosophers']

Commentary on an article in Pravda [Olyphant, PA], #36 which criticizes the actions of former supreme officer, Rev. Cornelius Laurisin.

A   XV (38): Oct 11, 1906; 3,4

2227 John Uhrin; "Vsîm počt. Bratstvam prynadležaščym do 'Soedynenija!'" [To all honorable lodges belonging to the 'Soedynenie!']

The enemies of the current supreme G.C.U. officers.

O   XV (39): Oct 18, 1906; 6,7

2228 [N.N.]; "Krasnŷj postup v s"orhanyzovaniju molodežy russkoj v Homsted, Pa." [Fine progress in the organization of young Rusyns in Homestead, PA]

The first G.C.U. juvenile lodges formed in Homestead, PA.

A   XV (40): Oct 25, 1906; 4,5

2229 John Uhrin; "Vsîm počt. Bratstvam do 'Soed.' prynadležaščym." [To all honorable lodges belonging to the 'Soedynenie']

    a. The publication of the General Convention's Protocol.
    b. The decisions of the G.C.U. overseeing commission.

O   XV (41): Nov 1, 1906; 4

2230 Rev. M. Jackovich, Michael Lucak; "Protokol" [Minutes]

Minutes of the first meeting of the G.C.U. Overseeing Committee held in New York City, October 9-10, 1906.

O   XV (41): Nov 1, 1906; 6

2231   Andrew Zbojan, Michael Bodrog; "Protokol" [Minutes]

Minutes of the G.C.U. Controllers Committee meeting held in
Homestead, PA, October 24-27, 1906.

O   XV (41): Nov 1, 1906; 9,10,11

2232   [N.N.]; "Ne na papery no v dîjstnosty" [Not on paper but in
reality]

The growth and status of the G.C.U.

A   XV (42): Nov 8, 1906; 2,3

2233   [N.N.]; "Slava y čest' uznavšym pravdu y spravedlyvost'" [Glory
and honor to those who recognize truth and justice]

Supporters of G.C.U. supreme president, John Uhrin's, policies regarding the administration of the organization.

A   XV (42): Nov 8, 1906; 4

2234   John Ihnat, Mary Várady; Leisenring, PA; Nov 11, 1906

Concerning Leisenring's two G.C.U. Juvenile Lodges.

L   XV (43): Nov 15, 1906; 2,3

2235   [N.N.]; "Parahraf 20-ŷj hol. statutov 'Soedynenija'" [Paragraph
(19) 20 of the supreme statutes of the 'Soedynenie']

Commentary on the G.C.U.'s controversial statute 19.

A   XV (44): Nov 22, 1906; 4,5

2236   Nicholas Pačuta, et al.; "Vsîm počt. Bratstvam prynadležaščym do
'Soedynenija' y vsîm Počt. hr. kat. Rusynam v Soed. Štatach
Sîv. Ameryky!" [To all honorable lodges belonging to the
'Soedynenie' and to all honorable Greek Catholic Rusyns in
the U.S. of North America!]

The celebration of St. Nicholas month.

O   XV (45): Dec 3, 1906; 2,3

2237   Redakcija; "Pereneslys'mesja! Redakcija, drukarnja y ofysŷ hl.
sekretarja y hl. pys'movodytelja uže pomîščenŷ v domî 'Soedynenija'. Ne ŷslo to lehko--Bor'ba s kontraktorom" [We have
moved! Editor, print shop and offices of the supreme secretary and supreme recording secretary have already moved into
the (new) building of the 'Soedynenie'. But it hasn't been
easy--Struggle with the building contractor]

The new G.C.U. building in Homestead, PA and the problems
with the building contractor.

E   XV (45): Dec 3, 1906; 4,5

2238   [N.N.]; "Prazdnyk Sv. O. Nykolaja" [Feastday of St. Nicholas]

        A   XV (46): Dec 13, 1906; 4,5

2239   [N.N.]; "Krasnŷj uspîch" [A fine success]

        G.C.U. juvenile lodges.

        A   XV (46): Dec 13, 1906; 6,7

2240   [N.N.]; "Svjato-Nykolaevskij Mîsjac" [Saint Nicholas Month]

        A   XV (47): Dec 20, 1906; 4

2241   [N.N.]; "Prazdnovanie Prazdnyka Sv. O. Nykolaja" [Celebration of
        the Feastday of St. Nicholas]

        A   XV (48): Dec 27, 1906; 4,5

2242   [N.N.]; "Na puty zakonnosty" [On the way of legality]

        Those in the G.C.U. who are opposed to the U.S. citizenship
        requirement for all supreme G.C.U. officers.

        A   XV (48): Dec 27, 1906; 4,5

2243   Nicholas Pačuta, John Uhrin; "Vsîm počt. tutoram y tutorkam hr.
        kat. russkych Junošeskych Bratstv, prynadležaščym do 'Soedy-
        nenija' do važnoho vnymanija!" [Important, attention all
        honorable tutors of the Greek Catholic Rusyn Juvenile Lodges
        belonging to the 'Soedynenie'!]

        Directions for the proper procedure in conducting the business
        of the juvenile lodges.

        O   XV (48): Dec 27, 1906; 6,7

2244   Rev. M. Jackovich, Michael Lucak; "Protokol" [Minutes]

        Protocol of the second meeting of the G.C.U. Overseeing
        Committee in Pottsville, PA, December 17, 1906.

        O   XV (48): Dec 27, 1906; 6,7

2245   Zsatkovich; "Odno krasnoe pamjatnoe toržestvo" [One beautiful
        memorable celebration]

        Tenth anniversary celebration of G.C.U. women's lodge #108
        in Braddock, PA.

        E   XV (49): Jan 3, 1907; 4,5

2246   "Prazdnovanie Prazdnyka Sv. O. Nykolaja, Patrona 'Soedynenija'"
        [Celebration of the feastday of St. Nicholas, patron of the
        'Soedynenie']

        Series of letters to the editor from the lodges relating local
        St. Nicholas Day celebrations.

        L   XVI (1): Jan 17, 1907; C-3, L-2&3

2247   John Uhrin; "Od hl. predsîdatelja 'Sojedinenija'" [From the
        supreme president of the 'Sojedinenie']

   G.C.U. statute #67 and the celebration of St. Nicholas feastday by the lodges.

   O   XVI (2): Jan 24, 1907; L-2

2248   John Uhrin; "Ot Hol. predsîdatelja 'Soedynenija'" [From the
        supreme president of the 'Soedynenie']

   a. The success of the St. Nicholas Day celebrations.
   b. Reports on the G.C.U. contribution of $274.00 to Rev.
      Theodore Demjanovics' orphan's fund in Trnovo nad Teresvou
      [Kökényes], Máramaros County, Hungary.
   c. The election of future supreme G.C.U. officers.

   O   XVI (3): Jan 31, 1907; L-2;
                                        XVI (4): Feb 7, 1907; C-2

2249   [N.N.]; "Smutnoe dokazatel'stvo duchovnoj slabosty--nevîžestva y
        nedozrilosty našoho naroda" [Sad evidence of the spiritual
        weakness--ignorance and immaturity of our people]

   Rusyn-American parents who fail to register their children in
   G.C.U. juvenile lodges.

                                        XVI (4): Feb 7, 1907; C-4

2250   John Uhrin, Nicholas Pačuta; "Od Hl. Uradu 'Sojedinenija'" [From
        the Supreme Administration of the 'Sojedinenie']

   a. The filing of death certificates from Europe (refers to
      G.C.U. statute 48)
   b. Procedure for sending dues from juvenile lodges to the
      main G.C.U. office.

   O   XVI (5): Feb 14, 1907; L-2

2251   Rev. John Szabo, et al.; "Protokol" [Minutes]

   Minutes of the G.C.U. supreme controllers' meeting held in
   Homestead and Braddock, PA, February 5-8, 1907.

   O   XVI (6): Feb 21, 1907; L-2

2252   Elizabeth Bašist; Rankin, PA; Feb 26, 1907

   Rankin's G.C.U. juvenile lodge.

   L   XVI (9): Mar 14, 1907; C-3, L-2

2253   Michael Yassem; Ford City, PA; Feb 27, 1907

   The activities of the Ford City's G.C.U. lodge.

   L   XVI (9): Mar 14, 1907; C-3, L-2&3

2254   John Uhrin; "Ot hol. predsîdatelja 'Soedynenija'" [From the supreme president of the 'Soedynenie']

        a. Guidelines for candidates seeking G.C.U. supreme officer positions.
        b. The G.C.U. juvenile lodges.

        O   XVI (9): Mar 14, 1907; C-6, L-6

2255   John Uhrin, Nicholas Pačuta; "Holovnoe čynovstvennoe sobranie 'Soedynenija'" [Supreme Officers' meeting of the 'Soedynenie']

        Meeting held May 27, 1907 in Norfolk, VA.

        O   XVI (14): Apr 18, 1907; C-1, L-1

2256   Ann Chila; Whiting, IN

        Activities of Whiting's G.C.U. juvenile lodge.

        L   XVI (18): May 23, 1907; C-2, L-2

2257   John Uhrin; "Ot hol. predsîdatelja 'Soedynenija'" [From the supreme president of the 'Soedynenie']

        Special collection fund contributed to by each parish and lodge for the support of the American Greek Catholic Bishop.

        O   XVI (19): May 30, 1907; C-2, L-2

2258   A.G.; Braddock, PA; May 21, 1907

        The dedication of Braddock's G.C.U. lodge's (#81) new banner.

        L   XVI (19): May 30, 1907; C-3, L-3

2259   [N.N.]; South Sharon, PA; Jun 6, 1907

        The dedication of South Sharon's G.C.U. lodge's (#258) two new banners.

        L   XVI (21): Jun 13, 1907; C-2&3, L-2

2260   [N.N.]; "Ročnoe Hl. Čynovnyčeskoe Sobranie" [Annual Supreme Officers' Meeting]

        Meeting in Norfolk, VA, June 3-6, 1907.

        O   XVI (21): Jun 13, 1907; C-4&5, L-4&5

2261   [N.N.]; "Protokol" [Minutes]

        Minutes of the G.C.U. supreme officers' annual meeting held in Norfolk, VA, June 4-7, 1907.

        Parts I-III: XVI (23-25): Jun 27-Jul 11, 1907; C-6&7, L-6

        Parts IV-V: XVI (27-28): Jul 25-Aug 1, 1907; C-6&7, L-6

        Parts VI-VII: XVI (30-31): Aug 15-22, 1907; C-2&6, L-2&6

        O

2262   John Uhrin; "Ot hol. predsîdatelja 'Soedynenija'" [From the
        supreme president of the 'Soedynenie']

    a. Commentary on those lodges who refuse to give transfer
            permits to members who request them.
    b. The tenth general G.C.U. convention.

        O   XVI (24): Jul 4, 1907; C-2, L-2

2263   Andrew Zsdišin; Bayonne, NJ

        Commentary on the juvenile branch of the G.C.U.

        L   XVI (25): Jul 11, 1907; C-3, L-3

2264   Nicholas Pačuta; "Ot hol. sekretarja 'Soedynenija'" [From the
        supreme secretary of the 'Soedynenie']

        Procedure for reporting G.C.U. juvenile lodge accounts to
        the general treasurer.

        O   XVI (27): Jul 25, 1907; C-6, L-6

2265   [N.N.]; New Castle, PA

        The organization of G.C.U. lodges in the New Castle vicinity.

        L   XVI (31): Aug 22, 1907; C-2&3, L-2

2266   John Uhrin; "Ot hol. predsîdatelja 'Soedynenija'" [From the
        supreme president of the 'Soedynenie']

        List of all lodges who haven't purchased tickets from the
        supreme spiritual director of the G.C.U.

        O   XVI (32): Aug 29, 1907; C-3, L-6

2267   Nicholas Pačuta; "Ot hol. sekretarja 'Soedynenija'" [From the
        supreme secretary of the 'Soedynenie']

        The payment of monthly dues on time by the lodges to the
        treasurer of the G.C.U.

        O   XVI (34): Sep 12, 1907; C-3, L-3

2268   [N.N.]; "Vŷsše 20,000" [More than 20,000]

        Growth of the G.C.U.

        A   XVI (35): Sep 19, 1907; C-4, L-4

2269   John Uhrin; "Ot hl. predsidatel'a 'Sojedinenija'" [From the
        supreme president of the 'Sojedinenie']

        The financial contributions by lodges to a general fund for
        the Bishop.

        O   XVI (38): Oct 10, 1907; L-3

2270   Rev. Nicholas Chopey, et al.; "Protokol" [Minutes]

Minutes and annual report of the G.C.U. Overseeing Committee
meeting held in Homestead, PA, November 12-13, 1907.

O   XVI (44): Nov 21, 1907; C-4, L-6

2271   Rev. John Sabo, et al.; "Protokol" [Minutes]

Minutes of the annual G.C.U. Controllers' meeting held in
Homestead and Braddock, PA, November 20-21, 1907.

O   XVI (44): Nov 21, 1907; C-4, L-6

2272   [N.N.]; "Ot hl. Urjadu 'Soedynenija'" [From the Supreme Administration of the 'Soedynenie']

Commentary on the G.C.U. during the past year and proposed
plans for the celebration of St. Nicholas Day.

O   XVI (45): Nov 28, 1907; C-2&3, L-2

2273   [N.N.]; "Protokol" [Minutes]

Minutes of the Council of the American Greek Catholic churches
meeting held in Homestead, PA, November 24, 1907.

O   XVI (46): Dec 5, 1907; C-1&2, L-2&3

2274   Ž.; "Čudesnŷy dîla, kotorŷy odnako zasluhujut na to, abŷ bŷly
vzjatŷ vo vnymanie" [Strange affairs, which all the same merit
attention]

Commentary on Magyar Záslo]Pittsburgh, PA] views that the
G.C.U. is an anti-Hungarian, Pan-Slavic organization.

E   XVII (6): Feb 20, 1908; C-4&5, L-5

2275   John Uhrin, Julius Egrecky; "Ot hl. urjadu 'Soedynenija Hreko Kat.
Russkych Bratstv.'" [From the supreme administration of the
G.C.U.]

The X General G.C.U. Convention to take place in Yonkers, NY.

O   XVII (12): Apr 2, 1908; C-2, L-4

2276   Nicholas Pačuta; "Ot hol. sekretarija 'Soedynenija'" [From the
supreme secretary of the 'Soedynenie']

The accounting of debts to the general treasury by all lodges
prior to April 30, 1900.

O   XVII (12): Apr 2, 1908; C-2, L-4

2277   [N.N.]; "X hl. Konvencija 'Soedyn.' y vŷbor delehatov" [X General
Convention of the 'Soedynenie' and the election of delegates]

A   XVII (13): Apr 9, 1908; C-4, L-4

2278   [N.N.]; "Buduščnost' Uhorskych Rusynov y X hl. Konvencija našoho 'Soed.'" [The future of the Uhro-Rusyns and the X General Convention of our 'Soedynenie']

     A   XVII (14): Apr 16, 1908; C-4, L-4

2279   John Uhrin, Julius Egrecky; "Ot hl. urjadu 'Soedynenija'" [From the supreme administration of the 'Soedynenie']

     a. The acceptance of new lodge members.
     b. The formation of new lodges.
     c. The selection of delegates to the X General G.C.U. Convention.

     O   XVII (15): Apr 23, 1908; C-4, L-4

2280   John Uhrin, Julius Egrecky; "Ot hl. urjadu 'Soedynenija Hreko Kat. Russkych Bratstv'" [From the supreme administration of the G.C.U.]

     Place and dates of the X General G.C.U. Convention.

     O   XVII (16): May 7, 1908; C-1, L-1

2281   [N.N.]; "O nas, pro nas" [About us, for us]

     G.C.U.'s position concerning the recent controversies involving the Greek Catholic Church in the nationality issue.

     A   XVII (16): May 7, 1908; C-4, L-4

2282   "Proektŷ počt. Bratstv na X hl. Konvenciju 'Soedynenija Hr. Kat. Russkych Bratstv'" [Proposals of the honorable lodges for the X General Convention of the G.C.U.]

     Part I: XVII (17): May 14, 1908; C-2&3, L-2&3
     Part II: XVII (18): May 21, 1908; C-3, L-2&3
     L

2283   Ž.; "X hl. Konvencija 'Soedynenija'" [X General Convention of the 'Soedynenie']

     Highlights of the X G.C.U. Convention.

     E   XVII (19): Jun 11, 1908; C-4&5, L-4&5

2284   Ž.; "Našoe 'Soedynenie' y eho X hl. Konvencija" [Our 'Soedynenie' and its X General Convention]

     Part I: XVII (20): Jun 18, 1908; C-1&2, L-1&2
     Part II: XVII (22): Jul 2, 1908; C-1&2, L-1&2
     E

2285   John Uhrin; "Ot hl. predsîdatelja 'Soedynenija'" [From the supreme
       president of the 'Soedynenie']

    a. The financial status and enemies of the organization.
    b. Advises newly elected supreme officers to present proof
       of U.S. citizenship prior to assuming office.

O   XVII (20): Jun 18, 1908; C-4, L-4

2286   John Petro, et al.; "Protokol" [Minutes]

    Minutes of the X General G.C.U. Convention held in Yonkers, NY
    May 25-30 and June 2-4, 1908.

    Parts I-IX   XVII (20-28): Jun 18-Aug 13, 1908

    Parts X-XII: XVII (30-32): Aug 27-Sep 10, 1908

    Part XIII: XVII (35): Oct 1, 1908; C-6, L-6

    Part XIV: XVII (37): Oct 15, 1908; C-6, L-6

    O

2287   [N.N.]; "Novoe pokušenie Ep. Ortŷn'skoho dlja nabŷtija sobî dajakoj
       vlasty" [Bishop Ortynsky's new attempt to acquire some power
       for himself]

    Bishop Ortynsky's efforts to ally the Roman Catholic hierarchy
    on his side in his struggle with the G.C.U.

A   XVII (21): Jun 25, 1908; C-4, L-4

2288   Nicholas Pačuta; "Ot hl. sekretarja 'Soedynenija'" [From the supreme
       secretary of the 'Soedynenie']

    a. Advises all adult sponsors of G.C.U. juvenile lodges to
       insure the contribution of 15¢ from every lodge member to
       the general treasury.
    b. The publication of new statutes for the juvenile lodges.

O   XVII (22): Jul 2, 1908; C-4, L-4

2289   [N.N.]; "Ot hl. urjadu 'Soedynenija Hr. Kat. Russkych Bratstv' v
       Soed. Statach Sîv. Ameryky" [From the supreme administration
       of the G.C.U. in the U.S. and North America]

    Expresses the desire to continue the work of the G.C.U. in the
    preservation of faith and nationality.

O   XVII (24): Jul 16, 1908; C-4, L-4

2290   Nicholas Pačuta; "Ot hl. sekretarja 'Soedynenija'" [From the supreme
       secretary of the 'Soedynenie']

    a. How to report a member's death to the main G.C.U. office.
    b. Advises each lodge to insure that each member is currently
       paid up.

O   XVII (24): Jul 16, 1908; C-7, L-7

2291 Nicholas Pačuta; "Počtennym Br. tutoram y sest. tutorkam vo
      vnymanie!'" [Attention honorable brother and sister tutors!]

      The payment of dues by juvenile lodges on time to the main
      office. Reminds adult tutors that they are responsible in
      ensuring the payment of dues by lodge members.

      O   XVII (24): Jul 16, 1908; C-7, L-7

2292 R.; "Epyskop Soter Stefan protyv 'Soedynenija Hr. Kat. Russkych
      Bratstv v Sîvernoj Amerykî'" [Bishop Soter Stefan (Ortynsky)
      is against the 'G.C.U. in North America']

      Commentary on the public statement Bishop Ortynsky made about
      the G.C.U. and its leaders.

      A   XVII (25): Jul 23, 1908; C-4, L-4

2293 Nicholas Pačuta; "Ot hl. sekretarja 'Soedynenija.' Otvît Č. 333
      v Vajtynh, Yndyana" [From the supreme secretary of the
      'Soedynenie.' Answer to lodge #333 in Whiting, Indiana]

      Reply to and commentary on a protest by lodge #333 against
      the ARV and its editor, P.J. Zsatkovich, in Slovak v Ameriki,
      August 18, 1908, #66.

      O   XVII (30): Aug 27, 1908; C-3, L-2

2294 George Gereg, et al.; "Vsîm hreko kat. Rusynam do Pensylvanijskoj
      Slov. Rymo y Hreko Kat. Ednotŷ prynadležaščym vo vnymanie!
      Protest" [To all Greek Catholic Rusyns belonging to the
      Pennsylvania Slovak Roman and Greek Catholic Union! A protest]

      Protest by lodge #128 of the P.R.G.C.U. against the actions of
      Bishop Ortynsky and his supporters.

      O   XVII (30): Aug 27, 1908; C-4, L-4

2295 Andrew Zbojan, et al.; "Ot hlavnych kontrollorov 'Soedynen.'"
      [From the supreme controllers of the 'Soedynenie']

      Fiscal accounting of G.C.U. funds and assets.

      O   XVII (31): Sep 3, 1908; C-4, L-2&3

2296 Rev. Nicholas Stecovich; "Otpovîd' Svobodî" [Reply to Svoboda]

      Defends the G.C.U. and the anti-Ukrainian Rusyns from the
      polemical articles in Svoboda.

      Part I: XVII (37): Oct 15, 1908; C-2, L-2

      Part II: XVII (38): Oct 22, 1908; C-1, L-2

      A

2297   [N.N.]; "Ot hl. urjadu 'Soedynenija hreko katolyčeskych russkych bratstv'" [From the supreme administration of the G.C.U.]

The past growth and future of the G.C.U. on the occasion of the celebration of St. Nicholas Day.

O   XVII (44): Dec 3, 1908; C-4&5, L-4&5

2298   [N.N.]; "Ot hlavnoho urjadu 'Soedynenija'" [From the supreme administration of the 'Soedynenie']

The celebration of "St. Nicholas Month" by all G.C.U. lodges.

O   XVII (46): Dec 17, 1908; C-2, L-2

2299   P.Ju. Zsatkovich; "'Soedynenie' y 'Sojuz'" [The 'Soedynenie' and the 'Sojuz']

The differences between these two competing organizations.

E, P   XVII (46): Dec 17, 1908; C-4,5,6, L-4&5

2300   Andrew Zbojan, et al.; "Ot hl. kontrolorov 'Soedynenija'" [From the supreme controllers of the 'Soedynenie']

Accounting of G.C.U. funds for the months of August, September, October, 1908.

O   XVII (46): Dec 17, 1908; C-10&11, L-10

2301   M. J.; "Díla dlja uhorskych Rusynov poderžanija dostojnŷ" [Matters deserving Uhro-Rusyns' support]

The G.C.U. and Uhro-Rusyns.

A   XVII (47): Dec 24, 1908; C-4, L-4

2302   "Prazdnovanie prazdnyka sv. O. Nykolaja, Patrona 'Soedynenie'" [Celebration of the feastday of St. Nicholas, patron of the 'Soedynenie']

Series of letters to the editor from the lodges relating local St. Nicholas Day celebrations.

L   XVII (48): Dec 31, 1908; C-2&3, L-2&3

2303   John Uhrin; "Ot hl. predsídatelja 'Soedynenija.' Pros'ba" [From the supreme president of the 'Soedynenie.' A request]

Requests donatiuns for a defense fund of G.C.U. lodge member, Paul Janoško who is accused of murder.

Req   XVIII (4): Feb 4, 1909; C-2, L-2

2304   [N.N.]; "Rezul'tat Svjato-Nykolaevskoho mísjaca" [Result of Saint Nicholas Month]

G.C.U. drive to recruit members during the annual celebration of St. Nicholas Month.

A   XVIII (5): Feb 11, 1909; C-2, L-4

2305   Nicholas Pačuta; "Smutnoe to dîlo, koly uže lyš' nepravdoju
       dokazujut" [It's a sad state of affairs, when they use only
       untruths to prove their point]

       Concerning P.R.G.C.U.'s allegations that the G.C.U. is a
       corrupt organization.

       A   XVIII (7): Feb 25, 1909; C-2, L-4

2306   John Uhrin; "Ot hl. Predsidatel'a 'Sojedin.'" [From the supreme
       president of the 'Sojedinenie']

       List of donations from various lodges for the defense fund of
       fellow lodge member Paul Janoško.

       Part I: XVIII (8): Mar 4, 1909; L-2

       Part II: XVIII (11): Mar 25, 1909; C-3, L-3

       Part III: XVIII (14): Apr 22, 1909; C-3, L-3

       O

2307   Michael Torhan; Mont Clare, PA; Mar 3, 1909

       "Zaslato" [Letter to the Editor]

       The polemics between the G.C.U. and the P.R.G.C.U.

       L   XVIII (8): Mar 4, 1909; L-2

2308   Andrew Zboyan, et al.; "Protokol Hl. Kontrollorov 'Soedynenija'"
       [Minutes of the Controller's (meeting) of the 'Soedynenie']

       Meeting held February 22-25, 1909 in Homestead, PA.

       O   XVIII (8): Mar 4, 1909; C-3, L-6

2309   Nicholas Pačuta; "Od hl. sekretarja 'Sojedinenija'" [From the
       supreme secretary of the 'Sojedinenie']

       Notice to members who have relatives in Europe and are members
       of the G.C.U. that death certificates must be filed with the
       Hungarian bureau of Vital Statistics and a copy sent to the
       U.S. General Consul in Budapest.

       O   XVIII (9): Mar 11, 1909; L-2

2310   Michael Cservinka; Pittsburgh, PA; Mar 9, 1909

       Commentary on the G.C.U. bond proposal.

       L   XVIII (9): Mar 11, 1909; C-2&3, L-2&3

2311   Nicholas Halyama; Pittsburgh, PA; Mar 15, 1909

       "Zaslato" [Letter to the Editor]

       Commentary on the G.C.U. bond proposal.

       L   XVIII (10): Mar 18, 1909; C-2&3, L-2

2312 Nicholas Pačuta; "Ot hl. sekretarja 'Soedynenija'" [From the
supreme secretary of the 'Soedynenie']

Reminder to all lodges to pay delinquent dues prior to the
end of the G.C.U.'s fiscal year, April 30, 1909.

O   XVIII (14): Apr 22, 1909; C-7, L-6

2313 John Uhrin; "Ot hl. predsîdatelja 'Soedynenija Hreko Kat. Bratstv'"
[From the supreme president of the G.C.U.]

Explains G.C.U. statute #65, in which members who reject
the Catholic faith, i.e., become orthodox, will lose their membership. Specifically refers to lodge #187 in Brook Side, AL.

O   XVIII (15): Apr 29, 1909; C-2, L-2

2314 Andrew Zboyan, et al.; "Protokol Hl. Kontrollorov 'Soedynenija'"
[Minutes of the Controller's (meeting) of the 'Soedynenie']

Meeting held May 17-20, 1909, in Homestead and Braddock, PA.

O   XVIII (19): May 27, 1909; C-3, L-3

2315 John Uhrin; "Ot hl. predsîdatelja 'Soedynenija Hreko Kat. Russkych
Bratstv'" [From the supreme president of the G.C.U.]

Announces the annual supreme officers' meeting to be held in
Milwaukee, WI, June 14-18, 1909.

O   XVIII (19): May 27, 1909; C-4, L-4

2316 [N.N.]; "Dobročynnŷy v vsepomoščestvujuščiy obščestva" [Charitable
and assistance societies]

Part I: Function of various fraternal and life insurance
organizations Rusyn-Americans should consider joining.

                              XVIII (20): Jun 3, 1909; C-2&3, L-2

Part II: "Jak upravljajutsja vspomohatel'nŷy y dobročynnŷy
obščestva?" [How are charitable and assistance societies
governed?]

                              XVIII (21): Jun 10, 1909; C-4, L-4

Part III: "Jak upravljajutsja vspomohatel'nŷy y dobročynnŷy
obščestva v fynansovom vzljadî?" [How are charitable and
assistance societies governed financially?]

                              XVIII (22): Jun 17, 1909; C-2, L-2

Part IV: "Jak ymijut upravljatysja dobročynnŷy y vspomohatel'-
nŷy obščestva v fynansovom vzhljadî" [How charitable and
assistance societies should be governed financially]

                              XVIII (23): Jun 24, 1909; C-4, L-4

A

2317　Ž.; "Ročnoe Hl. Čynovnyčeskoe Sobranie 'Soedynenija'" [Annual
　　　　meeting of the Supreme officers of the 'Soedynenie']

　　　　Commentary on the meeting in Milwaukee, WI, June 14-18, 1909.

　　　　E　　　　　　　　　　　　　　　　XVIII (21): Jun 10, 1909; C-4, L-4

2318　[N.N.]; "Ročnoe Holovnoe Čynovnyčeskoe Sobranie 'Soedynenija' v
　　　　Mylvakî, Vys" [Annual Meeting of the Supreme officers of the
　　　　'Soedynenie' in Milwaukee, WI]

　　　　A　　　　　　　　　　　　　　　　XVIII (23): Jun 24, 1909; C-2, L-2

2319　[N.N.]; "Protokol" [Minutes]

　　　　Minutes of the G.C.U. Supreme officers meeting held in
　　　　Milwaukee, WI, June 14-18, 1909.

　　　　Parts I-VII　　　　　　　　　　XVIII (24-30): Jul 1-Aug 12, 1909;
　　　　　　　　　　　　　　　　　　　　　　　　　　　　C-2&3, L-2&3

2320　John Uhrin; "Ot hl. predsîdatelja 'Soedynenija'" [From the Supreme
　　　　president of the 'Soedynenie']

　　　　The new administrative procedures to prevent lodge members from
　　　　embezzling the lodge's treasury.

　　　　O　　　　　　　　　　　　　　　　XVIII (33): Sep 2, 1909; C-4, L-4

2321　Andrew Zboyan, et al.; "Protokol Hl. Kontrollorov 'Soedynenija'"
　　　　[Minutes of the Controllers' (meeting) of the 'Soedynenie']

　　　　O　　　　　　　　　　　　　　　　XVIII (34): Sep 9, 1909; C-3, L-3

2322　[N.N.]; "Vozrastaeme" [We are growing]

　　　　The growth of the G.C.U.

　　　　A　　　　　　　　　　　　　　　　XVIII (35): Sep 16, 1909; C-4, L-4

2323　[N.N.]; "Zapomoha 'Soedynenija' Rusynam" [Assistance of the 'Soedy-
　　　　nenie' to Rusyns]

　　　　G.C.U. assistance to the needy, widowed and orphaned.

　　　　A　　　　　　　　　　　　　　　　XVIII (36): Sep 23, 1909; C-2, L-2

2324　John Uhrin, et al.; "Ot hl. urjadu 'Soedynenija Hreko Kat. Russkych
　　　　Bratstv'" [From the Supreme administration of the G.C.U.]

　　　　St. Nicholas Month celebrations.

　　　　O　　　　　　　　　　　　　　　　XVIII (46): Dec 2, 1909; C-4&5, L-4&5

2325　P. Ju. Zsatkovich; "Prazdnyk Sv. O. Nykolaja, pokrovytelja--patrona
　　　　'Soedynenija'" [Feastday of St. Nicholas, patron of the
　　　　'Soedynenie']

　　　　Growth of the G.C.U. during the past year.

　　　　E　　　　　　　　　　　　　　　　XVIII (48): Dec 16, 1909; C-1, L-1

2326   Andrew Gido; Hazleton, PA; Dec 9, 1909

Lodge #10 requests donations for John Gido and his seven
children.

L   XVIII (49): Dec 23, 1909

2327   "Prazdnovanie prazdnyka Sv. O. Nykolaja Pokrovytelja 'Soedynenija'"
[Celebration of the feastday of St. Nicholas, patron of the
'Soedynenie']

Series of letters to the editor from the lodges relating local
St. Nicholas Day celebrations.

L   XVIII (50): Dec 30, 1909; C-6&7, L-9&1(

2328   Andrew Zboyan, et al.; "Try mîsjačnoe spravozdanie Hl. Kontrollorov
'Soedynenija' na mîsjacŷ Avhust, Sentjabr' y Oktjabr' 1909"
[Tri-monthly report of the Supreme Controllers of the 'Soedy-
nenie' for the months of August, September and October 1909]

R   XVIII (50): Jan 6, 1910; L-11
                              XIX (1): Jan 13, 1910; C-2

2329   "Prazdnovanie Prazdnyka Pokrovytelja 'Soedynenija' Sv. O. Nykolaja"
[Celebration of the feastday of the patron of the 'Soedynenie,'
St. Nicholas]

Series of letters to the editor from the lodges relating local
St. Nicholas Day celebrations.

L   XIX (2): Jan 20, 1910; C-2&3, L-2

2330   Redakcija; "Našym sudyteljam" [To our judges]

Commentary on the critics of the G.C.U., ARV and the annual
almanac.

E   XIX (8): Mar 3, 1910; C-4, L-4

2331   John Uhrin; "Ot hl. urjadu 'Soedyn.'" [From the supreme administration of the 'Soedynenie']

Announces the resignation (effective March 19, 1910) of Nicholas
Pačuta from the post of G.C.U. supreme secretary.

O   XIX (11): Mar 24, 1910; C-2, L-4

2332   John Uhrin, et al.; "Ot hl. urjadu 'Soedynenie Hreko Kat. Russkych
Bratstv'" [From the supreme administration of the G.C.U.]

The XI G.C.U. Convention.

O   XIX (13): Apr 7, 1910; C-4&5, L-4

2333   John Uhrin, et al.; "Ot hl. urjadu 'Soedynenija'" [From the supreme administration of the 'Soedynenie']

Reminds lodges to pay all delinquent debts prior to April 30, 1910.

O   XIX (14): Apr 14, 1910; C-6, L-6

2334   Andrew Zboyan, et al.; "Spravozdanie Hl. Kontrollorov 'Soedynenija' o kontrollaciy, poderžannoj ot dnja 14-ho do 19-ho marta h. 1910" [Report of the Supreme Controllers of the 'Soedynenie' concerning the audit performed March 14-19, 1910]

R   XIX (16): Apr 28, 1910; C-6&6, L-6

2335   John Uhrin, et al.; "Ot hl. urjadu 'Soedynenija Hreko Kat. Russkych Bratstv'" [From the supreme administration of the G.C.U.]

Concerning the XI G.C.U. Convention.

O   XIX (18): May 19, 1910; C-6, L-6

2336   Andrew Oprisko; "Ot mîstnoho konvencional'n. komytetu" [From the local convention committee]

Information for delegates arriving in Chicago, IL to attend the XI G.C.U. Convention.

O   XIX (18): May 19, 1910; C-6, L-6

2337   "Proektŷ ot br. na XI hl. konvenciju 'Soedynenija'" [Proposals from the lodges for the XI General Convention of the 'Soedy-nenie']

Part I: XIX (18): May 19, 1910; C-6&7, L-6
Part II: XIX (19): May 26, 1910; C-2&3; L-2&3
Part III: XIX (20): Jun 2, 1910; C-2&3; L-2&3
L

2338   Paul J. Zsatkovich; "XI Hl. Konvencija 'Soedynenija'" [XI General Convention of the 'Soedynenie']

The G.C.U. and its XI Convention.

Part I: XIX (19): May 26, 1910; C-2, L-2
Part II: XIX (20): Jun 2, 1910; C-4, L-4
E

2339   John Uhrin; "Ot hl. predsîdatelja 'Soedynenija'" [From the supreme president of the 'Soedynenie']

a. A G.C.U. donation of $5,000.00 to a widow and orphan fund.
b. Commentary on Rev. Joseph Hanulya and his polemics against the G.C.U.

O   XIX (20): Jun 2, 1910; C-2, L-2

2340 John Uhrin, et al.; "Ot hl. urjadu 'Soedynenija Hreko Kat. Russkych Bratstv'" [From the supreme administration of the G.C.U.]

Instructions for delegates arriving in Chicago, IL to attend the XI G.C.U. Convention.

O   XIX (20): Jun 2, 1910; C-6, L-6

2341 John Drimak; "Vsîm počt. delehatam y delehatkam XI hl. Konvenciy v vnymanie!" [Attention all honorable delegates to the XI General Convention!]

Directions for arriving delegates.

O   XIX (20): Jun 2, 1910; C-6, L-6

2342 Andrew Zboyan, et al.; "Spravozdanie Hl. Kontrollorov 'Soedyn.' na mîsjacŷ mart y april' 1910" [Report of the Supreme Controllers of the 'Soedynenie' for the months of March and April, 1910]

R   XIX (20): Jun 2, 1910; C-6, L-6

2343 P. Ju. Zsatkovich; "Po XI hl. konvenciy našoho 'Soedynenija'" [After the XI General Convention of our 'Soedynenie']

E   XIX (21): Jun 16, 1910; C-2&3, L-4

2344 M. Mosurak; Allegheny, PA

The formation of the Gymnastic branch (Sokol) of the G.C.U. at the XI General Convention.

L   XIX (21): Jun 16, 1910; C-3&4, L-2

2345 John Uhrin; "Od hl. predsidatel'a 'Sojedinenija'" [From the supreme president of the 'Sojedinenije']

a. Reminds newly-elected supreme officers to post their bonds.
b. Thanks Chicago, IL lodge members for their help in making the XI Convention a success.

O   XIX (21): Jun 16, 1910; L-7

2346 Paul Ju. Zsatkovich, et al.; "Ot hl. urjadu 'Soed.'" [From the supreme administration of the 'Soodynenie']

The newly-formed branch of the G.C.U., Uhro-Rusyn Sokols.

O   XIX (22): Jun 23, 1910; C-2, L-2

2347 John Uhrin; "Ot hl. predsîdatelja 'Soedynenie'" [From the supreme president of the 'Soedynenie']

The newly-elected supreme officers of the G.C.U.

O   XIX (23): Jun 23, 1910; C-2, L-2

2348   [N.N.]; "Dobraja rada (sovît) posluchana" [Good advice has been
       heard]

       The friction between the G.C.U. and Bishop Ortynsky.

       A   XIX (23): Jun 23, 1910; C-4, L-4

2349   John Onofrej; Bridgeport, CT

       The G.C.U. Sokol lodges.

       L   XIX (24): Jul 7, 1910; C-2, L-2

2350   John Uhrin, et al.; "Protokol" [Minutes]

       Minutes of the XI G.C.U. General Convention held in Chicago, IL,
       June 6-11, 1910.

       Parts I-IV: XIX (25-28): Jul 14-Aug 4, 1910

       Parts V-X: XIX (30-36): Aug 18-Sep 29, 1910

       O

2351   Nicholas Rusinyak; "Dzešec ročny jubileum Sp. č. 210 v Dunbar, Pa."
       [Tenth anniversary of (G.C.U.) lodge #210 in Dunbar, PA]

       A   XIX (28): Aug 4, 1910; L-2

2352   Julius Egrecky; "Od hl. sekretara 'Sojedinenija Gr. Kat. Russkych
       Bratstv'" [From the supreme secretary of the G.C.U.]

       The payment of benefits to widows and orphans.

       O   XIX (32): Sep 1, 1910; L-6
                                  XIX (33): Sep 8, 1910; C-3

2353   Basil Rudišin; McKees Rocks, PA

       "Otvertŷj lyst O. Iossyfu Hanulja, redaktorovy hazetky, The
       Ruthenian" [Open letter to Rev. Joseph Hanulya, editor of
       the newspaper, Rusin]

       Rev. Hanulya's alleged responsibility in causing trouble
       between two G.C.U. lodges over a church function.

       L   XIX (35): Sep 22, 1910; C-2, L-3

2354   [N.N.]; "Osud 'Ruskoho Narodnoho sojuza' a od nedavna 'Grecko Kat.
       Rusjkoho Sojuza'" [The fate of the 'Rusyn National Union' and
       of late, the 'Greek Catholic Rusyn Union']

       Characterization of these two rival fraternal organizations.

       A   XIX (39): Oct 20, 1910; L-4

2355   Paul Ju. Zsatkovich, et al.; "Ot 'Soedynenija Hreko Kat. Russkych
       Bratstv'" [From the G.C.U.]

       The Sokol branch of the G.C.U.

       E   XIX (40): Oct 27, 1910; C-6, L-6

2356 [N.N.]; "Konvencija novoj Orhanyzaciy" [Convention of a new organization]

The convention of the R.N.U., held in Scranton, PA on October 25-26, 1910.

A   XIX (41): Nov 3, 1910; C-4, L-4

2357 John Koščak, et al.; Mingo Junction, OH; Oct 13, 1910

"Otvît. Komytetu 10-ho Odbora Nar. Slov. Spolku, na dopys' publykovanu v numerî 39-om Narodných Novyn s dnja 29-ho sentjabrja" [Answer. To the committee of the tenth section of the National Slovak Union, to the letter to the editor published in Národné Noviny, #39, September 29, 1910]

Relations between Ohio G.C.U. and N.S.U. lodges in jointly sponsored functions.

L   XIX (42): Nov 10, 1910; C-2&3, L-2&3

2358 Paul Ju. Zsatkovich; "Orhanyzovanie našoj moloděžy čerez Sokolskiy Bratstva" [Organization of our youth by means of the Sokol lodges]

E   XIX (44): Nov 24, 1910; C-4, L-4

2359 John Uhrin, et al.; "Ot hl. urjadu 'Soedynenija Hreko Kat. Russkych Bratstv'" [From the supreme administration of the G.C.U.]

The celebration of St. Nicholas Month by the lodges.

O   XIX (45): Dec 1, 1910; C-4&5, L-4&5

2360 John Uhrin; "Pomahajme bîdnŷm strajkeram" [Let us help the poor strikers]

Requests financial donations for striking Pennsylvanian G.C.U. lodge members.

Req   XIX (45): Dec 1, 1910; C-5, L-4

2361 Michzel Juhaz; "Spravozdanie Hl. Kontrollorov 'Soedynenija' o poslîdnoj kontrolî, poderžanoj 28-ho nojabrja 1910 y v slîdujuščych dnjach" [Report of the Supreme Controllers of the 'Soedynenie' concerning the last audit performed November 28, 1910 and on the following days]

R   XIX (47): Dec 15, 1910; C-2,3,6, L-2&3

2362 P. Ju. Ž.; "Prazdnyk 'Soedynenija'" [Feastday of the 'Soedynenie']

The celebration of St. Nicholas Day.

E   XIX (47): Dec 15, 1910; C-4, L-4

2363 [N.N.]; "Mîsjac svjato-Nykolaevskij" [St. Nicholas Month]

A   XIX (48): Dec 22, 1910; C-4, L-4

2364   John Uhrin, et al.; "Od uradu 'Sojedinen. Gr. Kat. Russk. Bratstv'"
       [From the supreme administration of the G.C.U.]

       The proper procedure for reporting a lodge member's death and
       filing for death benefits.

       O   XIX (49): Dec 29, 1910; L-4

2365   Nicholas Pačuta; "Ot predsîdatelja hl. suda 'Soed. Hr. Kat. Russkych
       Bratstv'" [From the president of the Supreme Court of the
       G.C.U.]

       Review of cases.

       O   XX (1): Jan 19, 1911; C-4, L-4

2366   [N.N.]; "Naš' Postup" [Our progress]

       The past and present state of the G.C.U.

       A   XX (1): Jan 19, 1911; C-4, L-4

2367   [N.N.]; "Sokolskiy upražnenija" [Sokol exercises]

       The March 10, 1911 athletic and gymnastic exhibition sponsored
       by the Pittsburgh, PA G.C.U. Sokol lodges.

       A   XX (2): Jan 26, 1911; C-4, L-4

2368   [N.N.]; "Sdîlaly mŷ ym radosty" [We made joy for them]

       The G.C.U. Christmas collection for striking miners in PA.

       A   XX (2): Jan 26, 1911; C-4, L-4

2369   Michael Macsuga, et al.; "XX Juvylejnoe Toržestvo" [XX Anniversary
       Celebration]

       The celebration of the Brooklyn, NY G.C.U. lodge #1's twentieth
       anniversary.

       A   XX (4): Feb 9, 1911; C-2, L-2

2370   Paul Čarnyj; St. Louis, MO

       Problems for the St. Louis G.C.U. lodge due to Rusyn-Ukrainian
       polemics.

       L   XX (6): Feb 23, 1911; C-2, L-2

2371   John Uhrin; "Ot hl. predsîdatelja 'Soedynenija'" [From the supreme
       president of the 'Soedynenije']

       The delegates from lodges #71 and #154 who did not have the
       chance to voice their opinions at the XI General G.C.U. Con-
       vention.

       O   XX (7): Mar 2, 1911; C-4, L-4

2372   John Hornyak; Pittsburgh-Oakland, PA

The G.C.U.'s largest lodge, #437 in Oakland.

L   XX (8): Mar 9, 1911; C-2, L-2

2373   Nicholas Pačuta; "Ot predsîdatelja hl. suda 'Soedynenija'" [From the president of the supreme court of the 'Soedynenie']

The May 24, 1911 meeting of the court.

O   XX (9): Mar 16, 1911; C-4, L-4

2374   Michael Juhas, et al.; "Spravozdanie Hl. Kontrollorov 'Soedynenija', o kontrollaciy poderžanoj 27-28-ho fevr. y 1-2-3-ho marta 1911, s poslîdnych trech mîsjacev: nojabr', dekabr' 1910 h. y janv. 1911" [Report of the Supreme Controllers of the 'Soedynenie', concerning the controller review held February 27-28 and March 1-3, 1911 for the last three months: November, December 1910 and January 1911]

Part I: XX (9): Mar 16, 1911; C-6, L-6

Part II: XX (10): Mar 23, 1911; C-6,7,8, L-6&7

R

2375   Michael Macsuga, et al.; Brooklyn, NY

The Brooklyn G.C.U. lodge's February 18, 1911 twentieth anniversary celebration.

L   XX (10): Mar 23, 1911; C-5, L-2&3

2376   John Uhrin; "Ot hl. predsîdatelja 'Soedynenija'" [From the supreme president of the 'Soedynenie']

a.   The sending of donations for the orphan fund to the main office.
b.   Payment of lodge members' funeral expenses.
c.   Postment of an insurance bond for newly elected supreme officers.
d.   Financial situation of the juvenile lodges.

O   XX (11): Mar 30, 1911; C-4, L-4

2377   John Uhrin; "Ot hl. predsîdatelja 'Soedynenija Hreko Kat. Russkych Bratstv'" [From the supreme president of the G.C.U.]

Annual supreme officers meeting will be held in Perth Amboy, NJ, June 26-30, 1911.

O   XX (15): May 4, 1911; C-9, L-9

2378   Nicholas Pačuta; "Ot predsîdatelja hl. suda 'Soedynenija'" [From the president of the supreme court]

a.   Requests that all complaints be sent to G.C.U. headquarters.
b.   Supreme court will meet in Perth Amboy, NJ June 26-30, 1911.

O   XX (15): May 4, 1911; C-9, L-9

2379   Michael A. Maczko; "Ot hl. pys'movodytelja 'Soedynenija'" [From
        the supreme recording secretary of the 'Soedynenie']

        Instructions for lodge officers in accepting new members.

        O   XX (15): May 4, 1911; C-9, L-9

2380   John Karafa, et al.; "Dvadcat' lîtnŷj juvylej čerkovnoho bratstva
        v Trentŷn, N.Dž." [Twenty year anniversary of the church lodge
        in Trenton, NJ]

        Lodge #33's twentieth anniversary celebration.

        A   XX (16): May 11, 1911; C-4&5, L-2

2381   [N.N.]; "Assekuracija žyznej est' ves'ma rozšyrena" [Life insurance
        is very widespread]

        Life insurance and life insurance companies.

        A   XX (18): May 25, 1911; C-4, L-4

2382   John Uhrin; "Ot hl. predsîdatelja" [From the supreme president]

        Requests all lodge members on strike in Westmoreland County, PA
        to apply for G.C.U. assistance.

        Req   XX (19): Jun 1, 1911; C-2&3, L-2

2383   [N.N.]; "Naš' odnoročnŷj postup" [Our yearly progress]

        Information on the past year financial and membership growth of
        the G.C.U.

        A   XX (22): Jun 22, 1911; C-4, L-4

2384   John Karafa, et al.; Trenton, NJ

        The Trenton lodge's May 30, 1911 twentieth anniversary celebra-
        tion.

        L   XX (22): Jun 22, 1911; C-5, L-2

2385   Michael Juhas, et al.; "Spravozdanie Hl. Kontrollorov 'Soedynenija'
        o kontrollaciy poderžanoj 5, 6, 7, 8, 9-ho junja, 1911, yz
        poslîdnych trech mîsjacev: Fevr., Mart y Aprîl 1911" [Report
        of the Supreme Controllers of the 'Soedynenie' concerning the
        controller review held June 5-9, 1911 for the last three months:
        February, March and April 1911]

        R   XX (22): Jun 22, 1911; C-6&7, L-6&7

2386   John Uhrin; "Ot hl. predsîdatelja 'Soedynenija'" [From the supreme
        president of the 'Soedynenie']

        Warns the lodges to beware of trouble makers in the G.C.U.

        O   XX (23): Jul 6, 1911; C-3, L-4

2387 Nicholas Pačuta; "Ot predsîdatelja hl. suda 'Soedynenija'" [From
the president of the supreme court of the 'Soedynenie']

Announces the convocation of a special session of the court to
discuss the problems of lodge #221 in Masontown, PA and lodge
#374 in Ronco, PA.

O   XX (24): Jul 13, 1911; C-4, L-4

2388 John Uhrin; "Protokol" [Minutes]

Minutes of the G.C.U. supreme officers meeting held in Perth
Amboy, NJ, June 26-30 and July 1, 1911.

Parts I-VI: XX (26-31): Jul 27-Aug 31, 1911

Part VII: XX (33): Sep 14, 1911; C-6, L-6

Part VIII: XX (35): Sep 28, 1911; C-6, L-6

Part IX: XX (37): Oct 12, 1911; C-6&7, L-6

Part X: XX (42): Nov 16, 1911; C-6, L-6

Part XI: XX (44): Nov 30, 1911; C-3, L-3

O

2389 [N.N.]; "Jakiy ymîjut bŷty vspomoščestvujuščiy obščestva?" [What
should relief associations be like?]

The G.C.U.'s function as a fraternal life insurance company.

A   XX (28): Aug 10, 1911; C-4, L-4

2390 Michael A. Maczko; "Ot hl. pys'movodytelja 'Soedynenija'" [From
the supreme recording secretary of the 'Soedynenie']

Procedures for the admittance of new lodge members.

O   XX (28): Aug 10, 1911; C-5, L-7

2391 [N.N.]; "Rozmnožujutsja orhanyzaciy--Brat'ja uhorskiy rusynŷ, bud'me
na straž'î" [Organizations are cropping up--Brother Uhro-Rusyns,
let us be on guard]

Warns Rusyns not to get involved with other fraternal organizations. Lists current Rusyn fraternals and their organs.

A   XX (33): Sep 14, 1911; C-4, L-4

2392 Nicholas Pačuta; "Ot predsîdatelja hl. suda 'Soedynenija'" [From the
president of the supreme court of the 'Soedynenie']

Court action on the recent cases it has heard.

O   XX (37): Oct 12, 1911; C-4, L-4

2393 [N.N.]; "Fynansiy našoho 'Soedynenija'" [Finances of our 'Soedynenie']

R   XX (38): Oct 19, 1911; C-4, L-4

2394 Michael Juhas, et al.; "Spravozdanie hl. kontrollorov 'Soedynenija'
      o kontrollaciy, poderžannoj 2-ho y v slîdujuščych dnjach
      oktjabrja, 1911" [Report of the supreme controllers of the
      'Soedynenie', concerning the controller review, held October 2,
      1911 and on the following days]

      R   XX (38): Oct 19, 1911; C-6,7,8, L-6,7,8

2395 [N.N.]; "Vozmožnŷjly postup v našom narodî?" [Is progress possible
      among our people?]

      The growth and development of the G.C.U. and its influence in
      the Rusyn communities.

      A   XX (39): Oct 26, 1911; C-4, L-4

2396 Michael Nemchik; Trenton, NJ

      Rusyns who give up their membership in the G.C.U. to join the
      R.N.U.

      L   XX (41): Nov 9, 1911; C-3, L-2&3

2397 John Uhrin, et al.; "Ot hl. urjadu 'Soedynenija hreko kat. russkych
      Bratstv'" [From the supreme administration of the G.C.U.]

      G.C.U. activities during the annual celebration of St. Nicholas
      Month.

      O   XX (44): Nov 30, 1911; C-4&5, L-4&5

2398 Andrew Lesko; Homestead, PA

      Homestead's G.C.U. Sokol lodge.

      L   XX (46): Dec 14, 1911; C-3, L-2

2399 [N.N.]; "Prazdnovanie prazdnyka sv. O. Nykolaja, pokrovytelja
      'Soedynenija' y svjato - Nykolaevskij mîsjac" [Celebration of
      the feastday of St. Nicholas, patron of the 'Soedynenie' and
      Saint Nicholas Month]

      A   XX (48): Dec 28, 1911; C-4, L-4

2400 [N.N.]; "V soedyneniy est' syla. Vnymaj na svjato-Nykolaevskij
      mîsjac!" [In union there is strength. Heed Saint Nicholas
      Month!]

      The celebration of St. Nicholas Month by the lodges.

      A   XX (49): Jan 4, 1912; C-4, L-4

2401 John Uhrin; "Ot hl. predsîdatelja 'Soedynenija'" [From the supreme
      president of the 'Soedynenie']

      Procedures for admitting new lodge members and forming new
      lodges.

      O   XXI (1): Jan 18, 1912; C-4, L-4

2402   Michael Nemchik; Trenton, NJ; Jan 27, 1912

"Zaslato" [Letter to the Editor]

Life insurance benefits received by members of the R.N.U.

L   XXI (3): Feb 1, 1912; C-2&3, L-2

2403   Joseph Petrovsky; Braddock, PA; Jan 25, 1912

"Krasnoe otlyčie odnoho našoho brata" [Beautiful distinction of one of our brethren]

Honors G.C.U. supreme treasurer, Peter Dzmura, for his eleven-year service to the organization.

L   XXI (4): Feb 8, 1912; C-2&3, L-2&3

2404   [N.N.]; "Den' 14-ho fevralja 1892-1912" [Day of February 14, 1892-1912]

Commemorates the twentieth anniversary of the G.C.U.

A   XXI (4): Feb 8, 1912; C-4, L-4

2405   John Kosty, et al.; McAdoo, PA; Feb 8, 1912

"Jubylejnoe toržestvo bratstva sv. Vladymira, čyslo v 'Soedyn.' 152" [Anniversary celebration of St. Vladimir lodge, #152 in the 'Soedynenie']

Commemorates the twentieth anniversary of lodge #152.

L   XXI (6): Feb 22, 1912; C-2&3, L-2&3

2406   Alexander Horoschak; Perth Amboy, NJ; Feb 5, 1912

"Nîskol'ko slov kasatel'no junošeskych bratstv, čysel v junošeskom otdîleniy 'Soedynenija' 31 y 32, a y prymîr našomu uhro-russkomu narodu" [Several words concerning juvenile lodges #31 and #32 in the juvenile branch of the 'Soedynenie', an example to our Uhro-Rusyn people]

L   XXI (6): Feb 22, 1912; C-4&5, L-3

2407   Michael Juhas and Michael Rushin; "Spravozdanie hl. kontrollorov 'Soedynenija' o kontrolljaciy poderžanoj 12-ho fevralja 1912 y [v] slîdujuščych dnjach" [Report of the supreme controllers of the 'Soedynenie' concerning the controllers review held February 12, 1912 and on the following days]

R   XXI (8): Mar 7, 1912; C-5,6,7,9, L-5,6,7

2408   John Bidransky; Strážské [Őrmezö], Zemplén county, Hungary; Jan 13, 1912

Thanks G.C.U. for insurance death benefits received by the brother of Peter Bidransky.

L, E   XXI (9): Mar 14, 1912; C-3, L-3

2409   [N.N.]; "Yspravlenie" [Correction]

Correction in the last report of the supreme controllers.
See: 2407

R   XXI (9): Mar 14, 1912; C-4, L-4

2410   John Uhrin; "Ot hl. urjada 'Soedynenija'" [From the supreme
administration of the 'Soedynenie']

Reminder for members to go to confession at least once a year.

O   XXI (10): Mar 21, 1912; C-4, L-4

2411   Julius Egreczky; "Ot hl. sekretarja 'Soedynenija'" [From the
supreme secretary of the 'Soedynenie']

Reminds lodges in all branches of the G.C.U. to pay all delinquent debts prior to the end of the G.C.U. fiscal year, April
30, 1912.

O   XXI (11): Mar 28, 1912; C-4, L-4

2412   [N.N.]; "Jako prazdnovaty sej naš' dvadcat' lîtnŷj juvylej?" [How
to celebrate our twentieth anniversary?]

The growth and development of the G.C.U. during the past twenty
years.

A   XXI (11): Mar 28, 1912; C-4, L-4

2413   John Uhrin, et al.; "Ot hl. urjada 'Soedynenija hreko kat. russkych
bratstv'" [From the supreme administration of the G.C.U.]

Instructions for delegates to the XII General Convention in
Homestead, PA.

O   XXI (12): Apr 4, 1912; C-4&5, L-4&5

2414   [N.N.]; "Nîskol'ko yskrennŷch slov y otporučanij po povodu XII hl.
konvenciy 'Soedynenija'" [Several sincere words and commenda-
tions on the occasion of the XII General Convention of the
'Soedynenie']

Parts I-V: XXI (13-17): Apr 18-May 16, 1912;
                                     C-4&5, L-4&5

A

2415   Nicholas Pačuta, et al.; "Protokol zasîdanija hl. suda 'Soedynenija
hreko kat. russkych bratstv' poderžannoho v mîstî klyvlŷnd, o.
v dnjach 12, 13 y 14-ho dekabrja 1911" [Minutes of the meeting
of the Supreme Court of the 'G.C.U.' held in Cleveland, OH,
December 12-14, 1911]

O   XXI (13): Apr 18, 1912; C-9&10

2416   John Uhrin; "Ot hl. predsîdatelja 'Soedynenija hr. kat. russkych bratstv'" [From the supreme president of the G.C.U.]

The twentieth anniversary celebration of the G.C.U. in Homestead, PA during the XII General Convention on July 2, 1912.

O   XXI (15): May 2, 1912; C-4, L-4

2417   John Uhrin, et al.; "Ot hl. urjada 'Soedynenija'" [From the supreme administration of the 'Soedynenie']

a. Where in Homestead, PA the XII General Convention will take place.
b. The May 27, 1912 pre-convention supreme officers meeting.

O   XXI (16): May 9, 1912; C-4, L-4

2418   "Proektŷ ot Bratstv na XII Hl. Konvenciju 'Soedynenija Hr. Kat. Russkych Bratstv'" [Proposals from the lodges for the XII General Convention of the G.C.U.]

Part I: XXI (17): May 16, 1912; C-2&3, L-2&3

Part II: XXI (18): May 23, 1912; C-9&10

Part III: XXI (19): May 30, 1912; C-3,6,7; L-3&6

L

2419   John Uhrin; "Ot hl. predsîdatelja 'Soedynenija'" [From the supreme president of the 'Soedynenie']

Requests all lodges to reply to the June 2, 1912 anniversary celebration invitations prior to May 28, 1912.

Req   XXI (18): May 23, 1912; C-4, L-4

2420   Julius Egreczky; "Ot hl. sekretarja 'Soedynenija'" [From the supreme secretary of the 'Soedynenie']

The procedure of reimbursing convention delegates' transportation expenses to Homestead, PA.

O   XXI (18): May 23, 1912; C-4, L-4

2421   [N.N.]; "Yspolnjajme dobrî svoju povynnost'" [Let us carry out well our obligation]

The XII General Convention of the G.C.U.

A   XXI (18): May 23, 1912; C-4&5, L-4&5

2422   O.; "Oproverženie odnoho velykoho cŷhanstva Ruthenian-a" [Refutation of a great lie in Rusin]

Commentary on the article by Rev. Hanulya in Rusin about ARV editor P.J. Zsatkovich's three sons.

A   XXI (19): May 30, 1912; C-2&3, L-2

2423   Michael Skurkay; "Odyn važnŷj proekt" [An important proposal]

A proposal submitted by lodge #188 in Monessen, PA for the XII General Convention.

A   XXI (19): May 30, 1912; C-3, L-2&3

2424   [N.N.]; "XII hl. konvencija 'Soedynenija'" [XII General Convention of the 'Soedynenie']

Proceedings of the XII General Convention.

A   XXI (20): Jun 13, 1912; C-2, L-2

2425   Michael Juhas and Michael Rushin; "Spravozdanie hl. kontrollorov 'Soedynenija', o kontrolljaciy poderzanoj 20-ho maja 1912 y v sľidujuščych dnjach" [Report of the supreme controllers of the 'Soedynenie' concerning the controllers review held May 20, 1912 and on the following days]

R   XXI (20): Jun 13, 1912; C-6&7, L-6&7

2426   [N.N.]; "Odnoe krasnoe bratskoe jubylejnoe toržestvo" [A beautiful lodge anniversary celebration]

Lodge #16's in DeLancey, PA twentieth anniversary celebration.

A   XXI (21): Jun 20, 1912; C-2, L-2

2427   John Bilak and John Škarupa; "Bratskiy predosterehajuščiy slova dlja vsîch členov bratstva č. v 'Soedyneniy' 290 v Alleheny, Pa." [Fraternal cautionary words for all members of lodge #290 in the 'Soedynenie' in Allegheny, PA]

Warns lodge members to be aware of Bishop Ortynsky's supporters during the XII General G.C.U. Convention. Editor's commentary follows.

A   XXI (22): Jun 27, 1912; C-2&3, L-2

2428   "Bratskoe y cerkovnoe toržestvo" [Lodge and church celebration]

Lodge #18's in Leisenring, PA twentieth anniversary celebration on July 4, 1912.

Ad   XXI (22): Jun 27, 1912; C-3, L-3

2429   Michael Juhas; "Ot predsîdatelja hl. kontrollorov 'Soedynenija'" [From the president of the supreme controllers committee of the 'Soedynenie']

The postment of personal bonds by newly elected supreme officers.

O   XXI (22): Jun 27, 1912; C-3, L-3

2430   [N.N.]; "Nîskol'ko slov o predkovencional'nych proektach" [Several words concerning the pre-convention proposals]

A   XXI (22): Jun 27, 1912; C-4, L-4

2431   [N.N.]; "Čto est' položenîyšym? Platyty vkladŷ dlja rozmeta, yly dlja vîka?" [What is more advisable? To pay deposits for term or life insurance?]

Life insurance policies offered by the G.C.U. and other organizations.

Parts I-III: XXI (22-24): Jun 27-Jul 11, 1912;
                                       C-4&5, L-4&5

A

2432   Paul J. Zsatkovich; "Kto est' otvîčatel'nŷm za Mackovo spravozdanie?" [Who is responsible for the Maczko report?]

Commentary on an anonymous report (published in _Rusin_), purportedly by G.C.U. supreme recording secretary, Michael Maczko, that puts the G.C.U. in a scandalous position during the XII General Convention.

E   XXI (23): Jul 4, 1912; C-2, L-2

2433   Jos. B. Krčmery; "Publyčnŷj otvît O. Iosyfu Hanulja, jak redaktoru _Rusyna_" [Public reply to Rev. Joseph Hanulya, editor of _Rusin_]

Commentary on a report about the G.C.U. which appeared in _Rusin_, #23, June 27, 1912.

A   XXI (23): Jul 4, 1912; C-2&3, L-2&3

2434   [N.N.]; "Protocol. XII hl. konvenciy 'Soedynenija hr. kat. russkych bratstv' v Soedynenŷch štatach Ameryky, poderžannoj v mîstî homsted, pa., v dnjach 2-12-ho junija, 1912" [Minutes of the XII General Convention of the G.C.U. in the U.S.A., held in the city of Homestead, PA, June 2-12, 1912]

Parts I-VI: XXI (23-28): Jul 4-Aug 8, 1912

Parts VII-XIII: XXI (31-38): Aug 29-Oct 17, 1912

Parts XIV-XVI: XXI (40-42): Oct 31-Nov 14, 1912;
                                         C-6, L-6

Part XVII: XXII (4): Feb 6, 1913; C-6, L-6

Parts XVIII-XXI: XXII (6-9): Feb 20-Mar 13, 1913;
                                         C-6, L-6

O

2435   [N.N.]; "Toržestva, kotorŷy ustroyvaly uhro-russkaja hreko kat. parafija y bratstva, do 'Soedynenija' prynadležaščiy v homsted, pa." [Celebration arranged by the Uhro-Rusyn Greek Catholic parish and lodge belonging to the 'Soedyenie' in Homestead, PA]

The activities celebrating the twentieth anniversary of the G.C.U.

A, P   XXI (24): Jul 11, 1912; C-2&3, L-2

2436   Paul J. Zsatkovich; "Novŷj hl. urjad 'Soedynenija'" [New supreme
        administration of the 'Soedynenie']

        E   XXI (24): Jul 11, 1912; C-4, L-4

2437   John Uhrin; "Ot hl. predsîdatelja 'Soedynenija'" [From the supreme
        president of the 'Soedynenie']

        Announces the suspension of women's lodge #297 in Allegheny, PA.
        All non-suspended members of this lodge have been transferred
        to lodge #542 in Allegheny.

        O   XXI (24): Jul 11, 1912; C-6, L-3

2438   Michael Rushin, et al.; "Ot novoho hl. urjada 'Soedynenija hreko
        kat. russkych bratstv'" [From the new supreme administration
        of the G.C.U.]

        Pledges to continue the good work of the G.C.U. in the realm
        of religious-national affairs.

        O   XXI (25): Jul 18, 1912; C-4, L-4

2439   [N.N.]; Lisbon Falls, ME

        The activities of the Lisbon Falls' Sokol lodge.

        L, P   XXI (26): Jul 25, 1912; C-2&3, L-2

2440   Ž.; "Odno bratskoe jubylejnoe toržestvo" [A fraternal lodge anni-
        versary celebration]

        The twentieth anniversary celebration of lodge #31 in Uniontown,
        PA.

        E   XXI (26): Jul 25, 1912; C-4, L-4

2441   Michael Rushin, et al.; "Ot hl. urjada 'Soedynenija Hreko Kat.
        Russkych Bratstv'" [From the supreme administration of the
        G.C.U.]

        Fate of lodge #290 in Allegheny, PA will be the topic of an
        August 18, 1912 meeting of G.C.U. supreme officers in
        Pittsburgh, PA.

        O   XXI (27): Aug 1, 1912; C-4, L-4

2442   Michael Rushin; "Ot predsîdatelja 'Soedynenija Hreko Kat. Russkych
        Bratstv'" [From the supreme president of the G.C.U.]

        Requests all lodges to send dues to Harry Savuliak in care of
        Shenandoah Trust Co. in Shenandoah, PA.

        Req   XXI (28): Aug 8, 1912; C-4

2443   [N.N.]; Homestead, PA

        The September 2, 1912 activities of the Homestead Sokol lodge.

        L   XXI (33): Sep 12, 1912; C-2, L-2&3

2444 Michael Rushin; "Ot hl. predsîdatelja 'Soedynenija'" [From the president of the 'Soedynenie']

Reminds newly elected supreme officers to present proof of U.S. citizenship prior to assuming office.

O   XXI (33): Sep 12, 1912; C-4, L-4

2445 Basil Ducar; Pleasant City, OH; Sept. 19, 1912

"Otvît na otvît rutenijana, vlastyvo eho redaktora" [Rebuttal to the rebuttal of Rusin, particularly its editor]

Accuses Rusin editor, Rev. Joseph Hanulya, of printing lies about the G.C.U.

L   XXI (34): Sep 19, 1912; C-2, L-2

2446 Michael Rushin; "Ot hl. predsîdatelja 'Soedynenija hreko kat. russkych bratstv'" [From the supreme president of the G.C.U.]

The dissention from lodges #560 and #653 in Brownsville, PA, over the G.C.U.'s decision to finance a delegation to Rome to petition for the establishment of a separate Uhro-Rusyn Greek Catholic Eparchy in America.

E   XXI (35): Sep 26, 1912; C-4, L-4

2447 John Smolnicky; "V zaščytî česty y pravdŷ" [In defense of honor and truth]

Dissention within the G.C.U. over the expenditure of $12,000.00 to send a delegation to Rome petition for a Uhro-Rusyn bishop for America.

A   XXI (36): Oct 3, 1912; C-2&3; L-2

2448 [N.N.]; "Neprijately 'Soedynenija' y uhro russkoho naroda svyrîpstvujut" [Enemies of the 'Soedynenie' and Uhro-Rusyn people go mad]

Issues behind the polemics over funds allocated by the G.C.U. to fight "trouble makers" in Rusyn communities.

Part I: XXI (36): Oct 3, 1912; C-4, L-4

Part II: XXI (37): Oct 10, 1912; C-4, L-4

A

2449 Redakcija; "Yspravlenie" [Correction]

Editor's commentary regarding the Smolnicky article and the G.C.U. funding of a delegation to Rome. See: 2447.

E   XXI (37): Oct 10, 1912; C-3, L-5

2450 John Uhrin, et al.; "Ot hr. kat. russkoho bratstva č. v 'Soedyneniy'
      26 v Homsted, Pa." [From the Greek Catholic Rusyn lodge #26
      in the 'Soedynenie' in Homestead, PA]

      Extract from the protocol of a lodge meeting held October 6,
      1912. Condems the action of G.C.U. lodges #560 and 653 in
      Brownsville, PA, in protesting the G.C.U.'s $12,000.00 alloca-
      tion for sending a delegation to Rome to petition for a Greek
      Catholic Uhro-Rusyn Bishop for America.

      O   XXI (38): Oct 17, 1912; C-2&3, L-2

2451 Rev. A.A.; "Narod naš dobrŷj, varujsja fal'šyvych prorokov, fal'šy-
      vych učytelej" [Our good people, beware false prophets, false
      teachers]

      Dissention within the G.C.U. concerning the expenditure of
      $12,000.00 for sending a delegation to Rome to petition for
      the appointment of a Uhro-Rusyn bishop for America.

      A   XXI (38): Oct 17, 1912; C-4&5, L-4

2452 Michael Juhas; "Spravozdanie hl. kontrollorov 'Soedynenija' o
      kontrollaciy, poderžanoj dnja 16-ho sentjabrja 1912 y [v]
      slîdujuščych dnjach" [Report of the supreme controllers of
      the 'Soedynenie' concerning the controllers review held Sep-
      tember 16, 1912 and on the following days]

      R   XXI (39): Oct 24, 1912; C-6&7, L-6&7

2453 Michael S. Rushin; "Ot hl. predsîdatelja 'Soedynenija Hreko Kat.
      Russkych Bratstv'" [From the supreme president of the G.C.U.]

      Announces the convocation of a meeting on November 24, 1912 in
      Allegheny, PA to discuss the selection of adult sponsors for
      juvenile lodges #17 and #18 in Allegheny, PA.

      O   XXI (42): Nov 14, 1912; C-4, L-4

2454 Andrew Lesso, et al.; "Protest ot bratstva blahovîščenija presv.
      Dîvŷ Mariy č. v 'Soedyneniy' 33" [Protest from St. Mary's
      Annunciation lodge #33 (Trenton, NJ) in the 'Soedynenie']

      Protest against G.C.U. lodge #560 in Brownsville, PA over the
      circulation of a flyer condemning the G.C.U. supreme officers'
      decision to send a delegation to Rome to request the appoint-
      ment of a Greek Catholic Uhro-Rusyn Bishop for America.

      A   XXI (43): Nov 21, 1912; C-4, L-4

2455 Michael S. Rushin; "Ot hl. predsîdatelja 'Soedynenija'" [From the
      supreme president of the 'Soedynenie']

      Requests financial donations from all lodges of the juvenile
      branch for the war effort of the Slavs in the Balkan War.

      Req   XXI (43): Nov 21, 1912; C-4, L-4

2456   George Z. Barany; "Bez polycmana balovaja zabava" [A (successful) dancing party without a policeman]

Lodge #96's in Bradenville, PA fifteenth anniversary celebration.

A   XXI (44): Nov 28, 1912; C-4&5, L-4

2457   Michael S. Rushin et al.; "Ot hl. urjada 'Soedynenija Hreko Kat. Russkych Bratstv'" [From the supreme administration of the G.C.U.]

The annual celebration of St. Nicholas Month.

O   XXI (45): Dec 5, 1912; C-4&5, L-4&5

2458   [N.N.]; "Svjato-Nykolaevskij Mîsjac" [Saint Nicholas Month]

A   XXI (48): Dec 26, 1912; C-4

2459   [N.N.]; "Švyndlerstvo, soveršenoe na škodu 'Soedynenija', lučše skazano na škodu členov, est' otkrŷtoe" [Embezzlement, which was caused to the detriment of the 'Soedynenie', better yet, to the detriment of the members is uncovered]

The embezzlement of G.C.U. funds by attorney William Vokolek.

A   XXII (1): Jan 16, 1913; C-4, L-4

2460   [N.N.]; "Našy 'prijately' opjat' dajut o sebî slŷšaty" [Our 'friends' make themselves heard again]

Commentary on an article concerning G.C.U. efforts to aid the Jugoslavs in Národné noviny [Pittsburgh, PA], #157.

A   XXII (1): Jan 16, 1913; C-4&5, L-4&5

2461   Michael Juhas, et al.; "Spravozdanie hl. kontrollorov 'Soedynenija' o kontrolljaciy poderžannoj 2-ho dekabrja y [v] slîdujuščych dnjach [Report of the supreme controllers of the 'Soedynenie' concerning the controllers review held December 2, 1912 and on the following days]

R   XXII (1): Jan 16, 1913; C-6&7, L-6&6

2462   Michael S. Rushin, et al.; "Ot Hl. Urjada 'Soedynenija Hreko Kat. Russkych Bratstv', jako Ynkvyrujuščoho Komyteta" [From the Supreme Administration of the G.C.U. as Inquiring Committee]

List of lodges and amount of funds involved in the Vokolek embezzlement.

O   XXII (2): Jan 23, 1913; C-4, L-4

2463 [N.N.]; "Vokolekovskiy švyndly" [Vokolek embezzlement]

Transcript (in English and Rusyn) of the confession of William Vokolek (accused of embezzling G.C.U. funds over a period of five years), taken January 10, 1913 at a Pittsburgh, PA police station.

A   XXII (2): Jan 23, 1913; C-4,5,6,7,
                                                    L-4,5,6,7

2464 Redakcija; "Vsîm poct. Bratstvam v laskavoe vnymanie!" [Attention all honorable lodges!]

The G.C.U. Jugoslav fund.

E   XXII (3): Jan 30, 1913; C-4, L-4

2465 Michael S. Rushin, et al.; "Ot hl. preds., preds. hl. kontrollorov, y preds. hl. sudu 'Soedynenija'" [From the supreme president, president of the supreme controllers and president of the supreme court of the 'Soedynenie']

The course of action by the supreme administration to deal with the Vokolek embezzlement.

O   XXII (4): Feb 6, 1913; C-4, L-4

2466 [N.N.]; "Narode uhro-russkij čytaj, sudy mudro, rozvažno dlja spravedlyvosty y sovîsty!" [Hungarian-Rusyn people read, judge reasonably, deliberately for justice and conscience!]

The embezzlement of G.C.U. funds by William Vokolek aided by former supreme secretary, Julius Egreczky.

Part I: XXII (5): Feb 13, 1913; C-4&5, L-4

Part II: XXII (6): Feb 20, 1913; C-2&3, L-2

A

2467 "Holosŷ naroda na zamîšatel'stva vozstavšiy vslîdstvie Vokolekov-skych švyndlej" [Opinions of the people regarding the confusion resulting from the Vokolek embezzlement]

Series of letters to the editor commenting on this issue.

L   XXII (6): Feb 20, 1913; C-2&3, L-2&3

2468 [N.N.]; "Čto to? Možet-ly každŷj zlomŷslennyk, buntovšcyk y špeku-lant napadovaty y očernjaty vedenie 'Soedynenija' y eho hl. urjadnykov?" [What's this? Is it permitted for every evil-thinker, instigator and speculator to attack and slander the direction of the 'Soedynenie' and its supreme administration?]

How the G.C.U. will prevent further embezzlements.

A   XXII (6): Feb 20, 1913; C-4, L-4

2469   [N.N.]; "Uhro-Russkoe Sokolstvo" [Uhro-Rusyn Sokols]

       A, P   XXII (6): Feb 20, 1913; C-9&10

2470   [N.N.]; "Čto ymîeme dîlaty s našymy Sokolamy?" [What do we have
       to do with our Sokols?]

       A   XXII (6): Feb 20, 1913; C-10

2471   [N.N.]; "Burenie y mest'" [Trouble-making and vengeance]

       Anti-G.C.U. activities of G.C.U. Sokol lodge founder, John
       Gocza.

       A   XXII (11): Mar 27, 1913; C-4, L-4

2472   John Uhrin, et al.; "Protokol zasîdanij hl. sudu 'Soedyenija Hreko-
       Kat. Russkych Bratstv', poderžanných v Homsted, Pa. 24-28-ho
       fevralja, 1913" [Minutes of the meeting of the supreme court
       of the G.C.U. held in Homestead, PA, February 24-28, 1913]

       Part I: XXII (11): Mar 27, 1913; C-6,9,10,11,12; L-6&7

       Part II: XXII (12): Apr 3, 1913; C-6&7

       O

2473   [N.N.]; "Zlomyšelna kritika" [Evil-minded criticism]

       The critics of the G.C.U. and its activities.

       A   XXII (12): Apr 3, 1913; L-2

2474   [N.N.]; "Nekvalyfykovannaja derzkaja smîlost'" [Incompetent,
       impudent boldness]

       Anti-G.C.U. activities of G.C.U. Sokol lodge founder, John
       Gocza.

       A   XXII (12): Apr 3, 1913; C-4, L-4

2475   Basil Kovalkovich, et al.; Philadelphia, PA; May 19, 1913

       "Otpovîd' h. Fedoru Šuda" [Answer to Mr. Theodore Shuda]

       Polemics among members of Philadelphia G.C.U. lodge #201.

       L   XXII (13): Apr 10, 1913; C-2, L-2

2476   [N.N.]; "Hosp. Ioann Hoca v službî čužych" [Mr. John Gocza in the
       service of foreigners]

       Anti-G.C.U. activities of John Gocza.

       A   XXII (13): Apr 10, 1913; C-4, L-4

2477   [N.N.]; "Novŷj adressar' našych Bratstv" [New directory of our
       lodges]

       The G.C.U. directory and statistics on the growth of the
       organization.

       A   XXII (15): Apr 24, 1913; C-4&5, L-4

2478   [N.N.]; "Sriadenie našoho Sokolstva" [Organization of our Sokols]

      A   XXII (15): Apr 24, 1913; L-9

2479   Michael Rushin; "Ot hl. predsîdatelja 'Soedynenija hreko kat. russkych bratstv'" [From the supreme president of the G.C.U.]

      The July 21-25, 1913 annual supreme officers meeting in Cleveland, OH.

      O   XXII (21): Jun 12, 1913; C-4, L-4

2480   Harry Savuliak; "Ot hl. kassiera 'Soedynenija hreko kat. russkych bratstv'" [From the supreme treasurer of the G.C.U.]

      Reminds lodges to pay all delinquent debts prior to publication of the G.C.U. financial report.

      O   XXII (21): Jun 12, 1913; C-4, L-4

2481   Michael J. Hanchin, et al.; "Protokol myttynha Uhro-Russkych Sokolov 'Soedynenija' na Pyttsbŷrhskoj okolycŷ sozvannoho učytelem y orhanyzatorom Uhro-Russkych Sokolov, dnja 20-ho aprîlja, 1913, v domî 'Soedynenija', v Homsted, Pa." [Minutes of the meeting of the Uhro-Rusyn Sokols of the 'Soedynenie' in the Pittsburgh vicinity sponsored by a teacher and organizer of the Uhro-Rusyn Sokols, on April 20, 1913 at the home of the 'Soedynenie' in Homestead, PA]

      O   XXII (22): Jun 19, 1913; C-9, L-9

2482   [N.N.]; "Praktyčnŷj patriotyzm" [Practical patriotism]

      The function of the Sokols in fostering good attitudes towards God, nationality and country.

      A   XXII (22): Jun 19, 1913; C-9&10, L-9&10

2483   Michael Juhas, et al.; "Spravozdanie hl. kontrollorov 'Soedynenija' o kontrolljaciy poderžanoj 26-ho maja y [v] slîdujuščych dnjach [Report of the supreme controllers of the 'Soedynenie' concerning the controllers review held May 26, 1913 and on the following days]

      Part I: XXII (22): Jun 19, 1913; C-10,11,12, L-10,11,12

      Part II: XXII (24): Jul 2, 1913; C-6,7,8, L-6&7

      R

2484   M.A. Maczko; "Ot hl. sekretarja 'Soed. hr. kat. russkych bratstv'" [From the supreme secretary of the G.C.U.]

      Reply to supreme treasurer, Harry Savuliak.
      See: 2480

      O   XXII (23): Jun 26, 1913; C-4, L-4

2485   Rev. Michael Jackovich; "Ot hl. duchovnoho upravytelja 'Soedynenija'"
[From the supreme spiritual advisor of the 'Soedynenie']

Lists lodges which have not sent in tickets.

O   XXII (27): Jul 31, 1913; C-2, L-2

2486   [N.N.]; "Ročnoe Hl. Čynovnyčeskoe Sobranie" [Annual Supreme
Officers Meeting]

The July 21-25, 1913 meeting in Cleveland, OH.

A   XXII (27): Jul 31, 1913; C-2, L-2

2487   Michael A. Maczko; "Ot hlavnoho sekretarija 'Soedynenija'" [From
the supreme secretary of the 'Soedynenie']

Lists Greek Catholic churches which have received financial
aid from the G.C.U.

O   XXII (31): Aug 28, 1913; C-4, L-4

2488   Paul Ju. Zsatkovich, et al.; "Ot komyteta yzbrannoho sehoročnym hl.
čynovnyčeskym sobraniem na ustanovlenie sokolskoho unyforma"
[From the committee selected by this year's supreme officers
meeting on the creation of a Sokol uniform]

O   XXII (31): Aug 28, 1913; C-4, L-4

2489   Rev. Michael Jackovich; "Ot holovnoho duchovnoho upravytelja
'Soedynenija'" [From the supreme spiritual advisor of the
'Soedynenie']

Lists lodges which have not purchased tickets.

O   XXII (32): Sep 4, 1913; C-2, L-2

2490   Michael Rushin, et al.; "Protokol ročnoho hl. čynovnyčeskoho
sobranija 'Soedynenija hr. kat. russkych bratstv v soed.
štatach ameryky', poderžannoho v mîstî klyvlŷnd, ohajo 21, 22,
23, 24 y 25-ho julija, 1913" [Minutes of the annual supreme
officers meeting of the 'G.C.U. of the U.S.A.' held in the
city of Cleveland, Ohio July 21-25, 1913]

Parts I-VII: XXII (32-38): Sep 4-Oct 16, 1913;
                                 C-6&7, L-6&7

O

2491   Michael Madzin; "Posvjaščenie Sokolskoho prapora y škol'nŷj yspŷt"
[Dedication of a Sokol banner and a school test]

Events took place September 1, 1913 in Braddock, PA.

A   XXII (34): Sep 18, 1913; C-5, L-4&5

2492   Michael S. Rushin; "Nîkol'ko prymîčanij na vspŷchnutija Rutenijana" [Several comments on the explosions by Rusin]

Commentary on an article about G.C.U. supreme president Rushin and the annual G.C.U. supreme officers meeting in Rusin, #36, September 11, 1913.

A   XXII (35): Sep 25, 1913; C-4, L-4

2493   [N.N.]; "Unyform Uhro-Russkych Sokolov 'Soedynenija'" [Uniform of the Uhro-Rusyn Sokols of the 'Soedynenie']

A, P   XXII (37): Oct 9, 1913; C-4, L-4

2494   Michael S. Rushin; "Ot hl. predsîdatelja 'Soedynenija'" [From the supreme president of the 'Soedynenie']

The nominations for the position of president of the supreme court left vacant by the death of John Uhrin.

O   XXII (38): Oct 16, 1913; C-4, L-4

2495   John Drimak; "Ot hl. pys'movodytelja 'Soedynenija hreko kat. russkych bratstv'" [From the supreme recording secretary of the G.C.U.]

New procedures for lodge secretaries to follow when filing for members' death benefits.

O   XXII (39): Oct 23, 1913; C-2&3, L-2

2496   Michael A. Maczko; "Ot hl. sekretarija 'Soedynenija'" [From the supreme secretary of the 'Soedynenie']

The costs of the Sokol uniforms.

O   XXII (41): Nov 6, 1913; C-4, L-4

2497   Michael Jaško; South Bethlehem, PA; Nov 9, 1913

"Zaslato" [Letter to the Editor]

The G.C.U.'s involvement in religious-nationality affairs.

L   XXII (42): Nov 13, 1913; C-2&3, L-2&3

2498   Rev. Michael Jackovich; "Ot hlavnoho duchovnoho upravytelja 'Soedynenija hr. kat. russkych bratstv'" [From the supreme spiritual advisor of the G.C.U.]

Lists lodges and members who have not purchased tickets.

O   XXII (43): Nov 20, 1913; C-2, L-2

2499   [N.N.]; "Unyform uhro-russkych sokolov 'Soedynenija'" [Uniform of the Uhro-Rusyn Sokols of the 'Soedynenie']

A, P   XXII (43): Nov 20, 1913; C-4, L-4

2500   Michael A. Maczko; "Ot hl. sekretarja 'Soedynenija hreko kat.
       russkych bratstv'" [From the supreme secretary of the G.C.U.]

       The costs of the Sokol uniforms.

       O   XXII (44): Nov 27, 1913; C-4, L-4

2501   Rev. Michael Jackovich, et al.; "Ot Hl. Urjadu 'Soedynenija Hreko
       Kat. Russkych Bratstv'" [From the Supreme Administration of
       the G.C.U.]

       The celebration of St. Nicholas Month by the lodges.

       O   XXII (47): Dec 18, 1913; C-4&5, L-4&5

2502   John Drimak; "Ot hl. pys'movodytelja 'Soedynenija'" [From the
       supreme recording secretary of the 'Soedynenie']

       The reward offered by the G.C.U. to any member who success-
       fully organizes a new lodge between August 15, 1913-1914.

       O   XXII (49): Jan 1, 1914; C-2

2503   P.J. Ž; "Paru uprimnych slov k otazke našoho uhro-russkoho Sokolstva"
       [Several sincere words concerning the question of our Uhro-
       Rusyn Sokols]

       Part I: XXIII (1): Jan 15, 1914; C-9

       Part II: XXIII (8): Mar 5, 1914; C-9

       E

2504   M.A. Maczko; "Ot hl. sekretarja 'Soedynenija'" [From the supreme
       secretary of the 'Soedynenie']

       Lists lodges that have debts to pay to the main office of the
       G.C.U.

       O   XXIII (2): Jan 22, 1914; C-4

2505   John Drimak; "Ot hl. pys'movodytelja 'Soedynenija'" [From the
       supreme recording secretary of the 'Soedynenie']

       The results of the G.C.U. membership drive during St. Nicholas
       Month, December 19, 1913 - January 19, 1913.

       O   XXIII (4): Feb 5, 1914; C-4

2506   Michael A. Maczko, et al.; "Ot hl. sekretarja y predsîdatelja hl.
       kontrollorov 'Soedynenija'" [From the secretary and president
       of the supreme controllers of the 'Soedynenie']

       Lists lodges which have debts to pay to the G.C.U.

       O   XXIII (5): Feb 12, 1914; C-4

2507   Michael Juhas; "Ot predsîdatelja hl. kontrollorov 'Soedynenija'"
        [From the president of the supreme controllers of the
        'Soedynenie']

        Requests lodge members, who attended the X General G.C.U.
        Convention in Chicago, IL and who donated to the orphan fund,
        to contact the G.C.U. main office.

        Req   XXIII (5): Feb 12, 1914; C-4

2508   Michael Juhas; "Spravozdanie hl. kontrollorov 'Soedynenija' yz
        kontroljaciy, perevedenoj dnja 19-ho janvarija 1914 y [v]
        slîdujuščych dnjach" [Report of the supreme controllers of
        the 'Soedynenie' from the controllers' review held January 19,
        1914 and on the following days]

        Parts I-II: XXIII (6-7): Feb 19-26, 1914; C-6&7
        R

2509   Michael S. Rushin; "Ot hl. predsîdatelja 'Soedynenija hreko kat.
        russkych bratstv'" [From the supreme president of the G.C.U.]

        The injunction of Theophile Zsatkovich, obtained against the
        G.C.U. supreme officers' raise in salary.

        O   XXIII (7): Feb 26, 1914; C-4

2510   Peter Dzmura; "Ot predsîdatelja hl. suda 'Soedynenija'" [From the
        president of the supreme court of the 'Soedynenie']

        Lists lodges which have not purchased tickets for the lenten
        season.

        O   XXIII (8): Mar 5, 1914; C-2&3

2511   Theophile A. Zsatkovich; "V zaščytî pravdŷ" [In defense of truth]

        Reply to supreme president Rushin concerning the court liti-
        gation brought to prevent increases in salary for supreme
        officers; lists what each officer receives currently in
        salary.
        See: 2509.

        A   XXIII (8): Mar 5, 1914; C-4&5

2512   Michael S. Rushin; "Ot hl. urjadu 'Soedynenija hreko kat. russkych
        bratstv'" [From the supreme administration of the G.C.U.]

        The plans for the XIII General G.C.U. Convention.

        O   XXIII (9): Mar 12, 1914; C-4

2513 "Holos naroda kasatel'no podvŷšenija plat hl. urjadnykov 'Soedynenija'" [Voice of the people concerning the increase in
salary of the supreme officers of the 'Soedynenie']

Series of letters to the editor about this G.C.U. matter.

Parts I-V: XXIII (9-13): Mar 12-Apr 9, 1914; C-4&5

Part VI: XXIII (16): May 7, 1914; C-3,4,5

L

2514 George Uram Hryšo; Lyndora, PA; Feb 21, 1914

"Zaslato" [Letter to the Editor]

Thanks G.C.U. for the $300.00 gift used to pay the Lyndora
parish's debts.

L XXIII (10): Mar 19, 1914; C-3

2515 "Pomošč dlja syrot y vdovyc' po polehšych v vojni Juho-Slavjanov
protyv Turkov" [Aid for orphans and widows of those who died
in the war of the Jugoslavs against the Turks]

Letters of thanks from the Jugoslavian Red Cross, Serbian and
Bulgarian Governments for the financial aid from the G.C.U.

LE XXIII (10): Mar 19, 1914; C-6

2516 "Proektŷ na XIII Hl. Konvenciju 'Soedynenija'" [Proposals for the
XIII General Convention of the 'Soedynenie']

Letters from the lodges proposing various agenda topics for
the convention.

Parts I-VII: XXIII (11-17): Mar 26-May 14, 1914

L

2517 John Drimak; "Ot hl. pys'movodytelja 'Soedynenija'" [From the
supreme recording secretary of the 'Soedynenie']

Lists lodges which have not sent in the names of their new
officers.

XXIII (11): Mar 26, 1914; C-4

2518 Michael Juhas; "Ot predsîdatelja hl. kontrollorov 'Soedynenija'"
[From the president of the supreme controllers of the 'Soedy-
nenie]

Warns lodges to pay dues directly to the main office and not
to persons who claim to be officers or representatives of the
G.C.U.

XXIII (11): Mar 26, 1914; C-4

2519   [N.N.]; "Nîskol'ko yskrennŷch slov pred XIII Konvencieju 'Soedyn.'"
[Several sincere words prior to the XIII Convention of the
'Soedynenie']

       A   XXIII (11): Mar 26, 1914; C-4

2520   [N.N.]; "Oproverženie" [Refutation]

       Denies allegations by the attorney handling the injunction
suit by Theophile A. Zsatkovich against the increase of salary
for G.C.U. supreme officers; attorney's letter in English.

       A   XXIII (12): Apr 2, 1914; C-2&3

2521   "Delehatŷ y Delehatky yzbranŷ na XIII Hlavnu Konvenciju 'Soedynenija'" [Delegates chosen for the XIII General Convention
of the 'Soedynenie']

       Part I: XXIII (13): Apr 9, 1914; C-6

       Part II: XXIII (15): Apr 30, 1914; C-7&8

       Part III: XXIII (16): May 7, 1914; C-6&7

       Part IV: XXIII (17): May 14, 1914; C-6

       O

2522   George Z. Baran'; "Protokol. Sobranija hreko kat. uhro-russkych
sokolskych reprezentantov yz okolycŷ Pyttsburhskoj otbŷvšohosja
dnja 29-ho marta 1914 h. popoludny ot 2-7 hodynî v domî slavnoho
'Soedynenija Hreko Kat. Russkych Bratstv' v Homsted, Pa."
[Minutes. Meeting of the Greek Catholic Uhro-Rusyn Sokol representatives from the vicinity of Pittsburgh, held March 29, 1914
from 2-7 p.m. in the home of the glorious 'G.C.U.' in Homestead,
PA]

       O   XXIII (13): Apr 9, 1914; C-9&10

2523   Michael S. Rushin; "Ot hl. predsîdatelja 'Soedynenija hreko kat.
russkych bratstv'" [From the supreme president of the G.C.U.]

       a. The salary increase for supreme officers.
       b. Sokol participation in the XIII General Convention.

       O   XXIII (15): Apr 30, 1914; C-4

2524   Michael S. Rushin; "Uhro-russkym sokolam v laskavoe vnymanie!"
[Attention Uhro-Rusyn Sokols!]

       Sokol participation in the XIII General Convention.

       O   XXIII (15): Apr 30, 1914; C-4

2525   Wilma Panca, et al.; Monessen, PA; April 23, 1914

       Monessen's G.C.U. lodge #188 joined the Orthodox "schism."

       L   XXIII (16): May 7, 1914; C-2&3

2526 P.J. Zsatkovich; "Nîskol'ko slov o našom Sokolstvi y o teperîšných
      bezporjadkach y buntach svyrîpstvujuščych v nem" [Several
      words concerning our Sokol lodges and the disorders and rebel-
      lion plaguing them]

      E   XXIII (16): May 7, 1914; C-9

2527 [N.N.]; "Brat Nykolaj Pačuta očystylsja yz pod žalobŷ, kotoraja bŷla
      podanna protyv neho v dîlî Šaradievskoj defravdaciy" [Brother
      Nicholas Pačuta has been exonerated from the indictment lodged
      against him in the Sarady embezzlement affair]

      See wanted poster in: XXIII (16): May 7, 1914; C-7.

      A   XXIII (17): May 14, 1914; C-4&5

2528 Paul J. Zsatkovich; "Nîskol'ko slov o tečeniy XIII Hl. Konvenciy
      'Soedynenija'" [Several words concerning the course of the
      XIII General Convention of the 'Soedynenie']

      The beginning of the convention. Due to a statute in the
      G.C.U. by-laws, ARV editor-in-chief is barred from attending
      the convention.

      E   XXIII (18): May 28, 1914; C-2

2529 Michael Juhas; "Spravozdanie hl. kontrollorov 'Soedynenija' dnja
      22-ho aprîlja 1914 y [v] slîdujuščych dnjach" [Report of the
      supreme controllers of the 'Soedynenie' April 22, 1914 and on
      the following days]

      O   XXIII (18): May 28, 1914; C-3&4

2530 [N.N.]; "XIII Hl. Konvencija 'Soedynenija'" [XIII General Convention
      of the 'Soedynenie']

      Major resolutions and proceedings of the convention.

      Part I: XXIII (19): Jun 4, 1914; C-4

      Part II: XXIII (20): Jun 11, 1914; C-4&5

      A

2531 Ž.; "Čto končyla XIII Hl. Konvencija kasatel'no uhro-russkoho
      Sokolstva" [What was the result of the XIII General Convention
      concerning the Uhro-Rusyn Sokols]

      The decision to create a supreme vice-president position for
      the Sokol lodges.

      E   XXIII (21): Jun 18, 1914; C-4

2532 Basil Kepenač; "Koe-čto o XIII hl. konvenciy našoho slavnoho 'Soedy-
      nenija' otbŷvšojsja v Skrentŷn, Pa." [Something about the XIII
      General Convention of our glorious 'Soedynenie' held in Scranton,
      PA]

      A   XXIII (21): Jun 18, 1914; C-4&5

2533   Michael S. Rushin, et al.; "Ot hl. urjada 'Soedynenija'" [From
the supreme administration of the 'Soedynenie']

Commentary by the newly elected supreme officers concerning
the future of the G.C.U.

O   XXIII (23): Jul 2, 1914; C-4

2534   [N.N.]; "Blahorodnŷy rîšenija XIII Konvenciy 'Soedynenija'"
[Noble decisions of the XIII Convention of the 'Soedynenie']

Part I: G.C.U. is dedicated to fight all who seek to destroy
the integrity of the Greek Catholic Church.

XXIII (24): Jul 9, 1914; C-4

Part II: The G.C.U. school fund for building a Catholic Rusyn
high school.

XXIII (25): Jul 16, 1914; C-4

Part III: The need for a Greek Catholic Orphanage.

XXIII (26): Jul 23, 1914; C-4

Part IV: The XIII General Convention.

XXIII (27): Jul 30, 1914; C-4

A

2535   Ann Kostura; "Ot hl. podpredsîdatel'ky 'Soedynenija'" [From the
supreme vice-president (of the women lodges) of the 'Soedynenie']

a. Women's roles as G.C.U. members.
b. Pledges to do her best to represent the women lodges in
all decision-making matters.

O   XXIII (25): Jul 16, 1914; C-4&5

2536   Michael Delyman, et al.; "Protokol XIII hl. konvenciy 'Soedynenija
Hreko Kat. Russkych Bratstv', otbŷvšojsja v dnjach 18-22-ho
maja, 1914 v Skrentŷn, Pa." [Minutes of the XIII General Convention of the G.C.U., held May 18-28, 1914 in Scranton, PA]

Parts I-XI: XXIII (25-35): Jul 16-Sep 24, 1914

Parts XII-XX: XXIII (37-45): Oct 8-Dec 3, 1914

Parts XXI-XXII: XXIV (11-12): Mar 18-25, 1915;
C-9&10, L-9&10

O

2537   John Drimak; "Ot hl. pys'movodytelja 'Soedynenija hreko kat. russkych
bratstv'" [From the supreme recording secretary of the G.C.U.]

New procedures for filing for death benefits by lodge secretaries.

O   XXIII (28): Aug 6, 1914; C-4

2538   Michael S. Rushin; "Ot hl. predsîdatelja 'Soedynenija hreko kat. russkych bratstv'" [From the supreme president of the G.C.U.]

Prerequisite in the selection of a site for the future Greek Catholic Rusyn Orphanage.

O   XXIII (29): Aug 13, 1914; C-4

2539   George Munčak and Michael Juhas; "Spravozdanie hlavnŷch kontrolorov 'Soedynenija' dnja 29-ho jun'ja y v slîdujuščych dnjach" [Report of the supreme controllers of the 'Soedynenie' (held) June 29, 1914 and on the following days]

R   XXIII (30): Aug 20, 1914; C-6&7

2540   Peter Stanyslav; Youngstown, OH

Commends the action taken by the XIII General Convention in retiring Paul J. Zsatkovich as ARV editor.

L   XXIII (31): Aug 27, 1914; C-11

2541   George Dandar; "Ot hl. kassiera 'Soedynenija'" [From the supreme treasurer of the 'Soedynenie']

Lists the supreme officers to whom checks can be made out by lodge officers for the payment of lodge debts.

O   XXIII (32): Sep 3, 1914; C-4

2542   [N.N.]; "Konvencija Narodnoho Sojuza" [Convention of the (Rusyn) National Union]

The convention was held in Buffalo, NY.

A   XXIII (34): Sep 17, 1914; C-4&5

2543   [N.N.]; "Odnoe vŷdarennoe toržestvo v Renkyn, Pa." [A successful celebration in Rankin, PA]

The September 20, 1914 dedication of the Rankin Sokol lodge's banner.

A   XXIII (35): Sep 24, 1914; C-2&3

2544   Michael S. Rushin; "Urjadnoe Ohološenie" [Official Announcement]

Requests lodges to donate a collection for war-stricken Rusyns in Europe.

Req   XXIII (35): Sep 24, 1914; C-4

2545   [N.N.]; "P. V. Baloh, neprijatel' dobroho ymeny 'Soedynenija'" [Rev. V. Balog, enemy of the good name of the 'Soedynenie']

Anti-G.C.U. activities of Rev. Balog.

A   XXIII (35): Sep 24, 1914; C-4

2546   George Komlos; "Ot hl. sekretarja 'Soedynenija'" [From the supreme secretary of the 'Soedynenie']

The procedures for filing for death benefits by lodge secretaries.

O   XXIII (37): Oct 8, 1914; C-4

2547   [N.N.]; "Serdce Naroda..." [Heart of the People...]

The efforts of Sokol and juvenile lodges to donate to the G.C.U.'s Rusyn war orphans fund.

A   XXIII (37): Oct 8, 1914; C-4

2548   [N.N.]; "Oborona O. Baloha a ešče koe-čto" [Defense of Rev. Balog and something else]

Rev. V. Balog's statement of his innocence from any alleged anti-G.C.U. activities; ARV reply to this defense.

A   XXIII (38): Oct 15, 1914; C-4&5

2549   John Drimak; "Ot hl. pys'movodytelja 'Soedynenija Hr. Kat. Russk. Bratstv'" [From the supreme recording secretary of the G.C.U.]

Requests lodge secretaries to send in the names of all members currently in Europe.

Req   XXIII (39): Oct 22, 1914; C-4

2550   Michael Pyllyšij; "Prijatel'-ly?" [Is he a friend?]

Questions Rev. V. Balog's remark that he never was an enemy of the G.C.U.

A   XXIII (42): Nov 12, 1914; C-4

2551   Rev. Valentine Balog; "Otpovîd' na statiju 'Prijatel'-ly?'" [Reply to the article 'Is he a friend?']
See: 2550.

A   XXIII (43): Nov 19, 1914; C-2&3

2552   John Drimak; "Ot hl. pys'movodytelja 'Soedynenija hreko kat. russkych bratstv'" [From the supreme recording secretary of the G.C.U.]

Statistics on membership in all three lodge branches as of October, 1914.

O   XXIII (43): Nov 19, 1914; C-4

2553   Rev. Alexander Dzubay, et al.; "Ot Hl. Urjadu 'Soedynenija'" [From the Supreme Administration of the 'Soedynenie']

The activities for the celebration of St. Nicholas Month.

O   XXIII (44): Nov 26, 1914; C-4&5

2554   Michael S. Rushin; "Uvydyme yly neuvydyme, Rusyne yly Rutenijane!"
        [We shall see or not see, Rusyn or Ruthenian!]

        Answer to the article in <u>Rusin</u>, #47 concerning certain G.C.U.
        lodges' encouragement of churches and other lodges to convert
        to Orthodoxy.

        A   XXIII (45): Dec 3, 1914; C-4

Chapter 3

Greek Catholic Church

3001   [N.N.]; "Boh Nebesnŷi ne ostavyt upovajuščych na Neho! Try kratnoe
slava! Vyl'ks Berskym našym brat'jam! Vyl'ks Berskiy Hr. kat.
Vîrnyky postaralys' o svoeho svjaščennyka! Vyl'ks Berskaja
parafija ne propala dlja nas, ona voskresla y zŷvet!" [God in
Heaven will not forsake those who hope in Him! Thrice Glory!
Our brothers in Wilkes Barre! Greek Catholic faithful of
Wilkes Barre got their priest! Wilkes Barre parish did not
fall away from us, it was resurrected and lives!]

After a brief Orthodox period, the Wilkes Barre parish returned
to Catholicism, with Rev. Michael Balog as the new pastor of
the parish.

A   III (6): Feb 6, 1894; C-1, L-9&10

3002   "Velykolîpnoe Toržestvo! Osvjaščenie dočasnoj mîstnosty dlja Hr.
kat. Bohosluž8enija v Vyl'ks Berach, Pa." [Splendid Celebration! The consecration of the temporary site for the Greek
Catholic services in Wilkes Barre, PA]

Consecration on February 25, 1894.

Ad   III (7): Feb 20, 1894; C-1, L-9

3003   Ju.; "Toržestvennoe posvjaščenie dočastnoj Hr. kat. Cerkovnoj
mîstnosty y doč. parochial'noho doma v Vylks Berach, Pa."
[Glorious consecration of the temporary site of the Greek
Catholic Church and temporary rectory in Wilkes Barre, PA]

Chronicles the return of the parish to Greek Catholicism.

E   III (9): Mar 6, 1894; C-2&3, L-9&10

3004   [N.N.]; "Vylks Berskij Hr. kat. russkiy vîrnyky začaly pravo protyvo
otobranoj ot nych cerkvy, parochial'noho doma y smyntara;
Poučenie dlja vsîch nas Amerykanskych Rusynov!" [The Greek
Catholic Ruthenian faithful of Wilkes Barre began legal proceedings against those who had taken the church, rectory, and
cemetery from them. A lesson for all of us American Rusyns!]

Describes the legal proceedings to obtain all church property
from the orthodox "schisists."

A   III (10): Mar 13, 1894; C-5, L-10

3005   Ju.; "Rešitel'nyi slova v spravî relihijno-narodnoho zabezpečenija
Amerykanskoj Rusy" [Decisive words on the matter of preserving
the religious-national heritage of American Rusyns]

Part VI: "Neotmînno nužno nam ymîty svoeho obrijada Episkopa!"
[We must, without fail, have our own Bishop!]

E   III (17): May 8, 1894; C-2&3, L-13

3006 "Osvjaščenie novoho Hr. kat. Russkoho Kladbyšča (cmyntarja)"
[Dedication of the new Greek Catholic Rusyn Cemetery]

Dedication in Mayfield, PA on June 23, 1894.

A   III (18): May 15, 1894; C-1

3007 G. Klembarsky, et al.; De Lancey, PA, Jun 25, 1894

Rusyn eparchies: in Europe and the need for one in America.

L   III (23): Jul 3, 1894; C-3, L-9

3008 "Osvjaščenie Nov. Altarja" [Dedication of a new Altar]

Dedication by Rev. Stephen Jaczkovich in McKeesport, PA on
August 5, 1894.

Ad   III (26): Jul 24, 1894; C-1, L-9

3009 "Ot upravytel'stva Hreko Kat. Cerkvy v Ameryki: Počtennŷm Hreko
kat. Cerkvy Vîrnykam v Hazletonî, Pa., y na okolycî!" [From
the ruling council of the Greek Catholic Church in America:
To the honorable Greek Catholic faithful in Hazleton, PA, and
surrounding vicinity!]

Reprint of an episcopal letter from Roman Catholic Bishop of
Scranton, PA, G.W.M. O'Hara, announcing the suspension of
Rev. Victor Martyak.

O   III (29): Aug 21, 1894; C-1, L-9

3010 Rev. Nicephor Chanath, V.R.; "Ot upravytel'stva Hreko kat. Russkoj
Cerkvy v Amerykî. Vsîm Vsečestnîjšym Otcam y Počtennŷm Hreko
kat. Vîrnykam v Soedynenŷch Štatach Sîvernoj Ameryky!" [From
the ruling council of the Greek Catholic Rusyn Church in
America. To all honorable fathers and faithful in the United
States and North America!]

A pastoral letter appealing for support of the Uniate Church
in America.

L   III (29): Aug 21, 1894; C-1, L-9

3011 Ju.; "Tolkovanija v spravach sumîstnych cerkovno-narodnŷch našych
ynteressov" [Interpretation of our mutual religious-national
interests]

Part VIII: Problem of "schism" among Greek Catholic Rusyns in
America and in Europe.

III (29): Aug 21, 1894; C-2

Part X: The Church: Position it occupies among Rusyns in
America and in Europe.

III (31): Sep 12, 1894; C-2

Part XI: The Church: Continued discussion of its importance to Rusyns in America and in Europe.

III (32): Sep 20, 1894; C-2

Part XII: The Church: Statistical information on the number of churches, priests and faithful in America (1894).

E III (33): Sep 27, 1894; C-2, L-13

3012 "Peremîna svjaščennykov" [Change of Priests]

Rev. V. Balog succeeds Rev. Alexander Shereghy (who returns to Europe) as pastor of the Scranton, PA parish.

R III (29): Aug 21, 1894; C-4

3013 [N.N.]; "Krokom (šahom) Vpered" [A Step Forward]

The appointment of Rev. Nicephor Chanath as head of the Greek Catholic clergy in America.

A III (29): Aug 21, 1894; C-4&5, L-13

3014 "Osvjaščenie novoj Hreko kat. Russkoj Cerkvy v Ionkersî, Nju. Jo." [Dedication of new Greek Catholic Rusyn Church in Yonkers, NY]

Dedication on October 2, 1894.

Ad III (31): Sep 13, 1894; C-2, L-9

3015 Alexander Kozubov; Hazleton, PA; Aug 18, 1894

Rusyn church, school and reading room in Hazleton, PA.

L III (32): Sep 20, 1894; C-4, L-13

3016 "Velykoe Toržestvo! Osvjaščenie uhol'naho (rohovoho) kamenja novo-budujuščoj Hr. kat. Russkoj Cerkvy v Hlen Lajn, Pa." [Solemn Celebration! Dedication of the corner stone of the new Greek Catholic Rusyn Church under construction in Glen Lyon, PA]

Dedication by Rev. M. Balog on October 28, 1894.

Ad III (34): Oct 4, 1894; C-1, L-9

3017 "Zaprošenie! Osvjaščenie kraeuhol'naho kamenja Hr. kat. Russkoj Cerkvy v Šeppton, Pa." [An invitation! Dedication of the corner stone of the Greek Catholic Rusyn Church in Sheppton, PA]

Dedication by Rev. N. Szteczovich on November 18, 1894.

Ad III (39): Nov 8, 1894; C-1, L-1

3018 "Toržestvennoe Osvjaščenie! Osvjaščenie 3-ech zvonov Hr. kat. Russkoj Cerkvy v Hazleton, Pa." [Solemn Dedication! Dedication of three bells for the Greek Catholic Rusyn Church in Hazleton, PA]

Dedication by Rev. N. Szteczovich on January 1, 1895.

Ad III (42): Nov 29, 1894; C-1, L-9

3019 Vasilievich; "Otkrovennŷy mnînija o napravleniy y stremlenijach
       <u>Am. Russkoho Vîstnyka</u>" [A candid opinion on the direction
       and aims of <u>ARV</u>]

       Part III: Priests and Religion in Hungary, Galicia, and
       America.

                              III (42): Nov 29, 1894; C-2, L-13

       Part IV: Priests and Religion: Statistical information on
       number of clergy in America.

       A   III (43): Dec 6, 1894; C-2&3, L-13

3020 "Toržestvo Osvjaščenija kraeuhol'noho kameny Hr. kat. Cerkvy v
       Filadelfia, Pa." [Dedication celebration of the corner stone
       of the Greek Catholic Church in Philadelphia, PA]

       Dedication by Rev. John Hrabar on December 25, 1894.

       Ad   III (45): Dec 20, 1894; C-1, L-9

3021 Rev. Nicephor Chanath, V.R.; "Ot upravytel'stva Hreko kat. Cerkvy
       v Amerykî. Vsîm Vsečestnîjsym Hr. kat. Svjaščennykom y
       Počtennŷm Hr. kat. Vîrnykam v Amerykî" [From the administra-
       tion of the Greek Catholic Church in America. To all honorable
       Greek Catholic priests and faithful in America]

       Reprint of an episcopal letter from Roman Catholic bishop of
       Scranton, PA, G.W.M. O'Hara, announcing the suspension and
       excommunication of Rev. Michael Balog (Wilkes Barre, PA).

       O   III (46): Dec 27, 1894; C-1, L-9

3022 [N.N.]; "Lechomŷslennyj postup" [A Flighty Action]

       Rev. Michael Balog's and the Wilkes Barre parish's "conversion"
       to Orthodoxy.

       A   III (46): Dec 27, 1894; C-2&3, L-13&14

3023 Paul Jurievich Žatkovich; "Otkrŷtŷj Lyst vsečestnîjšomu O. Alexiju
       Tovt v Vylkes Bery, Pa." [An open letter to honorable Rev.
       Alexis Toth in Wilkes Barre, PA]

       L   III (47): Jan 2, 1895; C-3

3024 "Toržestvennoe Osvjaščenie kraeuhol'naho kameny. Zaprošenie!"
       [An invitation to the solemn dedication of a corner stone!]

       Dedication by Rev. A. Dzubay in Kalumet, PA on January 13, 1895.

       Ad   III (47): Jan 2, 1895; C-4

3025 [N.N.]; "Pravoslavie y Scyzma" [Orthodoxy and Schism]

       Part I: The definition of Orthodoxy and its role in creating
       schism among Greek Catholic churches.

                              IV (4): Feb 7, 1895; C-2, L-13

Part II: The schismatic trend among uniate churches: a list of Greek Catholic clergy (identified by eparchy) in America who actively participated in the schismatic movement.

IV (5): Feb 14, 1895; C-2&3, L-3&4

Part III: The schismatic trend among Greek Catholic Churches.

IV (6): Feb 21, 1895; C-2, L-3

Part IV: Russian influences in the schismatic trend among Greek Catholics in America and in Europe.

IV (8): Mar 7, 1895; C-2, L-3

Part V: Orthodoxy and the Greek Catholic Church: Some fundamental arguments and explanations.

A   IV (9): Mar 14, 1895; C-2, L-3

3026 [N.N.]; "Rossija y Rymskiy Prestol" [Russia and the Roman See]

The impact upon Rusyns of the recent dialogues between the Russian government and the Papal See over the reunion of Orthodox and Catholic Churches.

A   IV (6): Feb 21, 1895; C-3

3027 Rev. Nicephor Chanath; "Ot Radŷ Hr. kat. Cerkvy Presv. Bohor. Mariy v Skrenton, Pa.; Uvîdomlenie" [Notification from the Church Council of St. Mary's Church in Scranton, PA]

Refutes charges that parishioners helped fund a death benefit collection for members of schismatic parishes.

O   IV (12): Apr 4, 1895; C-1, L-1

3028 [N.N.]; "Chrystos Voskrese!" [Christ is Risen!]

Statistics on number of churches, priests, faithful and G.C.U. members in America.

A   IV (13): Apr 14, 1895; C-1, L-1

3029 "Velykoe Toržestvo! Osvjaščenie novoj Hreko kat. Russkoj Cerkvy v Travher, Pa." [Great Celebration! Dedication of the new Greek Catholic Rusyn Church in Trauger, PA]

Dedication on April 28, 1895.

Ad   IV (14): Apr 25, 1895; C-1, L-1

3030 "Velykoe Toržestvo! Osvjaščenie novoj Hr. kat. Russkoj Cerkvy v Fyladel'fiy, Pa." [Great Celebration! Dedication of the new Greek Catholic Rusyn Church in Philadelphia, PA]

Dedication by Rev. John Hrabar on April 28, 1895.

Ad   IV (14): Apr 25, 1895; C-1, L-1

3031   Alexander Kozubov; "Otvorennŷj Lyst A. Tovtovy, šyzmatyckomu svjaščennyku v Vylkes Barre, Pa." [An open letter to A. Toth, schismatic priest in Wilkes Barre, PA]

    L   IV (14): Apr 25, 1895; C-2&3, L-2&3

3032   Ju.; "Svjatŷy Mîsta. Ponjatie, ystoryčnŷj počatok" [Holy Places. Idea, historical beginning]

Part I: "Cerkov'. Ymija, symvolyčnoe značenie, rodŷ" [The Church. Name, symbolic meaning, kinds]

IV (15): May 2, 1895; C-2&3, L-2

Part II: "Cerkovnaja Archytektura (Pravyla budovanija)" [Church architecture (Building rules)]

IV (16): May 9, 1895; C-2, L-2

Part III: Situation or placement of a church.

IV (17): May 16, 1895; C-2, L-2

Parts IV-VIII: Building styles.

IV (19-24): May 30-Jul 4, 1895; C-2&3, L-2&3

Part IX: Building styles and church artifacts.

IV (25): Jul 11, 1895; C-2&3, L-2

Part X: "I. Vnutrennoe ustroenie cerkvy. Prytvor" [I. Internal structure of a church. The Vestibule]

IV (26): Jul 18, 1895; C-2, L-2

Part XI: "Korabl' Cerkvy" [Nave of the Church]

IV (27): Jul 25, 1895; C-2, L-2

Part XII: "Chor-Altar. Ymija y sostavnŷy časty" [Choir-Altar. Name and component parts]

IV (29): Aug 8, 1895; C-2, L-2

Part XIII: Nyzšij chor, ykonostas" [Lower choir, iconostasis]

IV (30): Aug 15, 1895; C-3, L-2

Part XIII (Cont.): "Ykonostas" [Iconostasis]

IV (31): Aug 22, 1895; C-2&3, L-2

Part XIV: "Prestol. Vyd, ustroenie y symvolyčnoe značenie" [Altar. View, structure and symbolic meaning]

IV (32): Aug 29, 1895; C-2, L-2

Part XV: "Ustroenie sv. prestola" [Structure of the holy altar]

IV (34): Sep 12, 1895; C-2, L-2

Part XVI: "Symvolyčne značenie Prestola" [Symbolic meaning
of the Altar]

IV (35): Sep 19, 1895; C-2&3, L-2

Part XVII: "II. Vnîsňost' Cerkvy. Veža (turnjo)"
[II. Churches exterior. The Spire]

IV (36): Sep 26, 1895; C-2&3, L-2

Part XVII (Cont.): "Budova y osvjaščenie Cerkvy"
[Construction and Consecration of a Church]

IV (37): Oct 3, 1895; C-2;
IV (37&38): Oct 10, 1895; L-2

Part XVIII: "Pryčynŷ vslidstvie kotorŷch tratyt Cerkov'
osvjaščenie y blahoslovenie,--daže vslîdstvie kotorŷch
oskvernjaetsja Cerkov'" [The reasons by which a church
looses its consecration and blessing--and even becomes
desecrated]

IV (39): Oct 17, 1895; C-2&3, L-2

Part XIX: "Časovnî (kaplycî)" [Chapels]

IV (41): Oct 31, 1895; C-3, L-2&3

Part XX: "Kladbyšča (cmyntarî)" [Cemeteries]

A   IV (42): Nov 7, 1895; C-2&3, L-2

3033 "Velykoe Toržestvo! Osvjaščenie novoj Hr. kat. Russkoj Cerkvy sv.
      Vladymira v Alden, Pa." [Great Celebration! Dedication of
      the new Greek Catholic Church of Saint Vladimir in Alden, PA]

      Dedication on May 26, 1895.

      Ad   IV (16): May 9, 1895; C-1, L-1

3034 "Velykoe Toržestvo! Osvjaščenie rohovoho kamenja novobudujuščojsja
      Hr. kat. Russkoj Cerkvy v Punksutavnej, Pa." [Great Celebra-
      tion! Dedication of the corner stone of the new Greek Catholic
      Rusyn Church in Punxsutawney, PA]

      Dedication by Rev. John Szabo on May 12, 1895.

      Ad   IV (16): May 9, 1895; C-1, L-1

3035 "Blahoslovenie novoho kladbyšča (cmyntara)" [Blessing of a new
      cemetery]

      Dedication by Rev. Theodore Damjanovics in Trenton, NJ on
      June 2, 1895.

      Ad   IV (18): May 23, 1895; C-1, L-1

3036 [N.N.]; "Prymîčanija y Pojasnenija" [Notes and Explanations]

Part I: Issues of Orthodox schism.

IV (19): May 30, 1895; C-2, L-2&3

Part II: Greek Catholic church, theology, and clergy.

IV (20): Jun 6, 1895; C-2, L-2

Part III: Celibate clergy in Europe and in America.

IV (21&22): Jun 20, 1895; C-2, L-2

Part IV: Clergy in Europe and in America.

IV (23): Jun 27, 1895; C-2, L-2

Part V: Spirit of Catholicism among Rusyns in America.

IV (24): Jul 4, 1895; C-2, L-2

Part VI: Order of St. Basil the Great.

IV (25): Jul 11, 1895; C-2, L-2

A

3037 "Velykoe Toržestvo! Osvjaščenie novoj hr. kat. Russkoj Cerkvy v Punksutavnej, Pa." [Great Celebration! Dedication of the new Greek Catholic Rusyn Church in Punxsutawney, PA]

Dedication by Rev. John Szabo on July 4, 1895.

Ad   IV (20): Jun 6, 1895; C-1, L-1

3038 Ju.; "Nîskol'ko slov o kollektovaniy hrošej na cerkvy" [A few words about money collection for the Church]

E   IV (20): Jun 6, 1895; C-3

3039 [N.N.]; "Obščestvo hreko kat. svjaščennykov v Amerykî" [The Society of Greek Catholic priests in America]

Directives and aspirations of this organization formed in Hazleton, PA on June 11, 1895.

A   IV (21&22): Jun 20, 1895; C-11, L-11

3040 R...; Sátoraljaújhely [Ujhely], Zemplén County, Hungary, May 27, 1895

Religious problems in Europe.

L, E   IV (21&22): Jun 20, 1895; C-11&12, L-11

3041 John Veszek; Homestead, PA, Jul 6, 1895

Roman/Greek Catholic relations in U.S.

L   IV (26): Jul 18, 1895; C-2, L-2

3042 Rev. John Kelly, et al.; Král'ovce [Királynépe], Abaúj-Torna County, Hungary, Jul 15, 1895

Expresses gratitude to G.C.U. Lodge member, Michael Kelly, who sent financial aid for the construction of a church in Král'ovce.

L, E   IV (26): Jul 18, 1895; C-5, L-3

3043 "Velykoe Toržestvo! Osvjaščenie kraeuhol'naho (rohovoho) kamenja novobudujuščoj Cerkvy" [Great Celebration! Dedication of the cornerstone of a new church under construction]

Dedication in Beaver Meadows, PA on August 15, 1895.

Ad   IV (27): Jul 25, 1895; C-1, L-1

3044 O.J.S.; "Nado nam bol'šoj ènerhiy!" [We need more energy!]

Problems of the Greek Catholic Church in America.

A   IV (27): Jul 25, 1895; C-2, L-2

3045 F.; "Našy Cerkvy" [Our Churches]

Problems of the Greek Catholic Church in America.

Part I: IV (28): Aug 1, 1895; C-4&5, L-2&3

Part II: IV (29): Aug 8, 1895; C-2&3, L-2&3

A

3046 "Velykoe Toržestvo! Osvjaščenie Ykonostasa y novoho Parafial'naho doma" [Great Celebration! Dedication of an Iconostasis and a new rectory]

Dedication by Rev. A. Laurisin in Mahanoy City, PA on August 15, 1895.

Ad   IV (29): Aug 8, 1895; C-1, L-1

3047 Ja.; "Velykolîpnoe Cerkovnoe Toržestvo v Mahanoj Syty, Pa." [Magnificent Church Celebration in Mahanoy City, PA]

The dedication by Rev. Augustine Laurisin of the Mahanoy City Greek Catholic church's iconostasis and rectory on August 15, 1895.

A   IV (31): Aug 22, 1895; C-3, L-2&3

3048 Velykoe Toržestvo! Osvjaščenie Hreko. Kat. Russk. Cerkvy v Pytsburg, Pa." [Great Celebration! Dedication of the Greek Catholic Rusyn Church in Pittsburgh, PA]

Dedication on September 22, 1895.

Ad   IV (31): Aug 22, 1895; C-5, L-1

3049   .....K; Pittsburgh, PA; Sept. 25, 1895

Concerning the newly dedicated Greek Catholic Church in
Pittsburgh, PA. See: 3048.

L   IV (37): Oct 3, 1895; C-2
                                     IV (37&38): Oct 10, 1895; L-2

3050   "Velykolîpnoe Toržestvo. Toržestvennoe osvjaščenie rohovoho
kamenja novobudujuščoj hreko. kat. cerkvy v Džonstovn, Pa."
[Magnificent Celebration. Celebrational dedication of the
corner stone of the new Greek Catholic Church under construction in Johnstown, PA]

Dedication on October 13, 1895.

Ad   IV (38): Oct 13, 1895; C-1, L-1

3051   "Velykolîpnoe Toržestvo. Osvjaščenie hreko. kat. Russkoj Cerkvy
v Lansford, Pa." [Magnificent Celebration. Dedication of
the Greek Catholic Rusyn Church in Lansford, PA]

Dedication on November 28, 1895

Ad   IV (39): Oct 17, 1895; C-1, L-1

3052   J.Š.; Johnstown, PA; October 14, 1895

The dedication of the corner stone of the Greek Catholic Church
in Johnstown, PA. See: 3047.

L   IV (39): Oct 17, 1895; C-3, L-2&3

3053   Redakcija; "Protest y Prymičanie" [Protest and Comment]

Comments by Rev. Toth to ARV Editor concerning allegations
made in a letter to the Editor.

L   IV (39): Oct 17, 1895; C-4, L-4

3054   "Od Spolku sv. Pervomuč. Stephana v Leisenring, Pa. Pos'vecenie
novoho cintara" [From the Lodge of Saint Stephen in Leisenring, PA. Dedication of a new cemetery]

Dedication on November 3, 1895.

Ad   IV (41): Oct 31, 1895; L-1

3055   Rev. Cornelius Laurisin; Shenandoah, PA; Nov. 2, 1895

Shenandoah parish and schism.

L   IV (42): Nov 7, 1895; C-4&5, L-4&5

3056   [N.N.]; "Svjatŷy Vešcy (rîcy)" [Sacred objects]

Significance of religious symbols and objects in Greek Catholicism.

Part I: "A. Relyhijnŷy symboly" [A. Religious symbols]

IV (43): Nov 14, 1895; C-2, L-2

Part II: IV (44): Nov 21, 1895; C-2, L-2

A

3057 Ju.; "Radostnoe Russkoe Toržestvo" [Joyful Rusyn Celebration]

The dedication of the Lansford, PA Greek Catholic Church on November 28, 1895.

E   IV (47): Dec 11, 1895; C-2, L-2

3058 [N.N.]; "Poslîdstvija buntovanij bezdušnŷch ljudej. Dokazatel'stvo tomu, čto naš narod deržytsja svoych starodavnŷch sv. nrav y osuždaet buntŷ y balamučenija poodynokych zlodušnŷch špekuljantov." [Consequences of rebellion by people poor in spirit. Evidence that our people adhere to their own ancient, sacred laws and condemn rebellion and confusion by individual evil-minded speculators]

The Oldforge-Rendham, PA parish.

A   IV (48): Dec 18, 1895; C-2, L-2

3059 Paul Jurievich Žatkovich; "Otkrŷtŷj lyst ot Redaktora 'Am. Russk. Vistnyka.' Vsečest. Otcu Protoiereju Aleksiju Tovt v Vylks Bery, Pa." [An open letter from the Editor of ARV to Rev. Archpriest Alexis Toth in Wilkes Barre, PA]

Part I: IV (49): Dec 25, 1895; C-2&3, L-2&3

Part II: IV (50): Jan 2, 1896; C-3, L-4&5

L

3060 "Novŷj svjaščennyk--Zanjatie prychoda--Blahoslovenie Cerkvy" [New priest--Taking over a parish--Blessing of a Church]

a. Rev. Irenaeus Matyacko (Mukačevo [Munkács] Diocese) becomes the new pastor of Ramey, PA parish.
b. Rev. H. Dzubay dedicates the Johnstown, PA Greek Catholic Church.

Nr   IV (50): Jan 2, 1896; C-5, L-5

3061 "Velykolîpnoe Toržestvo. Osvjaščenie hreko kat. russkoj Cerkvy v Džonstovn, Pa." [Magnificent Celebration. Dedication of a Greek Catholic Rusyn Church in Johnotown, PA]

Dedication on January 28, 1896.

Ad   V (1): Jan 16, 1896; C-4, L-1

3062 [N.N.]; "Blahoslovenie cerkvy v Džonstovn, Pa." [Blessing of a church in Johnstown, PA]

A   V (4): Feb 6, 1896; C-2

3063 Most Rev. Smyrennŷj Nykolaj, Bishop of the Aleuts and Alaskans; San Francisco, CA; Jan. 22, 1896

   Clarifies the position of the Orthodox Mission in America regarding its policy of non-interference in the concerns of the American Greek Catholic Church.

   L   V (5): Feb 13, 1896; C-2&3

3064 Michael Dobrocki, Yonkers, NY, Feb. 15, 1896

   Conflict among parishioners of Yonkers Greek Catholic parish.

   L   V (8): Mar 12, 1896; C-2, L-2&3

3065 Rev. E. Satala; Passaic, NJ, Mar. 18, 1896

   Rebuttle to 3064.

   L   V (10): Mar 26, 1896; C-3, L-3

3066 "Cerkovnŷy Toržestva. Blahoslovenie zvona y novoj Hr. kat. Russkoj Cerkvy v Byver Medov, Pa." [Church Celebration. Blessing of a bell and the new Greek Catholic Rusyn Church in Beaver Meadow, PA]

   Dedication of: bell on April 12, 1896; church on May 30, 1896.

   Ad   V (12): Apr 9, 1896; C-1, L-1

3067 Rev. Acacius Kamensky; "Javnoe dokazatel'stvo lestyvoj ahytaciy." [Clear evidence of flattering agitation]

   Commentary on Rev. A. Toth's reply to 3063.

   A   V (12): Apr 9, 1896; C-2&3, L-2&3

3068 Edmund Lembick; Beaver Meadow, PA; April 15, 1896

   The dedication of the Greek Catholic Church in Beaver Meadow, PA. See 3066.

   L   V (14): Apr 23, 1896; L-2

3069 Redakcija, ARV; "Otpovîd', bŷvšemu uniatskomu, teper'-že neuniatskomu popovy, Hosp. Mychaylu Baloh v Brydžport, Konn." [Answer to the former uniate priest, Mr. Michael Balog in Bridgeport, CT]

   E   V (15): Apr 30, 1896; C-4, L-4

3070 Paul Jurievich Žatkovich; "Jak bŷ nam popravyty smutnoe cerkovnoe naše položenie?" [How should we mend our churches' sad situation?]

   Greek Catholic Church in America.

   E   V (18&19): May 21, 1896; C-10,11,12, L-10,11,12

3071   "Vîsty Cerkovnŷy" [Church News]

      a. First Divine Liturgy celebrated in Braddock, PA Greek
          Catholic Church on May 31, 1896.
      b. Rev. Nicholas Seregelly (Mukačevo [Munkács] Diocese)
          arrived in America from Europe.

                                       V (20): Jun 4, 1896; C-1, L-1

      c. Rev. Augustine Laurisin dedicates Minersville, PA Greek
          Catholic Church on July 4, 1896.
      d. Work on conversion of a building into a Greek Catholic
          Church in New York City began on May 25, 1896.
      e. Clergy meeting was held in the Shamokin, PA home of Rev.
          J. Konstankevič on June 3, 1896.

                                 V (21): Jun 11, 1896; C-1, L-1

      f. Rev. Nicholas Stecovich (Hazleton, PA) transferred to
          Braddock, PA.
      g. Rev. Acacius Kamensky (Wilkes Barre, PA) transferred to
          Hazleton, PA.
      h. Rev. Nicholas Seregelly assigned to Wilkes Barre, PA.

      Nr   V (22): Jun 18, 1896; C-1, L-1

3072   Edmund Lembick; Beaver Meadow, PA; June 5, 1896

      Church dedication in Beaver Meadow, PA, on May 30, 1896.

      L   V (22): Jun 18, 1896; L-3

3073   Rev. Acacius Kamensky; Hazleton, PA, June 16, 1896

      The recent transfers of clergy. See 3071f.-3071h.

      L   V (23): Jun 25, 1896; C-3, L-2&3

3074   "Vîsty Cerkovnŷy" [Church News]

      a. Rev. Cornelius Iljasevich (Mukačevo [Munkács] Diocese)
          arrived in America and assigned to Cleveland, OH.
      b. Rev. John Csurgovics (Cleveland, OH) returns to Europe.

      Nr   V (24): Jul 2, 1896; C-1, L-1

3075   [N.N.]; "Madjarskij Patriotyzm y Protoerej A. Tovt" [Magyar patriot-
        ism and archpriest A. Toth]

      Refers to 3067.

      A   V (24): Jul 2, 1896; C-3, L-2&3

3076   "Vîsty Cerkovnŷy" [Church News]

      a. New Greek Catholic Church has been organized in Homestead, PA.
      b. Wilkes Barre, PA Greek Catholic Church ended its brief period
          under "schismatic" control.

                                     V (25): Jul 9, 1896; C-1, L-1

c. Roman Catholic Bishop of Cleveland, Ohio refuses to accept married Greek Catholic clergy in his diocese.

Nr   V (27): Jul 23, 1896; C-1, L-1

3077 [N.N.]; "Hreko Katolyčeskiy Mad'jare y ych dvyženie o hr. kat. Mad'jarskaho epyskopstva na Uhorščyni" [Greek Catholic Magyars and their movement towards establishing a Greek Catholic Magyar eparchy in Hungary]

Magyar Greek Catholics in Szathmár and Szbolics counties in Hungary.

A   V (27): Jul 23, 1896; C-2&3, L-2&3

3078 "Vîsty Cerkovnŷy" [Church News]

a. Rev. Dr. Simon Szabo, doctor of theology and former professor of religious studies at Maramaroš Sighet (Máramarossziget) Gymnasium arrived in America on July 24, 1896.

V (28): Jul 30, 1896; C-1, L-1

b. ARV refutes allegations made by Svoboda [Mt. Carmel, PA] that four Greek Catholic priests were recalled to Europe by the Bishop of Mukačevo [Munkács].

c. New school and rectory of the Greek Catholic parish in Leisenring, PA, were dedicated.

V (29): Aug 6, 1896; C-1, L-1

d. Rev. N. Stecovich dedicates the Braddock, PA Greek Catholic Church on September 20, 1896.

V (30): Aug 13, 1896; C-1, L-1

e. Dedication of Trenton, NJ Greek Catholic Church iconostasis on September 6, 1896.

Nr   V (32): Aug 27, 1896; C-1, L-1

3079 John Jerabinecz, et al.; Johnstown, PA, Aug 10, 1896

The dedication of a cemetery in Johnstown, PA, on July 26, 1896.

L   V (32): Aug 27, 1896; C-3, L-2&3

3080 "Vîsty Cerkovnŷy" [Church News]

a. Cleveland, OH Greek Catholic parish sponsors a meeting for September 12, 1896 to discuss acquisition of property for a church.

b. Rev. Gabriel Martyak (Lansford, PA) left for Europe on September 3, 1896 to bring his wife and family to America.

V (34): Sep 10, 1896; C-1, L-1

c. Dedication of bells and altar of Minersville, PA Greek Catholic Church on September 30, 1896.

d. Passaic, NJ Greek Catholic parish hired George Kokajko on September 13, 1896 as Cantor.

    e. Rev. Dr. Simon Szabo assigned to Cleveland, OH.
    f. Rev. J. Csurgovics (Cleveland, OH) returned to Europe.
    g. Dedication of Mayfield, PA Greek Catholic Church's
       iconostasis on September 20, 1896.
    h. Mr. Michael Bodrog of Van Cortland, NY bought a $50.00
       set of vestments for Yonkers, NY Greek Catholic parish.

    Nr   V (35): Sep 17, 1896; C-1, L-1

3081 [N.N.]; Trenton, NJ; Sept. 6, 1896

      The dedication of the new iconostasis at the Trenton, NJ Greek
      Catholic Church on September 6, 1896. See 3078e.

      L   V (35): Sep 17, 1896; L-3

3082 [N.N.]; Miners Mills, PA, Sept. 10, 1896

      An immigrants' opinion on the Greek Catholic Church in America.

      L   V (35): Sep 17, 1896; C-3, L-4&5

3083 "Vîsty Cerkovnŷy" [Church News]

      Rev. Gabriel Martyak returned to America on October 9, 1896
      with his family.

      Nr   V (38): Oct 8, 1896; C-1, L-1

3084 Rev. John M. Szabo; "Slovo, skazannoe na posvjaščeniy cerkvy v
      Bradock, Pa., 20-ho sent. 1896." [Homily (given on the occa-
      sion) of the church dedication in Braddock, PA, Sept. 20, 1896]

      Parts I-III: V (38-40): Oct 8-Oct 22, 1896; C-6, L-6

      A

3085 "Vîsty Cerkovnŷy" [Church News]

      a. Rev. Gabriel Martyak returned to America with his wife and
         four children.
      b. Clergy meeting in Passaic, NJ on October 14, 1896 (names
         listed).
      c. New Rectory has been built for Johnstown, PA, parish.

                              V (40): Oct 22, 1896; C-1

      d. New Greek Catholic cemetery in Minersville, PA.

      Nr   V (41): Oct 29, 1896; C-, L-1

3086 Rev. Dr. Simeon Sabo; "Obchoždenie s eretykamy" [Treatment of
      heretics]

      Parts I-II: V (41-42): Oct 29-Nov 5, 1896; C-2, L-2

3087 "Vîsty Cerkovnŷy" [Church News]

      Dedication of the Scranton, PA Greek Catholic Church's
      iconostasis on November 1, 1896.

      Nr   V (42): Nov 5, 1896; C-1, L-1

3088 [N.N.]; Braddock, PA, Oct. 22, 1896

      List of financial and gift contributers who donated to the Braddock Greek Catholic Church. See 3078d.

      L   V (42): Nov 5, 1896; C-3, L-3

3089 "Vîsty Cerkovnŷy" [Church News]

      a. The first Divine Liturgy was celebrated in the Brooklyn, NY Greek Catholic Church on November 10, 1896 (List of participants).

                            V (43): Nov 12, 1896; C-1, L-1

      b. Rev. Anthony Hodobay (Prešov [Eperjes] Diocese) assigned to Ramey, PA.
      c. Rev. Julius Petrasovski (Prešov [Eperjes] Diocese) arrived in America.

      Nr   V (44): Nov 19, 1896; L-1

3090 Stephen Hudak, Ramey, PA, Nov. 15, 1896

      Information on the Greek Catholic parish in Ramey, PA, and Rev. Anthony Hodobay. See 3089b.

      L   V (44): Nov 19, 1896; L-5

3091 "Velykoe Toržestvo. Blahoslovenie obnovlennoj Cerkvy v Passayk, N. Dž." [Great celebration. Blessing of a renovated church in Passaic, NJ]

      Dedication on December 6, 1896.

      Ad   V (46): Dec 3, 1896; C-1, L-1

3092 [N.N.]; Passaic, NJ, Dec. 7, 1896

      The church dedication of the renovated church in Passaic, NJ. See 3091.

      L   V (47): Dec 10, 1896; L-2&3

3093 "Vîsty Cerkovnŷy" [Church News]

      Dedication of a Greek Catholic Church in Phoenixville, PA on May 1, 1897.

      Nr   V (50): Jan 6, 1897; C-5

3094 [N.N.]; "Hr. kat. Russk. Epyskop pry Ameryky" [Greek Catholic Bishop for America]

      The recent Vatican decision to create an eparchy in America for Greek Catholics.

      A   X (1): Jan 17, 1901; C-2, L-2

3095   John Jarabinec, et al.; Johnstown, PA; Jan 1901

       The purchase of two bells for the Johnstown Greek Catholic
       Church.

       L   X (2): Jan 24, 1901; C-7, L-7

3096   [N.N.]; "K voprosu o hreko slavjanskom obrjadî sredy zapadno-
       evropejskych slavjan" [On the question of a Greek Slavonic
       rite among West European Slavs]

       The Greek Catholic church as a viable spokesman for Slavs
       living in Austro-Hungary.

       Parts I-II: X (5-6): Feb 14-21, 1901; C-2&3, L-2&3

3097   Rev. Damaskin Polivka; "Do čoho steremyt naprjam dekotorŷch ljudej
       Amerykan'skoj Rusy!" [What the goals and aspirations of some
       Rusyn-Americans are!]

       Reply to an article by Rev. Nicholas Podhorec concerning the
       religiosity of Rusyn-Americans published in Svoboda, #3, 1901.

       A   X (7): Feb 28, 1901; C-2, L-2

3098   Nikolaj; Braddock, PA

       Problems in organizing a church choir.

       L   X (10): Mar 21, 1901; C-3, L-2&3

3099   "Cerkovnyja Spravŷ" [Church News]

       Donations are being collected for internal restoration of the
       Hazleton, PA Greek Catholic Church.

       Nr   X (12): Apr 4, 1901; C-6

3100   "Cerkovna Slavnosc, Slavnostne posvecanie novej gr. kat. russkej
       cerkvi v Northhampton, Pa." [Church celebration. Solemn
       dedication of the new Greek Catholic Rusyn church in North-
       hampton, PA]

       Dedication by Rev. D. Polivka on May 30, 1901.

       Ad   X (14): Apr 25, 1901; L-5

3101   Rev. H. Dzubay; "Toržestvennoe poblahoslovenie cerkvy v Džanstavn,
       PA" [Solemn blessing of a church in Johnstown, PA]

       A   X (15): May 2, 1901; C-4, L-4

3102   "Zaprošenie na slavnoe posvjaščenie cerkvy sv. Archanhela Mychayla
       v Pueblo, Kolorado" [Invitation to the glorious dedication of
       the church of St. Michael the Archangel in Pueblo, Colorado]

       Dedication by Rev. Nicholas Seregelly on June 2, 1901.

       Ad   X (16): May 9, 1901; C-3, L-6

3103 "Zaprošenie na Cerkovnoe Toržestvo v Lyndsy, Pa." [Invitation to a church celebration in Lindsey, PA]

Dedication of an iconostasis by Rev. John Szabo on May 30, 1901.

Ad   X (16): May 9, 1901; C-3, L-6

3104 "Slavnostne posvecanie novej gr. kat. russkej cerkvi v Johnstown, Pa." [Solemn dedication of a new Greek Catholic Rusyn Church in Johnstown, PA]

Dedication by Rev. Hilarion Dzubay on June 2, 1901.

Ad   X (16): May 9, 1901; L-6

3105 O.V.; "Popyky-Radykalŷ" [Young priests-radicals]

Seminarian and young priest radicals in Galicia.

A   X (17): May 16, 1901; C-4, L-4

3106 "Velykolîpnoe toržestvo. Toržestvennoe posvjaščenie novopokuplenoj hr. kat. russkoj cerkvy sv. Ioanna Krestytelja, altarja, kresta, vežy" [Magnificent celebration. Celebrational dedication of the newly purchased Greek Catholic Rusyn church of St. John the Baptist, altar, cross, spire]

Dedication in Pittsburgh, PA on June 9, 1901.

Ad   X (18): May 23, 1901; C-3, L-6

3107 "Velykoe cerkovnoe toržestvo na Zapadî-Vestach" [Great church celebration in the west]

Dedication of three bells for the Globeville, 'CO church by Rev. N. Seregelly on June 16, 1901.

Nr   X (18): May 23, 1901; C-3, L-6

3108 [N.N.]; "Odnoe velykolîpnoe cerkovnoe toržestvo" [One magnificent church celebration]

The dedication of the Northhampton Greek Catholic Church.

A   X (20): Jun 6, 1901; C-2&3, L-2&3

3109 "Toržestvo poblahoslovenija novoho Ykonostasa v Byver Mydov, Pa." [Blessing celebration of the new iconostasis in Beaver Meadow, PA]

Dedication by Rev. John Hal'ko on July 4, 1901.

Ad   X (20): Jun 6, 1901; C-7, L-6

3110 [N.N.]; Velykolîpnoe cerkovnoe toržestvo v Punksutavny-Lyndsy, Pa." [Magnificent church celebration in Punxsutawney-Lindsey, PA]

The church dedication on May 30, 1901.

A   X (21): Jun 13, 1901; C-2, L-2

3111   Rev. Damaskin Polivka; Northampton, PA; June 1, 1901

      "Podjaka" [Thanks]

      Expresses thanks concerning the dedication of the Northampton, PA Greek Catholic Church.

      L   X (21): Jun 13, 1901; C-3, L-2&3

3112   [N.N.]; Northampton, PA

      Commentary on the report of the May 30, 1901 Northampton, PA church dedication in Svoboda.

      L   X (21): Jun 13, 1901; C-4, L-4

3113   Rev. John Festorej; Stanča [Isztáncs], Zemplén County, Hungary; April 23, 1901

      Expresses gratitude to John Hasaralejk and John Šmajad of Trenton, NJ for $67.00 donation to Stanča parish.

      L, E   X (21): Jun 13, 1901; C-7

3114   Stephen Paczak; Pittsburgh, PA; June 10, 1901

      The June 9, 1901 dedication of the Pittsburgh, PA Greek Catholic Church.

      L   X (22): Jun 20, 1901; C-2, L-2

3115   "Velykoe Cerkovnoe Toržestvo v Majnersvyl, Pa." [Great church celebration in Minersville, PA]

      Dedication of church on July 4, 1901.

      Ad   X (22): Jun 20, 1901; C-7, L-7

3116   "Velykoe Cerkovnoe Toržestvo v Junhstavn, O" [Great church celebration in Youngstown, OH]

      Dedication of an altar by Rev. A. Mhley on July 4, 1901.

      Ad   X (22): Jun 20, 1901; C-7, L-7

3117   "Peremînŷ Duchovnykov" [Changes of Priests]

      a. Rev. Hilarion Dzubay (Johnstown, PA) returns to Europe at the request of his father, Rev. Stephen Dzubay.
      b. Rev. Julius Csucska, former editor of Nauka [Užhorod], has been assigned to Johnstown, PA.
      c. Rev. Victor Popovics (Stavné [Fenyvesvölgy], Ung County, Hungary) assigned to Oldforge-Rendham, PA.

      Nr   X (23): Jul 4, 1901; C-3, L-3

3118   [N.N.]; "Vmiste obektyvnaho opravdanijasja, bezstŷdnoe napadenie"
        [Instead of objective justification, shameless attack]

        Destruction of Rusyn spiritual morality by Galician priests
        and their supporters.

        A   X (24): Jul 11, 1901; C-2, L-2

3119   "Napomynanie" [Reminder]

        G.C.U. lodges are requested by Revs. Theodore Damjanovich and
        Gabriel Martyak to contribute to a fund to aid two poor
        parishes in Europe.

        Req   X (24): Jul 11, 1901; C-3, L-3

3120   "Peremînŷ Duchovnykov" [Change of priests]

        a. Rev. Stephen Jaczkovich (Pittsburgh, PA) returns to Europe.
        b. Rev. John Szabo (Lindsey, PA) temporarily assumes pastor-
            ship of the Pittsburgh, PA parish until Rev. Eugene Volkay
            can assume the vacancy left by Rev. Jaczkovich.
        c. Rev. Damaskin Polivka (Northampton, PA) transferred to
            Duquesne, PA.
        d. Rev. Julius Stankanyec (Duquesne, PA) returns to Europe.

        Nr   X (24): Jul 11, 1901; C-3, L-3

3121   J. Zahranysky; Minersville, PA, July 4, 1901

        "Toržestvennoe poblahoslovenie cerkvy" [Celebrational blessing
        of a Church]

        Concerning the July 4, 1901 dedication of the Minersville, PA
        Greek Catholic Church.

        L, P   X (24): Jul 11, 1901; C-2&3, L-2

3122   Stephen Paczak; Pittsburgh, PA; July 8, 1901

        "Peremînŷ Duchovnykov" [Change of priests]

        a. Rev. Stephen Jackovich (Pittsburgh, PA) returned to Europe.
        b. Rev. John Szabo (Lindsey, PA) assigned to Pittsburgh, PA
            parish.

        L, Nr   X (24): Jul 11, 1901; C-3, L-3

3123   V.Z.; Bridgeport, CT; June 7, 1901

        Troublemakers and schismatic trends in Bridgeport, CT parish.

        L   X (25): Jul 18, 1901; C-3, L-3

3124   [N.N.]; "Odnoe krasnoe cerkovnoe toržestvo" [One fine church cele-
        bration]

        The dedication of the Beaver Meadow, PA Greek Catholic Church
        iconostasis on July 4, 1901.

        A   X (26): Jul 25, 1901; C-2, L-2

3125   J.Č.; Phoenixville, PA; July 23, 1901

A Roman Catholic priest stirs up trouble among Greek Rusyn
Catholics and Slovak Roman Catholics.

L   X (27): Aug 1, 1901; C-3, L-2&3

3126   Rev. Theodore Obushkevich; "Otzŷv do naroda russkoho v Halyčynî y
Uhorščynî y do pročych Bratej Slavjan o skladku na sozdanie
yz tverdaho materijala cerkvy v Ust'ju Russkom [na Lemkach
Horlyckoho povîta v Halyčynî]" [Appeal to the Rusyn people
from Galicia and Hungary and other Slavic brethren about the
collection for the creation of a church from hard material in
Ustja Rus'ke (in the Lemko Land, Horlyci county, Galicia)]

Establishment of a Galician-Rusyn church fund.

A   X (29): Aug 15, 1901; C-4, L-4

3127   "Toržestvennoe poblahoslovenie kraeuhol'naho kameny novoj Hreko
kat. russk. Cerkvy v Vindber, Pa." [Celebrational blessing
of the corner stone of the new Greek Catholic Church in
Windber, PA]

Dedication on August 8, 1901.

Ad   X (29): Aug 15, 1901; C-6, L-6

3128   "Toržestvennoe poblahoslovenie novoj Hreko kat. russkoj cerkvy v
Paton, Pa." [Celebrational blessing of new Greek Catholic
Rusyn church in Patton, PA]

Dedication on September 2, 1901.

Ad   X (29): Aug 15, 1901; C-6, L-6

3129   "Toržestvennoe posvjaščenie novaho kolokola (zvona) hr. kat. cerkvy
Presv. Trojcŷ v Brydžport, Konn." [Celebrational blessing of
the new bell of the Greek Catholic church of the Holy Trinity
in Bridgeport, CT]

Dedication on September 2, 1901.

Ad   X (30): Aug 22, 1901; C-6, L-6

3130   "Yz kruha našych svjaščennykov" [From the circle of our priests]

a. Rev. Theodore Damjanovich (Brooklyn, NY) returned to
    Hungary to visit parents and relatives.
b. Rev. Cornelius Iljasevich (Wilkes Barre, PA) will sub-
    stitute for Rev. Theodore Damjanovich (currently visiting
    in Europe).
c. Rev. Eugene Volkay (Scranton, PA) assigned to Bridgeport, CT.
d. Rev. Anthony Izay, newly arrived from Europe, has been
    assigned temporarily to Wilkes Barre, PA.
e. Rev. George Gulovich (McAdoo, PA) assigned to Scranton, PA.
f. Rev. Victor Popovics (Oldforge-Rendham, PA) assigned to
    McAdoo, PA.

g. Rev. Nestor Dmytrov (Troy, NY) assigned to Northampton, PA.
h. Rev. Julius Medvecky (Lansford, PA) assigned to McKeesport, PA.
i. Rev. Myron Volkay (Northampton, PA) assigned to Plymouth, PA.

Nr   X (31): Aug 29, 1901; C-2, L-2

3131 "Hreko kat. Vîrnykam na okrestnosty Homsted, Pa., vo vnymanie"
      [Attention: Greek Catholic faithful in the vicinity of Home-
      stead, PA]

      Homestead Greek Catholic parish purchased land for a cemetery
      and is offering lots for sale.

      Ad   X (32): Sep 5, 1901; C-6, L-6

3132 "Toržestvennoe poblahoslovennie kraeuhol'naho kamene y Altarja novoj
      hr. kat. russkoj cerkvy sv. apost. Petra y Pavla v Avburn,
      Nju. Io." [Solemn blessing of the corner stone and altar of
      the new Greek Catholic Rusyn Church of Sts. Peter and Paul in
      Auburn, NY]

      Dedication by Rev. Eugene Volkay on October 9, 1901.

      Ad   X (34): Sep 19, 1901; C-6, L-6

3133 [N.N.]; "Konec odnoj smutnoj 'komediy'" [End of a sad 'comedy']

      Greek Catholic church troubles in Marblehead, OH.

      A   X (37): Oct 10, 1901; C-2

3134 [N.N.]; "S odnym humbuhom bol'še!" [One humbug more!]

      A proposal by Galician clergy and laity to convoke a meeting
      to discuss the formation of an American Greek Catholic Eparchy.

      A   XII (37): Oct 8, 1903; C-2, L-2

3135 [N.N.]; "Pros'ba odnoj Cerkovnoj Radŷ" [Request of one church
      council]

      Prosperity of Wilkes Barre, PA parish during and after the
      "schismatic" period.

      A   X (38): Oct 17, 1901; C-2, L-2

3136 "Cerkovnoe Toržestvo" [Church Celebration]

      Large cross for Wilkes Barre, PA Greek Catholic cemetery will
      be dedicated, October 20, 1901.

      Ad   X (38): Oct 17, 1901; C-7

3137 Michael Czuprik; McKeesport, PA; Oct 15, 1901

      The purchase of property for the McKeesport parish.

      L   X (39): Oct 24, 1901; C-2, L-2&3

3138   [N.N.]; "Povîrennŷj Halyčskaho Russkaho Mytropolytŷ v Amerykî"
       [Entrusted official of the Galician-Rusyn metropolitan is in
       America]

       Metropolitan Archbishop Andrew Sheptyts'kyi of L'viv sent a
       representative, Rev. Žoldak, to the U.S. and Canada to inquire
       about the welfare of Rusyn Greek Catholic Churches.

       A   X (41): Nov 7, 1901; C-2&3, L-2&3

3139   H.; McKeesport, Pa.; Oct 23, 1901

       On October 20, 1901, a fire destroyed the McKeesport Greek
       Catholic Church.

       L   X (41): Nov 7, 1901; C-3

3140   "Vîsty parafial'nŷ" [Parish news]

       a. Rev. Anthony Hodobay (Perth Amboy, NJ) returned with his
           family to Europe.
       b. Three new priests arrive in America from Europe:
           1. Rev. Anthony Kecskés (Mukačevo [Munkács] Diocese)
               formerly of parish in Sátoraljaújhely (Újhely),
               Zemplén county, assigned to Perth Amboy, NJ.
           2. Rev. Stephen Kulčicky (Przemyśl Diocese), formerly of
               parish in Sambor, Galicia, assigned to Ramey, PA.
           3. Rev. Michael Lengyel (Mukačevo Diocese), formerly of
               parish in Kostrina (Csontos), Ung County, Hungary,
               assigned to Oldforge-Rendham, PA.
       c. Rev. Victor Popovics transferred from Oldforge-Rendham, PA
           to McAdoo, PA.
       d. Rev. Nestor Volensky transferred from Pleasant City, OH
           to Youngstown, OH.
       e. Rev. Anthony Mhley transferred from Youngstown, OH to
           Lindsey-Punxsutawney, PA.
       f. Rev. George Gulovich, of St. Marys in Scranton, PA is
           very ill.
       g. John Danilovič is completing studies at a gymnasium in
           Hungary and plans to return to America and enter the
           seminary at Mt. Vernon, NY.

       Nr   X (42): Nov 14, 1901; C-3, L-3

3141   "Cerkovnoe Toržestvennoe poblahoslovenie kraeuhol'naho kamene novoj
       hr. kat. cerkvy v Salem, Mass." [Church Solemn blessing of the
       corner stone of the new Greek Catholic church in Salem, MA]

       Dedication by Rev. Eugene Volkay on November 28, 1901.

       Ad   X (42): Nov 14, 1901; C-6

3142   "Cerkovnŷja Toržestva. Poblahoslovenie novoho zvona" [Church
       celebration. Blessing of a new bell]

       Dedication in Charleroi, PA on November 28, 1901.

       Ad   X (42): Nov 14, 1901; C-6, L-3

3143 [N.N.]; Salem, MA; Dec 2, 1901

The November 28, 1901 dedication of the Salem, MA Greek Catholic Church.

L   X (45): Dec 5, 1901; C-2, L-3

3144 A.J. Machl'a; Bradenville, PA; Nov, 1901

The meetings organized for discussing construction of the Bradenville Greek Catholic Church.

L   X (45): Dec 5, 1901; C-2, L-3

3145 [N.N.]; "Vospomynanija o Hreko kat. Cerkovnoj Verchnosty v Amerykî" [Reminiscences about Greek Catholic church hierarchy in America]

Past successes and future goals of the American Greek Catholic Church, emphasizing the need for an established eparchy in America.

A   X (46): Dec 12, 1901; C-2, L-2

3146 "Vyzytator" [(Papal) Visitor]

The selection of a Papal Visitor from among the priests of the Prešov (Eperjes) and Mukačevo (Munkács) Dioceses to report on the conditions and growth of the Greek Catholic parishes in America.

A   XI (2&3): Jan 30, 1902; C-4

3147 H. Polynčak; Youngstown, OH; Feb 24, 1902

The purchase of a gospel book for the Youngstown parish.

L   XI (8): Mar 6, 1902; C-2

3148 "Cerkovnŷja Spravŷ" [Church Affairs]

a. Pleasant City, OH Greek Catholic church council meets March 23, 1902.
b. Monessen, PA Greek Catholic church meeting on March 9, 1902.

Ad   XI (8): Mar 6, 1902; C-7

3149 Rev. A. Petrašovich; Braddock, PA; Mar 4, 1902

"Otpovîd'" [Rebuttal]

To an article concerning Rusyn-American religious-nationality problems in Slovenski Denník, #164, October 4, 1901.

L   XI (9): Mar 13, 1902; C-3

3150 [N.N.]; "Ekskomunikacija (Ysključenie)-Ioann Ardan ekskomunykovan (ysključen) yz Cerkvy Katolyčeskoj" [Excommunication-John Ardan was excommunicated from the Catholic Church]

Reasons for and causes of Rev. John Ardan's (Olyphant, PA) excommunication.

A   XI (9): Mar 13, 1902; C-4

3151 "Yz kruha našych svjaščennykov" [From the circle of our priests]

a. Rev. Nicholas Stecovich returns to America from Europe and is assigned to Pleasant City, OH.
b. Rev. Michael Constantine Lengyel (Oldforge-Rendham, PA) has been transferred to St. Clair, PA, currently being administered by Rev. M. Jackovich (Lansford, PA).

Nr   XI (10): Mar 20, 1902; C-3

3152 Rev. John Szabo; Pittsburgh, PA

"Otpovid' na otpovid'" [Rebuttal to the rebuttal]
See: 3149.

L   XI (10): Mar 20, 1902; C-3

3153 [N.N.]; "Naša dîla y najnovšij attentat popykov-radykalov protyv Cerkvy Katolyčeskoj" [Our affairs and the latest attempt of the priest-radicals against the Catholic Church]

Persons and groups who seek to cause trouble among Rusyn-Americans.

Parts I-III: XI (10-12): Mar 20-Apr 3, 1902; C-4

3154 Simon Kapral, et al.; Bridgeport, CT; Mar 23, 1902

The financial support of the Bridgeport Church by parishioners.

L   XI (12): Apr 3, 1902; C-2

3155 Rev. A. Petrašovich; Braddock, PA; Mar 25, 1902

"Otpovîd' O. Sabov" [Rebuttal to Rev. Szabó]
See: 3152.

L   XI (12): Apr 3, 1902; C-2

3156 "Dva Lystŷ" [Two Letters]

Two letters to editor from Rusyn-Galicians in America commenting on a recent ARV article about the excommunication of Rev. John Ardan. The letters are followed by ARV rebuttal and a commentary on "radical" priests.
See: 3150.

L   XI (13): Apr 10, 1902; C-4

3157　[N.N.]; "Dȋlo ymenovanija vykarija dlja hr. Kat. v Amerykȋ soveršylos'. Teperȋšnyj Prazdnyk Svȋtloho Voskresenija naš Vykarij
budet uže u nas v Amerykȋ. Sv. O. Papa vykariem dlja Hreko
katolykov v Amerykȋ ymenoval: Vŷsokoprepodobnoho Otca Andreja
Hodobaja, krylošanyna-Kanonyka eparchiy Prjaševskoj" [Business
of naming the vicar for Greek Catholics in America completed.
On this year's Easter Sunday our vicar will already be with us
in America. The Holy Father, the Pope, named Very Rev. Andrew
Hodobay, canon of the Prešov Eparchy, to be vicar for Greek
Catholics in America]

Mission of Very Rev. Andrew Hodobay.

A　　　　　　　　　　　　　　　XI (14): Apr 17, 1902; C-4

3158　[N.N.]; "Pravda pobȋdyla" [Truth triumphs]

Rev. Alexis Toth's financial connection with Russian Orthodox
bishop, Nicholas.

L　　　　　　　　　　　　　　　XI (14): Apr 17, 1902; C-4

3159　[N.N.]; Jessup, PA; April 8, 1902

The suspension and excommunication of Rev. John Ardan.

L　　　　　　　　　　　　　　　XI (14): Apr 17, 1902; C-4

3160　Gregory Savuljak, et al.; Shenandoah, PA; April 4, 1902

The Shenandoah parish.

L　　　　　　　　　　　　　　　XI (15): Apr 24, 1902; C-2

3161　[N.N.]; "Želanie Amer. hr. kat. Rusynov yz časty uže soveršylos'"
[Wishes of the Greek Catholic Rusyns have been partially ful-
filled]

Very Rev. Andrew Hodobay and his mission as apostolic visitor
to America.

A, P　　　　　　　　　　　　　　XI (16): May 8, 1902; C-1&2

3162　[N.N.]; "Naš novŷj vykariat y našy protyvnyky" [Our new vicar and
our enemies]

Rusyn-American successes in establishing an American Greek
Catholic Eparchy and resulting problems.

A　　　　　　　　　　　　　　　XI (16): May 8, 1902; C-4

3163　[N.N.]; "Posȋščenija našoho vykarija, apost. vyzytatora" [Visits
of our vicar, apostolic visitor]

Very Rev. Andrew Hodobay's visit to Braddock, PA.

A　　　　　　　　　　　　　　　XI (17): May 15, 1902; C-2

3164 "Holosŷ yz Mykysport, PA, o posîščenijach našoho vykarija"
      [Voices from McKeesport, PA, about the visits of our vicar]

      L   XI (17): May 15, 1902; C-2

3165 John Ol'šavskij; Mahanoy City, PA; April 29, 1902

      Commentary on Rev. Basil Vološin's transfer from Mahanoy City
      to a newly-organized parish in Passaic, NJ.

      L   XI (17): May 15, 1902; C-3

3166 [N.N.]; "Bezsovîstnŷj yntryhator" [Unconscionable intriguer]

      Refutes arguments that apostolic visitor, Very Rev. A. Hodobay,
      was sent to America to act as a policeman over the American
      Greek Catholic Church.

      A   XI (17): May 15, 1902; C-4

3167 [N.N.]; "Naš Vŷsokoprepodobnŷj vykarij y eho dîjstvie" [Our Very
      Reverend vicar and his activities]

      A   XI (18): May 22, 1902; C-2

3168 John Dzubay; Charleroi, PA; April 29, 1902

      Commentary on the Charleroi parish and the apostolic visitor.

      L   XI (18): May 22, 1902; C-2

3169 a. "Toržestvennoe posvjaščenie cerkvy v Čarleroj, Pa." [Solemn
          dedication of a church in Charleroi, PA]

      Dedication by Rev. Eugene Homicko on May 30, 1902.

                                     XI (18): May 22, 1902; C-3

      b. "Posvjaščenie novoj hr. kat. russkoj cerkvy v Plesent Syty, O."
          [Dedication of new Greek Catholic Rusyn Church in Pleasant
          City, OH]

      Dedication on July 4, 1902.

                                     XI (18): May 22, 1902; C-3

      c. "Posvjaščenie novoj hr. kat. russkoj cerkvy v Toronto, O."
          [Dedication of new Greek Catholic Rusyn Church in Toronto, OH]

      Dedication on May 30, 1902.

      Ad   XI (18): May 22, 1902; C-3

3170 [N.N.]; "Naš vykarij y eho dîjstvovanie. Pervyj svjaščennyčeskij
      sobor pod predsîdatel'stvom našoho vykarija, apostol'skoho
      vyzytatora" [Our vicar and his activities. First clergy
      meeting under the chairmanship of our vicar, apostolic visitor]

      Meeting took place May 21, 1902 in Brooklyn, NY.

      A   XI (19): May 29, 1902; C-2

3171   [N.N.]; "Dal'šiy dijstvija Eho Vŷsokoprepodobija našeho vykarija" [Further activities of his Reverence, our vicar]

On May 22, 1902 Very Rev. Andrew Hodobay conferred with the apostolic delegate to America.

A   XI (19): May 29, 1902; C-2

3172   Rev. Orestes Zlockij; Hazleton, PA; May 31, 1902

The May 20, 1902 dedication of the Hazleton Greek Catholic Church.

L   XI (20): Jun 12, 1902; C-3

3173   [N.N.]; "Nynišnoe položenie y buduščnost' hr. kat. Rusynov v Amerykî" [Current situation and future of Greek Catholic Rusyns in America]

Part VII: "Pravoslavie yly shyzma" [Orthodoxy or schism]

A   XI (20): Jun 5, 1902; C-6

3174   [N.N.]; "Naš Vŷsokoprepodobnŷj Vykarij y eho dîstvovanie" [Our Very Reverend Vicar and his activities]

A   XI (21): Jun 12, 1902; C-2&3

3175   Rev. John Korotnoky; Allegheny, PA; May 27, 1902

The activities of the Apostolic Visitor, Very Rev. Andrew Hodobay.

L   XI (21): Jun 12, 1902; C-3

3176   [N.N.]; "Hreko katolyky" [Greek Catholics]

Explains who are Greek Catholics and includes a current list of Rusyn bishops and eparchies.

A   XI (21b): Jun 12, 1902; C-8

3177   "Cerkovnŷja Spravŷ" [Church Affairs]

        a. Rev. Cyril Gulovich dedicates the altar and iconostasis of the Barnesboro, PA Greek Catholic Church on July 4, 1902.
        b. Rev. Eugene Satala dedicates the altar of the Whiting, IN Greek Catholic Church on July 4, 1902.

Nr   XI (21): Jun 12, 1902; C-7

3178   [N.N.]; "Neponjatnoe postupanie vŷsokoprep. vyzytatora. Dîlaetsja vse bez vîdomosty naroda. Prava naroda, patrona cerkvej y parafij v Amerykî, v opasnosty. Vyzytator s nîkotorŷmy duchovnykamy chočet sbyty vse na korŷto starokraevoe. Naše 'Soedynenija' v ymeny svoem y vseho amerykanskoho hreko kat. russkoho naroda-protestuet" [Strange behavior of the Very Rev. visitor. All is done without the knowledge of the people. Rights of the people, the patrons of the churches and parishes

in America, are in danger. The visitor with several priests
wants to turn everything in the old country's direction.
Our 'Soedynenie' protests in the name of all American Greek
Catholic Rusyn people]

The clergy's plan to control church functions over the laity.

A   XI (25): Jul 17, 1902; C-2

3179   Michael Juhas, Nicholas Pačuta; "Ot Hl. Uradu 'Soedyn. Hr. Kat.
        Russk. Bratstv'" [From the Supreme Administration of G.C.U.]

        The need to preserve church property in the hands of the people
        and guarantee the autonomy of the American Greek Catholic Church.

        O   XI (25): Jul 17, 1902; C-2&3

3180   "Pereminy svjaščenykov" [Changes of Priests]

        a. Rev. Alexis Novak (Mukačevo Diocese) arrived in America
            and has been assigned to Mahanoy City, PA, currently
            administered by Rev. Basil Vološin (Passaic, NJ)
        b. Rev. John Ol'ševskij (Galicia) arrived in America and has
            been assigned to Mayfield, PA.
        c. Rev. Peter Keseliak (Cleveland, OH) was transferred to
            Yonkers, NY.
        d. Rev. Andrew Kaminsky (Yonkers, NY) transferred to Scranton,
            PA.

        Nr   XI (25): Jul 17, 1902; C-3

3181   [N.N.]; "Slovo o čynovstvî-uradî vyzytatora na osnovî-podstavî
        cerkovnoho prava" [Word about the office of the visitor on
        the basis of canon law]

        The European Greek Catholic church hierarchy's jurisdiction
        over the affairs of Greek Catholic churches in America and
        the idea of an independent Greek Catholic Church.

        Part I: XI (26): Jul 24, 1902; C-2

        Part II: "Kto možet bŷty apostol'skym vyzytatorom, jaku ymiet
        vlast', jakiy ymiet on prava?" [Who can become an Apostolic
        Visitor, how much power does he have, what kind of rights does
        he have?]

                                           XI (27): Jul 31, 1902; C-2
        Part III: XI (28): Aug 7, 1902; C-2

        A

3182   George Petryčko, Barnesboro, PA; Jul 12, 1902

        The July 4, 1902 church dedication in Barnesboro.

        L   XI (26): Jul 24, 1902; C-3

3183 Ju.; "Pochval'nŷj postup odnoj cerkovnoj našoj hromadŷ" [Praise-
      worthy action of one of our church communities]

      Commentary on the growth and development of the Perth Amboy,
      NJ Greek Catholic Church.

      E   XI (32): Sep 4, 1902; C-3

3184 [N.N.]; Windber, PA; Sept 2, 1902

      The dedication of the Windber church bells.

      L   XI (33): Sep 11, 1902; C-2&3

3185 "Yz kruha našych svjaščenykov" [From the circle of our clergy]

      a. Rev. Valentine Balog (Scranton, PA) returned to Europe
         July 29, 1902.
      b. Rev. Acacius Kamensky (Yonkers, NY) substitutes tempo-
         rarily for Rev. Balog.
      c. Rev. Michael Jackovich (Landsford, PA) has been assigned
         to St. John the Baptist Church.
      d. Rev. Orestes Zlockij (Hazleton, PA) assigned to Landsford,
         PA.
      e. Editors received an anonymous letter from Galicia informing
         them that the Congregation for the Propagation of Faith in
         Rome plans to send three Basilian priests (Revs. Dŷdyk,
         Tytla, Ieremija), a monk (brother Bîlan) and four nuns
         (Sisters Ambrozija, Tayda, Apolonija and Avhusta) to serve
         in the U.S. Date of arrival sometime in October 1902.

      Nr   XI (33): Sep 11, 1902; C-3

3186 "Cerkovnŷja Spravŷ" [Church Affairs]

      Dedication of Philadelphia, PA Greek Catholic Church's new
      rectory on September 28, 1902.

      Ad   XI (34): Sep 18, 1902; C-3

3187 [N.N.]; "Mistru 'Katolikovi'" [To Mr. 'Catholic']

      Commentary on an article about Greek Catholic Rusyn Americans
      published in American Slovak News (Slovensky American)
      (Pittsburgh, PA), #1000, September 24, 1902.

      A   XI (36): Oct 2, 1902; L-2

3188 [N.N.]; "Halyčeskiy duchovnyky y avtonomyčeskoe dvyženie načatoe
      nîskol'ko našymy duchovnykamy pod fyrmoju Vŷsokoprepod. O.
      A. Hodobaja" [Galician priests and the autonomous movement
      started by several of our priests under the auspices of Very
      Rev. A. Hodobay]

      Alleged movement by eleven priests (named) toward self-rule in
      all Greek Catholic American churches.

      A   XI (37): Oct 9, 1902; C-2&3

3189 [N.N.]; "Hezltonskaja konvencija otsročena!" [Hazleton Convention has been postponed!]

Convention for discussing formation of a Greek Catholic Eparchy in America postponed from October 21, 1902.

A XI (38): Oct 16, 1902; C-4

3190 "Peremîny Svjaščenykov" [Change of priests]

    a. Arrival of three new priests in America:
      1. Rev. Elias Gojdics (Prešov diocese) assigned to Bayonne City, NJ, currently administered by Rev. Theodore Stejfan.
      2. Rev. Victor Mirossay, not yet assigned.
      3. Rev. Acacius Kamensky (Mukačevo diocese) assigned to Kingston, PA.
    b. Rev. Theodore Stejfan (Bayonne, NJ) assigned to New Britain, CT.
    c. Rev. Damaskin Polivka (Duquesne, PA) assigned to Windber, PA.
    d. Rev. Eugene Satala (Whitney, IN) assigned to Duquesne, PA.
    e. Rev. John Parscouta (Oldforge-Rednham, PA) assigned to Whitney, IN.
    f. Rev. Vladimir Molchany (Kingston, PA) transferred to Cleveland, OH.
    g. Rev. Alexis Novak (Mahanoy City, PA) transferred to Scranton, PA.
    h. Rev. Theofane Obushkevich (Mayfield, PA) assigned to Mahanoy City, PA.
    i. Rev. J. Olševskij assigned to Mayfield, PA.
    j. Canadian Mission: Revs. Eyljas, Stockij, Dŷdyk, Zoldak and four nuns, all from the Metropolitan Diocese in Galicia, arrived in America on October 21, 1902. The priests and nuns are bound for Canada to serve Greek Catholic Rusyns there.

Nr XI (39): Oct 23, 1902; C-4&5

3191 Procopius Marfut; St. Louis, MO; Oct 20, 1902

The mission of Very Rev. Andrew Hodobay.

L XI (40): Oct 30, 1902; C-2

3192 Rev. Nicholas Stecovich; "Do otcev duchovných yz Halyčynŷ proyschodyvsŷch" [To the Reverend fathers (who come) from Galicia]

Reply to the idea of an independent American Greek Catholic church.

A XI (41): Nov 6, 1902; C-2

3193 "Cerkovnŷja Spravŷ" [Church Affairs]

Dedication of Saint Michael Greek Catholic Church's new altar in Windber, PA on November 23, 1902.

Ad XI (41): Nov 6, 1902; C-3

3194   [N.N.]; "Treba bŷty nam na čystom. Eho Vŷsokoprepodobie O. Andrej
Hodobaj dolžen uspokoyty vozvol'novavšyja smŷsly" [We must
get clear. His Very Reverend Andrew Hodobay should calm tur-
bulent minds]

       Very Rev. A. Hodobay and his mission to America. Reprint of
an article published in <u>Magyarok Csillaga</u> [McKeesport, PA],
#44, November 7, 1902.

       A   XI (42): Nov 13, 1902; C-2

3195   M.K. Lucak; Cleveland, OH; Oct 26, 1902

       The schism among Rusyn parishes allegedly caused by other
nationalities.

       L   XI (42): Nov 13, 1902; C-4

3196   "Cerkovnŷja Spravŷ" [Church Affairs]

       a. Dedication of Bradenville, PA Greek Catholic Church's
corner stone on November 30, 1902.
       b. Very Rev. Andrew Hodobay dedicates the bell and icono-
stasis of the Phoenixville, PA Greek Catholic church on
November 23, 1902.

       Ad   XI (42): Nov 13, 1902; C-5

3197   Anthony Monyč; New Britain, CT; Nov 15, 1902

       The construction of the New Britain Greek Catholic church.

       L   XI (44): Nov 27, 1902; C-2

3198   [N.N.]; "V zaščyt Vŷsokoprepodob. apostol. vyzytatora" [In defense
of the Very Reverend Apostolic visitor]

       Minutes of the November 25, 1902 clergy meeting in New York
City. Editor's commentary follows.

       A   XI (45): Dec 4, 1902; C-2

3199   [N.N.]; "Odno velykoe cerkovnoe toržestvo" [One magnificent church
celebration]

       The dedication of Bradenville, PA, church's corner stone on
November 30, 1902.

       A   XI (45): Dec 4, 1902; C-3

3200   Very Rev. Andrew Hodobay; Scranton, PA; Nov 14, 1902

       Reply of the Apostolic Visitor to several <u>ARV</u> articles con-
cerning his mission in America.

       L   XI (46): Dec 11, 1902; C-2&3

3201   Michael Dobrockij, et al.; Yonkers, NY; Dec 1, 1902

       The dedication of the Yonkers parish's new chalice.

       L   XI (46): Dec 11, 1902; C-3

3202   Rev. Elias Gojdics; Bayonne, NJ; Dec 13, 1902

       Correction in article. See 3198.

       L   XI (47): Dec 18, 1902; C-2

3203   Rev. A. Holosnyay; "Protokol" [Minutes]

       Minutes of the Mukačevo Diocese clergy association's meeting
on December 16, 1902 in Harrisburg, PA.

       O   XI (49): Jan 1, 1903; C-9

3204   Very Rev. Andrew Hodobay; Scranton, PA; Jan 5, 1903

       Apostolic visitor's commentary on the ARV's view and his own
position regarding the situation of the American Greek Catholic Church.

       L   XII (1): Jan 15, 1903; C-2&3, L-2&3

3205   Rev. Cornelius Laurisin; Shehandoah, PA; Feb 10, 1903

       "Zaslato" [Letter to the Editor]

       Reply to 3204.

       L   XII (5): Feb 12, 1903; C-2, L-2

3206   Michael Lucak; Cleveland, OH; Feb 23, 1903

       The formation of a church choir under the directorship of
Michael Sekerak.

       L   XII (6&7): Feb 26, 1903; C-11, L-2

3207   Mathew Soltis; Diamond, IN; May 13, 1903

       Diamond's Greek Catholic church activities.

       L   XII (10): Mar 19, 1903; C-3, L-3

3208   Alexander Kozubov; Perth Amboy, NJ

       The polemics among Perth Amboy parishioners.

       L   XII (11): Mar 26, 1903; C-3, L-3

3209   "Visty cerkovnŷy y duchovnyčeskiy" [Church and clergy news]

       a. Apostolic vicar and procurator representative of Greek
Catholic affairs in Rome, Rev. Alexander Ulicky, is being
sent to America to assess the situation of the Greek
Catholic churches there.

b. Rev. Nicholas Stecovich (Pleasant City, OH), transferred to Bradenville, PA to organize a new parish.

Nr   XII (12): Apr 2, 1903; C-3, L-3

3210   Rev. A. Petrašovich, et al.; "Dvyženie v dîlî amerykanskoj hreko Katolyčeskoj cerkovnoj verchnosty" [Movement concerning American Greek Catholic Church hierarchy]

Announces plans for calling a meeting of representatives from all parishes to discuss the establishment of a Greek Catholic Diocese in America.

A   XII (13): Apr 9, 1903; C-2, L-2

3211   B. Mikluščak, et al.; Duquesne, PA; April 14, 1903

The activities of the Duquesne Greek Catholic Church.

L   XII (15): Apr 30, 1903; C-2, L-2

3212   Rev. Michael Balogh; Trauger, PA; April, 1903

"Otkrŷtoe Pys'mo k. Vŷsokop. y Velykomožnomu Panu y Vyzytatoru Ameryk. Hr. Katolykov" [Open letter to the Very Rev. and Honorable Sir, [Apostolic] Visitor of the American Greek Catholics]

The mission of Very Rev. Andrew Hodobay.

L   XII (15): Apr 30, 1903; C-2&3, L-2

3213   [N.N.]; "Odyn jublej" [An anniversary]

Commemorates the twenty-fifth anniversary of Very Rev. Alexis Toth's ordination. Brief history of the Toth schism.

A   XII (15): Apr 30, 1903; C-4, L-4

3214   "Cerkovnŷja Spravŷ" [Church Affairs]

a. Rev. C. Lengyel dedicates the iconostasis of the Scranton, PA Greek Catholic church on May 24, 1903 (O.S.).
b. Dedication of the new Greek Catholic church in Bradenville, PA on May 30, 1903.

                                      XII (16): May 7, 1903; C-7, L-7

c. Rev. D. Polivka dedicates Windber, PA Greek Catholic church on May 30, 1903.
d. Rev. Nicholas Molchany dedicates the bells of the Passaic, NJ Greek Catholic church on May 31, 1903.

Nr   XII (17): May 14, 1903; C-7, L-3

3215   [N.N.]; "Odno ves'ma blahorodnoe predpryjatie" [A very worthwhile undertaking]

The activities of Rev. D. Polivka, who assisted in establishing a hospital, school and a convent of the Basilian sisters in Windber, PA.

A, P   XII (18): May 21, 1903; C-2, L-2

3216 [N.N.]; "Vŷsokoprep. O. Hodobay mol'čyt jak rŷba. Myssija eho v
Amerykî skončylas'. Y v koncy ne budem znaty, ož' dîjstno
čto on bŷl y dlja čeho bŷl v Amerykî" [Very Rev. Hodobay is
silent like a fish. His mission in America has ended. In
the end we will not know really who he was and the reason he
was in America]

The mission to America of the Very Rev. Andrew Hodobay,
Apostolic Visitor, ends May 20, 1903.

A   XII (18): May 21, 1903; C-4, L-4

3217 "Cerkovnŷja Spravŷ" [Church Affairs]

Dedication of the corner stone of the Homestead, PA Greek
Catholic Church on June 14, 1903.

Nr   XII (18): May 21, 1903; C-5, L-5

3218 [N.N.]; Windber, PA; Jun 4, 1903

The May 30, 1903 dedication of the Windber Greek Catholic
church.

L   XII (21): Jun 11, 1903; L-2&3

3219 Peter Dzmura; Braddock, PA; Jun 6, 1903

Reply to a letter to the editor in Cerkovnaja Nauka, #10,
concerning the polemics among parishioners of the Braddock
parish.

L   XII (21): Jun 11, 1903; L-3

3220 "Vîsty yz kruha našoho duchovenstva" [News from the circle of our
priests]

a. Revs. Antony Izay (Wilkes Barre, PA), Victor Popovich
(St. Clive, PA) and Cornelius Laurisin (Shenandoah, PA)
are leaving for Europe.
b. Revs. N. Chopey and P. Staurovsky arrived in America.
Rev. Chopey (Mukačevo diocese) assigned to Wilkes Barre,
PA. Rev. Staurovsky (Prešov diocese) assigned to
Monessen, PA.

Nr   XII (22): Jun 25, 1903; C-3, L-3

3221 [N.N.]; "Udostoenie našeho 'Soedynenija' duchovenstvom" [The clergy
honor our 'Soedynenie']

Clergy meeting in Scranton, PA, June 17-18, 1903.

A   XII (23): Jul 2, 1903; C-4, L-4

3222 Rev. A. Kecskés, et al.; "Zaslato" [Letter to the Editor]

Minutes of the clergy meeting which took place June 18, 1903
in Scranton, PA.

L   XII (24): Jul 9, 1903; C-2&3, L-2&3

3223   John Uhrin; Homestead, PA; Jun 20, 1903

The June 14, 1903 dedication of the Homestead Greek Catholic
Church.

L   XII (24): Jul 9, 1903; C-3, L-3

3224   [N.N.]; "Dolžno povynovatys' latynskym Epyskopam" [One should
submit to Latin-rite Bishops]

Rev. John Ardan's (Olyphant, PA) conversation with Roman
Catholic Bishop Hoban of Scranton, PA. From a partial reprint of an article in the Sun [New York], July 8, 1903.

A   XII (24): Jul 9, 1903; C-4, L-4

3225   Rev. Anthony Kecskés, et al.; "Memorandum"

Proceedings of the clergy meeting held in Scranton, PA on
June 18, 1903 was sent in a memorandum to a Bishop's committee in Europe.

A   XII (25): Jul 16, 1903; C-2, L-2

3226   "Cerkovnŷja Spravŷ" [Church Affairs]

a. Dedication of the Cleveland, OH parish's icon on August 30,
    1903.
b. Rev. Eugene Volkay dedicates Pleasant City, OH Greek Catho-
    lic Church on August 2, 1903.

Nr   XII (25): Jul 16, 1903; C-3, L-7

3227   George Vasyl'; "Otzŷv na sobranie duchovnykov v Skrenton, PA"
[Response to the clergy meeting in Scranton, PA]

A   XII (26): Jul 23, 1903; C-2, L-2

3228   Andrew Marko; Kingston, PA; Jul 17, 1903

The July 28, 1903 dedication of the Kingston Greek Catholic
Church's iconostasis and altar.

L   XII (26): Jul 23, 1903; C-3, L-2

3229   [N.N.]; "Memorandum predložennŷj ameryk. slovenskymy rymo-kat.
duchovnykamy Emynenciy Kardynalu Archiepyskopu, Vŷsokopreos-
vjaščennŷm, Archiepyskopam y Preosvjaščennŷm Epyskopam Soed.
Statov! Vylksbery, Pa. Dek. 1, 1903" [Memorandum proposed
by American Slovak Roman Catholic priests to the Eminent Cardinal Archbishop, Most Rev. Archbishops, and Bishops of the U.S.!
Wilkes Barre, PA. Dec 1, 1903]

The attempts by the Hungarian Government to control the church
affairs of Rusyns and Slovaks.

A   XII (28): Aug 6, 1903; C-2&3, L-2&3

3230   [N.N.]; "Krasnŷj prymîr čestnoj pracŷ v vŷderžannosty"
       [A beautiful example of honest work and steadfastness]

       The activities of St. Michael's parish in Passaic, NJ.

       A   XII (28): Aug 6, 1903; C-3, L-3

3231   Red.; Mt. Carmel, PA; Aug 10, 1903

       The August 6-7, 1903 Galician priest conference in Shamokin,
       PA.

       L   XII (29): Aug 13, 1903; C-2, L-2

3232   "Cerkovnŷja Spravŷ" [Church Affairs]

       Very Rev. A. Hodobay attends the dedication of the royal and
       deacon doors of the Wilkes Barre, PA church's iconostasis on
       August 30, 1903.

       Nr   XII (30): Aug 20, 1903; C-3, L-3

3233   [N.N.]; Allegheny, PA; Aug 18, 1903

       The August 9, 1903 dedication of the Allegheny Greek Catholic
       Church.

       L   XII (31): Aug 27, 1903; C-2, L-2

3234   [N.N.]; "O Epyskopa Pols'kaho v Amerykî" [Towards a Polish Bishop
       in America]

       Efforts by Polish Catholic immigrants to gain their own bishop.

       A   XII (32): Sep 3, 1903; C-2, L-3

3235   [N.N.]; "Vopros Amerykanskoho Hr. Katolyčeskoho Epyskopstva"
       [The question of an American Greek Catholic Bishopric]

       Part I: XII (34): Sep 17, 1903; C-2, L-2

       Part II: XII (37): Oct 8, 1903; C-2, L-2

       A

3236   Michael Grabany; Diamond, IN; Sep 8, 1903

       Rusyn communities in Indiana that lack parishes and G.C.U.
       lodges.

       L   XII (34): Sep 17, 1903; C-3, L-3

3237   Michael Korinko; Pottstown, PA; Sep 22, 1903

       The September 20, 1903 dedication of the Pottstown Greek
       Catholic Church's corner stone.

       L   XII (35): Sep 24, 1903; C-3, L-3

3238 [N.N.]; "Udaval pravoslavnaho Epyskopa" [He impersonated an
Orthodox Bishop]

A charlatan posing as Metropolitan Sefrim, an Orthodox Bishop,
was purportedly sent to America by the Tsar to collect money
for the construction of a monastery in Canada.

A   XII (35): Sep 24, 1903; C-4, L-4

3239 [N.N.]; "O Epyskopa Pol'skoho" [Towards a Polish Bishop]

The appointment of a Polish Bishop for Polish Roman Catholics
in America.

A   XII (36): Oct 1, 1903; C-2, L-2

3240 "Vîsty yz kruha našeho duchovenstva" [News from the circle of our
clergy]

   a. Rev. Julius Polyansky (Mukačevo Diocese) arrived in
America July 14, 1903. Rev. Polyansky (Techna [Dvorjanky],
Zemplén county, Hungary) has been assigned to St. Clive, PA.

   b. Rev. John Korotnoky (Allegheny, PA) has been named by the
Bishop of Prešov, Most Rev. Dr. John Valij, to the rank of
Monsignor and will be consulting advisor to the Bishop on
American Greek Catholic affairs.

Nr   XII (36): Oct 1, 1903; C-2, L-2

3241 [N.N.]; Windber, PA; Oct 4, 1903

The October 4, 1903 dedication of the Windber Greek Catholic
Church's two bells.

L   XII (37): Oct 8, 1903; C-2&3, L-2

3242 "Vîsty yz kruha našeho duchovenstva" [News from the circle of our
clergy]

   a. Ramey, PA Greek Catholic Church celebrates its tenth anniversary October 14, 1903.

   b. Rev. Ladomirsky (Jessup, PA) transferred to Youngstown, OH.

   c. Rev. Gabriel Chopey (Mukačevo Diocese) recently returned
from Europe and was assigned to the Jessup, PA.

   d. Rev. Nestor Volensky transferred from Youngstown, OH, however, at this time his new assignement is unknown.

   e. Rev. Emilian Seregelly (Mukačevo Diocese) arrived in
America November 4, 1903.

   f. Rev. A. Kecskés dedicates the corner stone of the New
Salem, PA Greek Catholic church on November 26, 1903.

Nr   XII (41): Nov 5, 1903; C-2, L-2

3243   Rev. Elias Gojdics; Bayonne, NJ; Nov 4, 1903

"Pros'ba" [Request]

Financial collection in honor of the Most Rev. John Valij's, Bishop of Prešov Diocese, 20th year anniversary.

L   XII (41): Nov 5, 1903; C-2, L-2

3244   a. "Toržestvennoe posvjaščenie novoj hr. kat. russkoj cerkvy v Potstovn, Pa." [Celebrational dedication of the new Greek Catholic Rusyn church in Pottstown, PA]

Dedication on November 22, 1903.

b. "Posvjaščenie novoho zvona v Bradenvyl, Pa." [Dedication of a new bell in Bradenville, PA]

Dedication on November 22, 1903.

Ad   XII (42): Nov 12, 1903; C-3, L-7

3245   [N.N.]; "Pravŷm podobaet pochvala! Dvadcjaty-Lîtnoe Blahoslovennoe y Dobročynnoe Dîstvovanie Eho Vŷsokopreosvjaščenstva D-ra Ioanna Valija, Hreko kat. Russkoho Epyskopa v Prjaševî na Uhorščynî" [Thy deserved praise! Twentieth year of the blessed and benevolent reign of his Most Rev. Dr. John Valij, Greek Catholic Rusyn Bishop in Prešov, Hungary]

Greek Catholic church in Europe and history of the Prešov diocese.

A, P   XII (44): Nov 26, 1903; C-1,2,3, L-1,2,3

3246   "Juvylejnŷy Cerk. Toržestva v Amerykî v čest' Vŷsokopresv. d-r Ioanna Valîja Preševskoho hr. kat. russk. Epyskopa-juvylanta" [Anniversary church celebrations in America in the honor of the Most Rev. Dr. John Valij's, Prešov Greek Catholic Bishop, anniversary]

Congratulatory letters to the editor on the occasion of the Most Rev. John Valij's twentieth year anniversary as Bishop of Prešov.

L   XII (45): Dec 3, 1903; C-2&3, L-2&3

3247   Michael Korinko; Pottstown, PA; Nov 25, 1903

The November 22, 1903 dedication of the Pottstown Greek Catholic Church

L   XII (46): Dec 10, 1903; C-2, L-2

3248   John Janossy; Bradenville, PA; Nov 27, 1903

The November 22, 1903 dedication of the Bradenville Greek Catholic Church's corner stone.

L   XII (46): Dec 10, 1903; C-2&3, L-2

3249   M. Nyahaj, et al.; Yonkers, NY; Nov 30, 1903

The November 26, 1903 dedication of the Yonkers Greek Catholic Church's corner stone.

L   XII (46): Dec 10, 1903; C-3, L-2&3

3250   [N.N.]; Toronto, OH; Nov 20, 1903

The November 29, 1903 dedication of the Toronto Greek Catholic Church's bells.

L   XII (46): Dec 10, 1903; C-3, L-3

3251   "Posvjaščenie novoj hr. kat. russkoj cerkvy v Homsted, Pa." [Dedication of the new Greek Catholic Rusyn church in Homestead, PA]

Dedication on November 27, 1903.

Ad   XII (46): Dec 10, 1903; C-6, L-7

3252   Rev. Nicholas Molchaney, et al.; Passaic, NJ; Dec 19, 1903

The Passaic parish.

L   XII (48): Dec 24, 1903; C-3, L-2&3

3253   John Uhrin; "Odno krasnoe cerkovnoe toržestvo" [A beautiful church celebration]

The December 27, 1903 dedication of the Homestead, PA Greek Catholic Church.

A, P   XIII (1): Jan 21, 1904; C-2, L-2

3254   John Kičinko; Monessen, PA; Feb 1, 1904

The conversion of Jacob Lieberman, a Jew from Hungary, to Christianity.

L   XIII (3): Feb 4, 1904; C-2, L-2

3255   "Vîsty cerkovnŷy" [Church affairs]

"Hr. kat. Russka cerkov v Bejon Syty, N'ju Dž. kotora dnja 19 janvarja pala žertvoju požara" [Greek Catholic Rusyn Church in Bayonne, NJ which on January 19 fell victim to fire]

Nr, P   XIII (3): Feb 4, 1904; C-4, L-4

3256   "Novosci zos kruhu našoho duchovenstva" [News from the circle of our priests]

      a. Rev. Dr. Theodosius Vasochik (Mukačevo Diocese) recently arrived in America and has been assigned to Hazleton, PA.
      b. Rev. Emilian Artimovich (Mukačevo Diocese) recently arrived in America and has been assigned to Jessup, PA.

Nr   XIII (4): Feb 11, 1904; L-3

3257   Rev. Elias Gojdics; "Publyčnaja pros'ba" [Public appeal]

Requests donations to rebuild the Bayonne, NJ church, destroyed by fire on January 19, 1904.

Req   XIII (9): Mar 17, 1904; C-2, L-2

3258   [N.N.]; "Putešestvie abbasa y apost. vyzytatora vŷsokoprep. O. Andreja Hodobaja v Rym" [Journey of the Apostolic Visitor, the Very Rev. Andrew Hodobay to Rome]

A   XIII (11): Mar 31, 1904; C-2, L-2

3259   [N.N.]; "Orhanyzacija Amerykanskoj Hreko Kat. Cerkvy" [Organization of the American Greek Catholic Church]

The past and future of the Greek Catholic Church in America.

Part I: XIII (12): Apr 7, 1904; C-2&3, L-2

Part II: XIII (13): Apr 21, 1904; C-2, L-2

A

3260   "Novosty yz kruhu našeho duchovenstva" [News from the circle of our clergy]

a. Rev. Irenaeus Janicky (Prešov Diocese) recently arrived in America and has been assigned to Alden, PA.
b. Rev. Anthony Kecskés (New Salem, PA) transferred to Bradenville, PA.
c. Rev. Nicholas Stecovich (Bradenville, PA) transferred to New Salem, PA.

Nr   XIII (12): Apr 7, 1904; C-3, L-3

3261   [N.N.]; "Jak starajutsja našy neprošenŷ opîkunŷ o našu Amer. hr. kat. Cerkov?" [How concerned are our uninvited tutors about our Greek Catholic Church?]

The Very Rev. Andrew Hodobay's mission to America and the reforms he wants to implement for the Church in America.

A   XIII (14): Apr 28, 1904; C-2, L-2

3262   Rev. Elias Gojdics; Bayonne, NJ; Apr 6, 1904

"Publyčnoe poblahodarenie" [Public thanks]

Pastor of the Bayonne parish expresses gratitude for donations received for the construction of a new church.

L   XIII (14): Apr 28, 1904; C-2, L-2

3263   Peter Duritza; Hawk Run, PA; Apr 6, 1904

The construction of the Hawk Run Greek Catholic Church.

L   XIII (14): Apr 28, 1904; C-2, L-2

3264   P — an.; "Naša relyhijno-narodna budučnost' v Amerykî" [Our
        religious-national future in America]

        The establishment of an American Greek Catholic Eparchy.

        A   XIII (15): May 5, 1904; C-2, L-2

3265   "Vel'ka Cerkovna Slavnosc" [Magnificent Church Celebration]

        Rev. Cornelius Laurisin dedicates the Brooklyn, NY Greek
        Catholic church on May 30, 1903.

        Ad   XIII (15): May 5, 1904; L-6

3266   "Vîsty Cerkovnŷy [Church Affairs]

        a. Dedication of Bradenville, PA parish's two church banners
            and icons on May 30, 1904.

                          XIII (15): May 5, 1904; C-7, L-6

        b. Dedication of the Perth Amboy, NJ church's corner stone
            on May 30, 1904.

                          XIII (17): May 19, 1904; C-7, L-7

        c. Rev. M.C. Lengyel dedicates Scranton, PA parish's large
            stone cross on May 30, 1904.

        Nr   XIII (17): May 19, 1904; C-3, L-3

3267   [N.N.]; Passaic, NJ; May 15, 1904

        The May 1, 1904 dedication of the Passaic Greek Catholic
        Church's banner.

        L   XIII (17): May 19, 1904; C-2, L-2

3268   Ann Macko; Toronto, OH; May 15, 1904

        The May 15, 1904 dedication of the Toronto Greek Catholic
        Church's "Plaščanyca."*

        L   XIII (17): May 19, 1904; C-3, L-2&3

3269   [N.N.]; "Bŷl-ly Vŷsokoprep. O. Andrej Hodobay v Rymî?" [Was the
        Very Rev. Andrew Hodobay really in Rome?]

        The Very Rev. A. Hodobay's mission to America and his trip to
        Rome afterwards.

        A   XIII (18): May 26, 1904; C-2&3, L-2

---

*A cloth upon which is a reproduction of Christ, considered to represent
the winding sheet, displayed during services in the post-Easter season.

3270 [N.N.]; "Dobrŷj sposob k rozvjazan'ju cerkovnoho našoho voprosa"
[A good method for solving our church question]

Former Apostolic Delegate to the U.S., Cardinal Satolli's
plan to discuss the formation of a Greek Catholic Eparchy in
America with the Holy Father in Rome.

A   XIII (19): Jun 2, 1904; C-2&3, L-2&3

3271 A. Z.; Perth Amboy, NJ; Jul 2, 1904

Activities of the Perth Amboy Greek Catholic Church and G.C.U.
lodge.

L   XIII (20): Jun 9, 1904; C-2&3, L-2&3

3272 "Vîsty Cerkovnŷy" [Church News]

a. Dedication of the Duquesne, PA church's corner stone on
   July 3, 1904.
b. Dedication of Phoenixville, PA Greek Catholic cemetery on
   July 12, 1904.

Nr   XIII (20): Jun 9, 1904; C-3, L-7

3273 Rev. Elias Gojdics; Bayonne, NJ; May 25, 1904

Thanks all lodges who contributed money for the reconstruction
of the Bayonne Greek Catholic Church.

L   XIII (20): Jun 9, 1904; C-3, L-6

3274 John Kuba, et al.; Bradenville, PA; Jun 7, 1904

Bradenville's Greek Catholic Church activities.

L   XIII (21): Jun 16, 1904; C-2&3, L-2

3275 Rev. Orestes Zlockij; Lansford, PA; Jul 15, 1904

Claims information in 3269 was presented incorrectly.

L   XIII (22): Jun 23, 1904; C-2, L-2

3276 John Czeperak; Phoenixville, PA; Jun 21, 1904

The activities of the Phoenixville Greek Catholic Church.

L   XIII (22): Jun 23, 1904; C-2, L-3

3277 Rev. Alexis Holosnyay; "Vozzvanio k všîm Amerykanskym Hreko
Katolykam" [Proclamation to all American Greek Catholics]

a. Commentary on the future of the American Greek Catholic
   Church.
b. The mission of the Very Rev. A. Hodobay.
c. Announces the convocation of the first (proposed) Greek
   Catholic Congress in America.

A   XIII (27): Aug 26, 1904; 4

3278 Ž.; "Odno krasnoe y velykoe cerkovnoe toržestvo" [One fine and magnificent church celebration]

Dedication of the Braddock, PA Greek Catholic church held on August 14, 1904.

E   XIII (27): Aug 26, 1904, 9,10

3279 "Vîsty Cerkovnŷy" [Church News]

Dedication of the Bayonne (or Perth Amboy), NJ Greek Catholic cemetery on September 5, 1904.

Nr   XIII (28): Sep 1, 1904; 7

3280 [N.N.]; "Nîskol'ko slov k vozzvaniju O. A. Holosnąja napravlennomu k vsîm ameryk. hreko katolykam" [A few words concerning the proclamation of Rev. Alexis Holosnyay directed to all American Greek Catholics]

The future of the Greek Catholic Church in America. See 3277.

Parts I-III: XIII (29-31): Sep 8-22, 1904; 4,9

A

3281 [N.N.]; St. Louis, MO; Sep 5, 1904

Dispells a rumor, caused by a letter to the editor of Svît [Madison, IL] claiming that the priest of the St. Louis Greek Catholic church placed the church under the jurisdiction of Russian Orthodox Bishop Tikon.

L   XIII (30): Sep 15, 1904; 9,10

3282 "Holosŷ o hr. kat. Konhressî" [Opinions about the Greek Catholic Congress]

Letters to the Editor from G.C.U. lodges and members commenting upon the proposal for a Greek Catholic Church Congress.

L   XIII (31): Sep 22, 1904; 4,5

3283 "Vîsty Cerkovnŷy" [Church News]

Dedication of the new Punxsutawney-Lindsey, PA Greek Catholic church on October 2, 1904.

Nr   XIII (31): Sep 22, 1904; 6

3284 Andrew Zbojan, et al.; Perth Amboy, NJ; Sep 9, 1904

The activities of the Perth Amboy Greek Catholic Church.

L   XIII (31): Sep 22, 1904; 9

3285 Simon Petrik, et al.; Hawk Run, PA; Sep 12, 1904

The September 5, 1904 dedication of the Hawk Run Greek Catholic church.

L   XIII (31): Sep 22, 1904; 9,10

3286   John Petrunyak; Patton, PA; Sep 12, 1904

        The purchase of a bell for the Patton Greek Catholic Church.

        L   XIII (31): Sep 22, 1904; 10

3287   Rev. A. Holosnyay; "Povtornoe Vozzvanie k Vsîm Ameryk. Hreko Kato-
        lykam!'" [A second proclamation to All Greek Catholics!]

        The proposed Greek Catholic Church Congress.

        A   XIII (32): Sep 29, 1904; 4

3288   Rev. Orestes Zlockij; Lansford, PA; Sep 16, 1904

        "Zaslato" [Letter to the Editor]

        The burial of Rev. Vladimir Molchany in a Protestant cemetery
        as sanctioned by the Very Rev. Andrew Hodobay.

        L   XIII (32): Sep 29, 1904; 6

3289   Rev. A. Holosnyay; "Našy svjaščennyky v Baltymor(î) y v Vašynhtonî"
        [Our priests in Baltimore, MD and Washington, D.C.]

        The formation of an American Greek Catholic Eparchy.

        A   XIII (34): Oct 13, 1904; 4,5

3290   Peter Budzilka; Donora, PA; Sep 13, 1904

        The September 4, 1904 dedication of the Donora Greek Catholic
        Church.

        L   XIII (34): Oct 13, 1904; 9

3291   [N.N.]; "Process o hr. kat. russku Cerkov v Dukejn, Pa" [Litiga-
        tion on the Greek Catholic Rusyn church in Duquesne, PA]

        Reprint of an article from the Slovenski Denník [Pittsburgh],
        October 17, 1904, regarding a court case between the Duquesne,
        PA and McKeesport, PA parishes over membership.

        A   XIII (35): Oct 20, 1904; 4

3292   "Vîsty Cerkovnŷy" [Church News]

        Rev. N. Stecovich dedicates New Salem, PA Greek Catholic
        church's altar on October 30, 1904.

        Nr   XIII (36): Oct 27, 1904; 7

3293   Rev. Orestes Zlocky; Lansford, PA; Oct 11, 1904

        "Zaslato" [Letter to the Editor]

        More information concerning the burial of Rev. Vladimir
        Molchany. Various questions concerning the event are directed
        to the Very Rev. Andrew Hodobay.

        L   XIII (36): Oct 27, 1904; 9,10

3294   "Vîsty Cerkovnŷy" [Church News]

      a.   Dedication of the Marble Head, OH Greek Catholic Church
          on November 24, 1904.

                                        XIII (37): Nov 3, 1904; 7

      b.   Dedication of the Perth Amboy, NJ Greek Catholic Church's
          new cross on November 20, 1904.

Nr   XIII (37): Nov 3, 1904; 7

3295   Redakcija; "Kto žadaet yskrenno učreždynie Hr. Kat. Epyskopstva v
       Amerykî?!" [Who really demands the establishment of a Greek
       Catholic Eparchy in America?!]

       Commentary on the proposed Greek Catholic Congress which would
       facilitate the establishment of an American Greek Catholic
       Eparchy.

E   XIII (37): Nov 3, 1904; 4,5

3296   Rev. A. Holosnyay; "Otvît O. Iosyfu Hanul'ovy y eho 'tovaryščam'"
       [An answer to Rev. Joseph Hanulya and his 'comrades']

       Refers to a letter (printed) by Rev. Joseph Hanulya on the
       question of an American Greek Catholic Eparchy.

L   XIII (38): Nov 10, 1904; 4,5,6

3297   Nicholas Pačuta; "Nîskol'ko otkrovenných slov k voprosu Ameryk. Hr.
       Kat. Konhressa" [A few candid remarks on the question of the
       American Greek Catholic Congress]

A   XIII (39): Nov 17, 1904; 4

3298   Michael Szemjan; Scranton, PA; Oct, 1904

       Commentary on an article in the <u>Scranton Times</u>, October 1,
       1904, p. 4, about the Scranton Greek Catholic Church. (<u>ARV</u>
       reprints the article in translation.)

L   XIII (39): Nov 17, 1904; 10

3299   Rev. Joseph Hanulya; "Opasnost' postupovanija O. Holosnjaja y 'eho
       tovaryščej'!" [Danger of the action of Rev. Holosnyay and
       'his comrades'!]

       Rev. Holosnyay's plans for a Greek Catholic Church Congress.

A   XIII (40): Nov 24, 1904; 2&3

3300   Rev. Orestes Zlockij; "K voprosu o našom Epyskopstvî" [On the
       question of our Bishopric]

       The establishment of an American Greek Catholic Eparchy.

A   XIII (41): Dec 1, 1904; 2,3

3301   And. Zbojan, et al.; Perth Amboy, NJ; Nov 28, 1904

The dedication of the Perth Amboy Greek Catholic Cemetery cross.

L   XIII (42): Dec 8, 1904; 2

3302   Rev. A. Holosnyay; "Odnym šahom vpered!" [One step forward!]

Reply to Holosnyay's critics (especially Rev. J. Hanulya) on the proposed basis for organizing an American Greek Catholic Eparchy.

A   XIII (42): Dec 8, 1904; 4,5

3303   Andrew Bussa; Binghampton, NY; Dec 7, 1904

Requests contributions to help finance the construction of the Binghampton Greek Catholic Church.

L   XIII (43): Dec 15, 1904; 2,3

3304   George Bučko, et al.; Marblehead, OH; Dec 6, 1904

The November 24, 1904 dedication of the Marblehead Greek Catholic Church.

L   XIII (43): Dec 15, 1904; 2,3

3305   J. Skakandy; Whiting, IN; Dec 3, 1904

The October 23, 1904 dedication of the Whiting Greek Catholic Cemetery.

L   XIII (43): Dec 15, 1904; 2,3

3306   Anthony Monics; New Britain, CT; Nov 26, 1904

The November 24, 1904 dedication of the New Britain Greek Catholic Church's corner stone.

L   XIII (43): Dec 15, 1904; 2,3

3307   Rev. Emil Kubek; "Nîskol'ko slov k voprosu o hr. kat. Epyskopstvî v Amerykî" [A few remarks on the question of a Greek Catholic Bishopric in America]

A   XIII (44): Dec 22, 1904; 9,11

3308   Rev. Gabriel Martyak; Bardejov [Bártfa], Sáros County, Hungary; Dec 13, 1904

Thanks all American Greek Catholics who contributed financially to the building of a church in Bardejov.

LE   XIII (46): Jan 5, 1905; 10,12

3309 [N.N.]; "Hr. Kat. Konhress y narod" [Greek Catholic Congress among the people]

The reception of the idea of a Greek Catholic Congress among the parishes.

A   XV (1): Jan 18, 1906; 2,3

3310 [N.N.]; "Protyv Konhressu-ly, yly tokmo protyv nîkotorŷch!? Y to ne ynde jak pravî na Konhressî!" [Against the Congress or only against some people!? And this only at the Congress!]

Commentary on those who are opposed to an autonomous Greek Catholic church in America as proposed by the Greek Catholic Congress.

A   XV (1): Jan 18, 1906; 4,5

3311 [N.N.]; "Hr. kat. Konhress y Narod. Protokol" [The Greek Catholic Congress and the people. Minutes]

Minutes of an all-parish meeting (held December 24, 1905 in Shenandoah, PA) discusses the ramifications of the proposals decided upon at the December 1905 Brooklyn, NY Greek Catholic Congress.

O   XV (2): Jan 25, 1906; 4,5

3312 Michael Jaško; Hazleton, PA; Jan 22, 1906

A raffle, conducted by the Hazleton parish, to raise money for the construction of a rectory.

L   XV (3): Feb 1, 1906; 2,3

3313 V. D.; Pleasant City, OH; Jan, 1906

The Pleasant City parish's problem of obtaining a priest to minister to them.

L   XV (3): Feb 1, 1906; 2,3,5

3314 [N.N.]; "Potreba vporjadkovanija cerkovnŷch našych dîl" [The necessity of putting our church affairs in order]

Arranging the American Greek Catholic Church to serve the needs of Rusyn-Americans rather than old country politics.

A   XV (3): Feb 1, 1906; 4,5

3315 Revs. A. Dzubay and Joseph Hanulya; "Ot ĕkzekut. komytetu V.C.N. sobranija" [From the Executive Committee of the Great Church-Laical Conference]

Plans for future meetings in organizing and presenting a proposal for a Greek Catholic Diocese in America to the Vatican.

O   XV (4): Feb 8, 1906; 2

3316 [N.N.]; "Dîlo Hr. Kat. Konhressa prodol'žaetsja" [Business of the Greek Catholic Congress continues]

More about the objectives of the Greek Catholic Congress.

A   XV (4): Feb 8, 1906; 4

3317 Elik Csura; "Radost' y smutok" [Happiness and sadness]

Commentary on the recent articles about the Greek Catholic Congress. Warns all concerned about "enemies" who would like to prevent Rusyn-Americans from having their own diocese.

A   XV (5): Feb 15, 1906; 4,5

3318 Rev. Michael Balog; Windber, PA; Feb 12, 1906

"Slovo k I. Amer. hr. kat. Konhressu" [A word concerning the First Greek Catholic Congress]

Opinions by members of the Windber parish about the Greek Catholic Congress.

L   XV (6): Feb 22, 1906; 4,5

3319 Revs. A. Dzubay and Joseph Hanulya; "Protokol" [Minutes]

Minutes of the executive committee meeting of the church-laical conference, held February 20, 1906 in McKeesport, PA.

O   XV (7): Mar 1, 1906; 2,3

3320 "Novosty yz kruhu našeho duchovenstva" [News from the circle of our priests]

a. Rev. Nicholas Szabados (Mukačevo Diocese) recently arrived in America and has been assigned to Patton, PA.
b. Rev. Nicholas Molchany (Passaic, NJ) assigned to Freeland, PA.
c. Revs Irenaeus Janicky (Freeland, PA) and Michael Mitro (Mt. Carmel, PA) were both assigned to Oldforge-Rendham, PA.
d. Rev. John Dorožinsky (New Britain, CT) assigned to Mt. Carmel, PA.
e. Rev. John Velihovsky (Olyphant, PA) assigned to Yonkers, NY.
f. Revs. Kamensky (current supreme spiritual of the G.C.U.) and Michael Jackovich (current controller of the G.C.U.) are both conducting a mission, February 6-9, 1906, in Virginia, visiting the communities of: Christiansburg, Richmond, Lynchburg, Bluefield and Roanoke.
g. Very Rev. Andrew Hodobay returned to Europe March 6, 1906.

Nr   XV (8): Mar 8, 1906; 2,3

3321 [N.N.]; "Konhress snov' otsročenyj" [Congress again postponed]

Greek Catholic Congress, scheduled to be held March 13, 1906, was postponed at the wish of U.S. Apostolic Delegate Most Rev. D. Falconio.

A   XV (8): Mar 8, 1906; 4,5

3322 [N.N.]; "Cerkovnaja Vlast' y Hreko Kat. Konhress" [Church authority and the Greek Catholic Congress]

The reasons for the postponement of the March 13, 1906 Greek Catholic Congress.

A   XV (9(): Mar 15, 1906; 4,5

3323 Revs. A. Dzubay and Joseph Hanulya; "Nît uže bol'še vŷhovorok!" [No excuses any more!]

The executive committee and the Greek Catholic Congress.

A   XV (11): Mar 29, 1906; 4,5

3324 "Vîsty Cerkovnŷy" [Church News]

Litigation by the McKeesport, PA parish against the Duquesne, PA parish, concerning parish membership, has been resolved by a court decision in favor of McKeesport.

Nr   XV (15): Apr 26, 1906; 2,4

3325 "Novosty yz kruha našeho duchovenstva" [News from the circle of our clergy]

     a. Very Rev. Andrew Hodobay assumed pastorship of the Braddock, PA parish April 22, 1906.
     b. Rev. Gabriel Chopey (Cleveland, OH) assigned to Perth Amboy, NJ.
     c. Rev. Alexis Novak (Perth Amboy, NJ) assigned to Cleveland, OH.
     d. Most Rev. Metropolitan Archbishop Andrew Sheptyts'kyi of L'viv [Lemberg] Diocese will visit America in the near future.

Nr   XV (16): May 3, 1906; 2,3

3326 "Vîsty Cerkovnŷy" [Church News]

     a. ARV denounces the Braddock, PA church council's decision to allow Very Rev. Andrew Hodobay to serve as the substitute for Rev. A. Petrassovich (currently in Europe). Rev. A. Hodobay is accused by the ARV of being an agent for the Hungarian Government, sent to America to spy upon the activities of Rusyns in America.
     b. Faithful in Mingo Junction, PA plan to build a Greek Catholic church.

Nr   XV (16): May 3, 1906; 2,3

3327 [N.N.]; "Pochval'nŷj postup našych brat'ev hr. kat. Rusynov v Čykaho, Yll" [Praiseworthy action of our Greek Catholic Rusyn brethren in Chicago, IL]

The accomplishments of the Chicago Greek Catholic parish.

A   XV (17): May 10, 1906; 2,3

3328   Michael Sabo; South Sharon, PA; May 19, 1906

The May 13, 1906 dedication of the South Sharon Greek Catholic Church's corner stone.

L   XV (21): Jun 14, 1906; 2,3

3329   "Novosty uz kruhu našeho duchovenstva" [News from the circle of our clergy]

a. Rev. Alexis Petrassovich (Braddock, PA) and his family returned to Europe. Very Rev. Andrew Hodobay has been assigned to the Braddock, PA parish.

b. It is rumored that Rev. Dr. Nicholas Demčuk (Archdiocese of L'viv [Lemberg], and present rector of St. Athanasius Seminary in Rome) has been named the first Greek Catholic Bishop for America. Small biography of Rev. Demčuk.

Nr, B   XV (22): Jun 21, 1906; 2

3330   "Vîsty Cerkovnŷy" [Church News]

Dedication of the Whiting, IN Greek Catholic parish's cemetery and cross in Hessville, IN July 4, 1906.

Nr   XV (23): Jun 28, 1906; 2,3

3331   Rev. Irenaeus Janicky; Passaic, NJ; Jun 7, 1906

"Zaslato. Otvît 'Korrespondentu' Pravdŷ!" [Letter to the Editor. Answer to the 'Correspondent' of Pravda!]

Refers to the article, "Lže-učytely y učenyky rozbysaky-mordercŷ" ("False teachers and pupils who are murderers") as a "godless" attack on a Greek Catholic priest.

L   XV (23): Jun 28, 1906; 2,3

3332   "Vîsty Cerkovnŷy" [Church News]

a. The Romanian Greek Catholic church in Cleveland, OH and its pastor, Rev. Dr. Epaminondás Lukač.

b. The Polish-American Bishop and the influence of the Poles in the Catholic church.

Nr   XV (24): Jul 5, 1906; 2

3333   Peter J. Maczko; "Nîskol'ko otkrovennŷch bratskych slov do našoj amerykanskoj bratiy russkoj hreko katolyčeskoj" [Some candid fraternal words to our American Greek Catholic brethren]

Calls for support of the Greek Catholic Congress.

A   XV (26): Jul 19, 1906; 2,3

3334   "Vîsty Cerkovnŷy" [Church News]

Rev. Emmanuel Pajkossy dedicates St. Clair, PA parish's three church towers on September 3, 1906.

Nr   XV (28): Aug 2, 1906; 12

3335 M.K. Lucák; Cleveland, OH; Jul 16, 1906

The July 1, 1906 dedication of the Cleveland Greek Catholic Church's corner stone.

L   XV (30): Aug 16, 1906; 2,3

3336 Redakcija; "Kohda už raz budet Konhress?" [When will finally the Congress be?]

The date for the meeting of the Greek Catholic Congress.

E   XV (30): Aug 16, 1906; 4,5

3337 "Vîsty Cerkovnŷy" [Church News]

Dedication of the Chicago, IL parish's new altar and cemetery on September 3, 1906.

Nr   XV (31): Aug 23, 1906; 5

3338 Ž.; "Katolyckij-Slovenskij Konhress" [Catholic-Slovak Congress]

Program of the congress held September 3, 1906 in Wilkes Barre, PA.

E   XV (32): Aug 30, 1906; 4,5

3339 "Vîsty Cerkovnŷy" [Church News]

a. Dedication of Toronto, OH parish's iconostasis on September 3, 1906. Rev. S. Polyansky dedicates Phoenixville, PA parish's altar, iconostasis and side altar September 16, 1906.

XV (32): Aug 30, 1906; 9,10

b. Rev. Nicholas Stecovich dedicates New Salem, PA parish's bell September 30, 1906.

Nr   XV (33): Sep 6, 1906; 9,11

3340 Rev. Michael; Toronto, OH; Sep 4, 1906

The dedication of the Toronto Greek Catholic Church's iconostasis.

L   XV (34): Sep 13, 1906; 2,3

3341 [N.N.]; "Slovenskij Kat. Konhress" [Slovak Catholic Congress]

Protocol and resolutions of the Wilkes Barre, PA Congress.

O   XV (34): Sep 13, 1906; 4,5

3342 "Vîsty Cerkovnŷy" [Church News]

Dedication of the Sevenville, PA Greek Catholic Church on September 23, 1906.

Nr   XV (34): Sep 13, 1906; 12

3343   "Novosty yz kruhu našeho duchovenstva" [News from the circle of
our clergy]

      a. Rev. Alexis Petrassovich returned to his Braddock, PA
parish following a two-month visit to Europe. Rev.
Petrassovich's substitute, Very Rev. Andrew Hodobay, went
to Philadelphia, PA from where he will return to Europe
October 2, 1906.

      b. Rev. A. Kamensky (Kingston, PA) returned to Europe Sep-
tember 27, 1906 to visit his family.

      c. Revs. Constantine Lengyel (Scranton, PA) and John Hrabar
(Philadelphia, PA) return to Europe with Very Rev. Andrew
Hodobay in October, 1906.

      d. Rev. Nicholas Strutinsky (Elizabeth, NJ) and Rev. N. Stech
(Olyphant, PA) will change parishes with each other.

      Nr   XV (35): Sep 20, 1906; 2,3

3344   "Vîsty Cerkovnŷy" [Church News]

      Dedication of the Sheffield, PA Greek Catholic church on
October 7, 1906.

      Nr   XV (37): Oct 4, 1906; 3

3345   Ž.; "Odyn yz najbol'šych renehatov, otrodylcev y zaprydatelej
bîdnoho uhro-russkoho naroda ydet v Ameryku" [One of the
biggest renegades, outcasts and traitors of the poor Uhro-
Rusyn people is coming to America]

      The arrival in America of Rev. Bartholomew Tutkovics (Prešov
Diocese), considered by the G.C.U. to be an agent for the
Hungarian Government.

      E   XV (38): Oct 11, 1906; 2,5

3346   [N.N.]; "Duchovenstvo pravoslavnoe (schyzmatyskoe) v Rosseiy"
[Orthodox priesthood in Russia]

      Attempts by the Russian Government to convert uniate priests
to Orthodoxy.

      A   XV (39): Oct 18, 1906; 4,5

3347   Andrew Bussa; Binghampton, NY; Nov 9, 1906

      The purchase of land for Binghampton's Greek Catholic Church.

      T,   XV (44): Nov 22, 1906; 2,3

3348   Paul Ju. Zsatkovich; "Redakciy Svît do laskavoj vîdomosty"
[Editor of Svît please note]

      Commentary on the viewpoint expressed in Svit regarding Rusyns
and Orthodoxy.

      E   XV (45): Dec 3, 1906; 4

3349 [N.N.]; "Propahanda Schyzmŷ y Podkarpatskiy Rusynŷ v Amerykî
(v otvît schyzmatyckomu orhanu Svît)" [Propagation of Schism
and the Subcarpathian Rusyns in America (in answer to the
schismatic organ Svît)]

Part I: XV (46): Dec 13, 1906; 4,5

Part II: XV (47): Dec 20, 1906; 4,5

Part III: XV (48): Dec 27, 1906; 4,5

A

3350 "Novosty yz kruhu našeho duchovenstva" [News from the circle of
our clergy]

a. Rev. Dr. J. Vasovčik (Mukačevo Diocese) recently arrived
in America and was assigned to Plymouth, PA.
b. Rev. Michael C. Lengyel (Scranton, PA) returns to Europe.
c. Rev. Michael Bendas (Plymouth, PA) has been assigned to
Scranton, PA.
d. Rev. Acacius Kamensky (Kingston, PA) returned to Europe
to visit his family.
e. Rev. Emil Mihályi (Bayonne, NJ) has been transferred.
f. Rev. T. Sabo (Hazleton, PA) assigned to Bayonne City, NJ.
g. Rev. Alexis Novak (Cleveland, OH) assigned to Hazleton, PA.
h. Rev. Burik (Pleasant City, OH) assigned to Cleveland, OH.

Nr XV (47): Dec 20, 1906; 3

3351 [N.N.]; "Zachranît, čto ešče zachranyty dastsja!" [Preserve what
one is still able to preserve!]

Magyar anti-clericalism disguised by the nationality laws.

A XV (49): Jan 3, 1907; 9,10

3352 [N.N.]; "Hrozné buducné vysledky našej l'ahostajnosci-nedbanlivosci"
[Terrible future results of our flightiness and carelessness]

Old world politics and schism among the American Greek Catholic
churches intensify the religious-nationality problems among
Rusyn-Americans.

A XVI (2): Jan 24, 1907; L-4

3353 Rev. Antonievič; "Dosyt uže my zdaly" [We have waited long enough]

Issues concerning the need for an American Greek Catholic
Eparchy.

A XVI (8): Mar 7, 1907; C-2, L-4

3354 [N.N.]; "Zavîščanie (testament) Pokojnoho Pol'skoho Archiepyskopa
D-ra Florijana Stableskija" [Last will of the late Polish
Archbishop Dr. Florian Stablewski (Archbishop of Poznań)]

A XVI (9): Mar 14, 1907; C-6, L-6

3355 Rev. A. Holosnyay; "Otvertoe Slovo do O. A. Petrasovyča, hr. kat.
duchovnyka v Bradoku, Pa." [A candid word to Rev. A. Petrassovich, Greek Catholic priest in Braddock, PA]

The alleged abuses of power by Rev. Petrassovich.

A   XVI (10): Mar 21, 1907; C-4, L-4

3356 Rev. A. Holosnyay; "Pros'ba do vŷsokopočtennŷch vîrnykov hr. kat.
russkoj parafiy v Bradok, Pa." [Request to the most honorable
faithful of the Greek Catholic Rusyn parish in Braddock, PA]

The boundaries between the Homestead and Braddock, PA parishes.

A   XVI (11): Mar 28, 1907; C-2, L-4

3357 [N.N.]; Hreko kat. russkij Epyskop pro Ameryku" [Greek Catholic
Rusyn Bishop for America]

A telegram from the Apostolic Delegate informs the G.C.U. that
Soter Stephen Ortynsky, O.S.B.M. has been named as the American
Greek Catholic Bishop.

A   XVI (11): Mar 28, 1907; C-2, L-4

3358 [N.N.]; Cleveland, OH; Mar 19, 1907

"Zaslato" [Letter to the Editor]

The polemics between the Roman and Greek Catholic churches in
Cleveland allegedly provoked by Very Rev. Andrew Hodobay.
Editor's commentary follows.

L   XVI (11): Mar 28, 1907; C-2&3, L-2

3359 [N.N.]; "Učinkovanie O. Bertalana Tutkovicsa podpada ne l'em
suspensacii, al'e aj excommunicacii-vilučeniu zos katol'ickej
Cerkvy" [The work of Rev. Bertalan Turkovics is subject to not
only suspension, but excommunication from the Catholic church]

The formation of a Hungarian Greek Catholic rite church by Rev.
Tutkovics is condemned by the Most Rev. Regis Canevin, Roman
Catholic Bishop of Pittsburgh, as independent and schismatic.

A   XVI (12): Apr 4, 1907; L-2

3360 Rev. J. Š.; Monessen, PA; April 2, 1907

Concerning the construction costs of the Monessen church.

L   XVI (12): Apr 4, 1907, L-3

3361 [N.N.]; "Amerik. Gr. kat. Russky Episkop" [American Greek Catholic
Rusyn Bishop]

Biographical information about Bishop Ortynsky and the events
leading to his appointment as the Greek Catholic Bishop for
America.

A   XVI (12): Apr 4, 1907; L-4

3362   [N.N.]; "Mad'arsky schizmatik na missii v gr. kat. russkej cerkvy"
[Magyar schismatic on a mission to the Greek Catholic Rusyn
church]

The activities of Rev. B. Tutkovics who seeks to organize a
Hungarian Greek Catholic Rite Church in America.

A   XVI (12): Apr 4, 1907; L-4

3363   V.H.; Hawk Run, PA; Mar 20, 1907

Hawk Run's Rusyn parish and community.

L   XVI (13): Apr 11, 1907; C-3, L-3

3364   [N.N.]; "Čto vseho možet zapryčynyty lehkomyslennost' odnoho
duchovnyka" [Look at what the lightmindedness of one priest
can cause]

How Rev. Tutkovics' plans for a Magyar Greek Catholic Rite
affects the Rusyn Greek Catholic Church in America.

A   XVI (13): Apr 11, 1907; C-4, L-4

3365   A.K.; "Duchovenstvo v narodî" [Clergy among the people]

Examines the unique relationship the Greek Catholic priest
has with his parishioners.

A   XVI (14): Apr 18, 1907; C-2, L-2

3366   [N.N.]; "Amer. Hreko Kat. Russkij Epyskop" [American Greek Catholic
Rusyn Bishop]

The reaction from various parts of the U.S. concerning the
appointment of the Most Rev. S.S. Ortynsky as the American
Greek Catholic Bishop.

A   XVI (14): Apr 18, 1907; C-4, L-4

3367   [N.N.]; "Prosvîščenie. Da prydet carstvie tvoe" [Enlightenment.
May thy kingdom come]

Trouble among members of the Braddock, PA parish.

A   XVI (14): Apr 18, 1907; C-4, L-4

3368   George Vasily; Mingo Junction, OH

The March, 1907 dedication of the Mingo Junction church bells.

L   XVI (16): May 2, 1907; C-2, L-2

3369   "Podjaka--blahodarenie yz staroho Kraju, yz Kamjunky spyšskoj
stolycŷ" [(Letter of) thanks from the old country, from
Kamjonka (Kövesfalva), Szépes County, (Hungary)]

Letter to Rev. Joseph Hanulya from Rev. Koman (pastor of
Kamjonka parish) thanking him for money received from Rusyn
Americans for the renovation of the Kamjonka church.

LE   XVI (16): May 2, 1907; C-4, L-4

3370   Rev. Cornelius Laurisin; "Bratskoe vozzvanie y zaprošenie do vsîch
Všečestnîjsych Otcev Duchovnŷch y do vsîch amer. hr. katolyčeskych parafij!" [Fraternal call and request to all honorable
fathers and to all American Greek Catholic parishes!]

Representatives from the G.C.U., R.N.U. and Obščestvo will meet
in Pittsburgh, PA on May 14, 1907 to discuss plans for welcoming
Bishop Ortynsky to America.

A   XVI (16): May 2, 1907; C-5, L-2

3371   [N.N.]; "Sobranie v dîlî pryvytanija novoymennoho našoho Epyskopa
Preosv. Stefana Ortŷn'skoho" [Meeting to discuss plans for
greeting our newly-named Bishop, the Most Rev. S. Stephen Ortynsky]

Meeting was held May 14, 1907 in Pittsburgh, PA.

Part I: XVI (17): May 16, 1907; C-4, L-4

Part II: XVI (19): May 30, 1907; C-4, L-4

A

3372   [N.N.]; "Vîsty y razsuždenie o[t] našoho Epyskopa" [News and
reflections from our Bishop]

Bishop Ortynsky's views on the nationality issue and the current
situation of the American Greek Catholic Church.

A   XVI (21): Jun 13, 1907; C-4, L-4

3373   "Posvjaščenie novoj hreko kat. russkoj cerkvy v Mynho Dzunkšyn, O."
[Dedication of the New Greek Catholic Rusyn Church in Mingo
Junction, OH]

Dedication on June 30, 1907.

Ad   XVI (21): Jun 13, 1907; C-5, L-7

3374   Joachim Homa; "Novŷj monastŷr' v Unhvarî" [New monastery in Užhorod]

The monastery of the Order of St. Basil the Great.

A   XVI (22): Jun 20, 1907; C-6, L-6

3375   Rev. Gabriel Chopey; "Ot Kassiera Komyteta dlja pryvytanija Epyskopa"
[From the Treasurer Committee for the welcoming of the Bishop]

List of donations contributed by various parishes and lodges.

Parts I-X: XVI (23-33): Jun 27-Sep 5, 1907

O

3376   [N.N.]; "O[t] našoho Epyskopa" [From our Bishop]

The activities of Bishop Ortynsky.

A   XVI (23): Jun 27, 1907; C-4, L-4

3377   "Toržestvennoe posvjaščenie novoho 'ykonostasa' hr. kat. russkoj
cerkvy" [Solemn dedication of a Greek Catholic Rusyn Church's
new iconostasis]

Dedication in Trauger, PA on July 4, 1907.

Ad   XVI (23): Jun 27, 1907; C-8, L-4

3378   [N.N.]; "Važnoe pered prychodom našoho Epyskopa" [Important matter
        prior to the arrival of our Bishop]

        Discusses the significance of Bishop Ortynsky to Rusyn-
        Americans.

        A   XVI (24): Jul 4, 1907; C-4, L-4

3379   [N.N.]; "Fantazija Halycijskych Vikrainciv. Halycijskiy Vkraincy
        želajut ymîty v lyčnosty Ameryk. hr. kat. russkoho Epyskopa ne
        cerkovnoho hl. načal'nyka, no hlavnoho načal'nyka vikrainskoho"
        [The fantasy of Galician-Ukrainians. Galician-Ukrainians wish
        to have in the person of the American Greek Catholic Bishop not
        a chief church leader, but a chief Ukrainian leader]

        A   XVI (26): Jul 18, 1907; C-2, L-2

3380   [N.N.]; "Odno velykolîpnoe cerkovnoe toržestvo" [A magnificent
        church celebration]

        The dedication of the Trauger, PA parish's new altar and
        iconostasis on July 4, 1907.

        A   XVI (26): Jul 18, 1907; C-2&3, L-3

3381   [N.N.]; "Ameryk. Hreko kat. Rusynŷ y Amerykanskoe Hreko Kat.
        Epyskopstvo" [American Greek Catholic Rusyns and the American
        Greek Catholic Bishopric]

        The struggle by Ruthenians in America to obtain their own
        eparchy.

        Part I: XVI (26): Jul 18, 1907; C-4, L-4

        Part II: XVI (29): Aug 8, 1907; C-4, L-4

        A

3382   Stephen Hrapčak; Bradenville, PA

        The July 4, 1907 dedication of the Bradenville church's new
        iconostasis.

        L   XVI (27): Jul 25, 1907; C-2&3, L-2&3

3383   [N.N.]; "Bezhranyčennaja bezstŷdnost'" [Unbounded shamelessness]

        Commentary on the article, 'Peršŷ Vykrain'sky Episkip v Americi'
        ('First Ukrainian Bishop in America') by Rev. O. Vasilijan,
        published in Katolickij Schid.

        A   XVI (27): Jul 25, 1907; C-4, L-4

3384   "Toržestvennoe posvjaščenie novoj russkoj hr. kat. cerkvy sv. Arch.
        Mychayla v Saut Fork, Pa." [Solemn dedication of the new Rusyn
        Greek Catholic Church of Saint Michael the Archangel in South
        Fork, PA]

        Dedication on September 2, 1907.

        Ad   XVI (27): Jul 25, 1907; C-5, L-7

3385   John Pavko; Rankin, PA

Efforts by Rankin's Rusyn community to raise money for their church.

L   XVI (28): Aug 1, 1907; C-2&3, L-2

3386   "Toržestvennoe posvjaščenie novoj hr. kat. russkoj cerkvy v Hlen Lajon, PA" [Solemn dedication of the new Greek Catholic Rusyn church in Glen Lyon, PA]

Dedication on September 2, 1907.

Ad   XVI (28): Aug 1, 1907; C-3, L-7

3387   [N.N.]; "Smutnŷy dîla, kotorŷy ne prynošajut nam nijakoj slavŷ, no tîm bol'še stŷda-han'bŷ" [Sad matters, which don't bring us glory, rather much shame-disgrace]

The Pittsburgh, PA church council's attempt to rid themselves of their present pastor, Rev. John Szabo. This process received much publicity and condemnation by Pittsburgh's Roman Catholic Bishop, the Most Rev. Regis Canevin.

A   XVI (28): Aug 1, 1907; C-4, L-4

3388   Stephen Janossy; Bradenville, PA

Commentary on the activities of the Bradenville parish.

L   XVI (29): Aug 8, 1907; C-2&3, L-2&3

3389   "Najnovijšiy vîsty o[t] našoho Epyskopa" [Latest news from our Bishop]

Rev. Joseph Chaplinsky (New York), secretary of the Bishop welcoming committee, states that Bishop Ortynsky is expected to arrive in New York from Europe on August 27, 1907.

Nr   XVI (29): Aug 8, 1907; C-4, L-4

3390   "Toržestvennoe posvjaščenie" [Solemn dedication]

Dedication of Toronto, OH parish's new rectory and school building on September 2, 1907.

Ad   XVI (29): Aug 8, 1907; C-5, L-6

3391   "V dîlî pryvytanija Epyskopa" [Concerning the welcome of the Bishop]

Program of events for the welcome of Bishop Ortynsky to America.

Nr   XVI (30): Aug 15, 1907; C-4, L-4

3392   Most Rev. S.S. Ortynsky; "Pervŷj Pastyr'skij Lyst pervoho amer. hr. kat. russkoho Epyskopa" [First Pastoral Letter of the first American Greek Catholic Rusyn Bishop]

L   XVI (31): Aug 22, 1907; C-4, L-4

3393   Rev. Joseph Chaplinsky; "Ot sekretarja Epyskopa pryvytajuščeho komytetu" [From the secretary of the Bishop's welcoming committee]

    a. Requests all priests to send their addresses to the welcoming committee.
    b. Invitation to priests and G.C.U. lodge members to attend the welcoming banquet.
    c. Those attending the banquet must send money to the committee treasurer, Rev. Gabriel Chopey.
    d. Bishop Ortynsky will stay at the Netherland Hotel in New York City.

O   XVI (31): Aug 22, 1907; C-4, L-4

3394   "Toržestvennoe posvjaščenie kraeuhol'noho kamene novoj hr. kat. russkoj cerkvy v Sajksvyl, Pa. Džeferson Konty" [Solemn dedication of the corner stone of the new Greek Catholic Rusyn church in Sykesville, PA Jefferson County]

Dedication on September 2, 1907.

Ad   XVI (31): Aug 22, 1907; C-8, L-3

3395   "Toržestvennoe Posvjaščenie kraeuhol'noho kamene novoj hr. kat. russkoj cerkvy v Čarleroj, Pa." [Solemn dedication of the corner stone of the new Greek Catholic church in Charleroi, PA]

Dedication on September 2, 1907.

Ad   XVI (31): Aug 22, 1907; C-8, L-3

3396   [N.N.]; "Naš Epyskop est' uže v Amerykî" [Our Bishop is already in America]

The arrival of Bishop Ortynsky in New York.

A   XVI (32): Aug 29, 1907; C-2, L-4

3397   [N.N.]; Kingston, PA

The problems among the parishioners of the Kingston parish.

L   XVI (32): Aug 29, 1907; C-2&3, L-2

3398   Andrew Varcholyk; Brook Side, AL

Requests donations to aid the construction of a Greek Catholic Church in Brook Side.

L   XVI (32): Aug 29, 1907; C-3, L-2

3399   [N.N.]; "Čto yz toho vŷjdet na dal'še?..." [What does this portend?...]

The reaction of Greek Catholic Rusyn Americans to having a Bishop from Galicia.

A   XVI (33): Sep 5, 1907; C-2, L-2

3400 [N.N.]; "Prijatie y pryvytanie našoho Epyskopa v N'ju Iorku"
      [Welcome of our Bishop in New York]

   The reception Bishop Ortynsky received when he arrived in
   New York.

   A   XVI (33): Sep 5, 1907; C-4, L-4

3401 [N.N.]; "Sytuacija ves'ma podozrîtel'na y nepochopytel'naja"
      [The situation is very suspicious and incomprehensible]

   Bishop Ortynsky's alleged pro-Ukrainian sentiments.

   A   XVI (34): Sep 12, 1907; C-2, L-4

3402 Michael Hrenyo; Charleroi, PA

   The September 2, 1907 dedication of the Charleroi Greek
   Catholic church's corner stone.

   L   XVI (34): Sep 12, 1907; C-3, L-2&3

3403 [N.N.]; "Rasporyženie epyskopskoe y vîsty o[t] našoho Epyskopa"
      [Episcopal decree and news from our Bishop]

   Series of announcements by Bishop Ortynsky concerning meeting
   with organization and church leaders over the establishment
   of the eparchy.

   A   XVI (34): Sep 12, 1907; C-4, L-4

3404 "Velykoe Cerkovnoe Toržestvo" [Magnificent Church Celebration]

   Dedication of the Greek Catholic church in Clairton, PA on
   October 6, 1907.

   Ad   XVI (35): Sep 19, 1907; C-5, L-3

3405 "Vîsty y dîla Cerkovnŷy" [News and church business]

   a. "Naš Preosv. Epyskop y zdîsnŷy rymo-kat. Epyskop" [Our
      Most Rev. Bishop and the local Roman Catholic Bishops]

   Bishop Ortynsky meets with the Roman Catholic Bishops of
   Altoona, Scranton and Pittsburgh, PA Dioceses.

   b. "Dîjatel'nost Preosvjaščennoho Sotera v Amerykî" [Affairs
      of the Most Rev. Soter (Ortynsky) in America]

   Bishop Ortynsky's schedule.

   Nɪ   XVI (36): Sep 26, 1907; C-3, L-4

3406 [N.N.]; "Mytynh Duchovnŷj" [Clergy Meeting]

   The clergy meeting proposed by Bishop Ortynsky to be held
   October 17-18, 1907.

   A   XVI (37): Oct 3, 1907; C-4, L-4

3407   Most Rev. Soter Ortynsky; "Ot Amer. Hreko Kat. Epyskopa" [From
       the American Greek Catholic Bishop]

     a. Announces a convention of all Greek Catholic priests in
       New York City October 15-16, 1907. Included is an agenda
       of topics to be discussed.
     b. Each parish is to send two delegates to a clergy meeting
       in New York City October 17-18, 1907.

    O   XVI (37): Oct 3, 1907; C-4, L-4

3408   John Uhrin; "Cyrkuljar hl. predsîdatelja 'Soedynenija'" [Circular
       of the supreme president of the 'Soedynenie']

       Catholic Congress and clergy meeting scheduled for October
       15-18, 1907.

    O   XVI (37): Oct 10, 1907; C-4, L-4

3409   John Uhrin; "Ot hol. predsîdatelja 'Soedynenija'" [From the
       supreme president of the 'Soedynenie']

       Bishop Ortynsky's proposed convention and clergy meeting
       scheduled for October 15-18, 1907 in New York City.

    O   XVI (38): Oct 10, 1907; C-2, L-2

3410   "Vîsty o našom Preosv. Epyskopî" [News about our Most Rev. Bishop]

       Bishop Ortynsky's schedule.

    Nr   XVI (38): Oct 10, 1907; C-4, L-4

3411   Anthony Monich; New Britain, CT

       The discord between the Uhro-Rusyn and Galician-Rusyn parish-
       oners in the New Britain parish.

    L   XVI (39): Oct 17, 1907; L-2

3412   John Drimak; Chicago, IL

       The new bells for the Chicago church.

    L   XVI (39): Oct 17, 1907; L-2

3413   [N.N.]; "Slabé karaktery" [Of weak character]

       Bishop Ortynsky's character, qualifications and selection as
       the American Greek Catholic Bishop.

    A   XVI (39): Oct 17, 1907; L-4

3414   [N.N.]; "Ne rjadnŷj Konhress, lyš' predvarytel'noe sovîtovanie-
       porada" [Not a regular Congress, only a preliminary meeting]

       The clergy meeting held October 15-18, 1907 in New York City.

    A   XVI (40): Oct 24, 1907; C-4&5, L-4&5

3415 "Cerkovnoe Toržestvo" [Church Celebration]

    a. Rev. E. Homich dedicates Passaic, NJ Greek Catholic Church on November 10, 1907.
    b. Rev. Irenaeus Matyacko dedicates Binghampton, NY Greek Catholic Church on November 17, 1907.

Ad   XVI (40): Oct 24, 1907; C-5, L-3

3416 John Uhrin; "Ot hol. predsîdatelja 'Soedynenija'" [From the supreme president of the 'Soedynenie']

John Uhrin's account of the special convention and clergy meeting (called for by Most Rev. S.S. Ortynsky) which he attended as a delegate of the Homestead, PA parish October 15-18, 1907.

O   XVI (41): Oct 31, 1907; C-2, L-2

3417 P. Ju. Zsatkovich; "O. Mychayl Baloh vmîsto toho, čtob uznaty svoy prevelykiy bludŷ y kajatysja, udaet nevynnoho holuba y zaslužennoho dîjatelja-faktora" [Rev. Michael Balog instead of acknowledging his great errors and repenting, feigns to be an innocent dove and praiseworthy activist]

The views held by the pastor of the Windber, PA parish.

E   XVI (41): Oct 31, 1907; C-2&3, L-2

3418 Vladimir Petrovsky; "Spravozdanie yz Konvenciy hr. kat. Svjaščen'stva Sîvernoj Ameryky s dnja 15 y 16 oktobra 1907 v N'ju Iorku" [Report of the Convention of the Greek Catholic Clergy of North America (held) October 15-16, 1907 in New York, NY]

O   XVI (41): Oct 31, 1907; C-4, L-4

3419 [N.N.]; "Papska bulla ob amerykanskych hreko kat. rusynach" [Papal Bull about the American Greek Catholic Rusyns]

Complete text of the Bull.

A   XVI (42): Nov 7, 1907; C-2&3, L-2&3

3420 "Cerkovnŷy Vîsty" [Church News]

    a. Most Rev. Bishop Ortynsky changes address from P.O. Box 543, South Fork, PA to 1105 N. 63 Street, Philadelphia, PA.
    b. Rev. Sylvester Lupis, O.S.B.M. arrived from Europe and was assigned to Sheffield, PA.

Nr   XVI (42): Nov 7, 1907; C-4, L-4

3421 [N.N.]; "Rozmyšlenia nad Papežskou Bullou o amer. gr. kat. Rusinach" [Reflection on the Papal Bull about the American Greek Catholic Rusyns]

A   XVI (43): Nov 14, 1907; L-2

3422   [N.N.]; "Strašna Komedija" [Terrible Comedy]

Commentary on the Papal Bull and the current and future situation of the American Greek Catholic Church.

A   XVI (44): Nov 21, 1907; C-2, L-2

3423   [N.N.]; "Čto y jak pyšut zdîšnŷy russkiy hazetŷ o Papskoj Bullî" [What the local Rusyn newspapers write about the Papal Bull]

Reports what Svoboda and Pravda have written in response to the Bull.

A   XVI (44): Nov 21, 1907; C-2&3, L-4

3424   [N.N.]; Hannastown, PA

The September 29, 1907 dedication of the Hannastown Greek Catholic Church's corner stone.

L   XVI (441): Nov 21, 1907; L-2&3

3425   [N.N.]; "Oborona protyv 'Papskoj Bullŷ'" [Defense against the 'Papal Bull']

How to protect the American Greek Catholic Church from the ideology expressed in the Papal Bull.

A   XVI (46): Dec 5, 1907; C-2&3, L-4

3426   "Cerkovnŷy Vîsty" [Church News]

"Peremîny" [Changes]

a. Rev. Michael Balog (Windber, PA) assigned to Pittsburgh, PA.
b. Rev. Joseph Hanulya (Duquesne, PA) assigned to Windber, PA.
c. Rev. Dr. Theodosius Vasochik (Plymouth, PA) assigned to Olyphant, PA.
d. Rev. John Szabo (Pittsburgh, PA) assigned to Plymouth, PA.
e. Rev. Theodore Ladomirsky (Youngstown, OH) assigned to Hazleton, PA.
f. Rev. Alexis Medvecky (McAdoo, PA) assigned to Youngstown, OH.
g. Rev. J. Martyak arrived in America from Europe and has been assigned to Toronto, OH.
h. Rev. Paul Staurovsky (Donora, PA) assigned to Trauger, PA.
i. Rev. Eugene Satala (Trauger, PA) returns to Europe.
j. Rev. Michael Biszaha (Chicago, IL) assigned to Donora, PA.
k. Rev. Basil Volosin (Trenton, NJ) assigned to New Britain, CT.
l. Rev. Cornelius Laurisin (Clairton, PA) assigned to Trenton, NJ.
m. Rev. Julius Csucska (Johnstown, PA) returns to Europe.
n. Rev. Nicholas Szabados (Patton, PA) assigned to Johnstown, PA
o. Rev. John Hrabar returned from Europe and has been assigned to Clairton, PA.
p. Rev. Eugene Volkay (New Britain, CT) assigned to Chicago, IL.
q. Rev. A. Kecskés (Phoenixville, PA) assigned to McKees Rocks, PA.

r. New priests from Galicia are expected to assume assign-
ments in Galician parishes.

s. Following parishes are without priests: Duquesne, PA;
Patton, PA; Phoenixville, PA; Rankin, PA; Pittsburgh-
Oakland, PA.

Nr   XVI (46): Dec 5, 1907; L-3

3427 [N.N.]; "Čto y jak sudjat čužiy o našom russkom Epyskopî, a voobšče
o teperîsnom položeniju Amerykanskych hreko katolykov" [How
foreigners judge our Rusyn Bishop, and in general, the current
situation of American Greek Catholics]

A   XVI (47): Dec 12, 1907; C-1&2, L-1&2

3428 [N.N.]; Chicago, IL

The November 10, 1907 dedication of the Chicago parish's cross
and bells.

L   XVI (47): Dec 12, 1907; L-2

3429 [N.N.]; Lansford, PA

The November 28, 1907 dedication of the Lansford Greek Catholic
Church.

L   XVI (47): Dec 12, 1907; L-2&3

3430 [N.N.]; "Prečudnŷy obstojatel'stva" [Strange circumstances]

The Greek Catholic church in America under Bishop Ortynsky.

A   XVI (48): Dec 19, 1907; C-2, L-4

3431 Nicholas Pačuta; "O. Hanulja snova staru notu spîvaet" [Rev.
Hanulya is singing that old tune again]

The suggestion to convoke another church congress to debate
the issues of church autonomy and the independence of the
various parishes.

A   XVI (48): Dec 19, 1907; C-2&3, L-2

3432 Basil Repinač; Hibernia, NJ; Dec 1, 1907

Commentary on the "Ea Semper" Papal Bull concerning the
American Greek Catholic Church.

L   XVI (48): Dec 19, 1907; L-2

3433 Michael Haragaly; Beaverdale, PA

The December 15, 1907 dedication of the Beaverdale Church's
two bells.

L   XVI (48): Dec 19, 1907; L-2

3434 [N.N.]; "O Bullî" [About the (Papal) Bull]

A   XVI (49): Dec 26, 1907; C-1&2, L-1&2

3435   Rev. Nicholas Chopey, et al.; "Protestŷ protyv Papskoj Bullŷ
          vŷdanoj Rymskoju Kurieju o nas, amer. hr. kat. Rusynach"
          [Protests against the Papal Bull issued by the Roman Curia
          concerning us, American Greek Catholic Rusyns]

          A   XVI (49): Dec 26, 1907; C-2&3, L-2&3

3436   John Uhrin; "Ot holovnoho urjadu 'Soedynenija'" [From the supreme
          administration of the 'Soedynenie']

          Discusses the limited powers of the Most Rev. S.S. Ortynsky
          as American Greek Catholic Bishop.

          O   XVII (1): Jan 16, 1908; C-1,2,3, L-1&2

3437   Rev. Nicholas Chopey; "O. N. Stefanovyču do laskavoho vnymanija"
          [To the attention of Rev. N. Stefanovič]

          The lack of protest against the Papal Bull by Galician priests
          and Bishop Ortynsky.

          A   XVII (1): Jan 16, 1908; C-4, L-4

3438   [N.N.]; "Epyskop v službî starokraevoj opasnoj polytyky" [A Bishop
          in the service of dangerous old country politics]

          Bishop Ortynsky and his Ukrainian sympathies.

          A   XVII (2): Jan 23, 1908; C-1,2,3, L-1,2,3

3439   Most Rev. S.S. Ortynsky; "Poslanie Pastŷrske" [Pastoral Message]

          Pastoral letter by Bishop Ortynsky preceeded by **ARV** commentary.

          L   XVII (4): Feb 6, 1908; C-1&2, L-1&2

3440   [N.N.]; "Otzŷv na 'Poslanie Pastŷrske'" [Answer to the Pastoral
          Message']

          Part İ: XVII (5): Feb 13, 1908; C-1&2, L-1

          Part II: XVII (7): Feb 27, 1908; C-1&2, L-1&2

          Part III: XVII (9): Mar 12, 1908; C-1&2, L-1

          Part IV: XVII (11): Mar 26, 1908; C-1&2, L-1&2

          A

3441   John Kurta; McKees Rocks, PA; Feb 10, 1908

          Bishop Ortynsky and the American Greek Catholic Church.

          L   XVII (5): Feb 13, 1908; L-2

3442   John Uhrin; "Ot hl. predsîdatelja 'Soedynenija'" [From the supreme
          president of the 'Soedynenie']

          The Greek Catholic Church in America and the titular position
          of Bishop Ortynsky.

          O   XVII (6): Feb 20, 1908; C-1&2, L-1

3443   Michael Volcsko, et al.; Whiting, IN; Feb 11, 1908

"Otvorenŷj Lyst O. Ioanovy Parskutovy" [Open Letter to Rev. John Parscouta]

The pastor of the Whiting parish.

L   XVII (6): Feb 20, 1908; C-2, L-3

3444   "Cerkovnŷy Vîsty" [Church News]

a. Rev. Valentine Balog (Mukačevo Diocese) recently arrived in America and was assigned to McKees Rocks, PA.
b. Rev. A. Kecskés (McKees Rocks, PA) transferred to Alexandria, PA.
c. Ten churches have signed their deeds over to the Most Rev. S.S. Ortynsky. They are as follows:

1. Manchester, NY
2. Syracuse, NY
3. Mc Kees Rocks, PA
4. New York City, NY
5. McAdoo, PA
6. Pittsburgh, PA
7. Pittsburgh, PA #2
8. Hazleton, PA #3
9. Pleasant City, OH
10. Bridgeport, CT

Nr   XVII (6): Feb 20, 1908; C-2, L-3

3445   Ž.; "Protest amer. hreko kat. russkoho naroda protyv Papskoj Bullŷ vŷdanoj dlja amer. hr. kat. Rusynov" [Protest of the American Greek Catholic Rusyn people against the Papal Bull issued for the American Greek Catholic Rusyns]

E   XVII (7): Feb 27, 1908; C-4&5, L-4

3446   Ž.; "Protest protyv našych cerkovnŷch hromad, amer. hreko kat. russkoho naroda, protyv Papskoj Bullŷ" [Protest of our churches, American Greek Catholic Rusyn people, against the Papal Bull]

Bishop Ortynsky's condemnation of those who are against the Papal Bull.

E   XVII (8): Mar 5, 1908; C-1&2, L-1&2

3447   G,T,; Duquesno, PA

A recent Duquesne parish meeting in which the current situation in the American Greek Catholic Church was discussed.

L   XVII (8): Mar 5, 1908; L-2&3

3448   [N.N.]; "Čudnŷy sredstva k osjahnen'ju cîly" [Strange means towards the achievement of a goal]

Rome's decision to give the Most Rev. Ortynsky full episcopal power.

A   XVII (9): Mar 12, 1908; C-2, L-4

3449   Ž.; "Predyvna chameleonska akcija" [A really strange chameleon action]

The change in attitude of Bishop Ortynsky and his supporters towards American Greek Catholics regarding the issue of nationality and control of the Greek Catholic Church in America.

E   XVII (11): Mar 26, 1908; C-2&3, L-4

3450   "Vîsty yz kruha cerkovnŷch" [News from the church circles]

a. Rev. Alexis Petrassovich (Braddock, PA) returned to America from Europe, however was rejected as the parish's priest by the church council. In a dispute with Most Rev. S.S. Ortynsky, the church council chose Rev. Anthony Kecskés (McKees Rocks, PA) as the new priest. In condemnation of this action, Bishop Ortynsky replies to the church council in a letter (reprinted). ARV commentary follows.
b. McKees Rocks, PA church council chose Rev. A. Kamensky (Kingston, OH) as their parish priest with the consent of the Roman Catholic Bishops of Scranton and Pittsburgh, PA.

Nr   XVII (11): Mar 26, 1908; C-3, L-3

3451   Ž.; "Velykoe cyvyl'no-cerkovnoe sobranie (konhress)" [Great laical-church meeting (congress)]

The formation of an all-Rusyn laical-church council which would decide issues of church jurisdiction, episcopal authority, as well as the nationality issue.

Parts I-III: XVII (12-14): Apr 2-16, 1908; C-1, L-1
E

3452   "Vîsty yz kruha cerkovnŷch" [News from the church circles]

"Treba mîsta 'vykrayncam'" [A place is necessary for the 'Ukrainians']

Commentary on the Most Rev. S.S. Ortynsky's and Mukačevo Bishop Julius Firczak's plan to recall twenty-two priests in America and replace them with Galicians.

Nr   XVII (12): Apr 2, 1908; C-2&3, L-2&3

3453   John Lezinsky; Scranton, PA; Mar 29, 1908

"Zaslato" [Letter to the Editor]

The Scranton parish's past and present problems over the religious-nationality issue. Editor's commentary follows.

L   XVII (13): Apr 9, 1908; C-2, L-2

3454 "Vîsty yz kruha cerkovných" [News from the church circles]

> a. Protest letter by Rev. Emil Kubek (Mahanoy City, PA) con-
>   cerning the "Ea Semper" Papal Bull.
> b. "Novŷj duchovnyk uhrorusskij y predyvna laska ukraynska"
>   [New Uhro-Rusyn priest and strange favors of Ukrainians]
>
> Rev. V. Suba (Mukačevo Diocese), brother-in-law of Rev.
> Nicholas Chopey, recently arrived in America and was assigned
> to the Hazleton, PA #6. ARV Commentary follows.
>
> Nr   XVII (13): Apr 9, 1908; C-2&3, L-2&3

3455 [N.N.]; "Jak sudjat o našych teperîšnŷch dîlach v starom kraju?"
     [What do they think about our current affairs in the old
     country?]

> Reprint of an article by Dr. Julius Hadžega on the Greek Catho-
> lic Church in America, in Görög Katolikus Szemle (Užhorod),
> #13, March 29, 1908. ARV commentary follows.
>
> A   XVII (13): Apr 9, 1908; C-4&5, L-4

3456 John Kipilo; Conemaugh, PA; Apr 18, 1908

> "Zaslato" [Letter to the Editor]
>
> The affect of Bishop Ortynsky's activities on the Conemaugh
> Rusyn community and parish.
>
> L   XVII (14): Apr 16, 1908; C-4&5, L-4&5

3457 [N.N.]; Pittsburgh-Oakland, PA

> The formation of a new parish in the Oakland vicinity.
>
> L   XVII (15): Apr 23, 1908; C-2, L-2

3458 Michael Hreno; Charleroi, PA

> Problems among parishioners of the Charleroi parish.
>
> L   XVII (15): Apr 23, 1908; C-2&3, L-2

3459 [N.N.]; "Nova tajna y javna akcija 'Ukraynsko-Radykal'noho Klyku'"
     [New secret and open action of the 'Ukrainian-Radical Clique]

> Bishop Ortynsky plans to transfer twenty-two Greek Catholic
> priests in America to Europe, replacing them with Galician
> clergy.
>
> A   XVII (15): Apr 23, 1908; C 4, L-4

3460 [N.N.]; "Ne na osnovî zakona y prava, no na osnovî postŷdnoj
     ahynaciy y terroryzma. Dva ynteresantnŷy zajavlenija" [Not
     on the basis of law and order, but on the basis of shameful
     agitation and terrorism. Two interesting declarations]

> The new approach by Bishop Ortynsky and his supporters to
> gain support for his policies.
>
> A   XVII (16): May 7, 1908; C-1&2, L-1&2

3461 [N.N.]; "Vozzvanie na cyvyl'no-cerkovnoe sobranie-konhress"
[Invitation to the laical-church meeting-congress]

Meeting is to be held in Braddock, PA May 14, 1908 and in
Scranton, PA May 23, 1908. List of sponsors-participants
and agenda topics.

O   XVII (16): May 7, 1908; C-4&5, L-5

3462 "Vîsty yz kruha cerkovnoho y yn'šiy" [News from the circle of
churches and other news]

a. The means the Most Rev. S.S. Ortynsky will use to obtain
full control over the parishes in America.
b. The conversion of ten churches (named) to Orthodoxy since
the activities of the Most Rev. S.S. Ortynsky began.
c. The formation of an independent Ukrainian Greek Catholic
Church in New York.

Nr   XVII (17): May 14, 1908; C-2, L-2

3463 [N.N.]; "Nîskol'ko otkrovennŷch slov pravdŷ pered X holovnoju
Konvencieju 'Soedynenija'" [Several candid words of truth
prior to the X General Convention of the 'Soedynenie']

The church-nationality problems among the Rusyn-Americans.

Parts I-II: XVII (17-18): May 14-21, 1908; C-4, L-4

3464 [N.N.]; "Amer. uhro-russkoe hr. kat. Epyskopstvo" [American Uhro-
Rusyn Greek Catholic Bishopric]

What constitutes a bishopric for Rusyn-Americans.

A, P   XVII (18): May 21, 1908; C-1

3465 [N.N.]; "Akcija Ukraynco-Radykalov y Pjatolyzunov" [Action of the
Ukrainian-Radicals and bootlickers]

Condemns Bishop Ortynsky and the Ukrainian movement in America.

A   VII (18): May 21, 1908; C-1&2, L-1&2

3466 [N.N.]; "Cyvyl'no-Cerkovnoe Sobranie (konhress) v Bradok, Pa."
[Laical-church meeting (congress) in Braddock, PA]

The first meeting of the Laical-church Congress held May 14,
1908 in Braddock.

A   XVII (18): May 21, 1908; C-2, L-2

3467 [N.N.]; "Duže važnoe!! Jak sudjat doma v starom kraju našy brat'ja
o dîstvovaniju tytuljarnoho Epyskopa Ortŷn'skoho?" [Very
important!! What do our brethren at home in the old country
think about the affairs of titular Bishop Ortynsky?]

Commentary on an article about the current troubles among
Greek Catholic Churches in America, which appeared in <u>Nauka</u>
(Užhorod), #17, May 7, 1908.

A   XVII (18): May 21, 1908; C-4, L-4

3468 "Cerkovnŷy Vîsty" [Church News]

    a. Dedication of the Rankin, PA parish's cross and hall on July 5, 1908.

                                  XVII (20): Jun 8, 1908; C-6, L-5

    b. Dedication of the Allentown, PA Greek Catholic church's corner stone on July 4, 1908.

                                  XVII (21): Jun 25, 1908; C-5, L-7

    c. Dedication of the Conemaugh, PA Greek Catholic church on June 28, 1908.

Nr   XVII (22): Jun 25, 1908; L-3

3469 [N.N.]; "Cerkovnŷy Toržestva" [Church Celebrations]

    a. The dedication of the Conemaugh, PA Greek Catholic church on June 28, 1908.
    b. The dedication of the Rankin, PA parish's cross and hall on July 5, 1908.

A   XVII (23): Jul 9, 1908; C-2&3, L-2&3

3470 George Fedorko, et al.; Whiting, IN; Jul 10, 1908

"Nadoslato. Dyvnŷy časŷ, dyvnŷy obstojatel'stva" [Letter to the Editor. Marvelous times, marvelous circumstances]

Polemics over religious-national issues among parishioners of the Whiting parish.

L   XVII (23): Jul 9, 1908; C-4, L-4

3471 [N.N.]; Johnstown, PA; Jul 14, 1908

"Zaslato" [Letter to the Editor]

The activities of church curator, Michael Kipilla.

L   XVII (24): Jul 16, 1908; C-2&3, L-2&3

3472 John Uhrin and John Smith; "Ot Eksekutyvnoho Komytetu Cerkovno-Cyvyl'noho Konhressu poderžanoho v Bradok y Skranton, Pa." [From the Executive Committee of the Laical-Church Congress which took place in Braddock and Scranton, PA]

The topics discussed at the two meetings of the Laical-Church Congress.

O   XVII (25): Jul 23, 1908; C-1&2, L-1&2

3473 "Cerkovnŷy Vîsty" [Church News]

Dedication of the Sheffield, PA Greek Catholic cemetery on August 2, 1908.

Nr   XVII (25): Jul 23, 1908; C-7, L-7

3474 [N.N.]; "Malo svîtla na bŷvšoe sostojanie zdorovlja Ep. Sotera Stefana Ortŷn'skoho" [A bit of light on the past health of Bishop Soter Stephen Ortynsky]

The mental condition of Bishop Ortynsky. From a Galician court transcript.

A   XVII (26): Jul 30, 1908; C-1&2, L-4&5

3475 [N.N.]; "Samooboronna praca musytsja provadyty jak najenerhyčnîjše y jak najskorše" [Self-defense actions must be carried out energetically and quickly]

The Laical-Church Congress's executive committee's plan of action against the Papal Bull and Bishop Ortynsky.

A   XVII (27): Aug 6, 1908; C-1&2, L-4

3476 "Cerkovnŷy Vîsty" [Church News]

a. Dedication of St. Clair, PA parish's iconostasis on September 7, 1908.

XVII (27): Aug 6, 1908; L-7
XVII (28): Aug 13, 1908; C-2

b. Rev. V. Kovaliczki (Barnesboro, PA) will be in Clymer, PA Sunday, August 30, 1908 to celebrate the Divine Liturgy.

Nr   XVII (28): Aug 13, 1908; C-2, L-3

3477 R.; "Sumnŷy, a otčasty y opastnŷy poslîdstvija" [Sad and somewhat dangerous consequences]

The division among Rusyn Greek Catholics in many parishes allegedly escalated by Bishop Ortynsky and his policies.

A   XVII (28): Aug 13, 1908; C-3, L-3

3478 [N.N.]; "Robljat jak chotjat. Ep. Ortŷn'skij pochvaljaet y odobrjaet vse" [They do as they wish. Bishop Ortynsky sings their praises and approves all]

The actions of Rev. Michael Balog, one of Bishop Ortynsky's zealous supporters.

A   XVII (29): Aug 20, 1908; C-2, L-2

3479 [N.N.]; "Strach čto robljat s narodom ukraynskiy duchovnyky pod protektoratstvom y za pozvaleniem Ep. Ortŷn'skoho" [The terrible evil that Ukrainian priests are doing among the people under the protection of and with the consent of Bishop Ortynsky]

Internal strife within a Philadelphia, PA parish allegedly caused by a supporter of Bishop Ortynsky, Rev. Simon Cziževicz.

A   XVII (30): Aug 27, 1908; C-2, L-2

3480   "Cerkovnŷy Vîsty" [Church News]

      a. Dedication of the Perth Amboy, NJ parish's iconostasis
         on September 7, 1908.

                           XVII (30): Aug 27, 1908; C-7, L-2

      b. Dedication of Alden, PA parish's stone cross on September
         27, 1908.

                           XVII (31): Sep 3, 1908; L-7
      Nr   XVII (32): Sep 10, 1908; C-3

3481   "Čto y jak hovoryt naš narod, y jak est' zadovolenŷj s teperîšnŷm
        položeniem cerkovnŷch dîl?" [What and how our people are
        saying and are the people satisfied with the current situa-
        tion of church affairs?]

        Series of letters to the editor commenting on Bishop Ortynsky
        and the Ukrainian national movement.

        Parts I-IV: XVII (33-36): Sep 17-Oct 8, 1908; C-2&3, L-2&3

        L

3482   M. B. K.; "Odnoe krasnoe y ympozantnoe cerkovnoe toržestvo" [One
        beautiful and impressive church celebration]

        The dedication of the Perth Amboy, NJ parish's iconostasis
        and altar on September 7, 1908.

        A   XVII (33): Sep 17, 1908; C-3, L-2&3

3483   Ž.; "Pervoe važnoe Sobranie Ekzekutyvnoho Komytetu Cerkovno-
        Cyvyl'noho Konhressu" [First important meeting of the Execu-
        tive Committee of the Church-Laical Congress]

        Meeting was held September 16, 1908 in Harrisburg, PA.

        E   XVII (33): Sep 17, 1908; C-4, L-4

3484   "Cerkovnŷy Vîsty" [Church News]

        Dedication of the Hannastown, PA church's bells on September 27,
        1908.

        Nr   XVII (33): Sep 17, 1908; C-7, L-7

3485   Ž.; "Najpaskudnîjšoe chameleonstvo. Šyren'e ukraynyzma, radykalyzma,
        da y anarchyzma pod tytulom katolyčestva" [The foulest chame-
        leon activities. The spreading of Ukrainianism, radicalism and
        even anarchism under the title of Catholicism]

        The activities of Bishop Ortynsky and his supporters.

        E   XVII (34): Sep 24, 1908; C-4&5, L-4

3486   "O. Ponjatyšyn ne lyš' dobrŷj chameleon, no y dobrŷj fynansysta"
        [Rev. Ponjatyšyn is not only a good chameleon, but a good
        financier]

Series of letters to the editor criticizing Rev. Ponjatyšyn, a supporter of Bishop Ortynsky.

L   XVII (35): Oct 1, 1908; C-4, L-4

3487 [N.N.]; "Strašnoe krovoprolytie v hr. kat. cerkvy v N'ju Brytejn', Konn." [Terrible bloodshed in the Greek Catholic Church in New Britain, CT]

The struggle between the Uhro-Rusyn and Galician-Ukrainian factions for control of the New Britain Greek Catholic Church.

Part I: XVII (37): Oct 15, 1908; C-5, L-5

Part II: XVII (38): Oct 22, 1908; C-4&5, L-4&5

A

3488 [N.N.]; "Od Executivnoho komitetu cerkovno-civilnoho kongressu potrimanoho v Braddock, Pa. i Scranton, Pa." [From the Executive Committee of the Ecclesiastical-Laical Congress held in Braddock, PA and Scranton, PA]

A six part series in Rusyn dialect and English about the current polemical situation existing among Greek Catholics in America.

Part I: The differences between Uhro-Rusyns and Galician Ukrainians.

                                 XVII (39): Oct 29, 1908; L-1&2

Part II: The causes of religious schism among Rusyns.

                                 XVII (40): Nov 5, 1908; L-1&2

Part III: The appointment of the Most Rev. S.S. Ortynsky as American Greek Catholic Bishop. An appointment, many claim, was due to the influence of old world politics.

                                 XVII (41): Nov 12, 1908; C-1,2,3, L-1&2

Part IV: Bishop Ortynsky: his early years as a monk in Galicia.

                                 XVII (42): Nov 19, 1908; C-1,2,3, L-1&2

Part V: The European politics in Galicia and Uhorska Rus'.

                                 XVII (44): Dec 3, 1908; C-1&2, L-1&2

Part VI: The arrival of Bishop Ortynsky to America in 1907.

O   XVII (47): Dec 24, 1908; C-1&2, L-1

3489 Michael Hanchin; "Propoved (Kazaňe) O. Michala Balogha v Pittsburgu So. Side i McKeesportsky diako-učitel'" [The sermon of Rev. Michael Balogh in the South Side Pittsburgh, PA (parish) and the McKeesport, PA (parish) sexton]

Rev. Michael Balogh and his politics.

A   XVII (39): Oct 29, 1908; L-4&5

3490   [N.N.]; "Strašné vysledky učinkovanie Ep. Ortynskyho" [Terrible results of the work of Bishop Ortynsky]

       The "schism" of several Greek Catholic churches resulting from Bishop Ortynsky's policies.

       A   XVII (40): Nov 5, 1908; L-4

3491   [N.N.]; "Ymiet-ly to bŷty znak našoj pobîdŷ, yly novŷj chytrŷj sposob v uspîch ukraynstva?" [Is it a sign of our victory or a new clever method in the success of Ukrainianism?]

       Priests and parishes who prefer to turn Orthodox rather than be under Bishop Ortynsky's jurisdiction.

       A   XVII (41): Nov 12, 1908; C-4, L-4

3492   [N.N.]; "Bîda dlja 'pjatolyzunov' Epyskop Ortŷn'skij ydet ym s pomoščiju" [Victory for the 'bootlickers,' Bishop Ortynsky helps them]

       The internal polemics in a Trenton, NJ parish over support of Bishop Ortynsky and his policies.

       A   XVII (42): Nov 19, 1908; C-4, L-4

3493   [N.N.]; "Ep. Ortŷn'skij v novom svîtlî" [Bishop Ortynsky in a new light]

       Bishop Ortynsky's moral and spiritual "fitness" to serve as the American Greek Catholic Bishop.

       A   XVII (43): Nov 26, 1908; C-1,2,3, L-1,2,3

3494   [N.N.]; "Akcija 'pjatolyzuna'" [Action of the 'bootlicker']

       The trouble among members of the Barnesboro, PA parish caused by Bishop Ortynsky's supporters.

       A   XVII (43): Nov 26, 1908; C-4, L-4

3495   Nicholas Val'čyšyn, et al.; "Po-čemu halyckiy Rusynŷ poprystavaly na schyzmu y prystajut v Embrydž', Pa." [Why Galician-Rusyns joined and are joining the schism in Embridge, PA]

       The polemical struggle between the trustees of the Embridge, PA parish and their pastor, Rev. Danilovich.

       A   XVII (43): Nov 26, 1908; C-4, L-4

3496   Michael Hanchin; "Ep. Ortŷn'skij, O. Horzo y djako-učytely. Otvît O. Horzovy" [Bishop Ortynsky, Rev. Gorzo and the sextons. Answer to Rev. Gorzo]

       A   XVII (45): Dec 10, 1908; C-4&5, L-4&5

3497   Joseph Fecko; Toronto, OH; Dec 8, 1908

"Klyvlandskij 'Pastŷrskij Lyst'" [Cleveland 'Pastoral Letter']

Commentary on Bishop Ortynsky's pastoral letter to Rusyn
parishes in Cleveland, OH and vicinity.

L   XVII (46): Dec 17, 1908; C-2&3, L-3

3498   [N.N.]; "Ot komytetu Uhro-Russkych Hreko Kat. Duchovnykov" [From
the committee of Uhro-Rusyn Greek Catholic Priests]

Warns of the harm being done to the Greek Catholic priesthood
by the Galician-Ukrainians and their polemics.

A   XVII (47): Dec 24, 1908; C-2, L-2

3499   John Uhrin and Michael Maczko; "Ot Ėkzekutyvnoho Komytetu Cerkovno-
Cyvyl'noho Konhressu poderžanoho v Bradok y Skrenton, Pa."
[From the Executive Committee of the Church-Lay Congress which
took place in Braddock and Scranton, PA]

The goals and aspirations of the Most Rev. S.S. Ortynsky
regarding the future of the American Greek Catholic Church.

O   XVII (48): Dec 31, 1908; C-9&10, L-9&10

3500   John Uhrin and Michael Maczko; "Ot Ėkzekutyvnoho Komytetu cyvyl'no-
cerkovnoho konhressu, poderžanoho v Bradok, Pa. y Skrenton, Pa."
[From the Executive Committee of the Laical-ecclesiastical
congress held in Braddock and Scranton, PA]

Bishop Ortynsky's plan of action to gain control of the American
Greek Catholic parishes.

O   XVIII (1): Jan 14, 1909; C-2&3, L-4

3501   John Kost'; McAdoo, PA

"Ukraynskoe panovanie" [Ukrainian domination]

The clergy who support Bishop Ortynsky.

L   XVIII (1): Jan 14, 1909; C-3, L-2

3502   Ž.; "Uhrorusskij narod ymîet podporovaty sbankrotovanŷ ukraynskiy
cerkvy" [Uhro-Rusyn people have to underwrite bankrupted
Ukrainian Churches]

Names churches in financial jeopardy due to a loss of members
because of Bishop Ortynsky's policies.

E   XVIII (2): Jan 21, 1909; C-2, L-2

3503   Š.; "Krasnŷj znak Pryznatel'nosty y Krasnŷy Roždestvennŷk Toržestvo"
[A beautiful sign of gratefulness and a beautiful Christmas
Celebration]

The Braddock, PA parish's solidarity in supporting its church council and pastor as well as the anniversary celebration on January 10, 1909.

A   XVIII (2): Jan 21, 1909; C-2, L-2

3504   Peter Dzmura, et al.; "Vŷtjah yz protokolu cerkovnoho mytynhu poderžanoho pry cerkvy sv. Petra y Pavla v Bradok, Pa. dnja 17-ho januara 1909" [Extract from the minutes of the church meeting held by the church of Sts. Peter and Paul in Braddock, PA January 17, 1909]

Resolution condemning Bishop Ortynsky and his policies.

O   XVIII (2): Jan 21, 1909; C-2, L-4

3505   M.C. Rushin; Minneapolis, MN

Bishop Ortynsky's visit to Minneapolis.

L   XVIII (2): Jan 21, 1909; C-2&3, L-2

3506   Michael Miterpak, et al.; Glen Lyon, PA

The effect Bishop Ortynsky's policies has had on the Glen Lyon parish.

L   XVIII (3): Jan 28, 1909; C-2, L-2

3507   John Procz, et al.; "Protokol Cerkovnoho Mytynhu poderžanoho v Donora, Pa. dnja 17 janvarja 1909, v dîlî cyrkuljara, vydanoho nîkym 'Komytetom yz Prjaševskoj dieceziy pochodjaščych duchovnykov'" [Minutes of the church meeting held in Donora, PA, January 17, 1909 concerning the matter of a circular, published by a 'Committee of priests from the Diocese of Prešov']

Opinion of the Donora parish about Bishop Ortynsky's policies.

A   XVIII (3): Jan 28, 1909; C-2, L-4

3508   John Boreczky; South Chicago, IL

The polemics among the parishioners of the Chicago parish allegedly sparked by Rev. Valentine Balog.

L   XVIII (3): Jan 28, 1909; C-3, L-2

3509   John Karaffa; Trenton, NJ

The Trenton parish's annual church meeting.

L   XVIII (3): Jan 28, 1909; C-3, L-2

3510   John Kuba; "Ne dajme zvestysja" [Let us not be led astray]

Warns Rusyn-American parishioners to disregard the appeal of Bishop Ortynsky to join a new church congress program.

A   XVIII (4): Feb 4, 1909; C-2&3, L-2

3511   [N.N.]; McAdoo, PA; Feb 4, 1909

      The formation of a new Uhro-Rusyn parish in McAdoo due to the loss of the old one to Bishop Ortynsky's supporters.

      L   XVIII (5): Feb 11, 1909; C-3, L-3

3512   [N.N.]; Gary, IN; Jan 25, 1909

      The competition between Rusyn and Ukrainian factions in Chicago and vicinity in organizing new parishes.

      L   XVIII (5): Feb 11, 1909; C-3, L-3

3513   John Uhrin and Michael Maczko; "Ot ĕkzekutyvnoho komytetu cyvyl'no-cerkovnoho konhressu, poderžanoho v Bradock, Pa. y Skrenton, Pa. Vozzvanie" [From the executive committee of the Laical-Church Congress held in Braddock and Scranton, PA. An appeal]

      Reminds all Rusyn-Americans to resist Ukrainian propaganda and Bishop Ortynsky's attempts to gain control of the parishes.

      O   XVIII (6): Feb 18, 1909; C-2, L-4

3514   John Drimak; Chicago, IL

      a. The February 14, 1909 fire which destroyed the Chicago church.
      b. The activities of the Ukrainian nationalists in the Chicago vicinity.

      L   XVIII (7): Feb 25, 1909; C-2&3, L-2

3515   Michael Babko; Bridgeport, CT; Feb 13, 1909

      The polemics among the Bridgeport parishioners.

      L   XVIII (9): Mar 11, 1909; C-3, L-3

3516   [N.N.]

      Rev. Ireneus Martyak and the Ukrainian national movement.

      L   XVIII (10): Mar 18, 1909; C-3, L-3

3517   [N.N.]; "Akcija ukrayncev y ej čudesnŷy ovoščy" [Action of the Ukrainians and its extraordinary fruit]

      Bishop Ortynsky and the Philadelphia, PA Greek Catholic parishes.

      A   XVIII (11): Mar 25, 1909; C-2&3, L-2

3518   Michael Labick; Duquesne, PA; Mar 21, 1909

      "Zaslato. Otvertoe Pys'mo O. Iosyfu Hanulja, bŷvšemu duchovnyku v Dukejn, Pa." [Letter to the Editor. Open letter to Rev. Joseph Hanulya, former pastor in Duquesne, PA]

      Member of Duquesne parish council requests Rev. Hanulya to account for missing church funds.

      L   XVIII (12): Apr 1, 1909; C-6, L-6

3519   [N.N.]; "Ukraynskiy ehomoscî chotîly ymîty dobrŷy žnyva"
        [Ukrainian priests wanted to have a good harvest]

        The attempts by Bishop Ortynsky and his supportive clergy to
        gain control of the Greek Catholic parishes.

        A   XVIII (12): Apr 1, 1909; C-6, L-6

3520   Rev. Joseph Hanulya; "Otvertaja Otpovîd'" [Candid rebuttal]

        See: 3518.

        L   XVIII (14): Apr 22, 1909; C-2&3, L-2

3521   Michael Labick; Duquesne, PA; Apr 19, 1909

        "Zajavlenie O. Iosyfu Hanulja!" [Notice to Rev. Joseph
        Hanulya!]

        Threatens legal action if missing church funds are not
        accounted for. See: 3518, 3520.

        L   XVIII (14): Apr 22, 1909; C-3, L-2&3

3522   John Hlivka; Duquesne, PA; Apr 19, 1909

        "Zaslato" [Letter to the Editor]

        Denies allegations in Svoboda that the Duquesne parish forced
        the transfer of Rev. John Hrabar.

        L   XVIII (14): Apr 22, 1909; C-3, L-3

3523   Ž.; "Nasylijam žestokostjam Ukraynskym Nablyžaetsja Konec" [The
        end of violations and cruelties by Ukrainians draws near]

        Stresses the need for a separate bishop and eparchy for Uhro-
        Rusyns in America.

        E   XVIII (15): Apr 29, 1909; C-3, L-3

3524   A. K.; Shenandoah, PA

        The indebtedness of the Shenandoah parish allegedly due to
        financial mismanagement by the parish priest and curators.

        L   XVIII (16): May 6, 1909; C-3, L-2&3

3525   [N.N.]; "Malo svîtla na černu y potaemnu akciju" [A bit of light
        on a black and secret action]

        Letters by a G.C.U. lodge secretary, Rev. Paul Staurovsky,
        Bishop Ortynsky and John Uhrin commenting on the situation
        of the Greek Catholic Church in America.

        A   XVIII (17): May 13, 1909; C-4&5, L-4&5

3526   John Minda, et al.; Clairton, PA; May 10, 1909

"Zaslato" [Letter to the Editor]

Problems among Clairton parishioners after "solving" the nationality question.

L   XVIII (17): May 13, 1909; C-6, L-2&3

3527   "Vel'ka Cerkovna Slavnosc" [Magnificent Church celebration]

Dedication of the Johnstown, PA parish's cross on June 6, 1909.

XVIII (17): May 13, 1909; L-7

Ad   XVIII (18): May 20, 1909; C-7

3528   Andrew Leško, et al.; Brooklyn, NY

The Brooklyn parish and the religious-nationality issue.

L   XVIII (18): May 20, 1909; C-2, L-2

3529   "Velykoe Cerkovnoe Toržestvo" [A magnificent church celebration]

Dedication of the Clymer, PA parish's bell on Monday, May 31, 1909.

Ad   XVIII (18): May 20, 1909; C-7, L-3

3530   [N.N.]; "Polnoe nezadovolenie protyv dîjstvovanija Epyskopa Ortŷn'skoho" [Complete dissatisfaction with the action of Bishop Ortynsky]

An article [reprinted] by a disgruntled Galician-Rusyn condemning the policies of Bishop Ortynsky.

A   XVIII (19): May 27, 1909; C-4, L-4

3531   John Kipilo; Conemaugh, PA; May 22, 1909

"Zaslato" [Letter to the Editor]

The effect Bishop Ortynsky's policies has had on the Conemaugh parish.

L   XVIII (20): Jun 3, 1909; C-3, L-2&3

3532   [N.N.]; "Protest Amerykanskoho Uhro-Russkoho Naroda" [Protest of the American Uhro-Rusyn People]

Against Bishop Ortynsky and his policies.

A   XVIII (20): Jun 3, 1909; C-4, L-4

3533   Stephen Senčak, et al.; "Velykij Uhro-russkij Narodnŷj Mytynh v Hery, Ynd." [Great National Uhro-Rusyn Meeting in Gary, IN]

Plan of action against Bishop Ortynsky and his supporters to be discussed at the June 19, 1909 meeting.

A   XVIII (20): Jun 3, 1909; C-4, L-4

3534   M. H.; Gary, IN

        The construction of a church for the Gary parish.

        L   XVIII (20): Jun 3, 1909; C-6, L-3

3535   John Popovich and Anthony Monich; "Pobîda pravdŷ nad nespravedly-
        vost'ju" [Victory of right over injustice]

        The formation of a new Uhro-Rusyn church in New Britain, CT.

        A   XVIII (21): Jun 10, 1909; C-3, L-3

3536   [N.N.]; "Odnoe ympozantnoe cerkovnoe toržestvo" [One impressive
        church celebration]

        The dedication of the Johnstown, PA parish's large cross on
        June 6, 1909.

        A   XVIII (21): Jun 10, 1909; C-3, L-3

3537   [N.N.]; "Odnoe uhro-russkoe cerkovnoe toržestvo" [Uhro-Rusyn church
        celebration]

        The May 31, 1909 dedication of the corner stone for the McAdoo,
        PA Greek Catholic church.

        A   XVIII (23): Jun 24, 1909; C-2&3, L-2

3538   [N.N.]; "Najnovîjšoe v cerkovnŷch dîlach amerykanskych hreko katoly-
        kov" [The latest concerning the church matters of the American
        Greek Catholics]

        Roman and Greek Catholic church relations in America; attitude
        of Rome toward the American Greek Catholic dilemma.

        A   XVIII (24): Jul 1, 1909; C-4, L-4

3539   John Hlivka; Duquesne, PA

        The financial situation of the Duquesne parish.

        L   XVIII (25): Jul 8, 1909; C-4&5, L-3

3540   [N.N.]; "Čoho požylsja uhro-russkij narod pry svoj čestnoj pracî y
        pry velykom svoem žertvoljubiju?" [What have the Uhro-Rusyn
        people ended up with despite their honorable work and great
        sacrifice?]

        Upheaval among the Greek Catholic parishes attributed to the
        Rusyn-Ukrainian polemics.

        A   XVIII (26): Jul 15, 1909; C-4, L-4

3541   [N.N.]; Clairton, PA

        The nationality issue among Clairton parishioners.

        L   XVIII (27): Jul 22, 1909; C-3, L-3

3542   "Novosty yz kruha našeho duchovenstva" [News from the circle of
        our clergy]

    a. Rev. Alexis Petrassovich (Braddock, PA) returned from an
        extended stay in Europe and was assigned to Cleveland, OH.
    b. Commentary on Rev. Emil (Emmanuel) Burik.

    Nr   XVIII (29): Aug 5, 1909; C-3, L-2&3

3543   "Cerkovnoe Toržestvo v Ionhstavn, O." [Church celebration in
        Youngstown, OH]

    Anniversary celebration on August 29, 1909.

    Ad   XVIII (29): Aug 5, 1909; C-7, L-3

3544   Andrew Ratica; Cleveland, OH

    The polemics among Cleveland parishioners allegedly caused by
    Rev. E. Burik.

    L   XVIII (30): Aug 12, 1909; C-2&3, L-2

3545   John Uhrin; "Ot Ekzekutyvnoho Komytetu Cerkovno-Cyvyl'noho Konhressu"
        [From the Executive Committee of the Church Laical Congress]

    Requests support from all parishes and lodges in the endeavor
    to safeguard the rights of individual parishes and preserve the
    integrity of the Uhro-Rusyn people.

    O   XVIII (31): Aug 19, 1909; C-2, L-2

3546   [N.N.]; "Orhan ukraynskoj verchnosty Dušpastŷr konaet. Ep.
        Ortŷn'skij spîšyt zachranyty, a chotja lyš' prodolžyty, eho
        žyvot" [Organ of the Ukrainian hierarchy Dušpastyr is dying.
        Bishop Ortynsky hurries to save it, or at least to prolong its
        life]

    A   XVIII (31): Aug 19, 1909; C-2&3, L-2

3547   "Novosty yz kruha našeho duchovenstva" [News from the circle of our
        clergy]

    "Bez plačenija pjat' procentov nît dyspenzaciy" [Without the
    payment of five percent no dispensation]

    Bishop Ortynsky requests an annual tithe of five percent from
    each parish's income. If payment is not forthcoming, Bishop
    Ortynsky could legally suspend the offending parish's priest.

    Nr   XVIII (31): Aug 19, 1909; C-3, L-2&3

3548   "Posvjaščenie novych zvonov" [Dedication of new bells]

    Dedication of the Charleroi, PA parish's bells on September 6,
    1909.

    Ad   XVIII (31): Aug 19, 1909; C-3, L-3

3549 John Uhrin and Michael Maczko; "Ot Ekzekutyvnoho Komytetu Cerkovno-Cyvyl'noho Konhressu" [From the Executive Committee of the Church-Laical Congress]

Requests support of the Galician-Rusyns of the old Rusyn party in the struggle with Bishop Ortynsky.

O   XVIII (32): Aug 26, 1909; C-2, L-2

3550 [N.N.]; "Brutal'nŷy postupovanija Ep. Ortŷn'skoho" [The brutal actions of Bishop Ortynsky]

The relations of the Windber, PA parish with Bishop Ortynsky.

A   XVIII (32): Aug 26, 1909; C-2&3, L-2&3

3551 Ž.; "27-ho Avhusta 1907" [August 27, 1907]

The second anniversary of Bishop Ortynsky's arrival in America.

E   XVIII (32): Aug 26, 1909; C-4, L-4

3552 "Poŝvecanie novoho cintira" [Dedication of a new cemetery]

Dedication in Clairton, PA on August 29, 1909.

Ad   XVIII (32): Aug 26, 1909; L-8

3553 [N.N.]; "Radostnŷy vîsty yz vsîch storon" [Joyful news from all sides]

The rumor Rome is considering the appointment of a bishop for the American Uhro-Rusyns.

A   XVIII (33): Sep 2, 1909; C-2, L-2

3554 [N.N.]; McAdoo, PA

The August 15, 1909 dedication of the McAdoo parish's three bells.

L   XVIII (34): Sep 9, 1909; C-2, L-2

3555 [N.N.]; "Pochval'noe dvyženie naŝoho duchovenstva v zaŝĉytî cerkvy y naroda" [Praiseworthy movement of our clergy in the preservation of church and nationality]

The Mukačevo and Prešov clergy societies meet in Harrisburg, PA September 23, 1909 to discuss the polemics which are causing trouble among the American Greek Catholic churches.

A   XVIII (34): Sep 9, 1909; C-4, L-4

3556 Andrew Ragan; Youngstown, OH

The August 29, 1909 Youngstown parish celebration.

L   XVIII (35): Sep 16, 1909; C-2&3, L-2&3

3557 "Zaprošenie na Cerkovnoe Toržestvo" [Invitation to a Church Cele-
bration]

Dedication of the Phoenixville, PA Greek Catholic church on
October 24, 1909.

Ad   XVIII (35): Sep 16, 1909; C-3, L-3

3558 Zsatkovich; "'Otvertoe pys'mo' O. A. Kečkejša do Vŷsokoprep. O.
A. Hodobaja" [An 'open letter' from Rev. A. Kecskés to the
Very Rev. A. Hodobay]

The appointment of a bishop and establishment of a Greek
Catholic Eparchy in America.

L   XVIII (35): Sep 16, 1909; C-4, L-4

3559 Rev. Cornelius Laurisin; "Velykoe Sobranie Uhro-Russkych Duchovnykov" [The great Uhro-Rusyn clergy meeting]

List of participants and agenda topics of the clergy meeting
held in Harrisburg, PA September 23, 1909.

O   XVIII (37): Sep 30, 1909; C-2, L-2

3560 John Uhrin and P. Ju. Zsatkovich; "Ot Ėkzekutyvnoho Komytetu
Cerkovno-Cyvyl'noho Konhressu" [From the Executive Committee
of the Church-Laical Congress]

List of donations for a special Church-Laical Congress.

O   XVIII (37): Sep 30, 1909; C-2, L-2

3561 Alexis Koscelnik; Charleroi, PA

The September 6, 1909 dedication of the Charleroi parish's
bells.

L   XVIII (37): Sep 30, 1909; C-3, L-2&3

3562 Zsatkovich; "Porozumînie meždu uhro-russkymy duchovnykamy kasatel'no
chranenijasja protyv ukraynskoj napasty" [Understanding among
Uhro-Rusyn clergy concerning the protection against the Ukrainian assault]

Resolutions of the September 23, 1909 clergy meeting held in
Harrisburg, PA, concerning the situation of the American Greek
Catholic Church.

E   XVIII (37): Sep 30, 1909; C-4, L-4

3563 Paul Hrivka; Youngstown, OH; Oct 4, 1909

"Zaslato" [Letter to the Editor]

The activities of Rev. Michael Balog.

L   XVIII (38): Oct 7, 1909; C-2, L-2

3564   Rev. Cornelius Laurisin; "Ot predsîdatelja komytetu duchovnykov"
       [From the president of the clergy committee]

       Condemns the action of Rev. Michael Balog.

       O   XVIII (39): Oct 14, 1909; C-2, L-2

3565   [N.N.]; "Ot Hr. Kat. Russkoj Parafiy Uspenija Presv. Bohorodycŷ v
       Ionhstavn, Ohajo. Protokol" [From the Greek Catholic parish
       of the Assumption in Youngstown, OH. Minutes]

       Parish meeting was held October 7, 1909.

       O   XVIII (39): Oct 14, 1909; C-2, L-2

3566   [N.N.]; "Pervoe zasîdanie komytetu duchovnykov. Akcija uhro-
       russkoho naroda, eho duchovenstvo y Ep. Ortŷn'skij" [First
       meeting of the committee of priests. Action of the Uhro-Rusyn
       people, its clergy and Bishop Ortynsky]

       Meeting was held October 21, 1909 in Philadelphia, PA.

       A   XVIII (41): Oct 28, 1909; C-4, L-4

3567   Š.; Bradenville, PA

       The October 17, 1909 dedication of the Bradenville parish's
       cross.

       L   XVIII (42): Nov 4, 1909; C-2&3, L-2

3568   [N.N.]; "Balamučenie našoho uhro-russkoho naroda ukrayncamy" [The
       confusion of our Uhro-Rusyn people by Ukrainians]

       Examines Rusyn solidarity amidst the polemical struggle with
       Bishop Ortynsky.

       A   XVIII (42): Nov 4, 1909; C-4&5, L-4&5

3569   Andrew Kisely; Phoenixville, PA; Nov 3, 1909

       "Žalobŷ naroda" [Complaints of the people]

       The effect Bishop Ortynsky's policies and supporters has had
       on the Phoenixville parish.

       L   XVIII (43): Nov 11, 1909; C-2, L-2

3570   "Velykoe Cerkovnoe Toržestvo" [A Magnificent Church Celebration]

       Dedication of the Duquesne, PA, Greek Catholic church on
       November 28, 1909

       Ad   XVIII (43): Nov 11, 1909; C-8, L-7

3571   [N.N.]; "Krajnoe krutîjstvo, podlaja lož'" [Extreme manipulation,
       a vile lie]

       Commentary on an article, about a separate bishop for Uhro-
       Rusyns, in Svoboda, #42, October 28, 1909.

       A   XVIII (44): Nov 18, 1909; C-2&3, L-2

3572   John Popovich, et al.; New Britain, CT

"Zaslato" [Letter to the Editor]

Polemics over the nationality issue among New Britain's parishioners.

L   XVIII (45): Nov 25, 1909; C-2, L-2

3573   Stephen Liska; East Youngstown, OH; Nov 15, 1909

"Zaslato" [Letter to the Editor]

The activities of Rev. Michael Balog.

L   XVIII (45): Nov 25, 1909; C-2&3, L-2

3574   "Novosty yz kruha našeho duchovenstva" [News from the circle of our clergy]

a. The health of Rev. Acacius Kamensky (Allentown, PA) has forced him to stay temporarily at a hospital. Rev. Stephen Janicky will be the administrator for the Allentown parish.

b. The Cleveland, OH Rusyn community's rejection of priests sent to them by Bishop Ortynsky.

Nr   XVIII (47): Dec 9, 1909; C-2, L-2

3575   [N.N.]; "Pered velykym Konhressom uhro-russkych y halycijsko-starorusskoj partiy hreko kat. parafiy" [Prior to the Congress of Greek Catholic parishes of Uhro-Rusyns and Galicians of the old Rusyn party]

The issues the Congress will discuss.

A   XVIII (47): Dec 9, 1909; C-4, L-4

3576   [N.N.]; Conemaugh, PA; Nov 29, 1909

"Akcija Epyskopa Ortŷn'skoho protyv Uhro-Russkych parafij" [Action (taken by) Bishop Ortynsky against Uhro-Rusyn parishes]

Bishop Ortynsky's alleged attempt to gain the deed to the Conemaugh church.

L   XVIII (48): Dec 16, 1909; C-2, L-2

3577   John Uhrin and Paul Ju. Zsatkovich; "Ot Ekzekutyvnoho Komytetu Cerkovno-Cyvyl'noho Konhressu Braddok-Skrentonskoho" [From the Executive Committee of the Church-Laical Congress of Braddock and Scranton, PA]

Announces the convocation of a Congress in Johnstown, PA January 11-12, 1910.

O   XVIII (49): Dec 23, 1909; C-4, L-4

3578   P. Ju. Zsatkovich; "Uhro-russkij Epyskop dlja uhorskych Rusynov v
       Amerykî" [A Uhro-Rusyn Bishop for Hungarian-Rusyns in America]

       A proposed candidate for the position as bishop of an American
       Uhro-Rusyn Diocese, is the Very Rev. Dr. Michael Artim (Prešov
       Diocese).

       E, P   XVIII (50): Dec 30, 1909; C-4, L-4

3579   [N.N.]; "Poblahoslonenie novoj hreko katolyčeskoj uhro-russkoj Cerkvy
       v Dukejn, Pa." [Blessing of the new Greek Catholic Uhro-Rusyn
       church in Duquesne, PA]

       Dedication held on November 28, 1910.

       A   XVIII (50): Dec 30, 1909; C-5, L-3

3580   Paul Ju. Zsatkovich; "Velykij vseobščij konhress uhro-russkych parafij"
       [Great universal congress of Uhro-Rusyn parishes]

       Congress held in Johnstown, PA, January 11-12, 1910.

       Parts I-III: XIX (2-4): Jan 20-Feb 3, 1910; C-2&3, L-2
       E

3581   Redakcija; "Za pravo y spravedlyvost' (dumŷ po našom konhressu)"
       [For truth and justice (thoughts after our congress)]

       Congress held in Johnstown, PA, January 11-12, 1910.

       E   XIX (2): Jan 20, 1910; C-4, L-4

3582   Andrew Lychvar, et al.; "Pros'ba. Ot Hreko Kat. Uhro-Russkoj Parafiy
       Sv. Trojcŷ v Nju Brytejn, Konn." [Request. From the Greek
       Catholic Parish of the Holy Ghost in New Britain, CT]

       Request for financial contributions for the support of the New
       Britain parish.

       Req   XIX (2): Jan 20, 1910; C-6, L-6

3583   John Uhrin, et al.; "Ot hl. urjadu 'Soedynenija'" [From the supreme
       administration of the 'Soedynenie']

       Requests financial aid from the lodges for the New Britain, CT
       parish.

       Req   XIX (2): Jan 20, 1910; C-6, L-6

3584   [N.N.]; "Položenie uhro-russkoj hreko kat. cerkvy Sošestvija Sv. Ducha
       v Oklŷnd-Pyttsburh, Pa." [(Financial) situation of the Greek
       Catholic Church, of the Descent of the Holy Ghost in Oakland-
       Pittsburgh, PA]

       A   XIX (3): Jan 27, 1910; C-7, L-3

3585   "Velykoe Cerkovnoe Toržestvo" [Great Church Celebration]

       Dedication of the Cleveland, OH Greek Catholic Church's corner
       stone on February 6, 1910.

       Ad   XIX (4): Feb 3, 1910; C-3, L-3

3586 P. Ju. Ž.; "Na dorozî lžy" [On the road of falsehood]

Bishop Ortynsky's opinions of the Johnstown, PA congress.

E   XIX (5): Feb 10, 1910; C-2, L-2

3587 T.; "Velykaja Nehoda. Brejdŷnvyllskaja hreko kat. uhro-russkaja
cerkov' zahorîla do tla" [Great misfortune. Bradenville,
(PA) Greek Catholic Church burned to the ground.

Fire occurred on February 8, 1910.

Nr   XIX (5): Feb 10, 1910; C-3, L-2&3

3588 John Uhrin and Paul Ju. Zsatkovich; "Ot Ekzekutyvnoho Komytetu
Džanstavnskoho Konhressu" [From the Executive Committee of
the Johnstown, PA Congress]

Announces the commencement of a concerted effort to recall
and replace Bishop Ortynsky.

O   XIX (6): Feb 17, 1910; C-2&3, L-2

3589 Z.H. Baran, et al.; "Ot tovaryščestva uhro-russkych d'jako-učytelej"
[From the society of Uhro-Rusyn cantors]

Supports the platform of the Uhro-Rusyn Congress in the preservation of Greek Catholic parish rights against the policies of
Bishop Ortynsky.

A   XIX (7): Feb 17, 1910; C-3, L-2

3590 [N.N.]; "Na dorozî lžy No. 2" [On the road of falsehood No. 2]

Answer to Bishop Ortynsky's commentary in an article which
appeared in Svoboda, #7.

Parts I-VI: XIX (7-12): Feb 24-Mar 31, 1910; C-2&3, L-2&3

A

3591 [N.N.]; "Koe-čto yz okolycŷ Ionhstavnskoj" [Something from the
vicinity of Youngstown, OH]

The slander court suit brought by Revs. M. Balog and Joseph
Fojtan against Rev. Alexis Medvecky.

Nr   XIX (7): Feb 17, 1910; C-3, L-2&3

3592 [N.N.]; Bradenville, PA; Mar 1, 1910

"Najnovîjšij slučaj skvernoj podkopnoj pracŷ Ukrayncev"
[Latest case of the bad undermining work of the Ukrainians]

The suggestion made by Bradenville Ukrainians that they and
the Rusyns join together to rebuild the fire-devastated Greek
Catholic Church.

L   XIX (8): Mar 3, 1910; C-2, L-2

3593   John Hlivka, et al.; Duquesne, PA

The settlement reached with the building contractor over the construction of the Duquesne church.

L   XIX (8): Mar 3, 1910; C-3, L-3

3594   [N.N.]; Cleveland, OH

The February 6, 1910 dedication of the Cleveland Greek Catholiç Church's corner stone.

L   XIX (8): Mar 3, 1910; C-3, L-3

3595   [N.N.]; "Bor'ba na žyt'e y smert' za 'Ukraynskuju Cerkov'!'" [The life and death struggle for a 'Ukrainian Church']

Bishop Ortynsky's struggle to gain the deeds to all Greek Catholic Churches in America.

A   XIX (9): Mar 10, 1910; C-2, L-2

3596   Redakcija; "Jakoe epyskopstvo chočeme ymîty mŷ Uhorskiy Rusynŷ v Amerykî?" [What kind of bishopric do we Uhro-Rusyns want to have in America?]

Reply to an article published in Slovenskị Dennîk, #2262.

E   XIX (9): Mar 10, 1910; C-4&5, L-4&5

3597   [N.N.]; Binghampton, NY

Rev. E. Petrasovich's friendship with Bishop Ortynsky.

L   XIX (12): Mar 31, 1910; C-3, L-3

3598   M.M.; Lyndora, PA

The co-existence of Galician-Ukrainians and Uhro-Rusyns in the Lyndora-Butler vicinity prior and after the arrival of Bishop Ortynsky in America.

L   XIX (13): Apr 7, 1910; C-3, L-2&3

3599   Andrew Bussa; Binghampton, NY; Apr 7, 1910

"Opravdanie" [Justification]

See 3597.

L   XIX (14): Apr 14, 1910; C-2&3, L-2

3600   ⌊N.N.⌋; Kingston, PA

The attendance of Galician-Ukrainians at the Kingston Greek Catholic Church due to the destruction of the Ukrainian church by fire.

L   XIX (14): Apr 14, 1910; C-3, L-3

3601 "Vîsty yz kruhu našeho uhro-russkoho hreko kat. duchovenstva"
[News from the circle of our Uhro-Rusyn Greek Catholic clergy]

    a. Rev. Basil Volosin (Toronto, OH) returns to Europe where
       he has been assigned to a parish in Szatmar County, Hungary.
    b. Rev. Emilian Seregelly (Charleroi, PA) returns to Europe.
    c. Several Rusyn priests [N.N.] will be arriving in America
       from Europe.
    d. "Peremîny" [Changes]
       1. Rev. A. Kamensky (Allentown, PA) assigned to Charleroi,
          PA.
       2. Rev. Alexis Petrassovich (South Sharon, OH) assigned
          to Chicago, IL.
       3. Rev. John Szabo (Duquesne, PA) assigned to Toronto, OH.
       4. Rev. Eugene Homichko (Carteret, NJ) assigned to
          Duquesne, PA.
       5. Rev. Victor Suba (Hazleton, PA #3) assigned to
          Carteret, NJ.
       6. Rev. Alexis Vajda (Newark, NJ) assigned to Hazleton,
          PA #3.

    Nr   XIX (15): Apr 21, 1910; C-3, L-3

3602 "Cerkovnoe Toržestvo" [Church Celebration]

Rev. N. Stecovich dedicates the New Salem, PA Greek Catholic
Church's stone cross on May 29, 1910.

    Ad   XIX (17): May 12, 1910; C-3, L-5

3603 John D. Hritz; Windber, PA; Apr 17, 1910

"Zaslato. Otvît odnomu yz 'Otkopnutŷch'" [Letter to the
Editor. Answer to one of the 'Kicked Away']

Commentary on Rev. D. Polivka.

    L   XIX (18): May 19, 1910; C-2, L-2

3604 Michael Bodrog; Yonkers, NY

Commentary on Rev. Basil Volosin.

                            XIX (18): May 19, 1910; L-2
    L   XIX (19): May 26, 1910; C-4&5

3605 John Guba, et al.; Marblehead, OH

The Marblehead parish's problem with propagators of "schism."

    L   XIX (19): May 26, 1910; L-2

3606 Š.; "Blahoslovenie osnovnoho kamenja novoj uhro-russkoj hr. kat.
cerkvy v Brejdŷnvyll" [Blessing of the foundation stone of
the new Uhro-Rusyn Greek Catholic Church in Bradenville, PA]

Dedication on May 22, 1910.

    A   XIX (20): Jun 2, 1910; C-4, L-2

3607   Michael Jurko, et al.; Cleveland, OH; May 31, 1910

      "Zaslato. Posvjaščenie Ukraynskoj-Katolyckoj Cerkvy v
      Klyvlŷnd, Ohajo" [Letter to the Editor. Dedication of the
      Ukrainian Catholic Church in Cleveland, OH]

      Dedication on May 29, 1910.

      L   XIX (21): Jun 16, 1910; C-3, L-2

3608   [N.N.]; North Catasauqua, PA

      The court litigation by Bishop Ortynsky to obtain the deed
      to the Northhampton church.

      L   XIX (21): Jun 16, 1910; C-3, L-2

3609   John Bubnash; Stocket, MT

      The visit of Rev. Alexander Kossey to Stockett.

      L   XIX (22): Jun 23, 1910; C-2, L-2

3610   [N.N.]; McKeesport, PA; Jul 2, 1910

      "Ukraynsko-rutenecko pjatolyzunskaja myssija" [Ukrainian-
      Ruthenian bootlicker mission]

      A clergy meeting at the rectory of the McKeesport parish.

      L   XIX (24): Jul 7, 1910; C-2, L-2

3611   Paul Ju. Zsatkovich; "Jak stoyt akcija uhro-russkoho naroda protyv
      ukraynskoj napasty" [How does the action of the Uhro-Rusyn
      people stand against the Ukrainian danger]

      Bishop Ortynsky, his supporters and the Ukrainian national
      movement in America.

      Part I: XIX (24): Jul 7, 1910; C-4&5, L-4

      Part II: XIX (25): Jul 14, 1910; C-1, L-4

      E

3612   "Vîsty yz kruha našeho uhrorusskoho hreko kat. duchovenstva"
      [News from the circle of our Uhro-Rusyn Greek Catholic clergy]

      a. Rev. Cornelius Laurisin (Trenton, NJ) assigned to a parish
          in Europe. ARV states that the assignment was at the re-
          quest of Bishop Ortynsky.
      b. Rev. Acacius Kamensky (Charleroi, PA) suffered a nervous
          breakdown.

      Nr   XIX (25): Jul 14, 1910; C-2&3, L-2&3

3613   [N.N.]; "Napadenie Svobodŷ" [Attack of Svoboda]

      Commentary on an article about Rev. Acacius Kamensky (Charleroi,
      PA) in Svoboda, #14.

      A   XIX (26): Jul 21, 1910; C-1, L-2

3614   [N.N.]; "Odnoe krasnoe cerkovnoe toržestvo" [A beautiful church celebration]

The July 4, 1910 tenth anniversary celebration of the Youngstown, OH Greek Catholic Church.

A   XIX (26): Jul 21, 1910; C-2, L-2

3615   John Uhrin and Paul Ju. Zsatkovich; "Ot Eksekutyvnoho Komytetu akciy Uhro-Russkoho Naroda protyv Ukraynskoj Napasty" [From the Executive Committee of the action of the Uhro-Rusyn people against the Ukrainian danger]

Part I: Urges Rusyns to unite and oppose Bishop Ortynsky, his supporters and Ukrainianism.

XIX (29): Aug 11, 1910; C-2, L-4

Part II: The arrival of Galician Archbishop Count Sheptyts'kyi in America.

XIX (30): Aug 18, 1910; C-2, L-4

Part III: Commentary on Rusin.

XIX (31): Aug 25, 1910; C-4, L-4

Part IV: The convocation of congress in Harrisburg, PA on September 8, 1910.

A   XIX (32): Sep 1, 1910; C-2, L-4

3616   Basil Rudišin, et al.; "Odnoe krasnoe cerkovnoe toržestvo" [A beautiful church celebration]

The July 31, 1910 dedication of the McKees Rocks, PA church's two bells.

A   XIX (30): Aug 18, 1910; C-2, L-2&3

3617   "Velykoe Cerkovnoe Toržestvo" [Great Church Celebration]

Dedication of the Cleveland, OH church's three bells on September 5, 1910.

Ad   XIX (31): Aug 25, 1910; C-3, L-8

3618   "Cerkovna Slavnosc!" [Church Celebration!]

Dedication of the Youngstown, OH Greek Catholic Church on August 28, 1910.

Ad   XIX (31): Aug 25, 1910; L-8

3619   Michael Marčisak; "Krasna cerkovna slavnosc" [A beautiful church celebration]

The August 28, 1910 dedication of the Leisenring, PA church's icon and altar.

A   XIX (32): Sep 1, 1910; L-2

3620   Andrew Koreny, et al.; Cleveland, OH

       The September 5, 1910 dedication of the Cleveland church's
       three bells.

       L   XIX (35): Sep 22, 1910; C-2&3, L-2&3

3621   "Vel'ka Cerkovna Slavnosc" [Great Church Celebration'

       Dedication of the Homestead, PA Greek Catholic Church and
       iconostasis on September 25, 1910.

       Ad   XIX (35): Sep 22, 1910; L-7

3622   Ž.; "Ympozantnoe cerkovnoe toržestvo v Homsted, Pa." [Impressive
       church celebration in Homestead, PA]

       The September 25, 1910 dedication of the Homestead church and
       its iconostasis.

       A   XIX (36): Sep 29, 1910; C-2&3, L-2&3

3623   John Cservinka; Trauger, PA

       The September 18, 1910 dedication of the Trauger Greek Catholic
       cemetery's cross.

       L   XIX (37): Oct 6, 1910; C-3, L-3

3624   Michael Kovaly, et al.; Glen Lyon, PA; Sep 26, 1910

       "Otvît ot uhro-russkoj parafiy y ot uhro-russkoho Bratstva č.
       v 'Soedyneniy' 28, v Hlen Lajyn, Pa." [Answer from the Uhro-
       Rusyn parish and lodge #28 in the 'Soedynenie' in Glen Lyon, PA]

       Reply to Rusin concerning Ukrainian-Rusyn polemics allegedly
       sparked by Bishop Ortynsky.

       L   XIX (37): Oct 6, 1910; C-5, L-5

3625   [N.N.]; "Slova naroda protyv ukraynstva y pjatolyzunstva" [People's
       words against Ukrainianism and bootlickers]

       Part I: Letters to the editor concerning the Ukrainization of
       the Butler-Lyndora, PA parish.

                       XIX (37): Oct 6, 1910; C-5, L-4&5

       Part II: Rusyn-Ukrainian polemics within the Cleveland, OH
       parish.

                       XIX (38): Oct 13, 1910; C-2&3, L-2

       Part III: Commentary on Rev. Joseph Hanulya.

       L, A   XIX (39): Oct 20, 1910; L-2&3

3626   Basil Fecurko; Pittsburgh (south side), PA; Sep 20, 1910

       Commentary on the Rusyn-Ukrainian polemics among the parish-
       ioners of the south side parish.

       L   XIX (38): Oct 13, 1910; C-3, L-3

3627 [N.N.]; "Nasledkom skvernoho zaobchadzania uhro-ukrainco-ruteneckoho
      'petolizača,' verniki odlučil'i se od starej cerkvi" [As a
      result of the evil behavior of a Uhro-Ukrainian-Ruthenian 'boot-
      licker,' the faithful left the old church]

      Ukrainian-Rusyn polemics with the Whiting, IN parish.

      A   XIX (39): Oct 20, 1910; L-3

3628 [N.N.]; "Ne rozumjat-ly nas, yly ne chotjat rozumîty?" [Either they
      do not understand us or they do not want to understand us?]

      How the Slovaks and Roman Catholics in America view the polemic
      struggle within the American Greek Catholic Church.

      A   XIX (40): Oct 27, 1910; C-4, L-4

3629 Joseph Meravcik; Peekskill, NY; Nov 1, 1910

      "Narîkanija našoho naroda na uhro-rutenijansko-ukraynskych
      Vytčykiv-pjatolyzunov" [Complaints of our people against the
      Uhro-Ruthenian-Ukrainian clergy-bootlickers]

      Polemics among the parishioners of the Peekskill parish.

      L   XIX (43): Nov 17, 1910; C-2&3, L-2&3

3630 [N.N.]; Barnesboro, Pa; Nov 13, 1910

      "Pered uhro-rutenecko-ukraynskym 'Vitčikom' zamknena cerkov'"
      [The church is closed for a Uhro-Ruthenian-Ukrainian 'priest']

      The activities of Barnesboro's pastor, Rev. Kovalicky.

      L   XIX (43): Nov 17, 1910; C-3, L-3

3631 "Vel'ka Cerkovna Slavnosc" [Great Church Celebration]

      Dedication of the Cleveland, OH parish's altar and service
      implements on November 27, 1910.

      Ad   XIX (43): Nov 17, 1910; L-8

3632 John Holniak, et al.; Pittsburgh-Oakland, PA

      The activities of the Oakland parish.

      L   XIX (44): Nov 24, 1910; C-3, L-3

3633 [N.N.]; McKeesport, PA; Nov 22, 1910

      "Narîkanie naroda na uhro-rutenecko-ukraynskych pjatolyzunov"
      [Complaints of the people against the Uhro-Ruthenian-Ukrainian
      bootlickers]

      Polemics among the parishioners of the McKeesport parish.

      L   XIX (45): Dec 1, 1910; C-2&3, L-2&3

3634 John Šepa, et al.; Sugar Creek, MO; Oct 30, 1910

    The organization of a parish in the Sugar Creek vicinity.

    L   XIX (45): Dec 1, 1910; C-4, L-3

3635 [N.N.]; "Halycijskij Mytropolyt, hraf Šeptyckij y akcija amer. uhro-russkoho naroda" [Galician Metropolitan (Archbishop), Count Sheptytz'kyi and the action of the American Uhro-Rusyn people]

    Metropolitan of L'viv, the Most Rev. Sheptyts'kyi's visit to America and his opinions concerning the polemics among Greek Catholics in America.

    A   XIX (47): Dec 15, 1910; C-4&5, L-4&5

3636 Emil Sarady; Gary, IN; Dec 12, 1910

    "Orhanyzovanie novoj uhro-russkoj parafiy" [Organization of a new Uhro-Rusyn parish]

    Greek Catholic parish in Gary.

    L   XIX (48): Dec 22, 1910; C-2&3, L-3

3637 [N.N.]; "Rutenijansko-ukraynsko-pjatolyzunskaja bezočlyvost'" [Ruthenian-Ukrainian-bootlicker impudence]

    Actions of Bishop Ortynsky and his supporters.

    A   XIX (49): Dec 29, 1910; C-2&3, L-2&3

3638 [N.N.]; "Uhorskiy Rusynŷ ne chotjat bŷty Rutencamy" [Uhro-Rusyns do not want to be Ruthenians]

    Letter to the editor about the disagreement over terminology between Rev. Joseph Hanulya and his Allegheny, PA parishioners; ARV opinion on the terminology debate follows.

    L, A   XIX (50): Jan 5, 1911; C-4&5, L-4

3639 Rev. Paul Bihun; "O Vašoj Bor'bî (pys'mo yz staroho kraju)" [About Your Struggle (letter from the old country)]

    The religious-nationality conflict among Rusyns in America from the viewpoint of an outsider.

    L   XX (2): Jan 26, 1911; C-3, L-2&3

3640 Sam Trochonovsky, et al.; Conemaugh, PA; Jan 16, 1911

    "Ročnyj parafijal'nyj mytynh v Konema, Pa." [Annual parish meeting in Conemaugh, PA]

    L   XX (2): Jan 26, 1911; C-3, L-3

3641 [N.N.]; "Korotkij otvît na dopys' 'Katolyka' yz Rankyn, Pa. publykovanu v 1005 č. Ednotŷ" [Short reply to the letter of a
'Catholic' from Rankin, PA published in issue 1005 (January 25,
1911) of Jednota]

The Greek Catholic priest in Rankin, PA.

L   XX (3): Feb 2, 1911; C-2, L-2

3642 [N.N.]; Allegheny, PA; Jan 23, 1911

"Zaslato" [Letter to the Editor]

a. Report on the annual parish meeting of the Allegheny church.
b. Commentary on the activities of pastor Rev. Joseph Hanulya.

L   XX (3): Feb 2, 1911; C-2&3, L-2

3643 Rev. Julius Sztankav; Rokosov (Rakasy), Ugocsa County, Hungary;
Jan 14, 1911

"Otkrŷtoe pys'mo k Amerykanskym Brat'jam" [Open letter to
American Brethren]

Appeals to Rusyn-Americans to resolve their religious discord.

LE   XX (3): Feb 2, 1911; C-4, L-4

3644 Rev. Dr. Theodosius Vasochik; "Spravozdanie Cerkovnoj Radŷ hr. kat.
uhro-russkoj cerkvy Sošestvija Sv. Ducha v Pyttsburh-Ovklŷnd,
Pa. o fynansijnom položeniy cerkvy s h. 1910" [Report of the
church council of the Greek Catholic Uhro-Rusyn church of the
descent of the Holy Ghost in Pittsburgh-Oakland, PA, concerning
the financial situation of the church during 1910]

R   XX (4): Feb 9, 1911; C-5, L-5

3645 [N.N.]; Bridgeport, CT; Feb 9, 1911

"Stučka Ukraynsko-Ruteneckaja ne vŷdarylasja" [Ukrainian-
Ruthenian trick failed]

The visit of Rev. Elias Gojdics to the Bridgeport parish.

L   XX (5): Feb 16, 1911; C-5, L-2&3

3646 [N.N.]; Whiting, IN

The disaster which befell Whiting's Ukrainian Greek Catholic
church during services on March 5, 1911.

L   XX (8): Mar 9, 1911; C-3, L-2

3647 M.L. Belejcak, et al.; Braddock, PA; Mar 7, 1911

"Zaslato" [Letter to the Editor]

Tri-monthly financial report of the Braddock Greek Catholic
church.

L   XX (8): Mar 9, 1911; C-3, L-3

3648 [N.N.]; "Cerkovnŷy dîla uhro-russkoho naroda, eho akcija y Ep. Ortŷn'skij" [Church business of the Uhro-Rusyn people, its actions and Bishop Ortynsky]

Latest information concerning the Greek Catholic parishes in America and their struggle with Bishop Ortynsky and his supporters.

Parts I-IV: XX (8-12): Mar 9-Apr 6, 1911; C-4, L-4

3649 [N.N.]; "Bor'ba uhorskych rusynov protyv dekorovannoho ukraynsko-ruteneckoho lakaja v Mykysport, Pa." [Struggle of the Uhro-Rusyns against the decorated Ukrainian-Ruthenian lackey in McKeesport, PA]

The legal battle between Rev. Valentine Gorzo and the McKeesport parish over the church property.

A   XX (9): Mar 16, 1911; C-2&3, L-2&3

3650 [N.N.]; New Castle, PA

The financial requirement to become a parishioner of the New Castle Greek Catholic church.

L   XX (11): Mar 30, 1911; C-3, L-3

3651 S.D. Mosurak, et al.; "Členam hreko katolyčeskoj cerkvy sv. Ducha" [To the members of the Greek Catholic Church of the Holy Ghost]

Adoption of by-laws incorporating the Pittsburgh, PA parish takes place at a church meeting on April 12, 1911.

A   XX (11): Mar 30, 1911; C-3, L-3

3652 G.Z. Barany; Cleveland, OH; Mar 15, 1911

"Zaslato" [Letter to the Editor]

The friendship between Cleveland pastor, Rev. Emil Burik and Bishop Ortynsky.

L   XX (13): Apr 13, 1911; C-2&3, L-3

3653 Michael Czibulya, et al.; Youngstown, OH; Apr 1, 1911

"Zaslato" [Letter to the Editor]

Letter from the Youngstown parish to a Cleveland Roman Catholic Slovak priest informing him of the issues behind the struggle within the American Greek Catholic Church.

L   XX (15): May 4, 1911; C-2&3, L-2

3654   Rev. A. Medvecky; Youngstown, OH; Apr 5, 1911

       "Zaslato" [Letter to the Editor]

       Letter to Youngstown Roman Catholic Slovak priest, Rev. Zlamal, informing him of the situation of the Greek Catholic Church.

       L   XX (15): May 4, 1911; C-3, L-2

3655   Theodore Czudjak, et al.; New Britain, CT; Apr 16, 1911

       "Zaslato" [Letter to the Editor]

       The activities of Rev. Chornyak.

       L   XX (15): May 4, 1911; C-4, L-2&3

3656   [N.N.]; Pittsburgh, PA (north side); May 24, 1911

       The court injunction against the parish meeting of the north side church, obtained by Gregory I. Zsatkovich on behalf of parishioners excluded from the meeting by pastor Rev. Joseph Hanulya.

       L   XX (18): May 25, 1911; C-2, L-2

3657   Joseph Slovensky; Brookside, AL

       The celebration of the Divine Liturgy in Brookside by Rev. M. Jackovics (Scranton, PA) on May 3, 1911.

       L   XX (18): May 25, 1911; C-2, L-2

3658   Peter Sekerak; Rock Springs, WY

       The celebration of the Divine Liturgy in Rock Springs by Rev. M. Jackovics (Scranton, PA) on May 10, 1911.

       L   XX (20): Jun 7, 1911; C-2, L-2

3659   [N.N.]; "Publyčnŷj protest duchovnykov protyv machynacij fyrmŷ Hanulja and Ko. Otkrŷtoe pys'mo k redaktomu _Rusyna_ y eho druham" [Public protest of the clergy against the machinations of the firm Hanulya and Co. Open letter to the editor of _Rusin_ and his friends]

       Letter is sponsored by sixteen priests of the Prešov Eparchy coalition.

       L   XX (21): Jun 15, 1911; C-1&2, L-2

3660   J. Hrabar; New Britain, CT

       Requests Rev. J. Hanulya to explain the differences over policy between the Holy See and the American Roman Catholic hierarchy concerning the American Greek Catholic Church.

       L   XX (21): Jun 15, 1911; C-5, L-2

3661 Rev. Cyril Constantine Gulovich; "Otkrŷtoe pys'mo do ukraynskoho
vîtčyka Hanuly v Alleheny, Pa., Ameryka. Sebezaščyta yz
staroho kraju. Bardiov (Šaryš-Uhorščyna) 29-ho maja 1911"
[Open letter to Ukrainian priest (Rev. J.) Hanulya in
Allegheny, PA, America. Self-defense from the old country,
Bardejov (Bártfa), Šaroš County, Hungary, May 29, 1911]

Letter from a former pastor of the Barnesboro, PA parish
condemning the activities of Rev. Hanulya.

LE   XX (23): Jul 6, 1911; C-1&2, L-1&2

3662 John Ihnat; Perth Amboy, NJ

The May 30, 1911 dedication of the Perth Amboy Greek Catholic
church's icon.

L   XX (24): Jul 13, 1911; C-2&3, L-2

3663 Michael Kovaly, et al.; Glen Lyon, PA

The June 5, 1911 dedication of the Glen Lyon Greek Catholic
cemetery and cross.

L   XX (24): Jul 13, 1911; C-3, L-2&3

3664 Rev. John Korotnoky; "Otvît redakciy Rusyna a osobenno sočynytelju
statiy 'Otvît 16 protestantam' O. Hanulî" [Answer to the
editor of Rusin and especially to the author of the article
'Answer to the 16 protesters' of Rev. Hanulya]

See: 3659

L   XX (25): Jul 20, 1911; C-2, L-2

3665 John Oleksa, et al.; Gary, IN; Jul 15, 1911

"Zaslato" [Letter to the Editor]

The purchase of land for the Gary Greek Catholic Church.

L   XX (25): Jul 29, 1911; C-2&3, L-3

3666 Julius Bakajsa; Duquesne, PA; Jul 11, 1911

"Odna krasna Uhro-Russkaja pobîda" [A beautiful Uhro-Rusyn
victory]

The efforts of Duquesne Rusyns to replace the church taken
from them by supporters of Bishop Ortynsky.

L   XX (25): Jul 20, 1911; C-4, L-2&3

3667 "Cerkovnoe Toržestvo" [Church Celebration]

Dedication of the Donora, PA Greek Catholic Church's corner
stone of September 4, 1911.

Ad   XX (27): Aug 3, 1911; C-8, L-8

3668 John Bučko, et al.; "Vsîm hreko katolykam na okolycî Jun'ŷntavn, Pa., vo važnoe vnymanie" [Attention all Greek Catholics in the vicinity of Uniontown, PA]

A meeting is slated for August 27, 1911 in Uniontown to discuss the organization of a parish.

Ad   XX (29): Aug 17, 1911; C-8, L-7

3669 Michael Hriczo, et al.; Duquesne, PA; Jul 20, 1911

"Zaslato" [Letter to the Editor]

The activities of the Duquesne parish under the pastorship of Rev. John Hrabar.

L   XX (30): Aug 24, 1911; C-2&3, L-2&3

3670 "Cerkovnoe Toržestvo" [Church Celebration]

Dedication of the Akron, OH Greek Catholic Church on September 4, 1911.

Ad   XX (30): Aug 24, 1911; C-5, L-3

3671 Rev. Cyril Constantine Gulovich; "Zaščyta česty yz staroho kraju. Vtoroe Otkrŷtoe Pys'mo ruteniano-ukraynskomu Vitčiku Hanulî v Alleheny, Pa. Ameryka" [Defense of honor from the old country. Second open letter to Ruthenian-Ukrainian priest, (Rev. J.) Hanulya in Allegheny, PA America]

Letter from Bardejov [Bártfa], Sáros County, Hungary.

Parts I-II: XX (31-32): Aug 31-Sep 7, 1911; C-4, L-4
LE

3672 [N.N.]; Allegheny, PA; Aug 14, 1911

"Ukraynsko-rutenijanskoe preslîdovanie" [Ukrainian-Ruthenian persecution]

The activities of Rev. Joseph Hanulya in Allegheny.

L   XX (32): Sep 7, 1911; C-2&3, L-2

3673 [N.N.]; McKeesport, PA; Aug 15, 1911

"Napast' Ort. Ukraynskaja" [Ortynsky Ukrainian assault]

The Ukrainian-Rusyn polemics among parishioners of the McKeesport parish.

L   XX (32): Sep 7, 1911; C-4&5, L-4&5

3674 [N.N.]; "Odnoe krasnoe cerkovnoe toržestvo" [A beautiful church celebration]

The September 4, 1911 dedication of the Donora, PA Greek Catholic Church's corner stone.

A   XX (34): Sep 21, 1911; C-2&3, L-2&3

3675 "Cerkovnoe Toržestvo" [Church Celebration]

Rev. A. Dzubay dedicates Leisenring's Greek Catholic Cemetery and cross on October 1, 1911.

Ad   XX (34): Sep 21, 1911; C-5, L-8

3676 [N.N.]; Newark, NJ

A Rusyn immigrant's account of trying to find the "correct" Greek Catholic Church in Newark to attend Sunday services.

L   XX (35): Sep 28, 1911; C-3, L-2&3

3677 "Cerkovnoe Toržestvo" [Church Celebration]

Date of the dedication of Leisenring's Greek Catholic Cemetery has been changed to October 29, 1911. See: 3675

Ad   XX (35): Sep 28, 1911; C-3, L-6

3678 [N.N.]; Podkopnaja akcija Ort. ukraynsko-ruteneckoj fyrmŷ 'Horzov-Hanulja Ko.'" [Undermining action of the Ortynsky Ukrainian-Ruthenian firm 'Gorzo-Hanulya Co.']

A   XX (35): Sep 28, 1911; C-4, L-4

3679 P. Ju. Ž.; "Slavenie Epyskopa Mukačevskoj Eparchiy, Julija Fyrčak" [In honor to Bishop of the Mukačevo Eparchy, Julius Firczak]

Editorial on the occasion of Bishop Firczak's fiftieth anniversary of his ordination.

E, P   XX (36): Oct 5, 1911; C-4, L-4

3680 Rev. John Szabo, et al.; Pittsburgh, PA

"Zaslato. Otvertŷj lyst' k blahočestyvŷm uhro-russkym hreko kat. vîrnykam v Rankyn, Pa." [To the editor. Open letter to the devout Uhro-Rusyn Greek Catholic faithful in Rankin, PA]

Requests Rankin parishioners to censure their pastor, Rev. John Parscouta, for alleged pro-Bishop Ortynsky activity.

L   XX (36): Oct 5, 1911; C-5, L-5

3681 Rev. Michael Szabados, et al.; Vojčice [Vécse], Zemplén County, Hungary; Aug 18, 1911

"Publyčnoe blahodarenie" [Public thanks]

Thanks Rusyn-Americans for donations received to help Vojčice residents rebuild their village church destroyed by fire.

LE   XX (37): Oct 12, 1911; C-3, L-3

3682 Joseph Fecko; Gary, IN

Progress report on the construction of the Gary Greek Catholic Church.

L   XX (37): Oct 12, 1911; C-3, L-3

3683 "Posvjaščenie zvona" [Dedication of a bell]

    Dedication of the Allentown, PA Greek Catholic Church's bell on November 12, 1911.

    Ad   XX (39): Oct 26, 1911; C-8, L-3

3684 [N.N.]; "Krutarstvo y slîplenie a nyč ynoho" [Confusion and blind-folding and nothing else]

    Commentary on an article [reprinted] about Bishop Ortynsky in Svoboda, #42.

    Part I: XX (40): Nov 2, 1911; C-4&5, L-4

    Part II: XX (42): Nov 16, 1911; C-4, L-4

    A

3685 "Zaprošenie" [An Invitation]

    Rev. John Danilovich dedicates the South Sharon, PA Greek Catholic Church's altar and icons on November 30, 1911.

    Ad   XX (40): Nov 2, 1911; C-8, L-7

3686 John Uram, et al.; McKees Rocks, PA; Oct 30, 1911

    "Zaslato. Ot uhro-russkoj parafiy Soš. sv. Ducha v Mykysraks, Pa." [Letter to the Editor. From the Uhro-Rusyn parish of the Descent of the Holy Ghost in McKees Rocks, PA]

    Refutes the allegation in Rusin, #40, that the McKees Rocks parish requested Bishop Ortynsky to appoint a new pastor for the parish.

    L   XX (41): Nov 9, 1911; C-2, L-2

3687 Alex Koscelnik, et al.; Charleroi, PA; Nov 4, 1911

    "Zaslato. Ot uhro-russkoj hreko kat. parafiy v Čarleroj, Pa." [Letter to the Editor. From the Uhro-Rusyn Greek Catholic parish in Charleroi, PA]

    Dispells rumors that a number of parishioners, dissatisfied with parish policy and administration, are planning to organize another parish.

    L   XX (41): Nov 9, 1911; C-2&3, L-2

3688 "Posvjaščenie" [A Dedidation]

    Dedication of the Mont Clare, PA Greek Catholic Church on November 19, 1911.

    Ad   XX (41): Nov 9, 1911; C-5, L-5

3689 Julius Bakajsa

"Zaslato. Ešče y slovenskiy plebanŷ vspomohajut Ort. ukr. ruteneckuju polytyku y preslîdujut zakonnuju akciju uhrorusskoho naroda" [Letter to the Editor. Slovak priests also aid Ortynsky Ukrainian Ruthenian politics and persecute the legitimate activities of the Uhro-Rusyn people]

L   XX (43): Nov 23, 1911; C-2&3, L-2

3690 John Maczko; Dunbar, PA; Nov 6, 1911

"Odnoe krasnoe cerkovnoe toržestvo" [A beautiful church celebration]

The October 29, 1911 dedication of the Leisenring, PA Greek Catholic Cemetery.

L   XX (43): Nov 23, 1911; C-3, L-2&3

3691 John Matyuk; Dunmore, PA; Dec 1, 1911

"Odnoe krasnoe cerkovnoe toržestvo" [A beautiful church celebration]

The November 30, 1911 dedication of the Dunmore Greek Catholic Church.

L   XX (45): Dec 7, 1911; C-2&3, L-2

3692 [N.N.]; "Krasnoe cerkovnoe toržestvo" [A beautiful church celebration]

The November 30, 1911 dedication of the South Sharon, PA Greek Catholic Church.

A   XX (46): Dec 14, 1911; C-2&3, L-2

3693 "Do vsîch hreko kat. rusynov na okolycî mononhahela syty, Pa." [To all Greek Catholic Rusyns in the vicinity of Monongahela, PA]

Dedication of the Monongahela Greek Catholic Chapel on December 24, 1911.

Ad   XX (46): Dec 14, 1911; C-3, L-7

3694 "Cerkovnoe Oznajmlenie" [Church Notice]

Dedication of the Gary, IN Greek Catholic Church on December 24, 1911.

Ad   XX (46): Dec 14, 1911; C-8, L-8

3695 [N.N.]; Sačurov [Szacsúr], Zemplén County, Hungary

The dedication of two bells for the Sačurov Greek Catholic Church on November 5, 1911.

LE   XX (48): Dec 28, 1911; C-2, L-2

3696   Theodore Glagola; Monongahela, PA

The December 24, 1911 dedication of the Monongahela Greek
Catholic Chapel.

L   XX (48): Dec 28, 1911; C-3, L-2

3697   "Cerkovnoe Toržestvo Hreko Kat. Russkoj Cerkvy Sv. Archystr.
Mychayla, Donora, Pa." [Church Celebration of the Greek
Catholic Rusyn Church of St. Michael the Archangel, Donora, PA]

Dedication of the church's bells on January 14, 1912.

Ad   XX (48): Dec 28, 1911; C-5, L-7

3698   [N.N.]; Shenandoah, PA; Jan 15, 1912

"Užasnoe bezpravie a ešče horšaja brutal'nost' Ep. Ortŷn'skoho"
[Terrible injustices and still worse brutality of Bishop
Ortynsky]

Polemics between the Shenandoah parish and Bishop Ortynsky and
his supporters.

L   XXI (1): Jan 18, 1912; C-3, L-3

3699   Joseph Fecko; Gary, IN; Jan 2, 1912

"Dvojnoe toržestvo" [Double celebration]

The December 24, 1911 dedication of the Gary Greek Catholic
Church.

L   XXI (1): Jan 18, 1912; C-3, L-2&3

3700   John Sandor, et al.; Conemaugh, PA; Jan 16, 1912

"Zaslato. Ot hreko kat. russkoj cerkovnoj radŷ v Konema, Pa."
[Letter to the Editor. From the Greek Catholic Rusyn Church
in Conemaugh, PA]

Reply to Revs. Hanulya and Gorzo, editors of Rusin, regarding
their opinions about the Conemaugh parish.

L   XXI (2): Jan 25, 1912; C-2, L-2

3701   Rev. Dr. Theo. M. Vasochik, et al.; "Rachunky y fynancijnoe položenie Uhro-Russkoj Hr. Kat. Cerkvy v Ovklŷnd-Pyttsbŷrh, Pa.
s h. 1911" [Accounts and financial situation of the Uhro-
Rusyn Greek Catholic Church in Oakland-Pittsburgh, PA for the
year 1911]

R   XXI (2): Jan 25, 1912; C-2&3, L-2&3

3702   [N.N.]; "Robota neprijatelej v polnom tečeniy" [Work of an enemy
in full swing]

The struggle between dissident clergy, Bishop Ortynsky and
the G.C.U.

A   XXI (2): Jan 25, 1912; C-4, L-4

3703 [N.N.]; "Pravda konečno pobîdyt!" [Truth will finally triumph!]

Concerning a rumor from Europe that Bishop Ortynsky will be transferred to Canada and a new bishop for the Uhro-Rusyns will be appointed soon.

A   XXI (7): Feb 29, 1912; C-1, L-1

3704 Michael Hriczo, et al.; Duquesne, PA; Jan 28, 1912

"Zaslato" [Letter to the Editor]

The polemics between supporters and non-supporters of Bishop Ortynsky.

L   XXI (7): Feb 29, 1912; C-2&3, L-2

3705 [N.N.]; "Krutar'stva y tî najskvernîjšiy pokušenija v dilî sochra-nenija ep. Ortŷn'skoho y eho hardŷ načalysja" [Falsehoods and the foul attempts in the matter of preserving Bishop Ortynsky and his entourage have begun]

The alleged transfer of Bishop Ortynsky to another country.

A   XXI (8): Mar 7, 1912; C-1, L-1

3706 John Karaffa; Trenton, NJ; Feb 27, 1912

"Obnovlennŷj attentat Ep. Ortŷn'skoho protyv našych parafij v štatî N'ju Džŷrsy" [Renewed attempt of Bishop Ortynsky against our parishes in the state of New Jersey]

Bishop Ortynsky's actions to obtain the deeds to Greek Catholic churches in NJ.

L   XXI (8): Mar 7, 1912; C-4, L-2

3707 [N.N.]; "O 'myssiy' kanonyka O. Barŷša kotorŷj prijšol v soedynenŷy štatŷ 'ratovaty' Ortŷnskoho y eho hardu" [On the 'mission' of Rev. Baryš, Canon who came to the U.S. to 'rescue' Bishop Ortynsky and his entourage]

Explanation of Rev. Baryš' mission to assess the situation of the American Greek Catholic Church.

A   XXI (9): Mar 14, 1912; C-1, L-1

3708 Rev. Joseph Papp; Nové Davidkovo (Újdávidháza), Bereg County, Hungary; Feb 15, 1912

Requests financial aid from American Greek Catholics to help rebuild the village church.

LE   XXI (9): Mar 14, 1912; C-3, L-3

3709 Rev. Eugene Homichko, et al.; "Rachunky y fynansijal'nŷj report hr. kat. uhro-russkoj cerkvy Sv. app. Petra y Pavla v Dukejn, Pa., s hoda 1911" [Accounts and financial report of the Greek Catholic Uhro-Rusyn Church of the Holy Apostles Peter and Paul in Duquesne, PA for the year 1911]

R   XXI (9): Mar 14, 1912; C-6, L-3

3710 [N.N.]; "Velykaja neudača, velykij fijasko, no ešče bol'šaja bezoč1yvost' Ort. ukr. ruteneckoj bandŷ" [Great failure, great fiasco, but still great impudence of the Ortynsky Ukrainian-Ruthenian band]

Issues behind the visit of Rev. Baryš, Canon from the Galician L'viv Diocese, to the U.S.

A   XXI (10): Mar 21, 1912; C-1, L-1

3711 [N.N.]; "Naš' narod est' ves'ma terpîlyvŷj, no y eho terpîlyvosty est' konec" [Our people are very patient, but their patience does have an end]

Some parishioners of the McKeesport, PA parish are trying to establish a new parish due to the polemics caused by Rev. V. Gorzo and supporters of Bishop Ortynsky.

A   XXI (10): Mar 21, 1912; C-2&3, L-2

3712 [N.N.]; Glassport, PA; Mar 25, 1912

"Nova uhro-russkaja hreko kat. parafija" [New Uhro-Rusyn Greek Catholic parish]

The organization of a parish in Glassport.

L   XXI (11): Mar 28, 1912; C-2, L-2

3713 "Posvjaščenie zvona" [Dedication of a bell]

Dedication of the Minersville Greek Catholic Church's bell on April 8, 1912.

Ad   XXI (12): Apr 4, 1912; C-3

3714 Theodore Glagola; Elizabeth, PA; Mar 20, 1912

"Otvît O. Nestoru Dmytrovu" [Reply to Rev. Nestor Dmytrov]

Commentary on an article by Rev. Dmytrov in Rusin, #12, concerning intra-parish strife among members of the Glassport, PA parish.

L   XXI (13): Apr 18, 1912; C-2&3

3715 [N.N.]; Dixonville, PA

The polemics among the parishioners of the Clymer, PA parish.

L   XXI (13): Apr 18, 1912; C-3

3716 John Ondish; Broderick, PA; Apr 4, 1912

"Otvît Mykysportskomu Rusynovy lučše Rutencovy kotorŷj chvalyt v 'Bratstvî' Ort. ukr. rutenskoho dzekana sovîtnyka y kanonyka Valentija Horzov" [Reply to the McKeesport, PA Rusyn better yet, Ruthenian, who praises in the 'Brotherhood' the Ortynsky Ukrainian-Ruthenian deacon, advisor and canon Rev. Valentine Gorzo]

L   XXI (14): Apr 25, 1912; C-3, L-2&3

3717 [N.N.]; "Narod naš' ymîet bŷty ves'ma ostorožnŷm vzljadom duchovnykov" [Our people should be on the lookout for priests]

Warns Rusyns to be careful of priests who support Bishop
Ortynsky.

A   XXI (15): May 2, 1912; C-2, L-2

3718 Jacob Kovalčik; Barton, OH

The efforts of Barton's Rusyn community to organize a parish.

L   XXI (15): May 2, 1912; C-2&3, L-2

3719 "Cerkovnoe Toržestvo" [Church Celebration]

a. Dedication of the Gary, IN Greek Catholic Church on May 30,
   1912.
b. Dedication of the Gary parish's bell on May 12, 1912.

Ad   XXI (15): May 2, 1912; C-5, L-3

3720 John Uhrin, et al.; "Narod ymîet opjat dokazaty svoju volju"
[People should again show their will]

Reports that Bishop Ortynsky's supporters are trying to prevent
his recall to Galicia. A strategy meeting is planned, to discuss Bishop Ortynsky's recall, for May 28, 1912 in Braddock, PA.

A   XXI (16): May 9, 1912; C-1, L-1

3721 "Cerkovnoe Toržestvo" [Church Celebration]

a. Dedication of the Uniontown, PA Greek Catholic Church's bell
   on July 4, 1912.
b. Dedication of the Rillton, PA Greek Catholic Church's corner
   stone on May 19, 1912.

Ad   XXI (16): May 9, 1912; C-5&8, L-7&8

3722 John Uhrin; "Sobranie našych parafij v Braddokî, Pa." [Meeting of
our parishes in Braddock, PA]

Topics on the agenda of the May 28, 1912 meeting in Braddock, PA.

A   XXI (17): May 16, 1912; C-4, L-4

3723 "Cerkovnoe Toržestvo" [Church Celebration]

Dedication of the Perth Amboy, NJ Greek Catholic Cemetery's
cross on May 30, 1912.

Ad   XXI (17): May 16, 1912; C-5, L-8

3724 [N.N.]; "Nykto naj ne dyvytsja tomu, čto ešče y do dnes' ne ymîeme
svoeho uhro-russkoho epyskopa" [Let no one be surprised by the
fact that to this very day we still do not have our own Uhro-
Rusyn bishop]

Obstacles to the appointment of a Uhro-Rusyn bishop for America.

A   XXI (18): May 23, 1912; C-1, L-1

3725   John Uhrin, et al.; "Ot urjadu ěksekutyvnoho komyteta akciy uhro-russkoho naroda" [From the officers of the executive committee of the action of the Uhro-Rusyn people]

The registration of parish delegates participating in the Braddock, PA parish congress on May 28, 1912.

O   XXI (18): May 23, 1912; C-4, L-4

3726   [N.N.]; "Sobranie našych parafij yz blyžajšych v otdalennîjšych okolyc Pyttsbŷrha, Pa. y Braddok, Pa." [Meeting of our parishes from near and outlying regions of Pittsburgh and Braddock, PA]

Meeting held May 28, 1912.

A   XXI (19): May 30, 1912; C-4, L-4

3727   Joseph Fecko; Gary, IN

The dedication of the Gary Greek Catholic Church.

L   XXI (20): Jun 13, 1912; C-2, L-2

3728   [N.N.]; Harazdovanie vitčikov vspomohajuščych polytyku Ep. Ortŷn'skoho" [Prosperity of priests who aid the politics of Bishop Ortynsky]

The trouble among Clairton, PA parishioners allegedly caused by Rev. Irenaeus Matyacko.

A   XXI (21): Jun 20, 1912; C-2, L-2

3729   Michael Andraš; Millville, NJ; Jun 12, 1912

"Vsîm rusynam v myllvyll, N. Dž. y na okolycî, v važnoe vnymanie" [Attention all Rusyns in Millville, NJ and vicinity]

The efforts by the Millville Rusyn community to build a church and parish school.

L   XXI (21): Jun 20, 1912; C-2&3, L-2

3730   "Bratskoe y cerkovnoe toržestvo" [Lodge and church celebration]

Rev. A. Dzubay dedicates the Leisenring, PA Greek Catholic Church's pulpit on July 4, 1912.

Ad   XXI (22): Jun 27, 1912; C-3, L-3

3731   "Cerkovnoe Toržestvo" [Church Celebration]

Dedication of the Rillton, PA Greek Catholic Church's corner stone on July 4, 1912.

Ad   XXI (22): Jun 27, 1912; C-8, L-8

3732 Paul Ju. Zsatkovich; "Nîskol'ko važných slov kasatel'no akciy uhro-
russkoho naroda v cîly oderžanija svoeho-uhro-russkoho epyskopa
y kasatel'no machynacij Ort. rutenskoj bandŷ" [Several important words concerning the action of the Uhro-Rusyn people in
the matter of obtaining their own Uhro-Rusyn bishop and the
machinations of the Ortynsky Ruthenian gang]

E   XXI (23): Jul 4, 1912; C-4, L-4

3733 [N.N.]; "Odnoe krasnoe cerkovnoe toržestvo" [A beautiful church
celebration]

The July 4, 1912 dedication of the Uniontown, PA Greek Catholic
Church's bell.

A   XXI (25): Jul 18, 1912; C-2&3, L-2&3

3734 Rev. Emil Burik; Bradenville, PA; Jul 15, 1912

"Otvertŷj lyst" [Open letter]

Addressed to Rev. Joseph Hanulya concerning an article published
in Rusin about the American Greek Catholic Church.

L   XXI (25): Jul 18, 1912; C-4, L-4

3735 Rev. Dr. Theodosius Vasochik, et al.; "Ot hr. kat. uhro-russkoj
cerkvy Soš. Sv. Ducha v Pyttsbŷrh-Ovklŷnd, Pa." [From the
Greek Catholic Uhro-Rusyn Church of the Holy Ghost in
Pittsburgh-Oakland, PA]

March-June, 1912 parish financial report.

R   XXI (27): Aug 1, 1912; C-3, L-3

3736 Rev. Joseph Papp; Nové Davidkoho (Újdávidháza), Bereg County, Hungary;
Jul 2, 1912

Report on receipt of financial aid sent by American Greek Catholics to help rebuild the village church.

LE   XXI (27): Aug 1, 1912; C-3, L-3

3737 John Uhrin, et al.; "Sobranie našych parafij v Vylkes Berry, Pa. y
v Pŷrt Amboj, N. Dž." [Meeting of our parishes in Wilkes Barre,
PA and in Perth Amboy, NJ]

The means to secure Bishop Ortynsky's transfer from America will
be discussed at the August 15-17, 1912 meetings.

A   XXI (27): Aug 1, 1912; C-4, L-4

3738 John Uhrin, et al.; "Ot urjada Eksekutyvnoho komyteta akciy uhro-
russkoho naroda" [From the officers of the Executive Committee
of the action of the Uhro-Rusyn people]

Concerning the meetings in Wilkes Barre, PA and Perth Amboy, NJ.

O   XXI (28): Aug 8, 1912; C-4, L-4

3739   "Slavnosta pošvecanka v Cleveland, O." [Solemn dedication in
Cleveland, OH]

Dedication of the South Brooklyn, OH Greek Catholic Cemetery
and cross on August 11, 1912.

Ad   XXI (28): Aug 8, 1912; L-8

3740   P. Ju. Ž.; "Pročto treba nam svoeho uhro-russkoho epyskopa?"
[Why do we need our own Uhro-Rusyn bishop?]

E   XXI (29): Aug 15, 1912; C-4, L-4

3741   [N.N.]; "Mad'jarsko-staro-hrečeskoe katolyčeskoe epyskopstvo v
Uhorščyni" [Magyar-old-Greek Catholic Bishopric in Hungary]

Creation of an all Magyar Greek Catholic Eparchy in Hungary
by Papal decree on July 8, 1912.

A   XXI (29): Aug 15, 1912; C-5, L-4&5

3742   "Zaprošenie na cerkovnoe toržestvo" [Invitation to a church cele-
bration]

Dedication of the Peekskill, NY Greek Catholic Church on
September 2, 1912.

Ad   XXI (30): Aug 22, 1912; C-3

3743   Michael Timcso, et al.; Sagamore, PA; Aug 15, 1912

"Zaslato" [Letter to the Editor]

Reply to a letter to the editor in Rusin, #29, concerning the
Sagamore parish.

L   XXI (30): Aug 22, 1912; C-3, L-2

3744   Paul Ju. Zsatkovich; "Sobranija našych parafij v Vylks Berry, Pa.
y Pyrt Amboj, N. Dz." [Meeting of our parishes in Wilkes
Barre, PA and Perth Amboy, NJ]

Resolutions of the August 15-17, 1912 meetings.

E   XXI (30): Aug 22, 1912; C-4, L-4

3745   [N.N.]; Allegheny, PA

The friction between Rev. Joseph Hanulya and the parishioners
of the Allegheny parish.

L   XXI (31): Aug 29, 1912; C-3, L-3

3746   P. Ju. Ž.; "Den' 27-ho avhusta 1907" [Day of August 27, 1907]

The fifth anniversary of Bishop Ortynsky's arrival in America.

E   XX (31): Aug 29, 1912; C-4, L-4

3747   Rev. Anthony Mhley; Punxsutawney, PA; Sep 2, 1912

"Zaslato. Otpovîd' na dopys' 'Krutarstvo Tychoho Otca,' v
hazetî Rutenijan, y na otpovîd na stat'ju 'Novyy Cerkvy-Farŷ'
v hazetî Bratstvo" [Letter to the Editor. Rebuttal to the
correspondence 'Falsehood of the Quiet Father' in the newspaper, Rusin, and to the rebuttal to the article 'New Parish-
Churches' in the newspaper Bratstvo]

L   XXI (32): Sep 5, 1912; C-2&3, L-2

3748   P. Ju. Ž.; "Ep. Ortyn'skyj, eho polytyka y Uhro-russkij narod"
[Bishop Ortynsky, his politics and the Uhro-Rusyn people]

E   XXI (32): Sep 5, 1912; C-4, L-4

3749   [N.N.]; "Čudesnaja, no y soblaznytel'naja propovîd' ukraynskoho
epyskopa" [Marvelous, but seductive sermon by the Ukrainian
bishop]

Letter to the editor commenting on a sermon delivered by
Bishop Ortynsky on September 2, 1912.

L   XXI (33): Sep 12, 1912; C-4, L-2

3750   [N.N.]; Allegheny, PA; Sep 16, 1912

"Otpovîd'redaktoru rutenijana na toe čto nababral v 34-om
seročnom numerî rutenijana" [Rebuttal to the editor of Rusin
to what he scribbled in issue 34 of this year's Rusin]

The movement on part of some Allegheny, PA parishioners to
begin a new parish.

L   XXI (34): Sep 19, 1912; C-3, L-2

3751   Rev. Nicholas Burik; Pleasant City, OH; Sep 16, 1912

"Otpovîd' O. Iosyfu Hanulja, redaktoru rutenijana" [Rebuttal
to Rev. Joseph Hanulya, editor of Rusin]

The activities of Rev. Hanulya.

L   XXI (35): Sep 26, 1912; C-2, L-2

3752   [N.N.]; "Novaja uhro-russkaja hreko kat. cerkov'" [New Uhro-Rusyn
Greek Catholic Church]

Commentary on the events leading the formation of another
Allegheny, PA Greek Catholic church.

A   XXI (36): Oct 3, 1912; C-3, L-2&3

3753   Rev. Dr. Theo. Vasochik, et al.; "Dochodŷ y Vŷdatky hreko kat. uhro-
russkoj cerkvy v Pyttsbŷrh-Ovklŷnd, Pa. ot 30-ho junija do 28-ho
sentjabrja 1912" [Revenues and expenses of the Greek Catholic
Uhro-Rusyn Church in Pittsburgh-Oakland, PA from June 30 to September 28, 1912]

R   XXI (36): Oct 3, 1912; C-3, L-8

3754 "Toržestvennoe posvjaščenie" [Solemn dedication]

Dedication of the Wilkes Barre, PA Greek Catholic Church's bell on October 29, 1912.

Ad   XXI (36): Oct 3, 1912; C-8, L-7

3755 P. Ju. Ž.; "Ort.-ukraynskaja partija vŷrukovala s otvorennŷmy kartamy" [Ortynsky-Ukrainian party openly shows its hand]

Commentary on an article about the nationality issue and the Greek Catholic Church in Duspastyr, #34.

E   XXI (37): Oct 10, 1912; C-1, L-1

3756 "Cerkovnoe Toržestvo" [Church Celebration]

Dedication of the Uniontown, PA Greek Catholic Cemetery and cross on October 20, 1912.

Ad   XXI (37): Oct 10, 1912; L-7

3757 John E. Sekerak; Cleveland, OH

The dedication of the Cleveland Greek Catholic Cemetery.

L   XXI (38): Oct 17, 1912; C-2&3, L-3

3758 Rev. Nicholas Molchany; "Ot hreko kat. parafiy Pokrova Presv. Dîvŷ Mariy v Kynhstŷn, Pa." [From the Greek Catholic parish of St. Mary's Protection in Kingston, PA]

The October 29, 1912 celebration of the Kingston parish's twentieth anniversary.

A   XXI (38): Oct 17, 1912; C-3, L-3

3759 Rev. Alexander Dzubay; "20-lîtnoe jubylejnoe toržestvo" [20-year anniversary celebration]

The November 13, 1912 celebration of the Leisenring, PA Greek Catholic Church's twentieth anniversary.

A   XXI (39): Oct 24, 1912; C-3, L-7

3760 "Toržestvo posvjaščenie zvona novovŷbudovannoj hr. kat. cerkvy v Ryllton, Pa." [Solemn dedication of the bell of the newly constructed Greek Catholic Church in Rillton, PA]

Dedication on November 23, 1912.

Ad   XXI (40): Oct 31, 1912; C-3, L-8

3761 [N.N.]; "Lykuet 'Schyzma'" ['Schism' rejoices]

The conversion of Philadelphia, PA Holy Ghost Church to Orthodoxy.

A   XXI (40): Oct 31, 1912; C-5, L-4

3762 [N.N.]; "Najnovijšiy vîsty, kotorŷy ves'ma sblyžij kasajutsja akciy uhro-russkoho naroda" [Latest news, which greatly concerns the actions of the Uhro-Rusyn people]

The rumor that Bishop Ortynsky is going to Rome to discuss the situation of the American Greek Catholic Church.

A   XXI (42): Nov 14, 1912; C-2, L-2

3763 [N.N.]; Kingston, PA

The October, 1912 twenty-fifth anniversary celebration of the Kingston parish.

L   XXI (42): Nov 14, 1912; C-3, L-3

3764 "Toržestvennoe posvjaščenie cerkvy v Braddok, Pa." [Solemn dedication of a church in Braddock, PA]

Dedication on November 17, 1912.

Ad   XXI (42): Nov 14, 1912; C-8, L-3

3765 Rev. M. Balog; "De ščo Ruthenian-u na 'neoplatitsja'" [Something to Rusin, so that 'it will not pay off']

Rev. J. Hanulya's rejection of some of his parishioners because they are anti-Ortynsky.

A   XXI (43): Nov 21, 1912; C-3, L-5

3766 "Ot novoj uhro-russkoj hreko kat. parafiy v Yri, Pa." [From the new Uhro-Rusyn Greek Catholic Parish in Erie, PA]

Dedication of the Erie Church on November 28, 1912.

Ad   XXI (43): Nov 21, 1912; C-5, L-3

3767 "Velykoe toržestvo y bal" [Magnificent celebration and ball]

Yonkers, NY Greek Catholic Church celebrates its twentieth anniversary on November 28, 1912.

Ad   XXI (43): Nov 21, 1912; C-6, L-3

3768 [N.N.]; "Krasnŷy ovoščy usylovnosty odnoj uhro-russkoj koloniy" [Beautiful fruits of labor of one Uhro-Rusyn colony]

The Braddock, PA Greek Catholic Church.

A   XXI (44): Nov 28, 1912; C 2, L 5

3769 John Samsin; Phoenixville, PA

The November 3, 1912 dedication of the Phoenixville Greek Catholic Church's bell towers and altar.

L   XXI (44): Nov 28, 1912; C-3, L-2

3770   P. Ju. Ž.; "Voznahraždenie sluh" [Rewarding of servants]

The appointment of Rev. Nicholas Chopey (Wilkes Barre, PA) as consistorial advisor to the Bishop of Mukačevo.

E, P   XXI (44): Nov 28, 1912; C-4, L-4

3771   [N.N.]; Trauger, PA

The October 20, 1912 dedication of the Trauger Greek Catholic Church.

L   XXI (46): Dec 12, 1912; C-3, L-2

3772   A. Labik; Duquesne, PA; Dec 2, 1912

"Ot uhro-russkoj hreko kat. parafiy Sv. Ap. Petra y Pavla" [From the Uhro-Rusyn Greek Catholic Parish of Sts. Peter and Paul]

Expresses thanks to former pastor, Rev. Eugene Homichko, and welcomes new pastor, Rev. Michael Balog.

L   XXI (47): Dec 19, 1912; C-2

3773   [N.N.]; "S odnoju uhro-russkoju hreko kat. cerkov'ju snov' bol'še" [There is one more Uhro-Rusyn Greek Catholic Church]

The November 28, 1912 dedication of the Erie, PA Greek Catholic Church.

A   XXI (49): Jan 2, 1913; C-4&5, L-2

3774   Rev. Dr. Theodosius Vasochik, et al.; "Rachunky Hreko Kat. Uhro-Russkoj Sošestvija Sv. Ducha v Pyttsbŷrh, Pa. Ovklŷnd, ot dnja 1-ho janvarja 1912 do dnja 21-ho dekabrja 1912" [Accounts of the Greek Catholic Rusyn Church of the Descent of the Holy Ghost in Pittsburgh-Oakland, PA from January 1, 1912 to December 21, 1912]

R   XXII (1): Jan 16, 1913; C-2, L-6

3775   "Cerkovnoe Toržestvo" [Church Celebration]

Rev. A. Medvecky dedicates the Elkhorn, WV Greek Catholic Church's corner stone on January 26, 1913.

Ad   XXII (1): Jan 16, 1913; C-5, L-3

3776   [N.N.]; Allegheny, PA

The polemics between Rev. Joseph Hanulya and his Allegheny parishioners.

L   XXII (2): Jan 23, 1913; C-3, L-2

3777   John Kovalkovich; "Bor'ba uhro-russkoho naroda s epysk. Ortŷn'skym v Fyladel'fiy, Pa." [Struggle of the Uhro-Rusyn people with Bishop Ortynsky in Philadelphia, PA]

A   XXII (4): Feb 6, 1913; C-4&5, L-4

3778   "Cerkovne Toržestvo" [Church Celebration]

Rev. Constantine Roskovich dedicates the Brownsville, PA Greek
Catholic Church's corner stone on March 2, 1913.

Ad   XXII (5): Feb 13, 1913; C-3, L-7

3779   [N.N.]; "Jak stoyme s našymy cerkovnŷmy dîlamy?" [How do we stand
with our church affairs?]

Commentary on the division among Greek Catholics in America.

A   XXII (6): Feb 20, 1913; C-4&5, L-4

3780   John Kovalkovich; Philadelphia, PA; Feb 4, 1913

"Otvît redaktoru Rutenian-a [Answer to the editor of Rusin]

Commentary on an article about a Greek Catholic Church in
Philadelphia, PA in Rusin, #5.

L   XXII (7): Feb 27, 1913; C-2, L-5

3781   Rev. Stephen Gulovich, et al.; "Rachunky Hreko Kat. Cerkvy Sv.
Ioanna Krestytelja v Jun'ŷnstavn, Pa. s hoda 1912" [Accounts
of the Greek Catholic Church of St. John the Baptist in Uniontown, PA for the year 1912]

R   XXII (7): Feb 27, 1913; C-3, L-3

3782   Andrew Lacko, et al.; "Hreko Kat. Russka Cerkov' Soš. Sv. Ducha v
Klyvlŷnd, O. v 14 ul. publykuet svoy cîloročnŷy rachunky"
[Greek Catholic Rusyn Church of the Descent of the Holy Ghost
on 14th street in Cleveland, OH publishes its accounts for the
whole year (1912)]

R   XXII (7): Feb 27, 1913; C-7

3783   John Gugava; McKeesport, PA; Feb 23, 1913

"Neslŷchanna ukr. rutenska derzost'" [Unheard of Ukrainian-
Ruthenian impudence]

Activities of Rev. V. Gorzo in the McKeesport parish.

L   XXII (8): Mar 6, 1913; C-3, L-2&3

3784   [N.N.]; "Cerkovnaja akcija amerykanskoho uhro-russkoho naroda"
[Church action of the American Uhro-Rusyn people]

The need of a separate Uhro-Rusyn bishopric for the American
Greek Catholic Church.

A   XXII (8): Mar 6, 1913; C-4, L-4

3785   Theodore Zub; "Kara Božaja" [God's punishment]

Problems of the New Britain, CT Greek Catholic Ukrainian Church.

A   XXII (9): Mar 13, 1913; C-2, L-2

3786   Frank Šuda; Philadelphia, PA; Mar 5, 1913

"Otpovîd' hosp. Ioannu Kovalkovyču" [Answer to Mr. John Kovalkovich]

Rusyn-Ukrainian polemics in Philadelphia. See: 3780.

L   XXII (9): Mar 13, 1913; C-2, L-2

3787   [N.N.]; "Konečnaja pobîda allehenskych uhorskych rusynov v bor'bî s rutenskym vytčykom Iosyfom Hanulja" [Final victory of the Allegheny, (PA) Uhro-Rusyns in the struggle with the Ruthenian priest, (Rev.) Joseph Hanulya]

The polemics between the Allegheny parishioners and their pastor, Rev. Joseph Hanulya.

A   XXII (9): Mar 13, 1913; C-4, L-4

3788   [N.N.]; "Nejasnost' u Ruthenian-î [Lack of clarity in Rusin]

Commentary on an article in Rusin concerning the creation of a Rusyn Greek Catholic Rite.

A   XXII (10): Mar 20, 1913; C-2, L-2

3789   [N.N.]; "Rekolekciy Ort. ukraynskoho y rutenskoho duchovenstva" [Religious retreat of the Bishop Ortynsky Ukrainian and Ruthenian clergy]

Commentary on a March 3-6, 1913 retreat as reported in Ameryka [New Britain, CT], #9. Participants listed.

A   XXII (10): Mar 20, 1913; C-4, L-4

3790   J.G.K.; Barnesboro, PA; Feb 23, 1913

"Narod uhro-russkij da ne dastsja zvesty" [May Uhro-Rusyn people not allow to be led astray]

The activities of Rev. Kovalicky in the Barnesboro parish which led to a court action.

L   XXII (10): Mar 20, 1913; C-4, L-4

3791   John Sekerak; Cleveland, OH

Rev. Michael Mitro, pastor of a Cleveland Greek Catholic parish.

L   XXII (11): Mar 27, 1913; C-3, L-2&3

3792   Theodore Glagola and Basil Pleša; Monongahela City, PA; Mar 24, 1913

"Napast' ne chodyt po licu, no meždu ljud'my" [An insult does not stay on the face, but goes among the people]

Polemics allegedly caused by Bishop Ortynsky's supporters in the vicinity of Monongahela City.

L   XXII (12): Apr 3, 1913; C-2, L-2

3793   John Magocs; McKeesport, PA; Mar 17, 1913

"Derzost' Ort. ukr. rutenska" [Ortynsky Ukrainian Ruthenian impudence]

Activities of Rev. Valentine Gorzo.

L   XXII (12): Apr 3, 1913; C-2, L-2

3794   [N.N.]; Lyndora, PA

The March 9, 1913 dedication of the Lyndora Greek Catholic Church's corner stone.

L   XXII (12): Apr 3, 1913; C-2, L-3

3795   Fred Miller, et al.; Cleveland, OH; Apr 2, 1913

"Otpovîd' Ioannu Sekerak of vîrnykov uhro-russkoj hr. kat. cerkvy soš. sv. ducha v Klyvlŷnd, Ohajo" [Answer to John Sekerak from the faithful of the Uhro-Rusyn Greek Catholic Church of the Descent of the Holy Ghost in Cleveland, Ohio]

Defense of parish's pastor, Rev. Michael Mitro. See: 3791.

L   XXII (14): Apr 17, 1913; C-2&3, L-2

3796   Rev. Dr. Theodosius Vasochik, et al.; "Spravozdanie za dochodŷ y vŷdatky hreko kat. uhro-russkoj cerkvy Sošestvija Sv. Ducha v Pyttsbŷrh-Ovklŷnd, Pa. ot 1-ho janvarja 1913, do 29-ho marta, 1913" [Report for disbursements and receipts of the Greek Catholic Uhro-Rusyn Church of the Descent of the Holy Ghost in Pittsburgh-Oakland, PA from January 1, 1913 to March 29, 1913]

R   XXII (14): Apr 17, 1913; C-3, L-7

3797   [N.N.]; McKeesport, PA; Apr 4, 1913

"Tjažkiy časŷ dlja uhorskych rusynov v Mykysportî, Pa." [Hard times for Uhro-Rusyns in McKeesport, PA]

Activities of Rev. V. Gorzo.

L   XXII (14): Apr 17, 1913; C-4&5, L-4&5

3798   P. Ju. Z.; "Rymskij sv. prestol dozvolyl hreko katolyčeskoe epyskopstvo dlja uhro-rusynov v Amerykî" [The Roman Holy See has granted a Greek Catholic Bishopric for Uhro-Rusyns in America]

Reprint of an article from Az Újság [Budapest], #94, April 20, 1913.

E   XXII (16): May 8, 1913; C-1&2, L-1

3799   [N.N.]; "Značenie hreko kat. Epyskopstva dlja uhro-russkoho naroda v Amerykî" [Significance of a Greek Catholic Bishopric for the Uhro-Rusyn people in America]

Part I: XXII (16): May 8, 1913; C-4, L-4

Part II: XXII (19): May 29, 1913; C-4, L-4

A

3800   "Cerkovnoe Toržestvo" [Church Celebration]

        a. Dedication of the Cleveland, OH Greek Catholic Church's corner stone on June 1, 1913.
        b. Dedication of the Monessen, PA Greek Catholic Church's iconostasis on June 29, 1913.

        Ad   XXII (17): May 15, 1913; C-3, L-2

3801   T.; "Cy treba do ameryky naraz dvoch epyskopov?" [Does America need simultaneously two bishops?]

        Commentary on the existence of Ukrainian and Uhro-Rusyn Greek Catholic eparchies in America.

        A   XXII (17): May 15, 1913; C-4, L-4

3802   Rev. A.A.; "K statiy, 'Cy treba nam dvuch epyskopov?'" [To the article, 'Do we need two bishops?']

        See: 3801.

        A   XXII (18): May 22, 1913; C-4, L-4

3803   [N.N.]; "Najnovîšiy avtentyčnŷy holosŷ o buduščoho samostojatel'noho uhro-russkoho hreko kat. Epyskopa v Amerykî" [Latest authentic opinions concerning the future independent Uhro-Rusyn Greek Catholic Bishop in America]

        Reprint of an article from Budapesti Hírlap [Budapest], May 14, 1913.

        A   XXII (19): May 29, 1913; C-1, L-1

3804   "Cerkovnoe Toržestvo" [Church Celebration]

        Dedication of the newly-painted Charleroi, PA Greek Catholic Church and icon on June 15, 1913.

        Ad   XXII (19): May 29, 1913; L-8

3805   [N.N.]; "Blahoslovennŷj plod čestnoj pracŷ y bor'bŷ" [Blessed fruit of honest work and struggle]

        Commentary on the transfer of Rev. Joseph Hanulya from the pastorate of the Allegheny, PA parish.

        A   XXII (20): Jun 5, 1913; C-2&3, L-2&3

3806   John Kobel'ak; Denver, CO

        The problem of Rusyn Greek Catholics in the Denver vicinity with Russian Orthodox "schism."

        L   XXII (21): Jun 12, 1913; C-2, L-2

3807 [N.N.]; "Dalšiy avtentyčnŷy vîsty kasatel'no pervoho uhro-russkoho hreko katolyčeskoho epyskopa v Amerykî" [Further authentic news concerning the first Uhro-Rusyn Greek Catholic Bishop in America]

Reprint of an article from <u>Katolikus Értesitő</u> [Budapest], July 1, 1913.

A   XXII (22): Jun 19, 1913; C-1, L-1

3808 [N.N.]; "Ympozantnoe cerkovnoe toržestvo v Monessŷn, Pa." [Impressive church celebration in Monessen, PA]

The June 26, 1913 dedication of the Monessen Greek Catholic Church and iconostasis.

A   XXII (23): Jun 26, 1913; C-2, L-2

3809 Rev. Dr. Theodosius Vasochik, et al.; "Spravozdanie za dochodŷ y vŷdatky hr. kat. uhro-russkoj cerkvy Sošestvija Sv. Ducha v Pyttsbŷrh-Ovklŷnd, Pa. ot 30-ho marta do 30-ho junija 1913" [Report of disbursements and receipts of the Greek Catholic Uhro-Rusyn Church of the Descent of the Holy Ghost in Pittsburgh-Oakland, PA from March 30 to June 30, 1913]

R   XXII (25): Jul 10, 1913; C-6, L-6

3810 John Haluska; Butler-Lyndora, PA

The July 4, 1913 dedication of the Butler Greek Catholic Church's bell.

L   XXII (26): Jul 17, 1913; C-3, L-3

3811 N. Mamrak; Dorchester, VA

Rev. Joseph Hanulya's friendship with Bishop Ortynsky.

L   XXII (28): Aug 7, 1913; C-3, L-3

3812 [N.N.]; "Blahorodnoe stremlenie" [Noble aspiration]

Commentary on the activities of Mukačevo Bishop, the Most Rev. A. Papp, in improving the well-being of the European Rusyns.

A   XXII (28): Aug 7, 1913; C-5, L-4&5

3813 [N.N.]; "Nîskol'ko slov k voprosu uporjadkovanija cerkovnŷch dîl uhro-russkoho hr. kat. naroda" [Several words on the question concerning the regulation of church affairs of the Uhro-Rusyn Greek Catholic people]

Commentary on the maintenance of a good church organization by the establishment of a Uhro-Rusyn Greek Catholic Eparchy in America.

A   XXII (31): Aug 28, 1913; C-4&5, L-4&5

3814　P. Ju. Ž.; "Udyvytel'nŷj perevorot v uporjadkovaniy cerkovnych dîl
ameryk. uhro-russkoho hreko kat. naroda" [Amazing turnabout
in the regulation of church affairs of the American Uhro-Rusyn
Greek Catholic people]

The obstacles preventing the appointment of a Uhro-Rusyn Bishop
for America.

E　　　　　　　　　　　　　　XXII (32): Sep 4, 1913; C-4&5, L-4

3815　"Cerkovnoe Ohološenie" [Church Announcement]

Dedication of the Cleveland, OH Greek Catholic Church's bells
on September 14, 1913.

Ad　　　　　　　　　　　　　　XXII (32): Sep 4, 1913; C-7, L-8

3816　P. Ju. Ž.; "Naroky uhro-russkoho naroda na svoe uhro-russkoe
epyskopstvo, sut'-ly spravnŷy? Esly da, ta tohda čto ymîet
dîlaty? Koe-čto v kratcî o našych otcev duchovnŷch" [Are
claims of the Uhro-Rusyn people for their own Uhro-Rusyn
bishopric, legitimate? If so, then what do they have to do?
Something in brief about our reverend clergy]

E　　　　　　　　　　　　　　XXII (33): Sep 11, 1913; C-4, L-4

3817　"Holosŷ našoho naroda kasatel'no epyskopstva" [Opinions of our
people concerning the bishopric]

Series of letters to the editor on this issue.

L　　　　　　　　　　　　　　XXII (33): Sep 11, 1913; C-4, L-4

3818　"Apellata y pros'bŷ v dîlî akciy uhro-russkoho hreko kat. naroda"
[Appeals and requests concerning the action by the Uhro-Rusyn
Greek Catholic people]

Four letters by the G.C.U. supreme officers requesting the
formation of a separate Uhro-Rusyn Greek Catholic Eparchy in
America.

L　　　　　　　　　　　　　XXII (34): Sep 18, 1913; C-1,2,3, L-1&2

3819　Michael Kucsak; New York, NY; Sep 1, 1913

"Velykoe nesčast'e" [Great misfortune]

On August 30, 1913 a fire destroyed the New York City Greek
Catholic Church.

L　　　　　　　　　　　　　　XXII (35): Sep 25, 1913; C-4&5, L-4

3820　P. Ju. Ž.; "Narod uhro-russkij, poka deržytsja v"edno, est' zavse
syl'nŷj y možet sochranyty svoy prava y buduščnost'" [Uhro-
Rusyn people, while they hold together are always strong and
can preserve their rights and future]

Requests Rusyns to wait a little longer for the appointment
of an Uhro-Rusyn bishop.

E　　　　　　　　　　　　　　XXII (36): Oct 2, 1913; C-4, L-4

3821   "Cerkovnoe Oholosenie" [Church Announcement]

> Dedication of the Williamstown, PA Greek Catholic Church's bell on October 12, 1913.

> Ad   XXII (36): Oct 2, 1913; C-5, L-3

3822   John Onačila; Cleveland, OH

> The September 14, 1913 dedication of the Cleveland Greek Catholic Church's bell.

> L   XXII (37): Oct 9, 1913; C-2&3, L-2&3

3823   Rev. Dr. Theodosius Vasochik, et al.; "Spravozdanie o dochodkach y vydatkach hreko katolyčeskoj uhro-russkoj cerkvy Sošestvija Sv. Ducha v Pyttsbŷrh-Ovklŷnd, Pa. ot 1-ho julija 1913 do 30-ho sentjabrja 1913" [Report concerning the disbursements and receipts of the Greek Catholic Uhro-Rusyn Church of the Descent of the Holy Ghost in Pittsburgh-Oakland, PA from July 1, 1913 to September 30, 1913]

> R   XXII (39): Oct 23, 1913; C-2, L-2&3

3824   Paul Ju. Zsatkovich; "Novŷj oborot v cerkovnŷch dîlach y čto ymîeme dîlaty v ochoronî uhro-russkoho naroda" [New turn in church affairs and what we have to do in the preservation of the Uhro-Rusyn people]

> The December 9-10, 1913 Congress in Johnstown, PA, at which the issues in obtaining the appointment of a Uhro-Rusyn bishop will be discussed.

> Parts I-II: XXII (39-40): Oct 23-30, 1913; C-4, L-4

> E

3825   Frank Shuda, et al.; Philadelphia, PA; Oct 19, 1913

> "Zaslato. Otvît h. Vasyliju Kovalkovyčovy" [Letter to the Editor. Rebuttal to Mr. Basil Kovalkovich]

> The polemics among parishioners of the Philadelphia Greek Catholic Church. See: 3780.

> L   XXII (40): Oct 30, 1913; C-2&3, L-2&3

3826   "Cerkovnoe Oholosenie" [Church Announcement]

> Most Rev. S.S. Ortynsky dedicates the Jennerstown, PA Greek Catholic Church's corner stone on November 22, 1913.

>   XXII (41): Nov 6, 1913; L-5
> Ad   XXII (42): Nov 13, 1913; C-8

3827 Paul J. Zsatkovich; "Povynosty y samoderžaniesja uhro-russkoho
naroda vslîdstvie novoho oborota kasatel'no cerkovnoj verchnosty" [Obligations and behavior of the Uhro-Rusyn people
in the face of the new turn concerning the church hierarchy]

Since Bishop Ortynsky received full diocesan power as a Greek
Catholic Bishop, Rusyns must work ever harder to procure their
own Rusyn bishop.

E   XXII (42): Nov 13, 1913; C-4, L-4

3828 "Cerkovnoe Ohološenie" [Church Announcement]

Dedication of the Greek Catholic Church of the Holy Virgin's
corner stone on November 23, 1913.

Ad   XXII (42): Nov 13, 1913; C-8, L-6

3829 Michael S. Rushin, et al.; "Ot hl. urjada 'Soedynenija hr. kat.
russkych bratstv' y ot èksekutyvnoho komiteta akciy uhro-
russkoho naroda" [From the supreme administration of the
G.C.U. and from the executive committee of the action of
the Uhro-Rusyn people]

Announces the convocation of a Church Congress for December
9-10, 1913 in Johnstown, PA.

O   XXII (43): Nov 20, 1913; C-1, L-1

3830 Koloman Čič Firla; East Port Chester, NY

The organization of a parish in the Port Chester vicinity.

L   XXII (43): Nov 20, 1913; C-2, L-2

3831 Paul J. Zsatkovich; "Narod uhro-russkij pered novoju problemoju"
[Uhro-Rusyn people facing a new problem]

Situation of the American Greek Catholic Church before the
Johnstown, PA Congress.

E   XXII (44): Nov 27, 1913; C-4, L-4

3832 Paul J. Zsatkovich; "Pred konhressom" [Before the congress]

The issues that will be discussed at the Johnstown, PA Congress.

E   XXII (45): Dec 4, 1913; C-1, L-1

3833 [N.N.]; "K relyhijno-narodnomu voprosu uhro-russkoho naroda"
[On the religious-national question of the Uhro-Rusyn people]

A   XXII (45): Dec 4, 1913; C-4, L-4

3834 George Gulyanics; New York, NY

The November 2, 1913 dedication of the New York Greek Catholic
Church.

L   XXII (46): Dec 11, 1913; C-2&3, L-2

3835   [N.N.]; "Konhress s bol'šoj časty otbŷlsja, s časty-že ešče vse deržyt" [Congress for the most part is over, (however) a part still continues]

Resolutions from the December 9-10, 1913 Church Congress held in Johnstown, PA.

A   XXII (46): Dec 11, 1913; C-4&5, L-4&5

3836   [N.N.]; "Krasnŷy uspichy Konhressa našych uhro-russkych parafij" [Beautiful successes of the Congress of our Uhro-Rusyn parishes]

Bishop Ortynsky's commentary on and approval of the resolutions of the Johnstown, PA Church Congress. This action brings peace to the American Greek Catholic Church for the first time in six years.

A   XXII (47): Dec 18, 1913; C-2, L-2

3837   "Cerkovnoe Ohološenie" [Church Announcements]

Dedication of the Canonsburg, PA Greek Catholic Church's bell on December 28, 1913.

Ad   XXII (47): Dec 18, 1913; C-5, L-3

3838   Michael Rushin, et al.; "Ot komyteta vŷbrannoho Džanstavnskym Cerkovno-Narodnŷm Konhressom" [From the committee chosen by the Johnstown, PA Church-Laical Congress]

Thirty-two point resolution approved by the Congress.

O   XXII (48): Dec 25, 1913; C-4&5, L-4

3839   Michael Kertis, et al.; Sutersville, PA

The organization of a parish in the Sutersville vicinity.

L   XXII (49): Jan 1, 1914; C-2

3840   [N.N.]; St. Louis, MO

The polemics among St. Louis parishioners over the annual parish meeting.

L   XXIII (2): Jan 22, 1914; C-2

3841   Rev. Joseph Papp; Nové Davidkovo (Újdávidháza); Bereg County, Hungary

List of donations sent by Rusyn-Americans for support of the Nove Davidkovo Church.

LE   XXIII (2): Jan 22, 1914; C-4&5

3842 Rev. Dr. Theodosius Vasochik, et al.; "Spravozdanie s dochodov y vydatkov hreko kat. uhro-russkoj cerkvy Sošestvija Sv. Ducha v Pyttsbŷrh-Ovklŷnd, Pa. (korn. Atvud y Bejts str.) s hoda 1913, čysljašče ot 1-ho janvarja 1913 do 31-ho dekabrja 1913" [Report on disbursements and receipts of the Greek Catholic Church of the Descent of the Holy Ghost in Pittsburgh-Oakland, PA (corner of Atwood and Bates Streets) from the year 1913, figured from January 1, 1913 to December 31, 1913]

  R   XXIII (3): Jan 29, 1914; C-5

3843 O.; "Do vsîch 'pravoslavnŷch!'" [To all 'Orthodox Christians!']

  Maintains that the Catholic church is the "true church."

  A   XXIII (4): Feb 5, 1914; C-2&3

3844 George Z. Baran'; "Protokol cyvyl'no-cerkovnoho konhressa uhro-russkych parafij, poderžannoho v dnjach 9-10-ho dekabrja, 1913 v džanstavn, Pa." [Minutes of the Laical church congress of Uhro-Rusyn parishes, held December 9-10, 1913 in Johnstown, PA]

  O   XXIII (6): Feb 19, 1914; C-2,3,4,5,8

3845 Basil Vyra; Pittsburgh-Frankstown, PA

  Commentary on the Frankstown parish.

  L   XXIII (7): Feb 26, 1914; C-3

3846 Rev. A. Stecjuk; "Yz kancellariy Amer. hr. kat. epyskopa" [From the office of the American Greek Catholic Bishop]

  Thursday is Bishop Ortynsky's day for public visits.

  O   XXIII (8): Mar 5, 1914; C-4

3847 Mathew Jalč, et al.; Pittsburgh-Frankstown, PA; Mar 3, 1914

  "Zaslato" [Letter to the Editor]

  Reply to 3844.

  L   XXIII (8): Mar 5, 1914; C-5

3848 Basil Kepenač; Glen Lyon, PA

  Commentary on the Glen Lyon Greek Catholic parish.

  L   XXIII (9): Mar 12, 1914; C-3

3849 Michael Mačkoš, et al.; Akron, OH

  The activities of a "schismatic" priest trying to collect money from Akron parishioners for the construction of a church.

  L   XXIII (11): Mar 26, 1914; C-2

3850   Rev. Joseph Papp; Nové Davidkovo (Újdávidháza), Bereg County, Hungary; Mar 17, 1914

Report on the use of donations sent by Rusyn-Americans for support of the village church.

LE   XXIII (12): Apr 2, 1914; C-3

3851   Most Rev. S. Ortynsky; "Epyskopskiy Rasporjaženija" [Episcopal Directives]

List of fifteen instructions for Greek Catholic Deacons. Reprinted from Eparchial'nŷi Vistnyk, #1.

A   XXIII (14): Apr 16, 1914; C-4

3852   John Karaffa; Trenton, NJ; May 1, 1914

"Nova uhro-russka hreko kat. cerkov' v Trentŷn, N'ju Dž." [New Uhro-Rusyn Greek Catholic Church in Trenton, NJ]

The construction of the $45,000.00 Trenton Greek Catholic Church.

L, P   XXIII (16): May 7, 1914; C-3

3853   [N.N.]; "Dîlo, kotoroe potrebuet obšyrnîjšoho pojasnenija" [A matter, which requires an extensive explanation]

The connection of G.C.U. funds embezzler, Emil Sarady, with the petition movement for the appointment of a Uhro-Rusyn Bishop.

Parts I-II: XXIII (16-17): May 7-14, 1914; C-4&5

A

3854   Stephen Zubal, et al.; "Spravozdanie kontrollorov Hreko Kat. Russkoj Cerkvy Sv. Ioanna Krestytelja v Jun'ynstavn, Pa. ot 1-ho janvarja do 31-ho dekabrja 1913" [Report of the controllers of the Greek Catholic Rusyn Church of St. John the Baptist in Uniontown, PA from January 1 to December 31, 1913]

R   XXIII (18): May 28, 1914; C-4

3855   [N.N.]; "Ot"îzd Preosv. S.S. Ortŷn'skoho v Rym" [Departure of Most Rev. S.S. Ortynsky for Rome]

Bishop Ortynsky left for Rome on June 2, 1914 to meet with the Holy Father and discuss the situation of the American Greek Catholic Church.

A   XXIII (20): Jun 11, 1914; C-4&5

3856   [N.N.]; "Prazdnykov. Prazdnyk v N'ju Iorku" [Feastday celebrated in New York]

The May 30, 1914 dedication of the New York, NY Greek Catholic Church.

A   XXIII (22): Jun 25, 1914; C-2&3

3857   "Cerkovnoe Toržestvo" [Church Celebration]

       Dedication of the Mingo Junction, OH Greek Catholic Cemetery
       on July 26, 1914.

       Ad   XXIII (24): Jul 9, 1914; C-3

3858   Gregory Šeptak; Elkhorn, WV

       a. On March 21, 1914 a fire destroyed the Elkhorn church.
       b. Commentary on Elkhorn's pastor, Rev. N. Szabo.

       L   XXIII (25): Jul 16, 1914; C-3

3859   Rev. Nicholas Szabo; Sheffield, PA; Jul 17, 1914

       "Zaslato" [Letter to the Editor]

       Reply to 3858.

       L   XXIII (26): Jul 23, 1914; C-2

3860   Rev. Theo Vasochik, et al.; "Dochodŷ y vŷdatky hr. kat. uhro-russkoj
       cerkvy Soš. Sv. Ducha v Pyttsbŷrh-Ovklŷnd, Pa." [Disbursements
       and receipts of the Greek Catholic Uhro-Rusyn Church of the
       Descent of the Holy Ghost in Pittsburgh-Oakland, PA]

       R   XXIII (27): Jul 30, 1914; C-3

3861   Albert Dzurovcak; Binghampton, NY

       The May 30, 1914 dedication of the Binghampton Greek Catholic
       Cemetery's cross.

       L   XXIII (29): Aug 13, 1914; C-2&3

3862   "Cerkovnoe Toržestvo" [Church Celebration]

       a. Dedication of the Trauger, PA Greek Catholic Church's
       corner stone on August 16, 1914.

                                       XXIII (29): Aug 13, 1914; C-8

       b. Dedication of the Punxsutawney, PA Greek Catholic Church
       on September 7, 1914.

       Ad   XXIII (30): Aug 20, 1914; C-2

3863   Alexander Harpas; "Odnoe radostnoe cerkovnoe toržestvo" [A joyful
       church celebration]

       The August 16, 1914 dedication of the Trauger, PA Greek Catho-
       lic Church's corner stone.

       A   XXIII (31): Aug 27, 1914; C-2&3

3864 [N.N.]; "Preosv. Epyskop prybŷl yz Evropŷ" [Most Rev. Ortynsky arrived from Europe]

Bishop Ortynsky returned to the U.S. on August 24, 1914. Commentary on the significance of his visit to Rome.

A   XXIII (31): Aug 27, 1914; C-4

3865 John Koščak; Mingo Junction, OH

The July 26, 1914 dedication of Mingo Junction's Greek Catholic Cemetery.

L   XXIII (32): Sep 3, 1914; C-2&3

3866 [N.N.]; "Vraču, yscîlysja..." [Doctor, heal thyself...]

Commentary on the problems plaguing the American Greek Catholic Church.

A   XXIII (33): Sep 10, 1914; C-4&5

3867 Most Rev. Soter S. Ortynsky; "Pryvît Eho Preosv. Epyskopa" [Greetings of his Most Rev. Bishop]

Commentary by Bishop Ortynsky on his trip to Rome and requests of donations for Rusyn war widows and orphans. Reprinted from an article in Ameryka.

A   XXIII (34): Sep 17, 1914; C-4

3868 "Velykolîpnoe Toržestvo" [A Magnificent Celebration]

Rev. Eugene Volkay dedicates a cross at St. Mary's Greek Catholic Church in Youngstown, OH on September 27, 1914.

Ad   XXIII (34): Sep 17, 1914; C-7

3869 [N.N.]; "Desjat'-lîtnŷj jubylej cerkvy punksutavnskoj" [Tenth anniversary of the Punxsutawney, PA church]

The September 7, 1914 anniversary celebration.

A   XXIII (35): Sep 24, 1914; C-2

3870 [N.N.]; "Travherskaja cerkov'" [Trauger, PA church]

The August 16, 1914 dedication of the Trauger Greek Catholic Church's corner stone.

A, P   XXITT (37): Oct 8, 1914; C-2

3871 George Huljanyč; "Konkurs" [Competition]

Commentary on an article by Rev. V. Balog, in Rusin, #39, about the competition for the position of cantor at the Whiting, IN parish.

A   XXIII (38): Oct 15, 1914; C-4&5

3872 G.Z. Barany; Bradenville, PA; Oct 5, 1914

"Otkrŷtoe pys'mo" [An open letter]

Reply to the article, "Schism and our cantors" by Joseph Hanulya in Rusin, #40.

L   XXIII (38): Oct 15, 1914; C-5

3873 Rev. Dr. Theo. Vasochik, et al.; "Dochodŷ hreko kat. uhro-russkoj cerkvy Sošestvija Sv. Ducha v Pyttsbŷrh-Ovklŷnd, Pa. ot 12-ho jul'ja 1914 do 3-ho oktjabrja, 1914" [Receipts of the Greek Catholic Uhro-Rusyn Church of the Descent of the Holy Ghost in Pittsburgh-Oakland, PA from July 12, 1914 to October 3, 1914]

R   XXIII (40): Oct 29, 1914; C-3

3874 John Rajčynec; East Chicago, IN

The efforts to organize a parish in East Chicago.

L   XXIII (40): Oct 29, 1914; C-3

3875 "Jubylejnoe toržestvo v Homsted, Pa." [Anniversary celebration in Homestead, PA]

Celebration of the Homestead Greek Catholic Church's twentieth anniversary on November 22, 1914.

Ad   XXIII (40): Oct 29, 1914; C-5

3876 Dr. A. D.; "Sud'ba Hreko Katolykov v Rossiy" [Fate of Greek Catholics in Russia]

Parts I-V: XXIII (41-45): Nov 5-Dec 3, 1914; C-2&3

A

3877 [N.N.]; "Yz Monessen do Monessen, Pa." [From Monessen to Monessen, PA]

Parish meeting slated for November 21, 1914 to discuss the parish's conversion to Orthodoxy.

A   XXIII (41): Nov 5, 1914; C-3

3878 Rev. Anthony Mhley; "Jubylejnoe toržestvo v N'ju Sejlem, Pa." [Anniversary celebration in New Salem, PA]

The November 29, 1914 tenth anniversary celebration of the New Salem Greek Catholic Church.

A   XXIII (42): Nov 12, 1914; C-5

3879 "Toržestvennoe osvjaščenie cerkovnŷch dzvonov" [Solemn dedication of church bells]

Dedication on November 21, 1914 in Jennerstown, PA.

Ad   XXIII (42): Nov 12, 1914; C-8

3880   [N.N.]; "Preosv. S.S. Ortŷn'skij v Homsted, Pa." [Most Rev.
       S.S. Ortynsky in Homestead, PA]

       Bishop Ortynsky will officiate at the twentieth anniversary
       celebration of the Homestead Greek Catholic Church on Novem-
       ber 22, 1914.

       A   XXIII (43): Nov 19, 1914; C-4

3881   [N.N.]; "Jubylejnoe toržestvo v Homsted, Pa." [Anniversary cele-
       bration in Homestead, PA]

       The November 22, 1914 twentieth anniversary celebration of
       the Homestead Greek Catholic Church.

       A   XXIII (44): Nov 26, 1914; C-5

3882   Most Rev. Soter S. Ortynsky; "Sv. Konhrehacija dlja rozšyrenija
       vîrŷ y dlja sprav vostočnych obrjadov" [Sacred Congregation
       for the Propagation of the Faith and for the Affairs of the
       Eastern Rites]

       Commentary on a decree published on Greek Catholics and clergy
       in America.

       A   XXIII (45): Dec 3, 1914; C-3

3883   [N.N.]; "Rus'kij Narodnŷj Zîzd v Fyladel'fija, Pa." [Rusyn
       National Meeting in Philadelphia, PA]

       December 8, 1914 meeting where the creation of a diocesan
       peoples council to arbitrate in matters of church and cultural
       affairs was discussed.

       A   XXIII (46): Dec 10, 1914; C-5

3884   [N.N.]; "Prošu slovo!" [May I have my say?]

       Condems the December 8, 1914 meeting in Philadelphia, PA,
       sponsored by Bishop Ortynsky, as a platform for Ukrainianism.
       Requests Rusyn-Americans to support the Uhro-Rusyn League.

       Parts I-II: XXIII (47-48): Dec 17-Dec 24, 1914; C-4&5
       A

3885   [N.N.]; "Narode uhro-russkij bud' na straži" [Uhro-Rusyn people
       be on guard]

       Warns Rusyn-Americans not to be persuaded that the Ukrainian
       propaganda from Bishop Ortynsky and his supporters is for the
       good of the Church and nationality.

       A   XXIII (47): Dec 17, 1914; C-5

3886   [N.N.]; "Protest protyv najnovîjšoj chytrosty Ukrayncev" [Protest against the latest cunning of the Ukrainians]

Commentary on the plan of Bishop Ortynsky and his supporters to create a special diocesan district to handle church and cultural affairs.

A   XXIII (48): Dec 24, 1914; C-4&5

3887   Michael Kertis, et al.; Sutersville, PA

The efforts to organize a parish in the Sutersville vicinity.

L   XXIII (49): Jan 1, 1914; C-2

3888   M.I.H.; "Kto končyt herostrateskuju zadaču?" [Who will fulfill Herostratus' task?]

Viewpoint about the religious nationality problem and commentary on Rev. Joseph Hanulya's representation of the Uhro-Rusyn people at the December 8, 1914 Philadelphia meeting.

E   XXIII (48): Dec 24, 1914; C-5

Chapter 4

Rusyn Social Issues and Developments

4001 A.Y.T., et al., advisor: Ju.; "Ystoryčeskoe heohrafyčeskoe korotkoe opysanye Halycko y Uhro-Russkych s vzhljadom na kul'turnoe rozvytie, na zvŷčaî y obŷcaî y druhiy znamenytnîšiy ych spravŷ; Rusynŷ Lemky (Halyckiy)" [Short historical and geographical description of Galician and Uhro-Rusyns examining their cultural development, customs and other significant aspects; Rusyn Lemky (of Galicia)]

Part IV: History of the Rusyn Lemky; Lemkian origins to their origins to their present situation under Habsburg rule.

III (1): Jan 2, 1894; C-6

Part V: Lemkian history.

III (2): Jan 9, 1894; C-6

Parts IX-X: Lemkian village life.

III (7-8): Feb 20-27, 1894; C-6

Part XII: Lemkian family life.

III (10): Mar 13, 1894; C-6

Part XIII: Lemkian village community: Institutions and social hierarchy.

A   III (11): Mar 20, 1894; C-6

4002 [N.N.]; "Vŷselenie Halycyskych y Uhorskych Rusynov v Ameryku y ych sorhanizovanie" [The immigration of Galician and Uhro-Rusyns to America and their organization]

Part IV: The early immigration of the clergy to America.

A   III (2): Jan 9, 1894; C-2, L-13

4003 [N.N.]; "Ne poškodyt malo bol'šoj ostorožnosty u našych ljudej!" [It would not hurt our people to be a bit more careful!]

Cautions Rusyn immigrants against contact with unethical businesses.

A   III (13): Apr 3, 1894; C-5

4004 M.P.K.; Leisenring, PA, Apr 12, 1894

Commentary on a strike in Western PA, involving several Slavic nationalities.

L   III (15): Apr 17, 1894; C-4

4005 [N.N.]; "Prymîrytel'naja akcija v Halyčynî" [A conciliatory action in Galicia]

Proceedings and resolutions of a Congress, organized by delegates of all Rusyn political parties in Austria, that took place in L'viv, Galicia.

Nr   III (16): Apr 29, 1894; C-3

4006 [N.N.]; "Vŷbralys' do kraju" [They went to the old country]

Six Rusyns returned to Europe after living in the U.S.

A   III (16): Apr 29, 1894; C-6

4007 M.P.K.; Leisenring, PA

"Strajk na okolycî Konnelsvyl'ja, Pa." [Strike in the
vicinity of Connelsville, PA]

Rusyn support for a general strike.

L   III (17): May 8, 1894; C-5, L-10

4008 [N.N.]; "Poljaky v Amerykî--yly--podražanija dostojnŷi prymîr,
jakto odnoj narodnosty naležytsja vozderžaty svoju vîru, svoju
narodnost', sochranjaty duch ystynnoho Patriotyzma!" [Poles
in America or an example worthy of following, of how a nationality should try to maintain its faith, nationality, and to
preserve the spirit of true patriotism!]

Description of the Polish immigrant's life in America. An
appeal is made to Rusyn-Americans to help maintain all immigrants' freedoms in America.

A   III (19): May 22, 1894; C-3, L-10

4009 M.P.K.; Leisenring, PA, May 10, 1894; May 12, 1894

Rusyn support for the general strike in the Connelsville, PA
vicinity.

L   III (19): May 22, 1894; C-5

4010 J.A. Smith and Paul Jurievich; "Spomahajmo nevynno terpjaščym
bratjam! Sčyroserdečnoe vozvanie do vsîch Bratstv naležaščych
do 'Soedynenija', do vsej Amerykanskoj Russkoj bratiy, y do
vsîch Vsec. Otcev našych Duchovnych! Brat'ja Rusyny!" [Let
us help those brethren who are innocently suffering! Sincere
requests to all lodges belonging to the 'Soedynenie' to all
American-Rusyn brethren and to all our honorable clergy!
Fellow Rusyns!]

Support for the general strike in the vicinity of Connelsville,
PA.

Req   III (19): May 22, 1894; supplement

4011 T.; Rogerstown, PA; Jun 14, 1894

Rusyn support for various strikes in Pennsylvania.

L   III (21): Jun 19, 1894; C-5

4012 Ju.; "Tolkovanija v spravach sumîstnych cerkovno-narodnŷch našych
ynteressov" [Interpretations of our mutual religious-national
interests]

Part I: Calls for greater unity among Rusyn-Americans in solving national and religious problems in America and in Europe.

III (22): Jun 26, 1894; C-2&3, L-13

Parts II-III: Need for unity among Rusyn-Americans.

A   III (23-24): Jul 3-10, 1894; C-2, L-13

4013   [N.N.]; "Spravedlyvoe zajavlenie mnînija" [Justified statement of opinion]

The American press and their news reports about various nationalities.

A   III (23): Jul 3, 1894; C-2&3

4014   M.P.K.; Leisenring, PA; Jul 11, 1894

Strike in the vicinity of Connelsville, PA.

L   III (25): Jul 17, 1894; C-2

4015   [N.N.]; "Lytvynŷ v Ameryki" [Lithuanians in America]

A   III (26): Jul 24, 1894; C-5

4016   Ju.; "Obezpečym sebe! Pozmahajmesja bŷty Amerykanskymy hraždanamy (sytyzenamy)!--Zakladajme kljubŷ polytyčnŷy! Pozmahajmesja poka pora (poka tomu čas)!" [Let's make ourselves secure! Let us strive to become American citizens!--Let us establish political clubs! Let us strive while there is time!]

A four part series discussing the process of becoming American citizens. Included is a discussion of the three major political parties a Rusyn-American can join.

Parts I-II: III (27-28): Jul 31-Aug 14, 1894; C-5, L-13&14

Part III: III (31): Sep 13, 1894; C-4, L-9&10

Part IV: III (33): Sep 27, 1894; C-2&3, L-13

E

4017   [N.N.]; "Bol'šaja čast' našeho naroda ne lyšaetsja svoŷch zlych nravov" [Most of our people have not lost their bad habits]

Deals with two vices common among Rusyns in America and in Europe: drunkenness and brawling

A   III (32): Sep 20, 1894; C-2&3, L-9

4018   [N.N.]; "Pred vŷboramy Urjadnykov Štatnŷch y Povîtovŷch" [Prior to the election of State and County Officials]

Stresses the duty of Rusyn-American Citizens to vote in the state and regional elections on November 6, 1894.

A   III (37): Oct 25, 1894; supplement to 37

4019   Rev. Alexander Dzubay; "Obezpečym sebja y material'no! Majže vsî
          narodnosty, zasîvšiy v Amerykî, zamahajutsja statys' tut
          vlastyteljamy nedvyžamaho (zemlja, dom) ymînija, tol'ko mŷ
          Rusyne stoymo nazadî!--Udobnŷj sposob dlja pokupky nedvyžymaho
          ymînija!'" [Let's make ourselves materially secure, too!
          Almost all of the nationalities who have settled in America
          are attempting to become owners of real property (land, homes).
          Only we Rusyns are backward in this respect!--A favorable way
          to buy real property!]

          Encourages Rusyn-Americans to invest their savings in real
          estate, businesses and other tangible property.

          A   III (38): Nov 1, 1894; C-2, L-13

4020   H.; Glen Lyon, PA; Oct 29, 1894

          Rusyn community in Glen Lyon, PA.

          L   III (39): Nov 8, 1894; C-2&3

4021   Ju.; "Koe-čto o p'jatyky y trezvosty" [A few words about drinking
          and sobriety]

          E   III (44): Dec 13, 1894; C-2, L-13

4022   Ju. Ch.; Olyphant, PA; Dec 6, 1894

          Commentary on Jews in America.

          L   III (44): Dec 13, 1894; C-2&3

4023   [N.N.]; "Čo-to O Falš'ivej Pris'ahi -- 'Ne Svedč Falečno!'" [Few
          words about perjury -- 'Don't witness falsely!']

          A   IV (1): Jan 16, 1895; L-9&10

4024   [N.N.]; "Jedno Dobroc'inne Naruc'enie v New Yorku" [A Beneficient
          Mission in New York]

          Philanthropic activities of a Hungarian organization.

          A   IV (1): Jan 16, 1895; L-13

4025   F.; "Charakterŷ" [Characters]

          Warns Rusyns against people who lack ethics especially in
          business and money transactions.

          A   IV (2): Jan 24, 1895; C-2, L-13

4026   Redakcija; "Vozvanie na pomoc k calej Russkej i Slovackej Nas'ej
          Bratiji!" [A call for support to all our Rusyn and Slovak
          brethren!]

          Support for Joseph Bezek's (a Croat national) conviction
          appeal.

          E   IV (2): Jan 24, 1895; L-9

4027   Redakcija; "Otklyk" [Response]

Commentary on the arrest of Rev. Victor Popoff in Pittsburgh, PA on the charge of disorderly conduct.

E   IV (9): Mar 14, 1895; C-5

4028   [N.N.]; "Korotkiy očerky ystoriy Halycko y Uhrorusskaho naroda. O drevnŷch (starodavnŷch) načalach slavjanstva y Rusynov. Kreščenie Rusy" [Short essays on the History of the Galician and Hungarian-Rusyn people. About the ancient beginnings of the Slavs and Rusyns. The Christianization of Rus']

Parts I-II: IV (10-11): Mar 21-28, 1895; C-2, L-3

A

4029   Ju.; "Koe-čto o kladbyščach (Cmyntarjach)" [Concerning cemeteries]

E   IV (15): May 2, 1895; C-2, L-2

4030   [N.N.]; "Antysemytŷ v Avstriy"   [Antisemites in Austria]

The antisemitic party in the Austrian Parliament.

A   IV (15): May 2, 1895; C-5, L-3

4031   [N.N.]; "A jak-to sudjat o našom zdîšnom položeniy ynŷ zdîšnŷy narodnosty?" [How do other peoples judge our local predicament?]

Reprint from a local newspaper [N.N.] of an article which discusses the problems of the Rusyn-American communities in America.

A   IV (17): May 16, 1895; C-2, L-2

4032   Rev. Theodosius Zlocky; Kopašnovo [Gernyés], Máramaros County, Hungary, Jun 12, 1895

Lauds the accomplishments of Rusyn-Americans.

LE   IV (24): Jul 4, 1895; C-3, L-2

4033   [N.N.]; "Socijalystŷ y žydŷ" [The Socialists and the Jews]

Commentary on the close association of Jews with socialist elements in European political circles.

A   IV (25): Jul 11, 1895; C-6, L-6

4034   [N.N.]; "Čto sudyty o davaniy dîtjam vyna y pyva" [What can one say about giving wine and beer to children]

A   IV (29): Aug 8, 1895; C-6, L-3

4035   [N.N.]; "Vot jak starajutsja ynŷ Amerykanskiy narodnosty o svoych starokraevŷch brat'jach. Nezavysymost' Yrljandiy. Ne humbuh-ovŷj ale ščyrŷj y dîjstvytel'nŷj patriotyzm. Svîtloe dokazatel'-stvo tomu čeho možno dobŷtys' pravdyvym sohlasiem. Anuž' brat'ja Amer. Rusynŷ, ne spîm, očukîmsja, podražajme prymîram ynŷch zdîšnŷch narodnostej!" [Here is how other American nationalities try (to help) their European brethren. Independence of Ireland. No humbug, but a sincere and real patriotism. Clear evidence of what can be achieved by real accord. Let us brother American Rusyns not be idle (but) come to our senses, let us imitate the examples of other local nationalities!]

Rusyn view of the Irish independence struggle.

A   IV (30): Aug 15, 1895; C-6, L-6

4036   [N.N.]; "Antysemytyzm" [Antisemitism]

A   IV (32): Aug 29, 1895; C-6, L-6

4037   Ju.; "Novoe y radostnoe narodno-relyhijnoe dvyženie Rusynov v Uhorščynî" [New and joyous national-religious movement of Rusyns in Hungary]

E   IV (33): Sep 5, 1895; C-2&3, L-2&3

4038   [N.N.]; "Konhress narodnostej v Budapeštî" [Congress of nationalities in Budapest]

Representatives of various Slavic nationalities in Hungary met on August 10, 1895 to discuss issues concerning their nationalities.

A   IV (34): Sep 12, 1895; C-3, L-3

4039   [N.N.]; "Vrah čelovîčestva" [The enemy of mankind]

Alcoholic abuse among Rusyns and other nationalities.

A   IV (36): Sep 26, 1895; C-3, L-2&3

4040   [N.N.]; "Žyd oboronjaet pol'skuju šljachtu yly raj žydov v Haliciy" [Jew defends Polish nobility or the Jewish paradise in Galicia]

A   IV (37): Oct 3, 1895; C-2

4041   [N.N.]; "Borba s pijanstvom" [A struggle with drunkenness]

Guidelines in preventing drunkenness; help for those with a drinking problem.

                                           IV (37): Oct 3, 1895; C-3
A   IV (37&38): Oct 10, 1895; L-2

4042   L.; Sheppton, PA; Oct 2, 1895

Rusyn community in Sheppton, PA.

L   IV (37&38): Oct 10, 1895; C-2&3, L-2&3

4043   [N.N.]; "Koe-čto o kolonyzaciy" [Something on colonization]

Part I: Rusyn immigrants' life in America verses misconceptions European-Rusyns have of American life.

                                           IV (40): Oct 24, 1895; C-2&3, L-2&3

Part II: "Nedostatok naklonnosty našych ljudej do kolonyzaciy. Slabosty našeho naroda" [An insufficient inclination of our people towards colonization. Weaknesses of our people]

IV (41): Oct 31, 1895; C-2, L-2

Part III: "Hdî y jak bŷ kolonyzovaty našych Rusynov?" [Where and how should we colonize our Ruthenians?]

IV (42): Nov 7, 1895; C-2, L-2

Part IV: "Vŷhodŷ y korŷsty čestnoj y položeniju našeho naroda otvîtnoj kolonyzaciy" [Profits and advantages of honest colonization suiting the situation of our people]

A   IV (43): Nov 14, 1895; C-2, L-2

4044 [N.N.]; "Smutnŷy javlenija v žyvobyt'ju našych Amerykanskych Rusynov y Slovakov" [Sad incidents in the lives of our American Rusyns and Slovaks]

Commentary on the "old country" attitudes Rusyn-Americans have toward their faith, nationality and the G.C.U.

Parts I-II: IV (44-45): Nov 21-28, 1895; C-2, L-2

Part III: IV (49): Dec 25, 1895; C-2, L-2

A

4045 L.H. and K.M.; Mayfield, PA; Oct, 1895

Commentary on national-religious issues in Europe and America.

Parts I-II: IV (44-45): Nov 21-28, 1895; C-2&3, L-2&3

Part III: IV (47): Dec 11, 1895; C-3, L-2&3

L

4046 [N.N.]; "Yz sudovoj halî" [From the Court]

Scranton, PA court cases; getting a lawyer.

A   IV (45): Nov 28, 1895; C-6, L-2&3

4047 Lucas Pyrch; Rudolph, WI; Nov 28, 1895

Rusyn colonization in America.

L   IV (46): Dec 5, 1895; C-2&3, L-2&3

4048 [N.N.]; "Deputacija russkych halyčan u cîsarija" [Galician Rusyn deputation at Court]

On December 16, 1895 various petitions were presented by a Rusyn deputation to Emperor Francis Joseph in Vienna.

A   V (1): Jan 16, 1896; C-3, L-2&3

4049   [N.N.]; "Smutnŷy javlenija sredy našych Rusynov y Slovakov v Amerykî; Svad'bŷ y balŷ" [Sad incidents among Rusyns and Slovaks in America; Weddings and balls]

Deplores the "uncivilized" behavior of Rusyns and Slovaks at weddings and balls.

A   V (2): Jan 23, 1896; C-2, L-2

4050   Hribovčan; Punxsutawney, PA; Jan 9, 1896

"Perehljad sedmyčnŷj na okolycy Punxsutawney, Pa." [Weekly review (of events) in the vicinity of Punxsutawney, PA]

L   V (2): Jan 23, 1896; C-2&3, L-2&3

4051   Michael K...; Pottstown, PA; Jan 13, 1896

An immigrant's opinion of Jews in Europe and America.

L   V (2): Jan 23, 1896; C-3, L-2

4052   [N.N.]; "Skol'ko ljudej priîchalo v 1895 hodu do Ameryky?" [How many people came to America in 1895?]

Immigration statistics for 1895.

A   V (2): Jan 23, 1896; C-3, L-3

4053   [N.N.]; "Upoznajme samych sebe" [Let us know ourselves]

Part I: Be true to your faith and nationality.

V (3): Jan 30, 1896; C-2

Part II: Rusyn-Americans.

V (4): Feb 6, 1896; C-2

Part III: "Položenie heohrafyčeskoe" [Geographical situation]

The affect of geography on Rusyn political and national development.

A   V (5): Feb 13, 1896; C-2

4054   Basil Žydnjak; St. Louis, MO; Jan 18, 1896

Concerning Rusyn colonization in America.

L   V (3): Jan 30, 1896; C-2&3

4055   Paul Čarny; St. Louis, MO; Jan 12, 1896

National-Religious problems among Rusyns in the St. Louis vicinity.

L   V (4): Feb 6, 1896; C-2&3

4056   [N.N.]; "Pijatyka jak najbol'šij vrah vseho čelovîčestva" [Liquor, the greatest enemy of all mankind]

A   V (10): Mar 26, 1896; C-2, L-2

4057   [N.N.]; "Novŷy predpoloženija v dîlî ohranyčenija êmyhraciy"
        [New proposals in the affairs of limiting immigration]

        Government statistics regarding immigration to America.

        A   V (11): Apr 2, 1896; C-2, L-2

4058   [N.N.]; Newark, NJ; Mar 23, 1896

        Rusyn community in Newark, NJ.

        L   V (11): Apr 2, 1896; C-3, L-3

4059   [N.N.]; "Zabotymsja (starajmesja) o sebî poka na to čas" [Let us
        take care of ourselves while there is still time]

        Immigration of Rusyns to America.

        A   V (13): Apr 16, 1896; C-2

4060   [N.N.]; "Uže y tut v Amerykî yskušajut nas" [Already here in
        America (there are) those who are tempting us]

        Hungarian government's offer of a consulate job to two Rusyn
        immigrants in the vicinity of Wilkes Barre, PA.

        A   V (13): Apr 16, 1896; C-2&3

4061   Michael Vilčak; Diamond, IN; Apr 12, 1896

        Rusyn community in Diamond, IN.

        L   V (14): Apr 23, 1896; C-3, L-2&3

4062   Joseph Potocsnyak; Passaic, NJ; Apr 16, 1896

        Rusyn community in Passaic, NJ.

        L   V (14): Apr 23, 1896; L-3

4063   [N.N.]; "Čeho možet 'byznes!'" [What business can achieve!]

        Commentary on a letter to the editor of a Hungarian newspaper
        [n.n.] in Hazleton, PA, concerning Rusyn religious-nationality
        problems in America.

        A   V (18&19): May 21, 1896; C-2&3, L-2&3

4064   [N.N.]; "Novŷj zakon dlja obmeženija êmyhraciy v Ameryku" [New law
        restricting immigration to America]

        A   V (20): Jun 4, 1896; C-2&3, L-2&3

4065   [N.N.]; "Pozabotîmsja (postarajmos') o našem suščestvovaniu v Amerykî"
        [Let us care about our existence in America]

        Part I: Immigration to America: Government restrictions on
        immigration.

                                   V (21): Jun 11, 1896; C-2, L-2

Part II: "Dîlajme tak, čtob uvažano nas v Amerykî" [Let us do so that we might be respected in America]

V (22): Jun 18, 1896; C-2, L-2

Part III: "Esly našy Rusynŷ stajutsja Amerykanskymy hraždanamy, vopros, vŷhodŷ yly vredŷ-ly proyschodjat yz toho dlja nych" [If Rusyns become American citizens, the question is, will it benefit them or not]

V (23): Jun 25, 1896; C-2, L-2

Part IV: "Pozmahajmesja uvelyčyty naše polytyčnoe vlijanie v Amerykî" [Let us strive to increase our political influences in America]

Advocates involvement by Rusyn-American citizens in politics.

A   V (24): Jul 2, 1896; C-2, L-2

4066   [N.N.]; New York, NY; May 30, 1896

Rusyn community in New York City and vicinity.

L   V (21): Jun 11, 1896; C-3, L-3

4067   Redakcija; "Otpovîd' y prymîčanie vkratcî" [Answer and comment in short]

Refers to 4063.

E   V (21): Jun 11, 1896; C-4, L-4

4068   [N.N.]; "Chrystijansko-narodnaja partija v Uhorščyni" [Christian-national party in Hungary]

Liberal political party in the Hungarian parliament.

A   V (22): Jun 18, 1896; C-2&3

4069   [N.N.]; "Pol'sko-katolyčeskij Konhres v Amerykî" [Polish-Catholic Congress in America]

A   V (25): Jul 9, 1896; C-2&3, L-2

4070   [N.N.]; "Co moz'e vykonac pravdiva l'ubov i scirosc ku svojej narodnosci" [What genuine love and sincerity can accomplish with regard to one's own nationality]

Polish community in Milwaukee, Wisconsin.

A   V (26): Jul 16, 1896; L-3

4071   [N.N.]; "Nîskol'ko ščyrych slov k našym russkym dîvycam y ženščynam" [Some sincere words to our Rusyn girls and women]

The female's role as Rusyns and Greek Catholics.

A   V (30): Aug 13, 1896; C-2, L-2

4072   Karpatov; "Uhorsky rusynŷ v tŷsjačo-lîte madjarskoj deržavŷ"
        [Uhro-Rusyns in the millenium of the Magyar state]

        A   V (30): Aug 13, 1896; C-2&3

4073   [N.N.]; "Nedostatok pravoj syly, ènerhiy y postojannosty u našych
        ljudej v dîlach orhanyzacijnŷch" [Our peoples' inadequate
        strength, energy and constancy in the affairs of the organi-
        zation]

        Part II: "Tolkovanie pryčyn èmyhraciy Podkarpatskych Rusynov
        v Ameryku" [Interpretations of the reasons for the immigra-
        tion of Subcarpathian Rusyns to America]

                      V (32): Aug 27, 1896; C-2, L-2

        Part III: "Položenie russko-narodnaho razvytija za pervŷch
        vremen èmyhraciy našeho naroda" [Situation of Rusyn national
        development prior to the first emigration of our people]

        A   V (33): Sep 3, 1896; C-2&3, L-2

4074   [N.N.]; "Odnoe sobŷtie, kotoroe možet služyty napomynaiem dlja vsîch
        nas" [One event, which can serve as a reminder for us all]

        Commentary on the American peoples' attitude toward immigrants,
        especially those in the labor force.

        A   V (32): Aug 27, 1896; C-2&3

4075   John Manchak; Pueblo, CO; Aug 15, 1896

        Rusyn communities in the American far west.

        L   V (32): Aug 27, 1896; C-3, L-3

4076   [N.N.]; "Duchovnaja temnota lyš' ne chočet mynuty" [Spiritual
        ignorance just would not go]

        Preference of many Rusyn-Americans for other faiths and
        nationalities.

        A   V (37): Oct 1, 1896; C-2

4077   [N.N.]; "Pol'sko-Katolicki Kongres v Amerikî" [Polish Catholic
        Congress in America]

        Congress met in Buffalo, NY, September 22-25, 1896.

        A   V (39): Oct 15, 1896; L-2

4078   [N.N.]; "Obraščennŷj socialysta y voobšče o socialystach"
        [A converted socialist and in general about socialists]

        Socialists in Poland and Galicia and their influence on Rusyns.

        A   V (45): Nov 26, 1896; C-2, L-2

4079   Edmund Lembick, Hazleton, PA, Nov 16, 1896

      Commentary on the issue of religion and nationality among
      Rusyns in America.

      L   V (45): Nov 26, 1896; C-2&3, L-2&3

4080   [N.N.]; "Pristehovalci (Emigranti)" [The immigrants]

      Statistical information on immigration to U.S., 1894-95.

      A   V (45): Nov 26, 1896; L-6

4081   [N.N.]; "Niskol'ko slov o kolonyzaciy" [A few words on coloniza-
      tion]

      A   V (46): Dec 3, 1896; C-3, L-2&3

4082   [N.N.]; "Soed. Statŷ protyvo emyhraciy" [U.S. against immigration]

      Discusses American attitudes against immigration to U.S.

      A   V (47): Dec 10, 1896; C-2, L-2

4083   [N.N.]; "Plochoe pyvo" [Bad beer]

      Problems associated with beer drinking in America.

      A   V (47): Dec 10, 1896; C-6, L-6

4084   [N.N.]; "Proti emigracii" [Against immigration]

      Proposed changes in U.S. immigration laws in a bill before
      Congress requiring literacy of new immigrants.

      A   V (48): Dec 17, 1896; L-2&3

4085   [N.N.]; "Byl ɇmyhracijnyi prijatŷj v senatî" [Immigration bill
      passes the senate]

      A Senate bill places restrictions on future immigrants to U.S.
      (restrictions enumerated). Repercussions of such a bill for
      future immigrant Rusyns.

      A   V (49): Dec 24, 1896; C-2, L-2

4086   [N.N.]; "Sohlasie" [Agreement]

      Calls for peace and unity among all Rusyn-Americans.

      A   V (49): Dec 24, 1896; C-2, L-2

4087   [N.N.]; "Brazylia" [Brazil]

      Travel log of this South American country with emphasis on the
      desirability of colonizing there by Rusyns.

      Part I: V (49): Dec 24, 1896; C-6, L-6

      Part II: V (50): Jan 6, 1897; C-6, L-6

      A

4088   [N.N.]; "Uhorskij prezes mynystrov ob uhorskych emyhrantach v Amerykî" [Hungarian prime minister on Hungarian immigrants in America]

      Partial reproduction of prime minister, Koloman Szél's December 17, 1900 speech before the Hungarian parliament.

      A   X (2): Jan 24, 1901; C-4, L-4

4089   [N.N.]; "Hrozna zaraza v Amer. Rusy yly rusynsko-radykal'nŷi socialyzm v Ameryki" [Dangerous epidemic among American Rusyns or Rusyn radical socialism in America]

      Several letters by Rusyn-Americans concerning their views on socialism.

      A, L   X (3): Jan 31, 1901; C-2, L-2

4090   Nicholaj; "Jak rodytely vospytajut svoy ditŷ" [How parents rear their children]

      Various opinions and suggestions for Rusyn-Americans on rearing children.

      Part I: X (3): Jan 31, 1901; C-2, L-2

      Part II: X (5): Feb 14, 1901; C-2, L-2

      A

4091   [N.N.]; "Bor'ba protyv pijanstva" [Struggle against drunkenness]

      A   X (4): Feb 7, 1901; C-2&3, L-2&3

4092   [N.N.]; "Narodnoe preuspîvanie-prohress" [National success-progress]

      Lauds Rusyn-American awareness of their national heritage and success in increasing material well-being.

      A   X (4): Feb 7, 1901; C-4, L-4

4093   [N.N.]; "Ob Ameryk. hraždanstvî" [About American citizenship]

      How Rusyn immigrants become American citizens.

      A   X (6): Feb 21, 1901; C-2, L-2

4094   Bert Hovrilo, Thomas Harčar; Pottsville, PA

      The strike in the vicinity of Hazleton and Wilkes Barre, PA.

      L   X (6): Feb 21, 1901; C-2&3, L-2&3

4095   [N.N.]; "Pamjatajte y 'na zadnŷja kolesa'" [Remember to mind your 'rear wheels']

      The need for Rusyn-Americans to remain independent and hard working, providing a better standard of life for themselves.

      A   X (6): Feb 21, 1901; C-4, L-4

4096   Ivan Ivanov; "Otzŷv na stat'ju 'Pamjatajte y na zadnŷja kolesa'"
       [Response to the article 'Remember to mind your rear wheels']
       A   X (7): Feb 28, 1901; C-4, L-4

4097   Basil Ostorožnyj; "Nîskol'ko skromných prymîčanij na statiju
       'Pamjatajte y na zadnŷja kolesa' y na ètu statiju podanŷj
       'Otzŷv'" [Some modest observations on the article 'Remember
       to mind your rear wheels' and on the 'Response' to that article]
       A   X (8): Mar 7, 1901; C-4, L-4

4098   J. Matta; Braddock, PA
       Political club named for George Washington organized February 25,
       1901 by Rusyn immigrants in Braddock, PA.
       L   X (9): Mar 14, 1901; C-3, L-3

4099   [N.N.]; "Neslŷchanno skandal'noe postupanie ehomoscov-radykalov yly
       Revoljucionernaja Lyha Pol'sko-Lytovsko-Rusynsko radykal'na"
       [Unheard of scandalous act of gentlemen-radicals or the revolu-
       tionary league of Polish-Lithuanian-Rusyn radicalism]
       Radical Rusyn workers in Pittsburgh, PA and vicinity.
       A   X (11): Mar 28, 1901; C-2&3, L-2&3

4100   [N.N.]; "V kochtjach zdyrcov" "In the clutches of exploiters]
       Cautions Rusyn immigrants to beware of unethical businesses.
       A   X (11): Mar 28, 1901; C-4, L-4

4101   [N.N.]; "Radykaly" [Radicals]
       Examines radical movements and organizations in America.
       Part I: X (12): Apr 4, 1901; C-2, L-2
       Parts II-VI: X (14-18): Apr 25-May 23, 1901; C-2, L-2&3
       Part VII: X (20): Jun 6, 1901; C-2, L-2
       A

4102   Nicholas Pačuta; "Ozvena ku 'Protestu'" [Answer to the 'Protest']
       Reply to 4099.
       A   X (14): Apr 25, 1901; L-4

4103   [N.N.]; "Sv. Krest y Žydŷ" [Holy Cross and Jews]
       Commentary on Jews in Hungary.
       A   X (16): May 9, 1901; C-2&3, L-2

4104   [N.N.]; "Dajte pozor na sebe" [Take care of yourselves]
       Rusyn-Americans who will not become American citizens.
       A   X (16): May 9, 1901; C-4, L-4

4105   [N.N.]; "Ovoščy lyberalyzmu v Uhorščyni" [Fruits of liberalism in Hungary]

Growth and influence of Jewish power in Hungary.

A   X (17): May 16, 1901; C-2&3, L-2&3

4106   Michael Pecuch; McAdoo, PA

Political club organized May 12, 1901 by Rusyn immigrants in McAdoo.

L   X (17): May 16, 1901; C-3, L-3

4107   Jacob Stefanišin, Pleasant Home, Canada; Apr 30, 1901

Commentary on 2068.

L   X (18): May 23, 1901; C-2&3, L-2

4108   [N.N.]; "Jak v Amerykî zaberajutsja zemli" [How they obtain land in America]

Homesteading in Oklahoma.

A   X (18): May 26, 1901; C-4, L-4

4109   John Vrabel'y; Gallup, NM; May 15, 1901

Organizing a miner's union in Northern New Mexico.

L   X (20): Jun 6, 1901; C-3, L-3

4110   [N.N.]; "Slava" [Glory]

Commentary on an article in <u>Ungvári Közlöny</u> (Užhorod), #20, May 16, 1901, concerning the use of the greeting "Slava Isusu Chrystu" by Rusyn students in State schools. Hungarian government considered the greeting subversive.

A   X (20): Jun 6, 1901; C-4, L-4

4111   [N.N.]; "Značenie ženščynŷ v rodynî y narodî" [Significance of women in the family and nation]

A   X (20): Jun 6, 1901; C-7, L-7

4112   [N.N.]; "Usylovnost' našeho naroda y eho buduščnost' v Amerykî" [Efforts of our people and their future in America]

Parts I-II: X (21-22): Jun 13-20, 1901; C-2, L 2

A

4113   [N.N.]; "Prepjatstvija dlja emyhraciy" [Obstacles for the immigration]

Secretary of U.S. Department of Immigration, Mr. Powderly, proposed an increase in the registration fee paid by newly arriving immigrants.

A   X (21): Jun 13, 1901; C-4, L-4

4114   John Vrabel'y; Gallup, NM; Jun 14, 1901

        Labor problems in New Mexico.

        L   X (22): Jun 20, 1901; C-2&3, L-2

4115   Michael Botun; Monessen, PA

        Working conditions in a Pittsburgh Steel Co. mill.

        L   X (23): Jul 4, 1901; C-3, L-3

4116   Mark Smetana, Elkhorn, WV

        The flood disaster in this small mining community.

        L   X (24): Jul 11, 1901; C-3, L-3

4117   [N.N.]; "Pročto ljudy yz Uhorščyný ĕmyhrujut?" [Why do people emigrate from Hungary?]

        Explanation of the Rusyn immigration to America.

        A   X (24): Jul 11, 1901; C-4, L-4

4118   [N.N.]; "Čestnota sčytaetsja zlodîjaniem-prestupleniem" [Honesty is considered a criminal offense]

        Commentary on the Hungarian Highlands Commission and its chairman, Edward Egan.

        A, P   X (24): Jul 11, 1901; C-4, L-4

4119   John Vrabel'y; Gallup, NM

        Outcome of a miner's strike in northern New Mexico.

        L   X (24): Jul 11, 1901; C-3, L-2&3

4120   [N.N.]; "Neblahodarnost' vladîet svîtom" [Ungratefulness rules the world]

        The evils in society.

        A   X (25): Jul 18, 1901; C-3, L-2

4121   [N.N.]; "Kapytal y praca" [Capital and labor]

        Industry and labor in America.

        A   X (25): Jul 18, 1901; C-4, L-4

4122   [N.N.]; "Osztrak-Magyar Munka Közvetitö Inteźet yly Avstro-Uhorskoe Robotu posredstvavajuščoe zavedenie" [Austro-Hungarian employment office]

        Attempts by the Austro-Hungarian Government to discourage immigration to America.

        A   X (26): Jul 25, 1901; C-4, L-4

4123   [N.N.]; "Yzmîna otečestvu" [Betrayal of the fatherland]

        Magyarization: Its effects on the Rusyn people and the
        support of it by some of the Greek Catholic clergy.

        A   X (27): Aug 1, 1901; C-2, L-2

4124   P.O.; "Hrŷzota sovîsty" [A pang of conscience]

        A Rusyn woman forsakes her faith and joins the Salvation Army.

        A   X (27): Aug 1, 1901; C-3

4125   [N.N.]; "Cîna farmerskoj pracŷ" [Price of farm work]

        Contrasts farm life in America and Europe.

        A   X (27): Aug 1, 1901; C-4, L-4

4126   [N.N.]; "Pol'skij katolyčesko-narodnyj konhress" [Polish Catholic
        National congress]

        Congress takes place September 24, 1901 in Buffalo, NY.

        A   X (28): Aug 8, 1901; C-2&3, L-2

4127   [N.N.]; "Bygamija" [Bigamy]

        Bigamy and Rusyn-Americans.

        A   X (29): Aug 15, 1901; C-2, L-2

4128   [N.N.]; "Narušenie prysjahy" [Breech of oath]

        Consequences of perjury.

        A   X (30): Aug 22, 1901; C-2, L-2

4129   [N.N.]; "Samostojatel'nost'" [Independence]

        The meaning of independence.

        A   X (30): Aug 22, 1901; C-2&3, L-2

4130   Y.....Y.; Youngstown, OH; Aug 19, 1901

        The industrial accident in the Youngstown National Steel Co.
        mill.

        L   X (30): Aug 22, 1901; C-3, L-3

4131   [N.N.]; "Pamjatajmo o molodežî našej" [Let us remember our young
        people]

        A   X (31): Aug 29, 1901; C-2, L-2

4132   [N.N.]; "Vzaymnost'" [Reciprocity]

        The need for Rusyn-Americans to stop bickering and show con-
        cern for each other.

        A   X (31): Aug 29, 1901; C-4, L-4

4133   [N.N.]; "Kto pobîdyt?" [Who will win?]

The issues involved in a great strike that crippled many
industrial factories in Pennsylvania.

A   X (32): Sep 5, 1901; C-4, L-4

4134   [N.N.]; "Robotnyky na kontrakt" [Workers on contract]

Rusyns who immigrate to America contracted to American companies as strike-breaking laborers.

A   X (32): Sep 5, 1901; C-4, L-4

4135   [N.N.]; "Robota (praca)" [Work]

Benefits of working for a living.

A   X (33): Sep 12, 1901; C-2, L-2

4136   M.K. Lucak; Cleveland, OH; Sep 8, 1901

The flood disaster in Cleveland.

L   X (33): Sep 12, 1901; C-3, L-2&3

4137   Michael Bovtun; Monessen, PA; Sep 6, 1901

The strike in a Monessen steel mill. See: 4115.

L   X (33): Sep 12, 1901; C-3, L-3

4138   [N.N.]; "Anarchysm" [Anarchy]

Public reaction to anarchy and anarchists in America and
Europe.

A   X (33): Sep 12, 1901; C-4, L-4

4139   [N.N.]; "Strajk" [Strike]

The strike affecting most factories and steel mills in the
Pittsburgh, PA vicinity.

A   X (35): Sep 26, 1901; C-2, L-2

4140   [N.N.]; "Nîskol'ko slov o robotî-pracî" [A few words about work]

Virtues of working for a living.

A   X (36): Oct 3, 1901; C-2, L-2

4141   U.; Lakewood, OH; Oct 1, 1901

Rusyn community in Lakewood.

L   X (36): Oct 3, 1901; C-3, L-3

4142 [N.N.]; "Poučenija yz poslîdnjaho strajku" [Lessons of the recent strike]

The strike which closed down several factories in the Pittsburgh, PA area.

A   X (36): Oct 3, 1901; C-4, L-4

4143 [N.N.]; "Neblahodarnŷj potomok" [Ungrateful descendent]

Commentary on a letter to the editor in _Jednota_ concerning problems among Rusyns and Slovaks in Illinois.

A   X (37): Oct 10, 1901; C-2, L-2

4144 [N.N.]; "Ne utîsnjajte syrot y vdovyc" [Do not oppress orphans and widows]

Commentary on unscrupulous people taking financial advantage of orphans and widows.

A   X (38): Oct 17, 1901; C-2, L-2

4145 [N.N.]; "Nedvyžymoe ymînie" [Immovable property]

Real estate in U.S.

A   X (39): Oct 24, 1901; C-2, L-2

4146 [N.N.]; "Planŷ na ohranyčenie ěmyhraciy" [Plans for the limitation of the immigration]

U.S. legislation to limit the influx of emigrants from Europe. Statistical information.

A   X (39): Oct 24, 1901; C-4, L-4

4147 [N.N.]; "Falošni proroci" [False prophets]

Ideology of anarchy and revolution.

A   X (40): Oct 31, 1901; L-2

4148 Bert Havrilla; Pottsville, PA

Coal miners strike in Oneida and Sheppton, PA.

L   X (40): Oct 31, 1901; L-2

4149 [N.N.]; "Polytyka" [Politics]

Rusyns and American politics.

A   X (41): Nov 7, 1901; C-4, L-4

4150 [N.N.]; "Umîrennost' y čystota" [Moderation and purity]

Two desirable virtues for Rusyn-Americans.

A   X (43): Nov 21, 1901; C-2&3, L-2

4151   J.V.; Passaic, NJ; Nov, 1901

        Rusyn-Slovak community in Passaic.

        L   X (43): Nov 21, 1901; C-3, L-2&3

4152   [N.N.]; "Podlecstvo najvŷsšoj stepeny" [Villany of the highest order]

        Commentary on individuals unconcerned with the welfare of their fellow workers and nationals.

        A   X (43): Nov 21, 1901; C-4, L-4

4153   [N.N.]; "Ėmyhracija" [The (Rusyn) emigration]

        A   X (44): Nov 28, 1901; C-4, L-4

4154   [N.N.]; "Ėmyhracija y lychva" [Emigration and usury]

        Usury practiced by Jews in Hungary: portrayed as a reason for the Rusyn immigration to America.

        A   X (45): Dec 5, 1901; C-4, L-4

4155   [N.N.]; "Bor'ba protyv ėmyhraciy" [Struggle against immigration]

        U.S. government is changing attitude towards the emigration of East Europeans in the aftermath of President McKinley's assassination.

        A   X (46): Dec 12, 1901; C-2, L-2

4156   [N.N.]; "Poslanie Prezydenta" [Message of the President]

        Theodore Roosevelt's address to Congress includes remarks about anarchy in U.S. and the emigration from Europe.

        A   X (46): Dec 12, 1901; C-4, L-4

4157   [N.N.]; "Pred bankrutom?" [Prior to bankruptcy?]

        Conditions in Hungary, especially in Budapest, which has a large percentage of unemployed workers.

        A   X (47): Dec 19, 1901; C-4, L-4

4158   [N.N.]; "Tol'ko vse vpered" [Always only forward]

        Encourages honest ambition and hard work to attain noble goals.

        A   X (48): Dec 26, 1901; C-4, L-4

4159   [N.N.]; "Porožna soloma?" [Empty straw?]

        The Slavic immigration to America.

        A   XI (1): Jan 16, 1902; C-4

4160 [N.N.]; "O sytuaciy našych brat'ev v starom kray, v Uhorščynî"
[About the situation of our brethren in the old country, in
Hungary]

Political and economic conditions in the Rusyn homeland.

A   XI (2&3): Jan 30, 1902; C-4&5

4161 [N.N.]; "Robota Žydov-Socialystov" [Work of Jews-Socialists]

Jews and socialism in the Austro-Hungarian and Russian empires.

A   XI (4): Feb 6, 1902; C-2&3

4162 [N.N.]; "Ne processujtesja!" [Don't litigate!]

Requests Rusyn-Americans to avoid court litigation in settling
arguments between themselves.

A   XI (4): Feb 6, 1902; C-4

4163 [N.N.]; "Moral'noe padenie ženŷ" [Moral downfall of a woman]

Commentary on a murderess and in general about the changing
attitudes of women in America.

A   XI (5): Feb 13, 1902; C-2

4164 [N.N.]; "Lžeslovie" [Lies]

Morality of false oaths.

A   XI (5): Feb 13, 1902; C-2

4165 [N.N.]; "Časŷ mînjajutsja a mŷ mînjaemsja s nymy" [Times change
and we change with them]

The past and present life of the Rusyn people.

A   XI (5): Feb 13, 1902; C-4

4166 [N.N.]; "Čuvstvo narodnaho sobstvennoho dostoynstva" [A sense of
national self-esteem]

Describes a useful and proper life.

A   XI (6&7): Feb 27, 1902; C-2

4167 [N.N.]; "Zlodîjstvo velykoj stepeny" [Large scale larceny]

Cheating people.

A   XI (6&7): Feb 27, 1902; C-4&5

4168 [N.N.]; "Ne opyvajtesja (udobna statija dlja velykopostnoho
čtenija)" [Don't drink too much (a suitable article for
reading during lent)]

Liquor indulgence during lent.

Parts I-IV: XI (9-12): Mar 13-Apr 3, 1902; C-2,3,7

A

4169   Joseph Fecko; Toronto, OH; Mar 29, 1902

        Rusyn community in Toronto.

        L   XI (12): Apr 2, 1902; C-2

4170   And. Ferenc; Helvetia, PA; Mar 28, 1902

        Rusyn community in Helvetia.

        L   XI (12): Apr 3, 1902; C-2&3

4171   [N.N.]; "Nŷnîšnoe položenie y buduščnost hr. kat. Rusynov v Amerykî"
        [Current situation and future of Greek Catholic Rusyns in
        America]

        Part I: XI (13): Apr 10, 1902; C-2

        Part II: "Proyschoždenie amer. Rusynov y ěmyhracija"
        [Origins of the American-Rusyns and the emigration]

                                  XI (14): Apr 17, 1902; C-2

        Part III: "Časŷ mînjajutsja, a s nymy mînjajutsja y ljude"
        [Times change and people change with them]

                                    XI (15): Apr 24, 1902; C-2

        Part IV: "Novoe dvyženie" [New movement]

                                  XI (16): May 8, 1902; C-6

        Part V: "Pryncypŷ (zasadŷ), napravlenie y prepjatstvie"
        [Principles, direction and obstacles]

                                  XI (17): May 15, 1902; C-2

        Part VI: "Nprošenŷ opekunŷ" [Uninvited guardians]

                                  XI (18): May 22, 1902; C-6

        Part VIII: "Pryvatnŷy ynteresy" [Private interests]

        A   XI (21b): Jun 12, 1902; C-6,7,8

4172   Peter Tyrpak; Hibernia, NJ

        Activities of Hibernia's Rusyn community.

        L   XI (15): Apr 24, 1902; C-2&3

4173   [N.N.]; "Jak Francuzŷ pracujut na sochraneniju svoeho narodnoho
        charaktera v Soedynenych Štatach" [How the French work for
        the preservation of their national character in the U.S.]

        A   XI (15): Apr 24, 1902; C-6&7

4174   [N.N.]; "Ubijstvo v Frylend, Pa." [Murder in Freeland, PA]

        An Irishman shot and killed a Rusyn at an Easter midnight
        procession at the Greek Catholic Church in Freeland.

        A   XI (16): May 8, 1902; C-2&3

4175   Andrew Marko; Kingston, PA; Apr 15, 1902

        Kingston's Rusyn community.

        L   XI (17): May 15, 1902; C-2

4176   [N.N.]; New Castle, PA; May 3, 1902

        New Castle's Rusyn community.

        L   XI (17): May 15, 1902; C-2

4177   Michael Ivan; Sheffield, PA; Apr 27, 1902

        Sheffield's Rusyn community.

        L   XI (17): May 15, 1902; C-2&3

4178   Michael Lucak; Cleveland, OH; May 18, 1902

        The growth of Cleveland's Rusyn community.

        L   XI (18): May 22, 1902; C-3

4179   [N.N.]; "Strajk" [Strike]

        Labor strikes in America.

        A   XI (18): May 22, 1902; C-4

4180   Michael Mylas; Loren, OH; Jun 1, 1902

        Loren's Rusyn community.

        L   XI (20): Jun 5, 1902; C-2

4181   [N.N.]; "Čîm voznesetsja slava naroda?" [By what means is a nation's glory enhanced?]

        Commentary on the qualities of the Rusyn nationality.

        A   XI (20): Jun 5, 1902; C-4

4182   [N.N.]; "Strajk" [Strike]

        Details about a mining strike in the vicinity of Wilkes Barre, PA.

        A   XI (?1): Jun 12, 1902; C-4&5

4183   [N.N.]; "Užasnaja katastrofa. Podzemoe nesčastie nadîlalo velykoe pustošenie na žyzny našych krajanov" [Terrible catastrophe. Underground accident decimated our countrymen's lives]

        List of dead [by name and nationality] from a steel company's mine disaster in Johnstown, PA, July 11-12, 1902.

        A   XI (25): Jul 17, 1902; C-4&5

4184 Andrew Ferenc; Helvetia, PA; Jul 24, 1902

   The recent U.M.W. resolution for Pennsylvania coal mines.

   L   XI (27): Jul 31, 1902; C-3

4185 [N.N.]; "Pervoe sraženie strajkerov s polycieju" [First battle
   of the strikers with police]

   Five thousand striking miners clashed with police trying to
   break the strike on July 30, 1902 in Shenandoah, PA.

   A   XI (27): Jul 31, 1902; C-4&5

4186 [N.N.]; "Pamjatnyk Ljudvyka Košuta y protyahytacija Slovakov a
   voobšče Slavjan v Klyvlandî, O" [Memorial of Lajos Kossuth
   and the contra-agitation of the Slovaks and in general the
   Slavs in Cleveland, OH]

   Cleveland Slovak community protests the city council's decision for permitting the Magyar community to erect a statue of
   Lajos Kossuth in a public square.

   A   XI (28): Aug 7, 1902; C-4

4187 [N.N.]; "Pora bŷ uže koe-čto robyty" [It's time to do something]

   Various nationalities and their organizations.

   A   XI (31): Aug 28, 1902; C-4

4188 [N.N.]; "Èmyhracijnyj Konhress v starom kray" [Emigration Congress
   in the old country]

   Results of a Congress, convened August 10, 1902 in Užhorod
   (Ungvár) to discuss causes of Rusyn emigration to America
   and other parts of the world.

   A   XI (32): Sep 4, 1902; C-2&3

4189 [N.N.]; "Mad'jarskaja choruhov'" [Magyar banner]

   Magyar immigrants and their organizations in America.

   A   XI (32): Sep 4, 1902; C-4&5

4190 [N.N.]; "Syla Robotnykov" [Strength of workers]

   The American labor movement.

   A   XI (33): Sep 11, 1902; C-4

4191 [N.N.]; "Trustŷ a robočij čelovîk" [Trusts and the working man]

   A   XI (34): Sep 18, 1902; C-4

4192 George Holodik Adamišin; Broderick, PA; Sep 21, 1902

   The coal miner's strike in the vicinity of Broderick and
   Wilkes Barre, PA.

   L   XI (35): Sep 25, 1902; C-3

4193   [N.N.]; "Slavjanskij den'" [Slavic day]

A proposed holiday to promote better understanding among the
Slavic nationalities in America.

A   XI (35): Sep 25, 1902; C-4

4194   Geo. Holodik Adamišin; Broderick, PA; Sep 29, 1902

The coal miner's strike in the vicinity of Broderick.

L   XI (36): Oct 2, 1902; C-2

4195   [N.N.]; "Nužno-ly nam amerykansk. hraždanstva-sytyzenstva?"
[Is American citizenship necessary for us?]

The pros and cons of American citizenship for Rusyn immigrants.

A   XI (37): Oct 9, 1902; C-3

4196   Stephen Janošy; Bradenville, PA; Sep 28, 1902

Commentary on a Pennsylvania coal miner's strike.

L   XI (37): Oct 9, 1902; C-4

4197   [N.N.]; "Buduščnost' robotnyka" [Worker's future]

Future of the American labor movement.

A   XI (37): Oct 9, 1902; C-4

4198   Rev. A. Kecskés; "Myr s namy!" [Peace among ourselves!]

Calls for Rusyns to stop bickering among themselves.

A   XI (38): Oct 16, 1902; C-2

4199   Andrew Ferenc; Helvetia, PA; Oct 3, 1902

The September 23, 1902 mining accident that claimed the lives
of two Rusyn miners.

L   XI (38): Oct 16, 1902; C-2&3

4200   [N.N.]; "Velykost' robotnyčestva" [The size of the working class]

The American labor movement.

A   XI (38): Oct 16, 1902; C-4

4201   [N.N.]; "Robotnyky y Socialyzm" [Workers and Socialism]

The association of workers with socialism in America and Europe.

A   XI (39): Oct 23, 1902; C-4

4202   [N.N.]; "Trustŷ y robočiy orhanyzaciy" [Trusts and labor organiza-
tions]

A   XI (41): Nov 6, 1902; C-4

4203   Nicholas Krajcn; Finley Park, IL; Oct, 1902

        Relief-aid for striking Pennsylvania coal miners.

        L   XI (42): Nov 13, 1902; C-4

4204   [N.N.]; "Prezydent Uniy Majnerskoj Myčel jako svîdok" [President
        of the Miners Union, (John) Mitchell, testifies]

        The arbitration talks in Scranton, PA, between mine owners
        and striking miners.

        A   XI (43): Nov 20, 1902; C-2&3

4205   [N.N.]; "Èmyhracijnŷj zakon" [Emigration law]

        Commentary on a law before the Hungarian parliament which
        restricts the immigration of Hungarian citizens to other
        countries, especially America.

        A   XI (43): Nov 20, 1902; C-4

4206   [N.N.]; "Katolyčeskij avtonomyč. konhress v Uhorščynî" [Autonomous
        Catholic Congress in Hungary]

        Resolutions adopted by the third Catholic Congress, October
        15-17, 1902 in Budapest.

        A   XI (44): Nov 27, 1902; C-2

4207   [N.N.]; "Socialyzm y robočiy orhanyzaciy" [Socialism and labor
        organizations]

        The coal miners strike in Scranton, PA and vicinity.

        A   XI (44): Nov 27, 1902; C-4

4208   [N.N.]; "Hroznŷy razmîrŷ" [Ominous dimensions]

        New military quotas established by the Hungarian army and the
        methods used by each Hungarian county to comply with the law.

        A   XI (45): Dec 4, 1902; C-4

4209   Joseph Dovalovskij; Cleveland, OH; Dec 7, 1902

        The December 4, 1902 meeting of an international Slav political
        club [n.n.].

        L   XI (46): Dec 11, 1902; C-3

4210   [N.N.]; "Jak pyšut o nas mad'jarskiy žurnalysty v starom kray"
        [What Magyar journalists write about us in the old country]

        What European Magyar newspapers report about Rusyns and Slovaks.
        Commentary on the article which appears in Magyar Híradó
        (Cleveland, OH).

        A   XI (46): Dec 11, 1902; C-4

4211   [N.N.]; "V porî osaždenija" [In time of siege]

The six month old coal miner's strike in Pennsylvania.

A   XI (47): Dec 18, 1902; C-4

4212   [N.N.]; "Myčel osterehaet pred socialyzmom" [Mitchell warns against socialism]

Commentary on John Mitchell, president of the United Mine Workers, and socialism in American Labor Unions.

A   XII (4): Feb 5, 1903; C-2, L-2

4213   Victor Petrassovich; Whitney, PA; Feb 6, 1903

The October 27, 1902 formation of a Hostetter, PA Rusyn political club.

L   XII (4): Feb 5, 1903; C-3, L-2

4214   [N.N.]; "Vŷvernený (Prevraščenny) razmîrŷ" [Distorted figures]

The situation of Rusyns in America and Europe.

Part I: XII (6): Feb 19, 1903; L-4, and
                     XII (6&7): Feb 26, 1903; C-4

Part II: XII (8): Mar 5, 1903; C-4, L-4

A

4215   [N.N.]; "Novŷj Ėmyhracijnŷj zakon" [New immigration law]

The new emigration restriction law before Congress which would prevent anarchists and former criminals from settling in America.

A   XII (9): Mar 12, 1903; C-4, L-4

4216   Nicholas Topol'an; Joliet, IL; Mar 14, 1903

Joliet's Rusyn community and activities.

L   XII (10): Mar 19, 1903; C-2&3, L-2&3

4217   [N.N.]; "Čest', Pravda y Alčnost'-Žadnost'" [Honor, Truth, and Greed]
Commentary on striving for wealth.

A   XII (10): Mar 19, 1903; C-4, L-4

4218   [N.N.]; "Poslîdnŷj otholos strajku" [Last echo of the strike]
Outcome of a six-month coal miner's strike in Pennsylvania.

A   XII (11): Mar 26, 1903; C-4, L-4

4219   [N.N.]; "Nezadovolenie meždu nîkotorŷmy majneramy na oblasty tverdoho uhlja" [Discontent among some miners in the anthracite region]

A   XII (12): Apr 2, 1903; C-4, L-4

4220 Nicholas Pačuta; Braddock, PA; Mar 31, 1903

The March 31, 1903 industrial accident that claimed the lives of several Rusyns (listed).

L   XII (13): Apr 9, 1903; C-3, L-3

4221 [N.N.]; "Obezpečenie buduščnosty am. hr. kat. Rusynov" [Assuring the future of American Greek Catholic Rusyns]

Examines the past 12-14 years of the Rusyn immigration to America and comments on the future of Rusyns in America.

Parts I-II: XII (14-15): Apr 16-30, 1903; C-2, L-2

Part III: XII (17): May 7, 1903; C-2, L-2

Part IV: XII (19): May 28, 1903; C-2, L-2

Part V: XII (21): Jun 11, 1903; C-2, L-2

A

4222 Rev. Irenaeus Matyaczko; St. Louis, MO; Apr 8, 1903

The Rusyn communities in the western states.

L   XII (14): Apr 16, 1903; C-2, L-2

4223 George Fejdelen; Hannastown, PA; Apr 17, 1903

The activities of the Hannastown Rusyn community.

L   XII (15): Apr 30, 1903; C-2, L-2

4224 M.G. Wilchak; Stewartsville, NJ; May 5, 1903

Stewartsville's Rusyn community and activities.

L   XII (16): May 7, 1903; C-3, L-3

4225 [N.N.]; "Nîmec-ly yly Russ?" [German or Russian?]

The politics of Eastern Europe where German and Russian interests conflict.

Parts I-III: XII (16-18): May 7-21, 1903; C-2&3, L-2&3

A

4226 [N.N.]; "Makedonija" [Macedonia]

The people, history and politics of this small Balkan country.

A   XII (16): May 7, 1903; C-4, L-4

4227 [N.N.]; "Proč' s Rymom" [Away with Rome]

The German anti-Catholic movement in Austria.

A   XII (17): May 14, 1903; C-4

4228   John Uhrin; Homestead, PA; May 9, 1903

        History and activities of Homestead's Rusyn community.

        L   XII (18): May 21, 1903; C-3, L-3

4229   [N.N.]; "Sîjaly vîter', žaly burju" [They sowed the wind, they reaped the storm]

        Jews in Bessarabia.

        A   XII (18): May 21, 1903; C-4

4230   George Macko; Dunbar, PA; May 17, 1903

        Dunbar's Rusyn community and activities.

        L   XII (19): May 28, 1903; C-2, L-2

4231   Basil Kepenač; Hibernia, NY; May 25, 1903

        Hibernia's Rusyn community.

        L   XII (19): May 28, 1903; C-2, L-2

4232   [N.N.]; "Otstupnyčestvo (Renehatstvo)" [Renegades]

        Rusyn-Americans who completely reject their faith and nationality.

        A   XII (19): May 28, 1903; C-4, L-4

4233   Michael Madzin; Scranton, PA; May 27, 1903

        Rusyn national-religious problems in America.

        L   XII (20): Jun 4, 1903; C-2&3, L-2&3

4234   [N.N.]; "Fal'šyva prysjaha" [False Oath]

        Commentary on breaking business agreements and promises.

        A   XII (24): Jul 9, 1903; C-4, L-4

4235   [N.N.]; "Dvyženie našych Russkych y Slovenskych naborščykov-drukarej" [A movement among our Rusyn and Slovak typesetters]

        Plans for a Rusyn-Slovak printers society to be discussed at a conference in New York City, July 18, 1903.

        A   XII (25): Jul 16, 1903; C-2, L-2

4236   Michael Sabo; South Sharon, PA; Jul 7, 1903

        Employment opportunities with the Sharon Steel Co.

        L   XII (25): Jul 16, 1903; C-2, L-2

4237   Michael Maczik; Streator, IL; Jul 18, 1903

        The damage done to Streator by a tornado.

        L   XII (26): Jul 23, 1903; C-2, L-2

4238 [N.N.]; "Neporjadky v Orhanyzacijach Robočych" [Disorders in
Worker Organizations]

Dishonesty and corruption of American union officials.

A   XII (27): Jul 30, 1903; C-2, L-2

4239 [N.N.]; "Vopros Emyhracijnŷj" [Immigration Question]

The fears of American officials that large numbers of immigrants cannot be Americanized and assimilated.

A   XII (30): Aug 20, 1903; C-2

4240 [N.N.]; "Predochranytel'noe protyvžydovskoe napravlenie v Rossiy"
[A precautionary anti-Jewish trend in Russia]

The treatment of Russian Jews.

Parts I-II: XII (30-31): Aug 20-27; C-2&3

4241 [N.N.]; "Help yourself"

The improvement of one's spiritual and material well-being in
America.

A   XII (30): Aug 20, 1903; L-4

4242 [N.N.]; "Pryncypŷ-Zasadŷ Chrystianskoho Socialyzma" [Principles
of Christian Socialism]

A   XII (31): Aug 27, 1903; C-2, L-2

4243 M.S. Rushin; Minneapolis, MN; Aug 26, 1903

Minneapolis' Rusyn community and activities.

L   XII (32): Sep 3, 1903; C-3, L-3

4244 [N.N.]; "Polytyčeskaja sytuacija v Uhorščynî" [Political situation
in Hungary]

Review of Austro-Hungarian political developments since the
revolution of 1848.

A   XII (33): Sep 10, 1903; C-2

4245 [N.N.]; "Zaščyta-ochorona pred anarchyzmom" [Protection from
anarchism]

The new American law designed to prevent anarchists from
immigrating to America.

A   XII (33): Sep 10, 1903; C-2, L-2

4246 [N.N.]; "Našy Brat'ja v Nju Iorku rušajutsja" [Our brethren in
New York are on the move]

The formation of a political club for Rusyns and Slovaks in
New York City.

A   XII (34): Sep 17, 1903; C-2&3, L-2&3

4247   [N.N.]; Bayonne, NJ; Sep 20, 1903

        Bayonne's Rusyn community and activities.

        L   XII (35): Sep 24, 1903; C-2&3, L-2

4248   [N.N.]; "Polytyčne s"orhanyzovanie našoho naroda" [Political organizations of our people]

        A   XII (37): Oct 8, 1903; C-4, L-4

4249   [N.N.]; "Bezpokojstvie na Uhorščynî" [Disquietude in Hungary]

        Current problems in Hungary.

        A   XII (37): Oct 8, 1903; C-6, L-6

4250   [N.N.]; "Žydovsko-Mad'jarskij patriotyzm" [Jewish-Magyar patriotism]

        Jewish influence in Hungary.

        A   XII (38): Oct 15, 1903; C-2&3, L-2&3

4251   George Luczo; St. Clair, PA; Oct 9, 1903

        "Zaslato. Nevîrna žena" [Letter to the Editor. Unfaithful wife]

        A Rusyn immigrant's trouble with his unfaithful wife.

        L   XII (38): Oct 15, 1903; C-3, L-4

4252   [N.N.]; "Situacija v Uhorščynî" [The situation in Hungary]

        Hungarian internal politics.

        A   XII (39): Oct 22, 1903; C-2, L-2

4253   George Koleszár; Yonkers, NY; Oct 18, 1903

        Yonkers' Rusyn community and activities.

        L   XII (39): Oct 22, 1903; C-2, L-2

4254   [N.N.]; "Proekt Vsîm Slavjanam vo vnymanie" [A proposal that merits the attention of all Slavs]

        The Pan-Slavic movement in Europe to help Slavs living under Turkish dominion.

        A   XII (39): Oct 22, 1903; C-4, L-4

4255   [N.N.]; "Najnovšiy narodno-hospodarskiy bor'bŷ" [The latest national-economic battles]

        The right of workers to organize unions and to strike.

        A   XII (40): Oct 29, 1903; C-4, L-4

4256   Stephen Tkač; Lindsey, PA; Nov 5, 1903

      Lindsey's Rusyn community and activities.

      L   XII (42): Nov 12, 1903; C-2, L-2

4257   George Kuchár; Lattimer, PA; Nov 8, 1903

      Lattimer's Rusyn community and activities.

      L   XII (42): Nov 12, 1903; C-2&3, L-2

4258   George Vasily; Mingo Junction, OH; Nov 16, 1903

      Mingo Junction's Rusyn-Slovak community and activities.

      L   XII (43): Nov 19, 1903; C-2, L-2

4259   Rev. John Parscouta; Whiting, IN; Nov 12, 1903

      "Zaslato" [Letter to the Editor]

      Letter to Rev. Pavčo, spiritual advisor of the F.C.S.U., in reply to his article about Rusyns and Slovaks in Jednota, #629.

      L   XII (43): Nov 19, 1903; C-2, L-2

4260   [N.N.]; "Našy Rusynŷ y Zapadnŷy Štatŷ-Vestŷ" [Our Rusyns and the Western States]

      Rusyn communities in the Western U.S.

      A   XII (44): Nov 26, 1903; C-4, L-4

4261   [N.N.]; "Pročto ne chotîl O. Iosyf Košalko pochoronyty p. Ahnesu Ambroze?" [Why didn't Rev. Joseph Košalko want to bury Mrs. Agnes Ambroze?]

      The death of the mother of A.C. Ambroze, president of the Slovak National Union fraternal organization, sparked controversy in the Slovak community. See: 6005.

      A   XII (44): Nov 26, 1903; C-4, L-4

4262   [N.N.]; "Sobŷtija povtorjajutsja" [Events repeat]

      The immigration of various Slavic nationalities to America.

      A   XII (45): Dec 3, 1903; C-4, L-4

4263   [N.N.]; "Mnoho ubytŷch" [Many killed]

      Breakdown of U.S. vital statistics for the fiscal year 1902-1903 of labor-related deaths.

      A   XII (46): Dec 10, 1903; C-2, L-2

4264   [N.N.]; "Polytyčnoe sdružovaniesja russkoho a voobšče slavjanskoho naroda v Amerykî" [The political organization of Rusyns and in general all Slavic people in America]

The formation of a Rusyn and Slavic political party in New York City.

A   XII (48): Dec 24, 1903; C-2, L-2

4265   [N.N.]; "Robotnystvo podvyzaetsja" [Workers become active]

The terrible working conditions in some parts of the U.S.

A   XII (49): Dec 31, 1903; C-2, L-2&3

4266   [N.N.]; "Umîrennost' nad vsîmy" [Moderation above all else]

Rusyn life in America and Europe.

A   XI (49): Jan 1, 1903; C-4

4267   [N.N.]; "Zadača Avstro-Uhorščynŷ v Europî" [The mission of Austro-Hungary in Europe]

The future of the Austro-Hungarian Empire.

A   XII (49): Dec 31, 1903; C-4, L-4

4268   Andrew Matviak; Phillipsburgh, NJ; Dec 27, 1903

Phillipsburgh's Rusyn community and activities.

L   XIII (1): Jan 21, 1904; C-2&3, L-2

4269   J. Skakandy; St. Clair, PA; Dec 19, 1903

Commentary on Rusyn-immigrants bad habits, chiefly drinking and wife beating.

L   XIII (1): Jan 21, 1904; C-3, L-2&3

4270   Jacob Slotta; Rouse, CO; Jan 4, 1904

Labor problems in Rouse.

L   XIII (1): Jan 21, 1904; C-3, L-3

4271   M. K. L.; Cleveland, OH; Jan 25, 1904

The industrial accident in Cleveland.

L   XIII (2): Jan 28, 1904; C-2, L-2

4272   John Pavlik; Big Soldier, PA; Feb 1, 1904

Big Soldier's Rusyn community and activities.

L   XIII (3): Feb 4, 1904; C-2, L-2

4273   John Mulik; Butler, PA; Feb 1, 1904

Living and working in Butler.

L   XIII (3): Feb 4, 1904; C-2, L-2

4274   John Krajnak; Berthelet, WI; Jan 18, 1904

       Berthelet's Rusyn community and activities.

       L   XIII (3): Feb 4, 1904; C-2, L-2

4275   [N.N.]; "Americko-vseslavianska schudza" [American all-Slavic
       conference]

       Conference in St. Louis, MO on February 1, 1904.

       A   XIII (4): Feb 11, 1904; L-2

4276   [N.N.]; "Nasilne prez Fiume (Rieku)" [Forced through Fiume
       (Rijeka)]

       A Rusyn immigrant's account of his journey from the homeland
       to America.

       A   XIII (4): Feb 11, 1904; L-4

4277   Milan Ballay; Allegheny, PA; Feb 15, 1904

       The formation of an all-Slav political club in Allegheny.

       L   XIII (5): Feb 18, 1904; L-2

4278   [N.N.]; "Pomadjarščenie men russkych valalov" [Magyarization of
       names of Rusyn villages]

       A   XIII (5): Feb 18, 1904; L-4

4279   John Koščak; Mingo Junction, OH; Feb 18, 1904

       The February 10, 1904 industrial accident in a steel mill
       which claimed the lives of several Rusyn workers (listed).

       L   XIII (6): Feb 25, 1904; L-2

4280   [N.N.]; "Otholos na Vozzvanie komytetu konvenciy ameryk. slav-
       janskych žurnalystov na St. Ljuîskoj svîtovoj vŷstavkî, yz
       storonŷ odnoj amer. madjarskoj hazetŷ" [Echo reaction to the
       appeal by the committee of the convention of American Slavic
       journalists at the St. Louis world exhibition, from the stand-
       point of one American Magyar newspaper]

       Reaction from the editor of <u>Magyar Hírmondó</u>, [Cleveland, OH]
       towards the Slav journalist meeting in St. Louis, MO.

       A   XIII (7): Mar 3, 1904; C-4, L-4

4281   [N.N.]; "Rossija ochoronyla Soedynenŷ Štatŷ. Zla otplata za to"
       [Russia protected the U.S. and is poorly repaid for it]

       The U.S. proposal to arbitrate in ending the Russo-Japanese
       War.

       A   XIII (8): Mar 10, 1904; C-2, L-2

4282   Stephen Jánossy, Paul Gefrovich; Bradenville, PA; Mar 6, 1904

        The March 5, 1904 industrial accident in Bradenville.

        L   XIII (8): Mar 10, 1904; C-2, L-2

4283   [N.N.]; "Sympatija amerykanskych Slavjan dlja Rossijan" [Sympathy
        of the American Slavs for the Russians]

        Resolution for the support of Russia against Japan.

        A   XIII (10): Mar 24, 1904; C-2, L-2

4284   Michael Krajňak; Berthelet, WI; Mar 13, 1904

        The activities of Berthelet's Rusyn community.

        L   XIII (11): Mar 31, 1904; C-2, L-2

4285   J. Skakandy; Whiting, IN; Mar 25, 1904

        Tornado damage in Whiting.

        L   XIII (11): Mar 31, 1904; C-3, L-2

4286   [N.N.]; Rockrab, CO; Mar 24, 1904

        The four month old miner's strike in the South-central area
        of Colorado.

        L   XIII (11): Mar 31, 1904; C-3, L-2&3

4287   [N.N.]; Bayonne, NJ; Mar 28, 1904

        The March 28, 1904 industrial accident in Bayonne.

        L   XIII (11): Mar 31, 1904; C-3, L-3

4288   [N.N.]; "Vopros poselenjasja èmyhrantov" [The question of settling
        immigrants]

        Information on how many and where immigrants settle in the U.S.

        A   XIII (11): Mar 11, 1904; C-4, L-4

4289   [N.N.]; "Volnenie v Uhorščynî" [Agitation in Hungary]

        Reasons for the immigration of Hungarians to America.

        A   XIII (13): Apr 21, 1904; C-4, L-4

4290   John Palyicka; Vel'ký Kazimir (Nagykázmer), Zemplén County, Hungary;
        Mar 7, 1904

        Flood disaster in Vel'ký Kazimir.

        A   XIII (15): May 5, 1904; C-2, L-2

4291   Helen Dzmura; Braddock, PA; Apr 27, 1904

       An explosion in Braddock that destroyed homes killing several people.

       L   XIII (15): May 5, 1904; C-2, L-2

4292   [N.N.]; "Bŷlo bŷ uže vremja vŷlîzty yz bolota" [It's about time to climb out of the swamp]

       The national-religious condition of Rusyns in America and Europe.

       A   XIII (16): May 12, 1904; C-2, L-2

4293   C. Z.; Bridgeport, CT; May 14, 1904

       Bridgeport's Rusyn community and activities.

       L   XIII (17): May 19, 1904; C-2, L-2

4294   [N.N.]; "Dobrŷ vyhljadŷ" [Good prospects]

       U.S. fiscal policy and the labor market.

       A   XIII (19): Jun 2, 1904; C-4, L-4

4295   P. Ju. Ž.; "Otvertŷ pys'ma do O. Yliy Hojdyča y eho edynomŷslennykov" [Open letters to Rev. Elias Gojdics and his partisans]

       Rusyns in America.

       Part I: XIII (20): Jun 9, 1904; C-2, L-2

       Part II: XIII (24): Jul 7, 1904; C-2, L-2

       L

4296   [N.N.]; "Publyčnoe napadenie madjarskoho pravytel'stva" [Public attack by the Magyar Government]

       Allegations of the Hungarian Government that the U.S. encourages the immigration to America.

       A   XIII (20): Jun 9, 1904; C-4, L-4

4297   Peter Budzilka; Donora, PA; Jun 8, 1904

       Donora's Rusyn community and activities.

       L   XIII (21): Jun 16, 1904; C-2, L-2

4298   [N.N.]; "Nedostatočnost' ystynnoho dobročynnoho Čuvstva v našom narodî" [Lack of real philanthropic sense in our people]

       Rusyn-American character flaws.

       A   XIII (22): Jun 23, 1904; C-2, L-2

4299   [N.N.]; "Opastna tychota" [Dangerous silence]

The past experiences and possible future encounters with persons and groups who seek to cause religious-national strife among Rusyn-Americans.

A   XIII (22): Jun 23, 1904; C-4, L-4

4300   M. K.; Philadelphia, PA; Jun 27, 1904

Past conflicts among the Rusyns in the Philadelphia vicinity.

L   XIII (23): Jun 30, 1904; C-2&3, L-3

4301   Joseph Fecko; Steubenville, OH; Jul 8, 1904

Toronto's Rusyn community and activities.

L   XIII (25): Jul 14, 1904; C-2, L-2

4302   Ž.; "Čto dolžnŷ bŷ ymîty hr. kat. Rusynŷ v Amerykî?" [What should Greek Catholic Rusyns have in America?]

Rusyn immigrant material wealth.

E   XIII (25): Jul 14, 1904; C-4, L-4

4303   Basil Soroka; Sugar Creek, MO; Aug 21, 1904

Sugar Creek's Rusyn community and activities.

L   XIII (28): Sep 1, 1904; 7

4304   Joseph Smiško; Glen Jean, WV; Aug, 1904

Glen Jean's Rusyn community and activities.

L   XIII (29): Sep 8, 1904; 9

4305   John Skakandy; Whiting, IN; Sep 2, 1904

Experiences of one Rusyn immigrant who came to America with difficulty due to Magyar officials.

L   XIII (29): Sep 8, 1904; 9

4306   [N.N.]; "Mežduparljamentarnŷj konhress v St. Ljuis, Mo." [Interparliamentary Congress in St. Louis, MO]

International representatives met in St. Louis on September 7, 1904 to discuss problems facing their respective governments.

A   XIII (30): Sep 15, 1904; 4

4307   M.G. Wilchak; Stewartsville, NJ; Sep 6, 1904

The Augustus 20, 1904 industrial accident in Stewartsville.

L   XIII (30): Sep 15, 1904; 9,10

4308   [N.N.]; "Objazannosty Pensylvanskych sytyzynov roždennŷch na čužynî" [Responsibilities of Pennsylvanian citizens born abroad]

Reminds American citizens to vote. <u>ARV</u> endorses incumbent President T. Roosevelt and republican party ticket for the November 1904 national, state and regional elections.

A   XIII (32): Sep 29, 1904; 5

4309   [N.N.]; "Vseslavjanskij y žurnalystyčnŷi S"îzd" [All-Slavic and journalists congress]

Proceedings from a Slavic journalist congress in St. Louis, MO September 20-23, 1904.

A   XIII (32): Sep 29, 1904; 4,5

4310   Rev. Emil Kubek; Mahanoy City, PA; Oct, 1904

"Zaslato" [Letter to the Editor]

Trouble makers among Rusyn-Americans.

L   XIII (35): Oct 20, 1904; 9

4311   [N.N.]; "Jak ynače teper' sudjat'" [How they judge differently now]

The opinions and attitudes of the Magyar delegation to the St. Louis, MO Inter-Parliamentary Congress on immigrants from Hungary in the U.S.

A   XIII (37): Nov 3, 1904; 9,10

4312   [N.N.]; "Korably Kunard Lyniy" [Ships of the Cunard Line]

The legal monopoly granted by the Hungarian government to the English shipping firm, Cunard Line, for the exclusive transportation of immigrants from Hungary to America.

A   XIII (40): Nov 24, 1904; 9,10

4313   John Onderišin; Hocking, IN; Dec 6, 1904

The death of a daughter at the hand of a fellow countryman whose marriage proposal was rebuffed by her.

L   XIII (44): Dec 22, 1904; 3

4314   [N.N.]; "Amerykanec o èmyhraciy" [An American on the emigration]

Commentary on an article by Ernest Crosby which describes the current emigration of foreigners from Europe to America, published in <u>The Arena</u>, December, 1904.

A   XIII (44): Dec 22, 1904; 4,5

4315   [N.N.]; "Svoj k svoemu" [Let's help our own]

The need for solidarity in matters of faith and nationality among all Rusyns.

A   XII (50): Jan 7, 1904; C-4, L-4

4316   [N.N.]; "Jak unia podporuje majnerskych robotnikov" [How the union supports the miners]

The United Mine Workers Union [U.M.W.].

A   XV (1): Jan 18, 1906; 12

4317   [N.N.]; "Mynuvšost', teperîšnost' y buduščnost' Avstro-Uhorščyny" [Past, present and future of Austro-Hungary]

History, politics and economics of the Austro-Hungarian Empire.

A   XV (2): Jan 25, 1906; 2,3

4318   [N.N.]; "Poradŷ majnerov y vlastytelej majn" [Consultation of the miners and mine owners]

Current contract negotiations between the U.M.W. and mine owners in Indianapolis, IN.

A   XV (3): Feb 1, 1906; 2,3

4319   [N.N.]; "Chyba v èmyhraciy" [Mistake in the immigration]

The settlement of immigrants in the eastern states each year.

A   XV (3): Feb 1, 1906; 4,5

4320   [N.N.]; "Russkiy socialystŷ-mužyky (zemledîlcŷ)" [Russian socialist peasants]

Socialist movement in the Russian Empire.

A   XV (3): Feb 1, 1906; 6,7

4321   [N.N.]; "Sud'ba majnerov" [The fate of the miners]

More on the issues involved in the contract negotiations in Indianapolis, IN.

A   XV (5): Feb 8, 1906; 2,3

4322   [N.N.]; "Obžalovan'e protyv mad'jarskoho pravytel'stva" [Grievance against the Magyar government]

Immigration specialist, Marcus Brown's August 12, 1905 mission to Budapest to ascertain why unusually high numbers of Hungarian citizens immigrate to the U.S.

A   XV (4): Feb 8, 1906; 4,5

4323   Michael Pliško; Elizabethport, NJ; Feb 9, 1906

Elizabethport's Rusyn community and activities.

L   XV (5): Feb 15, 1906; 2,3

288

4324 [N.N.]; "Rusin kandidovany na mesticky urad" [Rusyn candidate for city council]

G.C.U. Supreme recording secretary Julius Egrecky's bid for the directorship of the Homestead, PA city school district.

A   XV (5): Feb 15, 1906; 3

4325 [N.N.]; "Ubijstvo pod plaščom zakona" [Murder under the mantle of the law]

The Magyar police execution of Rusyn peasants suspected of anti-government activity.

A   XV (5): Feb 15, 1906; 4,5

4326 [N.N.]; "Najnovijšoe o majnerach" [Latest about the miners]

Recent news about the U.M.W. contract negotiations.

A   XV (6): Feb 22, 1906; 2,3

4327 [N.N.]; "Polytyčnoe položenie v Uhorščyni" [The political situation in Hungary]

Part I: XV (6): Feb 22, 1906; 6,7

Parts II-III: XV (12-13): Apr 5-12, 1906; 4,5

A

4328 Danil Kuzmiak; Alden, PA; Feb 9, 1906

Alden's Rusyn community and activities.

L   XV (6): Feb 22, 1906; 6,7

4329 Peter J. Maczkov; "O nas pro nas" [About us for us]

1. Election results for the position of Homestead, PA school director in which supreme recording secretary, Julius Egrecky, was a candidate.
2. First Greek Catholic Congress.

A   XV (7): Mar 1, 1906; 6,7

4330 Ž.; "Pijatyka, jak najbol'šij vrach vseho čelovîčestva" [Liquor, the biggest enemy of all mankind]

Rusyn-Americans' drinking problems.

E   XV (8): Mar 8, 1906; 2

4331 [N.N.]; "Položenie majnerov" [Situation of the miners]

The anthracite miners convention in Indianapolis, IN where negotiations between the U.M.W. and mine owners were conducted on contract agreements.

Parts I-V: XV (10-14): Mar 22-Apr 19, 1906

Part VI: XV (16): May 3, 1906; 4,5

Part VII: "Strach pered vseobščym strajkom na oblasty tverdoho uhlja mynul" [Fear of a general strike in the anthracite region passes]

A   XV (17): May 10, 1906; 4,5

4332   [N.N.]; "Mad'jaronstvo" [Magyarophilism]

The effects of magyarization on Rusyns and Slovaks in Hungary.

A   XV (12): Apr 5, 1906; 4,5

4333   [N.N.]; "Protest Robotnykov v Ameryki" [Protest of workers in America]

A memorandum, sponsored by various labor organizations, was sent to President Roosevelt and Congress protesting anti-labor practices by business.

A   XV (12): Apr 5, 1906; 6,7

4334   [N.N.]; "Emyhracija vozrastaet" [The immigration is growing]

Immigration statistics for March, April, May, and June, 1905.

A   XV (12): Apr 5, 1906; 7

4335   [N.N.]; "Sposobnost' dlja neuniových ljudej" [(Employment) opportunity for non-union people]

A   XV (13): Apr 12, 1906; 8

4336   Andrew Matviak; Phillipsburg, NJ; Apr 6, 1906

Phillipsburg's Rusyn community and activities.

L   XV (14): Apr 19, 1906; 2,3

4337   [N.N.]; "Popravka visty v dili krovoprolytija v Vyndber, Pa." [Correction of the news concerning the bloodshed in Windber, PA]

In 4331, Part V, ARV reported incorrectly the attack on striking miners by authorities in Windber, PA.

A   XV (15): Apr 26, 1906; 4

4338   [N.N.]; "Žertva toj neščastnoj pijatyky" [A victim of the unfortunate drunkenness]

Alcoholic abuse among Rusyn-Americans.

A   XV (16): May 3, 1906; 2,3

4339   M.S. Rushin; Minneapolis, MN; Apr 27, 1906

Minneapolis' Rusyn community and activities.

L   XV (17): May 10, 1906; 2,3

4340   [N.N.]; "Pokrok našoho naroda" [Progress of our people]

George Vaško, a Rusyn-American, was elected to the Bayonne
City, NJ city council.

A   XV (19): May 27, 1906; 3

4341   Rev. Orestes Zlockij; "Vozzvanie k amerykanskym Rusynam" [Request
to American Rusyns]

Requests donations of $1.60 (8 crowns) from Rusyn-Americans
to support a European charity fund for Rusyn poor, to be sent
to Rev. A. Vološin, Nauka publishing office, Maramaroš Sighet
[Máramarossziget], Maramaroš County, Hungary.

Req   XV (19): May 24, 1906; 4,5

4342   [N.N.]; "Deševŷj čelovîčeskij žyvot" [Cheap human life]

Pennsylvania State inspector John C. Delaney's inspection of
the dangerous working conditions in factories and railroad
facilities throughout the state.

A   XV (23): Jun 28, 1906; 2,3

4343   [N.N.]; "Novŷj naturalyzacijnŷj-sytyzenskij zakon" [The new
naturalization and citizen law]

Legislation by Congress on the naturalization process for new
citizens.

A   XV (26): Jul 19, 1906; 6,7

4344   Michael Trojan; Pleasant City, OH; Jul 27, 1906

The mining accident in the vicinity of Pleasant City.

L   XV (28): Aug 2, 1906; 2,3

4345   P. V.; Philadelphia, PA; Aug 1, 1906

Polemical situation in the Rusyn community in Philadelphia.

L   XV (29): Aug 9, 1906; 2,3

4346   Rev. Orestes Zlockij; "Čy može bŷty chrystianyn socialystom?"
[Is it possible for a Christian to be socialist?]

Commentary on an article about social democracy and religion,
which appeared in Volja, #9, May 1, 1906.

A   XV (32): Aug 30, 1906; 2,3

4347   John Miterko; Hawk Run, PA; Sep 4, 1906

Hawk Run's Rusyn community and activities.

L   XV (34): Sep 13, 1906; 2,3

4348   [N.N.]; "Demoralyzacija posredstvom separatyzmu" [Demoralization
       by means of separatism]

       The chief problems among Rusyns in Europe and America.

       A   XV (36): Sep 27, 1906; 4,5

4349   [N.N.]; "Potreba emyhrantov" [The necessity of immigrants]

       Why immigrants are important to America and its future.

       A   XV (36): Sep 27, 1906; 6,7

4350   [N.N.]; "Talijane v Amerykî" [Italians in America]

       A   XV (36): Sep 27, 1906; 6,7

4351   [N.N.]; Braddock, PA; Oct 1, 1906

       Braddock's Rusyn community and activities.

       L   XV (37): Oct 4, 1906; 2,3

4352   [N.N.]; Allentown, PA; Sep 26, 1906

       The polemics among Allentown Rusyns.

       L   XV (37): Oct 4, 1906; 2,3

4353   [N.N.]; "Jak zaobchoždalysja s emyhrantamy pered rokamy" [How
       emigrants were dealt with in previous years]

       Foreign immigration to America during the early 1800's.

       A   XV (39): Oct 18, 1906; 2,3

4354   [N.N.]; "Ratujme do nesčast'ja popavšoho našoho brata" [Let us
       aid our unfortunate brethren]

       Helping Rusyn-Americans in difficulty.

       A   XV (39): Oct 18, 1906; 4,5

4355   Ž.; "Žertvujme bol'še bratskoj zabotlyvosty našym brat'jam y sestram
       prychodjaščym do Amerykî" [Let us offer more fraternal con-
       sideration to our brothers and sisters who are coming to America]

       The need to care for other Rusyn immigrants as they disembark at
       Ellis Island in New York.

       E   XV (43): Nov 15, 1906; 6,7

4356   [N.N.]; "Jak pracujut Japoncŷ v Soed. Štatach" [How the Japanese
       work in the U.S.]

       Japanese immigration and its effect on the labor market in
       America.

       A   XV (49): Jan 3, 1907; 4,5

4357   [N.N.]; "Platŷ robotnykov y dorohotnja prožyvlenija" [Wages of workers and the high costs of living]

The need for a cost of living increase in all workers salaries.

A   XVI (1): Jan 17, 1907; C-8, L-6

4358   Ž.; "Indignačné Protestujucé Schodzi" [Indignant Protest Meeting]

Slovak organizations sponsor a series of meetings, to take place in February, 1907 to protest Magyar tyranny in the homeland.

                                   XVI (3): Jan 31, 1907; L-4
E   XVI (4): Feb 7, 1907; C-4&5

4359   [N.N.]; "Nîmaja Tyšyna" [Mute silence]

General apathy of Rusyn-American communities in response to events of religious-national importance.

A   XVI (5): Feb 14, 1907; C-2, L-4

4360   [N.N.]; "Yndyhnacijnŷy-Protestujuščiy Vîča-Sobranija" [Indignant Protest Assemblies]

More about the meetings organized by Slovak organizations to protest Magyar tyranny.

A   XVI (5): Feb 14, 1907; C-2&3, L-2

4361   [N.N.]; "Preporodzenie Austro-Uhorsku" [Regeneration of Austro-Hungary]

Slovak leaders discussed the current situation of their people under Magyar rule at a February 13, 1907 meeting in Vidnava [Weidenau].

A   XVI (6): Feb 21, 1907; L-4

4362   [N.N.]; "Velykij yndyhnacijnŷj Konhress Slovakov v Čykaho, Yll." [Great indignant Congress of the Slovaks in Chicago, IL]

Meeting of the Slovak Congress on February 17, 1907 to discuss what can be done in response to Magyar tyranny in the Slovak homeland.

A   XVI (7): Feb 28, 1907; C-2, L-4

4363   "Smutnyj dokaz surovosty i dykosty velykoj časty našeho naroda" [Sad evidence of primitivism and savagery of a large part of our people]

Series of letters to the editor about "old country" attitudes of many Rusyn-Americans toward their faith, nationality and each other.

                                   XVI (7): Feb 28, 1907; L-2&3
L   XVI (8): Mar 7, 1907; C-3

4364 [N.N.]; "Nîkotorŷy statnopravnŷy najnovšiy ydey" [Some of the latest state-law ideas]

A series of personal and state rights proposed by the Hungarian Government for its citizens.

             XVI (8): Mar 7, 1907; L-2&3
A   XVI (9): Mar 14, 1907; C-6

4365 Adolph Černy; "Yz bor'bŷ halyskych Rusynov" [From the struggle of the Galician-Rusyns]

Nationality problems among Rusyns in Galicia.

A   XVI (9): Mar 14, 1907; C-4, L-4

4366 Paul Pacuda; "Našym krajanam ne ymîjuščym pracŷ, yly dobroj pracŷ, vo vnymanie!" [Attention to our countrymen who are unemployed or do not have good jobs!]

Employment opportunities with the Windber While Coal Mining Company in the strike affected region of Windber, PA.

A   XVI (10): Mar 21, 1907; C-2, L-3

4367 John Skurka; Brook Side, AL; Mar 5, 1907

Brook Side's Rusyn community and activities.

L   XVI (10): Mar 21, 1907; C-2&3, L-2

4368 Peter Kimak; St. Louis, MO; Mar 7, 1907

Employment opportunities in St. Louis and vicinity for newly arrived Rusyn immigrants.

L   XVI (10): Mar 21, 1907; C-3, L-3

4369 [N.N.]; "Vseobšča nuzda o robotnykov v Amerykî" [The general demand for workers in America]

American labor situation.

A   XVI (10): Mar 21, 1907; C-6, L-6

4370 Basil Hegediis; Sugar Creek, MO; Mar 8, 1907

Employment opportunities in the vicinity of Sugar Creek and Kansas City for Rusyn immigrants.

L   XVI (11): Mar 28, 1907; L-3

4371 [N.N.]; "Vyznamosc indignančnych schodzoch. Kto ne je s narodom, ten je proti ňemu!" [Significance of the indignant meetings. He who is not with the people is against them!]

Meeting in McKeesport, PA on April 7, 1907 to discuss the plight of the Slovak and Rusyn people under Magyar rule.

A   XVI (11): Mar 28, 1907; L-6

4372   [N.N.]; "Americké indignačné schodzy Slavianov" [American indig-
        nant meeting of Slavs]

        The McKeesport, PA meeting on April 7, 1907.

        A   XVI (12): Apr 4, 1907; L-6

4373   A. T.; "Yndyhnacijnoe sobranie v Mykysport, Pa." [Indignant meeting
        in McKeesport, PA]

        Meeting took place April 7, 1907.

        A   XVI (13): Apr 11, 1907; C-2, L-2

4374   Michael Hulič; Sykesville, PA; Mar 24, 1907

        Sykesville's Rusyn community and activities.

        L   XVI (13): Apr 11, 1907; C-3, L-3

4375   Ignatius Ladna; Baltimore, MD

        Baltimore's Rusyn community and activities.

        L   XVI (16): May 2, 1907; C-2, L-2

4376   Basil Kepinač; Hibernia, NJ

        Hibernia's Rusyn community.

        L   XVI (17): May 16, 1907; C-2, L-2

4377   Redakcij; "Proekt na snyščenie Rusy" [Project on the destruction
        of Rus']

        Rusyn faith and nationality in Europe.

        E   XVI (17): May 16, 1907; C-6&7; L-6

4378   [N.N.]; "Vlasnoručnŷj lyst cîsarja Franc Iosyf y eho značenie"
        [Personal letter of Emperor Francis Joseph and its significance]

        A letter written by the Austro-Hungarian emperor for the occasion
        of his April 29, 1907 visit to Prague, discuss the relationship
        between the Slavs and the Germans in the Empire.

        L   XVI (17): May 16, 1907; C-6&7, L-6

4379   [N.N.]; "Dostalys'me slîdujuščoe vozzvanie y pryhlašenie" [We've
        just received the following appeal and invitation]

        A convention, comprised of representatives from various Slavic-
        nationality newspapers (listed), to take place May 26, 1907 in
        Cleveland, OH.

        A   XVI (18): May 23, 1907; C-4, L-4

4380 [N.N.]; "Slovenskij narodnŷj Konhress otbŷlsja neoźydanno krasno"
      [The Slovak National Congress went unexpectedly well]

      Congress met May 26, 1907 in Cleveland, OH.

      A   XVI (19): May 30, 1907; C-2, L-2

4381 [N.N.]; "Socialyzm" [Socialism]

      A Rusyn viewpoint.

      A   XVI (19): May 30, 1907; C-3, L-6

4382 [N.N.]; "Naśy ahytatorŷ" [Our agitators]

      The "enemies" of the Rusyn people in America and in Europe.

      A   XVI (19): May 30, 1907; C-4, L-4

4383 Michael Nemčik; "Yndyhnacijnoe sobranie v Trenton, Nju Dź.,
      podarylosja krasno" [Indignant meeting in Trenton, NJ went
      well]

      Meeting on May 19, 1907.

      A   XVI (20): Jun 6, 1907; C-2, L-2

4384 Peter Paytas; Dixonville, PA

      Dixonville's and Clymer's Rusyn community.

      L   XVI (22): Jun 20, 1907; C-2, L-2

4385 Joseph B-p; "Nuže do pracŷ, nespîm" [Let's go to work, not sleep!]

      Commentary on Rusyn-Americans helping unfortunate brethren in
      Europe.

      A   XVI (23): Jun 27, 1907; C-2, L-2

4386 [N.N.]; "Yndyhnacijnoe Sobranie v Monesen, Pa." [Indignant Meeting
      in Monessen, PA]

      Meeting on June 30, 1907.

      A   XVI (24): Jul 4, 1907; C-4, L-4

4387 [N.N.]; "Buduščnost' Avstro-Uhroščyny" [The future of Austro-
      Hungary]

      Politics and nationality problems of the Empire.

      A   XVI (25): Jul 11, 1907; C-2&3, L-2

4388 [N.N.]; "Protyv P'janstva" [Against Drunkenness]

      A   XVI (25): Jul 11, 1907; C-4, L-4

4389   [N.N.]; "O edynstvî russkoho naroda" [On the unity of the Rusyn people]

Pan-Slavic and Ukrainian ideologies and their effect on the Rusyns.

Parts I-IV: XVI (26-29): Jul 18-Aug 8, 1907; C-2, L-2

A

4390   Simeon Brilla; Hawk Run, PA

The Rusyn community and parish in Hawk Run.

L   XVI (27): Jul 25, 1907; C-3, L-3

4391   John Bilunka; Pittsburgh, PA

Alcoholic abuse among Rusyns.

L   XVI (27): Jul 25, 1907; C-3, L-3

4392   [N.N.]; "Narodnostynŷj vopros na socialystyčnom konhressî" [Nationality question at the socialist congress]

Issues discussed during a European German-Magyar socialist congress, June 29-30, 1907.

A   XVI (27): Jul 25, 1907; C-4, L-4

4393   [N.N.]; Lisbon Falls, ME

Lisbon Falls' Rusyn community and activities.

L   XVI (30): Aug 15, 1907; C-2&3, L-2

4394   [N.N.]; "Co še robilo na Ellis Islandu?" [What happened on Ellis Island?]

Inspection procedures by immigration officials on New York's Ellis Island.

A   XVI (34): Sep 12, 1907; L-3

4395   [N.N.]; "Akcija v pol'zu uniy" [Action in favor of union]

A congress, which took place in a Moravian monastery, proposes the union of all Slavic peoples under Russian rule.

A   XVI (34): Sep 12, 1907; C-6, L-6

4396   [N.N.]; "Emyhracija yz Uhorščynŷ" [Emigration from Hungary]

The costs of immigrating to America from Hungary.

A   XVI (34): Sep 12, 1907; C-6, L-6

4397   [N.N.]; "Socialyzm y Patriotyzm (otečestvennost')" [Socialism and Patriotism]

Socialist movement in Europe.

A   XVI (35): Sep 19, 1907; C-6, L-6

4398   [N.N.]; "Ljude k obstojatel'stvam prysposobljajuščiysja" [People adjusting to the circumstances]

Nationality issue among Rusyn-Americans.

A   XVI (36): Sep 26, 1907; C-2&3, L-2

4399   [N.N.]; "Jak smyšl'aju poriadni Mad'are" [What honest Magyars think]

Elections in Hungary.

A   XVI (36): Sep 26, 1907; L-2&3

4400   [N.N.]; "Terajšie položenie politicke v Uhorsku" [Current political situation in Hungary]

Serbo-Croatian politics in Hungary.

A   XVI (36): Sep 26, 1907; L-6

4401   [N.N.]; "Boj za vseobecne tajne hlasovanie v Uhorsku" [Struggle for universal and secret suffrage in Hungary]

A   XVI (36): Sep 26, 1907; L-6

4402   Redakcija; "Otvertoe Pys'mo do O. Mychayla Baloha, v Vyndber, Pa." [Open letter to Rev. Michael Balog in Windber, PA]

Commentary on Rev. Balog's letter written in defense of Bishop Ortynsky's views on Rusyn nationality.

L   XVI (37): Oct 3, 1907; C-2, L-2

4403   [N.N.]; "Russko-židovska emigracia" [Russian-Jewish emigration]

Immigration of Russian Jews and other Jews from areas of Eastern Europe to America.

A   XVI (39): Oct 17, 1907; L-6

4404   [N.N.]; "Čto chotîly zrobyty yz Rossiy" [What they wanted to make out of Russia]

Jews in Russia.

Parts I-II: XVI (41-42): Oct 1-Nov 7, 1907; C-4, L-4
A

4405   [N.N.]; "Data o vražde v Černovej" [Information about the murder in Černova (Lipto County, Hungary)]

The mass murder of villagers in Černova by Hungarian soldiers, as reported in the Slovak newspaper Národné Noviny.

A   XVI (43): Nov 14, 1907; L-2

4406   [N.N.]; "Uhorski Rusini i Ukrainism" [Hungarian Rusyns and Ukrainianism]

The nationality issue among Rusyn-Americans.

A   XVI (43): Nov 14, 1907; L-4

4407   [N.N.]; "Obman'čyvŷy Aljarmŷ" [Deceptive Alarms]

How speculators deceive the unsuspecting immigrant about the "bad times" that await them in America.

A   XVI (45): Nov 28, 1907; C-3, L-4

4408   [N.N.]; "Užasnaja katastrofa. Vŷsše 550 majnerov zahynulo vslîdstvie eksploziy hazov v Mononhah, statî Zapadnoj Vîrdžyniy" [Terrible catastrophe. More than 550 miners perished on account of an explosion of gases in Monongah, in the state of West Virginia]

Necrology list of Rusyn and Slovakian miners.

A   XVI (47): Dec 12, 1907; C-3, L-4

4409   [N.N.]; "Užasnaja katastrofa. V majnî v Džejakobs Kryk, Pa." [Terrible catastrophe. In the mine at Jacobs Creek, PA]

The December 19, 1907 mine explosion that claimed 300 lives. Necrology list of Rusyn miners.

A   XVI (49): Dec 26, 1907; C-1&2, L-5

4410   [N.N.]; "Den' O. Nykolaja" [St. Nicholas Day]

Commentary on the mining disaster at Jacobs Creek, PA as reported in the <u>Pittsburgh Dispatch</u>, December 20, 1907 citing coincidence that many Rusyn lives were saved because St. Nicholas day holiday was the same day as the disaster.

A   XVI (49): Dec 26, 1907; C-3, L-4

4411   [N.N.]; "'V nebî est' spravedlyvost'!'..." ['In heaven there is justice!'...]

The 1907 mining disasters in Monongah, WV and Jacobs Creek, PA.

A   XVII (2): Jan 23, 1908; C-1&3, L-4

4412   [N.N.]; "'Ukraynstvo' začalo dîjstno svyrîpstvovaty" ['Ukrainianism' really began to rampage]

The Ukrainian national movement and Rusyn-Americans.

A   XVII (3): Jan 30, 1908; C-1,2,3, L-1,2,3

4413   Vladimir Marušin; "Žal'" [Pity]

The 1907 Monongah, WV and Jacobs Creek, PA mining disasters.

A   XVII (5): Feb 13, 1908; C-2, L-4

4414   Joseph Ridilla; Dawson, PA; Feb 1, 1908

"Zaslato" [Letter to the Editor]

Requests Rusyn-Americans to stop their bickering and work together for the glory and honor of their nationality and religion.

L   XVII (6): Feb 20, 1908; C-2, L-3

4415   George Chukala; Hazleton, PA

        Commentary on 4414.

        L   XVII (8): Mar 5, 1908; L-3

4416   Ž.; "Jak sudza našo bratia Rusini v Galicii o vikraincach-vikrainu,
        vikrainizm?" [How do our brother Rusyns in Galicia feel about
        Ukrainians, Ukraine, Ukrainianism?]

        Part I: XVII (8): Mar 5, 1908; L-4

        Part II: "Ukrainska nevol'a (otroctvo)" [Ukrainian bondage]

        E   XVII (9): Mar 12, 1908; L-2

4417   [N.N.]; "Teperîšnŷy plochiy časŷ" [Current hard times]

        Current employment situation for miners and laborers with
        retrospect to the last panic in 1893-94.

        A   XVII (9): Mar 12, 1908; C-2&3, L-2&3

4418   Andrew Matviak, Carbonado, WA

        Carbonado's Rusyn community and activities.

        L   XVII (9): Mar 12, 1908; L-3

4419   John Kulamer; "Vozzvanie k vsîm russko-slovenskym polytyčeskym
        orhanyzaciam y hraždanam okruha Aleheny, Pa." [Notice to all
        Rusyn Slovak political organizations and members in the
        vicinity of Allegheny, PA]

        Announces the formation of general political council to meet
        in Homestead, PA April 11, 1908.

        A   XVII (10): Mar 19, 1908; C-2, L-2

4420   [N.N.]; "Po voprosu ěmyhraciy" [About the question of the emigra-
        tion]

        Current trend among legislators to pass laws restricting the
        immigration of foreigners]

        A   XVII (10): Mar 19, 1908; C-4, L-4

4421   [N.N.]; "Slavjanskij vopros" [The Slavic question]

        The influence of Russian political power in Europe and the
        issue of Pan-Slavism.

        A   XVII (10): Mar 19, 1908; C-4, L-4

4422   [N.N.]; "Dokolî ljude budut pyty op'janjajuščiy napoy?" [How long
        yet will people drink alcoholic beverages?]

        A   XVII (14): Apr 16, 1908; C-2, L-2

4423   Andrew V. Zsoffcsak; Vanderbilt, PA

        Political clubs and elections.

        L   XVII (15): Apr 23, 1908; C-3, L-2&3

4424   [N.N.]; "Ubijstvo namîstnyka Halyciy" [Murder of the Galician governor]

        Commentary on the murder of Governor Andrew Potocki as reported in Kuryer Polsky.

        A   XVII (15): Apr 23, 1908; C-6, L-6

4425   [N.N.]; "Duchoborcŷ" [Doukhobors]

        About a group of Doukhobors (a Russian religious sect which denies the divinity of the Holy Spirit) who emigrated to Canada at the turn of the twentieth century.

        A   XVII (17): May 14, 1908; C-6, L-6

4426   [N.N.]; "Jak ščadytsja v Amerykî" [How to be thrifty in America]

        Commentary on immigrant's spending habits in America; from an article in the North American Review, [n.d.].

        A   XVII (19): Jun 11, 1908; C-2&3, L-3

4427   [N.N.]; "Slavjanskaja vzaymnost'" [Slavic mutuality]

        Commentary on a Pan-Slavic article in Moskovskija Vîdomosty.

        A   XVII (19): Jun 11, 1908; C-6, L-6

4428   [N.N.]; "Pročto robyty rozdîlenie" [Why cause division]

        Commentary on an article about foreigners in America, a Pittston, PA English language newspaper [n.n.].

        A   XVII (20): Jun 18, 1908; C-2, L-2

4429   [N.N.]; "Banka a bankár" [Bank and banker]

        The types of banks in America and how banks can help an individual.

        A   XVII (26): Jul 30, 1908; L-2

4430   [N.N.]; "Ňerobce haňbu" [Don't create shame]

        The problem of drunkenness and brawling among Rusyn and Slovak workers.

        A   XVII (27): Aug 6, 1908; L-2

4431   [N.N.]; "Polytyka" [Politics]

        Comparison of American-style politics with European politics.

        A   XVII (28): Aug 13, 1908; C-4, L-4

4432   M.G. Wilchak; Belvidere, NJ

        The peaceful co-existence of Hungarian and Galician Rusyns in Belvidere.

        L   XVII (30): Aug 27, 1908; C-2, L-2

4433   Michael Kerestan; Monessen, PA; Aug 21, 1908

        Formation of a political club and employment opportunities in Monessen.

        L   XVII (30): Aug 27, 1908; C-2, L-2

4434   [N.N.]; "Prišol učytysja" [He came to learn]

        The mission of Hungarian Emigration Committee representative, Joseph Madaras, who came to the U.S. to learn about the resettlement of Hungarian emigrants in America.

        A   XVII (30): Aug 27, 1908; C-3, L-3

4435   Ž.; "Otčajanna akcija ukrayncev y radykalov" [Desperate action of the Ukrainians and radicals]

        Bishop Ortynsky's alleged involvement with the Hungarian Government.

        E   XVII (31): Sep 3, 1908; C-1&2, L-4

4436   John Drimak; Chicago, IL; Aug 22, 1908

        "Poslîdstvija ahytaciy ukrayncev y radykalov meždu Uhorskymy Rusynamy" [Consequences of agitation by Ukrainians and radicals among Uhro-Rusyns]

        L   XVII (31): Sep 3, 1908; C-2, L-2

4437   M.B.; Cleveland, OH; Sep 2, 1908

        "Kto vynovatŷj?...? [Who's guilty?...]

        The polemics between Ukrainians and Rusyns in Cleveland.

        L   XVII (32): Sep 10, 1908; C-2, L-2

4438   [N.N.]; "Kel'o krajov, tel'o obyčajov" [As many customs as there are countries]

        The experience of one Rusyn immigrant in America.

        Λ   XVII (32): Зєр 10, 1908; L-2

4439   [N.N.]; "Postŷdna, bezlyčna ahytacija ukraynsko-radykal'nŷch voždej meždu uhorskymy Rusynamy" [Shameful, impudent agitation of Ukrainian-radical leaders among Uhro-Rusyns]

        The internal strife within Rusyn-American communities escalated by the Ukrainian national movement.

        A   XVII (32): Sep 10, 1908; C-4, L-4

4440   Paul Karaffa; Pittsburgh, PA; Sep 14, 1908

A drunken brawl between several Rusyns that resulted in murder.

L   XVII (33): Sep 17, 1908; C-3

4441   Rev. Cornelius Laurisin; "Pros'ba v ynteresî odnoho nesčastnoho našoho brata-Rusyna" [Request on behalf of one of our unfortunate brother-Rusyns]

Requests financial and moral support for Paul Herman, a Rusyn immigrant from New Brunswick, NJ, accused of murder.

Req   XVII (36): Oct 8, 1908; C-2, L-2

4442   [N.N.]; "Cyhan'stva-lžy y klevetŷ, jako sredstva k budovan'ju v Amerykî Ukraynŷ y k obezpečeniju ukraynskoho Epyskopstva" [Lies and slander as the means for the construction of a Ukraine in America and for the assurance of a Ukrainian Bishopric]

The political and religious aspirations of Ukrainian nationalists in America.

Parts I-II: XVII (37-38): Oct 15-22, 1908; C-2,4, L-4

A

4443   [N.N.]; "Vov prospech majnerov" [To the advantage of the miners]

The current labor situation among American miners.

A   XVII (39): Oct 29, 1908; L-4

4444   [N.N.]; "Strašna katastrofa v majny" [Terrible catastrophe in a mine]

Mining disaster in Marianna, PA which claimed many Rusyn and Slovak lives (listed).

A   XVII (44): Dec 3, 1908; C-2, L-2

4445   [N.N.]; "Olehčen'ja dlja ĕmyhrantov" [Relief for immigrants]

The situation of immigrants working in America.

A   XVII (47): Dec 24, 1908; C-4&5, L-4

4446   [N.N.]; "Čarovnaja syla zolotoho kraju" [The bewitching strength of the golden land]

How tales of wealth in America lures emigrants from Hungary.

A   XVIII (3): Jan 28, 1909; C-3, L-2

4447   Joseph Biskup; Craig Root Co., CO

Employment and homesteading opportunities for Rusyns in Colorado.

L   XVIII (4): Feb 4, 1909; C-3, L-2

4448   [N.N.]; "Predpaschal'naja (Velykodennaja) Sv. Yspovîd' y ukraynsko-
        radykal'na akcija" [Lenten confession and the Ukrainian-
        radical action]

        Ukrainian nationalism in the western states of the U.S.

        A   XVIII (6): Feb 18, 1909; C-2&3, L-2

4449   [N.N.]; "Ukrayncŷ svyrîpstvujut" [Ukrainians are rampaging]

        Ukrainianism, Bishop Ortynsky and his policies, and the news-
        paper, Dušpastyr.

        A   XVIII (10): Mar 18, 1909; C-4, L-4

4450   [N.N.]; "Obraz yz žyzny Kanadijskych Rusynov" [A scene from the
        life of the Canadian-Rusyns]

        Partial reprint of an article from Kanadijskaja Nyva
        [Manitoba], March 15, 1909.

        A   XVIII (11): Mar 25, 1909; C-4&5, L-4

4451   [N.N.]; "Protyv èmyhraciy" [Against the immigration]

        U.S. policies in restricting immigration.

        A   XVIII (12): Apr 1, 1909; C-4, L-4

4452   Rev. Emil Kubek; "Naša pradîdnaja kljatva..." [Our ancestral
        oath...]

        Commentary on topics concerning schism, morality and nation-
        ality problems among Rusyns in America.

        Parts I-X: XVIII (12-21): Apr 1-Jun 10, 1909; C-2&3, L-2&3
        A

4453   [N.N.]; "Nasylijam y Žestokostjam Ukraynskym Nablyžaetsja Konec"
        [The End of Violations and Cruelties by Ukrainians Draws Near]

        Rusyn-Ukrainian polemics.

        A   XVIII (16): May 6, 1909; C-2&3, L-2

4454   Michael Onderak; Newburg, OH

        Newburg's Rusyn community and activities.

        L   XVIII (16): May 6, 1909; C-3, L-3

4455   John Boreczky; South Chicago, IL

        The activities of Galician-Ukrainians in Chicago and vicinity.

        L   XVIII (16): May 6, 1909; C-3, L-3

4456   [N.N.]; "Klyčut nas domoj" [They call us home]

        Life in Europe and the immigration of Rusyns to America.

        A   XVIII (16): May 6, 1909; C-4, L-4

4457   [N.N.]; "V svobodnoj kraynî" [In the free country]

Rusyn immigrant's opinion about the advantages of living in America.

A   XVIII (18): May 20, 1909; C-4, L-4

4458   [N.N.]; "Strohost' ymmyhracijnoho zakona" [Strictness of the immigration law]

The current 1909 immigration law.

A   XVIII (25): Jul 8, 1909; C-4, L-4

4459   [N.N.]; Cleveland, OH

The polemics between Rusyns and Ukrainians in Cleveland.

L   XVIII (26): Jul 15, 1909; C-3, L-3

4460   Michael Kosch; South Loren, OH

Polemics between Rusyns and Ukrainians in South Loren.

L   XVIII (27): Jul 22, 1909; C-3, L-3

4461   [N.N.]; "Amerykanskiy Hazetŷ-Pressa y Ėmyhrantŷ" [The American Press and the Emigrants]

Commentary on American press coverage of the immigration of foreigners to America.

A   XVIII (27): Jul 22, 1909; C-4, L-4

4462   [N.N.]; "Velykij strajk v Mykysraks, Pa. y Botlŷr, Pa." [Strike in McKees Rocks and Butler, PA]

Strike against the Pressed Steel Car Company began July 14, 1909.

A   XVIII (27): Jul 22, 1909; C-4&5, L-4&5

4463   [N.N.]; "Nŷnîšnoe položenie v Soedynenŷch Štatach" [The current situation in the U.S.]

The American labor movement and the immigration.

A   XVIII (28): Jul 29, 1909; C-4, L-4

4464   [N.N.]; "Poščečyna ynostrancam" [Slap in the face of foreigners]

A strike affecting several Pittsburgh, PA companies and the union condemnation of immigrant "scab" laborers.

A   XVIII (30): Aug 12, 1909; C-4, L-4

4465   [N.N.]; "Strajk v Mykysraks" [Strike in McKees Rocks, PA]

Developments in the strike against the Pressed Steel Car Company.

A   XVIII (31): Aug 19, 1909; C-4, L-4

4466   John Uhrin; "Ot hl. predsîdatelja 'Soedynenija'" [From the supreme
        president of the 'Soedynenie']

        The strike against the Pressed Steel Car Company in McKees
        Rocks, PA.

        O   XVIII (32): Aug 26, 1909; C-2, L-2

4467   [N.N.]; "Strašnoe krovoprolytie v Mykysraks, Pa" [Terrible blood-
        shed in McKees Rocks, PA]

        The strike against the Pressed Steel Car Company.

        A   XVIII (32): Aug 26, 1909; C-4&5, L-4&5

4468   Elias Demeter; "Amerykanskij Russkij Vavylon" [American Rusyn
        Babylon]

        Discussion of polemics and differences between Uhro-Rusyns,
        Ukrainians and Orthodox Rusyns.

        Parts I-III: XVIII (33-35): Sep 2-16, 1909; C-2&3, L-2
        A

4469   [N.N.]; "Mynulosja-ly uže rabstvo?" [Is slavery really over with?]

        The working conditions in many American companies.

        A   XVIII (33): Sep 2, 1909; C-4&5, L-4

4470   [N.N.]; "Rabstvo v Mykysraks, Pa" [Slavery in McKees Rocks, PA]

        The court injunction against strikers of the Pressed Steel Car
        Company.

        A   XVIII (33): Sep 2, 1909; C-5, L-5

4471   [N.N.]; "Konec uže blyžytsja" [The end is close]

        Negotiations between management and striking workers to settle
        the strike against the Pressed Steel Car Company in McKees
        Rocks, PA.

        A   XVIII (34): Sep 9, 1909; C-4&5, L-4

4472   [N.N.]; "Bud'te na strazî" [Be on the guard]

        Strike against the Pressed Steel Car Company in McKees Rocks, PA.

        A   XVIII (35): Sep 16, 1909; C-4&5, L-4

4473   [N.N.]; "Novota na Ellis Islandu" [New ways on Ellis Island]

        The new immigrant registration procedure on Ellis Island.

        A   XVIII (35): Sep 16, 1909; L-6

4474   [N.N.]; "Praca y bor'ba uhro-russkoho naroda y eho protyvnyky"
        [Work and struggle of the Uhro-Rusyn people and their opponents]

        A   XVIII (36): Sep 23, 1909; C-4, L-4

4475   [N.N.]; "Chrance svojo životy" [Protect your lives]

Safety precautions for Rusyns employed in hazardous occupations.

A   XVIII (39): Oct 14, 1909; C-4

4476   [N.N.]; "Koe-čto o 'Uhro-Russkoj Narodnoj Lyhî'" [Something about the 'Uhro-Rusyn Peoples League']

A   XVIII (40): Oct 21, 1909; C-2, L-2

4477   John Molčan, et al.; Struthers, OH; Nov 1, 1909

"Zaslato. Ukraynskaja franja na okolycî Ionhstavnskoj" [Letter to the Editor. Ukrainian devilry in the vicinity of Youngstown, (OH)]

The polemics in the Youngstown Rusyn community over the nationality issue.

L   XVIII (42): Nov 4, 1909; C-2, L-2

4478   [N.N.]; "Obohaščeniesja narodov" [(Numerical) enrichment of peoples]

The numerical growth of Rusyns and other nationalities in America.

A   XVIII (42): Nov 4, 1909; C-4&5, L-4&5

4479   [N.N.]; "Koe čto o ὲmyhraciy" [Something about the emigration]

The Rusyn immigration to America.

A   XVIII (44): Nov 18, 1909; C-4, L-4

4480   [N.N.]; "Buduščnost' Uhorščynŷ" [The future of Hungary]

Hungarian politics.

A   XVIII (47): Dec 9, 1909; C-4&5, L-4&5

4481   [N.N.]; "Velykaja Ymmyhracija yz Avstro-Uhorščynŷ" [The great immigration from Austro-Hungary]

A   XVIII (48): Dec 16, 1909; C-4, L-4

4482   [N.N.]; "Epyskop Ortŷn'skij obkradenŷi" [Bishop Ortynsky was robbed]

List of items taken from Bishop Ortynsky's Philadelphia, PA residence as reported by a Philadelphia Magyar daily [n.n., n.d.].

A   XVIII (49): Dec 23, 1909; C-2, L-2

4483   Trofim Han; Clarksburgh, WV

Clarksburgh's Rusyn community and activities.

L   XIX (3): Jan 27, 1910; C-3, L-3

4484   [N.N.]; "Opjat' protyv ymyhrantov" [Again against the immigrants]
       American opinion concerning the immigration.

       A   XIX (3): Jan 27, 1910; C-4, L-4

4485   [N.N.]; "Peklo Rusynov v Haliciy" [The hell of Rusyns in Galicia]
       Ukrainian movement in Galicia.

       Parts I-II: XIX (4-5): Feb 3-10, 1910; C-2&3, L-2
       A

4486   [N.N.]; "Novŷi 'narodnŷi opor'" [New 'national resistance']
       Growing national consciousness among Rusyns in Hungary.

       A   XIX (4): Feb 3, 1910; C-4, L-4

4487   [N.N.]; "Otvîčatel'nost' pracŷdavatelej" [Responsibilities of
       employers]

       The struggle between labor and management.

       A   XIX (5): Feb 10, 1910; C-4, L-4

4488   Michael Scserbik; New Alexandria, PA

       Polemics over the nationality issue among Rusyns in New
       Alexandria.

       L   XIX (10): Mar 17, 1910; C-2, L-3

4489   [N.N.]; "K perepysy obŷvatelej Soedynenŷch Štatov" [Concerning
       the census of inhabitants of the United States]

       a.   1910 U.S. census.
       b.   The procedures of the census takers.
       c.   ARV advice to Rusyns on answering questions pertaining
            to nationality.

       Parts I-III: XIX (11-13): Mar 24-Apr 7, 1910
       A

4490   Redakcija; "Perepyščyk obyvatel'stva" [Census taker]

       Advice to Rusyns in Homestead, PA and vicinity on answering
       questions pertaining to nationality.

       E   XIX (13): Apr /, 1910; C-6, L-6

4491   [N.N.]; Northampton, PA

       The nationality issue among Rusyn-Americans raised by the
       1910 U.S. census.

       L   XIX (14): Apr 14, 1910; C-3, L-2&3

4492   [N.N.]; "Zavtra, dnja 15-ho aprîlja, načnetsja perepys' ljudej (census)" [Tomorrow, April 15, begins the census]

Procedures census takers are to follow regarding the classification of foreigners and immigrants.

A   XIX (14): Apr 14, 1910; C-4, L-4

4493   [N.N.]; Youngstown, OH

"Ukraynskiy neščastnyky na okolycî Ionhstavn, Ohajo" [Ukrainian wretches in the vicinity of Youngstown, OH]

Ukrainian-Rusyn polemics.

L   XIX (15): Apr 21, 1910; C-2&3, L-2&3

4494   [N.N.]; "Yz Verchovynŷ. Ešče raz o vyborach" [From the Highlands. Once again about elections]

Commentary on an article about Rusyns in Hungary and their right to suffrage in Alkotamány [Budapest], #82, April 7, 1910.

A   XIX (15): Apr 21, 1910; C-4, L-4

4495   John Drimak; Chicago, IL; Apr 20, 1910

"Uhorskiy Rusynŷ v Čykaho, Yll" [Hungarian-Rusyns in Chicago, IL

Ukrainian-Rusyn polemics in Chicago.

L   XIX (17): May 12, 1910; C-2, L-2

4496   George Ragan; Berwick, PA; Apr 25, 1910

"Bezočlyvost' ukraynskaja y ej poslîdstvija" [Ukrainian impudence and its consequences]

L   XIX (17): May 12, 1910; C-2, L-2

4497   P. Ch.; Cambridge, OH

Rusyn-Ukrainian polemics.

                                     XIX (18): May 19, 1910; L-2
L   XIX (19): May 26, 1910; C-4

4498   [N.N.]; "Uznanie našoj relyhijno-narodnoj pracŷ, y smutnoe položenie uhro-russkoho naroda v starom kraju" [Recognition of our religious-national achievements, and the sad situation of the Uhro-Rusyn people in the old country]

Commentary on an article in Nauka [Užhorod], #14, March 25, 1910, which compares Rusyn life in Europe and America.

A   XIX (18): May 19, 1910; C-4, L-4

4499   Anthony Katrina; Yukon, PA

        The coal miners' strike in the Yukon vicinity.

        L   XIX (21): Jun 16, 1910; L-3

4500   [N.N.]; "Ljudej pustošaščiy fabryky. Klyvlyndskij avstro-uhorskij konzul podal do statu pros'bopys' v zaščytî robotnykov ymmyhrantov" [Factories destroying people. Cleveland, OH Austro-Hungarian consul sent to the state (of Ohio) a request in the defense of the immigrant workers]

        Immigrant labor problems in Cleveland.

        A   XIX (22): Jun 23, 1910; C-2, L-2

4501   [N.N.]; "Čto nam prynesla taja perepys' - census?" [What the census brought us?]

        Commentary on the 1910 U.S. census.

        A   XIX (22): Jun 23, 1910; C-4, L-4

4502   Tom Zurik; Letrobe, PA; Jun 27, 1910

        "Napomynaet robotnykov čtob ne chodyly za robotoju hdî strajkuetsja" [Reminding workers not (to search) for employment where (others) are on strike]

        Requests unemployed Rusyns not to scab against strikers in the Letrobe vicinity.

        L   XIX (23): Jun 30, 1910; C-3

4503   [N.N.]; Bradenville, PA

        Requests unemployed Rusyns not to scab against strikers in the Bradenville-Letrobe vicinity.

        L   XIX (23): Jun 30, 1910; C-3, L-3

4504   [N.N.]; "Bor'ba za chlîb nasuščnŷj" [Struggle for daily bread]

        The miners' strike in Pennsylvania.

        A   XIX (24): Jul 7, 1910; C-2, L-2

4505   [N.N.]; "Ukraynyzm v Halyciy" [Ukrainianism in Galicia]

        A   XIX (27): Jul 28,,1910; C-1, L-4

4506   [N.N.]; Butler-Lyndora, PA; Jul 20, 1910

        "Uhorskiy Rusynŷ na okolycî Botlyr-Lyndora, Pa." [Hungarian Rusyns in the vicinity of Butler-Lyndora, PA]

        Polemics among Rusyns and Ukrainians in Butler.

        L   XIX (27): Jul 28, 1910; C-2, L-2

4507   J.D.; Bradenville, PA; Jul 26, 1910

"Zos okol'ici strajku" [From the vicinity of the strike]

The affect the strike in Bradenville is having on Rusyn workers and their families.

L   XIX (27): Jul 28, 1910; L-2

4508   [N.N.]; "Jedna zos hlavnych pričin nepripuscenie immigrantov do Spojenych Statov" [One of the main reasons that immigrants are not admitted to the United States]

The minimum financial requirement of $25.00 each immigrant must meet prior to being processed for entry into the U.S.

A   XIX (28): Aug 4, 1910; L-4

4509   [N.N.]; "Demoralyzuem-ly my narod?" [Are we demoralizing the people?]

The polemics among Rusyn-Americans over the nationality issue.

A   XIX (29): Aug 11, 1909; C-2&3, L-4&5

4510   [N.N.]; "Moral'nost' ymmyhrantov" [Morality of immigrants]

The lack of morals among immigrant males in America.

A   XIX (33): Sep 8, 1910; C-4, L-4

4511   [N.N.]; "Zasidanie eksekutyvnoho komyteta akciy uhro-russkoho naroda protyv halycijsko-ukraynskoj y radykal'noj napasty" [Meeting of the Executive Committee for the action of the Uhro-Rusyn people against the Galician-Ukrainian and radical offensive]

Meeting in Harrisburg, PA on September 8, 1910.

Part I: XIX (34): Sep 15, 1910; C-4, L-4

Part II: XIX (36): Sep 29, 1910; C-4, L-4

R

4512   Paul Ju. Zsatkovich; "Majnerskiy strajkerŷ v bîdnom položeniy" [Striking miners are in a poor situation]

Requests donations for striking miners in the vicinity of Erven and Greensburg, PA.

E, Req   XIX (37): Oct 6, 1910; C-4&5, L-4

4513   [N.N.]; "V zaščytî ymyhrantov" [In defense of the immigrants]

The attitudes of Anglo-Americans towards immigrants.

A   XIX (40): Oct 27, 1910; C-4&5, L-4

4514   [N.N.]; "Snov' lyš' protyv ynostrancev" [Again only against
       foreigners]

       Commentary on one of the issues of the November state and
       regional elections -- restrictions on immigration.

       A   XIX (41): Nov 3, 1910; C-4, L-4

4515   [N.N.]; "Ymmyhraciju chotjat ešče bolîe ohranyčyty" [They want to
       limit the immigration even more]

       Proposed changes in the U.S. immigration law.

       A   XIX (42): Nov 10, 1910; C-4, L-4

4516   [N.N.]; "Amerykance darujut vnymanija ymyhrantam" [Americans are
       paying attention to the immigrants]

       The Y.M.C.A.'s involvement in helping newly arrived immigrants.

       A   XIX (43): Nov 17, 1910; C-4&5, L-4

4517   Joseph Feczko; Gary, IN

       Gary's Rusyn community and activities.

       L   XIX (44): Nov 24, 1910; C-3, L-3

4518   G.K.; Bradenville, PA; Nov 21, 1910

       "Holosŷ yz okolycî strajku" [Opinions from the vicinity of
       the strike]

       The affect an eight-month long coal miners' strike is having
       on Rusyn coal miners and their families.

       L   XIX (45): Dec 1, 1910; C-3, L-3

4519   [N.N.]; "Lyš' remeslennykov chotjat prypustyty" [They only want
       to admit craftsmen]

       Proposed amendments to the 1907 Immigration Act.

       A   XIX (46): Dec 8, 1910; C-5, L-5

4520   [N.N.]; "Ešče vse protyv ymmyhrantov" [Everyone is still against
       the immigrants]

       The results of a study sponsored by the U.S. Immigration
       Commission on curbing the large immigration to the U.S.

       A   XIX (47): Dec 15, 1910; C-4&5, L-5

4521   [N.N.]; Bradenville, PA; Dec 14, 1910

       "Yz okolycŷ strajku" [From the vicinity of the strike]

       Progress report on the strike by Rusyn coal miners in PA.

       L   XIX (48): Dec 22, 1910; C-3, L-3

4522   [N.N.]; "Smutnaja statystyka" [Sad statistics]

Statistics from the Allegheny County, PA coroner's office on 1910 industrial and mining accidents.

A   XX (1): Jan 19, 1911; C-2&3, L-2

4523   [N.N.]; "Vnymaime na hrošy" [Let us pay attention to money]

Financial transactions between Rusyn immigrants and lending institutions.

A   XX (1): Jan 19, 1911; C-4&5, L-4

4524   Michael Regec, et al.; "Slovo k skebam v Vestmorlynd Ko., Pa." [A word to the scabs in Westmoreland County, PA]

Two letters to the editor expressing displeasure at scabs undermining the strike in Westmoreland County.

L   XX (2): Jan 26, 1911; C-2, L-2

4525   [N.N.]; "Jak obezpečyty bankovŷy depozytŷ?" [How to insure bank deposits?]

Practical advice on banking.

A   XX (3): Feb 2, 1911; C-4, L-4

4526   [N.N.]; McKeesport, PA; Jan 30, 1911

"Ukraynsko-Ruteneckaja napast' v Mykysportî, Pa." [Ukrainian-Ruthenian assault in McKeesport, PA]

Ukrainian-Rusyn polemics.

L   XX (3): Feb 2, 1911; C-4&5, L-4

4527   [N.N.]; "Snov' odyn bankar' pošol svîtom" [Again another banker went broke]

How bank closures affect Rusyn-Americans.

A   XX (4): Feb 9, 1911; C-4, L-4

4528   Basil Kepinacs; "Dolja uhro-russkoho naroda tut v Amerykî y v starom krajî" [The fate of the Uhro-Rusyn people here in America and in the old country]

A   XX (6): Feb 23, 1911; C-2, L-2

4529   John Pavliak; Sykesville, PA

The formation of a Rusyn Slovak political club.

L   XX (6): Feb 23, 1911; C-3, L-2

4530   [N.N.]; "Kazarskiy chytrosty" [Khazar wiliness]

        Financial dealings with Jews. Reprint of an article by Rev.
        Julius Sztankaj in Görög Katolikus Szemle [Užhorod].

        A   XX (6): Feb 23, 1911; C-5

4531   O.; "Brutal'nosty ukraynsko-hetmanskiy y ukraynsko-rutenecko-
        hetmančukovskiy" [Ukrainian-Hetmanate and Ukrainian-
        Ruthenian-Hetmanide brutalities]

        Ukrainian nationalism and how it has affected the Rusyn
        communities in America.

        A   XX (7): Mar 2, 1911; C-4, L-4

4532   John Mitro; Youngstown, OH; Mar 8, 1911

        "Zaslato" [Letter to the Editor]

        Commentary on the condition of the Rusyn people in Europe
        and America.

        L   XX (9): Mar 16, 1911; C-3, L-3

4533   [N.N.]; "Na zaščyty ymmyhrantov" [In defense of the immigrants]

        a. The outlawing of immigrant contract labor.
        b. Proposals for the limitation of employing immigrants in
            New York state.

        A   XX (9): Mar 16, 1911; C-4&5, L-4

4534   [N.N.]; "Ot koho ymîem učytysja?" [From whom should we learn?]

        Commentary on Jews and freemasons.

        A   XX (10): Mar 23, 1911; C-4&5, L-4&5

4535   [N.N.]; "Tajnoe anarchystyčnoe obščestvo rutencov-ukrayncov"
        [Secret anarchist society of Ruthenian-Ukrainians]

        Secret Galician organization 'Siczynski'.

        A   XX (13): Apr 13, 1911; C-4, L-4

4536   Basil Fecurka, et al.; Pittsburgh-Frankstown, PA; Mar 25, 1911

        "Zaslato" [Letter to the Editor]

        Commentary on the polemics in Pittsburgh's south side Rusyn
        community.

        L   XX (13): Apr 13, 1911; C-4&5, L-2&3

4537   John Zavacky; Lyndora, PA

        Commentary on Rusyn-Ukrainian polemics.

        L   XX (14): Apr 20, 1911; C-3, L-2&3

4538   [N.N.]; "Opjat' lyš' protyv ymyhraciy" [Again only against the immigration]

        a. The efforts of the New York Missionary and Immigration Aid Society.
        b. Commentary on the anti-immigration viewpoint of Cornell University professor, Dr. J.V. Enks.

        A   XX (14): Apr 20, 1911; C-4&5, L-4

4539   George Hanusz; Murray City, OH

        Murray City's Rusyn community and activities.

        L   XX (15): May 4, 1911; C-3, L-3

4540   [N.N.]; "Yz mîst na farmŷ" [From the cities to the farms]

        Commentary on the American farmer and why farming is an attractive alternative for Rusyn industrial workers.

        A   XX (15): May 4, 1911; C-6, L-5

4541   John Drutarovsky; Bradenville, PA; May 5, 1911

        "Yz okolycŷ strajku" [From the vicinity of the strike]

        The situation among striking Rusyn coal miners in Westmoreland County, PA.

        L   XX (17): May 18, 1911; C-3, L-3

4542   [N.N.]; Lisbon Falls, ME; May 3, 1911

        Lisbon Falls' Rusyn community.

        L   XX (18): May 25, 1911; C-2, L-2

4543   Michael Danko, Harriman, TN; May 14, 1911

        Farming opportunities for Rusyn immigrants in the vicinity of Harriman.

        L   XX (18): May 25, 1911; C-2&3, L-2

4544   Mary Stefanov; Johnstown, PA

        Farming opportunities for Rusyn immigrants in the vicinity of Johnstown.

        L   XX (19): Jun 1, 1911; C-3, L-3

4545   [N.N.]; "Padenie moral'nosty" [Decline of morality]

        Commentary on the lower standards of morality among the world's populace, especially among Rusyn-Americans.

        A   XX (19): Jun 1, 1911; C-4, L-4

4546 John Uhrin; "Resul'tat holosovanija na zapomohu majnerskym
strajkeram" [Result of the voting to aid the striking miners
(in Westmoreland County, PA)]

A   XX (20): Jun 7, 1911; C-2&3, L-2&3

4547 Michael Pillisi; Whiting, IN

The Ukrainian-Rusyn polemics in Whiting's Rusyn community.

L   XX (21): Jun 15, 1911; C-4, L-2

4548 [N.N.]; "Nevol'nyky v kraynî svobodŷ" [Slaves in the land of the
free]

Commentary on the situation of labor in the U.S.

A   XX (21): Jun 15, 1911; C-4, L-4

4549 John Uhrin, et al.; "Vŷkaz rozdîlenija hrošej otholosovannŷch y
žertvovannych dlja strajkerov na Vestmorlŷndskoj okolycî
[Report on the distribution of the money voted and donated
for the strikers in Westmoreland County (PA)]

R   XX (25): Jul 20, 1911; C-6, L-6

4550 O.A.P.; Medzilaborce (Mezŏlaborcz), Zemplén County, Hungary, Jul 7,
1911

A fire destroyed the village of Habura (Laborczbŏ), Zemplén
County.

LE   XX (26): Jul 27, 1911; C-4, L-3

4551 [N.N.]; "Sdyranie uhorskych rusynov v Velykom" [The rip-off of
Uhro-Rusyns in Velikŷ]

Commentary on the conditions of Rusyns in Hungary.

A   XX (30): Aug 24, 1911; C-3

4552 [N.N.]; "Narodnŷy parlamentŷ" [National parliaments]

Comparison of parliamentary government in Hungary with that
of other nations.

A   XX (30): Aug 24, 1911; C-4&5, L-4&5

4553 [N.N.]; "Ešče odnoe nebezpečenstvo dlja ymmyhrantov" [One more
danger for the immigrants]

The proposed clause in the U.S. Immigration Act requiring all
immigrants to be literate.

A   XX (33): Sep 14, 1911; C-4, L-4

4554 Frank Shuda, et al.; Philadelphia, PA

Philadelphia's first Rusyn-Slovak Republican Party Club.

L   XX (35): Sep 28, 1911; C-3, L-3

4555 [N.N.]; "Načynajut razmyšljaty nezavysmo" [They are beginning to think independently]

Commentary on U.S. elections.

A   XX (41): Nov 9, 1911; C-4, L-4

4556 John Bučko; "Čto nas dîlyt, čto nas soedynyt?" [What divides us, what unites us?]

Rusyn-Ukrainian polemics.

A   XX (43): Nov 23, 1911; C-4, L-4

4557 John Ontko, et al.; Uniontown, PA; Jan 16, 1912

"Krasnŷj postup našych Brat'ev v Jun'yntavn, Pa." [Beautiful progress of our brethren in Uniontown, PA]

L   XXI (1): Jan 18, 1912; C-2&3, L-2

4558 [N.N.]; "Opjat' hrozyt nebezpečenstvo" [Again danger threatens]

Legislation before Congress restricting immigration.

A   XXI (1): Jan 18, 1912; C-4&5, L-4

4559 Michael Nemchik; Trenton, NJ

Trenton's Rusyn political club.

L   XXI (2): Jan 25, 1912; C-2, L-2

4560 [N.N.]; "Uhro-russkoj narod ymîet byty na strazî" [Uhro-Rusyn people should be on guard]

Concerning the dangers Rusyn-Americans face from trouble-makers.

Part I: XXI (3): Feb 1, 1912; C-4, L-4

Part II: XXI (6): Feb 22, 1912; C-4, L-4

Part III: XXI (7): Feb 29, 1912; C-4&5, L-4

A

4561 [N.N.]; "Verchovyna" [Highlands]

Rusyn situation in Hungary.

A   XXI (3): Feb 1, 1912; C-4&5, L-4&5

4562 [N.N.]; "Bankar' Rozett sbankrutoval" [Banker Morris Rozett went bankrupt]

Six banks owned by Morris Rozett were closed. Loss is especially difficult due to the large number of Rusyns and Slovaks who banked with Rozett.

A   XXI (9): Mar 14, 1912; C-4&5, L-4

4563   [N.N.]; "Pomošč' ymmyhrantam" [Help for the immigrants]

Efforts of several groups in the Pittsburgh, PA area to help
immigrants to settle in America.

A   XXI (11): Mar 28, 1912; C-4, L-4

4564   A.Z.; Bridgeport, CT

Bridgeport's Rusyn community and activities.

L   XXI (11): Mar 28, 1912; C-3, L-3

4565   [N.N.]; "Bor'by za prava naroda" [Struggle for civil rights]

The civil rights struggle in America and other nations.

A   XXI (20): Jun 13, 1912; C-4, L-4

4566   John Bubnash; Stockett, MT

Stockett's Rusyn community and activities.

L   XXI (22): Jun 27, 1912; C-3, L-3

4567   [N.N.]; "Važnoe dlja vsîch a tak y dlja nas" [Important for all
and thus for us too]

Employment opportunities for immigrants published by the U.S.
Bureau of Immigration.

A   XXI (25): Jul 18, 1912; C-4, L-4

4568   B.M. Kovalkovich; Philadelphia, PA; Aug 17, 1912

"Slavjanskij narodnŷj bank" [Slavic people's bank]

Philadelphia's First Russian-Slavish Bank.

L   XXI (28): Aug 8, 1912; C-2, L-2

4569   John Borč; Mingo Junction, OH

Mingo Junction's Rusyn community and activities.

L   XXI (30): Aug 22, 1912; C-2&3, L-2

4570   [N.N.]; "Kolonyzacija" [Colonization]

Commentary on the desirability of Rusyn immigrants forming
communities in certain regions of the U.S.

A   XXI (33): Sep 12, 1912; C-4, L-4

4571   [N.N.]; "Korotkaja ystorija ymmyhraciy" [A short history of the
immigration]

General statistical information concerning the immigration of
foreigners to the U.S. from 1820-1912.

A   XXI (39): Oct 24, 1912; C-4, L-4

4572   Basil Strojin; Minersville, PA

      Polemics over the nationality issue among Minersville's
      Rusyns.

      L   XXI (40): Oct 31, 1912; C-2, L-2

4573   John Papovich; New Britain, CT

      Living and working in the New England area.

      L   XXI (41): Nov 7, 1912; C-2&3, L-2

4574   Michael Breza, Jr., et al.; Roebling, NJ

      Roebling's Rusyn community and activities.

      L   XXI (42): Nov 14, 1912; C-2&3, L-2

4575   Gregory Savuliak; Shenandoah, PA; Nov 18, 1912

      A special collection by Rusyns for the Balkan Slavs involved
      in the Balkan Wars.

      L   XXI (43): Nov 21, 1912; C-3, L-3

4576   Gregory Savuliak; Shenandoah, PA; Dec 5, 1912

      "Žertvy̆ na vspomoščestvovanie syrot y vdovyc ostavšych po
      polehšych v teperîšnoj vojnî Juho-Slavjanov s Turkom"
      [Donations for the aid of orphans and widows who were left
      by those killed in the current war of the south Slavs with
      the Turks]

      Part I: XXI (45): Dec 5, 1912; C-2, L-2

      Part II: XXI (47): Dec 19, 1912; C-3

      Part III: XXI (49): Jan 2, 1913; C-3, L-3

      R

4577   [N.N.]; "Jak rozmyšljajut doma, v Uhorsščynî o vojnî?" [What do
      they think at home, in Hungary, about the war?]

      Magyar and Rusyn public opinion regarding the Balkan Wars.

      A   XXI (49): Jan 2, 1913; C-4, L-4

4578   Harry Savuliak; "Vspomoščestvovanie syrot y vdovyc po pavšych v
      vojnî našych brat'ev juho-slavjanov" [Charity-aid for orphans
      and widows of those killed in the war of our brethren, southern
      Slavs]

      Report on donations received for the support of the Jugoslavian
      cause.

      Part I: XXII (1): Jan 16, 1913; C-5, L-2

      Part II: XXII (5): Feb 13, 1913; C-5, L-3

      Part III: XXII (7): Feb 27, 1913; C-3, L-3

Part IV: XXII (9): Mar 13, 1913; C-3, L-3

Part V: XXII (14): Apr 17, 1913; C-5

Part VI: XXII (16): May 8, 1913; C-3, L-4

R

4579   [N.N.]; "Bŷrnett-Dyllynhhemovŷj zakonoproekt" [Burnett-Dillingham
        bill]

        The bill before Congress that would restrict the immigration
        of illiterate foreigners.

        A   XXII (2): Jan 23, 1913; C-2, L-2

4580   [N.N.]; "Ešče koe-čto o tom Bŷrnett-Dyllynhhemovom Zakonoproektî"
        [Something more about that Burnett-Dillingham Bill]

        A   XXII (3): Jan 30, 1913; C-4, L-4

4581   [N.N.]; "Prymîrŷ poučajut ljudej" [Examples teach people]

        Embezzlement in America.

        A   XXII (3): Jan 30, 1913; C-4, L-4

4582   [N.N.]; "Zaslužennoe otlyčie odnoho ščyroho prijatelja našoho naroda"
        [Well deserved distinction of a sincere friend of our people]

        Commends the care and service given to Rusyn customers of the
        Homestead Savings Bank by employee, Bartholomew Ranky.

        A   XXII (5): Feb 13, 1913; C-4, L-4

4583   [N.N.]; "Syzmatyckî brechnî u Rutenian-î" [Schismatic lies in Rusin]

        Commentary on the article about Rusyns in America in Rusin, #6.

        A   XXII (6): Feb 20, 1913; C-3

4584   [N.N.]; "Bŷrnett-Dyllynhhemovŷj zakonoproekt propal" [Burnett-
        Dillingham bill lost]

        The defeat by Congress of an anti-immigration bill.

        A   XXII (6): Feb 20, 1913; C-6, L-3

4585   Andrew Matviak; Carbonado, WA

        Carbonado's Rusyn and Slavic community.

        L   XXII (9): Mar 13, 1913; C-3, L-3

4586   [N.N.]; "Padenie moral'nosty" [Decline of morality]

        A   XXII (10): Mar 20, 1913; C-4, L-4

4587 Michael Lomaga, et al.; Perryopolis, PA; Mar 24, 1913

"Narod uhro-russkij naj varuetsja (storožytsja) Ort. ukr.
rutencov" [Let the Uhro-Rusyn people be aware of the
Ortynsky Ukrainian-Ruthenians]

Rusyn-Ukrainian polemics in Perryopolis.

L   XXII (11): Mar 27, 1913; C-2, L-2

4588 [N.N.]; "Prybŷl novŷj ambassador" [New ambassador has arrived]

Dr. Constantine Dumba, new Austro-Hungarian ambassador to the
U.S.

A   XXII (15): Apr 24, 1913; C-5, L-4

4589 Rev. Joseph Papp; Nové Davidkoho (Újdávidháza), Bereg County,
Hungary; Mar 19, 1913

Thanks Rusyn-Americans for financial aid sent to some of the
villagers in Nové Davidkoho.

LE   XXII (17): May 15, 1913; C-3, L-2

4590 [N.N.]; "Opjat' ymmyhrantnŷj vopros" [Again the immigrant question]

The activities of U.S. Senator Dillingham in sponsoring anti-
immigration legislation in Congress.

A   XXII (20): Jun 5, 1913; C-4, L-4

4591 [N.N.]; "Reform naturalyzacijnoho zakona" [Reform of the naturalization law]

The several changes in the law effective January 1, 1914.

A   XXII (20): Jun 5, 1913; C-4, L-4

4592 [N.N.]; "Mylost' na smert' osuždennomu krajanovy" [Mercy on our
countryman condemned to death]

Commentary on the August 6, 1911 murder of Frank Bezek by
Frank Maly.

A   XXII (22): Jun 19, 1913; C-2, L-2

4593 [N.N.]; "Nova proba protyv ynostrancev" [New attempt against the
foreigners]

The claims by anti-immigration U.S. Congressman Burnett and
Senator Dillingham, that immigrants cannot be assimilated
fully into the mainstream of American life.

A   XXII (22): Jun 19, 1913; C-4, L-4

4594 [N.N.]; "Uhorskaja ĕmyhracija" [Hungarian emigration]

Reasons for the massive Rusyn immigration to America.

A   XXII (22): Jun 19, 1913; C-4, L-4

4595   George Fejdelem; Ernest, PA

The availability of work in Ernest.

L   XXII (25): Jul 10, 1913; C-3, L-3

4596   G.V.; "Novŷj Svît" [New World]

Living in America.

A   XXII (27): Jul 31, 1913; C-2, L-2

4597   [N.N.]; "Čechija pered kryzoju" [Bohemia prior to a crisis]

Czechs in the Austro-Hungarian Empire.

A   XXII (29): Aug 14, 1913; C-2&3, L-2

4598   John Drobniak, et al.; Braverville, MN

Braverville's Rusyn community and activities.

L   XXII (30): Aug 21, 1913; C-2, L-2

4599   [N.N.]; "Dolja našoho naroda v starom kray" [Fate of our people
in the old country]

A   XXII (30): Aug 21, 1913; C-4, L-4

4600   [N.N.]; "Cholera v starom kray" [Cholera in the old country]

Report on the cholera epidemic in the Rusyn counties of
Hungary purportedly brought by reservists returning from the
Balkan wars.

Parts I-IV: XXII (34-37): Sep 18-Oct 9, 1913; C-5, L-4&5

A

4601   John Drobniak; Braverville, MN

The availability of farm land in the vicinity of Braverville.

L   XXII (38): Oct 16, 1913; C-3, L-2&3

4602   Paul J. Zsatkovich; "Plochoe ponjatie sohlasija meždu našym narodom
y yz toho proyschodjašciy neprijatnosty" [Poor understanding
of agreement between our people and the ensuing misfortunes]

The constant bickering among Rusyn-Americans.

E   XXII (41): Nov 6, 1913; C-4, L-4

4603   H.; "Uvahy na 'Novŷj Hod'" [Observations on the 'New Year']

The future of Rusyns in Europe and America.

A   XXIII (1): Jan 15, 1914; C-4

4604   [N.N.]; "Dîla robočiy" [Workers' affairs]

Labor problems and the working conditions in industry.

A   XXIII (2): Jan 22, 1914; C-4

4605   [N.N.]; "Ohranyčenie ymmyhraciy" [Restriction of the immigration]

The bill before Congress (sponsored by Rep. Burnett [D.-AL]) which calls for immigration quotas.

Part I: XXIII (4): Feb 5, 1914; C-4&5

Part II: XXIII (5): Feb 12, 1914; C-4

A

4606   H.; "Charakter" [Character]

The good and bad characteristics of the Rusyn people.

A   XXIII (5): Feb 12, 1914; C-5

4607   A...D...; Chandler, CO

The miners strike in Rockville County.

L   XXIII (21): Jun 18, 1914; C-3

4608   [N.N.]; "Svjata Rus'..." [Holy Rus...]

Rusyn nation and nationality.

A   XXIII (26): Jul 23, 1914; C-4&5

4609   H.; "Na porozî svîtovoj vojnŷ" [On the threshold of world war]

The events which began World War I.

A   XXIII (28): Aug 6, 1914; C-4&5

4610   Michael Mychlyk; Hartshorne, OK

Employment opportunities for Rusyn immigrants in OK.

L   XXIII (31): Aug 27, 1914; C-11

4611   George Šutljak, et al.; Maynard, OH

The five month old coal miners strike in Maynard.

L   XXIII (33): Sep 10, 1914; C-3

4612   [N.N.]; "Pervaja počta" [First letter (from Europe)]

The affect of World War I on the communication between relatives in America and Europe.

A   XXIII (33): Sep 10, 1914; C-4

4613   George Penzenyk, et al.; "Koho dolžny mŷ spomoščestvovaty?"
       [Whom should we aid?]

       Financially aiding Rusyns in Europe suffering from the ravages
       of the World War.

       A   XXIII (35): Sep 24, 1914; C-4

4614   John Hornyak, et al.; "Jakym sposobom dolžny mŷ spomoščestvovaty
       pokalîcennŷch v vojnî, jak tože syroty y vdovŷ po polehšych
       našych brat'ev?" [How should we aid those crippled in the
       war as well as orphans and widows of our dead brethren?]

       A   XXIII (35): Sep 24, 1914; C-5

4615   [N.N.]; "Voennaja lyteratura" [War literature]

       Hungarian government activity to increase support and patriotism
       for Hungary's involvement in World War I.

       A   XXIII (36): Oct 1, 1914; C-2

4616   [N.N.]; "Mylodarŷ hlavnŷch urjadnykov y robotnykov drukarny 'Soedy-
       nenija'" [Donations from the supreme officers and workers of
       the print shop of the 'Soedynenie']

       List of donations for the aid-relief of war-stricken European
       Rusyns.

       R   XXIII (36): Oct 1, 1914; C-4

4617   M.I.H.; "Blahočestyvŷj uhro-russkij narode!" [Pious Uhro-Rusyn
       people!]

       Requests donations from G.C.U. lodges and parishes for war-
       stricken Rusyns in Europe.

       Req   XXIII (36): Oct 1, 1914; C-4&5

4618   "Starokraevaja počta" [Letters (from) the old country]

       Several letters to the editor from Europe relating news of the
       war.

       LE   XXIII (36): Oct 1, 1914; C-5&6

4619   [N.N.]; "Na russkoj zemly" [On the Rusyn land]

       Russian military action in Galicia.

       A   XXIII (37): Oct 8, 1914; C-2&3

4620   George Dandar; "Uhro-russkij voennyj fond" [Uhro-Rusyn war fund]

       Report on donations received from lodges and parishes for
       aiding Rusyn war widows and orphans.

       Parts I-VIII: XXIII (37-44): Oct 8-Dec 3, 1914; C-3,5,6
       Parts IX-X: XXIII (47-48): Dec 17-24, 1914; C-3,5
       R

4621   Elizabeth Šuba, et al.; "K blahorodnŷm supruham uhro-russkych
               Vsečest. Otcev Duchovnych" [To the noble wives of Uhro-Rusyn
               priests]

               Requests donations for Rusyn war widows, orphans and the
               International Red Cross.

               Req   XXIII (37): Oct 8, 1914; C-4

4622   Basil Nastyč; Zimon? (Zemlin?), Hungary; Sep 7, 1914

               War effort in Uhorska Rus'.

               LE   XXIII (37): Oct 8, 1914; C-4&5

4623   [N.N.]; "K učytel'kam ručnych prac" [To teachers of manual labor]

               Requests Rusyn teachers in Hungary to support the war effort.

               A   XXIII (38): Oct 15, 1914; C-2

4624   Rev. A. Holosnyay; "Voennŷj fond supruhov uhro-russkych Vsečestnij-
               šych Otcev duchovnych" [War fund of wives of Uhro-Rusyn clergy]

               Parts I-II: XXIII (38-39): Oct 15-22, 1914; C-3

               Parts III-IV: XXIII (41-42): Nov 5-12, 1914; C-2,3,5

               R

4625   Mara; Vyšní or Nižní Olčvar (Felsö or Alsó Olcsvar), Abauj-Torna
               County, Hungary; Sep 8, 1914

               War effort in Uhorska Rus'.

               LE   XXIII (38): Oct 15, 1914; C-3

4626   [N.N.]; "Potîcha v pečaly" [Consolation in (times of) grief]

               Rusyn-American efforts to aid their war-stricken European
               brethren.

               A   XXIII (38): Oct 15, 1914; C-4

4627   O...; "Čaša terpînija perepolnena..." [Cup of suffering runneth
               over...]

               Expresses hope for a Russian victory over Austro-Hungary in
               the world war.

               A   XXIII (39): Oct 22, 1914; C-4

4628   [N.N.]; "Lyca nad polem vojnŷ" [Faces on the field of war]

               The affect of the world war on Rusyns in Europe and America.

               A   XXIII (39): Oct 22, 1914; C-4

4629 John Koščak; Mingo Junction, OH

The efforts of Mingo Junction Rusyn community to donate to the various Rusyn war widow and orphan funds.

L   XXIII (40): Oct 29, 1914; C-2&3

4630 Redakcija; "Prymîčanija k statiy 'Čaša terpînija perepolena'" [Remarks on the article 'Cup of suffering runneth over']

Editor's commentary/historical analysis.

E   XXIII (40): Oct 29, 1914; C-4&5

4631 G.Z. Barany; Bradenville, PA; Oct 28, 1914

"Niskol'ko slov k Rutenijanu" [Several words to Rusin]

Reply to Rev. Hanulya's remarks about G.Z. Barany in Rusin.

L   XXIII (40): Oct 29, 1914; C-5

4632 [N.N.]; "Kollekta na voennŷj fond s Mynha Džonkšŷn, Ohajo, v cerkvy Sv. Andreja" [Collection for the war (widows and orphans) fund from Mingo Junction, Ohio, St. Andrew's Church]

R   XXIII (41): Nov 5, 1914; C-3

4633 Joseph Borys; "Doloj syto s očej" [Down with the veil from the eyes]

Warns Rusyn-Americans to beware of Ukrainianism.

A   XXIII (41): Nov 5, 1914; C-4

4634 Katherine Černeha; Huta (Unghuta), Ung County, Hungary; Sep 22, 1914

"Pys'mo yz staroho kraja" [Letter from the old country]

Letter from a wife to her husband in America relating news of the war and death of friends and relatives.

LE   XXIII (41): Nov 12, 1914; C-5

4635 [N.N.]; "Dîty vojakov" [Children of soldiers]

The fate of Rusyn families whose menfolk are serving in the army during World War I.

A   XXIII (43): Nov 19, 1914; C-4&5

4636 John Harahal'; Somewhere in Bosnia

"Pys'mo yz staroho kraja" [Letter from the old country]

Letter from a Rusyn in the Hungarian army to a brother in America relating news about himself and action on the Balkan front.

LE   XXIII (43): Nov 19, 1914; C-5

4637   O...; "Ne sohlašajuščymsja s stat'ej: 'Čaša terpînija perepolnena'"
[To those who do not agree with the article: 'Cup of suffering
runneth over']

A   XXIII (44): Nov 26, 1914; C-4&5

4638   Rev. Dr. Vasochik; "Pys'mo starokraevoho uhro-russkoho epyskopa"
[Letter from the Uhro-Rusyn bishop in the old country]

Letter of thanks from Mukačevo Bishop, Most Rev. Anthony Papp,
for financial aid received for Rusyn war widows and orphans.

LE   XXIII (46): Dec 10, 1914; C-4

4639   Ylona Tehza-Bilak; Máramaros County, Hungary

"Pys'mo yz staroho kraja" [Letter from the old country]

Letter from a wife to her husband in America relating news of
the war in Máramaros County.

LE   XXIII (46): Dec 10, 1914; C-5

4640   Zajaroš Andrew; Nižnia Olšava (Alsóolsva), Zemplén County, Hungary

Letter to a brother in America concerning the war in Europe.

LE   XXIII (46): Dec 10, 1914; C-5

4641   O...; "Zajavlenie" [Declaration]

Requests Rusyn-Americans to consider Russia as the Rusyn homeland and to support the war effort on its behalf.

A   XXIII (47): Dec 17, 1914; C-2

Chapter 5

Rusyn Culture and Education

5001   [N.N.]; "Našy Koljadŷ y Koljadnyky" [Our Christmas Carols and Carolers]

The religious-cultural significance of Christmas carols and the custom of caroling in Carpatho Rus'.

A   III (1): Jan 2, 1894; C-9&10, L-15

5002   A.Y.T., et al., advisor: Ju.; "Ystoryčeskoe heohrafyčeskoe korotkoe opysanye Halycko y Uhro-Russkych s vzhljadom na kul'turnoe rozvytie, na zvŷčaî y obŷčaî y druhiy znamenytnîšiy ych spravŷ, Rusynŷ Lemky (Halyckiy)" [Short historical and geographical descriptions of Galician and Uhro-Rusyns, examining their cultural development, customs and other significant aspects; Rusyn Lemky (of Galicia)]

Parts VI-VII: Lemkian daily life and folk customs.

                 III (3-4): Jan 16-23, 1894; C-6

Part VIII: Lemkian folk and religious music.

                 III (5-6): Jan 30-Feb 6, 1894; C-6

Part XI: The annual holidays celebrated by the Lemky.

                 III (9): Mar 6, 1894; C-6

Parts XIV-XV: Lemkian peasant dress.

                 III (12-13): Mar 27-Apr 3, 1894; C-6

Part XVI: Slovak influences on the cultural development of the Rusyn-Lemky.

                 III (14): Apr 10, 1894; C-6

Parts XVII-XVIII: The language of the Lemky.

A   III (15-16): Apr 17-29, 1894; C-6

5003   [N.N.]; "Zakladajmo Čytal'nŷ!" [Let us Establish Reading Rooms!]

Necessity of establishing reading rooms to facilitate education and promote literacy among the Rusyn immigrants in America.

A   III (5): Jan 30, 1894; C-2, L-13

5004   [N.N.]; "Jak bŷ to nam najlekše založyty čytal'nŷ?" [What is the easiest way for us to establish reading rooms?]

Information for Rusyn-Americans on setting up a reading room in their community.

A   III (6): Feb 6, 1894; C-3, L-13

5005   [N.N.]; "Čytalnja y Bratstvo" [The Reading Room and the Brotherhood]

Establishment of reading rooms as beneficial to the G.C.U.

A   III (7): Feb 20, 1894; C-2, L-13

5006 M. C.; "Nîskol'ko slov k voprosu zakladanija Čytalen'" [A few
words on the question of establishing Reading Rooms]

A   III (8): Feb 27, 1894; C-2, L-13

5007 [N.N.]; "Razluky meždu hazetamy" [The differences between news-
papers]

The desirability of reading only newspapers (n.n.) offering
complete and accurate information.

A   III (9): Mar 6, 1894; C-2

5008 Ju.; "Čtože nam dîlaty v spravach zabezpačenija russkoj nauky y
russkoho prosvîščenija?" [What must we do to preserve Rusyn
learning and culture (in America)?]

E   III (10): Mar 13, 1894; C-2, L-13

5009 Ju.; "Rešitel'nyi slova v spravî relihijno-narodnoho zabezpačenija
Amerykanskoj Rusy" [Decisive words on the matter of preserving the religious-national heritage of American-Rusyns]

Part I: III (12): Mar 27, 1894; C-2, L-13

Part II: "Sohlasie, vednomŷslie y l'ubov" [Cooperation,
unity in thought, and love]

                                 III (13): Apr 3, 1894; C-2, L-13

Part III: "Vzaymnoe stremlenie" [Mutual aspirations]

E   III (14): Apr 10, 1894; C-2, L-13

5010 [N.N.]; "Chrystos Voskres!" [Christ is Risen!]

Lit-Poetry   III (16): Apr 17, 1894; C-2

5011 [N.N.]; "Popa nam nanjaly" [They hired a priest for us]

Lit-Poetry   III (16): Apr 17, 1894; C-2

5012 [N.N.]; "Nîkotorŷy suevîrya y vorožbŷ soključennŷ s svîtlŷm
Voskreseniem v Uhro Russach" [Some superstitions and fortune-
telling associated with Easter among the Uhro-Rusyns]

A   III (16): Apr 29, 1894; C-2

5013 [N.N.]; "Svîtloe voskresenie na Uhorskoj Rusy" [Holy Easter Sunday
in Hungarian Rus']

A   III (16): Apr 29, 1894; C-2, L-9&10

5014 [N.N.]; "Zamach na Russkuju pys'mennost' y na Russkoe prosvîščenie
v Halyčynî y Uhorščynî" [Assaults on Rusyn literature and
enlightenment in Galicia and Hungary]

Includes several excerpts from literature of Hungarian Rus'
and Galicia.

A   III (17): May 8, 1894; C-6

5015   [N.N.]; "Poučytel'noe y Vozbudytel'noe! Vot pryznanie y vosch-
        valenie našych relyhijno-narodnŷch stremlenij!" [Instructive
        and Inspiring! This is the acknowledgement and praise of our
        religious-national aspirations!]

        Contrasts a Rusyn immigrant's life in America with life in
        Europe.

        A   III (18): May 15, 1894; C-2, L-13

5016   [N.N.]; "Nastavlenija Obščestva ymenem Mich. Kačkovskoho o slavî y
        zabezpačeniy myloj sv. Rusy v Halyčynî, Uhorščyni y Bukovynî"
        [The Mich. Kačkovskij Society's instructions concerning the
        glory and preservation of hallowed Rus' in Galicia, Hungary
        and Bukovina]

        A   III (18): May 15, 1894; C-6

5017   [N.N.]; "Naš' jazŷk" [Our language]

        Rusyn language.

        A   III (21): Jun 19, 1894; C-6

5018   Ju.; "Tolkovanija v spravach sumîstnych cerkovno-narodnych našych
        ynteressov" [Interpretations of our mutual religious-national
        interests]

        Part IV: Unity can be maintained only through education.
        Eliminate illiteracy among Rusyns in America and in Europe.

                                    III (25): Jul 17, 1894; C-2
                                    III (26): Jul 24, 1894; L-3

        Part V: Rusyn national heritage can be preserved in America
        through the establishment of schools, theaters, etc. Rusyn
        immigrants must take a lesson from other nationally conscious
        immigrant groups if Rusyn culture is to survive in America.

                                    III (26): Jul 24, 1894; C-2
                                    III (27): Jul 31, 1894; L-13

        Part VI: A priority project for immigrant Rusyns is to
        organize a school for Rusyn children for the preservation of
        the national heritage.

                                    III (27): Jul 31, 1894; C-2

        Part VII: Problems and causes of separatism among Rusyn groups
        and communities in Europe and in America.

                                    III (28): Aug 14, 1894; C-2

        Part XIII: Preservation of Rusyn culture in America as a joint
        effort by clergy and laity.

                                    III (34): Oct 4, 1894; C-2, L-13

Part XIV: All Rusyns must become educated to insure the survival of the national heritage in America.

III (35): Oct 11, 1894; C-2, L-13

Part XV: The Rusyn intelligentsia in Europe.

III (36): Oct 18, 1894; C-2&3, L-13

Part XVI: Rusyn-Americans must help their less fortunate brethren in Europe.   Rusyn-Americans have the ability to become leaders in Rusyn culture in Europe and in America.

III (37): Oct 25, 1894; C-2, L-13

Part XVII: The establishment of a religious-national school for Rusyn immigrant children to ensure survival of Rusyn culture in America.

E   III (39): Nov 8, 1894; C-2, L-13

5019   Ieronym Anonym; "Russkaja Dolja: Povist'" [The Rusyn Fate: A Narrative Tale]

Parts I-XVII: III (31-47): Sep 13, 1894-Jan 2, 1895; C-6

Parts XVIII-XXIX: IV (1-12): Jan 16-Apr 4, 1895; C-6

Lit-Prose

5020   [N.N.]; "Sobranie členov Obščestva ym. Mich. Kačkovskoho vo L'vovî" [Meeting of the members of the Mich. Kačkovskij Society in L'viv]

Proceedings and resolutions of the September 18, 1894 meeting of the Kačkovskij Society.

Parts I-IV: III (36-39): Oct 18-Nov 8, 1894; C-2,3

A

5021   [N.N.]; "Muzykal'no-deklamatorskij večer, otbŷvšijsja 18-ho sep. yz slučaja Hl. Sobr. Obšč. ym. Kačkovskoho" [An evening musical-recital September 18 on the occasion of the General Meeting of the Kačkovskij Society]

A   III (40): Nov 15, 1894; C-3

5022   Ju.; "Znanie ystoriy, jako hlavnŷi motyv (Pobudytel'čaja pryčyna) vozderžanija y uvaženija svoej narodnosty" [Knowledge of history, the main motive for preservation and respect of one's nationality]

E   IV (12): Apr 4, 1895; C-2, L-3

5023   [N.N.]; "Na predaniach (tradiciach) osnovujucé nektoré zvyc'aji. Prazdnik Svietloho Voskresenia" [Some Easter Sunday customs based on traditions]

A   IV (13): Apr 14, 1895; L-2

5024   D.M.; "Na Polonynach"   [In the Mountain-Valleys]

      Lit-Poetry   IV (13): Apr 14, 1895; C-6

5025   Ju.; "Sybyr'skiy Yzhnannyky: Povîst" [Siberian Exiles: A Narrative Tale]

      Lit-Prose   IV (13): Apr 14, 1895; C-6

5026   [N.N.]; "Yz Halycko y Uhrorusskych narodnych pîsnej" [Folk songs of Galicia and Hungarian-Rus']

     1.   "Uhelju, Uhelju, nesčesnŷj Uhelju!"
     2.   "Ked ty moy vlasŷ"
     3.   "Kalyno, malyno, hotova kolîba"
     4.   "Upav snîžok mežy horŷ"

                        IV (14): Apr 25, 1895; C-6, L-6

     5.   "Byda mi siroty z'iti"

                        IV (15): May 2, 1895; L-6

     6.   "Poniže Ternavy potoček kervavy"
     7.   "Ked som išol od Ungvara do Tal'i"
     8.   "Mojo žalty vlasy z mene zostrihal'i"

                        IV (16): May 9, 1895; L-6

     9.   "Ej, l'esy, zeleny l'esy"
    10.   "Mamko moja, mamko"

                        IV (17): May 16, 1895; L-3

    11.   "Ked jem išol prez milenkej sjiny"
    12.   "Dole moja, dole"

                        IV (18): May 23, 1895; L-6

    13.   "O Bože moj! Co mam robic?"
    14.   "Velo pšenic, ma'o žit"

                        IV (20): Jun 6, 1895; L-6

    15.   "Bereza, bereza"

                        IV (21&22): Jun 20, 1895; L-6

    16.   "Ej, bida mi z krasnou ženou"
    17.   "Ja takoho muža maju"

                        IV (24): Jul 4, 1895; L-6

    18.   "Letiv orel ponad more"
    19.   "Stupaj konik, stupaj konik"
    20.   "Mamko moja, mamko"

                        IV (25): Jul 11, 1895; L-6

    21.   "Gazda že ja, gazda"
    22.   "Krasša ja, Ivanku, jako ty"
    23.   "U bohatych djivoček"
    24.   "Do kostela pošov"

                        IV (27): Jul 25, 1895; L-6

25. "Oj naš' bat'ko Revucha"

                                 IV (27): Jul 25, 1895; C-6

26. "Ej, keby mi ňe hora"

Fs   IV (29): Aug 8, 1895; L-6

5027   L.H.; "Do Vesnŷ" [To the Spring]

       Lit-Poetry   IV (15): May 2, 1895; C-6

5028   Ju. L.; "Tuha za Otčynoju" [Pining for the Mother Land]

       Lit-Poetry   IV (15): May 2, 1895; C-6

5029   I.I.O.; "Holos nad Prut" [Voice over the River Prut]

       Lit-Poetry   IV (16): May 9, 1895; C-6

5030   Ieronym Anonym; "Počtovŷj Rožok (Počtovaja Truba): Rozskaz"
       [The Postal Horn: A Short Story]

       Parts I-VII: IV (16-23): May 9-Jun 27, 1895; C-6

       Lit-Prose

5031   [N.N.]; "Nauka starym i mladym" [Teachings for the old and young]

       1. Collection of eleven proverbs.

                                  IV (16): May 9, 1895; L-6

       2. Collection of twenty-four proverbs.

       Pro   IV (41): Oct 31, 1895; L-6

5032   A.P.; "Pîsn' pod-Karpatskoho Rusyna" [Song of the Subcarpathian
       Rusyn]

       Lit-Poetry   IV (17): May 16, 1895; C-6

5033   A.--B.; "Husljar'" [The Fiddler]

       Lit-Poetry   IV (19): May 30, 1895; C-6

5034   [N.N.]; "Sčastie Žyzny" [Fortune of a Life]

       Lit-Poetry   IV (19): May 30, 1895; C-6

5035   Rev. Alexander Duchnovich; "Ja Rusin byl..." [I have been a Rusyn...]

       Lit-Poetry   IV (19): May 30, 1895; L-6

5036   [N.N.]; "Dumka" [Elegy]

       Lit-Poetry   IV (20): Jun 6, 1895; C-6

5037   E.C.; "Praščan'e s bratom" [Parting with a Brother]

       Lit-Poetry   IV (21&22): Jun 20, 1895; C-6 (misnumbered as C-3)

5038   Y.N.; "Žal'" [Pity]

        Lit-Poetry   IV (24): Jul 4, 1895; C-6

5039   P.L.; "Lîta moy moloden'ky!..." [My Young Years!...]

        Lit-Poetry   IV (25): Jul 11, 1895; C-6

5040   K.P.; "Nadîja" [Hope]

        Lit-Poetry   IV (26): Jul 18, 1895; C-6

5041   [N.N.]; "Možem y mŷ, Amer. Rusynŷ, yz toho poučytys'!"
       [We American-Rusyns can also learn from this!]

       Rusyns in America, like some of their brethren in Europe,
       should do their best to preserve faith, language and nation-
       ality.

       A   IV (28): Aug 1, 1895; C-2&3

5042   [N.N.]; "Podkarpatskaja Rus' predstavlenna na Čechsko-Slavjanskoj
       vŷstavkî v Prahî" [Subcarpathian Rus' featured at the Czecho-
       Slavic exhibition in Prague]

       A   IV (34): Sep 12, 1895; C-3, L-3

5043   [N.N.]; "Mytropolyt Sembratovyč o fonetycî" [(Sylvester Cardinal)
       Metropolitan Sembratovych (writes) on phonetics]

       A   IV (37): Oct 3, 1895; C-2&3

5044   [N.N.]; "Na Jarmarku (povîstka yz staroho kraju); Rozhovor Nykolaja
       s Mychalom" [At the Fair (A narrative tale from the old
       country); Nicholas' conversation with Michael]

       Part I: IV (38): Oct 10, 1895; C-6

       Part II (Conclusion):   IV (39): Oct 17, 1895; C-6

       Lit-Prose

5045   Ju.; "Proukažme Bratskuju Ščyrost'! Starokraevŷy našy brat'ja
       trebujut ot nas, Amer. Rusynov pomoščy" [Let us display
       brotherly sincerity! Our European brethren need help from
       us, American Rusyns]

       Refers to 4037, commenting on the preservation of Rusyn cul-
       ture in Europe and America.

       E   IV (39): Oct 17, 1895; C-2, L-2

5046   O.O.K.; "Babskoe Lito, po narodnomu povîrju" [Indian Summer,
       according to folk belief]

       Parts I-II: IV (40-41): Oct 24-31, 1895; C-6

       Lit-Prose

5047 [N.N.]; "Ctym y vozslavym nad vsîmy našu vîru y narodnost'!"
[Let us honor and glorify above all (else) our faith and
nationality!]

Preservation of faith and nationality among Rusyn-Americans.

Part I: V (7): Mar 5, 1896; L-2

Part II: V (9): Mar 19, 1896; C-2, L-2

A

5048 [N.N.]; "Pripovidki" [Proverbs]

Collection of twenty-one proverbs.

Pro   V (9): Mar 19, 1896; L-6

5049 [N.N.]; "Vasyl y Onufrij" [Basil and Onufry]

A 24 part fictional conversation between two Rusyns who discuss
various topics concerning the nationality-religious problems
and the G.C.U.

Parts I-XIX: V (12-31): Apr 9-Aug 20, 1896; C-6, L-6
Lit-Prose

5050 [N.N.]; "Radostnŷy javlenija v razsuždenijach našeho naroda"
[Joyful occurrences in the thinking of our people]

The progress Rusyns in America are making in realizing their
national-religious heritage.

A   V (18&19): May 21, 1896; C-2, L-2

5051 [N.N.]; "Pochval'nŷj relyhijno-narodnŷj prohres" [Commendable
religious-nationality progress]

Progress made by Rusyn-Americans in advancing religious and
national self-awareness among Rusyns.

A   V (26): Jul 16, 1896; C-2&3, L-2&3

5052 [N.N.]; "Dîjstvytel'nŷy dokazatel'stva zabotlyvosty y žertvoljubija
našeho naroda v pol'zu svoej vîrŷ, obrjada y narodnosty"
[Real evidence of care and self-sacrifice of our people in the
interest of their faith, rite and nationality]

A   V (28): Jul 30, 1896; C-2, L-2&3

5053 [N.N.]; "Telehrama" [The Telegram]

Lit-Prose   V (42): Nov 5, 1896; C-6, L-6

5054 [N.N.]; "Nužda bol'šoj nauky" [The need for more education]

Rusyn immigrant education in America.

A   V (47): Dec 10, 1896; C-6, L-6

5055   Č.; "Russkomu Jazŷku" [To the Rusyn Language]

Lit-Poetry   X (6): Feb 21, 1901; C-7

5056   [N.N.]; "Svîtloe Voskresenie na Podkarpatskoj Rusy" [Holy Easter
       Sunday in Subcarpathian Rus']

A   X (13): Apr 11, 1901; C-2&3, L-2&3

5057   [N.N.]; "Odno krasnoe škol'noe toržestvo" [One fine school celebra-
       tion]

Lauds the successes of the Trenton, NJ Greek Catholic parish
school.

A   X (25): Jul 18, 1901; C-2, L-2&3

5058   [N.N.]; "Škola y obrazovanie dîtej" [School and education of
       children]

The importance of education for Rusyn-American children.

A   X (32): Sep 5, 1901; C-2, L-2

5059   [N.N.]; "Pokrok" [Progress]

Lauds the ability of Rusyn-Americans to obtain an education
and contribute to the glory of their national heritage.

A   X (40): Oct 31, 1901; C-4

5060   [N.N.]; "V Prazd. sv. O. Nykolaja" [On the feastday of Saint
       Nicholas]

Lit-Poetry   X (47): Dec 19, 1901; C-2, L-2

5061   [N.N.]; "Narodnaja hordos'" [(Rusyn) National Pride]

A   X (47): Dec 19, 1901; C-2, L-2

5062   [N.N.]; "Pochval'noe y radostnoe preuspîvanie našeho naroda"
       [Praiseworthy and joyful successes of our people]

The national-religious consciousness of Rusyn-Americans.

A   XI (1): Jan 16, 1902; C-2

5063   [N.N.]; "Odno krasnoe škol'noe Toržestvo" [One fine school cele-
       bration]

The accomplishments of the Rusyn Greek Catholic parish school
in Shenandoah, PA.

A   XI (1): Jan 16, 1902; C-2&3

5064   [N.N.]; "Hej Rusynŷ!" [Hey Rusyns!]

Lit-Poetry   XI (1): Jan 16, 1902; C-5

5065   [N.N.]; "Pochval'noe dvyženie" [Praiseworthy movement]

The efforts of Vladimir Fabian, cantor for the Greek Catholic parish in Pittsburgh, PA, toward organizing a cultural society.

A   XI (2&3): Jan 30, 1902; C-2

5066   [N.N.]; "Fel'eton" [Newspaper Satire]

"Jak našy ljude hovorjat v Amerykî?" [How do our people speak in America?]

Lit-Prose   XI (4): Feb 6, 1902; C-6&7

5067   Rev. Theophane A. Obushkevich; Mayfield, PA; Feb 10, 1902

A fund drive to collect donations for Galician-Lemko-Rusyn students attending the University of L'viv in Galicia.

L   XI (5): Feb 13, 1902; C-3

5068   [N.N.]; "Fel'eton" [Newspaper Satire]

"Nespoznavsja (yz ust ljudej napysav Lemko)" [He didn't get it (written down from the lips of the people by a Lemko)]

Lit-Prose   XI (5): Feb 13, 1902; C-6&7

5069   [N.N.]; "Otzŷv k brat'jam Rusynam yz Halyčynŷ y Uhorščyny o sobyraniju žertv dlja russkych unyversytetskych studentov v L'vovî" [Appeal to brother Rusyns from Galicia and Hungary, concerning the collection of donations for Rusyn university students in L'viv]

Cultural and financial information on Rusyn students at L'viv university.

A   XI (6&7): Feb 27, 1902; C-4

5070   Rev. Theophane Obushkevich; Mayfield, PA; May 24, 1902

The fund drive to raise financial aid for Rusyn students at L'viv University in Galicia.

L   XI (12): Apr 3, 1902; C-3

5071   Rev. Theophane Obushkevich; Mayfield, PA; Apr 11, 1902

List of those who sent or pledged financial aid for the L'viv University Rusyn student fund.

L   XI (14): Apr 17, 1902; C-3

5072   "Cerkovnyja Spravy" [Church Affairs]

First Rusyn Theater opens its season with the play, Arendar at the Joseph Hadekovaj hall in Perth Amboy, NJ April 28, 1902.

Ad   XI (15): Apr 24, 1902; C-5

5073   Rev. Theophane Obushkevich; Mayfield, PA; May 29, 1902

      The fund drive for L'viv University Rusyn students.

      L   XI (20): Jun 5, 1902; C-2&3

5074   [N.N.]; "Anhlijskiy hazetŷ y vospytanie-vŷchova ditej" [English-
      language newspapers and the rearing of children]

      Tells Rusyn-American parents to safeguard their children's
      upbringing by watching what they read and explain the differ-
      ences in customs in America with regard to their own faith
      and nationality.

      A   XI (29): Aug 14, 1902; C-7

5075   [N.N.]; "Novŷj škol'nŷj hod" [New school year]

      American schools and the importance of education for Rusyn-
      American children.

      A   XI (34): Sep 18, 1902; C-2&3

5076   [N.N.]; "Fel'eton" [Newspaper Satire]

      "Pohl'ad na zem Rusynov" [View of the Rusyn lands]

      Lit-Prose   XI (36): Oct 2, 1902; C-7

5077   J.Č.; "Krajanam na Roždestvo Chrystovo" [To our countrymen for
      Christmas]

      Lit-Poetry   X (49): Jan 2, 1902; C-3, L-3

5078   [N.N.]; "Fel'eton" [Newspaper Satire]

      "Obrazčyky yz dušpastŷrstva russkoho duchovenstva v Halyčynî"
      [Cameos from the pastoral activity of Rusyn priests in Galicia]

      Part I: XII (6&7): Feb 26, 1903; C-6

      Part II: XII (9): Mar 12, 1903; C-8

      Lit-Prose

5079   [N.N.]; "Nedostatok narodnoho ducha, čuvstva y soznanija"
      [Insufficient national spirit, feeling and consciousness]

      Rusyn national consciousness in America.

      A   XII (29): Aug 13, 1903; C-2, L-2

5080   P. Ju. Ž.; "Jak nam - Rusynam ymenovatysja?" [What should we -
      Rusyns call ourselves?]

      Examination of the term Ruthenian-Rusyn.

      E   XII (31): Aug 27, 1903; C-4, L-4

5081 [N.N.]; "Novŷj škol'nŷj hod" [New school year]

The importance of education for Rusyn-Americans.

A   XII (32): Sep 3, 1903; C-4, L-4

5082 [N.N.]; "Lyteratura" [Literature]

Review of a book written by Baron Shram, entitled <u>Grof Raday</u>, published by Joseph V. Rožko of Cleveland, OH.

A   XIII (9): Mar 17, 1904; C-2, L-2

5083 [N.N.]; "Svîtlŷj prazdnyk Voskresenija Chrystova na Uhorskoj Rusy" [Easter Sunday in Hungarian Rus']

A   XII (12): Apr 7, 1904; C-6, L-6

5084 [N.N.]; "Fel'eton" [Newspaper Satire]

a. "Preslîdovanie žydov v Rossiy" [Persecution of Jews in Russia (Pogroms)]

        XIII (19): Jun 2, 1904; C-6, L-6

b. "Ženščyna v Rossiy" [Women in Russia]

        XIII (20): Jun 9, 1904; C-6, L-6

c. "Slavjanskij svît" [The Slavic world]

        XIII (22): Jun 23, 1904; C-6, L-6

Lit-Prose

5085 [N.N.]; "Rus' Amerykanska podnosytsja" [Rusyn-Americans make progress]

The opening, on September 15, 1904, of a Rusyn National House and School (123 Sussex Street, Jersey City, NJ) for students ten and older.

A   XIII (27): Aug 26, 1904; 11

5086 [N.N.]; "Pry pomoščy sej tablycŷ každŷj, kto ne znaet čytaty po russky, s malŷm trudom možet naučytys'" [With the help of this table, everyone who doesn't know how to read (Cyrillic) can teach himself with little difficulty]

Cyrillic and Latin script equivalency table.

Tab   XIII (27): Aug 26, 1904; 12

5087 [N.N.]; "Narodnŷ školŷ v Pensylveniy" [Elementary schools in Pennsylvania]

Statistical information on the Pennsylvanian elementary school system.

A   XIII (33): Oct 6, 1904; 9

5088   [N.N.]; "Potreba Lyteraturŷ" [The need for literature]

The importance of Rusyn-American writings in preserving Rusyn culture in America.

A   XIII (36): Oct 27, 1904; 9

5089   [N.N.]; "Novŷj škol'nŷj zakon y narodnosty na Uhorščynî" [New school law and the nationalities in Hungary]

Concerning the new law, introduced into parliament by Hungarian cultural minister, Adalbert Berzeviczy, requiring all state schools to use Magyar as the language of instruction.

A   XIII (44): Dec 22, 1904; 9,11

5090   Nicholas Pačuta; "Svatŷj večer' v Zemplynskom okolo Vranova" [Christmas Eve in Zemplén (county) near Vranov nad Topl'ov (Varannó)]

A   XIII (46): Jan 5, 1905; 4,5

5091   [N.N.]; "Čytaj Kume Maksyme!" [Read Brother Maksim!]

Review of a play performed by a Rusyn-Slovak theatrical group in Homestead, PA on January 29, 1906.

A   XV (5): Feb 15, 1906; 2,3

5092   [N.N.]; "Pochval'nŷj postup" [Praiseworthy action]

The Homestead and Braddock, PA parish choral societies founded in December, 1905.

A   XV (6): Feb 22, 1906; 2,3

5093   [N.N.]; "Svîtloe Voskresenija na Uhorskoj Rusy" [Easter Sunday in Hungarian Rus']

A   XV (13): Apr 12, 1906; 6,7

5094   Rev. Joseph Hanulya; "Symfonija" [Symphony]

Review of the first Rusyn Symphonic concert held May 15, 1906 in Homestead, PA.

A   XV (19): May 24, 1906; 4,5

5095   [N.N.]; "Nîskol'ko bratskych slov moym brat'jam Rusynam v Monessen, Pa." [Some fraternal words to my brother Rusyns in Monessen, PA]

The education of Rusyn youth in Rusyn parish schools.

A   XV (23): Jun 28, 1906; 4,5

5096   Rev. Michael J. Biszaha; "Chranenie jazŷka" [Custody of the language]

Commentary on the Rusyn language.

A   XV (29): Aug 9, 1906; 4,5

5097   Rev. Joseph P. Hanulya; "Staroslavjanskij Slovar'" [Old-Slavonic Dictionary]

Review of an Old-Slavonic dictionary with Rusyn, Hungarian, and German equivalents published by Unió Könyvnyomda Részvény Társaság Užhorod [Ungvár], Hungary.

A   XV (33): Sep 6, 1906; 4,5

5098   Redakcija; "Odna duže polezna knyha" [A very useful book]

Review of a ten-part liturgical music anthology written by Rev. John Boksay a Greek Catholic priest of the Mukačevo Diocese and Mr. Joseph Malinics, professor of ritual music at the Greek Catholic teacher's school in Užhorod and cantor of the Mukačevo Diocese Cathedral.

A   XV (35): Sep 20, 1906; 4,5

5099   [N.N.]; "Jaka est' nahoroda?" [What is the reward?]

Preserving the religious-national character of Rusyn-Americans.

A   XVI (6): Feb 21, 1907; C-2, L-4

5100   [N.N.]; "Kratky obšah memoranduma rumunskych neuniatskych uhorskych epyskopov" [Short contents of a memorandum of the Rumanian non-uniate Hungarian Bishops]

Memorandum protests the reform act of the national schools in Hungary.

A   XVI (11): Mar 28, 1907; C-2&3

5101   George Koleszar; "Podderžujme russkost'" [Let us preserve (our) Rusynness]

Preservation of Rusyn national character in America.

A   XVI (14): Apr 18, 1907; C-2, L-2

5102   [N.N.]; "Vseslavjanskij jazŷk" [All-Slavic language]

The Old Bulgarian and Church Slavonic language.

A   XVI (14): Apr 18, 1907; C-3

5103   [N.N.]; "Kto ne ljubyt svoju narodnost y svoj materynskiy jazŷk, tot hrîšyt protyv Boha" [He who does not love his nationality and maternal tongue sins against God]

Rusyn national consciousness.

A   XVI (22): Jun 20, 1907; C-4, L-4

5104   [N.N.]; "Novŷj škol'nŷj hod" [New school year]

Education for Rusyn-American children.

A   XVI (34): Sep 12, 1907; C-4, L-4

5105   [N.N.]; "Časŷ, ljude y ubîẑdenija mînjajutsja" [Times, people and convictions change]

Rusyn linguistics and some of the polemical implications that can be derived from its study.

A   XVI (35): Sep 19, 1907; C-2, L-2

5106   [N.N.]; "Jak dolho mohut žyty Slavjane v Amerykî" [How long can Slavs live in America]

Preservation of Slavic language and culture in America amidst the pressures of assimilation.

A   XVI (40): Oct 24, 1907; C-2, L-2

5107   [N.N.]; "Anglicka škola pre dospelych" [English (language) school for adults]

The night class program of English language, American History and American Law for non-English speaking foreigners conducted in Homestead, PA.

A   XVII (27): Aug 6, 1908; L-2

5108   [N.N.]; "Našy parochial'nŷy školŷ" [Our parochial schools]

The future of Greek Catholic parish schools in light of the nationality issue.

A   XVII (32): Sep 10, 1908; C-2, L-2

5109   [N.N.]; "Uhro-Russkaja Narodna Lyha" [Uhro-Rusyn National League]

Cultural organization formed in Homestead, PA October 6, 1907. Lists organization's statutes.

Parts I-II: XVII (46-47): Dec 17-24, 1908

A

5110   [N.N.]; "Pîsny na roždestvo Chrystovo" [Christmas Carols]

Fs   XVII (48): Dec 31, 1908; C-6, L-6

5111   [N.N.]; "Obščestvennaja žyzn' d'jako-učytelej" [Social life of a cantor-teacher]

The role of the cantor in a Greek Catholic parish. Information about a society of cantors in America.

A   XVIII (7): Feb 25, 1909; C-2, L-2

5112   [N.N.]; "Odnoe krasnoe škol'noe toržestvo" [One beautiful school celebration]

The Taylor, PA Greek Catholic parish school.

A   XVIII (26): Jul 15, 1909; C-2&3, L-2&3

5113   [N.N.]; New Salem, PA; Jun 26, 1909

"Škol'noe Toržestvo" [School celebration]

The New Salem parish school's end of the year exams.

L   XVIII (28): Jul 29, 1909; C-2, L-2

5114   [N.N.]; "Fel'eton" [Newspaper Satire]

"Perechyščrennŷj. Oriental'naja ystorija poslî nîmeckaho
O. Emylij A. Kubek" [The outwitted. An oriental story taken
from the German by Rev. Emil A. Kubek]

Lit-Prose   XVIII (32): Aug 26, 1909; C-6, L-6

5115   [N.N.]; "Odnoe krasnoe škol'noe toržestvo" [One beautiful school
celebration]

The Hawk Run, PA Greek Catholic parish school.

A   XVIII (33): Sep 2, 1909; C-3, L-3

5116   [N.N.]; "Škol'noe toržestvo" [School celebration]

The Homestead, PA Greek Catholic parish school.

A   XVIII (36): Sep 23, 1909; C-2, L-2

5117   [N.N.]; "Snov' odnoe krasnoe škol'noe toržestvo" [Another beautiful school celebration]

The Scranton, PA Greek Catholic parish school.

A   XVIII (37): Sep 30, 1909; C-2, L-2

5118   [N.N.]; "Bol'šytsja naša yntellyhencija" [Growth of our intelli-
gentsia]

Report on the higher education progress of G.I. Zsatkovich;
V.P. Dzmura; J.A. Smith, Jr.; A.S. Prokopovitch; and
A.P. Dzmura, all sons of Rusyn immigrants.

A   XVIII (41): Oct 28, 1909; C-2, L-2

5119   [N.N.]; "Est'-ly nam potrebna 'Uhro-Russkaja Narodnaja Lyha'?"
[Is the 'Uhro-Rusyn Peoples League' a necessity for us?]

A   XVIII (41): Oct 28, 1909; C-2, L-2

5120   [N.N.]; "Vsetaky ešče žiem" [All the same we are still living]

Commentary on an article about the existance and development
of Rusyn national culture in Budapesti Hírlap [Budapest].

A   XVIII (43): Nov 11, 1909; C-4, L-4

5121 [N.N.]; "Hospodynam d'jako-učyteljam v bratskoe vnymanie"
[Fraternal attention to all cantors]

Advocates the formation of a cantor society for Rusyn American cantors.

A   XVIII (44): Nov 18, 1909; C-2, L-2

5122 M. Hanchin; "Ymîeme-ly potrebu na 'Uhro-Russkuju Lyhu'?" [Do we need a 'Uhro-Rusyn League'?]

The reasons for a Uhro-Rusyn League.

A   XVIII (45): Nov 25, 1909; C-2, L-2

5123 Basil Kepinač; Glen Lyon, PA

The Uhro-Rusyn League.

L   XVIII (46): Dec 2, 1909; C-2, L-2

5124 George Z. Baran, et al.; "Protokol yz sobranija uhro-russkych d'jako-učytelej, poderžanoho dnja 23-ho nojabr'ja 1909 hoda v mîstî Braddock, Pa." [Minutes of the Uhro-Rusyn cantor meeting, held November 23, 1909 in the town of Braddock, PA]

O   XVIII (49): Dec 23, 1909; C-2, L-2

5125 B. Sulin; Braddock-Homestead, PA

The formation of a young people's choir and theatrical club.

L   XIX (6): Feb 17, 1910; C-3, L-2&3

5126 John Majernik; South Sharon, PA

The formation of a choir and theatrical club.

L   XIX (6): Feb 17, 1910; C-3, L-3

5127 [N.N.]; "Ymmyhranty y školy" [Immigrants and schools]

The assimilation of immigrants into the mainstream of American life through education.

A   XIX (15): Apr 21, 1910; C-4, L-4

5128 [N.N.]; "Sochranîm našiy krasnŷy relyhijno-narodnŷy obŷčay" [Let us preserve our beautiful religious-national customs]

A   XIX (16): Apr 28, 1910; C-2, L-2

5129 Rev. M. Jackovics; "Vozzvanie y pros'ba k uhro-russkomu duchovenstvu y k uhro-russk. pîvco-učyteljam!" [Notice and request to Uhro-Rusyn clergy and cantors!]

Requests $5.00 donations for a scholarship fund established in the memory of Dr. Alexander Mikita in Mukačevo (Munkács).

Req   XIX (31): Aug 25, 1910; C-2, L-3

5130   Sigismund Barany; "Ot predsîdatelja Tovaryščestva Uhro-Russkych
       D'jako-učytelej" [From the president of the Society of Uhro-
       Rusyn Cantors]

       Membership fees and the second convention of the organization,
       slated for February, 1911.

       O   XIX (43): Nov 17, 1910; C-6, L-3

5131   [N.N.]; "Po koncertî" [After the Concert]

       Review of a concert, sponsored by the YMCA, at Carnegie Hall
       in Pittsburgh, PA on December 2, 1910. Various nationalities,
       including the Carpatho-Rusyns, took part.

       A   XIX (46): Dec 8, 1910; C-4&5, L-4&5

5132   [N.N.]; "Narodné zvyčaje v prazdnik Roždestva Christovoho, osobitno
       v Sviaty Ščedry večar" [National customs at Christmas, espe-
       cially on Christmas Eve]

       A   XIX (50): Jan 5, 1911; L-2&3

5133   [N.N.]; "Jakoe est' prosvîščenie narodov?" [What is the state of
       education of peoples?]

       Commentary on education and the literacy level of various
       immigrant nationalities.

       A   XX (6): Feb 23, 1911; C-4&5, L-4&5

5134   [N.N.]; "Svîtloe Voskresenie na Uhorskoj Rusy" [Holy Easter Sunday
       in Hungarian Rus']

       A   XX (14): Apr 20, 1911; C-2, L-2

5135   Peter J. Macko; Toronto, OH; Apr 7, 1911

       "Zaslato" [Letter to the Editor]

       The term "Ruthenian" is discussed.

       L   XX (14): Apr 20, 1911; C-3, L-3

5136   [N.N.]; "Pisomnictvo" [Literature]

       Review of Niva.

       A   XX (23): Jul 6, 1911; L-4

5137   [N.N.]; "Tajnosc pokroku človeka" [The mystery of human progress]

       Review of Niva.

       A   XX (25): Jul 20, 1911; L-4

5138   [N.N.]; "Na načalî škol'noho hoda" [At the beginning of the school
       year]

       The importance of education to Rusyns.

       A   XX (34): Sep 21, 1911; C-4, L-4

5139   G.Z. Baran, et al.; "Ot hreko kat. uhro-russkoho d'jako-učytel'skoho
       tovaryščestva" [From the Greek Catholic Uhro-Rusyn cantor
       society]

       a. Membership dues.
       b. Position of the Cantor Society with regards to the struggle
           between supporters and non-supporters of Bishop Ortynsky.

       O   XX (39): Oct 26, 1911; C-2&3, L-2

5140   [N.N.]; "Takoe koe-čto dîlaet nam radost'" [Something like this
       makes us happy]

       The high level of literacy among Rusyn-Americans.

       A   XX (39): Oct 26, 1911; C-4, L-4

5141   [N.N.]; "Nove čislo Nivy" [New issue of Niva]

       A   XX (41): Nov 9, 1911; L-6

5142   [N.N.]; "Pîvčij koncert vsîch narodov" [Choral concert of all
       nations]

       Participation of Rusyns and other nationalities in a March 1,
       1912 international choral concert in Pittsburgh, PA.

       A   XXI (3): Feb 1, 1912; C-5, L-5

5143   M.A.M.; Homestead, PA

       Review of a play, Bludar, performed January 29, 1912 by members
       of the Homestead parish.

       A   XXI (5): Feb 15, 1912; C-3, L-2&3

5144   [N.N.]; "Koncerty pîvčych obščestv (chorov)" [Concert of choral
       societies]

       The March 1, 1912 international choral concert in Pittsburgh, PA.

       A   XXI (6): Feb 15, 1912; C-3, L-5

5145   [N.N.]; "Koncert pîvčych obščestv" [Concert of choral societies]

       The March 1, 1912 international choral concert in Pittsburgh, PA.

       A   XXI (6): Feb 22, 1912; C-4, L-4

5146   [N.N.]; "Prohramma koncerta" [Program of the concert]

       The March 1, 1912 international choral concert in Pittsburgh, PA.

       A   XXI (7): Feb 29, 1912; C-4&5, L-4&5

5147   [N.N.]; "Po koncertî" [After the concert]

       Review of a March 1, 1912 international choral concert in
       Pittsburgh, PA.

       A   XXI (8): Mar 7, 1912; C-4, L-4

5148   Paul J. Zsatkovich; "Jak sudyt naš uhro-russkij narod o poymenovaniy: 'Ruthenian, Ruthen'?" [What do our Uhro-Rusyn people think about the name: 'Ruthenian, Ruthene'?]

Several letters to the editor commenting on this subject.

E, L   XXI (14): Apr 25, 1912; C-2&3, L-2

5149   [N.N.]; "Otčyty dlja tîch kotorŷy chotjat statysja horožanamy" [Lectures for those who want to become citizens]

The citizenship program for immigrants, sponsored by the Pittsburgh, PA area Y.M.C.A.

A   XXI (15): May 2, 1912; C-4, L-4

5150   [N.N.]; "Horožanstvo" [Citizenship]

The citizenship program for immigrants sponsored by the Pittsburgh, PA area Y.M.C.A.

A   XXI (18): May 23, 1912; C-5, L-5

5151   [N.N.]; "Snov' odnoe toržestvo ynostrancev" [Another celebration for foreigners]

A June 6, 1912 event sponsored by the Pittsburgh, PA area Y.M.C.A.

A   XXI (20): Jun 13, 1912; C-4, L-4

5152   Rev. Nicholas Danyko, et al.; Svidník [Szvidnik], Sáros County, Hungary

Thanks American Greek Catholics for financial aid for the establishment of a village reading room.

LE   XXI (22): Jun 27, 1912; C-3, L-2

5153   [N.N.]; "Narodoprosvîščenie" [Public education]

A night school program for Pittsburgh, PA area immigrants.

A   XXI (34): Sep 19, 1912; C-4, L-4

5154   [N.N.]; "Nîskol'ko slov o narodnom spîvî" [Several words about (Rusyn) folk songs]

A   XXI (42): Nov 7, 1912; C-5&6, L-4&5

5155   Rev. Emil A. Kubek; "Velykij Sŷn" [The Great Son]

Lit-Prose   XXI (43): Nov 21, 1912; C-2&3, L-2&3

5156   [N.N.]; "Aleksandr Duchnovyč" [Alexander Duchnovich]

The G.C.U. sponsored Rusyn choir, 'Alexander Duchnovich.'

A   XXI (43): Nov 21, 1912; C-4&5, L-4&5

5157　[N.N.]; "Čto prynadležyt ešče k cîly pîvčoho obščestva
A. Duchnovyča?" [What more is the aim of the choral society,
A. Duchnovich?]

　　　　A　　　　　　　　　　　　XXI (46): Dec 12, 1912; C-2&3, L-5

5158　M.H.; "Na Roždestvo (obraz yz Zemplynskoj)" [On the occasion of
Christmas (scene from Zemplén)]

　　　　A　　　　　　　　　　　　XXI (49): Jan 2, 1913; C-2, L-2

5159　[N.N.]; "Pervŷj koncert y teatral'noe predstavlenie" [First concert
and theatrical presentation]

Program of a concert to be given by the Alexander Duchnovich
Choir in Homestead, PA on February 24, 1913.

　　　　A　　　　　　　　　　　　XXII (4): Feb 6, 1913; C-3, L-3

5160　[N.N.]; "Pervŷj publyčnŷj vystup chora ymeny 'Aleksandr Duchnovyč'"
[First public performance of the 'Alexander Duchnovich Choir']

Performance in Homestead, PA.

　　　　A　　　　　　　　　　　　XXII (6): Feb 20, 1913; C-4&5, L-4

5161　I.P.; "Zadzvonyly vo vsî dzvonŷ..." [They rang all the bells...]

　　　　Lit-Poetry　　　　　　　　XXII (6): Feb 20, 1913; C-11

5162　[N.N.]; "Fele'ton" [Newspaper Satire]

G. Hárdonyi; "Daleko dotolî yly jak vabjatsja našy ljude v
starom kray v Ameryku a yz Ameryky nazad v kraj" [A long way
to go, or how our people in the old country are enticed to
America and from America back to Europe]

　　　　Part I:　　　　　　　　　XXII (6): Feb 20, 1913; C-11&12

　　　　Part II:　　　　　　　　　XXII (15): Apr 24, 1913; C-9&10, L-9&10

　　　　Lit-Prose

5163　[N.N.]; "Pervŷj koncert y tejatral'noe predstavlenie chora ymeny
'Aleksander Duchnovyč'" [First concert and theatrical presentation of the 'Alexander Duchnovich Choir']

Review of the concert held in Homestead, PA, February 24, 1913.

　　　　A　　　　　　　　　　　　XXII (7): Feb 27, 1913; C-4&5, L-4&5

5164　[N.N.]; "Koncert narodov" [Concert of nations]

Program of third annual international choral concert, sponsored
by the Pittsburgh, PA area Y.M.C.A. Concert takes place April
10, 1913.

　　　　A　　　　　　　　　　　　XXII (9): Mar 13, 1913; C-4&5, L-4

5165   Michael J. Hanchin; "K počt. čytateljam" [To honorable readers]

The topics discussed at the annual meeting of the Alexander Duchnovich Choral Society.

A   XXII (10): Mar 20, 1913; C-3, L-2

5166   Rev. Michael Jackovich; "Koncert narodov" [Concert of nations]

Protest by the supreme spiritual advisor over the participation of the Alexander Duchnovich Choir in a Y.M.C.A. sponsored choral concert during the lenten season.

A   XXII (12): Apr 3, 1913; C-4, L-4

5167   Michael Hanchin; "Prymičanija na vŷšeudannuju stat'ju hl. duch. upravytelja 'Soedynenija', O. Mych. Jackovyča 'Koncert narodov'" [Commentary on the article of supreme spiritual advisor of the 'Soedynenie', Rev. Michael Jackovich, 'Concert of nations', published above]

A   XXII (12): Apr 3, 1913; C-4&5, L-4

5168   [N.N.]; "'Pobîda' O. Jackovyča, duchovnoho upravytelja 'Soedynenija', nad chorom 'A. Duchnovyč'" ['Victory' of Rev. Jackovich, spiritual advisor of the 'Soedynenie', over the choir 'A. Duchnovich']

Condemnation by Rev. Jackovich of the Y.M.C.A. and the participation of the Alexander Duchnovich Choir in the Y.M.C.A.'s program of choral music.

A   XXII (14): Apr 17, 1913; C-4, L-4

5169   Basil Sulin; "Duchnovyču" [To (Alexander) Duchnovich]

Lit-Poetry   XXII (15): Apr 24, 1913; C-2, L-2

5170   [N.N.]; "Svîtloe Voskresenie na Uhorskoj Rusy" [Holy Easter Sunday in Hungarian Rus']

A   XXII (15): Apr 24, 1913; C-2&3, L-2&3

5171   [N.N.]; "Pervoe produkovaniesja našoho uhro-russkoho chora na okolycî pyttsbŷrhskoj ymeny 'Aleksandr Duchnovyč' pered šyršoju publykoju" [First performance of our Uhro-Rusyn 'Alexander Duchnovich Choir' in the vicinity of Pittsburgh, PA before a large public audience]

Concert in Pittsburgh, PA on May 11, 1913.

A   XXII (17): May 15, 1913; C-4, L-4

5172   [N.N.]; "Koncert, teatral'noe predstavlenie y bal" [Concert, theatrical presentation and ball]

The program of a choral concert and play to be given by the Alexander Duchnovich Choir in Braddock, PA on May 26, 1913.

A   XXII (17): May 15, 1913; C-5, L-5

5173   [N.N.]; "Počtennoj uhro-russkoj publykî na Pyttsbŷrhskoj okolycî"
        [To the honorable Uhro-Rusyn public in Pittsburgh, PA and
        vicinity]

        The performances on May 26 and May 30, 1913 by the Alexander
        Duchnovich Choir in Braddock and Homestead, PA.

        A   XXII (18): May 22, 1913; C-2, L-2

5174   Rev. Nicholas Chopey; "Protocol Pîvco-Učytel'skoho Sobora, otbŷvša-
        hosja v Hejzeltŷn, Pa., ulyca Nort Pajn pod čyslom 138, dnja
        27-ho marta 1913 hoda" [Minutes of the Cantors' meeting held
        in Hazleton, PA at 138 North Pine St. on March 27, 1913]

        O   XXII (22): Jun 19, 1913; C-6&7, L-6

5175   Michael Juhas, et al.; "Vo vnymanie!!! Vsîm uhro-russkym pîvco-
        učyteljam, žijuščym v Ameryk. Soedynenŷch Štatach"
        [Attention!!! To all Uhro-Rusyn cantors living in the U.S.A.]

        The July 15, 1913 cantors convention in Luzerne, PA.

        O   XXII (24): Jul 3, 1913; C-2, L-2

5176   Dimitri Bellej, et al.; Uniontown, PA

        Uniontown's parish school.

        L   XXII (31): Aug 28, 1913; C-2, L-2

5177   Michael Juhas and David Sočka; "Protocol p-učytel'skoho sobora
        soključennoho s škol'nym prepodavaniem, otbŷvšohosja v
        Kynhstŷn, Pa. dnja 15-ho julja, 1913 hoda" [Minutes of the
        Cantors meeting, with the inclusion of school teaching, in
        Kingston, PA July 15, 1913]

        Part I: XXII (37): Oct 9, 1913; C-2&3, L-2

        Parts II-III: XXII (39-40): Oct 23-30, 1913; C-6,7,8, L-6

        O

5178   Michael Juhas; "Ot predsîdatelja tovaryščestva p.-učytel'skoho"
        [From the president of the cantor society]

        The November 27, 1913 meeting in St. Clair, PA.

        O   XXII (43): Nov 20, 1913; C-2&3, L-3

5179   [N.N.]; "Obrazovanie narodov" [Education of peoples]

        The U.S. government's encouragement of literacy for all
        Americans.

        A   XXII (43): Dec 4, 1913; C-5, L-4&5

5180 [N.N.]; "Novŷj znak žyznesposobnosty chora 'O. A. Duchnovyč'"
[New sign of vitality of the choir 'Rev. A. Duchnovich']

The past achievements and future prospects of this Pittsburgh,
PA based choir.

A   XXII (45): Dec 4, 1913; C-5, L-4&5

5181 M.J.H.; "Pora bŷ mŷ dalysja do vseobščoj revyziy našych bîdnych
škol'nŷch snošenij" [It's time for us to start a general
revision of our poor school affairs]

The poor attitude Rusyn-Americans have toward the education
of themselves and their offspring.

A   XXII (48): Dec 25, 1913; C-4&5, L-5

5182 [N.N.]; "Protocol III-ho okružnoho p.-učytel'skoho sobora,
soključennoho s škol'nŷm prepodavaniem, otbŷvšohosja v Sent
Klejr, Pa. 27-ho dekabrja 1912" [Minutes of the III district
(meeting) of Cantors, with school teaching, held in St. Clair,
PA, December 27, 1913]

Part I: XXII (49): Jan 1, 1914; C-2

Part II: XXIII (2): Jan 22, 1914; C-5

Part III: XXIII (5): Feb 12, 1914; C-4&5

Part IV: XXIII (7): Feb 26, 1914; C-2&3
                    O

5183 V.M.; "Polovica vina, polovica vody (vesalohra v 1 akte od Kostu
Trifkovica)" [Half wine, half water (one act comedy by Kosta
Trifkovič)]

Lit-Play   XXIII (1): Jan 15, 1914; C-10&11

5184 P.J.Ž.; "Prohress Katolycyzma yly jak rabotajut samosoznatel'nŷy
anhlijskiy, ajryšskiy y nîmeckiy rymo-katolyky v vŷššom
vŷučovaniy svoj molodežy" [Progress of Catholicism or how
self-conscious English, Irish and German Roman Catholics work
toward the higher education of their young people]

E   XXIII (4): Feb 5, 1914; C-4

5185 [N.N.]; "Kto chopnŷj oduševljatys' pry pamjaty predkov, tot stupyt
v ych slîd" [He who is capable of being inspired by the
memory of ancestors, will follow in their footsteps]

Review of a collection of poems, by the late Rev. Alexander
I. Pavlovich, Vinec, (Užhorod: Unio, 1914).

A   XXIII (7): Feb 26, 1914; C-4&5

5186 [N.N.]; "Uhro-Russky Narodny Hymn" [Uhro-Rusyn National Anthem]

"Ja Rusyn byl" by Rev. A. Duchnovich.

Lit-Poetry   XXIII (8): Mar 5, 1914; C-10

5187 Basil Kepenač; Glen Lyon, PA

Commentary on Rev. A. Pavlovich's <u>Vinec</u> (Užhorod: Unio, 1914).

L   XXIII (10): Mar 19, 1914; C-2&3

5188 George Z. Baran' and Basil Slyvka; "Protokol sobranija D'jako-
Učytel'skoho Tovaryščestva Pyttsbŷrhskoj okolycŷ pod ochoronju
Sv. App. Kyrylla y Metodija poderžannoho v Homsted, Pa., dnja
12-ho marta, 1912" [Minutes of the meeting of the Cantor
Society of Sts. Cyril and Methodius in the Pittsburgh vicinity,
held in Homestead, PA, March 12, 1914]

O   XXIII (10): Mar 19, 1914; C-5

5189 Michael Nejmet and Alexis Šandor; "Protokol. IV-ho p.-učytel'skoho
sobora soključennaho s škol'nŷm prepodavaniem, otbŷvšohosja v
Pert Amboj, N. Dž. dnja 25-ho marta, 1914 hoda" [Minutes of
the IV Cantor's meeting, including school teaching, held in
Perth Amboy, NJ, March 25, 1914]

Part I: XXIII (15): Apr 30, 1914; C-6

Parts II-V: XXIII (19-22): Jun 4-25, 1914; C-2&3

Part VI: XXIII (25): Jul 16, 1914; C-2&3

Parts VII-VIII: XXIII (28-29): Aug 6-13, 1914; C-2,3,6

Parts IX-X: XXIII (31-32): Aug 27-Sep 3, 1914; C-2&3

O

5190 John Hebor, et al.; St. Clair, PA

End of the year activities of the St. Clair Greek Catholic
parish school.

L   XXIII (23): Jul 2, 1914; C-2&3

5191 Basil Muska; Wilkes Barre, PA

"Zaslato. Beryt prymîr yz seho!" [Letter to the Editor. Take
an example from this!]

Final examinations of the Wilkes Barre Greek Catholic parish
school.

L   XXIII (24): Jul 9, 1914; C-2&3

5192 [N.N.]; "Yzdajut vtoru čast' slovarja O. Mytraka" [The second part
of Rev. Mitrak's dictionary is being published]

Review of part II of the late Rev. Alexander Mitrak's Hungarian-
Russian dictionary (Užhorod: Unio).

A   XXIII (25): Jul 16, 1914; C-5

5193 [N.N.]; "Nîskol'ko slov k d'jako-učyteljam hljadajuščym stanovyšče"
[Several words to cantors who are looking for positions]

A   XXIII (27): Jul 30, 1914; C-4&5

5194   [N.N.]; "School Days..."

       The importance of education for Rusyn-Americans.

       A   XXIII (32): Sep 3, 1914; C-4

5195   Nikita Mykla; Duquesne, PA

       The August 19, 1914 Duquesne Greek Catholic parish's school celebration.

       L   XXIII (34): Sep 17, 1914; C-2

5196   John Sopko, et al.; Minersville, PA

       The August 22, 1914 Minersville Greek Catholic parish's school celebration.

       L   XXIII (34): Sep 17, 1914; C-2&3

5197   M.S.S.; Pittsburgh, PA

       The August 19, 1914 Pittsburgh Greek Catholic parish's school celebration.

       L   XXIII (35): Sep 24, 1914; C-3

5198   Nicholas Nad; "Prošu krasno" [Please]

       Lit-Poetry   XXIII (37): Oct 8, 1914; C-2

5199   [N.N.]; "Proektŷ Statutov D'jako-Učytel'skoho Tovaryščesta Hreko Kat. Russkoj Diecesiy Soedynenŷch Štatov Sîvernoj Ameryky" [Draft Statutes of the Cantor Society of the Greek Catholic Rusyn Diocese of the United States of America]

       The September 30, 1914 Cantor and Diocesan school teachers meeting.

       A   XXIII (40): Oct 29, 1914; C-2&3

5200   O...; "Vtoroe otčestvo" [The second fatherland]

       How Rusyn-Americans have been able to preserve their culture in America whereas in Europe this has not been the case.

       A   XXIII (40): Oct 29, 1914; C-5

5201   [N.N.]; "Sobor učytel'skij" [Teachers' meeting]

       The October 10, 1914 Greek Catholic teachers meeting held in St. Clair, PA.

       Part I: XXIII (41): Nov 5, 1914; C-3

       Part II: XXIII (42): Nov 12, 1914; C-3

       A

5202   Theodore Y. Racyn; "Zamîtky yz 5-ho učytel'skoho sobora" [Notes
        on the 5th (Greek Catholic parish) teachers' meeting]

      The October 10, 1914 meeting in St. Clair, PA.

      O   XXIII (41): Nov 5, 1914; C-4&5

5203   George Huljanyč; "Soedynenŷj koncert" [United concert]

      A November 29, 1914 choral concert, sponsored by several Greek
        Catholic parishes in Yonkers, NY, for the benefit of the Rusyn
        war widows and orphans fund.

      A   XXIII (43): Nov 19, 1914; C-3

5204   Michael Juhas; "Harmonija meždu učyteljamy y verchnost'ju"
        [Harmony between teachers and hierarchy]

      The agreement reached between parish priests and Greek Catholic
        parish teachers over wages and teaching conditions.

      Part I: XXIII (44): Nov 26, 1914; C-2&3

      Part II: XXIII (46): Dec 10, 1914; C-2

      Part III: XXIII(48): Dec 24, 1914; C-2&3

      A

Chapter 6

Rusyn Individuals

- A -

6001	Adzima, Theodore	L	XI (28): Aug 7, 1902; C-3
6002	Adzima, Mary	N	X (31): Aug 29, 1901; C-7, L-7
6003	Adzima, Michael	N	V (30): Aug 13, 1896; C-4, L-4
6004	Almas, John	N	IV (47): Dec 12, 1895; C-4, L-4
6005	Ambroze, Agnes	B A	XII (43): Nov 19, 1903; C-4, L-4 4621
6006	Andrejčak, Andrew	N	V (41): Oct 29, 1896; C-4
6007	Andrejčik, M.	L	XVI (13): Apr 11, 1907; C-2&3, L-3
6008	Andrejkanics, George	L	XVIII (20): Jun 3, 1909; C-3, L-3
6009	Andryš, Thomas	L	XXI (28): Aug 8, 1912; C-3, L-3

- B -

6010	Bač, Michael	L	XXI (7): Feb 29, 1912; C-3, L-3
6011	Bak, Ann	L	XXI (27): Aug 1, 1912; C-2&3, L-2
6012	Bakajsa, Suzanna	L	XIII (18): May 26, 1904; C-3, L-2&3
6013	Bakoš, Dimitri	N	XI (4): Feb 6, 1902; C-6
6014	Balanda, Basil	L	XIII (46): Jan 5, 1905; 9,11
6015	Balint, Andrew	L	X (29): Aug 15, 1901; C-3, L-3
6016	Balla, M.	L	XVI (13): Apr 11, 1907; C-2&3, L-3
6017	Balog, Ann	N	III (32): Sep 20, 1894; C-4, L-9
6018	Balog, Joseph	L	XXII (32): Sep 4, 1913; C-3, L-3
6019	Balugyanszki, Mary	N	IV (17): May 16, 1895; C-4, L-4
6020	Bango, John	N L	X (14): Apr 25, 1901; L-7 X (9): Mar 14, 1901; C-3, L-3
6021	Barbuščak, Matthew	L	XII (25): Jul 16, 1903; C-3, L-3

6022	Bardiovska, Verona	N	IV (44): Nov 21, 1895; C-4, L-4
6023	Barna, Joseph	L	XVII (14): Apr 16, 1908; L-3
6024	Barna, Paul	N	III (2): Jan 9, 1894; C-4, L-9
6025	Barňas, Michael	L	XIII (6): Feb 25, 1904; L-2
6026	Barnej, Stephen	L	XVII (3): Jan 30, 1908; L-5
6027	Basaral, Michael	N	X (24): Jul 11, 1901; C-6, L-6
6028	Bazili, Ann	N	X (40): Oct 31, 1901; L-7
6029	Becz, Andrew	L	XII (13): Apr 9, 1903; C-3, L-3
6030	Begy, John	N	X (49): Jan 2, 1902; C-6, L-6
6031	Bekeč, Michael	N	XI (14): Apr 17, 1902; C-7
6032	Belej, John	N	XI (17): May 15, 1902; C-7
6033	Belejčak, Paul	L	XIX (2): Jan 20, 1910; C-3, L-2&3
6034	Benicki, Joseph	N	V (38): Oct 8, 1896; C-4, L-4
		L	V (39): Oct 15, 1896; L-3
6035	Benjak, Elizabeth	N	XI (21): Jun 12, 1902; C-7
6036	Bezeghy, Anthony	B	XV (44): Nov 22, 1906; 9,10
6037	Biczko, Andrew	L	XX (16): May 11, 1911; C-2&3, L-3
6038	Bidnik, Anthony	N	V (14): Apr 23, 1896; L-4
6039	Bidransky, Peter	LE	XXI (9): Mar 14, 1912; C-3, L-3
6040	Billi, Mary	N	X (31): Aug 29, 1901; C-7, L-7
6041	Billo, Basil	L	XXII (12): Apr 13, 1913; C-2&3, L-3
6042	Birovcsak, John	N	V (39): Oct 15, 1896; L-4
6043	Biszaha, Eugenia	B	XXII (41): Nov 6, 1913; C-4, L-4
6044	Blaňar, John	N	X (19): May 30, 1901; C-7, L-7
6045	Bobal, Joseph	L	XII (13): Apr 9, 1903; C-3, L-3
6046	Bochin, Peter	L	XXII (19): May 29, 1913; C-2&3, L-2&3
6047	Bolgarsky, Dmitri	N	X (45): Dec 5, 1901; C-6, L-6

6048   Bomberovyč, John   L   XI (47): Dec 18, 1902; C-2

6049   Bonczevski, Rev. Anthony   B   XI (4): Feb 5, 1903; C-2, L-2

6050   Borovski, Mary   N   V (36): Sep 24, 1896; C-4, L-4

6051   Borsuk, Theodosius   N   III (23): Jul 3, 1894; C-4, L-9

6052   Bovtun, Katherine   N   XI (9): Mar 13, 1902; C-6

6053   Breyan, Hilarion   L   XXI (20): Jun 13, 1912; C-2, L-2

6054   Breza, Michael   N   V (12): Apr 9, 1896; C-4, L-4
                                    L   V (25): Jul 9, 1896; C-3, L-3

6055   Brinkač, John   N   V (7): Mar 5, 1896; L-4

6056   Brojelovič, Thaddeus   L   XVIII (18): May 20, 1909; C-3, L-3

6057   Bryndza, Andrew   N   XI (9): Mar 13, 1902; C-6

6058   Bubelinyi, Joseph   L   XII (13): Apr 9, 1903; C-3, L-3

6059   Bubnash, George   L   XVIII (23): Jun 24, 1909; C-3, L-3

6060   Bučko, Ann   L   XXII (17): May 15, 1913; C-2, L-2

6061   Budaj, Stephen   L   XXI (6): Feb 22, 1912; C-3, L-3

6062   Budzinkay, Michael   N   X (14): Apr 25, 1901; L-7

6063   Bujdos, Suzanne   N   IV (50): Jan 2, 1895; C-4

6064   Bumba, George   N   IV (42): Nov 7, 1895; C-4, L-4
                                    L   IV (45): Nov 28, 1895; C-3, L-4&5

6065   Bumbera, Andrew   N   XI (21): Jun 12, 1902; C-7

6066   Bundža, Basil   N   XI (9): Mar 13, 1902; C-6
                                    L   XI (4): Feb 6, 1902; C-3

6067   Burak, Julia   N   X (45): Dec 5, 1901; C-6, L-6

6068   Buraly, Mary   N   V (18&19): May 21, 1896; C-4, L-4

6069   Buša, Andrew   L   XV (9): Mar 15, 1906; 2,3

6070   Bušanič, Paul   N   X (7): Feb 28, 1901; C-6

6071   Bydnyk, Anthony   N   V (14): Apr 23, 1896; C-4

6072   Bŷstrŷj, Andrew   L   XXIII (3): Jan 29, 1914; C-2

- C -

6073	Cap, Joseph	N	IV (32): Aug 29, 1895; C-2&3, L-4
6074	Capik, George	L	XXI (11): Mar 28, 1912; C-2&3, L-2&3
6075	Čarko, Mary	N	XI (17): May 15, 1902; C-6
6076	Čegin, Michael	L	XX (11): Mar 30, 1911; C-3, L-3
6077	Čerivka, John	L	XIII (8): Mar 10, 1904; C-2&3, L-2
6078	Červenjak, Ann	N	XI (14): Apr 17, 1902; C-7
6079	Chajka, Michael	N	V (14): Apr 23, 1896; C-4, L-4
6080	Chanat, Rev. Nicephor	B	X (2): Jan 24, 1901; C-1, L-1
6081	Chlebach, George	N	XI (17): May 15, 1902; C-7
6082	Chmelnicki, Michael	N	V (9): Mar 19, 1896; C-4, L-4
6083	Choleva, Margaret	N	XI (9): Mar 13, 1902; C-6
6084	Chovanec, Leško	L	XI (28): Aug 7, 1902; C-3
6085	Chvasta, John	L	XIII (1): Jan 21, 1904; C-3, L-3
6086	Cibul'a, George	L	XII (13): Apr 9, 1903; C-3, L-3
6087	Cibul'ak, Matthew	L	XII (13): Apr 9, 1903; C-3, L-3
6088	Činčar, Michael	L	XIII (6): Feb 25, 1904; L-2
6089	Cincul'a, Suzanne	N	X (14): Apr 25, 1901; L-7
6090	Cióka, Joseph	N	X (14): Apr 25, 1901; L-7
6091	Cip, John Sr.	L	XX (16): May 11, 1911; C-2&3, L-3
6092	Čisar, Louis	N	V (32): Aug 27, 1896; C-4
6093	Čorej, Michael	N	XI (21): Jun 12, 1902; C-7
		A	XI (15): Apr 24, 1902; C-6&7
6094	Cseperak, John	N	X (40): Oct 31, 1901; L-7
6095	Csucska, Rev. Cyril	N	X (11): Mar 28, 1901; C-6, L-6
		B	X (1): Jan 17, 1901; C-2&3, L-2
		B	X (4): Feb 7, 1901; C-5, L-5
		B	X (10): Mar 21, 1901; C-2, L-2

- D -

6096	Dančo, Alexis	L	XX (15): May 4, 1911; C-3, L-3
6097	Danko, John	L	XIX (3): Jan 27, 1910; C-3, L-3
6098	Danko, John	L	XX (22): Jun 22, 1911; C-4&5, L-2
6099	Danyo, Michael	N	X (24): Jul 11, 1901; C-6, L-6
6100	Demčak, Ann	N	X (35): Aug 29, 1901; C-7, L-7
6101	Demčuk, Rev. Dr. Nicholas	B	XV (22): Jun 21, 1906; 2
6102	Demjanovič, Mary	N	III (9): Mar 6, 1894; C-4, L-9
6103	Demjan, John	L	XXIII (1): Jan 15, 1914; C-3
6104	Demko, Mary	N	XI (21): Jun 12, 1902; C-7
6105	Demun, Michael	L	XVIII (41): Oct 28, 1909; C-3, L-2
6106	Derbiš, Michael	L	XXII (19): May 29, 1913; C-2&3, L-2&3
6107	Derkač, John	N	XV (2): Jan 25, 1906; 4&5
6108	Desčičk, Joseph	L	XIX (13): Apr 7, 1910; C-3, L-3
6109	Despot, Dora	N	V (18&19): May 21, 1896; C-4, L-4
6110	Dikun, Basil	N	X (35): Sep 26, 1901; C-7, L-7
6111	Dijarko, John	L	XVIII (40): Oct 21, 1909; C-3, L-2
6112	Djuhoš, Joseph	N	XI (4): Feb 6, 1902; C-6
6113	Djuryca, George	L	XI (42): Nov 13, 1902; C-4
6114	Doboš, Mary	L	XVI (16): May 2, 1907; C-2, L-2
6115	Dobroczki, Joseph	N	V (14): Apr 23, 1896; C-4, L-4
6116	Dohan, Michael	L	XXI (26): Jul 25, 1912; C-3, L-2&3
6117	Dohanič, Matthew	N	X (11): Mar 28, 1901; C-6, L-6
6118	Dokožokovsky, Aftan	L	XII (13): Apr 9, 1903; C-3, L-3
6119	Dolinsky, Andrew	N	X (49): Jan 2, 1902; C-6, L-6
6120	Domoraczki, Andrew	N	IV (34): Sep 12, 1895; C-4, L-4

6121	Drap, Andrew	N	X (35): Sep 26, 1901; C-7, L-7
6122	Drobniak, Andrew	N	IV (32): Aug 29, 1895; C-2&3, L-4
6123	Drohobeczky, Most Rev. Julius	B	XVII (18): May 21, 1908; C-1, L-1
6124	Drotar, Nicholas	N	IV (15): May 2, 1895; C-4, L-4
		L	IV (15): May 2, 1895; C-3, L-2&3
6125	Drotar, Veronica	N	X (3): Jan 31, 1901; C-6, L-6
6126	Ducar, Michael	L	XIX (41): Nov 3, 1910; C-2&3, L-2
6127	Ducs, Michael	L	XVI (22): Jun 20, 1907; C-2, L-2
6128	Dudinsky, Rev. Alexis	B	XVIII (39): Oct 14, 1909; C-2&3, L-3
6129	Dunda, George	L	XV (43): Nov 15, 1906; 2,3
6130	Durkal, George	L	XII (36): Oct 1, 1903; C-2, L-2
6131	Durkovič, Ann	N	X (49): Jan 2, 1902; C-6, L-6
6132	Durniak, Nicholas	N	III (1): Jan 2, 1894; C-4, L-11
6133	Dziak, Michael	N	X (40): Oct 31, 1901; L-7
6134	Dzijak, John	L	XVIII (28): Jul 29, 1909; C-3, L-3
6135	Dzijak, John	B	XXI (5): Feb 5, 1912; C-2&3, L-2
6136	Dzmura, Andrew	B	XXI (22): Jun 27, 1912; C-5, L-5
6137	Dzmura, Victor P.	B	XXII (25): Jul 10, 1913; C-2&3, L-2
6138	Dzubay, Rev. Alexander	B	XV (10): Mar 22, 1906; 2,3
6139	Dzubay, George	N	X (27): Aug 1, 1901; C-6, L-6
6140	Džupin, John	N	X (45): Dec 5, 1901; C-6, L-6
6141	Dzurovčak, Ann	L	XXIII (8): Mar 5, 1914; C-3

- E -

6142	Egan, Edward	B	X (37): Oct 10, 1901; C-4&5, L-4
6143	Emrich, Irene	L	XVI (47): Dec 12, 1907; L-2

6144	Enik, Michael	L	X (5): Feb 14, 1901; C-3, L-2&3
6145	Eštok, George	L	XX (7): Mar 2, 1911; C-2, L-3
6146	Eštok, John	N	X (3): Jan 31, 1901; C-6, L-6

- F -

6147	Fabula, Michael	N	X (31): Aug 29, 1901; C-7, L-7
6148	Fabyš, Michael	L	XVI (41): Oct 31, 1907; C-3, L-3
6149	Fajder, Suzanne	N	XI (25): Jul 17, 1902; C-6
6150	Fazekas, John	N	IV (31): Aug 22, 1895; C-4, L-4
6151	Feckanin, Joseph	L	XXII (4): Feb 6, 1913; C-3, L-2
6152	Fecsie, Peter	L	XVIII (36): Sep 23, 1909
6153	Fedor, Ann	N	X (3): Jan 31, 1901; C-6, L-6
6154	Fedor, Mary	N	X (27): Aug 1, 1901; C-6, L-6
6155	Fedorov, Mary	N	IV (16): May 9, 1895; C-4, L-4
6156	Fejedelem, Paul	N	V (34): Sep 10, 1896; C-4, L-4
		L	V (34): Sep 10, 1896; C-4&5, L-5
6157	Felehiy, Mrs. John	L	XXIII (32): Sep 3, 1914; C-2
6158	Fencik, John	N	X (49): Jan 2, 1902; C-6, L-6
6159	Fencyk, Rev. Eugene	B	XIII (1): Jan 21, 1904; C-4, L-4
6160	Ferenc, Andrew	L	XII (1): Jan 15, 1903; C-3, L-3
6161	Ferencz, George		XIX (3): Jan 27, 1910; C-3, L-2
6162	Fiffick, John R.	L	XVI (3): Jan 31, 1907; L-2
			XVI (4): Feb 7, 1907; C-3
6163	Figel, Ann	L	XIX (17): May 12, 1910; C-2&3, L-2
6164	Firczak, Most Rev. Julius	B	XX (36): Oct 5, 1911; C-1&2, L-1&2
		B,P	XXI (21): Jun 20, 1912; C-1&2, L-1
6165	Fizejr, Sofia	L	XXI (47): Dec 19, 1912; C-2

6165	Fizejr, Sofia	L	XXI (47): Dec 19, 1912; C-2
6166	Fljak, Michael	N	XI (9): Mar 13, 1902; C-6
6167	Földy, Basil	L	XVIII (24): Jul 1, 1909; C-3, L-3
6168	Fuga, Peter	L	XXII (19): May 29, 1913; C-2&3, L-2&3
6169	Furčanyk, Ann	L	XI (22): Jun 26, 1902; C-3
6170	Fusčič, Michael	L	XVIII (18): May 20, 1909; C-3, L-3
6171	Fusčin, Michael		(See: Fusčič, Michael)
6172	Fyhelij, Andrew	N	XI (4): Feb 6, 1902; C-6

- G -

6173	Gabaly, Eve	N	V (45): Nov 26, 1896; C-4, L-4
6174	Gabor, Mary	N	IV (37&38): Oct 3, 1895; C-4, L-4
6175	Gajda, Stephen	N	X (31): Aug 29, 1901; C-7, L-7
6176	Gajdoš, Michael	L	XXI (12): Apr 4, 1912; C-2, L-2
6177	Galya, George	L	XIX (2): Jan 20, 1910; C-3, L-2&3
6178	Gamrat, Andrew	N	X (7): Feb 28, 1901; C-7, L-7
6179	Garančovsky, George	L	XXII (28): Aug 7, 1913; C-3, L-3
6180	Gbur, Andrew	N	X (19): May 30, 1901; C-7, L-7
6181	Geci, John	L	XX (35): Sep 28, 1911; C-2, L-2
6182	Geczy, John	L	XXII (19): May 29, 1913; C-2&3, L-2&3
6183	Gelan, Michael	N	X (40): Oct 31, 1901; L-7
6184	Gera, Joseph	L	XVI (32): Aug 29, 1907; C-3, L-2
6185	Gergely, Joseph	L	XVIII (20): Jun 3, 1909; C-3, L-3
6186	Gernat, Ann	N	X (31): Aug 29, 1901; C-7, L-7
6187	Gnar, Mary	N	IV (10): Mar 21, 1895; C-4, L-1
6188	Gócs, Mary	N	X (27): Aug 1, 1901; C-6, L-6

6189	Gratko, Mary	N	V (47): Dec 10, 1896; C-4, L-4
6190	Grega, Julia	N	IV (31): Aug 22, 1895; C-4, L-4
6191	Grip, Julianna	N	III (1): Jan 2, 1894; C-4, L-11
6192	Grosik, John	L	XV (34): Sep 13, 1906; 3,6
6193	Gulovich, Rev. George	N	X (49): Jan 2, 1902; C-6, L-6
		B	X (42): Nov 14, 1901; C-1
		B	X (43): Nov 21, 1901; C-2, L-2
6194	Gulyaša, J.	L	XV (3): Feb 1, 1906; 2,3
6195	Guman, John	N	X (24): Jul 11, 1901; C-6, L-6

- H -

6196	Habasik, Andrew	L	XIX (29): Aug 11, 1910; C-3, L-2
6197	Habla, Constantine	L	XVI (10): Mar 21, 1907; C-2, L-2
6198	Hajdoščyk, Erža	N	XI (4): Feb 6, 1902; C-6
6199	Hajduk, Michael	N	X (31): Aug 29, 1901; C-7, L-7
6200	Hajtko, Sydor	N	XI (9): Mar 13, 1902; C-6
6201	Halahan, Andrew	N	X (11): Mar 28, 1901; C-6, L-6
6202	Haluška, George	L	XX (12): Apr 6, 1911; C-3, L-3
6203	Hamila, Ann	L	XVIII (44): Nov 18, 1909; C-3, L-2
6204	Hančyšyn, John	N	XI (14): Apr 17, 1902; C-7
6205	Haňkevič, Pauline	N	V (38): Oct 8, 1896; C-1, L-4&5
6206	Hanulya, Rev. Joseph	B	XIX (17-19): May, 1910; C-4, L-4
6207	Hardiho, John	L	XIII (2): Jan 28, 1904; C-2, L-2
6208	Harhala, Michael	N	XI (14): Apr 17, 1902; C-7
6209	Haščak, Theodore	N	XI (17): May 15, 1902; C-7
6210	Haspryk, Ymro	N	XI (14): Apr 17, 1902; C-7
6211	Haurilo, John	L	XVII (14): Apr 16, 1908; L-3

6212	Haurillo, Stephen	N	IV (32): Aug 29, 1895; C-2&3, L-4
6213	Havril, Andrew	L	XV (28): Aug 2, 1906; 2,4
6214	Havrillo, John	L	XXII (19): May 29, 1913; C-2, L-2
6215	Hazobit, Elizabeth	N	X (11): Mar 28, 1901; C-6, L-6
6216	Hegedis, Barbara	N	X (40): Oct 31, 1901; L-7
6217	Heletka, Eve	N	XI (25): Jul 17, 1902; C-6
6218	Herko, George	N	X (11): Mar 28, 1901; C-6, L-6
6219	Herko, Havrilo	L	X (8): Mar 7, 1901; C-3, L-2&3
6220	Herman, John	L	XII (13): Apr 9, 1903; C-3, L-3
6221	Herman, Paul	A	XVIII (14): Apr 22, 1909; C-2, L-2
6222	Hertnek, Ann	L	XV (39): Oct 18, 1906; 2&3
6223	Hertnik, John	N	X (45): Dec 5, 1901; C-6, L-6
6224	Hnapyk, Karl	L	XVI (17): May 16, 1907; C-2, L-2
6225	Hnatišin, Helen	N	X (40): Oct 31, 1901; L-7
6226	Hocman, Joseph	N	X (3): Jan 31, 1901; C-6, L-6
6227	Hodobay, Very Rev. Andrew	B B	XI (16): May 8, 1902; C-1&2 XXII (40): Oct 29, 1914; C-4
6228	Holey, Suzanne	N	X (27): Aug 1, 1901; C-6, L-6
6229	Holik, Simko	N	X (24): Jul 11, 1901; C-6, L-6
6230	Holitka, Joseph	N	III (20): Jun 12, 1894; C-5, L-9
6231	Holodik, George	L	X (9): Mar 14, 1901; C-3, L-3
6232	Honda, John	L	XX (6): Feb 23, 1911; C-3, L-2
6233	Horbala, Alexander	L	XXIII (25): Jul 16, 1914; C-2&3
6234	Horna, John	L	XIX (5): Feb 10, 1910; C-3, L-3
6235	Hornyak, Andrew	L	XIII (4): Feb 11, 1904; L-3
6236	Horvat, Alexis	N	XI (17): May 15, 1902; C-7
6237	Hospodar, Mary	N	XI (9): Mar 13, 1902; C-6

6238	Hostetter, Michael	L	XXII (48): Dec 25, 1913; C-3, L-2
6239	Hreha, John	L	XVI (48): Dec 19, 1907; L-2
6240	Hovanecz, Ann	N	V (17): May 14, 1896; L-4
6241	Hreno-Tončikova, Ann	L	XIII (37): Nov 3, 1904; 11
6242	Hricz, Rev. George	L	XXI (27): Aug 1, 1912; C-2, L-2
6243	Hriczak, Mrs. Michael	L	XVIII (43): Nov 11, 1909; C-2, L-2
6244	Hromcsak, Simon	N	IV (36): Sep 26, 1895; C-4, L-4
6245	Hryn'o, John	N	XI (4): Feb 6, 1902; C-6
6246	Hučko, Basil	N	V (22): Jun 18, 1896; C-4, L-4
6247	Hudak, Basil	N	X (11): Mar 28, 1901; C-6, L-6
6248	Humenik, George	L	XVI (31): Aug 22, 1907; C-3, L-2
6249	Húrdos, Michael Maczko	N	X (45): Dec 5, 1901; C-6, L-6
6250	Hurňy, John	N	X (14): Apr 25, 1901; L-7
6251	Hužvar, Joseph	N	IV (14): Apr 25, 1895; C-4, L-4
6252	Hyblar, Joseph	L	XXIII (20): Jun 11, 1914; C-3

- I -

6253	Ihnat, Ann	N	X (49): Jan 2, 1902; C-6, L-6
6254	Ihnat, John	N	III (2): Jan 9, 1894; C-4, L-9
6255	Isaysky, John	L	XX (14): Apr 20, 1911; C-2, L-2
6256	Ivan, George	N	X (45): Dec 5, 1901; C-6, L-6
6257	Ivančo, Ann	N	X (11): Mar 28, 1901; C-6, L-6

- J -

| 6258 | Jackaňin, Mary | N | X (3): Jan 31, 1901; C-6, L-6 |
| 6259 | Jaczina, John | N | X (35): Sep 26, 1901; C-7, L-7 |

6260	Jacob, Ann	N	III (40): Nov 15, 1894; C-4, L-9
6261	Jakubcsak, John	N	III (19): May 22, 1894; C-4, L-9
6262	Jankura, George	N	X (24): Jul 11, 1901; C-6, L-6
6263	Janoščik, John	N L	V (30): Aug 13, 1896; C-4, L-4 V (29): Aug 6, 1896; L-3
6264	Janoško, Peter	E,P	XXII (16): May 8, 1913; C-2&3, L-2&3
6265	Janossy, Stephen	L	XVIII (10): Mar 18, 1909; C-3, L-3
6266	Jarosik, John	L	XXI (40): Oct 31, 1912; C-6, L-3
6267	Jarusinsky, Ann	N	V (42): Nov 5, 1896; C-4, L-4
6268	Jaščur, Andrew	L	XXII (37): Oct 9, 1913; C-3, L-3
6269	Jašo, Michael	L	XXII (19): May 29, 1913; C-2&3, L-2&3
6270	Javyljak, Ann	N	V (5): Feb 13, 1896; C-4
6271	Jenik, Michael	N	X (7): Feb 28, 1901; C-7, L-7
6272	Judik, Basil	L	XVIII (18): May 20, 1909; C-3, L-2
6273	Juhasz, Mary	N	X (35): Sep 26, 1901; C-7, L-7
6274	Juhaz, Paul	L	XIII (19): Jun 2, 1904; C-3, L-3
6275	Jura, Michael	N	IV (32): Aug 29, 1895; C-2&3, L-4
6276	Jurcs, Andrew	N	IV (42): Nov 7, 1895; C-4, L-4
6277	Jurkanič, George	L	XXI (17): May 16, 1912; C-3, L-3

- K -

6278	Kachur, Michael	L	XIX (31): Aug 25, 1910; L-2
6279	Kačmarik, John Jr.	L	X (13): Apr 11, 1901; C-4, L-3
6280	Kačur, Barbara	N	IV (1): Jan 16, 1895; L-9
6281	Kalvin, Michael	L	XXI (10): Mar 21, 1912; C-3, L-2&3
6282	Kaminsky, Rev. Victor	B	XII (48): Dec 24, 1903; C-4&5, L-4&5
6283	Kanya, Eve	N	IV (40): Oct 25, 1895; C-4, L-4

6284	Kapinos, Michael	N	IV (32): Aug 29, 1895; C-2&3, L-4
6285	Kapitan, Simon	L	XVIII (18): May 20, 1909; C-3, L-3
6286	Kapko, Mary	N	XI (17): May 15, 1902; C-7
6287	Kapral, Basil	L	XV (42): Nov 8, 1906; 2,4
6288	Kapusta, Julia	N	X (14): Apr 25, 1901; L-7
6289	Karafa, John	L	XVI (16): May 2, 1907; C-3, L-2&3
6290	Karafa, Mary	N	IV (50): Jan 2, 1896; C-4
6291	Karahut, Michael	L	XII (5): Feb 12, 1903; C-3, L-3
6292	Kažimir, Andrew	L	XX (5): Feb 16, 1911; C-3, L-3
6293	Kecskés, Very Rev. Anthony	B	XII (24): Jul 9, 1903; C-2, L-2
6294	Kelly, George	N	X (27): Aug 1, 1901; C-6, L-6
6295	Kerpač, Andrew	L	XIX (29): Aug 11, 1910; L-2
6296	Keselyšča, Ann		(See: Dzurovčak, Ann)
6297	Kičanich, George	N	X (35): Sep 26, 1901; C-7, L-7
6298	Kimack, Basil	L	XVIII (16): May 6, 1909; C-3, L-3
6299	Kingya, Mary	N L	V (33): Sep 3, 1896; C-4, L-4 V (34): Sep 10, 1896; C-5, L-5
6300	Klazan, John	N	IV (28): Aug 1, 1895; C-4, L-4
6301	Klembarsky, George		XV (48): Dec 27, 1906; 3
6302	Klinger, Katherine	N	III (40): Nov 15, 1894; C-4, L-9
6303	Kluzsinski, Joseph	N	IV (28): Aug 1, 1895; C-4, L-4
6304	Kmecz, Michael	N	X (31): Aug 29, 1901; C-7, L-7
6305	Kmetz, John	L	XII (13): Apr 9, 1903; C-3, L-3
6306	Kočerha, Michael	L	XIII (22): Jun 23, 1904; C-2, L-2&3
6307	Kocserga, Theodore	L	XXI (2): Jan 25, 1912; C-2, L-2
6308	Koczur, John	L	XVI (29): Aug 8, 1907; C-3, L-3
6309	Kodak, Joseph	L	XII (13): Apr 9, 1903; C-3, L-3

6310	Kohut, Katherine	N	IV (48): Dec 19, 1895; C-4, L-4
6311	Kohut, Nicholas	L	XX (11): Mar 30, 1911; C-2&3, L-3
6312	Kohut, Verona	N	XI (21): Jun 12, 1902; C-7
6313	Kol, Phillip	N	V (3): Jan 30, 1896; C-4
6314	Kolcun, George	L	XV (21): Jun 14, 1906; 2,3
6315	Koleszar', George	N	X (27): Aug 1, 1901; C-6, L-6
6316	Komaneczki, John	N	III (30): Sep 4, 1894; C-4, L-9
6317	Komyčak, George	L	XXIII (31): Aug 27, 1914; C-10
6318	Kopač, John	L	XIII (12): Apr 7, 1904; C-3, L-3
6319	Korčhjak, John	L	XXIII (19): Jun 4, 1914; C-3
6320	Kordijak, Andrew	L	XXII (4): Feb 6, 1913; C-3, L-2
6321	Kordos, John	N	X (35): Sep 26, 1901; C-7, L-7
6322	Korman, Michael	L	XX (3): Feb 2, 1911; C-3, L-3
6323	Kormoš, George	L	XVIII (18): May 20, 1909; C-3, L-3
6324	Korpaš, Michael	L	XVIII (41): Oct 28, 1909; C-2&3, L-2
6325	Kostecky, Ann	N	III (4): Jan 23, 1894; C-4, L-9
6326	Kostyč, Basil	N	XI (4): Feb 6, 1902; C-6
6327	Kotansky, George Jr.	L	XXII (22): Jun 19, 1913; C-10, L-10
6328	Kotis, Wencho	L	XVII (9): Mar 12, 1908; L-3
6329	Kotulya, John	N	X (40): Oct 31, 1901; L-7
6330	Kovač, Joseph	N	XI (14): Apr 17, 1902; C-7
6331	Kovach, George	L	XVIII (24): Jul 1, 1909; C-3, L-3
6332	Kovachy, Adalbert	B	XV (29): Aug 9, 1906; 4,5
6333	Kovacs, Mary	N	X (24): Jul 11, 1901; C-6, L-6
6334	Kovacs, John	L	XXII (18): May 22, 1913; C-3, L-3
6335	Kovalčik, Ann	N	X (14): Apr 25, 1901; L-7
6336	Krajňak, Stephen	N	X (3): Jan 31, 1901; C-6, L-6

6337	Kral'ovyč, John	N	XI (14): Apr 17, 1902; C-7
6338	Krehely, Helen	N	X (19): May 30, 1901; C-7, L-7
6339	Krup, Peter	L	XX (48): Dec 28, 1911; C-2&3, L-2
6340	Kruška, Rev. John	L	XXI (27): Aug 1, 1912; C-2, L-2
6341	Kružel'ak, Ann	N	X (14): Apr 25, 1901; L-7
6342	Kuba, Mary Lolen	L	XVIII (12): Apr 1, 1909; C-6, L-6
6343	Kubiňa, Katherine	N	X (40): Oct 31, 1901; L-7
6344	Kucsar, Peter	N	III (43): Dec 6, 1894; C-4, L-9
6345	Kudl'ja, John	L	X (6): Feb 21, 1901; C-3, L-3
6346	Kudljak, John	N L	XI (4): Feb 6, 1902; C-6 XI (1): Jan 16, 1902; C-2
6347	Kuki, Ann	N	V (24): Jul 2, 1896; C-4, L-4
6348	Kupeč, John	L	XVIII (41): Oct 28, 1909; C-3, L-3
6349	Kurečko, John	N	V (24): Jul 2, 1896; C-4, L-4
6350	Kurucz, Nicholas	N	X (49): Jan 2, 1902; C-6, L-6
6351	Kusnicki, Ann	N	V (48): Dec 17, 1896; L-4
6352	Kuzma, Andrew	N	V (30): Aug 13, 1896; C-4, L-4
6353	Kuzma, Michael	N	XI (17): May 15, 1902; C-7
6354	Kuzsnyir, Peter	L	XVIII (40): Oct 21, 1909; C-3, L-2&3
6355	Kycko, Mary	N	III (15): Apr 17, 1894; C-4, L-9

- L -

6356	Labisak, Hric	N	X (31): Aug 29, 1901; C-7, L-7
6357	Lacko, George	N	X (7): Feb 28, 1901; C-7, L-7
6358	Ladomirsky, Imrich	L	XV (2): Jan 25, 1906; 2,3
6359	Lakatos, Elizabeth	N	IV (17): May 16, 1895; C-4, L-4
6360	Landsman, Michael	N	V (7): Mar 5, 1896; L-4

6361	Lašinsky, Andrew	N	X (45): Dec 5, 1901; C-6, L-6
6362	Lazorchik, John	L	XIX (2): Jan 20, 1910; C-3, L-3
6363	Lazorik, Katherine	N	V (26): Jul 16, 1896; C-4, L-4
6364	Lažo, Peter	N	X (45): Dec 5, 1901; C-6, L-6
6365	Lebeda, Mary	N	III (11): Mar 20, 1894; C-4, L-9
6366	Lelekač, Basil	L	XXI (40): Oct 31, 1912; C-6, L-3
6367	Lelekač, M.	L	XVI (13): Apr 11, 1907; C-2&3, L-3
6368	Lend'el, John	N L	XI (17): May 15, 1902; C-7 XI (12): Apr 3, 1902; C-3
6369	Lendovsky, John	L	X (32): Sep 5, 1901; C-3, L-3
6370	Lengyel, Rev. Michael	B	XVI (42): Nov 7, 1907; C-4, L-4
6371	Lenik, Michael	L	XXI (7): Feb 29, 1912; C-3, L-3
6372	Leščišin, Ivan	L	XII (19): May 28, 1903; C-2, L-2
6373	Leščišin, John	L	XIX (5): Feb 10, 1910; C-3, L-3
6374	Leško, Michael	N	IV (42): Nov 7, 1895; C-4, L-4
6375	Libertin, John	N L	X (35): Sep 26, 1901; C-7, L-7 X (30): Aug 22, 1901; C-3, L-3
6376	Ligus, John	L	XIX (3): Jan 27, 1910; C-3, L-3
6377	Limar, Theodore	N	X (27): Aug 1, 1901; C-6, L-6
6378	Lobada, Elizabeth	N	XI (9): Mar 13, 1902; C-6
6379	Locsmany, Peter	N	X (27): Aug 1, 1901; C-6, L-6
6380	Lois, John	N	XV (37): Oct 4, 1906; 4
6381	Lopuch, Basil	N	V (17): May 14, 1896; L-4
6382	Locmandij, Michael	N	XI (4): Feb 6, 1902; C-6
6383	Loy, John Jr.	L	XIII (14): Apr 28, 1904; C-2, L-2
6384	Lučkay, Joseph	N	IV (32): Aug 29, 1895; C-2&3, L-4
6385	Lukacsena, Stephen	N	V (47): Dec 10, 1896; C-4
6386	Lutaš, Michael	L	XXIII (19): Jun 4, 1914; C-3

6387	Lyisak, Theodore	N	X (27): Aug 1, 1901; C-6, L-6
6388	Lynko, Daniel	N	XI (9): Mar 13, 1902; C-6

- M -

6389	Mačala, Joseph	N	X (31): Aug 29, 1901; C-7, L-7
6390	Mackovjak, John	L	XX (21): Jun 15, 1911; C-5, L-2&3
6391	Mačuga, Ann	N	V (38): Oct 8, 1896; C-4, L-4
6392	Maczko, Michael	L	XVI (16): May 2, 1907; C-2&3, L-2
		L	XVI (17): May 16, 1907; C-2&3, L-2
6393	Maczura, Nicholas	N	V (46): Dec 3, 1896; C-4, L-4
		L	V (45): Nov 26, 1896; C-2, L-2
6394	Madzej, Anthony	N	XI (9): Mar 13, 1902; C-6
6395	Maguska, George	N	X (11): Mar 28, 1901; C-6, L-6
6396	Maisel, Mary	N	IV (47): Dec 12, 1895; C-4, L-4
6397	Makara, Joseph	N	V (31): Aug 20, 1896; C-4, L-4
6398	Malend, George		XIII (15): May 15, 1904; C-2, L-2
6399	Maliňak, Photij	N	X (24): Jul 11, 1901; C-6, L-6
6400	Malinyak, Michael	L	XVI (22): Jun 20, 1907; C-2, L-2
6401	Mamrosh, Theodosia	N	X (11): Mar 28, 1901; C-6, L-6
6402	Mancosh, Michael	L	XV (16): May 3, 1906; 2,3
6403	Mancoš, Ann	L	XV (44): Nov 22, 1906; 2,3
6404	Marcin, John	N	X (40): Oct 31, 1901; L-7
6405	Maskarynec, Basil	N	XI (9): Mar 13, 1902; C-6
6406	Matejovsky, John	N	III (27): Jul 31, 1894; C-4, L-9
6407	Matyas, Ann	N	IV (16): May 9, 1895; C-4, L-4
6408	Matyijcsak, Eve	N	III (32): Sep 20, 1894; C-4, L-9
6409	Medvecky, Rev. Julius	N	XVI (49): Dec 26, 1907; L-4

6410	Medvedy, Andrew	L	XXI (32): Sep 5, 1912; C-3, L-2&3
6411	Meglész, Mary	N	X (14): Apr 25, 1901; L-7
6412	Meszaros, Frank	N	IV (21): Jun 20, 1895; C-4, L-4
6413	Meszaroš, Paul	L	XVI (6): Feb 21, 1907; L-3
6414	Mezey, Michael	L	XXII (19): May 29, 1913; C-2&3, L-2&3
6415	Michalči, George	L	XIII (47): Jan 12, 1905; 2,3
6416	Mihalyi, Michael	N	V (36): Sep 24, 1896; C-5, L-4
6417	Mikita, Dr. Alexander	B	XIX (24): Jul 7, 1910; C-3, L-2
6418	Mikita, Michael	L	XII (17): May 14, 1903; C-3, L-3
6419	Mika, John	N	IV (32): Aug 29, 1895; C-2&3, L-4
6420	Mikloš, John	L	XII (48): Dec 24, 1903; C-3, L-3
6421	Milenkyho, Michael	L	XVI (16): May 2, 1907; C-3, L-3
6422	Minna, Michael	L	XXII (14): Apr 17, 1913; C-3, L-3
6423	Mirmak, John	N L	X (24): Jul 11, 1901; C-6, L-6 X (13): Apr 11, 1901; C-3
6424	Mizerak, Matthew	L	XIX (48): Dec 22, 1910; C-3, L-3
6425	Mochnacky, Michael	N	X (49): Jan 2, 1902; C-6, L-6
6426	Mohnač, Michael	N	X (31): Aug 29, 1901; C-7, L-7
6427	Mojzes, Mary	N	V (23): Jun 25, 1896; C-4, L-4
6428	Mokriš, Mary	L	XXII (3): Jan 30, 1913; C-3, L-2
6429	Molčan, Joseph	L	XV (46): Dec 13, 1906; 2,3
6430	Molchany, Rev. Vladimir	B	XIII (30): Sep 15, 1904; 4
6431	Mulesa, Michael	L	XXI (47): Dec 19, 1912; C-2&3
6432	Murajka, Anthony	N	X (27): Aug 1, 1901; C-6, L-6
6433	Murjanko, Ann	N	III (12): Mar 27, 1894; C-4, L-9
6434	Myšanyn, John	N	XI (9): Mar 13, 1902; C-6
6435	Myšyk, Anthony	L	XXIII (21): Jun 18, 1914; C-3

6436 Myterko, Peter   N   XI (25): Jul 17, 1902; C-6

- N -

6437 Nižankovski, Rev. Vladimir B   XII (20): Jun 4, 1903; C-4, L-4

6438 Nohay, Louis   L   XIX (3): Jan 27, 1910; C-3, L-2

6439 Novak, Rev. Alexis   B   XXII (10): Mar 19, 1914; C-4&5

6440 Novak, Joseph   N   IV (24): Jul 4, 1895; C-4, L-4
                                L   IV (24): Jul 4, 1895; C-5, L-4

6441 Novak, Stephen   L   XII (13): Apr 9, 1903; C-3, L-3

6442 Novotni, Ann   N   III (25): Jul 17, 1894; C-4, L-9

6443 Novotnij, Mary   N   XI (4): Feb 6, 1902; C-6

6444 Nyhaj, Michael   L   XIII (25): Jul 14, 1904; C-2&3, L-2&3

- O -

6445 Olah, Michael   N   X (45): Dec 5, 1901; C-6, L-6

6446 Olejnik, Joseph   L   XII (18): May 21, 1903; C-3, L-3

6447 Ondko, Ann   N   IV (4): Feb 7, 1895; C-4, L-9

6448 Ondovčik, Ann   N   X (40): Oct 31, 1901; L-7

6449 Onuška, Michael   L   X (33): Sep 12, 1901; C-2&3
                                N   X (40): Oct 31, 1901; C-7

6450 Ortynsky, Most Rev.   B   XVI (12): Apr 4, 1907; L-4
         Soter S.   B   XVII (42): Nov 19, 1908; C-1,2,3,
                                                            L-1&2

6451 Ovszak, Andrew   B   XXII (28): Aug 7, 1913; C-2&3, L-2

6452 Ozimok, Katherine   N   III (17): May 8, 1894; C-4, L-9

- P -

6453	Pacan, Michael	L	XXII (23): Jun 26, 1913; C-3, L-2
6454	Pajtaš, Ann		(See: Figel, Ann)
6455	Papik, George	L	XV (11): Mar 29, 1906; 2,3
6456	Parimuha, Jacob	L	XXI (12): Apr 4, 1912; C-3, L-2
6457	Parscouta, Rev. John	L	XI (26): Jul 24, 1902; C-3
6458	Parymucha, Katherine	N	XI (21): Jun 12, 1902; C-7
6459	Pastirčik, Mary	N	X (45): Dec 5, 1901; C-6, L-6
6460	Patryljak, John	N	XI (4): Feb 6, 1902; C-6
6461	Pavlisčak, Michael	L	XXII (7): Feb 27, 1913; C-3, L-2
6462	Pavlyk, Michael	L	XV (11): Mar 29, 1906; 2
6463	Pecuch, Michael	N	X (35): Sep 26, 1901; C-7, L-7
		L	X (29): Aug 15, 1901; C-2&3, L-2
6464	Pekar', Andrew	L	XVI (30): Aug 15, 1907; C-3, L-3
6465	Perhacs, Ann	N	IV (35): Sep 19, 1895; C-4, L-4
6466	Petraš, Michael	L	XIX (5): Feb 10, 1910; C-3, L-3
6467	Petrig, John	L	XIX (18): May 19, 1910; L-2
			XIX (19): May 26, 1910; C-4
6468	Petrik, Ann	N	X (49): Jan 2, 1902; C-6, L-6
6469	Petriško, Stephen	N	X (19): May 30, 1901; C-7, L-7
6470	Petrovskij, Elizabeth	L	XXIII (33): Sep 10, 1914; C-2
6471	Petyko, Andrew	N	X (49): Jan 2, 1902; C-6, L-6
6472	Pilar, John	L	XII (13): Apr 9, 1903; C-3, L-3
6473	Pirhala, Suzanne	L	XX (33): Sep 14, 1911; C-2, L-2
6474	Pizur, Michael	L	XXII (11): Mar 27, 1913; C-2&3, L-3
6475	Pjatak, George	N	IV (27): Jul 25, 1895; L-4
6476	Pjatak, Michael	N	X (7): Feb 28, 1901; C-7, L-7

6477	Plackoň, Barbara	N	X (7): Feb 28, 1901; C-7, L-7
6478	Plavecky, Ann	N	X (40): Oct 31, 1901; L-7
6479	Pohut, Katherine	L	XI (42): Nov 13, 1902; C-4
6480	Polačok, Ann	N	X (35): Sep 26, 1901; C-7, L-7
6481	Polkabla, Joseph	L	XX (46): Dec 14, 1911; C-3, L-2&3
6482	Polyvka, Ann	N	X (5): Feb 14, 1901; C-5
6483	Pondjak, Michael	N	IV (29): Aug 8, 1895; C-4, L-4
6484	Popik, George	L	XV (11): Mar 29, 1906; 2,3
6485	Popovich, Anthony	L	XXIII (31): Aug 27, 1914; C-10
6486	Popyk, Michael	N	XI (14): Apr 17, 1902; C-7
6487	Porvaznik, Michael	L	XXI (40): Oct 31, 1912; C-6, L-3
6488	Pouchan, Justina	L	XVIII (23): Jun 24, 1909; C-3, L-2&3
6489	Pravlocsak, John	N	V (50): Jan 6, 1897; C-4
6490	Prec, Ann	L	XXIII (7): Feb 26, 1914; C-2&3
6491	Pribilsky, Paul	N	X (14): Apr 25, 1901; L-7
6492	Pristas, George	N	V (27): Jul 23, 1896; C-4, L-4
		LE	V (41): Oct 29, 1896; C-4&5
6493	Pristaš, Katherine	L	XIX (26): Jul 21, 1910; C-4, L-2&3
6494	Proc, Ann		(See: Prec, Ann)
6495	Prokopovič, Michael	N	IV (32): Aug 29, 1895; C-2&3, L-4
6496	Pruzinsky, Gregory	N	III (2): Jan 9, 1894; C-4, L-9
6497	Pusztay, Joseph	N	X (14): Apr 25, 1901; L-7
6498	Pyroško, Michael	N	XI (14): Apr 17, 1902; C-7

- R -

| 6499 | Racsicza, George | N | IV (49): Dec 26, 1895; C-4, L-4 |
| 6500 | Radasky, Joseph | L | XII (18): May 21, 1903; C-3, L-3 |

6501	Rapko, Stephen	N	V (3): Jan 30, 1896; C-4
6502	Raš, Stephen	L	XXI (41): Nov 7, 1912; C-3, L-2&3
6503	Redaly, Michael	N	IV (46): Dec 5, 1895; C-4, L-4
6504	Reday, John	N	X (40): Oct 31, 1901; L-7
6505	Remeneckij, Elizabeth	N	XI (9): Mar 13, 1902; C-6
6506	Repak, Rev. Dr. Eugene	B	XIX (44): Nov 24, 1910; C-5, L-5
6507	Riško, Anastasia	N	X (11): Mar 28, 1901; C-6, L-6
6508	Rod'om, Michael	N	XI (25): Jul 17, 1902; C-6
6509	Rojko, George	L	XX (29): Aug 17, 1911; C-2&3, L-2
6510	Romanko, Basil	N L	X (31): Aug 29, 1901; C-7, L-7 X (26): Jul 25, 1901; C-3, L-2
6511	Romanko, George	L	XIX (14): Apr 14, 1910; C-3, L-3
6512	Roška, John	L	XIII (12): Apr 7, 1904; C-3, L-3
6513	Rushin, Elizabeth	B	XXII (21): Jun 18, 1914; C-2&3
6514	Rusiňak, John	N	X (24): Jul 11, 1901; C-6, L-6
6515	Rusynjak, Mary	N	XI (4): Feb 6, 1902; C-6
6516	Rusynjak, Michael	N	XI (21): Jun 12, 1902; C-7
6517	Rymar, John	N	XI (17): May 15, 1902; C-7

- S -

6518	Sabol, Peter	L	XX (11): Mar 30, 1911; C-3, L-3
6519	Sadlovsky, Lenora	N	X (31): Aug 29, 1901; C-7, L-7
6520	Šagan, Mary	N	X (19): May 30, 1901; C-7, L-7
6521	Šalak, George	L	XIX (6): Feb 17, 1910; C-3, L-3
6522	Saloni, Katherine	L	XXII (13): Apr 10, 1913; C-3, L-2
6523	Saloni, Michael	L	XXII (6): Feb 20, 1913; C-3, L-3
6524	Šandor, Stephen	N	XI (25): Jul 17, 1902; C-6

6525	Šarady, Sofia	L	XX (33): Sep 14, 1911; C-3, L-3
6526	Savko, John	N	X (19): May 30, 1901; C-7, L-7
6527	Savulak, Elias	N L	V (47): Dec 10, 1896; C-4, L-4 V (47): Dec 10, 1896; C-2, L-2
6528	Sčeremžak, Joseph	L	XXII (8): Mar 10, 1904; C-2, L-2
6529	Šeeš, Elizabeth	N	XI (9): Mar 13, 1902; C-6
6530	Šefchik, Alexis	L	XVIII (24): Jul 1, 1909; C-3, L-3
6531	Sekerak, John	L	XX (14): Apr 20, 1911; C-2&3, L-2
6532	Sekerek, John		(See: Sekerak, John)
6533	Seman, Stephen	N	X (7): Feb 28, 1901; C-7, L-7
6534	Šestak-Svistak, John	LE	XV (35): Sep 20, 1906; 2,3
6535	Sewczik, Xenia	N	X (19): May 30, 1901; C-7, L-7
6536	Sheregellyi, Rev. Nicholas	B	XII (10): Mar 19, 1903; C-2, L-2
6537	Sičak, John	L	XV (25): Jul 12, 1906; 2,3
6538	Sidun, Andrew	L	XX (15): May 4, 1911; C-3, L-3
6539	Sidriak, Nicholas	L	XIII (7): Mar 3, 1904; C-3, L-2&3
6540	Siket, Michael	L	XX (8): Mar 9, 1911; C-3, L-2&3
6541	Šikora, Mary	N	X (49): Jan 2, 1902; C-6, L-6
6542	Sikora, Petronella	L	XVI (35): Sep 19, 1907; C-3, L-2&3
6543	Simka, George	L	XVI (47): Dec 12, 1907; L-2
6544	Šinovič, Michael	L	XII (13): Apr 9, 1903; C-3, L-3
6545	Sirak, John	L	XVIII (41): Oct 28, 1909; C-3, L-2&3
6546	Sivik, Michael	N	V (5): Feb 13, 1896; C-4
6547	Skitka, Michael	N	X (24): Jul 11, 1901; C-6, L-6
6548	Sklinčo, Suzanne	N	III (22): Jun 26, 1894; C-4, L-9
6549	Škodák, John	L	XII (13): Apr 9, 1903; C-3, L-3
6550	Škonda, John	N	IV (32): Aug 29, 1895; C-2&3, L-4

6551	Skorodynskij, John	N	XI (21): Jun 12, 1902; C-7
6552	Skunda, John	L	XII (13): Apr 9, 1903; C-3, L-3
6553	Škut, George	L	XIII (46): Jan 5, 1905; 9,10,11,12
6554	Slanyk, Mary	L	XV (32): Aug 30, 1906; 2
6555	Smeriha, George Jr.	L	XXI (29): Aug 15, 1912; C-3, L-3
6556	Smetana, Michael	N	III (5): Jan 30, 1894; C-4, L-9
6557	Smij, Alex	N	IV (12): Apr 4, 1895; C-4, L-1
6558	Smiško, Joseph	L	XVIII (43): Nov 11, 1909; C-2&3, L-2
6559	Smith, John Andrew	B	III (20): Jun 12, 1894; C-3
		B	IV (14): Apr 25, 1895; C-4&5, L-4&5
6560	Smutko, Joseph	L	XIII (5): Feb 18, 1904; L-2
6561	Sninsky, Michael	N	X (31): Aug 29, 1901; C-7, L-7
6562	Soban, Michael	N	XI (25): Jul 17, 1902; C-6
6563	Soltak, Ann		(See: Hreno-Tončikova, Ann)
6564	Soltis, Ann	N	III (27): Jul 31, 1894; C-4, L-9
6565	Šoltis, Elias	L	XX (43): Nov 23, 1911; C-3, L-3
6566	Somskij, Tom	L	XI (28): Aug 7, 1902; C-3
6567	Somsky, Elizabeth	N	X (49): Jan 2, 1902; C-6, L-6
6568	Somsky, Michael	L	XVIII (18): May 20, 1909; C-3, L-3
6569	Sontak, Elizabeth	N	III (17): May 8, 1894; C-4, L-9
6570	Soroka, Dmitri	N	IV (44): Nov 21, 1895; C-4, L-4
		L	IV (43): Nov 14, 1895; C-2&3, L-2
6571	Soval, Stephen	N	V (3): Jan 30, 1896; C-4
6572	Sovič, Ann	L	XVI (15): Apr 25, 1907; C-2, L-2
6573	Spak, John	L	XV (36): Sep 27, 1906; 2,3
6574	Spilcsak, Peter	L	XIX (3): Jan 27, 1910; C-3, L-2
6575	Spirňak, Michael	N	X (7): Feb 28, 1901; C-7, L-7

6576	Špontak, George	L	XIX (6): Feb 17, 1910; C-3, L-3
6577	Stančak, John	L	XXIII (12): Apr 2, 1914; C-3
6578	Stec, Paraska	N	V (24): Jul 2, 1896; C-4, L-4
6579	Stecz, Michael		(See: Svecy, Michael)
6580	Stefan, George	N	XI (21): Jun 12, 1902
6581	Stefan, Paul	L	XXII (8): Mar 6, 1913; C-3, L-3
6582	Stefanisin, George	N	X (45): Dec 5, 1901; C-6, L-6
6583	Stefuš, Paul		(See: Stefan, Paul)
6584	Stroka, John	L	XII (4): Feb 5, 1903; C-2, L-2
6585	Stuljakovyč, Joseph	B	XXII (48): Dec 24, 1914; C-2
6586	Sugar, George	N	X (35): Sep 26, 1901; C-7, L-7
6587	Sulik, Adam	N	X (19): May 30, 1901; C-7, L-7
6588	Sut'ak, Peter	N	X (49): Jan 2, 1902; C-6, L-6
6589	Šutjak, Mary	N	XI (14): Apr 17, 1902; C-7
6590	Svap, Basil	N	X (24): Jul 11, 1901; C-6, L-6
6591	Svecy, Michael	L	XIII (36): Oct 27, 1904; 10
6592	Sveda, John	L	XIX (5): Feb 10, 1910; C-3, L-3
6593	Svitanich, Michael	L	XXII (6): Feb 20, 1913; C-3, L-3
6594	Sydork, Mary	N L	XI (21): Jun 12, 1902; C-7 XI (20): Jun 5, 1902; C-2
6595	Symko, Paul	L	XII (1): Jan 15, 1903; C-3, L-3
6596	Syn, Peter	L	XI (47): Dec 18, 1902; C-2
6597	Syvak, John	N	XI (17): May 15, 1902; C-7
6598	Szabadoš, John	L	XIII (35): Oct 20, 1904; 9&10
6599	Szabo, Rev. John	B	XX (46): Dec 14, 1911; C-2, L-2
6600	Szabolik, Mary	N	X (45): Dec 5, 1901; C-6, L-6
6601	Szakac, Katherine	N	IV (1): Jan 16, 1895; L-9

6602	Szakaczki, Michael	N	IV (27): Jul 25, 1895; L-4
6603	Szerencsa, George	N	V (33): Sep 3, 1896; C-4, L-4
6604	Szilvašy, George	N	X (31): Aug 29, 1901; C-7, L-7
6605	Szinicza, Leško	N	IV (33): Sep 5, 1895; C-4, L-4
6606	Szoganics, Michael	N	X (45): Dec 5, 1901; C-6, L-6
6607	Szucha, Michael	L	XVIII (43): Nov 11, 1909; C-2, L-2
6608	Szulik, Helen	N	IV (14): Apr 25, 1895; C-4, L-4

- T -

6609	Timko, John	L	XXII (19): May 29, 1913; C-2&3, L-2&3
6610	Timko, Mary	L	X (16): May 9, 1901; C-3, L-3
6611	Timko, Paul	N	V (7): Mar 5, 1896; L-4
6612	Tirnak, Makarij	L	XXIII (1): Jan 15, 1914; C-2
6613	Tokar, George	N	XI (9): Mar 13, 1902; C-6
6614	Tokarčik, Michael	L	XIII (30): Sep 15, 1904; 9,10
6615	Tolenčik, Michael	L	XVI (15): Apr 25, 1907; C-2, L-2
6616	Tomčak, Mary	N	X (14): Apr 25, 1901; L-7
6617	Tomka, M.K.	L	XVII (29): Aug 20, 1908; C-2&3, L-2
6618	Tomko, Andrew	L	XIX (28): Aug 4, 1910; C-2, L-3
6619	Tomko, Mary	L	XXII (46): Dec 11, 1913; C-2, L-2
6620	Toriš, John	N	X (11): Mar 28, 1901; C-6, L-6
6621	Toth, Rev. Alexis	B	XVIII (17): May 13, 1909; C-3, L-3
6622	Tovt, Frank	N	XI (25): Jul 17, 1902; C-6
6623	Tretynyk, Ann	N	XI (9): Mar 13, 1902; C-6
6624	Trojan, Michael	L	XVIII (33): Sep 2, 1909; C-3, L-3
6625	Tulenčik, Michael		(See: Tolenčik, Michael)

6626	Turčan, John Pacak	L	XX (33): Sep 14, 1911; C-2&3, L-2
6627	Turk, Peljahija	N	XI (17): May 15, 1902; C-7
6628	Uhaly, George	N	X (19): May 30, 1901; C-7
6629	Uhl'ar, Elizabeth	N	X (35): Sep 26, 1901; C-7, L-7
6630	Uhrin, Andrew	L	XVI (44): Nov 21, 1907; L-2
6631	Uhrin, John	B,P B	XXII (38): Oct 16, 1913; C-1,2,3, L-1 XXII (38): Oct 16, 1913; C-4, L-4
6632	Urban, Elizabeth	N	IV (44): Nov 21, 1895; C-4, L-4

- V -

6633	Vagaski, John	N	IV (32): Aug 29, 1895; C-2&3, L-4
6634	Valij, Most Rev. Dr. John	B B	XII (44): Nov 26, 1903; C-2, L-2 XX (45): Dec 7, 1911; C-1, L-1
6635	Valyko, Andrew	L	XIII (41): Dec 1, 1904; 4
6636	Vanšyk, Michael	N	XI (14): Apr 17, 1902; C-7
6637	Vanyk, John	L	XV (41): Nov 1, 1906; 2,3
6638	Varcha, John	N	IV (32): Aug 29, 1895; C-2&3, L-4
6639	Varchol, Elias	N	V (17): May 14, 1896; L-4
6640	Varga, John	N	X (3): Jan 31, 1901; C-6, L-6
6641	Varga, Nicholas	N	X (27): Aug 1, 1901; C-6, L-6
6642	Varga, Stephen	L	XVIII (40): Oct 21, 1909; C-3, L-2
6643	Varha, Andrew	N	XI (14): Apr 17, 1902; C-7
6644	Vasil, Paul	N	IV (31). Aug 22, 1895; C-4, L-4
6645	Vasilindev, John Jr.	L	XX (20): Jun 2, 1910; C-2, L-2
6646	Vasily, George	L	XXI (40): Oct 31, 1912; C-6, L-3
6647	Vaško, Michael	N	XI (21): Jun 12, 1902; C-7
6648	Vaverčak, Mary	L	XVI (9): Mar 14, 1907; C-3, L-3

6649	Vavrek, Joseph	N	XI (4): Feb 6, 1902; C-6
6650	Vazily, Andrew	L	XIX (41): Nov 3, 1910; C-3, L-2&3
6651	Venhry, Joseph	N	X (19): May 30, 1901; C-7, L-7
6652	Vereš, George	L	XVI (17): May 16, 1907; C-2, L-2
6653	Vilda, Clementine	N	III (28): Aug 14, 1894; C-4, L-9
6654	Visčak, Basil	L	XIX (25): Jul 14, 1910; L-3
6655	Viszlay, John	N	X (24): Jul 11, 1901; C-6, L-6
6656	Vlasacs, George	L	XX (32): Sep 7, 1911; C-3, L-3
6657	Vojtovič, John	L	III (36): Oct 1, 1903; C-2, L-2
6658	Volk, Lucas	L	XVI (6): Feb 21, 1907; L-3
6659	Vološin, Rev. Basil	L	XIX (18): May 19, 1910; L-2 XIX (19): May 26, 1910; C-4&5
6660	Volovar, Michael	L	XII (1): Jan 15, 1903; C-3, L-3
6661	Vorek, Paul	L	X (8): Mar 7, 1901; C-3, L-3
6662	Vrabel', Mary	N	X (14): Apr 25, 1901; L-7
6663	Vrabel', Dimitri	L	XXIII (18): May 28, 1914; C-3
6664	Vrabely, Mary	N	X (27): Aug 1, 1901; C-6, L-6
6665	Vydransky, Paul	L	XX (2): Jan 26, 1911; C-6, L-3

- W -

6666	Wasilčak, Andrew	L	XVI (18): May 23, 1907; C-2, L-2
6667	Wayeuš, John	L	XVII (9): Mar 12, 1908; L-3
6668	Wirostok, Elizabeth	N	III (2): Jan 9, 1894; C-4, L-9

- Z -

6669	Zajac, Julia	N	XI (4): Feb 6, 1902; C-6
6670	Zajac, Basil	N	XI (25): Jul 17, 1902; C-6
6671	Zamborij, Mary	N	XI (17): May 15, 1902; C-7
6672	Zarnaj, Elizabeth	N	XI (14): Apr 17, 1902; C-7
6673	Zavacky, Ann	N	III (4): Jan 23, 1894; C-4, L-9
6674	Zavacky, Simon	L	XIX (14): Apr 14, 1910; C-3, L-3
6675	Zbojan, Michael	N	V (14): Apr 23, 1896; C-4, L-4
6676	Zbojovski, Ann	N	V (48): Dec 17, 1896; L-4
6677	Zboray, John	N	IV (32): Aug 29, 1895; C-2&3, L-4
6678	Zelep, John	L	XX (32): Sep 7, 1911; C-3, L-3
6679	Zidik, Rev. Peter	L	XXI (27): Aug 1, 1912; C-2, L-2
6680	Zmijak, [?]	L	XV (36): Sep 27, 1906; 2,3
6681	Zozulak, Adam	N	X (40): Oct 31, 1901; L-7
6682	Zozul'ak, Ann	N	X (35): Sep 26, 1901; C-7, L-7
6683	Zsatkovich, Gregory I.	B,P B	XIX (38): Oct 13, 1910; C-4, L-4 XXI (21): Jun 20, 1912; C-4&5, L-4
6684	Zubal', Elias	L	XXIII (5): Feb 12, 1914; C-2
6685	Zubal', Joseph	L	XXII (18): May 22, 1913; C-3, L-2

Appendices

APPENDIX I

SUPREME OFFICERS OF THE GREEK CATHOLIC UNION
AND THEIR TENURE

Elected at the founding convention in Wilkes Barre, PA

for the term of February 14, 1892 - May 31, 1893

Supreme President: John A. (Žinčak) Smith

Supreme Vice-President: Anthony Kostik

Supreme Secretary: Simon Fedorovsky

Supreme Recording Secretary: Rev. Eugene Volkay

Supreme Treasurer: Theodore Talpash (Talpaš)

Supreme Controller: Rev. Augustine Laurisin

Overseeing Committee: Rev. Theophane Obushkevich
                       Rev. Stephen Jackovich
                       Michael Kravčik
                       John Martahus

Elected at the second general convention in Scranton, PA

for the term of June 1, 1893 - May 31, 1894

Supreme President: John A. Smith

Supreme Vice-President: Alexis Shljanta (Shlanta)

Supreme Secretary: Paul Jurievich Zsatkovich (Žatkovich)

Supreme Recording Secretary: Dionisius Pirč (Pyrch)

Supreme Treasurer: Anthony Onushchak (Onuščak)

Supreme Controller: Rev. Augustine Laurisin

Supreme Overseeing Committee: Rev. Theophane Obushkevich
                               Rev. Alexander Shereghy
                               Peter Bokšay (Bokša)
                               Andrew Andrejcin (Andrejczin)
                               Paul Matyaš
                               John Ihnat
                               Michael Terepan

Elected at the third general convention in Shenandoah, PA
for the term of June 1, 1894 - May 31, 1896

Supreme President: John A. Smith

Supreme Vice-President: Alexis Shljanta

Supreme Secretary: Rev. Cornelius Laurisin

Supreme Recording Secretary: Rev. John Szabo (Šabov)

Supreme Treasurer: Anthony Onushchak

Supreme Controller: Anthony Kostik

Supreme Overseeing Committee: Rev. Alexander Dzubay - Committee Head
Andrew Kosar
George Vretjak (Vretiak)
Paul Matyaš
Jacob (Jacko) Kurillo
Peter Bokšay

Elected at the fourth general convention in New York, NY
for the term of June 1, 1896 - May 31, 1897

Supreme President: John A. Smith

Supreme Secretary: August B. Bessenyey

Supreme Recording Secretary: Paul Jurievich Zsatkovich

Supreme Treasurer: George Vretjak

Supreme Spiritual Advisor: Rev. Dr. Simon Szabo (Šabov)

Supreme Controllers: Joseph Potočnjak (Potocsnyak)
Rev. Theodore Damjanovics (Demjanovich)

Supreme Overseeing Committee: <u>Committee Heads</u>

Rev. Alexander Dzubay
Stephen Metely (Metelij)

<u>Committee Members</u>

Anthony Kostik
Michael Juhas (Yuhasz)
John Kušnirik
Rev. Valentine Balog (Balogh)
Rev. Cornelius Laurisin
Joseph Potočnjak

Director of Printing Department: Rev. Theodore Damjanovics

Elected at the fifth general convention in Braddock, PA

for the term of June 1, 1897 - May 31, 1899

Supreme President: John A. Smith
            Rev. Cornelius Laurisin

Supreme Vice-President: George Kokajko
            John Hatrak

Supreme Secretary: August B. Bessenyey

Supreme Recording Secretary: Paul Jurievich Zsatkovich

Supreme Treasurer: Peter Dzmura

Supreme Spiritual Advisor: Rev. Theodore Damjanovics
            Rev. Simon Szabo

Supreme Controller: Michael Juhas

Supreme Overseeing Committee: Committee Heads

            Rev. Alexander Dzubay
            Stephen Metely

            Committee Members

            Rev. Gabriel Martyak
            Anthony Kostik
            Rev. Andrew Kaminsky
            John Kušnirik
            John Lend'el
            Michael Juhas
            Michael D'jurik

Director of Printing Department: Rev. Theodore Damjanovics

Elected at the sixth general convention in Cleveland, OH

for the term of June 1, 1899 - May 31, 1902

Supreme President: Rev. Theodore Damjanovics (transferred to Europe
            shortly after election)

Supreme Vice-President: Michael Juhas (succeeded Rev. Damjanovics)

Supreme Secretary: August B. Bessenyey

Supreme Recording Secretary: Rev. Alexis Holosnyay

Supreme Treasurer: Peter Dzmura

Supreme Spiritual Advisor: Rev. Cornelius Laurisin

Supreme Controller: Rev. John Hal'ko (Haljko, Halyko)

```
Supreme Overseeing Committee:   Committee President
                                Rev. Gabriel Martyak
                                Committee Members
                                Rev. John Ardan
                                Michael Smutko
                                John Dziak (Dzijak)
                                Ann Hreňa (Hrenja)
ARV Editor-in-Chief:   Paul Jurievich Zsatkovich*
```

Elected at the seventh general convention in Cleveland, OH
for the term of June 1, 1902 - June 30, 1904

Supreme President: Michael Juhas

Supreme Vice-President: Michael Fedorko

Supreme Secretary: August B. Bessenyey

Supreme Recording Secretary: Nicholas Pačuta (Pachuta)

Supreme Treasurer: Peter Dzmura

Supreme Spiritual Advisor: Rev. Damaskin (Damascene) Polivka

Supreme Controllers: Joseph Ždi (Ždy)
Peter Kozub
Michael K. Lucak

```
Supreme Overseeing Committee:   Committee President
                                Michael Ocelovany
                                Committee Members
                                John Chuba
                                Simon Kavasnyak (Kavasnak)
                                Michael Molnar
                                Helen Marinčak (Marincik)
Supreme Tribunal:   Tribunal President
                    Michael Sabo
                    Tribunal Secretary
                    John Dziak
```

---

* The office of ARV Editor-in-Chief was not considered an official supreme
officer position, however the editor was generally present at any meeting
or conference held by the supreme officers and voiced opinions on decision-
making questions. For this reason, the ARV editorship is considered part
of this listing.

Tribunal Members

Andrew Marko
Andrew Russnak
Michael Gošpar (Gaspar)
John Sofranko
Ann Bejda

ARV Editor-in-Chief: Paul Jurievich Zsatkovich

Elected at the eighth general convention in Trenton, NJ
for the term of July 1, 1904 - June 30, 1906

Supreme President: Michael Juhas

Supreme Vice-President: John Dziak

Supreme Woman Vice-President: Helen Marinčak

Supreme Secretary: Nicholas Pačuta

Supreme Recording Secretary: Julius Egrecky (Egreczky)

Supreme Treasurer: Peter Dzmura

Supreme Spiritual Advisor: Rev. Damaskin Polivka
                            Rev. Acacius Kamensky

Supreme Controllers: Rev. Michael Jackovich
                      John Uhrin
                      George Galya (Gulya)

Supreme Overseeing Committee: Committee President
                               Joseph Ždi

                               Committee Members
                               Michael Jaško
                               Michael Sabo
                               John Kobulnicky
                               Michael K. Lucak
                               John Zidik
                               John Kacik
                               George Macko
                               Ann Bejda
                               Emil Fecko

Elected at the ninth general convention in Wilkes Barre, PA
for the term of July 1, 1906 - June 30, 1908

Supreme President: John Uhrin

Supreme Vice-President: John Dziak

Supreme Woman Vice-President: Helen Marinčak

Supreme Secretary: Nicholas Pačuta

Supreme Recording Secretary: Julius Egrecky

Supreme Treasurer: Peter Dzmura

Supreme Spiritual Advisor: Rev. Nicholas Chopey

Supreme Controllers: Rev. Nicholas Strutinsky (succeeded by Rev. John Szabo)
                      Andrew Zbojan (Zboyan)
                      Michael Bodrog

Supreme Overseeing Committee: <u>Committee President</u>

                                Rev. Michael Jackovich

                                <u>Committee Members</u>

                                John Drimak (Drymak)
                                Michael Mačuga (Machuga)
                                Michael Breza (Breznaly), Jr.
                                Michael K. Lucak
                                George Bandurich (succeeded by George Galya)
                                Ignatius Ladna (succeeded by Thomas Strich)
                                Michael Jaško
                                Caroline Levendovsky (Levandovsky)
                                Ann Beres (Bires)

Supreme Attorney: John F. Cox

Supreme Physician: Dr. August Korchnak

Director of Printing Department: Rev. Joseph Hanulya (succeeded by Rev.
                                  Cornelius Laurisin)

Supreme Standard Bearer: John Lois

<u>ARV</u> Editor-in-Chief: Paul Jurievich Zsatkovich

Elected at the tenth general convention in Yonkers, NY
for the term of July 1, 1908 - June 30, 1910

Supreme President: John Uhrin

Supreme Vice-President: George Šepelyak

Supreme Woman Vice-President: Mary Holub

Supreme Secretary: Nicholas Pačuta

Supreme Recording Secretary: Julius Egrecky

Supreme Treasurer: Peter Dzmura

Supreme Spiritual Advisor: Rev. Nicholas Stecovich (Szteczovich)

Supreme Controllers: Andrew Zbojan
                           Michael Juhas
                           Michael Bodrog

Supreme Overseeing Committee: Committee President

                           Gregory Savuliak

                           Committee Members

                           Michael Mačuga
                           John Kipila (Kipilla)
                           John Hatrak
                           Joseph Fecko (Feczko)
                           John Praschak
                           George Bandurich
                           Ann Dzurinda
                           Caroline Levendovsky

Supreme Physician: Dr. August Korchnak

Director of Printing Department: Rev. Alexis Holosnyay

Supreme Standard Bearer: George Dandar

Elected at the eleventh general convention in Chicago, IL
for the term of July 1, 1910 - June 30, 1912

Supreme President: John Uhrin

Supreme Vice-President: George Šepelyak

Supreme Woman Vice-President: Helen Marinčak

Supreme Secretary: Julius Egrecky

Supreme Recording Secretary: Michael Maczko (Macko)

Supreme Assistant Recording Secretary: John Drimak

Supreme Treasurer: Gregory Savuliak

Supreme Spiritual Advisor: Rev. Michael Jackovich

Supreme Controllers: Michael Juhas
                       John Dziak
                       Michael S. Rushin

Supreme Tribunal: Tribunal President

                   Nicholas Pačuta

                   Tribunal Members

                   John Hatrak
                   George Bandurich
                   Ann Dzurinda
                   Joseph Ždi

<u>Tribunal Members</u> (cont'd)

John Vrabely (Vrabel)
Mary Jevčak (Yevcak)
John Virostko
John Oleksa
John Borecky (Boreczky)
Elizabeth Zafian

Supreme Physician: Dr. August Korchnak

Director of Printing Department: Rev. Alexis Holosnyay

Supreme Standard Bearer: George Dandar

Organizer of the Uhro-Rusyn Sokols: Paul Jurievich Zsatkovich

Elected at the twelfth general convention in Homestead, PA
for the term of July 1, 1912 - June 30, 1914

Supreme President: Michael S. Rushin

Supreme Vice-President: George Dandar

Supreme Woman Vice-President: Mary Nemeth

Supreme Secretary: Julius Egrecky

Supreme Recording Secretary: Michael A. Maczko

Supreme Assistant Recording Secretary: John Drimak

Supreme Treasurer: Gregory Savuliak

Supreme Spiritual Advisor: Rev. Michael Jackovich

Supreme Controllers: Michael Juhas
George Šepelyak
George Kondor

Supreme Tribunal: <u>Tribunal President</u>

John Uhrin

<u>Tribunal Members</u>

George Bandurich
Michael Mocsary (Mochary)
Andrew Ragan
Joseph Ždi
John Konkus
John Borecky
Michael Pilissy (Pillisy)
S.D. Mošurak
John F. Leško
John Korman
John Barilich

Tribunal Members (cont'd)

Ann Kužila (Kuzsila)
Mary Jevčak
Mary Holub
Helen Marinčak
Alexis Kostelnik (Koscelnik)
John Vrabely

Director of Printing Department: Rev. Alexis Holosnyay

Supreme Standard Bearer: Joseph Petrovsky

Supreme Flag Bearer: George Selepecz

ARV Editor-in-Chief: Paul Jurievich Zsatkovich

ARV Assistant Editors: Theophile A. Zsatkovich (Žatkovich)
Michael J. Hanchin

ARV Expeditor: Michael Timko

Elected at the thirteenth general convention in Scranton, PA
for the term of July 1, 1914 - June 30, 1916

Supreme President: Michael S. Rushin

Supreme Vice-President: George Kondor

Supreme Woman Vice-President: Ann Kostura

Supreme Sokol Vice-President: Alexis Kostelnik

Supreme Financial Secretary: George G. Komloš

Supreme Recording Secretary: John Drimak

Supreme Assistant Recording Secretary: Michael Kolecsar

Supreme Sokol Recording Secretary: Michael Deliman

Supreme Treasurer: George Dandar

Supreme Spiritual Advisor: Rev. Alexander Dzubay

Supreme Controllers: George Munchak (Munčak)
Michael Nejmet (Nemeth)

Supreme Tribunal: Tribunal President

Michael Bodrog

Tribunal Recording Secretary

John Kozic (Kozich)

Tribunal Members

John Slivka
John Korman

<u>Tribunal Members</u> (cont'd)

Suzanne Plaskon
Helen Marinčak
John Oleksa
Ann Dzurinda
Elizabeth Besterci (Bestercy)
Michael Pilissy
Elizabeth Volčko (Volchko)
John Borecky
John Virostko
John Luco

Supreme Legal Advisor: Joseph E. Myers

Manager of Printing Department: Michael J. Juhas (Yuhasz), Jr.

Supreme Standard Bearer: Stephen Bakoš

<u>ARV</u> Editor-in-Chief: Michael J. Hanchin

<u>ARV</u> Assistant Editors: Peter J. Maczkov
Nicholas Pačuta

<u>ARV</u> Expeditor: Michael Timko

APPENDIX II

MEMBERSHIP STATISTICS OF THE GREEK CATHOLIC UNION, G.C.U. YOUTH LODGES, AND G.C.U. SOKOL LODGES

G.C.U. -- Membership Statistics 1894

Members	Suspensions	Source
3,042		III (1): Jan 2, 1894; C-4, L-10
3,056		III (3): Jan 16, 1894; C-5, L-9
3,153		III (4): Jan 23, 1894; C-4, L-9
3,154 [misprint 3,145]		III (5): Jan 30, 1894; C-4, L-9
3,188		III (6): Feb 6, 1894; C-4, L-9
3,205		III (8): Feb 27, 1894; C-4, L-9
3,206		III (9): Mar 6, 1894; C-4, L-9
3,239		III (10): Mar 13, 1894; C-4, L-9
3,235		III (11): Mar 20, 1894; C-4, L-9
3,245		III (12): Mar 27, 1894; C-4, L-9
3,227	29	III (13): Apr 3, 1894; C-4, L-9
3,220	29	III (14): Apr 10, 1894; C-4, L-9
3,200	29	III (15): Apr 17, 1894; C-4, L-9
3,171	29	III (16): Apr 29, 1894; C-4, L-9
3,147	390	III (17): May 8, 1894; C-4, L-9
3,137	390	III (18): May 15, 1894; C-4, L-9
3,054	390	III (19): May 22, 1894; C-4, L-9
2,712	390	III (22): Jun 26, 1894; C-4, L-9
2,525	390	III (25): Jul 17, 1894; C-5, L-9

G.C.U. -- Membership Statistics 1896

Members	Suspensions	Source
4,085		V (25): Jul 9, 1896; C-4, L-4
4,153		V (29): Aug 6, 1896; C-2, L-4
4,226		V (33): Sep 3, 1896; C-4, L-4
4,249		V (42): Nov 5, 1896; C-4, L-4
4,285		V (47): Dec 10, 1896; C-4, L-4

G.C.U. -- Membership Statistics 1901

Month	Number of Lodges	Number of Members from Previous Month	Number of New Members	Number of Members Who Transferred Lodges	Number of Deaths	Number of Members Who Left G.C.U. for Various Reasons	Total Number of Members	Source
Dec, 1900	221	8,364	500	19	4	162	8,717	X (1): Jan 17, 1901; C-3, L-3
Jan, 1901	221	7,833	559	30	8	154	9,156	X (7): Feb 28, 1901; C-9, L-3
Feb, 1901	222	9,157	240	18	9	143	9,261	X (11): Mar 28, 1901; C-3, L-3
Mar, 1901	228	9,265	235	23	6	149	9,368	X (14): Apr 25, 1901; L-3
Apr, 1901	233	9,364	211	10	8	119	9,458	X (19): May 30, 1901; C-3, L-3
May, 1901	234	9,453	259	24	9	232	9,495	X (22): Jun 20, 1901; C-3, L-3
Jun, 1901	239	9,496	453	26	10	238	9,727	X (26): Jul 25, 1901; C-3, L-3
Jul, 1901	240	9,741	268	67	11	282	9,783	X (31): Aug 29, 1901; C-3, L-3
Aug, 1901	243	9,779	238	31	5	249	9,794	X (35): Sep 26, 1901; C-3, L-3
Sep, 1901	248	9,792	272	24	10	257	9,831	X (40): Oct 31, 1901; L-3
Oct, 1901	252	9,817	244	54	8	242	8,865	X (44): Nov 28, 1901; C-3, L-3
Nov, 1901	254	9,878	188	25	4	139	9,948	X (48): Dec 26, 1901; C-3, L-3

G.C.U. -- Membership Statistics 1902

Month	Number of Lodges	Number of Members from Previous Month	Number of New Members	Number of Members Who Transferred Lodges	Number of Deaths	Number of Members Who Left G.C.U. for Various Reasons	Total Number of Members	Source
Dec, 1901	260	9,937	526	27	6	237	10,246	XI (2&3): Jan 30, 1902; C-3
Jan, 1902	262	10,225	480	20	13	188	10,524	XI (7): Feb 27, 1902; C-3
Feb, 1902	268	10,507	346	34	9	191	10,687	XI (11): Mar 27, 1902; C-3
Mar, 1902	271	10,687	220	22	7	219	10,703	XI (15): Apr 24, 1902; C-9
Apr, 1902	272	10,698	153	25	6	186	10,684	XI (19): May 29, 1902; C-3
May, 1902	273	10,684	247	18	4	284	10,661	XI (21): Jun 12, 1902; C-9
Jun, 1902	276	10,771	531	12	17	447	10,850	XI (31): Aug 28, 1902; C-6
Aug, 1902	278	10,748	222	14	3	138	10,843	XI (35): Sep 25, 1902; C-6
Sep, 1902	283	10,678	206	29	5	168	10,740	XI (40): Oct 30, 1902; C-6
Oct, 1902	285	10,824	211	35	10	178	10,882	XI (44): Nov 27, 1902; C-6
Nov, 1902	287	10,898	202	37	2	153	10,982	XI (49): Jan 1, 1903; C-12

G.C.U. -- Membership Statistics 1903

Month	Number of Lodges	Number of Members from Previous Month	Number of New Members	Number of Members Who Transferred Lodges	Number of Reinstated Members	Number of Deaths	Number of Members Who Left G.C.U. for Various Reasons	Total Number of Members	Source
Dec, 1902	289	10,984	337	27	38	7	203	11,176	XII (2&3): Jan 29, 1903; C-10&11, L-6
Feb, 1903	299	11,885	333	13	37	13	230	12,026	XII (9): Mar 12, 1903; C-3, L-3
Mar, 1903	303	12,026	331	54	40	15	306	12,130	XII (15): Apr 30, 1903; C-3, L-3
Apr, 1903	306	12,130	128	26	27	8	409	11,894	XII (19): May 28, 1903; C-3, L-3
May, 1903	307	11,826	198	36	35	12	383	11,699	XII (22): Jun 25, 1903; C-12, L-3
Jun, 1903	307	11,707	146	17	22	5	284	11,610	XII (27): Jul 30, 1903; C-3, L-3
Jul, 1903	307	11,610	195	21	27	10	405	11,438	XII (31): Aug 27, 1903; C-3, L-3
Aug, 1903	311	11,438	292	41	28	5	212	11,582	XII (36): Oct 1, 1903; C-3, L-3
Sep, 1903	311	11,582	192	29	20	22	171	11,630	XII (43): Nov 19, 1903; C-3, L-3

G.C.U. -- Membership Statistics 1904

Month	Number of Lodges	Number of Members from Previous Month	Number of New Members	Number of Members Who Transferred Lodges	Number of Reinstated Members	Number of Deaths	Number of Members Who Left G.C.U. for Various Reasons	Total Number of Members	Source
Jan, 1904	328	11,574	833	31	38	9	295	12,172	XIII (3): Feb 4, 1904; C-3, L-3
Feb, 1904	330	12,174	197	28	47	11	227	12,206	XIII (9): Mar 17, 1904; C-3, L-3
Mar, 1904	331	12,206	195	36	53	7	308	12,175	XIII (14): Apr 28, 1904; C-3, L-3
Apr, 1904	331	12,175	115	30	29	13	269	12,067	XIII (16): May 12, 1904; C-3, L-3
May, 1904	336	12,067	219	40	25	7	199	12,145	XIII (21): Jun 16, 1904; C-3, L-3
Jul, 1904	345	12,199	276	37	20	13	232	12,287	XIII (29): Sep 8, 1904; 10
Sep, 1904	345	12,259	203	29	24	9	192	12,314	XIII (33): Oct 6, 1904; 2
Oct, 1904	348	12,311	312	55	24	11	211	12,480	XIII (38): Nov 10, 1904; 11
Nov, 1904	351	12,467	252	31	21	9	217	12,545	XIII (42): Dec 8, 1904; 11

G.C.U. -- Membership Statistics 1906

Month	Number of Lodges	Number of Members from Previous Month	Number of New Members	Number of Members Who Transferred Lodges	Number of Reinstated Members	Number of Deaths	Number of Members Who Left G.C.U. for Various Reasons	Total Number of Members	Source
Dec, 1905	394	14,990	702	47	17	19	190	15,547	XV (3): Feb 1, 1906; 11
Jan, 1906	399	15,547	943	29	8	14	234	16,299	XV (6): Feb 22, 1906; 11-12
Feb, 1906	400	16,299	282	48	18	8	266	16,373	XV (9): Mar 15, 1906; 11-12
Mar, 1906	402	16,373	337	31	20	12	275	16,474	XV (16): May 3, 1906; 12
Apr, 1906	403	16,474	267	91	23	15	347	16,493	XV (18): May 17, 1906; 7-8
May, 1906	404	16,493	302	39	18	9	241	16,602	XV (23): Jun 28, 1906; 11-12
Jun, 1906	406	16,602	318	51	18	12	280	16,602	XV (26): Jul 19, 1906; 11-12
Jul, 1906	409	16,697	388	54	16	12	269	16,874	XV (30): Aug 16, 1906; 11-12
Aug, 1906	412	16,874	366	54	23	8	322	16,987	XV (34): Sep 13, 1906; 11-12
Sep, 1906	419	16,937	399	48	25	14	216	17,229	XV (38): Oct 11, 1906; 11-12
Oct, 1906	422	17,229	334	72	20	10	204	17,441	XV (43): Nov 15, 1906; 11-12
Nov, 1906	427	17,441	378	57	21	12	217	17,668	XV (46): Dec 13, 1906; 11-12

G.C.U. -- Membership Statistics 1907

Month	Number of Lodges	Number of Members from Previous Month	Number of New Members	Number of Members Who Transferred Lodges	Number of Reinstated Members	Number of Deaths	Number of Members Who Left G.C.U. for Various Reasons	Total Number of Members	Source
Dec, 1906	431	17,668	761	70	4	16	262	18,225	XVI (1): Jan 17, 1907; C-6&7 XVI (2): Jan 24, 1907; L-6&7
Jan, 1907	437	18,225	878	31	25	12	194	18,953	XVI (4): Feb 7, 1907; C-7&8 XVI (5): Feb 14, 1907; L-7&8
Feb, 1907	446	18,953	628	44	16	18	252	18,371	XVI (9): Mar 14, 1907; C-7,8 XVI (8): Mar 7, 1907; L-6&7
Mar, 1907	448	19,371	358	69	22	16	227	19,577	XVI (13): Apr 11, 1907; C-6,7, L-6&7
Apr, 1907	451	19,577	396	69	24	17	309	19,470	XVI (18): May 23, 1907; C-6,7, L-6&7
May, 1907	454	19,740	291	37	14	13	213	19,856	XVI (21): Jun 13, 1907; C-6,7, L-6&7
Jun, 1907	457	19,856	393	63	23	9	350	19,976	XVI (26): Jul 18, 1907; C-6&7, L-6&7
Jul, 1907	460	19,976	390	51	32	8	341	20,100	XVI (31): Aug 31, 1907; C-6&7, L-6&7
Aug, 1907	466	20,100	509	77	29	15	292	20,408	XVI (33): Sep 5, 1907; C-6&7, L-6&7
Sep, 1907	469	20,408	400	78	20	17	275	20,624	XVI (38): Oct 10, 1907; C-6&7, L-6&7
Oct, 1907	473	20,624	439	70	24	14	290	20,853	XVI (43): Nov 14, 1907; L-6&7

G.C.U. -- Youth Lodges' Membership Statistics 1907

Month	Number of Lodges	Number of Members from Previous Month	Number of New Members	Number of Members Who Transferred Lodges	Number of Reinstated Members	Number of Deaths	Number of Members Who Left G.C.U. for Various Reasons	Total Number of Members	Source
Mar, 1907	60	1,313	137					1,449	XVI (14): Apr 18, 1907; C-8, L-7
Jun, 1907	69	1,697	81			1	6	1,768	XVI (25): Jul 11, 1907; C-7, L-7
Jul, 1907	70	1,768	85	1		1	20	1,833	XVI (30): Aug 15, 1907; C-7, L-7
Aug, 1907	73	1,833	102	3		1	11	1,926	XVI (34): Sep 12, 1907; C-7, L-7
Oct, 1907	85	2,196	156				8	2,344	XVI (42): Nov 7, 1907; C-7, L-7
Nov, 1907	91	2,344	144	2		1	14	2,475	XVI (45): Nov 28, 1907; L-7
Dec, 1907	93	2,474	82	3			14	2,545	XVI (50): Jan 2, 1908; C-7, L-7

G.C.U. -- Membership Statistics 1908

Month	Number of Lodges	Number of Members from Previous Month	Number of New Members	Number of Members Who Transferred Lodges	Number of Reinstated Members	Number of Deaths	Number of Members Who Left G.C.U. for Various Reasons	Total Number of Members	Source
Nov, 1907	476	20,853	359	77	31	20	329	20,971	XVII (1): Jan 16, 1908; C-6&7, L-6&7
Dec, 1907	483	20,971	693	85	35	18	442	21,324	XVII (2): Jan 23, 1908; L-6&7
Jan, 1908	487	21,324	580	55	35	26	444	21,544	XVII (6): Feb 20, 1908; C-6&7; XVII (5): Feb 13, 1908; L-6&7
Feb, 1908	489	21,544	227	80	15	22	488	21,349	XVII (10): Mar 19, 1908; C-6&7, L-6&7
May, 1908	495	20,829	130	41	11	13	345	20,653	XVII (21): Jun 25, 1908; C-6&7, L-6&7
Jul, 1908	501	20,486	276	89	26	12	441	20,424	XVII (28): Aug 13, 1908; C-6&7, L-6&7
Aug, 1908	503	20,424	242	66	30	11	437	20,314	XVII (33): Sep 17, 1908; C-6&7, L-6&7
Sep, 1908	508	20,314	333	84	29	5	307	20,408	XVII (41): Nov 12, 1908; C-6&7, L-6&7
Oct, 1908	509	20,408	217	58	31	12	258	20,454	XVII (42): Nov 19, 1908; C-6&7
Nov, 1908	514	20,454	354	53	16	16	289	20,672	XVII (47): Dec 24, 1908; C-6&7, L-6&7

G.C.U. -- Youth Lodges' Membership Statistics 1908

Month	Number of Lodges	Number of Members from Prev-ous Month	Number of New Members	Number of Members Who Transferred Lodges	Number of Reinstated Members	Number of Deaths	Number of Members Who Left G.C.U. for Various Reasons	Total Number of Members	Source
Jan, 1908	99	2,545	181	2	2		15	2,715	XVII (6): Feb 20, 1908; C-7 XVII (5): Feb 13, 1908; L-7
Feb, 1908	99	2,715	64	2	1	1	26	2,754	XVII (10): Mar 19, 1908; C-7, L-7
May, 1908	106	2,869	54	1	2		18	2,906	XVII (21): Jun 25, 1908; C-7, L-7
Jul, 1908	106	2,955	356			2	33	3,276	XVII (28): Aug 13, 1908; C-7, L-7
Sep, 1908	117	3,564	244	4		1	44	3,767	XVII (41)::Nov 12, 1908; C-7, L-7
Oct, 1908	124	3,767	308	3	2	1	67	4,012	XVII (42): Nov 19, 1908; L-7

G.C.U. -- Membership Statistics 1909

Month	Number of Lodges	Number of Members from Previous Month	Number of New Members	Number of Members Who Transferred Lodges	Number of Reinstated Members	Number of Deaths	Number of Members Who Left G.C.U. for Various Reasons	Total Number of Members	Source
Dec, 1908	519	20,674	896	40	22	15	221	21,396	XVIII (3): Jan 28, 1909; L-6&7
Jan, 1909	532	21,463	984	60	23	23	187	22,253	XVIII (6): Feb 18, 1909; L-8; XVIII (10): Mar 18, 1909; C-6&7
Feb, 1909	535	22,253	305	60	20	18	258	22,362	XVIII (11): Mar 25, 1909; C-6&7, L-7&8
Mar, 1909	537	22,362	355	69	29	14	314	22,487	XVIII (14): Apr 22, 1909; C-7&8, L-7&8
Apr, 1909	540	22,487	217	45	20	15	194	22,460	XVIII (18): May 20, 1909; C-7&8, L-7&8
May, 1909	542	22,460	327	65	26	18	280	22,517	XVIII (24): Jul 1, 1909; C-6&7, L-6&7
Jun, 1909	543	22,517	342	49	37	17	323	22,605	XVIII (28): Jul 29, 1909; C-6&7, L-6&7
Jul, 1909	543	22,605	277	60	41	22	303	22,658	XVIII (30): Aug 12, 1909; C-6&7, L-6&7
Aug, 1909	548	22,658	376	67	32	10	354	22,769	XVIII (34): Sep 9, 1909; C-6&7, L-6&7
Sep, 1909	556	22,769	480	89	36	20	357	22,997	XVIII (38): Oct 7, 1909; C-6&7, L-6&7
Oct, 1909	559	22,997	393	83	27	21	283	23,196	XVIII (43): Nov 11, 1909; C-6&7, L-6&7
Nov, 1909	562	23,196	358	52	34	20	259	23,361	XVIII (49): Dec 23, 1909; C-6&7, L-6&7

G.C.U. -- Youth Lodges' Membership Statistics 1909

Month	Number of Lodges	Number of Members from Previous Month	Number of New Members	Number of Members Who Transferred Lodges	Number of Reinstated Members	Number of Deaths	Number of Members Who Left G.C.U. for Various Reasons	Total Number of Members	Source
Dec, 1908	135	4,264	181	4	3		37	4,445	XVIII (4): Feb 4, 1909; L-7
Jan, 1909	146	4,445	342	2		2	22	4,765	XVIII (6): Feb 18, 1909; L-8
Feb, 1909	155	4,765	295		2		24	5,038	XVIII (12): Apr 1, 1909; C-8, L-8
Mar, 1909	160	5,038	268	5		2	55	5,254	XVIII (15): Apr 29, 1909; C-7, L-7
Apr, 1909	163	5,254	161	3	1	1	34	5,384	XVIII (20): Jun 3, 1909; C-8, L-8
May, 1909	168	5,384	255	3	1		64	5,579	XVIII (25): Jul 8, 1909; C-6
Jun, 1909	170	5,579	187		1	4	70	5,693	XVIII (28): Jul 29, 1909; C-3, L-7
Jul, 1909	170	5,693	127	1	1	2	56	5,764	XVIII (30): Aug 12, 1909; C-8, L-8
Aug, 1909	171	5,764	163	10	2	2	56	5,881	XVIII (34): Sep 9, 1909; C-8, L-3
Sep, 1909	171	5,881	109	2			32	5,960	XVIII (38): Oct 7, 1909; C-8, L-7
Oct, 1909	171	5,960	191		3	1	61	6,092	XVIII (44): Nov 18, 1909; C-6, L-6

G.C.U. -- Membership Statistics 1910

Month	Number of Lodges	Number of Members from Previous Month	Number of New Members	Number of Members Who Transferred Lodges	Number of Reinstated Members	Number of Deaths	Number of Members Who Left G.C.U. for Various Reasons	Total Number of Members	Source
Dec, 1909	565	23,361	1,161	69	59	21	319	24,310	XIX (1): Jan 13, 1910; C-6&7, L-6&7
Jan, 1910	568	24,310	952	76	43	23	226	25,132	XIX (6): Feb 17, 1910; C-6&7, L-6&7
Feb, 1910	572	25,133	413	78	24	19	260	25,369	XIX (9): Mar 10, 1910; C-6&7, L-6&7
Mar, 1910	574	25,369	355	107	28	17	360	25,482	XIX (17): May 12, 1910; C-6&7, L-6&7
Apr, 1910	577	25,482	387	42	20	18	274	25,635	XIX (18): May 19, 1910; C-9&10, L-9&10
May, 1910	579	25,635	290	42	16	17	251	25,715	XIX (22): Jun 23, 1910; C-6&7, L-6&7
Jun, 1910	581	25,715	361	80	30	24	339	25,823	XIX (24): Jul 7, 1910; C-6&7, L-6&7
Jul, 1910	584	25,823	388	99	37	18	384	25,945	XIX (31): Aug 25, 1910; C-6&7; XIX (29): Aug 11, 1910; L-6&7
Aug, 1910	592	25,945	486	95	24	17	361	26,172	XIX (33): Sep 8, 1910; C-6&7, L-6&7
Sep, 1910	596	26,172	390	78	36	12	286	26,378	XIX (38): Oct 13, 1910; C-6&7, L-6&7
Oct, 1910	599	26,378	403	71	36	14	331	26,543	XIX (44): Nov 24, 1910; C-6&7, L-6&7
Nov, 1910	608	26,543	554	150	30	18	350	26,909	XIX (47): Dec 15, 1910; C-7&8, L-6&7

G.C.U. -- Youth Lodges' Membership Statistics 1910

Month	Number of Lodges	Number of Members from Previous Month	Number of New Members	Number of Members Who Transferred Lodges	Number of Reinstated Members	Number of Deaths	Number of Members Who Left G.C.U. for Various Reasons	Total Number of Members	Source
Nov, 1909	173	6,092	136	6	1		27	6,208	XIX (1): Jan 13, 1910; C-7, L-7
Jan, 1910	178	6,386	161	10	3	3	50	6,507	XIX (6): Feb 17, 1910; C-7, L-7
Feb, 1910	178	6,507	108	2	6		29	6,594	XIX (10): Mar 17, 1910; C-7, L-7
Mar, 1910	180	6,594	169	23	9	1	44	6,750	XIX (18): May 19, 1910; C-10, L-10
Apr, 1910	181	6,750	144	23	1	4	68	6,846	XIX (19): May 26, 1910; C-8, L-7
May, 1910	182	6,846	85	2	1	1	15	6,918	XIX (22): Jun 23, 1910; C-8, L-3
Jul, 1910	184	7,031	146	5	5		45	7,142	XIX (31): Aug 25, 1910; C-8 XIX (27): Jul 28, 1910; L-7
Aug, 1910	184	7,141	180	12	4	6	71	7,260	XIX (34): Sep 15, 1910; C-8 XIX (33): Sep 8, 1910; L-7
Sep, 1910	184	7,261	180	8	2	1	40	7,410	XIX (37): Oct 6, 1910; C-7, L-7
Oct, 1910	184	7,410	140	5			21	7,524	XIX (40): Oct 27, 1910; C-7, L-7
Nov, 1910	190	7,514	316	6	1	2	52	7,784	XIX (46): Dec 8, 1910; C-8, L-8

G.C.U. -- Membership Statistics 1911

Month	Number of Lodges	Number of Members from Previous Month	Number of New Members	Number of Members Who Transferred Lodges	Number of Reinstated Members	Number of Deaths	Number of Members Who Left G.C.U. for Various Reasons	Total Number of Members	Source
Dec, 1910	615	26,909	1,028	114	40	15	410	27,666	XX (1): Jan 19, 1911; C-6&7, L-6&7
Jan, 1911	622	27,666	999	73	31	21	306	28,442	XX (4): Feb 9, 1911; C-6&7, L-6&7
Feb, 1911	626	28,442	453	57	30	19	322	28,641	XX (8): Mar 9, 1911; C-6&7, L-6&7
Mar, 1911	630	28,641	404	101	31	21	512	28,644	XX (15): May 4, 1911; C-15&16, L-15&16
Apr, 1911	634	28,644	266	110	21	21	334	28,686	XX (16): May 11, 1911; C-6&7, L-6&7
May, 1911	634	28,686	317	109	29	22	459	28,660	XX (20): Jun 7, 1911; C-6&7, L-6&7
Jun, 1911	637	28,660	350	82	36	23	87	28,718	XX (24): Jul 13, 1911; C-6&7, L-6&7
Jul, 1911	639	28,718	332	99	36	24	446	28,707	XX (28): Aug 10, 1911; C-6&7, L-6&7
Aug, 1911	640	28,707	318	66	39	25	399	28,706	XX (34): Sep 21, 1911; C-6&7, L-6&7
Sep, 1911	642	28,706	360	80	43	17	368	28,804	XX (39): Oct 26, 1911; C-6&7, L-6&7
Oct, 1911	648	28,804	336	86	30	27	310	28,919	XX (41): Nov 9, 1911; C-6&7, L-6&7
Nov, 1911	650	28,919	277	59	19	16	296	28,962	XX (47): Dec 21, 1911; C-6&7, L-6&7

G.C.U. -- Youth Lodges' Membership Statistics 1911

Month	Number of Lodges	Number of Members from Previous Month	Number of New Members	Number of Members Who Transferred Lodges	Number of Reinstated Members	Number of Deaths	Number of Members Who Left G.C.U. for Various Reasons	Total Number of Members	Source
Dec, 1910	193	7,784	189		4	2	41	7,934	XX (3): Feb 2, 1911; C-8, L-8
Jan, 1911	197	7,934	272				53	8,153	XX (5): Feb 16, 1911; C-8, L-7
Feb, 1911	204	8,153	315	6	1	1	57	8,417	XX (9): Mar 16, 1911; C-8, L-8
Mar, 1911	206	8,417	228	4	3	1	65	8,586	XX (15): May 4, 1911; C-16, L-16
Apr, 1911	206	8,586	338	19		4	90	8,849	XX (17): May 18, 1911; C-6
May, 1911	215	8,849	176	8		2	64	8,967	XX (21): Jun 15, 1911; C-7, L-8
Jul, 1911	219	9,108	173	2	6	1	60	9,228	XX (36): Oct 5, 1911; C-7, L-8
Aug, 1911	219	9,228	119	7	3	1	49	9,307	XX (37): Oct 12, 1911; C-8, L-8
Sep, 1911	220	9,307	196	4	3	2	109	9,399	XX (40): Nov 2, 1911; C-7, L-7
Oct, 1911	226	9,399	224	6	5	3	54	9,577	XX (42): Nov 16, 1911; C-7, L-7

G.C.U. -- Sokol Lodges' Membership Statistics 1911

Month	Number of Lodges	Number of Members from Previous Month	Number of New Members	Number of Members Who Transferred Lodges	Number of Reinstated Members	Number of Deaths	Number of Members Who Left G.C.U. for Various Reasons	Total Number of Members	Source
Feb, 1911	27	462	97	7		1	18	547	XX (9): Mar 16, 1911; C-8, L-8
Mar, 1911	31	547	52	4	1		21	583	XX (15): May 4, 1911; C-16, L-16
Apr, 1911	34	583	82	12		1	40	636	XX (18): May 25, 1911; C-6
May, 1911	34	636	19	1			25	631	XX (21): Jun 15, 1911; C-7, L-8
Jul, 1911	36	656	34	1	1	1	21	670	XX (36): Oct 5, 1911; C-7, L-8
Aug, 1911	37	670	52	3		1	48	676	XX (37): Oct 12, 1911; C-8, L-8
Sep, 1911	38	676	32	1			15	694	XX (40): Nov 2, 1911; L-7
Oct, 1911	38	694	6	2	2		24	680	XX (42): Nov 16, 1911; C-7, L-7

G.C.U. -- Membership Statistics 1912

Month	Number of Lodges	Number of Members from Previous Month	Number of New Members	Number of Members Who Transferred Lodges	Number of Reinstated Members	Number of Deaths	Number of Members Who Left G.C.U. for Various Reasons	Total Number of Members	Source
Dec, 1911	653	28,962	868	80	47	22	331	29,604	XXI (3): Feb 1, 1912; C-6&7, L-6&7
Jan, 1912	660	29,604	887	95	27	37	341	30,255	XXI (5): Feb 15, 1912; C-6&7, L-6&7
Feb, 1912	664	30,255	461	82	26	26	328	30,470	XXI (10): Mar 21, 1912; C-6&7, L-6&7
Mar, 1912	666	30,470	317	76	20	26	384	30,473	XXI (14): Apr 25, 1912; C-6&7, L-6&7
Apr, 1912	668	30,473	262	57	27	17	416	30,386	XXI (18): May 23, 1912; C-10&11
May, 1912	668	30,386	294	80	27	22	417	30,348	XXI (21): Jun 20, 1912; C-6&7, L-6&7
Jun, 1912	669	30,371	274	134	31	22	422	30,366	XXI (25): Jul 18, 1912; C-6&7, L-6&7
Jul, 1912	676	30,366	401	157	27	21	464	30,466	XXI (29): Aug 15, 1912; C-6&7, L-6&7
Aug, 1912	679	30,466	351	88	35	13	413	30,514	XXI (33): Sep 12, 1912; C-6&7, L-6&7
Sep, 1912	688	30,514	454	125	33	22	326	30,778	XXI (37): Oct 10, 1912; C-6&7, L-6&7
Oct, 1912	689	30,791	352	102	19	21	353	30,890	XXI (43): Nov 21, 1912; C-6&7, L-6&7
Nov, 1912	693	30,890	375	84	21	26	284	30,060	XXI (48): Dec 26, 1912; C-6&7

G.C.U. -- Youth Lodges' Membership Statistics 1912

Month	Number of Lodges	Number of Members from Previous Month	Number of New Members	Number of Members Who Transferred Lodges	Number of Reinstated Members	Number of Deaths	Number of Members Who Left G.C.U. for Various Reasons	Total Number of Members	Source
Dec, 1911	232	9,800	225	34	4	3	65	9,993	XXI (4): Feb 8, 1912; C-6, L-6
Jan, 1912	240	9,993	312	20	2	5	55	10,267	XXI (6): Feb 22, 1912; C-6, L-6
Feb, 1912	240	10,267	189	10	3	2	111	10,356	XXI (11): Mar 28, 1912; C-8, L-8
Mar, 1912	248	10,356	339	8	3	5	92	10,609	XXI (15): May 2, 1912; C-8, L-8
Apr, 1912	251	10,609	220	9	2	3	95	10,472	XXI (18): May 23, 1912; C-6, L-6
May, 1912	253	10,742	186	22	7	5	64	10,861	XXI (22): Jun 27, 1912; C-6, L-6
Jun, 1912	254	10,861	200	12	6	5	53	11,021	XXI (26): Jul 25, 1912; C-8, L-8
Jul, 1912	259	11,023	228	16	2	7	89	11,173	XXI (30): Aug 22, 1912; C-7, L-7
Aug, 1912	261	11,173	203	5	25		91	11,315	XXI (34): Sep 19, 1912; C-8, L-8
Sep, 1912	267	11,313	294	4	1	3	97	11,512	XXI (39): Oct 24, 1912; C-8, L-8
Oct, 1912	269	11,512	230	17	2	3	91	11,667	XXI (44): Nov 28, 1912; C-6, L-6

G.C.U. -- Sokol Lodges' Membership Statistics 1912

Month	Number of Lodges	Number of Members from Previous Month	Number of New Members	Number of Members Who Transferred Lodges	Number of Reinstated Members	Number of Deaths	Number of Members Who Left G.C.U. for Various Reasons	Total Number of Members	Source
Dec, 1911	41	71?	61	1			25	748	XXI (4): Feb 8, 1912; C-6, L-6
Jan, 1912	41	748	35		2		20	765	XXI (6): Feb 22, 1912; C-6, L-6
Feb, 1912	41	765	31	6		1	16	785	XXI (11): Mar 28, 1912; C-8, L-6
Mar, 1912	44	785	84	9	1	1	29	849	XXI (15): May 2, 1912; C-8, L-7
Apr, 1912	45	849	46	18		1	14	898	XXI (18): May 23, 1912; C-11, L-6
May, 1912	46	898	50	2	2		19	933	XXI (22): Jun 27, 1912; C-6, L-6
Jun, 1912	48	933	80		1		12	1002	XXI (26): Jul 25, 1912; L-7
Jul, 1912	51	1002	94	1	2		29	1070	XXI (30): Aug 22, 1912; C-7, L-7
Aug, 1912	52	1070	64	8	3	1	27	1117	XXI (34): Sep 19, 1912; C-7, L-7
Sep, 1912	58	1117	251	11	2		46	1331	XXI (38): Oct 17, 1912; C-7, L-7
Oct, 1912	61	1335	136	5	1	1	20	1456	XXI (44): Nov 28, 1912; C-6, L-6

G.C.U. -- Membership Statistics 1913

Month	Number of Lodges	Number of Members from Previous Month	Number of New Members	Number of Members Who Transferred Lodges	Number of Reinstated Members	Number of Deaths	Number of Members Who Left G.C.U. for Various Reasons	Total Number of Members	Source
Dec, 1912	694	31,060	886	123	30	28	336	31,735	XXII (3): Jan 30, 1913; C-6&7, L-6&7
Jan, 1913	701	31,735	972	68	26	26	287	32,488	XXII (5): Feb 13, 1913; C-6&7, L-6&7
Feb, 1913	703	32,488	423	104	18	24	280	32,729	XXII (10): Mar 20, 1913; C-6&7, L-6&7
Mar, 1913	706	32,729	366	123	12	28	368	32,834	XXII (13): Apr 10, 1913; C-6&7, L-6&7
Apr, 1913	709	32,834	320	121	19	29	376	32,889	XXII (17): May 15, 1913; C-6&7, L-6&7
May, 1913	709	32,889	257	88	8	27	385	32,830	XXII (21): Jun 12, 1913; C-6&7, L-6&7
Jun, 1913	712	32,830	307	75	15	35	342	32,850	XXII (26): Jul 17, 1913; C-6&7, L-6&7
Jul, 1913	714	32,850	383	90	9	21	412	32,899	XXII (29): Aug 14, 1913; C-6&7, L-6&7
Aug, 1913	718	32,899	329	102	26	35	341	32,980	XXII (42): Nov 13, 1913; C-6, L-7
Sep, 1913	719	32,980	356	98	13	26	309	33,442	XXII (44): Nov 27, 1913; C-6, L-6

G.C.U. -- Youth Lodges' Membership Statistics 1913

Month	Number of Lodges	Number of Members from Previous Month	Number of New Members	Number of Members Who Transferred Lodges	Number of Reinstated Members	Number of Deaths	Number of Members Who Left G.C.U. for Various Reasons	Total Number of Members	Source
Nov, 1912	272	11,667	224	14	8	5	84	11,844	XXII (6): Feb 20, 1913; C-12
Jan, 1913	277	12,024	258	25	2	2	72	12,230	XXII (7): Feb 27, 1913; C-8, L-7
Mar, 1913	285	12,431	333	9	6	1	97	12,681	XXII (16): May 8, 1913; C-7, L-7
Apr, 1913	289	12,631	240	10	4	5	88	12,842	XXII (19): May 29, 1913; C-6, L-6
May, 1913	289	12,842	168	31	1	5	80	12,957	XXII (20): Jun 5, 1913; C-6, L-6
Jun, 1913	293	12,957	271	5	3	4	100	13,132	XXII (25): Jul 10, 1913; C-6&7, L-6&7
Jul, 1913	294	13,132	248	11		5	93	13,298	XXII (27): Jul 31, 1913; C-7, L-7
Aug, 1913	297	13,298	282	18	3	5	137	13,459	XXII (31): Aug 28, 1913; C-6, L-7
Sep, 1913	300	13,459	308	14	4	2	85	13,698	XXII (41): Nov 6, 1913; C-6, L-7
Oct, 1913	301	13,693	282	4	5	2	68	13,919	XXII (45): Dec 4, 1913; C-6, L-6

G.C.U. -- Sokol Lodges' Membership Statistics 1913

Month	Number of Lodges	Number of Members from Previous Month	Number of New Members	Number of Members Who Transferred Lodges	Number of Reinstated Members	Number of Deaths	Number of Members Who Left G.C.U. for Various Reasons	Total Number of Members	Source
Nov, 1912	62	1456	84	9	3		32	1520	XXII (6): Feb 20, 1913; C-12
Jan, 1913	68	1540	133	2	2	1	35	1640	XXII (8): Mar 6, 1913; C-8, L-7
Mar, 1913	70	1673	107	5			38	1749	XXII (14): Apr 17, 1913; C-6, L-7
Apr, 1913	73	1747	82	8		2	26	1809	XXII (19): May 29, 1913; C-6, L-6
May, 1913	74	1809	74	10	1	2	42	1850	XXII (20): Jun 5, 1913; C-6, L-6
Jun, 1913	79	1850	111	7	2	2	40	1928	XXII (25): Jul 10, 1913; C-7, L-7
Jul, 1913	82	1928	95	4	2		37	1992	XXII (27): Jul 31, 1913; C-7, L-7
Aug, 1913	84	1992	112	7	3		72	2042	XXII (31): Aug 28, 1913; C-6, L-7
Sep, 1913	85	2042	71	5	1		61	2058	XXII (41): Nov 6, 1913; C-6, L-7
Oct, 1913	87	2058	107	12	2	1	54	2124	XXII (45): Dec 4, 1913; C-6, L-6
Nov, 1913	88	2124	72	10			50	2156	XXII (48): Dec 25, 1913; C-6, L-6

G.C.U. -- Membership Statistics 1914

Month	Number of Lodges	Number of Members from Previous Month	Number of New Members	Number of Members Who Transferred Lodges	Number of Reinstated Members	Number of Deaths	Number of Members Who Left G.C.U. for Various Reasons	Total Number of Members	Source
Oct, 1913	721	33,112	349	87	13	20	333	33,208	XXIII (1): Jan 15, 1914; C-6
Nov, 1913	725	33,208	302	124	13	25	293	33,329	XXIII (2): Jan 22, 1914; C-6
Dec, 1913	726	33,329	706	94	22	26	102	33,723	XXIII (4): Feb 5, 1914; C-6
Jan, 1914	734	33,723	796	159	10	21	377	34,290	XXIII (5): Feb 12, 1914; C-6
Feb, 1914	737	34,290	294	59	4	21	344	34,282	XXIII (8): Mar 5, 1914; C-6
Mar, 1914	739	34,282	276	85	15	28	414	34,216	XXIII (19): Jun 4, 1914; C-6&7
Apr, 1914	743	34,216	254	56	9	24	299	34,212	XXIII (21): Jun 18, 1914; C-6
May, 1914	744	34,212	242	90	5	22	394	34,133	XXIII (24): Jul 9, 1914; C-6
Jun, 1914	745	34,133	284	130	12	35	455	34,019	XXIII (31): Aug 27, 1914; C-11&12
Jul, 1914	746	34,019	224	67	14	19	373	33,932	XXIII (37): Oct 8, 1914; C-6
Aug, 1914	747	33,932	200	75	28	21	311	33,903	XXIII (43): Nov 19, 1914; C-11&12
Sep, 1914	748	33,903	256	96	17	17	251	34,004	XXIV (1): Jan 7, 1915; C-6, L-6
Oct, 1914	752	34,004	328	76	6	27	232	34,155	XXIV (3): Jan 21, 1915; C-6, L-6
Nov, 1914	756	34,155	303	51	4	27	209	34,277	XXIV (4): Jan 28, 1915; C-6, L-6
Dec, 1914	758	34,277	1,194	85	9	22	232	35,311	XXIV (5): Feb 4, 1915; C-6, L-6

G.C.U. -- Youth Lodges' Membership Statistics 1914

Month	Number of Lodges	Number of Members from Previous Month	Number of New Members	Number of Members Who Transferred Lodges	Number of Reinstated Members	Number of Deaths	Number of Members Who Left G.C.U. for Various Reasons	Total Number of Members	Source
Nov, 1913	304	13,919	247	13	5	1	120	14,063	XXIII (1): Jan 15, 1914; C-12
Dec, 1913	307	14,063	232	13	2	2	74	14,234	XXIII (3): Jan 29, 1914; C-6
Jan, 1914	309	14,234	294	6	5	6	96	14,437	XXIII (8): Mar 5, 1914; C-12
Feb, 1914	320	14,437	445	20	1	5	154	14,744	XXIII (16): May 7, 1914; C-8
Mar, 1914	321	14,744	283	21	1	1	140	14,908	XXIII (19): Jun 4, 1914; C-7
Apr, 1914	323	14,908	236	8	5	3	100	15,054	XXIII (21): Jun 18, 1914; C-7
May, 1914	325	15,054	289	7			84	15,266	XXIII (25): Jul 16, 1914; C-8
Jun, 1914	331	15,266	340	18		5	97	15,522	XXIII (28): Aug 6, 1914; C-6&7
Jul, 1914	335	15,522	654	20		2	103	16,094	XXIII (43): Nov 19, 1914; C-12
Aug, 1914	342	16,094	808	10		1	138	16,779	XXIV (5): Feb 4, 1915; C-7, L-7
Sep, 1914	344	16,779	607	17	1	7	84	17,313	XXIV (6): Feb 11, 1915; C-7, L-7
Oct, 1914	348	17,313	580	21	7	4	103	17,814	XXIV (7): Feb 18, 1915; C-7, L-6&7
Nov, 1914	352	17,814	491	16	8	8	118	18,195	XXIV (12): Mar 25, 1915; C-12, L-12
Dec, 1914	354	18,195	336	9	1	3	122	18,416	XXIV (24): Jun 17, 1915; C-6&7, L-6

G.C.U. -- Sokol Lodges' Membership Statistics 1914

Month	Number of Lodges	Number of Members from Previous Month	Number of New Members	Number of Members Who Transferred Lodges	Number of Reinstated Members	Number of Deaths	Number of Members Who Left G.C.U. for Various Reasons	Total Number of Members	Source
Dec, 1913	88	2156	30	4	3	3	43	2147	XXIII (1): Jan 15, 1914; C-12
Jan, 1914	90	2147	71	10	4		94	2138	XXIII (3): Jan 29, 1914; C-6
Feb, 1914	95	2138	148	14			62	2238	XXIII (8): Mar 5, 1914; C-12
Mar, 1914	99	2238	120	19	1	1	68	2309	XXIII (11): Mar 26, 1914; C-12
Apr, 1914	102	2309	122	13	1	1	39	2405	XXIII (21): Jun 18, 1914; C-7
May, 1914	102	2405	55	9	1		50	2420	XXIII (25): Jul 16, 1914; C-8
Jun, 1914	106	2420	106	9	1	2	58	2476	XXIII (26): Jul 23, 1914; C-8

APPENDIX III

FINANCIAL STATUS OF THE GREEK CATHOLIC UNION, G.C.U. YOUTH LODGES, AND G.C.U. SOKOL LODGES

G.C.U. -- Financial Status 1901

Month	Old Debts	Policy Dues	Monthly Collection	St. Nicholas Fund	New Member Fees	Reserve Fund	Legal Fund	Almanac Fund	ARV & Print Fund	Postage Expenses	Monthly Total	Source
Dec, 1900	$185.28	$5,527.35	$819.90	$168.42	$36.50	$102.95	$ 2.50	$	$1.50	$ 9.50	$6,853.90	X (1): Jan 17, 1901; C-7, L-7
Jan, 1901	23.45	6,150.54	874.20	180.26	28.00	132.25		6.40	3.85	9.00	7,407.95	X (7): Feb 25, 1901; C-7, L-7
Feb, 1901	97.34	6,822.12	851.20	175.98	73.50	64.99	22.18	1.70	1.75		8,110.76	X (11): Mar 28, 1901; C-7, L-7
Mar, 1901	15.96	6,141.78	866.00	175.80	86.00	45.25	20.30	14.00	1.50		7,336.59	X (14): Apr 25, 1901; L-6
Apr, 1901	24.19	7,230.46	871.20	175.72	92.00	45.50	451.44	309.75	5.70	3.00	9,208.96	X (19): May 30, 1901; C-6, L-6
May, 1901	19.00	8,781.48	981.50	201.72	122.50	83.00	111.17	68.70	9.00	28.50	10,406.57	X (22): Jun 20, 1901; C-6, L-6
Jun, 1901	16.24	6,024.26	825.48	166.89	123.00	60.50	16.89	14.50			7,247.76	X (26): Jul 25, 1901; C-6, L-6
Jul, 1901	83.71	8,471.30	962.00	186.53	163.50	96.75	16.00	31.20	1.50	5.00	10,027.49	X (31): Aug 29, 1901; C-6, L-6
Aug, 1901	25.23	8,813.35	947.95	191.87	98.50	47.00	19.50	17.30	1.50	18.00	10,130.20	X (35): Sep 26, 1901; C-6, L-6
Sep, 1901	21.07	9,106.92	924.94	191.82	89.50	51.25	22.67	5.00	1.00	4.50	10,416.67	X (40): Oct 31, 1901; L-6&7
Oct, 1901	32.18	8,544.69	909.05	185.96	84.50	46.75	6.91				9,810.04	X (44): Nov 28, 1901; C-6&7, L-6&7
Nov, 1901	49.20	8,576.83	852.90	171.62	90.00	43.00	26.50	23.30		4.50	9,837.85	X (48): Dec 26, 1901; C-6&7, L-6&7

G.C.U. -- Financial Status 1902

Month	Old Debts	Policy Dues	Monthly Collection	St. Nicholas Fund	New Member Fees	Reserve Fund	Legal Fund	Almanac Fund	Misc.	Monthly Total	Source
Dec, 1901	$60.19	$10,232.69	$ 982.30	$198.26	$64.50	$ 96.00	$27.35	$	$	$11,661.29	XI (2&3): Jan 30, 1902; C-6&7
Jan, 1902	82.36	8,867.96	908.30	187.03	55.00	120.00	58.00	13.00	96.00	10,387.70	XI (7): Feb 27, 1902; C-6&7
Feb, 1902	33.87	7,896.79	1,001.30	203.75	98.00	78.55	25.90	26.25	20.90	9,385.31	XI (11): Mar 27, 1902; C-6&7
Mar, 1902	40.48	8,964.36	1,019.20	211.56	115.00	50.75	3.40	5.00	26.30	10,442.05	XI (15): Apr 24, 1902; C-10&11
Apr, 1902	54.06	8,971.21	995.70	203.59	69.50	31.80	14.93	24.90	57.53	10,423.22	XI (19): May 29, 1902; C-6&7
May, 1902	47.22	8,878.72	1,128.08	218.41	92.27	167.60	11.20	166.00	495.02	11,195.02	XI (21): Jun 12, 1902; C-10&11
Jun & Jul 1902	90.74	10,066.51	1,635.11	365.56	207.85	91.02	115.50	111.10	117.01	12,800.65	XI (31): Aug 28, 1902; C-7&8
Aug, 1902	13.44	6,026.77	669.49	169.26	84.50	41.87	.17		2.25	7,007.75	XI (35): Sep 25, 1902; C-7&8
Sep, 1902	3.49	9,937.91	736.80	194.21	104.50	51.00	.51		28.91	11,084.33	XI (40): Oct 30, 1902; C-7&8
Oct, 1902	74.17	10,565.87	817.25	207.56	92.00	43.75	21.78		144.85	11,967.23	XI (44): Nov 27, 1902; C-7&8
Nov, 1902	53.55	10,442.12	816.61	207.44	77.25	65.40	.17		27.55	11,690.48	XI (49): Jan 1, 1902; C-10&11

* First National Bank, Braddock, PA
** Braddock Trust Company Bank
\+ Lincoln National Bank, Pittsburgh, PA
  German National Bank, Pittsburgh, PA
  Union National Bank, Braddock, PA

G.C.U. -- Financial Status 1903

Month	Monthly Money Received By Treasury	Monthly Money Paid Out By Treasury	Total Amount Received	Total Amount Paid Out	Monthly Balance	Total Balance*	Assets in Bank**+	Total G.C.U. Assets	
Dec, 1902	$12,592.98	$ 9,497.02	$	$	$	$	$	$	XII (2&3): Jan 29, 1903; C-11&12, L-7&8
Jan, 1903	9,717.23	10,784.18							XII (5): Feb 12, 1903; C-6&7, L-6&7
Feb, 1903	.14,291.82	9,619.50	36,602.03	29,900.70	6,701.33	42,396.82	49,098.15		XII (9): Mar 12, 1903; C-6&7, L-6&7
Mar, 1903	16,415.17								XII (15): Apr 30, 1903; C-6&7, L-6&7
Apr, 1903	12,721.29								XII (19): May 28, 1903; C-6&7, L-6&7
May, 1903	10,590.08								XII (22): Jun 25, 1903; C-7&8, L-11&12
Jun, 1903	12,357.12	10,885.96							XII (27): Jul 30, 1903; C-6&7, L-6&7
Jul, 1903	7,880.69	43,896.64							XII (31): Aug 27, 1903; C-6&7, L-6&7
Aug, 1903	11,248.39	5,802.24							XII (39): Oct 22, 1903; C-6&7, L-6&7
Sep, 1903	7,267.04	11,836.94							XII (43): Nov 19, 1903; C-6, L-6
Oct, 1903	7,609.56	6,148.45							XII (48): Dec 24, 1903; C-6&7, L-6&7
Nov, 1903	9,384.90	5,763.68	105,622.86	84,331.91		21,288.95	30,000.00	51,288.95	XII (49): Dec 31, 1903; C-6&7, L-6&7
									XII (48): Dec 24, 1903; C-6, L-7

G.C.U. -- Financial Status 1904

*Union National Bank, Braddock, PA
Lincoln National Bank, Pittsburgh, PA
German National Bank, Pittsburgh, PA

Month	Amount Received Monthly By Treasury	Balance from Previous Month	Total Monthly Income	Total Monthly Debts	New Balance	Total Amount Invested in Three Banks*	Total G.C.U. Assets	Source
Dec, 1903	$13,323.85	$21,288.95	$	$7,210.80	$27,402.02	$30,000.00	$57,402.02	XIII (3): Feb 4, 1904; C-6&7, L-6&7
Feb, 1904	10,496.47	28,306.33		9,131.20	1,365.27			XIII (9): Mar 17, 1904; C-6&7, L-6&7
Mar, 1904	14,522.20	34,069.13		8,759.40	34,069.13	30,000.00	64,069.13	XIII (14): Apr 28, 1904; C-6&7, L-6&7
Apr, 1904	12,057.89	34,906.52		11,220.50	34,906.52	30,000.00	64,906.52	XIII (16): May 12, 1904; C-6&7, L-6&7
May, 1904	14,411.93	34,906.52		9,501.66	39,816.79	30,000.00	69,816.79	XIII (21): Jun 16, 1904; C-6&7, L-6&7
Aug, 1904	12,212.64	32,138.89	44,351.53	7,492.70	36,858.83	30,000.00		XIII (30): Sep 15, 1904; 11, 12
Sep, 1904	13,650.82	36,858.83	50,509.65	13,631.06	36,878.59	30,000.00		XIII (35): Oct 20, 1904; 11, 12
Oct, 1904	12,519.90	36,878.59	49,398.49	12,414.28	36,984.21	30,000.00		XIII (38): Nov 10, 1904; 12, 13
Nov, 1904	15,674.67	36,984.21	52,658.88	9,899.01	42,759.87	30,000.00		XIII (42): Dec 8, 1904; 12, 13

G.C.U. -- Financial Status 1906

*Lincoln National Bank, Pittsburgh, PA
German National Bank, Pittsburgh, PA
Union National Bank, Braddock, PA
First National Bank, Braddock, PA

Month	Amount Received Monthly By Treasury	Balance from Previous Month	Total Monthly Income	Total Monthly Debts	New Balance	Total Amount Invested in Four Banks*	Total G.C.U. Assets	Source
Dec, 1905	$	$36,298.78	$57,775.78	$15,215.18	$42,560.60	$	$	XV (3): Feb 1, 1906; 12
Jan, 1906	20,271.95	42,560.60	62,832.55	16,209.49	46,623.06			XV (6): Feb 22, 1906; 12
Feb, 1906	22,608.19	46,623.25	69,231.25	26,593.58	42,637.67			XV (10): Mar 22, 1906; 12
Mar, 1906	19,400.19	42,637.67	62,037.86	22,927.45	39,110.41			XV (16): May 3, 1906; 12
Apr, 1906	19,597.56	39,110.41	58,707.97	15,261.03	43,446.94	43,288.52	86,735.46	XV (18): May 17, 1906; 12
May, 1906	16,144.48	43,446.94	59,591.42	18,136.40	41,455.02	43,288.52	84,743.54	XV (23): Jun 28, 1906; 12
Jun, 1906	19,964.74		35,890.89	19,605.54	35,531.69			XV (31): Aug 23, 1906; 12
Sep, 1906	17,172.56	40,495.64	60,465.72	19,094.98	41,370.74			XV (40): Oct 25, 1906; 12
Oct, 1906	21,573.43	41,370.74	62,994.17	16,189.04	46,850.13			XV (44): Nov 22, 1906; 8

G.C.U. -- Financial Status 1907

Month	Amount Received Monthly By Treasury	Balance from Previous Month	Total Monthly Income	Total Monthly Debts	New Balance	Source
Dec, 1906		LISTS ONLY WHAT EACH LODGE PAID NO FINANCIAL BREAKDOWN			$27,826.49	XVI (4): Feb 7, 1907; C-8 XVI (3): Jan 31, 1907; L-8
Jan, 1907	$22,8?2.17	$24,259.72	$47,071.84	$19,245.40	27,188.72	XVI (7): Feb 28, 1907; L-8
Feb, 1907	22,033.92	27,826.49	49,860.41	22,671.69	16,939.45	XVI (11): Mar 28, 1907; L-7
Mar, 1907	23,458.46	27,188.72	50,647.18	33,707.73	20,789.70	XVI (17): May 16, 1907; C-8, L-7
Apr, 1907	29,129.33	16,939.45	46,068.78	25,279.08	17,465.58	XVI (19): May 30, 1907; C-8, L-8
May, 1907	25,372.08	20,789.70	46,161.78	28,696.20	16,225.73	XVI (28): Aug 1, 1907; C-8, L-6&7
Jun, 1907	24,847.56	17,465.58	42,313.14	26,087.41	14,427.87	XVI (29): Aug 8, 1907; L-6
Jul, 1907	18,673.93	16,225.73	34,904.66	20,476.79	19,779.52	XVI (33): Sep 5, 1907; C-3 XVI (32): Aug 29, 1907; L-6&7
Aug, 1907	22,337.57	14,427.87	36,765.44	16,985.92	26,393.60	XVI (36): Sep 26, 1907; L-6
Sep, 1907	24,485.17	19,899.52	44,384.69	17,991.03	28,877.36	XVI (39): Oct 17, 1907; L-7
Oct, 1907	25,902.04	26,393.66	52,295.70	23,418.34	31,139.01	XVI (45): Nov 28, 1907; L-7
Nov, 1907	24,871.92	28,877.36	53,749.28	22,610.27		XVI (49): Dec 26, 1907; L-6

G.C.U. -- Youth Lodges' Financial Status 1907

Month	Total Monthly Income	Balance from Previous Month	Total Monthly Debts	New Balance	Source
Jul, 1907	$1,412.65		$200.00	$1,212.65	XVI (30): Aug 15, 1907; C-8, L-7
Aug, 1907	383.05	$1,212.65		1,595.70	XVI (37): Oct 3, 1907; C-6 XVI (36): Sep 26, 1907; L-7
Sep, 1907	226.90	1,595.70	300.00	1,522.60	XVI (38): Oct 10, 1907; C-7, L-7
Oct, 1907	336.30	1,522.60		1,858.90	XVI (47): Dec 12, 1907; L-7
Nov, 1907	346.65	1,858.90		2,205.55	XVI (49): Dec 26, 1907; L-7

G.C.U. -- Financial Status 1908

Month	Amount Received Monthly By Treasury	Balance from Previous Month	Total Monthly Income	Total Monthly Debts	New Balance	Source
Dec., 1907	$28,976.25	$31,139.01	$60,115.27	$20,569.37	$39,545.90	XVII (3): Jan 30, 1908; L-6
Jan, 1908	26,373.80	39,545.90	65,919.70	27,513.87	38,405.83	XVII (7): Feb 27, 1908; C-6, L-7
Mar, 1908	30,687.93	36,696.37	67,384.30	29,964.01	37,420.29	XVII (16): May 7, 1908; C-6, L-7
May, 1908	16,653.08	41,697.04	58,350.12	32,346.10	26,004.02	XVII (22): Jul 2, 1908; C-8, L-7
Jun, 1908	27,342.09	26,004.02	53,346.11	25,718.27	27,627.84	XVII (27): Aug 6, 1908; C-4, L-7
Jul, 1908	31,044.78	27,627.86	58,712.64	25,917.39	32,795.25	XVII (29): Aug 20, 1908; C-7, L-7
Aug, 1908	23,556.76	32,795.25	56,352.01	28,153.48	28,198.53	XVII (35): Oct 1, 1908; C-7, L-7
Sep, 1908	20,571.26	28,198.53	48,769.74	19,936.55	29,633.24	XVII (40): Nov 5, 1908; L-7
Oct, 1908	18,317.92	29,633.24	49,276.12	23,294.04	25,982.08	XVII (44): Dec 3, 1908; C-7, L-7
Nov, 1908	19,423.95	25,982.08	45,406.03	14,892.43	30,513.60	XVII (48): Dec 31, 1908; C-11, L-11

G.C.U. -- Youth Lodges' Financial Status 1908

Month	Total Monthly Income	Balance from Previous Month	Total Monthly Debts	New Balance	Source
Dec, 1907	$236.40	$2,205.55		$2,441.95	XVII (1): Jan 16, 1908; C-7, L-7
Jan, 1908	228.65	2,441.95		2,670.60	XVII (6): Feb 20, 1908; C-5, L-7
Feb, 1908	382.30	2,670.60	$150.00	2,902.90	XVII (9): Mar 12, 1908; L-7
Mar, 1908	243.95	2,902.90	300.00	2,846.85	XVII (17): May 14, 1908; C-6, L-6
Jun, 1908	521.65	2,834.70		3,355.90	XVII (28): Aug 13, 1908; C-8 XVII (27): Aug 6, 1908; L-7
Oct, 1908	619.20	3,865.15	600.00	4,900.15	XVII (45): Dec 10, 1908; C-6, L-6

G.C.U. -- Financial Status 1909

Month	Amount Received Monthly By Treasury	Balance from Previous Month	Total Monthly Income	Total Monthly Debts	New Balance	Source
Dec, 1908	$25,756.60	$30,513.60	$56,270.20	$19,523.73	$36,746.47	XVIII (2): Jan 21, 1909; L-6
Jan, 1909	23,134.08	36,746.47	59,880.55	23,588.78	36,291.77	XVIII (7): Feb 25, 1909; L-8
Feb, 1909	27,237.43	25,982.08	63,529.25	32,513.83	31,015.42	XVIII (10): Mar 18, 1909; C-8, L-7
Mar, 1909	34,943.47	31,015.42	65,958.89	32,613.00	33,345.89	XVIII (15): Apr 29, 1909; C-8, L-8
Apr, 1909	24,202.19	33,345.89	65,958.89	30,802.74	26,745.34	XVIII (19): May 27, 1909; C-7, L-8
May, 1909	27,723.96	26,745.34	54,469.30	22,220.07	32,249.23	XVIII (24): Jul 1, 1909; C-8, L-8
Jun, 1909	27,069.17	32,249.23	59,318.40	27,561.80	31,756.60	XVIII (28): Jul 29, 1909; C-8, L-8
Jul, 1909	24,916.54	31,756.60	56,673.14	24,683.45	31,989.69	XVIII (31): Aug 19, 1909; C-8, L-8
Aug, 1909	35,024.94	31,989.69	67,014.63	23,856.97	42,957.66	XVIII (36): Sep 23, 1909; C-6, L-6
Sep, 1909	22,874.65	42,957.66	65,832.31	31,953.20	33,879.11	XVIII (40): Oct 21, 1909; C-8 / XVIII (39): Oct 14, 1909; L-8
Oct, 1909	28,283.04	23,879.11	52,162.15	18,319.16	33,842.99	XVIII (45): Nov 25, 1909; C-3, L-6
Nov, 1909	31,087.20	33,842.99	64,930.19	28,741.05	36,189.14	XVIII (50): Dec 30, 1909; L-12

G.C.U. -- Youth Lodges' Financial Status 1909

Month	Total Monthly Income	Balance from Previous Month	Total Monthly Debts	New Balance	Source
Nov, 1908 Dec, 1908 Jan, 1909		NO FIGURES REPORTED			
Feb, 1909	$727.60	$6,049.75	$600.00	$6,177.35	XVIII (7): Feb 25, 1909; L-8
Mar, 1909	864.00	6,177.35	300.00	6,741.35	XVIII (10): Mar 18, 1909; C-7 XVIII (9): Mar 11, 1909; L-7
Apr, 1909	833.65	6,741.35	600.00	6,975.00	XVIII (16): May 6, 1909; C-8, L-8
May, 1909	813.20	1,975.00		2,788.20	XVIII (20): Jun 3, 1909; C-8, L-8
Jul, 1909	999.50	3,586.88		4,586.38	XVIII (27): Jul 22, 1909; C-8, L-7 XVIII (25): Jul 18, 1909; L-7
Aug, 1909	921.50	4,586.38	1,800.00	3,707.88	XVIII (35): Sep 16, 1909; C-7, L-7
Sep, 1909	797.80	3,707.88	600.00	3,905.68	XVIII (36): Sep 23, 1909; C-8, L-8
Oct, 1909	875.50	3,905.68		4,780.18	XVIII (40): Oct 21, 1909; C-7, L-8 XVIII (46): Dec 2, 1909; C-6, L-6

G.C.U. -- Financial Status 1910

Month	Amount Received Monthly By Treasury	Balance from Previous Month	Total Monthly Income	Total Monthly Debts	New Balance	Source
Nov, 1909	$31,087.20	$33,842.99	$64,930.19	$28,741.05	$36,189.14	XIX (1): Jan 13, 1910; C-8
Dec, 1909	34,740.94	36,189.14	70,930.08	30,325.37	40,604.71	XIX (4): Feb 3, 1910; C-7, L-6
Jan, 1910	29,247.01	40,604.71	69,851.77	35,318.64	34,335.08	XIX (9): Mar 10, 1910; C-3, L-3
Feb, 1910	29,532.45	34,533.08	64,065.53	29,381.87	34,683.66	XIX (11): Mar 24, 1910; C-7, L-7
Mar, 1910	35,085.59	34,683.66	69,769.25	28,450.16	41,319.09	XIX (18): May 19, 1910; C-16, L-16
Apr, 1910	28,379.45	41,319.09	69,698.54	41,542.14	28,156.14	XIX (19): May 26, 1910; C-6, L-6
May, 1910	29,729.09	28,156.40	57,885.49	26,908.04	30,977.45	XIX (25): Jul 14, 1910; L-7
Jun, 1910	25,547.90	30,977.45	56,525.35	35,648.45	20,876.90	XIX (30): Aug 18, 1910; L-8
Jul, 1910	35,672.30	20,876.90	56,559.20	27,338.50	29,220.70	XIX (41): Nov 3, 1910; C-7, L-7
Aug, 1910	34,303.73	29,220.70	63,524.43	35,118.12	28,406.31	XIX (42): Nov 10, 1910; C-7, L-7
Sep, 1910	31,169.31	28,406.31	59,575.62	27,431.23	32,144.39	XIX (43): Nov 17, 1910; L-7
Oct, 1910	26,914.43	32,134.06	59,048.49	24,785.19	34,263.30	XIX (45): Dec 1, 1910; C-8, L-8

G.C.U. -- Youth Lodges' Financial Status 1910

Month	Total Monthly Income	Balance from Previous Month	Total Monthly Debts	New Balance	Source
Nov, 1909	$932.25	$1,781.18	$2,600.00	$113.43	XIX (1): Jan 13, 1910; C-8, L-3
Dec, 1909	909.80	113.43		1,023.23	XIX (4): Feb 3, 1910; C-6, L-7
Jan, 1910	983.75	1,023.23	1,200.00	806.98	XIX (11): Mar 24, 1910; C-8, L-6
Feb, 1910	975.25	806.98		1,782.23	XIX (13): Apr 7, 1910; C-8, L-6

G.C.U. -- Financial Status 1911

Month	Amount Received Monthly By Treasury	Balance from Previous Month	Total Monthly Income	Total Monthly Debts	New Balance	Source
Nov, 1910	$24,315.60	$34,264.30	$58,579.90	$23,142.98	$35,436.92	XX (5): Feb 16, 1911; C-7, L-7
Dec, 1910	38,670.36	35,436.92	74,107.28	33,775.69	40,331.59	XX (6): Feb 23, 1911; C-6, L-6
Jan, 1911	28,695.72	40,331.59	69,027.31	33,370.00	35,657.31	XX (7): Mar 2, 1911; C-6, L-6
Feb, 1911	34,315.84	35,657.31	69,973.15	28,149.38	41,823.77	XX (15): May 4, 1911; C-14, L-14
Mar, 1911	34,795.10	41,823.77	76,618.87	30,762.17	45,856.70	XX (17): May 18, 1911; C-6, L-6
Apr, 1911	29,058.88	45,856.70	74,915.58	28,490.19	46,425.39	XX (18): May 25, 1911; C-6, L-6
May, 1911	40,638.07	46,425.39	87,063.46	38,401.34	48,662.12	XX (29): Aug 17, 1911; C-7, L-7
Jun, 1911	40,061.09	48,662.12	88,723.21	36,676.42	52,046.79	XX (30): Aug 24, 1911; C-7, L-7
Jul, 1911	36,307.44	52,046.79	88,354.23	35,735.65	52,618.58	XX (32): Sep 7, 1911; C-6, L-6
Aug, 1911	41,745.77	52,618.58	94,364.35	47,238.92	47,125.43	XX (48): Dec 28, 1911; C-6, L-6
Sep, 1911	41,203.76	47,125.43	88,329.19	48,817.20	39,511.99	XX (49): Jan 4, 1912; C-6, L-6

G.C.U. -- Youth Lodges' Financial Status 1911

Month	Total Monthly Income	Balance from Previous Month	Total Monthly Debts	New Balance	Source
Jan, 1911	$3,533.05	$8,251.25	$1,517.30	$6,733.95	XX (11): Mar 30, 1911; C-8, L-8
Feb, 1911	1,272.80		75.73		
Mar, 1911	1,223.45		373.90		
Apr, 1911	1,175.61	6,733.95	79.65	9,876.53	XX (18): May 25, 1911; C-6, L-6
May, 1911	1,481.35	9,877.45	376.88		
Jun, 1911	1,308.00	10,981.92	1,572.40		
Jul, 1911	1,351.35	10,717.52	1,630.32	10,438.55	XX (40): Nov 2, 1911; C-8, L-7

G.C.U. -- Sokol Lodge Financial Status 1911

Month	Total Monthly Income	Balance from Previous Month	Total Monthly Debts	New Balance	Source
Jan, 1911	$208.90				
Feb, 1911	317.00				
Mar, 1911	404.55				
Apr, 1911	385.90			$1,316.35	XX (19): Jun 1, 1911; C-8, L-7

G.C.U. -- Financial Status 1912

Month	Amount Received Monthly By Treasury	Balance from Previous Month	Total Monthly Income	Total Monthly Debts	New Balance	Source
Oct, 1911	$38,547.53	$39,511.99	$78,059.52	$25,156.39	$52,903.13	XXI (1): Jan 18, 1912; C-6, L-6
Nov, 1911	40,475.83	52,903.13	147,738.91*	101,943.92	45,794.99	XXI (2): Jan 25, 1912; C-6, L-6
Dec, 1911	35,010.13	45,794.99	80,805.12	58,265.82	22,539.30	XXI (4): Feb 8, 1912; C-6, L-6
Jan, 1912	34,447.15	22,539.30	56,986.45	33,088.32	23,898.13	XXI (6): Feb 22, 1912; C-6, L-6
Feb, 1912	46,141.23	23,898.13	70,039.36	30,732.57	39,306.79	XXI (13): Apr 18, 1912; C-6
Mar, 1912	44,853.31	39,306.79	84,160.10	45,053.87	39,106.23	XXI (16): May 9, 1912; C-6, L-6
Apr, 1912	49,729.11	39,106.23	88,835.34	55,178.18	33,657.16	XXI (18): May 23, 1912; C-12
May, 1912	32,214.19	33,657.16	65,871.35	36,750.65	29,120.70	XXI (31): Aug 29, 1912; C-8, L-7
Jun, 1912	32,620.59	29,120.70	61,741.29	34,930.19	26,811.10	XXI (32): Sep 5, 1912; C-8, L-7
Jul, 1912	45,018.20	26,811.10	71,829.30	34,571.58	37,257.72	XXI (34): Sep 19, 1912; C-7, L-7
Aug, 1912	39,997.44	37,257.72	77,255.16	35,410.22	41,844.94	XXI (45): Dec 5, 1912; C-6, L-6
Sep, 1912	31,423.67	41,844.94	73,268.61	32,959.45	40,309.16	XXI (46): Dec 12, 1912; C-6, L-6
Oct, 1912	43,022.14	40,309.16	83,331.30	28,198.57	55,132.73	XXI (47): Dec 19, 1912; C-6

*Inclusion of funds in the following saving accounts:

First National Bank, Braddock, PA	$ 7,803.32
	15,636.98
Homestead Savings & Trust Co., Homestead, PA	2,110.13
Lincoln National Bank, Pittsburgh, PA	3,864.97
Farmers National Bank, Pittsburgh, PA	5,918.00
German National Bank, Pittsburgh, PA	3,738.52
German Savings Bank, Pittsburgh, PA	3,514.86
	11,773.17

G.C.U. -- Youth Lodges' Financial Status 1912

Month	Total Monthly Income	Balance from Previous Month	Total Monthly Debts	New Balance	Source
Feb, 1912	$1,643.60		$373.68		
Mar, 1912	1,715.70		1,287.60		
Apr, 1912	1,583.30		1,577.80	$3,085.88	XXI (18): May 23, 1912; C-11&12

G.C.U. -- Sokol Lodge Financial Status 1912

Month	Total Monthly Income	Balance from Previous Month	Total Monthly Debts	New Balance	Source
Jan, 1912	$568.60				
Feb, 1912	458.80				
Mar, 1912	611.05				
Apr, 1912	631.55		$197.00	$6,035.11	XXI (18): May 23, 1912; C-12

G.C.U. -- Financial Status 1913

Month	Amount Received Monthly By Treasury	Balance from Previous Month	Total Monthly Income	Total Monthly Debts	New Balance	Source
Nov, 1912	$37,737.34	$55,132.73	$92,870.07	$54,433.48	$38,436.59	XXII (12): Apr 3, 1913; L-6
Dec, 1912	47,442.13	38,436.59	85,878.72	49,228.57	36,650.15	XXII (14): Apr 17, 1913; C-6, L-6
Jan, 1913	41,344.76	36,650.15	77,994.91	45,305.69	32,689.22	XXII (15): Apr 24, 1913; C-6, L-6
Feb, 1913	53,508.21	32,689.22	85,997.43	42,474.75	43,522.68	XXII (16): May 8, 1913; C-6, L-6
Mar, 1913	37,364.47	43,522.68	80,887.15	42,610.14	38,277.01	XXII (17): May 15, 1913; C-3, L-3
Apr, 1913	40,413.19	38,277.01	78,690.20	34,815.65	43,874.55	XXII (18): May 22, 1913; C-6, L-6
May, 1913	52,939.63	43,874.55	96,814.18	36,999.91	59,814.27	XXII (23): Jun 26, 1913; C-6, L-6
Jun, 1913	46,357.65	59,814.27	106,171.92	44,602.78	61,569.14	XXII (27): Jul 31, 1913; C-6, L-6
Jul, 1913	48,339.20	61,569.14	109,908.34	65,801.68	44,106.66	XXII (30): Aug 21, 1913; C-6, L-6
Aug, 1913	46,671.87	44,106.66	90,778.53	44,447.20	46,331.33	XXII (38): Oct 16, 1913; C-7, L-7
Sep, 1913	44,186.38	46,331.33	90,517.71	42,457.02	48,039.79	XXII (39): Oct 23, 1913; C-6, L-7
Oct, 1913	51,434.59	48,039.79	99,474.38	41,253.55	58,220.83	XXII (43): Nov 20, 1913; C-6, L-6

G.C.U. -- Financial Status 1914

Month	Amount Received Monthly By Treasury	Balance from Previous Month	Total Monthly Income	Total Monthly Debts	New Balance	Source
Nov, 1913	$38,560.14	$58,220.83	$96,780.97	$42,481.94	$54,299.03	XXIII (2): Jan 22, 1914; C-7
Dec, 1913	43,419.41	54,299.03	97,718.44	40,005.11	57,713.33	XXIII (5): Feb 12, 1914; C-7
Jan, 1914	46,370.96	57,713.33	104,084.29	41,508.31	62,575.98	XXIII (9): Mar 12, 1914; C-6
Feb, 1914	41,959.98	62,575.98	104,535.96	54,161.73	50,374.23	XXIII (11): Mar 26, 1914; C-6
Mar, 1914	41,088.23	50,374.23	91,462.46	38,433.17	53,029.29	XXIII (16): May 7, 1914; C-12
Apr, 1914	44,067.39	53,029.29	97,096.68	43,606.43	53,490.25	XXIII (22): Jun 25, 1914; C-6
May, 1914	35,486.11	53,490.25	88,976.36	44,633.85	44,342.51	XXIII (23): Jul 2, 1914; C-6
Jun, 1914	43,036.95	44,342.51	87,379.46	85,738.81	1,640.65	XXIII (27): Jul 30, 1914; C-6
Jul, 1914	50,395.37	1,660.26	52,055.63	36,782.88	15,272.75	XXIII (32): Sep 3, 1914; C-6
Aug, 1914	48,723.93	15,272.75	63,996.69	50,206.69	13,789.99	XXIII (36): Oct 1, 1914; C-6&7
Sep, 1914	38,646.09	13,789.99	52,436.08	39,159.34	13,276.74	XXIII (39): Oct 22, 1914; C-6&7
Oct, 1914	35,800.05	13,276.74	49,076.79	32,868.02	16,208.77	XXIII (43): Nov 19, 1914; C-9&10
Nov, 1914	37,674.65	16,208.77	53,883.42	28,347.90	25,535.52	XXIII (48): Dec 24, 1914; C-6
Dec, 1914	43,022.68	25,535.92	68,557.60	37,819.67	30,737.93	XXIV (3): Jan 21, 1915; C-7, L-6&7

G.C.U. -- Youth Lodges' Financial Status 1914

Month	Total Monthly Income	Balance from Previous Month	Total Monthly Debts	New Balance	Source
Apr, 1914	$2,153.79	$9,670.19	$5,674.00	$6,149.98	XXIII (22): Jun 25, 1914; C-8
May, 1914	2,015.41	6,149.98	116.25	8,049.14	XXIII (23): Jul 2, 1914; C-7
Jun, 1914	2,284.55	8,049.14	1,176.44	10,333.69	XXIII (26): Jul 23, 1914; C-8
Jul, 1914	2,478.75	9,157.25	1,589.00	10,047.00	XXIII (34): Sep 17, 1914; C-7
Aug, 1914	2,759.95	10,047.00	1,022.00	11,784.95	XXIII (35): Sep 24, 1914; C-7
Sep, 1914	2,677.65	11,784.95	72.00	14,390.60	XXIII (40): Oct 29, 1914; C-6&7
Oct, 1914	2,612.50	14,390.60	1,525.50	15,477.60	XXIII (43): Nov 19, 1914; C-10&11
Nov, 1914	2,252.15	15,477.60	939.00	17,091.25	XXIII (46): Dec 10, 1914; C-6
Dec, 1914	3,112.75	17,091.25	2,527.00	17,677.00	XXIV (2): Jan 14, 1915; C-7, L-6

G.C.U. -- Sokol Lodge Financial Status 1914

Month	Total Monthly Income	Balance from Previous Month	Total Monthly Debts	New Balance	Source
Apr, 1914	$1,352.55	$6,427.25	$5,684.50	$2,095.30	XXIII (22): Jun 25, 1914; C-8
May, 1914	1,271.00	2,095.30	406.70	2,959.60	XXIII (23): Jul 2, 1914; C-7
Jun, 1914	1,588.05	2,959.60	911.85	3,635.80	XXIII (26): Jul 23, 1914; C-8

Indices

PHOTOGRAPH INDEX

I. Personalia

1.	Artim, Very Rev. Dr. Michael	XVIII (50): Dec 30, 1909; C-4, L-4
2.	Bessenyey, August B.	XI (21b): Jun 12, 1902; C-2
3.	Bodrog, John	XVII (46): Dec 17, 1908; C-7
4.	Chopey; Rev. Nicholas	XXI (44): Nov 28, 1912; C-4
5.	Drohobeczky, Most Rev. Julius	XI (21b): Jun 12, 1902; C-7 XVII (18): May 21, 1908; C-1
6.	Dzijak, John	XI (21b): Jun 12, 1902; C-2
7.	Dzubay, Rev. Alexander	XI (21b): Jun 12, 1902; C-3
8.	Dzmura, Peter	X (2): Jan 24, 1901; C-8 XI (21b): Jun 12, 1902; C-2
9.	Egrecky (Egreczky), Julius	XVII (46): Dec 17, 1908; C-4
10.	Fecko (Feczko), Joseph	XVII (24): Jul 16, 1908; C-8
11.	Fedorko, Michael	XI (30): Aug 21, 1902; C-1
12.	Firczak, Most Rev. Julius	XI (21b): Jun 12, 1902; C-6 XX (36): Oct 5, 1911; C-1 XXI (21): Jun 20, 1912; L-1
13.	Gocza, John	XXI (26): Jul 25, 1912; L-2
14.	Hodobay, Very Rev. Andrew	XI (16): May 8, 1902; C-1 XI (21b): Jun 12, 1902; C-5
15.	Holosnyay, Rev. Alexis	XI (21b): Jun 12, 1902; C-2 XIII (1): Jan 21, 1904; C-1 XVII (46): Dec 17, 1908; C-3
16.	Hreňa (Hrenja), Ann	XI (21b): Jun 12, 1902; C-3
17.	Juhas (Yuhasz), Michael Sr.	XI (22): Jun 26, 1902; C-1
18.	Janoško, Peter	XXII (16): May 8, 1913; C-3, L-3
19.	Kacik, John	XII (35): Sep 24, 1903; C-1, L-1
20.	Kaminsky, Rev. Victor	XII (48): Dec 24, 1903; C-5, L-4

21. Kecskés, Rev. Anthony   XII (23): Jul 2, 1903; C-1, L-1

22. Laurisin, Rev. Cornelius   XI (21b): Jun 12, 1902; C-2

23. Lucak, Michael K.   XI (21b): Jun 12, 1902; C-2

24. Obushkevich, Rev. Theophane A.   XI (21b): Jun 12, 1902; C-2

25. Pačuta, Nicholas   XVII (46): Dec 17, 1908; C-4
                                  XIX (36): Sep 29, 1910; C-7

26. Polivka, Rev. Damascene   XI (22): Jun 26, 1902; C-1
     (Damaskin)

27. Rushin, Michael S.   XXI (24): Jul 11, 1912; L-1

28. Smith, John A. (Zinčak)   III (20): Jun 12, 1894; C-1

29. Sheptytz'kyi, Most Rev. Andrew   XI (21b): Jun 12, 1902; C-6

30. Mother Theophile   XII (18): May 21, 1903; C-2, L-2

31. Uhrin, John   XIII (13): Apr 21, 1904; L-3
                                  XVII (46): Dec 17, 1908; C-3
                                  XXII (38): Oct 16, 1913; C-1

32. Valij, Most Rev. John   XI (21b): Jun 12, 1902; C-7
                                  XII (44): Nov 26, 1903; C-1, L-1

33. Vasko, George   XV (19): May 24, 1906; 3

34. Volkay, Rev. Eugene   XI (21b): Jun 12, 1902; C-3

35. Zsatkovich, Paul Jurievich   XVII (46): Dec 17, 1908; C-5

36. Zsatkovich, Gregory Ignatius XIX (38): Oct 31, 1910; C-4

II. Churches

1. Bayonne, NJ Greek Catholic   XIII (3): Feb 4, 1904; C-1, L-1
    Church

2. Homestead, PA Greek Catholic XIII (1): Jan 21, 1904; C-1
    Church and Rectory

3. Mahanoy City, PA Greek   XII (48): Dec 24, 1903; C-1, L-1
    Catholic Church

4. Trauger, PA Greek Catholic   XXIII (37): Oct 8, 1914; C-9
    Church

5. Trenton, NJ Greek Catholic Church

XXIII (16): May 7, 1914; C-1

6. Wilkes Barre, PA Greek Catholic Church and Rectory

XXI (44): Nov 28, 1912; C-4

III. Greek Catholic Union

1. Advertisement for the tenth anniversary edition

XL (21b): Jun 12, 1902; C-1

2. Assistants to ARV editor [N.N.]

XVII (46): Dec 17, 1908; C-5

3. ARV editor's office

XVII (46): Dec 17, 1908; C-6

4. G.C.U. account books and office

XVII (46): Dec 17, 1908; C-6

5. G.C.U. Homestead, PA Headquarters Building Exterior

XVII (46): Dec 17, 1908; C-4

6. G.C.U. Sokol Lodge Uniforms

XXII (6): Feb 20, 1913; C-9
XXII (37): Oct 9, 1913; C-4
XXII (43): Nov 20, 1913; C-4

7. Paper stores for the ARV

XVII (46): Dec 17, 1908; C-8

8. Print shop and presses of the ARV

XVII (46): Dec 17, 1908; C-6

EDITORIAL INDEX

The following is a chronological reference to all editorial entries listed in this volume.

LETTERS TO THE EDITOR INDEX (EUROPE)

The following is a chronological reference to all letters to the editor from Europe entries listed in this volume.

LETTERS TO THE EDITOR INDEX (AMERICA)

The following is a chronological reference to all letters to the editor from America entries listed in this volume.

1902	1903	1904	1906
3200	3237	4293	6358
3201	6130	3267	6194
4209	6657	2169	3312
6048; 6596	3241	3268	4323
3202	4251	6012	3318
2138	4253	6274	4328
2139	3243	4295	6069
	4256	3271	6484
1903	4257	3273	6462
	4259	4297	4336
3204	4258	3274	6402
6160; 6660; 6595	3246	3275	4339
2141	3247	6306	2200
6584	3248	2173	6314
4213	3249	3276	3328
3205	3250	4300	3331
6291	3252	2174	6537
3206	6420	2175	6213
4216	2163	4301	4344
3207		6444	4345
3208	**1904**	4303	3335
4220		4304	1049
4222	4268	4305	2220
3211	4269	4307	6554
4223	2164	3281	3340
3212	6085	3282	4347
4224	4270	3284	2222
2147	6207	3285	6192
6418	4271	3286	6573
4228	4272	3288	6680
6446	4273	3290	4351
6500	3254	4310	4352
4230	4274	6598	6222
4231	6235	3293	6637
6372	4277	6591	6287
4233	4279	6241	2234
3218	6539	3296	6129
3219	4282	3298	6403
3222	6077	6635	3347
3223	4284	3301	6429
4236	4285	3303	6301
2151	4286	3304	
6021	4287	2185	
4237	6318	3305	**1907**
3228	6512	3306	
3231	3262	4313	2246
3233	3263	6014	6162
4243	6383	6553	6413
3236	4291	6415	6658
4247	6398	2187	4363
			2252

1907	1907	1909	1909
2253	3412	3508	6324
6648	6148	3509	6105
6197	1055	4447	6348
4367	6630	3511	6545
4368	3424	3512	4477
3355	6534	3514	3567
3358	6143	2307	3569
4370	3428	2310	6607
3360	3429	3515	6243
6007; 6016; 6367	3432	2311	6558
3363	3433	6265	6203
4374	6239	3516	3572
6615		6342	3573
6572		3518	5123
3368	1908	3520	3576
4375	6026	3521	2326
6114	3439	3522	2327
6392	3441	3524	
6421	4414	4454	
6289	3443	4455; 6298	1910
6224	3447	3526	2328
4376; 6652	4415	3528	6033; 6177
6392	4418	6272	6362
4378	6667; 6328	6056; 6323; 6568; 6285	6438; 6574
2256	3453		6161
6666	3456	6170	4483
2258	6211	3531	6376
2259	6023	6185	6097
6400	3457	6008	6592
4384	3458	3534	6466
6127	4423	6488	6373; 6234
2263	2282	6059	5125
3382	3470	6530; 6167; 6331	5126
4390	3471	3539	6521; 6576
4391	6617	4459	3592
3385	4432	3541	3593
3388	4433	4460	3594
6308	4436	5113	4488
4393	4437	6134	3597
6464	3481	3544	3598
2265	4440	6624	3599
6248	3486	3554	4491
3392	1059	3556	3600
3397	3497	3558	6674
6184	2302	6152	6511
3398		3561	4493
3402	1909	3563	4495
6542	3501	1063	4496
4402	3505	6111; 6642	6163
3411	3506	6354	3603

1910	1911	1911	1912
2337	4526	6678	2418
4497; 6467	6292	3673	6277
3604	3645	6473	6053
3605	2370	6626	3727
6645	4529; 6232	6525	3729
3607	6145	6181	4566
3608	2372	3676	3734
2344	3646	4554	2439
4499	6540	3680	6116
3609	3647	3682	6242; 6340;
4502	4532	3686	6679
4503	2375	3687	6011
3610	3650	2396	4568
2349	6311	3689	6009
1065	6518; 6076	3690	6555
6654	1071	6565	4569
4506	6202	3691	3743
4507	3652	2398	3745
6618	4536	6481	3747
6196	6255	6339	6410
6295	6531	3696	2443
6278	4537		2445
3620	5135	**1912**	3749
2353	3653	4557	3750
3623	3654	3698	3751
3624	6096	3699	3757
3625	4539	4559	4572
3626	6091; 6037	6307	6366; 6646;
1069	4541	3700	6487;
6126	3656	2402	6266
6650	4542	2403	4573
2357	3657	5143	6502
3629	4543	2405	4574
3630	4544	2406	3763
1070	3658	3704	4575
4517	3659	6010	3769
3632	4547	6371	4576
3633	3660	3706	3771
4518	6390	6281	3772
3634	6098	3712	6165
3636	2384	6074	6431
4521; 6424	3662	4564	
3638	3663	6176	
	3664	6456	**1913**
1911	3665	3714	3776
4524	1075	1079	6428
3640	3666	3715	6151; 6320
6665	6509	5148	2467
3642	3669	3716	6523; 6593
6322	3672	3718	3780
	6656		

1913			1914
6461			6612
3783			6103
6581			3840
3786			6072
4585			6684
3790			6490
4587			3845
6474			6141
3791			3847
3792			3848
3793			2513
3794			5187
6041			2514
2475			3849
6522			2516
3795			6577
6422			2525
3797			3852
6060			6663
6685			6319
6334			6386
6214			6252
6609;	6046;	6106;	6435
	6168;	6182;	4607
	6269;	6414	5190
3806			5191
6327			6233
6453			3858
4595			3859
3810			1089
6179			1090
3811			3861
4598			6485
5176			6317
6018			2540
3817			4610
3818			6157
3819			3865
3822			6470
6268			4611
4601			5195
3825			5196
2497			5197
3830			3872
6619			4629
3834			3874
6238			4631
3839			

SUBJECT INDEX

Stecovich, Rev. Nicholas [also: Szteczovich], Supreme Spiritual Advisor for the Greek Catholic Union, 3017, 3018, 3071f, 3078d, 3151a, 3209b, 3260c, 3292, 3339b, 3602; Appendix I, p. 396

Stejfan, Rev. Theodore, 3190a-1, 3190b

Stewartsville, NJ: Rusyn community, 4224

Stockett, MT: Greek Catholic Mission, 3609; Rusyn community, 4566

Rev. Stockij, 3190j

Streator, IL: tornado damage in, 4237

Strich, Thomas, member of Supreme Overseeing Committee of the Greek Catholic Union, Appendix I, p. 396

Strikers, aid for, 4203, 4512

Strikes (Labor) in: America, 4179; Bradenville, PA, 4503, 4521, affect of on Rusyn families in, 4507, 4518; Broderick, PA, 4192, 4194; Butler, PA, 4462; Colorado, 4286; Connelsville, PA, 4004, 4007, 4009, 4010, 4014; Erven, PA, 4512; Greensburg, PA, 4512; Hazleton, PA, 4094; Letrobe, PA, 4502, 4503; McKees Rocks, PA, 4462, 4465, 4466, 4467, 4470, 4471, 4472; Monessen, PA, 4137; New Mexico, 4109, 4114, 4119; Oneida, PA, 4148; Pennsylvania, 4011, 4133, 4196, 4211, 4218, 4504; Pittsburgh, PA, 4139, 4142, 4464; Rockville County, CO, 4607; Scranton, PA, 4204, 4207; Shenandoah, PA, 4185; Sheppton, PA, 4148; Westmoreland County, PA, 4524, 4541, 4546, 4549; Wilkes Barre, PA, 4094, 4182, 4192; Windber, PA, 4337, 4366. See also: Coal Miners, Industry, Labor, United Mine Workers of America

Strutinsky, Rev. Nicholas, Supreme Controller of the Greek Catholic Union, 3343d; Appendix I, p. 396

Stupaj konik, stupaj konik, 5026-19

Suba, Rev. Victor, 3454b, 3601d-5

Subcarpathian Rus', 5042

Sugar Creek, MO: Greek Catholic Church, 3634; Rusyn community, 4303

Sun, newspaper, [published in New York, NY], 3224

Sutersville, PA: Greek Catholic Church, 3839, 3887

Svidník [Szvidnik], Sáros County, Hungary: village reading room, 5152

Svît, newspaper, [published in Madison, IL], 3281, 3348, 3349

Svoboda, organ of the Rusyn National Union, [published in Jersey City, NJ]: 1003, 1006, 1007, 1019, 1023, 1033, 1054, 1055, 1058, 1091, 2296, 3097, 3112, 3522, 3571, 3590, 3613, 3684; commentary on, 1002, 1004, 1008, 1010, 1017, 1018, 1022, 1024, 1026, 1027, 1028, 1030, 1032, 1057; endorsements by, 3134; falsified letters to the editor of, 1060; on the "Ea Semper" Papal Bull, 3423; Rusyn nationality, as defined by, 1001

Sybyr'skiy Yzhannyky: povîst, 5025

Sykesville, PA: Greek Catholic Church, 3394; Rusyn community, 4374

Syracuse, NY: Greek Catholic Church, 3444c-2

Szabados, Rev. Nicholas, 3320a, 3426n

Szabo, Rev. John [also: Szabov], Supreme Recording Secretary and Supreme Controller of the Greek Catholic Union, 2001, 2120, 2131,

AUTHOR INDEX